File Structures

An Object-Oriented Approach with C++

File Structures

An Object-Oriented
Approach with C++

Michael J. Folk
University of Illinois

Bill Zoellick
CAP Ventures

Greg Riccardi
Florida State University

ADDISON-WESLEY

Addison-Wesley is an imprint of Addison Wesley Longman, Inc.

Reading, Massachusetts • Harlow, England • Menlo Park, California
Berkeley, California • Don Mills, Ontario • Sydney
Bonn • Amsterdam • Tokyo • Mexico City

Acquisitions Editor: Susan Hartman
Associate Editor: Katherine Harutunian
Production Editors: Patricia A. O. Unubun / Amy Willcutt
Production Assistant: Brooke D. Albright
Design Editor: Alwyn R. Velásquez
Senior Marketing Manager: Tom Ziolkowski
Interior Design and Composition: Greg Johnson, Art Directions
Cover Designer: Eileen Hoff

Library of Congress Cataloging-in-Publication Data

Folk, Michael J.

   File structures: an object-oriented approach with C++/ Michael J. Folk, Bill Zoellick, Greg Riccardi.

   p.   cm.

   Includes bibliographical references and index.

   ISBN 0-201-87401-6

   1. C++ (Computer program language) 2. File organization (Computer science) I. Zoellick, Bill. II. Riccardi, Greg. III. Title.

QA76.73.C153F65   1998

005.74'1—dc21

                                              97-31670

                                                CIP

Access the latest information about Addison-Wesley titles from our World Wide Web site: http://www.awl.com/cseng

The programs and applications presented in this book have been included for their instructional value. They have been tested with care but are not guaranteed for any purpose. The publisher does not offer any warranties or representations, nor does it accept any liabilities with respect to the programs or applications.

Many of the designations used by manufacturers and sellers to distinguish their products are claimed as trademarks. Where those designations appear in this book, and Addison-Wesley was aware of a trademark claim, the designations have been printed in initial caps or all caps.

Reprinted with corrections, March 1998.

Printed in the United States of America.

3 4 5 6 7 8 9 10-MA-01009998

Dedication

To Pauline and Rachel
To Karen, Joshua, and Peter
and
To Ann, Mary, Christina, and Elizabeth

Preface

The first and second editions of *File Structures* by Michael Folk and Bill Zoellick established a standard for teaching and learning about file structures. The authors helped many students and computing professionals gain familiarity with the tools used to organize files.

This book extends the presentation of file structure design that has been so successful for twelve years with an object-oriented approach to implementing file structures using C++. It demonstrates how the object-oriented approach can be successfully applied to complex implementation problems. It is intended for students in computing classes who have had at least one programming course and for computing professionals who want to improve their skills in using files.

This book shows you how to design and implement efficient file structures that are easy for application programmers to use. All you need is a compiler for C++ or other object-oriented programming language and an operating system. This book provides the conceptual tools that enable you to think through alternative file structure designs that apply to the task at hand. It also develops the programming skills necessary to produce quality implementations.

The coverage of the C++ language in this book is suitable for readers with a basic knowledge of the language. Readers who have a working familiarity with C++ should have no problem understanding the programming examples. Those who have not programmed in C++ will benefit from access to an introductory textbook.

The first programming examples in the book use very simple C++ classes to develop implementations of fundamental file structure tools.

One by one, advanced features of C++ appear in the context of implementations of more complex file structure tools. Each feature is fully explained when it is introduced. Readers gain familiarity with inheritance, overloading, virtual methods, and templates and see examples of why these features are so useful to object-oriented programming.

Organization of the Book

The first six chapters of this book give you the tools to design and implement simple file structures from the ground up: simple I/O, methods for transferring objects between memory and files, sequential and direct access, and the characteristics of secondary storage. The last six chapters build on this foundation and introduce you to the most important high-level file structure tools, including indexing, cosequential processing, B-trees, B+ trees, hashing, and extendible hashing.

The book includes extensive discussion of the object-oriented approach to representing information and algorithms and the features of C++ that support this approach. Each of the topics in the text is accompanied by object-oriented representations. The full C++ class definitions and code are included as appendices and are available on the Internet. This code has been developed and tested using Microsoft Visual C++ and the Gnu C++ compilers on a variety of operating systems including Windows 95, Windows NT, Linux, Sun Solaris, and IBM AIX.

You can find the programming examples and other materials at the Addison-Wesley Web site: http://www.awl.com/cseng/titles/0-201-87401-6/.

Object-Oriented File Structures

There are two reasons we have added the strong object-oriented programming component to this book. First, it allows us to be more specific, and more helpful, in illustrating the tools of file structure design. For each tool, we give very specific algorithms and explain the options that are available to implementers. We are also able to build full implementations of complex file structure tools that are suitable for solving file design problems. By the time we get to B-tree indexing, for instance, we are able to use previous tools for defining object types, moving data between memory and files, and simple indexing. This makes it possible for the B-tree classes to have simple implementations and for the book to explain the features of B-trees as enhancements of previous tools.

The second purpose of the programming component of the book is to illustrate the proper use of object-oriented methods. Students are often exposed to object-oriented techniques through simple examples. However, it is only in complex systems that the advantages of object-oriented techniques become clear. In this book, we have taken advantage of the orderly presentation of file structure tools to build a complex software system as a sequence of relatively simple design and implementation steps. Through this approach, students get specific examples of the advantages of object-oriented methods and are able to improve their own programming skills.

A Progressive Presentation of C++

We cover the principles of design and implementation in a progressive fashion. Simple concepts come first and form the foundation for more complex concepts. Simple classes are designed and implemented in the early chapters, then are used extensively for the implementation topics of the later chapters. The most complex file structure tools have simple implementations because they extend the solid foundation of the early chapters.

We also present the features of C++ and the techniques of object-oriented programming in a progressive fashion. The use of C++ begins with the simplest class definitions. Next comes the use of stream classes for input and output. Further examples introduce inheritance, then virtual functions, and finally templates.

Each new feature is introduced and explained in the context of a useful file structure application. Readers see how to apply object-oriented techniques to programming problems and learn firsthand how object-oriented techniques can make complex programming tasks simpler.

Exercises and Programming Problems

The book includes a wealth of new analytical and programming exercises. The programming exercises include extensions and enhancements to the file structure tools and the application of those tools. The tools in the book are working software, but some operations have been left as programming problems. The deletion of records from files, for instance, is discussed in the text but not implemented. Specific programming problems fill in the gaps in the implementations and investigate some of the alternatives that are presented in the text.

An application of information processing is included as a series of programming projects in the exercise sets of appropriate chapters. This application begins in Chapter 1 with the representation of students and course registrations as objects of C++ classes. In Chapter 2, the project asks for simple input and output of these objects. Later projects include implementing files of objects (Chapter 4), indexes to files (Chapter 7), grade reports and transcripts (Chapter 8), B-tree indexes (Chapter 9), and hashed indexes (Chapter 12).

Using the Book as a College Text

The first two editions of *File Structures* have been used extensively as a text in many colleges and universities. Because the book is quite readable, students typically are expected to read the entire book over the course of a semester. The text covers the basics; class lectures can expand and supplement the material. The professor is free to explore more complex topics and applications, relying on the text to supply the fundamentals.

A word of caution: It is easy to spend too much time on the low-level issues presented in the first six chapters. Move quickly through this material. The relatively large number of pages devoted to these matters is not a reflection of the percentage of the course that should be spent on them. The intent is to provide thorough coverage in the text so the instructor can assign these chapters as background reading, saving precious lecture time for more important topics.

It is important to get students involved in the development of file processing software early in the course. Instructors may choose some combination of file tool implementation problems from the programming exercises and applications of the tools from the programming projects. Each of the programming problems and projects included in the exercises is intended to be of short duration with specific deliverables. Students can be assigned programming problems of one to three weeks in duration. It is typical for one assignment to depend on previous assignments. By conducting a sequence of related software developments, the students finish the semester with extensive experience in object-oriented software development.

A Book for Computing Professionals

We wrote and revised this book with our professional colleagues in mind. The style is conversational; the intent is to provide a book that you can read over a number of evenings, coming away with a good sense of how to approach file structure design problems. Some computing professionals may choose to skip the extensive programming examples and concentrate on the conceptual tools of file structure design. Others may want to use the C++ class definitions and code as the basis for their own implementations of file structure tools.

If you are already familiar with basic file structure design concepts and programming in C++, skim through the first six chapters and begin reading about indexing in Chapter 7. Subsequent chapters introduce you to cosequential processing, B-trees, B+ trees, hashing, and extendible hashing. These are key tools for any practicing programmer who is building file structures. We have tried to present them in a way that is both thorough and readable.

The object-oriented C++ design and the implementation included throughout the book provide an extensive tour of the capabilities of the language and thorough examples of object-oriented design. If you need to build and access file structures similar to the ones in the text, you can use the C++ code as class libraries that you can adapt to your needs. A careful reading of the design and implementation examples can be helpful in enhancing your skills with object-oriented tools. All of the code included in the book is available on the Internet.

If you are not already a serious Unix user, the Unix material in the first eight chapters will give you a feel for why Unix is a powerful environment in which to work with files.

Supplementary Materials

The following supplementary materials are available to assist instructors and students. Links to these supplements are on the book's official World Wide Web page at http://www.awl.com/cseng/titles/0-201-87401-6/.

An Instructors' Guide including answers to exercises will be available. Instructors should contact their Addison-Wesley local sales representative for information on the Guide's availability.

Programming examples and code will also be available via anonymous ftp at ftp.aw.com/cseng/authors/riccardi

Acknowledgments

It is a pleasure to acknowledge the outstanding work of Mike Folk and Bill Zoellick. As one who taught from the original work, I am pleased to add my contribution to its evolution.

There are many people I would like to thank for help in preparing this revision of *File Structures*. The staff of the Computer and Engineering Publishing Group of Addison-Wesley was extremely helpful. Editor Susan Hartman approached me to revise this excellent book and add a C++ programming component. She was responsible for getting all of the complex pieces put together. Katherine Harutunian, associate editor, was helpful and good-humored during the long and stressful process. The production staff of Patricia Unubun, Brooke Albright, and Amy Willcutt worked with me and were able to get the book finished on time.

I am particularly appreciative of the reviewers: H.K. Dai, Ed Boyno, Mary Ann Robbert, Barbara L. Laguna, Kenneth Cooper, Jr., and Mathew Palakal. Their comments and helpful suggestions showed me many ways to improve the book, especially in the presentation of the programming material.

My greatest debt is to my wife, Ann, and my daughters, Mary, Christina, and Elizabeth, for giving me the time to work on this project. It was their support that allowed me to carry this project to completion.

Greg Riccardi
Tallahassee, Florida
riccardi@cs.fsu.edu

Contents

Chapter 3 Secondary Storage and System Software   43

Chapter 4   Fundamental File Structure Concepts   117

Chapter 5   Managing Files of Records   153

Chapter 6   Organizing Files for Performance   201

Chapter 7 Indexing   247

Chapter 8 Cosequential Processing and the Sorting of Large Files   289

Chapter 9   Multilevel Indexing and B-Trees   369

Chapter 10   Indexed Sequential File Access and Prefix B⁺ Trees   423

Chapter 11   Hashing   463

Appendix A   Designing File Structures for CD-ROM   **565**

Appendix B   ASCII Table   **579**

Appendix C   Formatted Output with C++ Stream Classes   **581**

Appendix D Simple File Input/Output Examples   585

Appendix E Classes for Buffer Manipulation   591

Appendix F A Class Hierarchy for Buffer Input/Output   607

Appendix G   Single Level Indexing of Records by Key   637

Appendix H   Cosequential Processing   659

Appendix I   Multi-level Indexing with B-Trees   677

Appendix J   Extendible Hashing   689

File Structures

An Object-Oriented
Approach with C++

1

Introduction to the Design and Specification of File Structures

❖ Introduce the primary design issues that characterize file structure design.

❖ Survey the history of file structure design, since tracing the developments in file structures teaches us much about how to design our own file structures.

❖ Introduce the notions of file structure literacy and of a *conceptual toolkit* for file structure design.

❖ Discuss the need for precise specification of data structures and operations and the development of an object-oriented toolkit that makes file structures easy to use.

❖ Introduce classes and overloading in the C++ language.

1.1 The Heart of File Structure Design

Disks are slow. They are also technological marvels: one can pack thousands of megabytes on a disk that fits into a notebook computer. Only a few years ago, disks with that kind of capacity looked like small washing machines. However, relative to other parts of a computer, disks are slow.

How slow? The time it takes to get information back from even relatively slow electronic random access memory (RAM) is about 120 nanoseconds, or 120 billionths of a second. Getting the same information from a typical disk might take 30 milliseconds, or 30 thousandths of a second. To understand the size of this difference, we need an analogy. Assume that memory access is like finding something in the index of this book. Let's say that this local, book-in-hand access takes 20 seconds. Assume that accessing a disk is like sending to a library for the information you cannot find here in this book. Given that our "memory access" takes 20 seconds, how long does the "disk access" to the library take, keeping the ratio the same as that of a real memory access and disk access? The disk access is a quarter of a million times longer than the memory access. This means that getting information back from the library takes 5 million seconds, or almost 58 days. Disks are *very* slow compared with memory.

On the other hand, disks provide enormous capacity at much less cost than memory. They also keep the information stored on them when they are turned off. The tension between a disk's relatively slow access time and its enormous, nonvolatile capacity is the driving force behind file structure design. Good file structure design will give us access to all the capacity without making our applications spend a lot of time waiting for the disk.

A *file structure* is a combination of representations for data in files and of operations for accessing the data. A file structure allows applications to read, write, and modify data. It might also support finding the data that matches some search criteria or reading through the data in some particular order. An improvement in file structure design may make an application hundreds of times faster. The details of the representation of the data and the implementation of the operations determine the efficiency of the file structure for particular applications.

A tremendous variety in the types of data and in the needs of applications makes file structure design very important. What is best for one situation may be terrible for another.

1.2   A Short History of File Structure Design

Our goal is to show you how to think creatively about file structure design problems. Part of our approach draws on history: after introducing basic principles of design, we devote the last part of this book to studying some of the key developments in file design over the last thirty years. The problems that researchers struggle with reflect the same issues that you confront in addressing any substantial file design problem. Working through the approaches to major file design issues shows you a lot about how to approach new design problems.

The general goals of research and development in file structures can be drawn directly from our library analogy.

- Ideally, we would like to get the information we need with one access to the disk. In terms of our analogy, we do not want to issue a series of fifty-eight-day requests before we get what we want.

- If it is impossible to get what we need in one access, we want structures that allow us to find the target information with as few accesses as possible. For example, you may remember from your studies of data structures that a binary search allows us to find a particular record among fifty thousand other records with no more than sixteen comparisons. But having to look sixteen places on a disk before finding what we want takes too much time. We need file structures that allow us to find what we need with only two or three trips to the disk.

- We want our file structures to group information so we are likely to get everything we need with only one trip to the disk. If we need a client's name, address, phone number, and account balance, we would prefer to get all that information at once, rather than having to look in several places for it.

It is relatively easy to come up with file structure designs that meet these goals when we have files that never change. Designing file structures that maintain these qualities as files change, grow, or shrink when information is added and deleted is much more difficult.

Early work with files presumed that files were on tape, since most files were. Access was sequential, and the cost of access grew in direct proportion to the size of the file. As files grew intolerably large for unaided sequential access and as storage devices such as disk drives became available, indexes were added to files. The indexes made it possible to keep a list of keys and pointers in a smaller file that could be searched more quickly. With the key and pointer, the user had direct access to the large, primary file.

Unfortunately, simple indexes had some of the same sequential flavor as the data files, and as the indexes grew, they too became difficult to manage, especially for dynamic files in which the set of keys changes. Then, in the early 1960s, the idea of applying tree structures emerged. Unfortunately, trees can grow very unevenly as records are added and deleted, resulting in long searches requiring many disk accesses to find a record.

In 1963 researchers developed the tree, an elegant, self-adjusting binary tree structure, called an AVL tree, for data in memory. Other researchers began to look for ways to apply AVL trees, or something like them, to files. The problem was that even with a balanced binary tree, dozens of accesses were required to find a record in even moderate-sized files. A method was needed to keep a tree balanced when each node of the tree was not a single record, as in a binary tree, but a file block containing dozens, perhaps even hundreds, of records.

It took nearly ten more years of design work before a solution emerged in the form of the *B-tree*. Part of the reason finding a solution took so long was that the approach required for file structures was very different from the approach that worked in memory. Whereas AVL trees grow from the top down as records are added, B-trees grow from the bottom up.

B-trees provided excellent access performance, but there was a cost: no longer could a file be accessed sequentially with efficiency. Fortunately, this problem was solved almost immediately by adding a linked list structure at the bottom level of the B-tree. The combination of a B-tree and a sequential linked list is called a *B+ tree*.

Over the next ten years, B-trees and B+ trees became the basis for many commercial file systems, since they provide access times that grow in proportion to $\log_k N$, where N is the number of entries in the file and k is the number of entries indexed in a single block of the B-tree structure. In practical terms, this means that B-trees can guarantee that you can find one file entry among millions of others with only three or four trips to the disk. Further, B-trees guarantee that as you add and delete entries, performance stays about the same.

Being able to retrieve information with just three or four accesses is pretty good. But how about our goal of being able to get what we want with a single request? An approach called *hashing* is a good way to do that with files that do not change size greatly over time. From early on, hashed indexes were used to provide fast access to files. However, until recently, hashing did not work well with volatile, dynamic files. After the development of B-trees, researchers turned to work on systems for extendible, dynamic hashing that could retrieve information with one or, at most, two disk accesses no matter how big the file became.

1.3   A Conceptual Toolkit: File Structure Literacy

As we move through the developments in file structures over the last three decades, watching file structure design evolve as it addresses dynamic files first sequentially, then through tree structures, and finally through direct access, we see that the same design problems and design tools keep emerging. We decrease the number of disk accesses by collecting data into buffers, blocks, or buckets; we manage the growth of these collections by splitting them, which requires that we find a way to increase our address or index space, and so on. Progress takes the form of finding new ways to combine these basic tools of file design.

We think of these tools as *conceptual* tools. They are methods of framing and addressing a design problem. Each tool combines ways of representing data with specific operations. Our own work in file structures has shown us that by understanding the tools thoroughly and by studying how the tools have evolved to produce such diverse approaches as B-trees and extendible hashing, we develop mastery and flexibility in our own use of the tools. In other words, we acquire literacy with regard to file structures. This text is designed to help readers acquire file structure literacy. Chapters 2 through 6 introduce the basic tools; Chapters 7 through 11 introduce readers to the highlights of the past several decades of file structure design, showing how the basic tools are used to handle efficient sequential access—B-trees, B+ trees, hashed indexes, and extendible, dynamic hashed files.

1.4   An Object-Oriented Toolkit: Making File Structures Usable

Making file structures usable in application development requires turning this conceptual toolkit into application programming interfaces— collections of data types and operations that can be used in applications. We have chosen to employ an object-oriented approach in which data types and operations are presented in a unified fashion as *class* definitions. Each particular approach to representing some aspect of a file structure is represented by one or more classes of objects.

A major problem in describing the classes that can be used for file structure design is that they are complicated and progressive. New classes are often modifications or extensions of other classes, and the details of the data representations and operations become ever more complex. The most effective strategy for describing these classes is to give specific representations in the simplest fashion. In this text, use the C++ programming language to give precise specifications to the file structure classes. From the first chapter to the last, this allows us to build one class on top of another in a concise and understandable fashion.

1.5   Using Objects in C++

In an object-oriented information system, data content and behavior are integrated into a single design. The objects of the system are divided into classes of objects with common characteristics. Each class is described by its *members*, which are either data attributes *(data members)* or functions *(member functions* or *methods)*. This book illustrates the principles of object-oriented design through implementations of file structures and file operations as C++ classes. These classes are also an extensive presentation of the features of C++. In this section, we look at some of the features of objects in C++, including class definitions, constructors, public and private sections, and operator overloading. Later chapters show how to make effective use of inheritance, virtual functions, and templates.

An example of a very simple C++ class is `Person`, as given below.

```
class Person
{ public:
    // data members
    char LastName [11], FirstName [11], Address [16];
    char City [16], State [3], ZipCode [10];
    // method
    Person ();   // default constructor
};
```

Each `Person` object has first and last names, address, city, state, and zip code, which are declared as members, just as they would be in a C `struct`. For an object `p` of type `Person`, `p.LastName` refers to its `LastName` member.

The `public` label specifies that the following members and methods are part of the interface to objects of the class. These members and methods can be freely accessed by any users of `Person` objects. There are three levels of access to class members: `public`, `private`, and `protected`. The last two restrict access and will be described later in the book. The only significant difference in C++ between `struct` and `class` is that for `struct` members the default access is `public`, and for `class` members the default access is `private`.

Each of these member fields is represented by a character array of fixed size. However, the usual style of dealing with character arrays in C++ is to represent the value of the array as a null-delimited, variable-sized string with a maximum length. The number of characters in the representation of a string is one more than the number of characters in the string. The `LastName` field, for example, is represented by an array of eleven characters and can hold a string of length between 0 and 10. Proper use of strings in C++ is dependent on ensuring that every string variable is initialized before it is used.

C++ includes special methods called *constructors* that are used to provide a guarantee that every object is properly initialized.[1] A constructor is a method with no return type whose name is the same as the class. Whenever an object is created, a constructor is called. The two ways that objects are created in C++ are by the declaration of a variable (automatic creation) and by the execution of a `new` operation (dynamic creation):

---

1. A *destructor* is a method of a class that is executed whenever an object is destroyed. A destructor for class `Person` has definition `~Person ()`. Examples of destructors are given in later chapters.

```
Person p; // automatic creation
Person * p_ptr = new Person; // dynamic creation
```

Execution of either of the object creation statements above includes the execution of the `Person` constructor. Hence, we are sure that every `Person` object has been properly initialized before it is used. The code for the `Person` constructor initializes each member to an empty string by assigning 0 (null) to the first character:

```
Person::Person ()
{ // set each field to an empty string
   LastName [0] = 0; FirstName [0] = 0; Address [0] = 0;
   City [0] = 0; State [0] = 0; ZipCode [0] = 0;
}
```

The symbol :: is the *scope resolution operator.* In this case, it tells us that `Person()` is a method of class `Person`. Notice that within the method code, the members can be referenced without the dot (.) operator. Every call on a member function has a pointer to an object as a hidden argument. The implicit argument can be explicitly referred to with the keyword `this`. Within the method, `this->LastName` is the same as `LastName`.

Overloading of symbols in programming languages allows a particular symbol to have more than one meaning. The meaning of each instance of the symbol depends on the context. We are very familiar with overloading of arithmetic operators to have different meanings depending on the operand type. For example, the symbol + is used for both integer and floating point addition. C++ supports the use of overloading by programmers for a wide variety of symbols. We can create new meanings for operator symbols and for named functions.

The following class `String` illustrates extensive use of overloading: there are three constructors, and the operators = and == are overloaded with new meanings:

```
class String
{public:
   String (); // default constructor
   String (const String&); //copy constructor
   String (const char *); // create from C string
   ~String (); // destructor
   String & operator = (const String &); // assignment
   int operator == (const String &) const; // equality
   char * operator char*() // conversion to char *
      {return strdup(string);} // inline body of method
private:
```

```
    char * string; // represent value as C string
    int MaxLength;
};
```

The data members, `string` and `MaxLength`, of class `String` are in the `private` section of the class. Access to these members is restricted. They can be referenced only from inside the code of methods of the class. Hence, users of `String` objects cannot directly manipulate these members. A conversion operator (`operator char *`) has been provided to allow the use of the value of a `String` object as a C string. The body of this operator is given *inline*, that is, directly in the class definition. To protect the value of the `String` from direct manipulation, a copy of the string value is returned. This operator allows a `String` object to be used as a `char *`. For example, the following code creates a `String` object `s1` and copies its value to normal C string:

```
String s1 ("abcdefg"); // uses String::String (const char *)
char str[10];
strcpy (str, s1); // uses String::operator char * ()
```

The new definition of the assignment operator (`operator =`) replaces the standard meaning, which in C and C++ is to copy the bit pattern of one object to another. For two objects `s1` and `s2` of class `String`, `s1 = s2` would copy the value of `s1.string` (a pointer) to `s2.string`. Hence, `s1.string` and `s2.string` point to the same character array. In essence, `s1` and `s2` become aliases. Once the two fields point to the same array, a change in the string value of `s1` would also change `s2`. This is contrary to how we expect variables to behave. The implementation of the assignment operator and an example of its use are:

```
String & String::operator = (const String & str)
{ // code for assignment operator
     strcpy (string, str.string);
     return *this;
}
String s1, s2;
s1 = s2; // using overloaded assignment
```

In the assignment `s1 = s2`, the hidden argument (`this`) refers to `s1`, and the explicit argument `str` refers to `s2`. The line `strcpy (string, str.string);` copies the contents of the string member of `s2` to the string member of `s1`. This assignment operator does not create the alias problem that occurs with the standard meaning of assignment.

To complete the class `String`, we add the copy constructor, which is used whenever a copy of a string is needed, and the equality operator (`operator ==`), which makes two `String` objects equal if the array contents are the same. The predefined meaning for these operators performs pointer copy and pointer comparison, respectively. The full specification and implementation of class `String` are given in Appendix G.

SUMMARY

The key design problem that shapes file structure design is the relatively large amount of time that is required to get information from a disk. All file structure designs focus on minimizing disk accesses and maximizing the likelihood that the information the user will want is already in memory.

This text begins by introducing the basic concepts and issues associated with file structures. The last half of the book tracks the development of file structure design as it has evolved over the last thirty years. The key problem addressed throughout this evolution has been finding ways to minimize disk accesses for files that keep changing in content and size. Tracking these developments takes us first through work on sequential file access, then through developments in tree-structured access, and finally to relatively recent work on direct access to information in files.

Our experience has been that the study of the principal research and design contributions to file structures—focusing on how the design work uses the same tools in new ways—provides a solid foundation for thinking creatively about new problems in file structure design. The presentation of these tools in an object-oriented design makes them tremendously useful in solving real problems.

Object-oriented programming supports the integration of data content and behavior into a single design. C++ class definitions contain both data and function members and allow programmers to control precisely the manipulation of objects. The use of overloading, constructors, and private members enhances the programmer's ability to control the behavior of objects.

KEY TERMS

AVL tree. A self-adjusting binary tree structure that can guarantee good access times for data in memory.

B-tree. A tree structure that provides fast access to data stored in files. Unlike binary trees, in which the branching factor from a node of the tree is two, the descendants from a node of a B-tree can be a much larger number. We introduce B-trees in Chapter 9.

B+ tree. A variation on the B-tree structure that provides sequential access to the data as well as fast-indexed access. We discuss B+ trees at length in Chapter 10.

Class. The specification of the common data attributes (members) and functions (methods) of a collection of objects.

Constructor. A function that initializes an object when it is created. C++ automatically adds a call to a constructor for each operation that creates an object.

Extendible hashing. An approach to hashing that works well with files that over time undergo substantial changes in size.

File structures. The organization of data on secondary storage devices such as disks.

Hashing. An access mechanism that transforms the search key into a storage address, thereby providing very fast access to stored data.

Member. An attribute of an object that is included in a class specification. Members are either data fields or functions (methods).

Method. A function member of an object. Methods are included in class specifications.

Overloaded symbol. An operator or identifier in a program that has more than one meaning. The context of the use of the symbol determines its meaning.

Private. The most restrictive access control level in C++. Private names can be used only by member functions of the class.

Public. The least restrictive access control level in C++. Public names can be used in any function.

Sequential access. Access that takes records in order, looking at the first, then the next, and so on.

FURTHER READINGS

There are many good introductory textbooks on C++ and object-oriented programming, including Berry (1997), Friedman and Koffman (1994), and Sessions (1992). The second edition of Stroustrup's book on C++ (1998) is the standard reference for the language. The third edition of Stroustrup (1997) is a presentation of the Draft Standard for C++ 3.0.

PROGRAMMING PROJECT

This is the first part of an object-oriented programming project that continues throughout the book. Each part extends the project with new file structures. We begin by introducing two classes of data objects. These projects apply the concepts of the book to produce an information system that maintains and processes information about students and courses.

1. Design a class `Student`. Each object represents information about a single student. Members should be included for identifier, name, address, date of first enrollment, and number of credit hours completed. Methods should be included for initalization (constructors), assignment (overloaded "=" operator), and modifying field values, including a method to increment the number of credit hours.

2. Design a class `CourseRegistration`. Each object represents the enrollment of a student in a course. Members should be included for a course identifier, student identifier, number of credit hours, and course grade. Methods should be included as appropriate.

3. Create a list of student and course registration information. This information will be used in subsequent exercises to test and evaluate the capabilities of the programming project.

The next part of the programming project is in Chapter 2.

Fundamental File Processing Operations

2

❖ Describe the process of linking a *logical file* within a program to an actual *physical file* or device.

❖ Describe the procedures used to create, open, and close files.

❖ Introduce the C++ input and output classes.

❖ Explain the use of overloading in C++.

❖ Describe the procedures used for reading from and writing to files.

❖ Introduce the concept of *position* within a file and describe procedures for *seeking* different positions.

❖ Provide an introduction to the organization of hierarchical file systems.

❖ Present the Unix view of a file and describe Unix file operations and commands based on this view.

CHAPTER OUTLINE

2.1 Physical Files and Logical Files

When we talk about a file on a disk or tape, we refer to a particular collection of bytes stored there. A file, when the word is used in this sense, physically exists. A disk drive might contain hundreds, even thousands, of these *physical files*.

From the standpoint of an application program, the notion of a file is different. To the program, a file is somewhat like a telephone line connected to a telephone network. The program can receive bytes through this phone line or send bytes down it, but it knows nothing about where these bytes come from or where they go. The program knows only about its own end of the phone line. Moreover, even though there may be thousands of physical files on a disk, a single program is usually limited to the use of only about twenty files.

The application program relies on the operating system to take care of the details of the telephone switching system, as illustrated in Fig. 2.1. It could be that bytes coming down the line into the program originate from a physical file or that they come from the keyboard or some other input device. Similarly, the bytes the program sends down the line might end up in a file, or they could appear on the terminal screen. Although the program often doesn't know where bytes are coming from or where they are going, it does know which line it is using. This line is usually referred to as the *logical file* to distinguish it from the *physical files* on the disk or tape.

Before the program can open a file for use, the operating system must receive instructions about making a hookup between a logical file (for example, a phone line) and some physical file or device. When using operating systems such as IBM's OS/MVS, these instructions are provided through job control language (JCL). On minicomputers and microcomputers, more modern operating systems such as Unix, MS-DOS, and VMS provide the instructions within the program. For example, in Cobol,[1] the association between a logical file called `inp_file` and a physical file called `myfile.dat` is made with the following statement:

```
select inp_file assign to "myfile.dat".
```

This statement asks the operating system to find the physical file named `myfile.dat` and then to make the hookup by assigning a logical file (phone line) to it. The number identifying the particular phone line that is assigned is returned through the variable `inp_file`, which is the file's *logical name*. This logical name is what we use to refer to the file inside the program. Again, the telephone analogy applies: My office phone is connected to six telephone lines. When I receive a call I get an intercom message such as, "You have a call on line three." The receptionist does not say, "You have a call from 918-123-4567." I need to have the call identified *logically*, not *physically*.

2.2   Opening Files

Once we have a logical file identifier hooked up to a physical file or device, we need to declare what we intend to do with the file. In general, we have two options: (1) open an *existing* file, or (2) create a *new* file, deleting any existing contents in the physical file. Opening a file makes it ready for use by the program. We are positioned at the beginning of the file and are

---

1. These values are defined in an "include" file packaged with your Unix system or C compiler. The name of the include file is often `fcntl.h` or `file.h`, but it can vary from system to system.

Figure 2.1 The program relies on the operating system to make connections between logical files and physical files and devices.

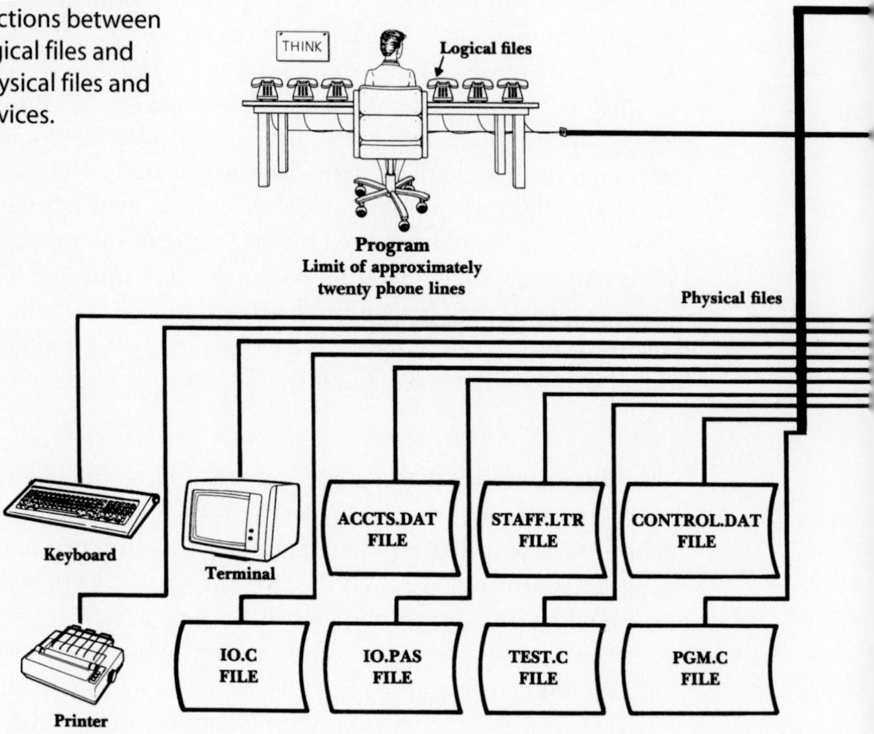

ready to start reading or writing. The file contents are not disturbed by the open statement. Creating a file also opens the file in the sense that it is ready for use after creation. Because a newly created file has no contents, writing is initially the only use that makes sense.

As an example of opening an existing file or creating a new one in C and C++, consider the function open, as defined in header file fcntl.h. Although this function is based on a Unix system function, many C++ implementations for MS-DOS and Windows, including Microsoft Visual C++, also support open and the other parts of fcntl.h. This function takes two required arguments and a third argument that is optional:

```
fd = open(filename, flags [, pmode]);
```

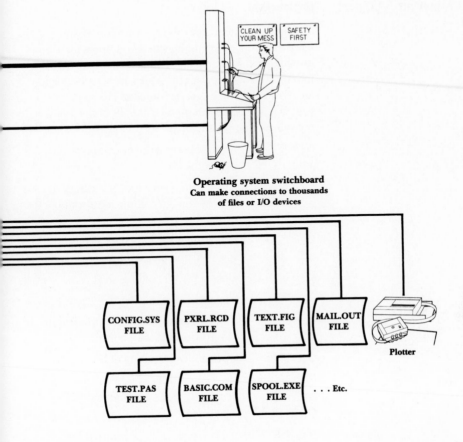

Operating system switchboard
Can make connections to thousands
of files or I/O devices

The return value `fd` and the arguments `filename`, `flags`, and `pmode` have the following meanings:

Argument	Type	Explanation
`fd`	`int`	The file descriptor. Using our earlier analogy, this is the phone line (logical file identifier) used to refer to the file within the program. It is an integer. If there is an error in the attempt to open the file, this value is negative.
`filename`	`char *`	A character string containing the physical file name. (Later we discuss pathnames that include directory information about the file's location. This argument can be a pathname.)

(continued)

Argument	Type	Explanation
flags	int	The flags argument controls the operation of the open function, determining whether it opens an existing file for reading or writing. It can also be used to indicate that you want to create a new file or open an existing file but delete its contents. The value of flags is set by performing a bit-wise OR of the following values, among others.

O_APPEND	Append every write operation to the end of the file.
O_CREAT	Create and open a file for writing. This has no effect if the file already exists.
O_EXCL	Return an error if O_CREATE is specified and the file exists.
O_RDONLY	Open a file for reading only.
O_RDWR	Open a file for reading and writing.
O_TRUNC	If the file exists, truncate it to a length of zero, destroying its contents.
O_WRONLY	Open a file for writing only.

Some of these flags cannot be used in combination with one another. Consult your documentation for details and for other options.

Argument	Type	Explanation
pmode	int	If O_CREAT is specified, pmode is required. This integer argument specifies the protection mode for the file. In Unix, the pmode is a three-digit octal number that indicates how the file can be used by the owner (first digit), by members of the owner's group (second digit), and by everyone else (third digit). The first bit of each octal digit indicates read permission, the second write permission, and the third execute permission. So, if pmode is the octal number 0751, the file's owner has read, write, and execute permission for the file; the owner's group has read and execute permission; and everyone else has only execute permission:

```
                    r w e   r w e   r w e
pmode = 0751 =      1 1 1   1 0 1   0 0 1
                    owner   group   world
```

Given this description of the open function, we can develop some examples to show how it can be used to open and create files in C. The following function call opens an existing file for reading and writing or creates a new one if necessary. If the file exists, it is opened without change; reading or writing would start at the file's first byte.

```
fd = open(filename, O_RDWR | O_CREAT, 0751);
```

The following call creates a new file for reading and writing. If there is already a file with the name specified in filename, its contents are truncated.

```
fd = open(filename, O_RDWR | O_CREAT | O_TRUNC, 0751);
```

Finally, here is a call that will create a new file only if there is not already a file with the name specified in filename. If a file with this name exists, it is not opened, and the function returns a negative value to indicate an error.

```
fd = open(filename, O_RDWR | O_CREAT | O_EXCL, 0751);
```

File protection is tied more to the host operating system than to a specific language. For example, implementations of C running on systems that support file protection, such as VAX/VMS, often include extensions to standard C that let you associate a protection status with a file when you create it.

2.3   Closing Files

In terms of our telephone line analogy, closing a file is like hanging up the phone. When you hang up the phone, the phone line is available for taking or placing another call; when you close a file, the logical file name or file descriptor is available for use with another file. Closing a file that has been used for output also ensures that everything has been written to the file. As you will learn in a later chapter, it is more efficient to move data to and from secondary storage in blocks than it is to move data one byte at a time. Consequently, the operating system does not immediately send off the bytes we write but saves them up in a buffer for transfer as a block of data. Closing a file ensures that the buffer for that file has been flushed of data and that everything we have written has been sent to the file.

Files are usually closed automatically by the operating system when a program terminates normally. Consequently, the execution of a close statement within a program is needed only to protect it against data loss in the event that the program is interrupted and to free up logical filenames for reuse.

Now that you know how to connect and disconnect programs to and from physical files and how to open the files, you are ready to start sending and receiving data.

2.4 Reading and Writing

Reading and *writing* are fundamental to file processing; they are the actions that make file processing an *input/output* (I/O) operation. The form of the read and write statements used in different languages varies. Some languages provide very high-level access to reading and writing and automatically take care of details for the programmer. Other languages provide access at a much lower level. Our use of C and C++ allows us to explore some of these differences.[2]

2.4.1 Read and Write Functions

We begin with reading and writing at a relatively low level. It is useful to have a kind of systems-level understanding of what happens when we send and receive information to and from a file.

A low-level read call requires three pieces of information, expressed here as arguments to a generic Read function:

```
Read (Source_file, Destination_addr, Size)
```

Source_file   The Read call must know where it is to read from. We specify the source by logical file name (phone line) through which data is received. (Remember, before we do any reading, we must have already opened the file so the connection between a logical file and a specific physical file or device exists.)

Destination_addr   Read must know where to place the information it reads from the input file. In this generic function we specify the destination by giving the first address of the memory block where we want to store the data.

Size   Finally, Read must know how much information to bring in from the file. Here the argument is supplied as a byte count.

---

2. To accentuate the differences and view I/O operations at something close to a systems level, we use the fread and fwrite functions in C rather than the higher-level functions such as fgetc, fgets, and so on.

A `Write` statement is similar; the only difference is that the data moves in the other direction:

```
Write(Destination_file, Source_addr, Size)
```

`Destination_file`	The logical file name that is used for sending the data.
`Source_addr`	`Write` must know where to find the information it will send. We provide this specification as the first address of the memory block where the data is stored.
`Size`	The number of bytes to be written must be supplied.

2.4.2 Files with C Streams and C++ Stream Classes

I/O operations in C and C++ are based on the concept of a stream, which can be a file or some other source or consumer of data. There are two different styles for manipulating files in C++. The first uses the standard C functions defined in header file `stdio.h`. This is often referred to as *C streams* or *C input/output*. The second uses the stream classes of header files `iostream.h` and `fstream.h`. We refer to this style as *C++ stream classes*.

The header file `stdio.h` contains definitions of the types and the operations defined on C streams. The standard input and output of a C program are streams called `stdin` and `stdout`, respectively. Other files can be associated with streams through the use of the `fopen` function:

```
file = fopen (filename, type);
```

The return value `file` and the arguments `filename` and `type` have the following meanings:

Argument	Type	Explanation
`file`	`FILE *`	A pointer to the file descriptor. Type `FILE` is another name for `struct _iobuf`. If there is an error in the attempt to open the file, this value is null, and the variable `errno` is set with the error number.
`filename`	`char *`	The file name, just as in the Unix open function.
`type`	`char *`	The `type` argument controls the operation of the open function, much like the flags argument to open. The following values are supported:

`"r"`	Open an existing file for input.
`"w"`	Create a new file, or truncate an existing one, for output.

> "a"   Create a new file, or append to an existing
>   one, for output.
>
> "r+"   Open an existing file for input and output.
>
> "w+"   Create a new file, or truncate an existing one,
>   for input and output.
>
> "a+"   Create a new file, or append to an existing
>   one, for input and output.

Read and write operations are supported by functions `fread`, `fget`, `fwrite`, and `fput`. Functions `fscanf` and `fprintf` are used for formatted input and output.

Stream classes in C++ support open, close, read, and write operations that are equivalent to those in `stdio.h`, but the syntax is considerably different. Predefined stream objects `cin` and `cout` represent the standard input and standard output files. The main class for access to files, `fstream`, as defined in header files `iostream.h` and `fstream.h`, has two constructors and a wide variety of methods. The following constructors and methods are included in the class:

```
fstream (); // leave the stream unopened
fstream (char * filename, int mode);
int open (char * filename, int mode);
int read (unsigned char * dest_addr, int size);
int write (unsigned char * source_addr, int size);
```

The argument `filename` of the second constructor and the method `open` are just as we've seen before. These two operations attach the `fstream` to a file. The value of `mode` controls the way the file is opened, like the `flags` and `type` arguments previously described. The value is set with a bit-wise or of constants defined in class `ios`. Among the options are `ios::in` (input), `ios::out` (output), `ios::nocreate` (fail if the file does not exist), and `ios::noreplace` (fail if the file does exist). One additional, nonstandard option, `ios::binary`, is supported on many systems to specify that a file is binary. On MS-DOS systems, if `ios::binary` is not specified, the file is treated as a text file. This can have some unintended consequences, as we will see later.

A large number of functions are provided for formatted input and output. The overloading capabilities of C++ are used to make sure that objects are formatted according to their types. The infix operators >>(extraction) and <<(insertion) are overloaded for input and output, respectively. The header file `iostream.h` includes the following overloaded definitions of the insertion operator (and many others):

```
ostream& operator<<(char c);
ostream& operator<<(unsigned char c);
ostream& operator<<(signed char c);
ostream& operator<<(const char *s);
ostream& operator<<(const unsigned char *s);
ostream& operator<<(const signed char *s);
ostream& operator<<(const void *p);
ostream& operator<<(int n);
ostream& operator<<(unsigned int n);
ostream& operator<<(long n);
ostream& operator<<(unsigned long n);
```

The overloading resolution rules of C++ specify which function is selected for a particular call depending on the types of the actual arguments and the types of the formal parameters. In this case, the insertion function that is used to evaluate an expression depends on the type of the arguments, particularly the right argument. Consider the following statements that include insertions into cout (an object of class ostream):

```
int n = 25;
cout << "Value of n is "<< n << endl;
```

The insertion operators are evaluated left to right, and each one returns its left argument as the result. Hence, the stream cout has first the string "Value of n is " inserted, using the fourth function in the list above, then the decimal value of n, using the eighth function in the list. The last operand is the I/O manipulator endl, which causes an end-of-line to be inserted. The insertion function that is used for << endl is not in the list above. The header file iostream.h includes the definition of endl and the operator that is used for this insertion.

Appendix C includes definitions and examples of many of the formatted input and output operations.

2.4.3 Programs in C++ to Display the Contents of a File

Let's do some reading and writing to see how these functions are used. This first simple file processing program opens a file for input and reads it, character by character, sending each character to the screen after it is read from the file. This program includes the following steps:

1. Display a prompt for the name of the input file.
2. Read the user's response from the keyboard into a variable called filename.

3. Open the file for input.
4. While there are still characters to be read from the input file,

   a. read a character from the file;

   b. write the character to the terminal screen.
5. Close the input file.

Figures 2.2 and 2.3 are C++ implementations of this program using C streams and C++ stream classes, respectively. It is instructive to look at the differences between these implementations. The full implementations of these programs are included in Appendix D.

Steps 1 and 2 of the program involve writing and reading, but in each of the implementations this is accomplished through the usual functions for handling the screen and keyboard. Step 4a, in which we read from the input file, is the first instance of actual file I/O. Note that the fread call using C streams parallels the low-level, generic Read statement we described earlier; in truth, we used the fread function as the model for our low-level Read. The function's first argument gives the *address* of a character variable used as the *destination* for the data, the second and third arguments are the element size and the number of elements (in this case the size is 1 byte, and the number of elements is one), and the fourth argument gives a pointer to the file descriptor (the C stream version of a logical file name) as the *source* for the input.

```
// listc.cpp
// program using C streams to read characters from a file
// and write them to the terminal screen
#include <stdio.h>
main( ) {
   char ch;
   FILE * file; // pointer to file descriptor
   char filename[20];
   printf("Enter the name of the file: ");    // Step 1
   gets(filename);                             // Step 2
   file =fopen(filename, "r");                 // Step 3
   while (fread(&ch, 1, 1, file) != 0)         // Step 4a
     fwrite(&ch, 1, 1, stdout);                // Step 4b
   fclose(file);                               // Step 5
}
```

Figure 2.2 The file listing program using C streams (listc.cpp).

```
// listcpp.cpp
// list contents of file using C++ stream classes
#include <fstream.h>
main () {
   char ch;
   fstream file; // declare unattached fstream
   char filename[20];
   cout <<"Enter the name of the file: " // Step 1
      <<flush; // force output
   cin >> filename;                         // Step 2
   file . open(filename, ios::in);       // Step 3
   file . unsetf(ios::skipws);// include white space in read
   while (1)
   {
      file >> ch;                         // Step 4a
      if (file.fail()) break;
      cout << ch;                         // Step 4b
   }
   file . close();                       // Step 5
}
```

Figure 2.3 The file listing program using C++ stream classes (listcpp.cpp).

The arguments for the call to operator >> communicate the same information at a higher level. The first argument is the logical file name for the input source. The second argument is the name of a character variable, which is interpreted as the address of the variable. The overloading resolution selects the >> operator whose right argument is a char variable. Hence, the code *implies* that only a single byte is to be transferred. In the C++ version, the call file.unsetf(ios::skipws) causes operator >> to include white space (blanks, end-of-line, tabs, and so on). The default for formatted read with C++ stream classes is to skip white space.

After a character is read, we write it to standard output in Step 4b. Once again the differences between C streams and C++ stream classes indicate the range of approaches to I/O used in different languages. Everything must be stated explicitly in the fwrite call. Using the special assigned file descriptor of stdout to identify the terminal screen as the destination for our writing,

```
fwrite(&ch, 1, 1, stdout);
```

means: "Write to standard output the contents from memory starting at the address &ch. Write only one element of one byte." Beginning C++ programmers should pay special attention to the use of the & symbol in the `fwrite` call here. This particular call, as a very low-level call, requires that the programmer provide the starting *address* in memory of the bytes to be transferred.

`Stdout`, which stands for "standard output," is a pointer to a struct defined in the file `stdio.h`, which has been included at the top of the program. The concept of standard output and its counterpart standard input are covered later in Section 2.8 "Physical and Logical Files."

Again the C++ stream code operates at a higher level. The right operand of operator `<<` is a character value. Hence a single byte is transferred to `cout`.

```
cout << ch;
```

As in the call to operator `>>`, C++ takes care of finding the *address* of the bytes; the programmer need specify only the name of the variable ch that is associated with that address.

2.4.4 Detecting End-of-File

The programs in Figs. 2.2 and 2.3 have to know when to end the `while` loop and stop reading characters. C streams and C++ streams signal the end-of-file condition differently. The function `fread` returns a value that indicates whether the read succeeded. However, an explicit test is required to see if the C++ stream `read` has failed.

The `fread` call returns the number of elements read as its value. In this case, if `fread` returns a value of zero, the program has reached the end of the file. So we construct the `while` loop to run as long as the `fread` call finds something to read.

Each C++ stream has a state that can be queried with function calls. Figure 2.3 uses the function `fail`, which returns true (1) if the previous operation on the stream failed. In this case, `file.fail()` returns false if the previous read failed because of trying to read past end-of-file. The following statement exits the `while` loop when end-of-file is encountered:

```
if (file.fail()) break;
```

In some languages, including Ada, a function `end_of_file` can be used to test for end-of-file. As we read from a file, the operating system keeps track of our location in the file with a *read/write pointer*. This is necessary: when the next byte is read, the system knows where to get it. The `end_of_file` function queries the system to see whether the read/write pointer has moved past the last element in the file. If it has, `end_of_file` returns true; otherwise it returns false. In Ada, it is necessary to call `end_of_file` before trying to read the next byte. For an empty file, `end_of_file` immediately returns `true`, and no bytes can be read.

2.5 Seeking

In the preceding sample programs we read through the file *sequentially,* reading one byte after another until we reach the end of the file. Every time a byte is read, the operating system moves the read/write pointer ahead, and we are ready to read the next byte.

Sometimes we want to read or write without taking the time to go through every byte sequentially. Perhaps we know that the next piece of information we need is ten thousand bytes away, so we want to jump there. Or perhaps we need to jump to the end of the file so we can add new information there. To satisfy these needs we must be able to control the movement of the read/write pointer.

The action of moving directly to a certain position in a file is often called *seeking*. A *seek* requires at least two pieces of information, expressed here as arguments to the generic pseudocode function `Seek`:

```
Seek(Source_file, Offset)
```

`Source_file` The logical file name in which the seek will occur.

`Offset` The number of positions in the file the pointer is to be moved from the start of the file.

Now, if we want to move directly from the origin to the 373d position in a file called `data`, we don't have to move sequentially through the first 372 positions. Instead, we can say

```
Seek(data, 373)
```

2.5.1 Seeking with C Streams

One of the features of Unix that has been incorporated into C streams is the ability to view a file as a potentially very large *array of bytes* that just happens to be kept on secondary storage. In an array of bytes in memory, we can move to any particular byte using a subscript. The C stream seek function, fseek, provides a similar capability for files. It lets us set the read/write pointer to any byte in a file.

The fseek function has the following form:

```
pos = fseek(file, byte_offset, origin)
```

where the variables have the following meanings:

pos   A long integer value returned by fseek equal to the position (in bytes) of the read/write pointer after it has been moved.

file   The file descriptor of the file to which the fseek is to be applied.

byte_offset   The number of bytes to move from some origin in the file. The byte offset must be specified as a long integer, hence the name fseek for long seek. When appropriate, the byte_offset can be negative.

origin   A value that specifies the starting position from which the byte_offset is to be taken. The origin can have the value 0, 1, or 2[3]

0–fseek from the beginning of the file;

1–fseek from the current position;

2–fseek from the end of the file.

The following definitions are included in stdio.h to allow symbolic reference to the origin values.

```
#define SEEK_SET    0
#define SEEK_CUR    1
#define SEEK_END    2
```

The following program fragment shows how you could use fseek to move to a position that is 373 bytes into a file.

```
long pos;
fseek(File * file, long offset, int origin);
File * file;
.
.
pos=fseek(file, 373L, 0);
```

---

3. Although the values 0, 1, and 2 are almost always used here, they are not guaranteed to work for all C implementations. Consult your documentation.

2.5.2 Seeking with C++ Stream Classes

Seeking in C++ stream classes is almost exactly the same as it is in C streams. There are two mostly syntactic differences:

- An object of type `fstream` has two file pointers: a get pointer for input and a put pointer for output. Two functions are supplied for seeking: `seekg` which moves the get pointer, and `seekp` which moves the put pointer. It is not guaranteed that the pointers move separately, but they might. We have to be very careful in our use of these seek functions and often call both functions together.

- The seek operations are methods of the stream classes. Hence the syntax is `file.seekg(byte_offset,origin)` and `file.seekp(byte_offset,origin)`. The value of origin comes from class ios, which is described in more detail in Chapter 4. The values are ios::beg (beginning of file), ios::cur (current position), and ios::end (end of file).

The following moves both get and put pointers to a byte 373:

```
file.seekg(373, ios::beg);
file.seekp(373, ios::beg);
```

2.6   Special Characters in Files

As you create the file structures described in this text, you may encounter some difficulty with extra, unexpected characters that turn up in your files with characters that disappear and with numeric counts that are inserted into your files. Here are some examples of the kinds of things you might encounter:

- On many computers you may find that a Control-Z (ASCII value of 26) is appended at the end of your files. Some applications use this to indicate end-of-file even if you have not placed it there. This is most likely to happen on MS-DOS systems.

- Some systems adopt a convention of indicating end-of-line in a text file[4] as a pair of characters consisting of a carriage return (CR: ASCII

---

4. When we use the term "text file" in this text, we are referring to a file consisting entirely of characters from a specific standard character set, such as ASCII or EBCDIC. Unless otherwise specified, the ASCII character set will be assumed. Appendix B contains a table that describes the ASCII character set.

value of 13) and a line feed (LF: ASCII value of 10). Sometimes I/O procedures written for such systems automatically expand single CR characters or LF characters into CR-LF pairs. This unrequested addition of characters can cause a great deal of difficulty. Again, you are most likely to encounter this phenomenon on MS-DOS systems. Using flag "b" in a C file or mode ios::bin in a C++ stream will suppress these changes.

■ Users of larger systems, such as VMS, may find that they have just the opposite problem. Certain file formats under VMS *remove* carriage return characters from your file without asking you, replacing them with a *count* of the characters in what the system has perceived as a line of text.

These are just a few examples of the kinds of uninvited modifications that record management systems or that I/O support packages might make to your files. You will find that they are usually associated with the concepts of a line of text or the end of a file. In general, these modifications to your files are an attempt to make your life easier by doing things for you automatically. This might, in fact, work out for those who want to do nothing more than store some text in a file. Unfortunately, however, programmers building sophisticated file structures must sometimes spend a lot of time finding ways to disable this automatic assistance so they can have complete control over what they are building. Forewarned is forearmed: readers who encounter these kinds of difficulties as they build the file structures described in this text can take some comfort from the knowledge that the experience they gain in disabling automatic assistance will serve them well, over and over, in the future.

2.7   The Unix Directory Structure

No matter what computer system you have, even if it is a small PC, chances are there are hundreds or even thousands of files you have access to. To provide convenient access to such large numbers of files, your computer has some method for organizing its files. In Unix this is called the *file system*.

The Unix file system is a tree-structured organization of *directories*, with the *root* of the tree signified by the character /. All directories, including the root, can contain two kinds of files: regular files with programs and

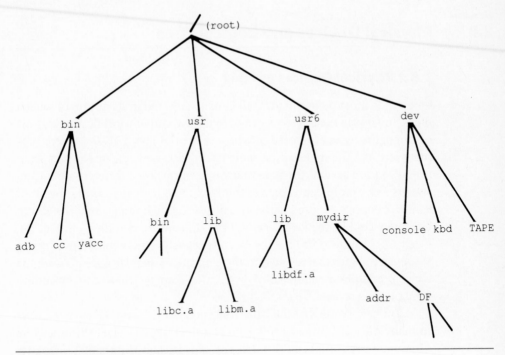

Figure 2.4 Sample Unix directory structure.

data, and directories (Fig. 2.4). Since devices such as tape drives are also treated like files in Unix, directories can also contain references to devices, as shown in the `dev` directory in Fig. 2.4. The file name stored in a Unix directory corresponds to what we call its physical name.

Since every file in a Unix system is part of the file system that begins with the root, any file can be uniquely identified by giving its *absolute pathname*. For instance, the true, unambiguous name of the file "addr" in Fig. 2.4 is `/usr6/mydir/addr`. (Note that the / is used both to indicate the root directory and to separate directory names from the file name.)

When you issue commands to a Unix system, you do so within a directory, which is called your *current directory*. A pathname for a file that does not begin with a / describes the location of a file relative to the current directory. Hence, if your current directory in Fig. 2.4 is `mydir`, `addr` uniquely identifies the file `/usr6/mydir/addr`.

The special filename . stands for the current directory, and .. stands for the parent of the current directory. Hence, if your current directory is `/usr6/mydir/DF`, `../addr` refers to the file `/usr6/mydir/addr`.

2.8 Physical Devices and Logical Files

2.8.1 Physical Devices as Files

One of the most powerful ideas in Unix is reflected in its notion of what a file is. In Unix, a file is a sequence of bytes without any implication of how or where the bytes are stored or where they originate. This simple conceptual view of a file makes it possible to do with very few operations what might require several times as many operations on a different operating system. For example, it is easy to think of a magnetic disk as the source of a file because we are used to the idea of storing such things on disks. But in Unix, devices like the keyboard and the console are also files—in Fig. 2.4, /dev/kbd and /dev/console, respectively. The keyboard produces a sequence of bytes that are sent to the computer when keys are pressed; the console accepts a sequence of bytes and displays their corresponding symbols on a screen.

How can we say that the Unix concept of a file is simple when it allows so many different physical things to be called files? Doesn't this make the situation more complicated, not less so? The trick in Unix is that no matter what physical representation a file may take, the logical view of a Unix file is the same. In its simplest form, a Unix file is represented logically by an integer—the file descriptor. This integer is an index to an array of more complete information about the file. A keyboard, a disk file, and a magnetic tape are all represented by integers. Once the integer that describes a file is identified, a program can access that file. If it knows the logical name of a file, a program can access that file without knowing whether the file comes from a disk, a tape, or a connection to another computer.

Although the above discussion is directed at Unix files, the same capability is available through the stdio functions fopen, fread, and so on. Similar capabilities are present in MS-DOS, Windows, and other operating systems.

2.8.2 The Console, the Keyboard, and Standard Error

We see an example of the duality between devices and files in the listc.cpp program in Fig. 2.2:

```
file =fopen(filename, "r");          // Step 3
while (fread(&ch, 1, 1, file) != 0)  // Step 4a
   fwrite(&ch, 1, 1, stdout);        // Step 4b
```

The logical file is represented by the value returned by the `fopen` call. We assign this integer to the variable `file` in Step 3. In Step 4b, we use the value `stdout`, defined in `stdio.h`, to identify the console as the file to be written to.

There are two other files that correspond to specific physical devices in most implementations of C streams: the keyboard is called `stdin` *(standard input)*, and the error file is called `stderr` *(standard error)*. Hence, `stdin` is the keyboard on your terminal. The statement

```
fread(&ch, 1, 1, stdin);
```

reads a single character from your terminal. `Stderr` is an error file which, like `stdout`, is usually just your console. When your compiler detects an error, it generally writes the error message to this file, which normally means that the error message turns up on your screen. As with `stdin`, the values `stdin` and `stderr` are usually defined in `stdio.h`.

Steps 1 and 2 of the file listing program also involve reading and writing from `stdin` or `stdout`. Since an enormous amount of I/O involves these devices, most programming languages have special functions to perform console input and output—in list.cpp, the C functions `printf` and `gets` are used. Ultimately, however, `printf` and `gets` send their output through `stdout` and `stdin`, respectively. But these statements hide important elements of the I/O process. For our purposes, the second set of read and write statements is more interesting and instructive.

2.8.3 I/O Redirection and Pipes

Suppose you would like to change the file listing program so it writes its output to a regular file rather than to `stdout`. Or suppose you wanted to use the output of the file listing program as input to another program. Because it is common to want to do both of these, operating systems provide convenient shortcuts for switching between standard I/O (`stdin` and `stdout`) and regular file I/O. These shortcuts are called *I/O redirection* and *pipes*.[5]

I/O redirection lets you specify at execution time alternate files for input or output. The notations for input and output redirection on the command line in Unix are

```
< file               (redirect stdin to "file")
> file               (redirect stdout to "file")
```

---

5. Strictly speaking, I/O redirection and pipes are part of a Unix shell, which is the command interpreter that sits on top of the core Unix operating system, the kernel. For the purpose of this discussion, this distinction is not important.

For example, if the executable file listing program is called "list.exe," we redirect the output from `stdout` to a file called "myfile" by entering the line

```
list.exe > myfile
```

What if, instead of storing the output from the list program in a file, you wanted to use it immediately in another program to sort the results? Pipes let you do this. The notation for a pipe in Unix and in MS-DOS is |. Hence,

```
program1 | program2
```

means take any `stdout` output from program1 and use it in place of any `stdin` input to program2. Because Unix has a special program called `sort`, which takes its input from `stdin`, you can sort the output from the list program, without using an intermediate file, by entering

```
list | sort
```

Since `sort` writes its output to `stdout`, the sorted listing appears on your terminal screen unless you use additional pipes or redirection to send it elsewhere.

2.9   File-Related Header Files

Unix, like all operating systems, has special names and values that you must use when performing file operations. For example, some C functions return a special value indicating end-of-file (EOF) when you try to read beyond the end of a file.

Recall the flags that you use in an `open` call to indicate whether you want read-only, write-only, or read/write access. Unless we know just where to look, it is often not easy to find where these values are defined. Unix handles the problem by putting such definitions in special header files such as `/usr/include`, which can be found in special directories.

Header files relevant to the material in this chapter are `stdio.h`, `iostream.h`, `fstream.h`, `fcntl.h`, and `file.h`. The C streams are in `stdio.h`; C++ streams in `iostream.h` and `fstream.h`. Many Unix operations are in `fcntl.h` and `file.h`. EOF, for instance, is defined on many Unix and MS-DOS systems in `stdio.h`, as are the file pointers `stdin`, `stdout`, and `stderr`. And the flags O_RDONLY,

O_WRONLY, and O_RDWR can usually be found in `file.h` or possibly in one of the files that it includes.

It would be instructive for you to browse through these files as well as others that pique your curiosity.

2.10   Unix File System Commands

Unix provides many commands for manipulating files. We list a few that are relevant to the material in this chapter. Most of them have many options, but the simplest uses of most should be obvious. Consult a Unix manual for more information on how to use them.

`cat` *filenames*	Print the contents of the named text files.
`tail` *filename*	Print the last ten lines of the text file.
`cp` *file1 file2*	Copy file1 to file2.
`mv` *file1 file2*	Move (rename) file1 to file2.
`rm` *filenames*	Remove (delete) the named files.
`chmod` *mode filename*	Change the protection mode on the named files.
`ls`	List the contents of the directory.
`mkdir` *name*	Create a directory with the given name.
`rmdir` *name*	Remove the named directory.

SUMMARY

This chapter introduces the fundamental operations of file systems: Open, Create, Close, Read, Write, and Seek. Each of these operations involves the creation or use of a link between a *physical file* stored on a secondary device and a *logical file* that represents a program's more abstract view of the same file. When the program describes an operation using the *logical file name,* the equivalent physical operation gets performed on the corresponding physical file.

The six operations appear in programming languages in many different forms. Sometimes they are built-in commands, sometimes they are functions, and sometimes they are direct calls to an operating system.

Before we can use a physical file, we must link it to a logical file. In some programming environments, we do this with a statement (`select`/`assign` in Cobol) or with instructions outside of the program (operating system shell scripts). In other languages, the link between the physical file and a logical file is made with open or create.

The operations create and open make files ready for reading or writing. Create causes a new physical file to be created. Open operates on an already existing physical file, usually setting the read/write pointer to the beginning of the file. The close operation breaks the link between a logical file and its corresponding physical file. It also makes sure that the file buffer is flushed so everything that was written is actually sent to the file.

The I/O operations `Read` and `Write`, when viewed at a low systems level, require three items of information:

- The *logical name* of the file to be read from or written to;
- An *address* of a memory area to be used for the "inside of the computer" part of the exchange;
- An indication of *how much data* is to be read or written.

These three fundamental elements of the exchange are illustrated in Fig. 2.5.

`Read` and `Write` are sufficient for moving sequentially through a file to any desired position, but this form of access is often very inefficient. Some languages provide seek operations that let a program move directly to a certain position in a file. C provides direct access by means of the `fseek` operation. The `fseek` operation lets us view a file as a kind of large array, giving us a great deal of freedom in deciding how to organize a file.

Another useful file operation involves knowing when the end of a file has been reached. End-of-file detection is handled in different ways by different languages.

Much effort goes into shielding programmers from having to deal with the physical characteristics of files, but inevitably there are little details about the physical organization of files that programmers must know. When we try to have our program operate on files at a very low level

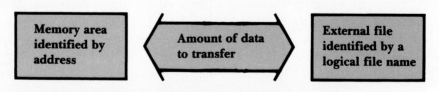

Figure 2.5 The exchange between memory and external device.

(as we do a great deal in this text), we must be on the lookout for little surprises inserted in our file by the operating system or applications.

The Unix file system, called the *file system,* organizes files in a tree structure, with all files and subdirectories expressible by their *pathnames.* It is possible to navigate around the file system as you work with Unix files.

Unix views both physical devices and traditional disk files as files, so, for example, a keyboard (`stdin`), a console (`stdout`), and a tape drive are all considered files. This simple conceptual view of files makes it possible in Unix to do with a very few operations what might require many times the operations on a different operating system.

I/O redirection and *pipes* are convenient shortcuts provided in Unix for transferring file data between files and *standard I/O. Header files* in Unix, such as `stdio.h`, contain special names and values that you must use when performing file operations. It is important to be aware of the most common of these in use on your system.

KEY TERMS

Access mode. Type of file access allowed. The variety of access modes permitted varies from operating system to operating system.

Buffering. When input or output is saved up rather than sent off to its destination immediately, we say that it is *buffered.* In later chapters, we find that we can dramatically improve the performance of programs that read and write data if we buffer the I/O.

Byte offset. The distance, measured in bytes, from the beginning of the file. The first byte in the file has an offset of 0, the second byte has an offset of 1, and so on.

Close. A function or system call that breaks the link between a logical file name and the corresponding physical file name.

Create. A function or system call that causes a file to be created on secondary storage and may also bind a logical name to the file's physical name—see Open. A call to create also results in the generation of information used by the system to manage the file, such as time of creation, physical location, and access privileges for anticipated users of the file.

End-of-file (EOF). An indicator within a file that the end of the file has occurred, a function that tells if the end of a file has been encountered (`end_of_file` in Ada), or a system-specific value that is returned by file-processing functions indicating that the end of a file has been encountered in the process of carrying out the function (EOF in Unix).

File descriptor. A small, nonnegative integer value returned by a Unix `open` or `creat` call that is used as a logical name for the file in later Unix system calls. This value is an index into an array of `FILE` structs that contain information about open files. The C stream functions use `FILE` pointers for their file descriptors.

File system. The name used in Unix and other operating systems to describe a collection of files and directories organized into a tree-structured hierarchy.

Header file. A file that contains definitions and declarations commonly shared among many other files and applications. In C and C++, header files are included in other files by means of the "#include" statement (see Figs. 2.2 and 2.3). The header files `iostream.h`, `stdio.h`, `file.h`, and `fcntl.h` described in this chapter contain important declarations and definitions used in file processing.

I/O redirection. The redirection of a stream of input or output from its normal place. For instance, the operator > can be used to redirect to a file output that would normally be sent to the console.

Logical file. The file as seen by the program. The use of logical files allows a program to describe operations to be performed on a file without knowing what physical file will be used. The program may then be used to process any one of a number of different files that share the same structure.

Open. A function or system call that makes a file ready for use. It may also bind a logical file name to a physical file. Its arguments include the logical file name and the physical file name and may also include information on how the file is expected to be accessed.

Pathname. A character string that describes the location of a file or directory. If the pathname starts with a /, then it gives the *absolute pathname*—the complete path from the root directory to the file. Otherwise it gives the *relative pathname*—the path relative to the current working directory.

Physical file. A file that actually exists on secondary storage. It is the file as known by the computer operating system and that appears in its file directory.

Pipe. A Unix operator specified by the symbol | that carries data from one process to another. The originating process specifies that the data is to go to stdout, and the receiving process expects the data from stdin. For example, to send the standard output from a program makedata to the standard input of a program called usedata, use the command makedata | usedata.

Protection mode. An indication of how a file can be accessed by various classes of users. In Unix, the protection mode is a three-digit octal number that indicates how the file can be read, written to, and executed by the owner, by members of the owner's group, and by everyone else.

Read. A function or system call used to obtain input from a file or device. When viewed at the lowest level, it requires three arguments: (1) a Source file logical name corresponding to an open file; (2) the Destination address for the bytes that are to be read; and (3) the Size or amount of data to be read.

Seek. A function or system call that sets the read/write pointer to a specified position in the file. Languages that provide seeking functions allow programs to access specific elements of a file *directly*, rather than having to read through a file from the beginning *(sequentially)* each time a specific item is desired. In C, the fseek function provides this capability.

Standard I/O. The source and destination conventionally used for input and output. In Unix, there are three types of standard I/O: *standard input* (stdin), *standard output* (stdout), and stderr *(standard error)*. By default stdin is the keyboard, and stdout and stderr are the console screen. I/O redirection and pipes provide ways to override these defaults.

Write. A function or system call used to provide output capabilities. When viewed at the lowest level, it requires three arguments: (1) a Destination file name corresponding to an open file; (2) the Source address of the bytes that are to be written; and (3) the Size or amount of the data to be written.

FURTHER READINGS

Introductory textbooks on C and C++ tend to treat the fundamental file operations only briefly, if at all. This is particularly true with regard to C, since there are higher-level standard I/O functions in C, such as the read operations fget and fgetc. Some books on C and/or UNIX that do provide treatment of the fundamental file operations are Kernighan and Pike (1984) and Kernighan and Ritchie (1988). These books also provide discussions of higher-level I/O functions that we omitted from our text.

An excellent explanation of the input and output classes of C++ is found in Plaugher (1995), which discusses the current (C++ version 2) and proposed draft standard for C++ input and output.

As for Unix specifically, as of this writing there are many flavors of Unix including Unix System V from AT&T, the originators of Unix, BSD (Berkeley Software Distribution) Unix from the University of California at Berkeley, and Linux from the Free Software Foundation. Each manufacturer of Unix workstations has its own operating system. There are efforts to standardize on either Posix, the international standard (ISO) Unix or OSF, the operating system of the Open Software Foundation. All of the versions are close enough that learning about any one will give you a good understanding of Unix generally. However, as you begin to use Unix, you will need reference material on the specific version that you are using. There are many accessible texts, including Sobell (1995) which covers a variety of Unix versions, including Posix, McKusick, et al (1996) on BSD, and Hekman (1997) on Linux.

EXERCISES

1. Look up operations equivalent to `Open`, `Close`, `Create`, `Read`, `Write`, and `Seek` in other high-level languages, such as Ada, Cobol, and Fortran. Compare them with the C streams or C++ stream classes.

2. For the C++ language:

    a. Make a list of the different ways to perform the file operations Create, Open, Close, Read, and Write. Why is there more than one way to do each operation?

    b. How would you use `fseek` to find the current position in a file?

    c. Show how to change the permissions on a file `myfile` so the owner has read and write permissions, group members have execute permission, and others have no permission.

    d. What is the difference between `pmode` and O_RDWR? What `pmodes` and O_RDWR are available on your system?

    e. In some typical C++ environments, such as Unix and MS-DOS, all of the following represent ways to move data from one place to another:

```
scanf        fgetc        read        cat (or type)
fscanf       gets         <           main (argc, argv)
getc         fgets        |
```

Describe as many of these as you can, and indicate how they might be useful. Which belong to the C++ language, and which belong to the operating system?

3. A couple of years ago a company we know of bought a new Cobol compiler. One difference between the new compiler and the old one was that the new compiler did not automatically close files when execution of a program terminated, whereas the old compiler did. What sorts of problems did this cause when some of the old software was executed after having been recompiled with the new compiler?

4. Consult a C++ reference and describe the values of the io_state of the stream classes in C++. Describe the characteristics of a stream when each of the state bits is set.

5. Design an experiment that uses methods `seekg`, `seekp`, `tellg`, and `tellp` to determine whether an implementation of C++ supports separate get and put pointers for the stream classes.

6. Look up the Unix command `wc`. Execute the following in a Unix environment, and explain why it gives the number of files in the directory.

   ls | wc -w

7. Find `stdio.h` on your system, and find what value is used to indicate end-of-file. Also examine `file.h` or `fcntl.h`, and describe in general what its contents are for.

PROGRAMMING EXERCISES

8. Make the `listcpp.cpp` program of Appendix D work with your compiler on your operating system.

9. Write a program to create a file and store a string in it. Write another program to open the file and read the string.

10. Implement the Unix command `tail -n`, where *n* is the number of lines from the end of the file to be copied to `stdout`.

11. Change the program `listcpp.cpp` so it reads from `cin`, rather than a file, and writes to a file, rather than `cout`. Show how to

execute the new version of the program in your programming environment, given that the input is actually in a file called `instuff`.

12. Write a program to read a series of names, one per line, from standard input, and write out those names spelled in reverse order to standard output. Use I/O redirection and pipes to do the following:

    a. Input a series of names that are typed in from the keyboard, and write them out, reversed, to a file called file1.

    b. Read the names in from `file1`; then write them out, re-reversed, to a file called `file2`.

    c. Read the names in from `file2`, reverse them again, and then sort the resulting list of reversed words using `sort`.

13. Write a program to read and write objects of class String. Include code that uses the assignment operator and the various constructors for the class. Use a debugger to determine exactly which methods are called for each statement in your program.

PROGRAMMING PROJECT

This is the second part of the programming project begun in Chapter 1. We add methods to read objects from standard input and to write formatted objects to an output stream for the classes of Chapter 1.

14. Add methods to class `Student` to read student field values from an input stream and to write the fields of an object to an output stream, nicely formatted. You may also want to be able to prompt a user to enter the field values. Use the C++ stream operations to implement these methods. Write a driver program to verify that the class is correctly implemented.

15. Add methods to class `CourseRegistration` to read course registration field values from an input stream and to write the fields of an object to an output stream, nicely formatted. You may also want to be able to prompt a user to enter the field values. Use the C++ stream operations to implement these methods. Write a driver program to verify that the class is correctly implemented.

The next part of the programming project is in Chapter 4.

CHAPTER

Secondary Storage and System Software

3

CHAPTER OBJECTIVES

❖ Describe the organization of typical disk drives, including basic units of organization and their relationships.

❖ Identify and describe the factors affecting disk access time, and describe methods for estimating access times and space requirements.

❖ Describe magnetic tapes, give an example of current high-performance tape systems, and investigate the implications of block size on space requirements and transmission speeds.

❖ Introduce the commercially important characteristics of CD-ROM storage.

❖ Examine the performance characteristics of CD-ROM, and see that they are very different from those of magnetic disks.

❖ Describe the directory structure of the CD-ROM file system, and show how it grows from the characteristics of the medium.

❖ Identify fundamental differences between media and criteria that can be used to match the right medium to an application.

❖ Describe in general terms the events that occur when data is transmitted between a program and a secondary storage device.

❖ Introduce concepts and techniques of buffer management.

❖ Illustrate many of the concepts introduced in the chapter, especially system software concepts, in the context of Unix.

CHAPTER OUTLINE

Good design is always responsive to the constraints of the medium and to the environment. This is as true for file structure design as it is for carvings in wood and stone. Given the ability to create, open, and close files, and to seek, read, and write, we can perform the fundamental operations of file *construction*. Now we need to look at the nature and limitations of the devices and systems used to store and retrieve files in order to prepare ourselves for file design.

If files were stored just in memory, there would be no separate discipline called file structures. The general study of data structures would give us all the tools we need to build file applications. But secondary storage devices are very different from memory. One difference, as already noted, is that accesses to secondary storage take much more time than do accesses to memory. An even more important difference, measured in terms of design impact, is that not all accesses are equal. Good file structure design uses knowledge of disk and tape performance to arrange data in ways that minimize access costs.

In this chapter we examine the characteristics of secondary storage devices. We focus on the constraints that shape our design work in the chapters that follow. We begin with a look at the major media used in the storage and processing of files, magnetic disks, and tapes. We follow this with an overview of the range of other devices and media used for secondary storage. Next, by following the journey of a byte, we take a brief look at the many pieces of hardware and software that become involved when a byte is sent by a program to a file on a disk. Finally, we take a closer look at one of the most important aspects of file management—buffering.

3.1 Disks

Compared with the time it takes to access an item in memory, disk accesses are always expensive. However, not all disk accesses are *equally* expensive. This has to do with the way a disk drive works. Disk drives[1] belong to a class of devices known as *direct access storage devices* (DASDs) because they make it possible to access data *directly*. DASDs are contrasted with *serial devices*, the other major class of secondary storage devices. Serial devices use media such as magnetic tape that permit only serial access, which means that a particular data item cannot be read or written until all of the data preceding it on the tape have been read or written in order.

Magnetic disks come in many forms. So-called *hard disks* offer high capacity and low cost per bit. Hard disks are the most common disk used in everyday file processing. *Floppy* disks are inexpensive, but they are slow and hold relatively little data. Floppies are good for backing up individual files or other floppies and for transporting small amounts of data. Removable disks use disk cartridges that can be mounted on the same drive at different times, providing a convenient form of backup storage that also makes it possible to access data directly. The Iomega Zip (100 megabytes per cartridge) and Jaz (1 gigabyte per cartridge) have become very popular among PC users.

Nonmagnetic disk media, especially optical discs, are becoming increasingly important for secondary storage. (See Sections 3.4 and 3.5 and Appendix A for a full treatment of optical disc storage and its applications.)

3.1.1 The Organization of Disks

The information stored on a disk is stored on the surface of one or more platters (Fig. 3.1). The arrangement is such that the information is stored in successive *tracks* on the surface of the disk (Fig. 3.2). Each track is often divided into a number of *sectors*. A sector is the smallest addressable portion of a disk. When a `read` statement calls for a particular byte from a disk file, the computer operating system finds the correct surface, track, and sector, reads the entire sector into a special area in memory called a *buffer*, and then finds the requested byte within that buffer.

---

1. When we use the terms *disks* or *disk drives,* we are referring to *magnetic* disk media.

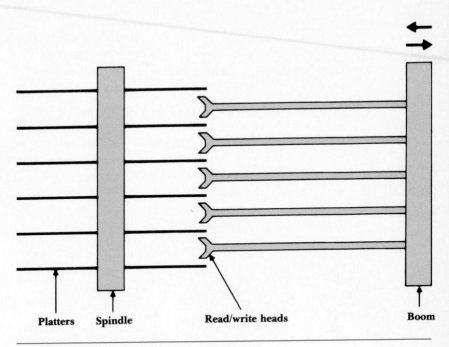

Figure 3.1 Schematic illustration of disk drive.

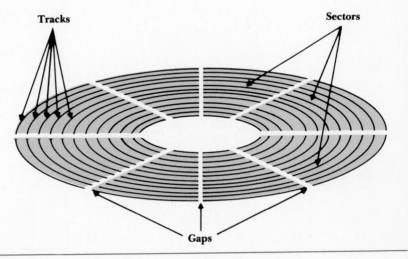

Figure 3.2 Surface of disk showing tracks and sectors.

Disk drives typically have a number of platters. The tracks that are directly above and below one another form a *cylinder* (Fig. 3.3). The significance of the cylinder is that all of the information on a single cylinder can be accessed without moving the arm that holds the read/write heads. Moving this arm is called *seeking*. This arm movement is usually the slowest part of reading information from a disk.

3.1.2 Estimating Capacities and Space Needs

Disks range in storage capacity from hundreds of millions to billions of bytes. In a typical disk, each platter has two surfaces, so the number of tracks per cylinder is twice the number of platters. The number of cylinders is the same as the number of tracks on a single surface, and each track has the same capacity. Hence the capacity of the disk is a function of the number of cylinders, the number of tracks per cylinder, and the capacity of a track.

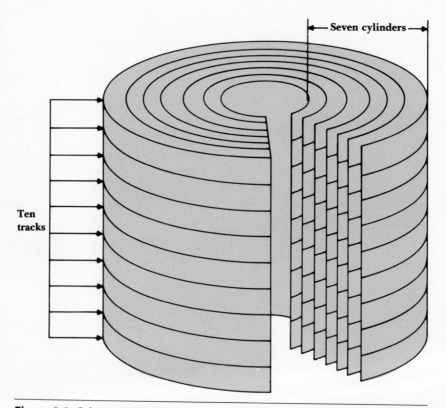

Figure 3.3 Schematic illustration of disk drive viewed as a set of seven cylinders.

The amount of data that can be held on a track and the number of tracks on a surface depend on how densely bits can be stored on the disk surface. (This in turn depends on the quality of the recording medium and the size of the read/write heads.) In 1991, an inexpensive, low-density disk held about 4 kilobytes on a track and 35 tracks on a 5-inch platter. In 1997, a Western Digital Caviar 850-megabyte disk, one of the smallest disks being manufactured, holds 32 kilobytes per track and 1,654 tracks on each surface of a 3-inch platter. A Seagate Cheetah high performance 9-gigabyte disk (still 3-inch platters) can hold about 87 kilobytes on a track and 6526 tracks on a surface. Table 3.1 shows how a variety of disk drives compares in terms of capacity, performance, and cost.

Since a cylinder consists of a group of tracks, a track consists of a group of sectors, and a sector consists of a group of bytes, it is easy to compute track, cylinder, and drive capacities.

Track capacity = number of sectors per track × bytes per sector
Cylinder capacity = number of tracks per cylinder × track capacity
Drive capacity = number of cylinders × cylinder capacity.

Table 3.1 Specifications of the Disk Drives

Characteristic	Seagate Cheetah 9	Western Digital Caviar AC22100	Western Digital Caviar AC2850
Capacity	9000 MB	2100 MB	850 MB
Minimum (track-to-track) seek time	0.78 msec	1 msec	1 msec
Average seek time	8 msec	12 msec	10 msec
Maximum seek time	19 msec	22 msec	22 msec
Spindle speed	10000 rpm	5200 rpm	4500 rpm
Average rotational delay	3 msec	6 msec	6.6 msec
Maximum transfer rate	6 msec/track, or 14 506 bytes/msec	12 msec/track, or 2796 bytes/msec	13.3 msec/track, or 2419 bytes/msec
Bytes per sector	512	512	512
Sectors per track	170	63	63
Tracks per cylinder	16	16	16
Cylinders	526	4092	1654

If we know the number of bytes in a file, we can use these relationships to compute the amount of disk space the file is likely to require. Suppose, for instance, that we want to store a file with fifty thousand fixed-length data records on a "typical" 2.1-gigabyte small computer disk with the following characteristics:

$$\text{Number of bytes per sector} = 512$$
$$\text{Number of sectors per track} = 63$$
$$\text{Number of tracks per cylinder} = 16$$
$$\text{Number of cylinders} = 4092$$

How many cylinders does the file require if each data record requires 256 bytes? Since each sector can hold two records, the file requires

$$\frac{50\,000}{2} = 25\,000 \text{ sectors}$$

One cylinder can hold

$$63 \times 16 = 1008 \text{ sectors}$$

so the number of cylinders required is approximately

$$\frac{25\,000}{1008} = 24.8 \text{ cylinders}$$

Of course, it may be that a disk drive with 24.8 cylinders of available space does not have 24.8 *physically contiguous* cylinders available. In this likely case, the file might, in fact, have to be spread out over dozens, perhaps even hundreds, of cylinders.

3.1.3 Organizing Tracks by Sector

There are two basic ways to organize data on a disk: by sector and by user-defined block. So far, we have mentioned only sector organizations. In this section we examine sector organizations more closely. In the following section we will look at block organizations.

The Physical Placement of Sectors

There are several views that one can have of the organization of sectors on a track. The simplest view, one that suffices for most users most of the time, is that sectors are adjacent, fixed-sized segments of a track that happen to hold a file (Fig. 3.4a). This is often a perfectly adequate way to view a file *logically*, but it may not be a good way to store sectors *physically*.

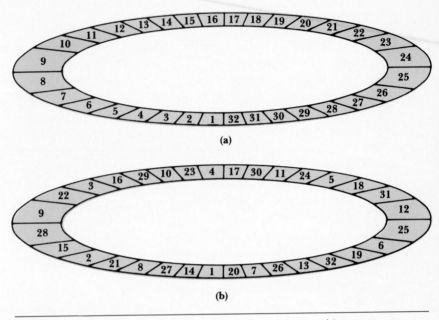

Figure 3.4 Two views of the organization of sectors on a thirty-two-sector track.

When you want to read a series of sectors that are all in the same track, one right after the other, you often cannot read *adjacent* sectors. After reading the data, it takes the disk controller a certain amount of time to process the received information before it is ready to accept more. If *logically* adjacent sectors were placed on the disk so they were also *physically* adjacent, we would miss the start of the following sector while we were processing the one we had just read in. Consequently, we would be able to read only one sector per revolution of the disk.

I/O system designers have approached this problem by *interleaving* the sectors: they leave an interval of several physical sectors between logically adjacent sectors. Suppose our disk had an *interleaving factor* of 5. The assignment of logical sector content to the thirty-two physical sectors in a track is illustrated in Fig. 3.4(b). If you study this figure, you can see that it takes five revolutions to read the entire thirty-two sectors of a track. That is a big improvement over thirty-two revolutions.

In the early 1990s, controller speeds improved so that disks can now offer 1:1 interleaving. This means that successive sectors are physically adjacent, making it possible to read an entire track in a single revolution of the disk.

Clusters

Another view of sector organization, also designed to improve performance, is the view maintained by the part of a computer's operating system that we call the *file manager*. When a program accesses a file, it is the file manager's job to map the logical parts of the file to their corresponding physical locations. It does this by viewing the file as a series of *clusters* of sectors. A cluster is a fixed number of contiguous sectors.[2] Once a given cluster has been found on a disk, all sectors in that cluster can be accessed without requiring an additional seek.

To view a file as a series of clusters and still maintain the sectored view, the file manager ties logical sectors to the physical clusters they belong to by using a *file allocation table* (FAT). The FAT contains a list of all the clusters in a file, ordered according to the logical order of the sectors they contain. With each cluster entry in the FAT is an entry giving the physical location of the cluster (Fig. 3.5).

On many systems, the system administrator can decide how many sectors there should be in a cluster. For instance, in the standard physical disk structure used by VAX systems, the system administrator sets the cluster size to be used on a disk when the disk is initialized. The default value is 3 512-byte sectors per cluster, but the cluster size may be set to any value between 1 and 65 535 sectors. Since clusters represent physically contiguous groups of sectors, larger clusters will read more sectors without seeking, so the use of large clusters can lead to substantial performance gains when a file is processed sequentially.

Extents

Our final view of sector organization represents a further attempt to emphasize physical contiguity of sectors in a file and to minimize seeking even more. (If you are getting the idea that the avoidance of seeking is an important part of file design, you are right.) If there is a lot of free room on a disk, it may be possible to make a file consist entirely of contiguous clusters. When this is the case, we say that the file consists of one *extent:* all of its sectors, tracks, and (if it is large enough) cylinders form one contiguous whole (Fig. 3.6a on page 54). This is a good situation, especially if the file is to be processed sequentially, because it means that the whole file can be accessed with a minimum amount of seeking.

---

2. It is not always *physically* contiguous; the degree of physical contiguity is determined by the interleaving factor.

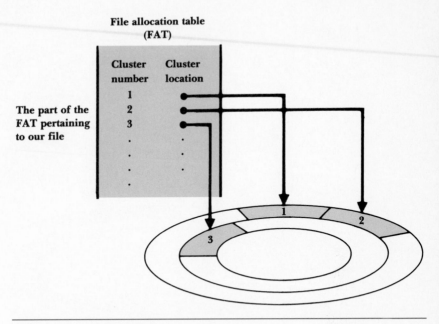

Figure 3.5 The file manager determines which cluster in the file has the sector that is to be accessed.

If there is not enough contiguous space available to contain an entire file, the file is divided into two or more noncontiguous parts. Each part is an extent. When new clusters are added to a file, the file manager tries to make them physically contiguous to the previous end of the file, but if space is unavailable, it must add one or more extents (Fig. 3.6b). The most important thing to understand about extents is that as the number of extents in a file increases, the file becomes more spread out on the disk, and the amount of seeking required to process the file increases.

Fragmentation

Generally, all sectors on a given drive must contain the same number of bytes. If, for example, the size of a sector is 512 bytes and the size of all records in a file is 300 bytes, there is no convenient fit between records and sectors. There are two ways to deal with this situation: store only one record per sector, or allow records to *span* sectors so the beginning of a record might be found in one sector and the end of it in another (Fig. 3.7).

The first option has the advantage that any record can be retrieved by retrieving just one sector, but it has the disadvantage that it might leave an enormous amount of unused space within each sector. This loss of space

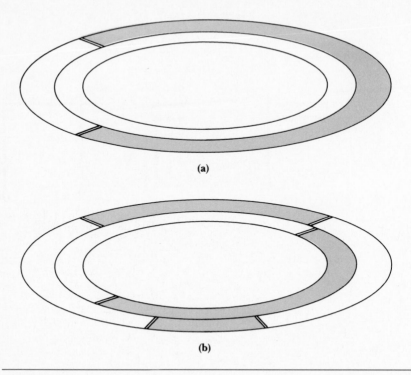

(a)

(b)

Figure 3.6 File extents (shaded area represents space on disk used by a single file).

within a sector is called *internal fragmentation.* The second option has the advantage that it loses no space from internal fragmentation, but it has the disadvantage that some records may be retrieved only by accessing two sectors.

Another potential source of internal fragmentation results from the use of clusters. Recall that a cluster is the smallest unit of space that can be allocated for a file. When the number of bytes in a file is not an exact multiple of the cluster size, there will be internal fragmentation in the last extent of the file. For instance, if a cluster consists of three 512-byte sectors, a file containing 1 byte would use up 1536 bytes on the disk; 1535 bytes would be wasted due to internal fragmentation.

Clearly, there are important trade-offs in the use of large cluster sizes. A disk expected to have mainly large files that will often be processed sequentially would usually be given a large cluster size, since internal fragmentation would not be a big problem and the performance gains might be great. A disk holding smaller files or files that are usually accessed only randomly would normally be set up with small clusters.

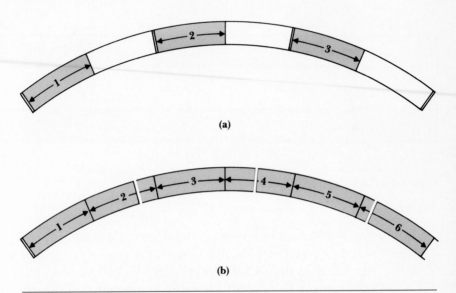

(a)

(b)

Figure 3.7 Alternate record organization within sectors (shaded areas represent data records, and unshaded areas represent unused space).

3.1.4 Organizing Tracks by Block

Sometimes disk tracks are *not* divided into sectors, but into integral numbers of user-defined *blocks* whose sizes can vary. (*Note:* The word *block* has a different meaning in the context of the Unix I/O system. See Section 3.7 for details.) When the data on a track is organized by block, this usually means that the amount of data transferred in a single I/O operation can vary depending on the needs of the software designer, not the hardware. Blocks can normally be either fixed or variable in length, depending on the requirements of the file designer and the capabilities of the operating system. As with sectors, blocks are often referred to as physical records. In this context, the physical record is the smallest unit of data that the operating system supports on a particular drive. (Sometimes the word *block* is used as a synonym for a sector or group of sectors. To avoid confusion, we do not use it in that way here.) Figure 3.8 illustrates the difference between one view of data on a sectored track and that on a blocked track.

A *block* organization does not present the sector-spanning and fragmentation problems of sectors because blocks can vary in size to fit the logical organization of the data. A block is usually organized to hold an integral number of logical records. The term *blocking factor* is used to indicate the number of records that are to be stored in each block in a file.

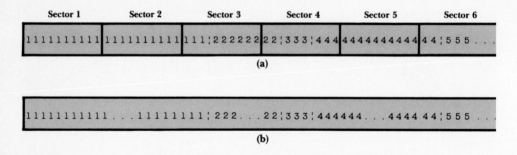

Figure 3.8 Sector organization versus block organization.

Hence, if we had a file with 300-byte records, a block-addressing scheme would let us define a block to be some convenient multiple of 300 bytes, depending on the needs of the program. No space would be lost to internal fragmentation, and there would be no need to load two blocks to retrieve one record.

Generally speaking, blocks are superior to sectors when it is desirable to have the physical allocation of space for records correspond to their logical organization. (There are disk drives that allow both sector addressing and block addressing, but we do not describe them here. See Bohl, 1981.)

In block-addressing schemes, each block of data is usually accompanied by one or more *subblocks* containing extra information about the data block. Typically there is a *count subblock* that contains (among other things) the number of bytes in the accompanying data block (Fig. 3.9a). There may also be a *key subblock* containing the key for the last record in the data block (Fig. 3.9b). When *key* subblocks are used, the disk controller can search a track for a block or record identified by a given key. This means that a program can ask its disk drive to search among all the blocks on a track for a block with a desired key. This approach can result in much more efficient searches than are normally possible with sector-addressable schemes, in which keys generally cannot be interpreted without first loading them into primary memory.

3.1.5 Nondata Overhead

Both blocks and sectors require that a certain amount of space be taken up on the disk in the form of *nondata overhead*. Some of the overhead consists of information that is stored on the disk during *preformatting*, which is done before the disk can be used.

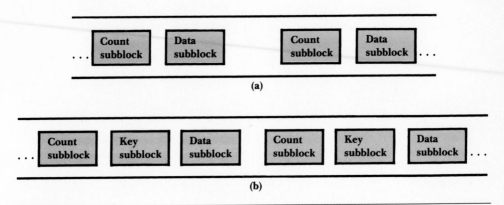

(a)

(b)

Figure 3.9 Block addressing requires that each physical data block be accompanied by one or more subblocks containing information about its contents.

On sector-addressable disks, preformatting involves storing, at the beginning of each sector, information such as sector address, track address, and condition (whether the sector is usable or defective). Preformatting also involves placing gaps and synchronization marks between fields of information to help the read/write mechanism distinguish between them. This nondata overhead usually is of no concern to the programmer. When the sector size is given for a certain drive, the programmer can assume that this is the amount of actual data that can be stored in a sector.

On a block-organized disk, some of the nondata overhead is invisible to the programmer, but some of it must be accounted for. Since subblocks and interblock gaps have to be provided with every block, there is generally more nondata information provided with blocks than with sectors. Also, since the number and size of blocks can vary from one application to another, the relative amount of space taken up by overhead can vary when block addressing is used. This is illustrated in the following example.

Suppose we have a block-addressable disk drive with 20 000 bytes per track and the amount of space taken up by subblocks and interblock gaps is equivalent to 300 bytes per block. We want to store a file containing 100-byte records on the disk. How many records can be stored per track if the blocking factor is 10? If it is 60?

1. If there are ten 100-byte records per block, each block holds 1000 bytes of data and uses 300 + 1000, or 1300, bytes of track space when overhead is taken into account. The number of blocks that can fit on a 20 000-byte track can be expressed as

$$\frac{20\ 000}{1300} = 15.38 = 15$$

So fifteen blocks, or 150 records, can be stored per track. (Note that we have to take the *floor* of the result because a block cannot span two tracks.)

2. If there are sixty 100-byte records per block, each block holds 6000 bytes of data and uses 6300 bytes of track space. The number of blocks per track can be expressed as

$$\frac{20\ 000}{6300} = 3$$

So three blocks, or 180 records, can be stored per track.

Clearly, the larger blocking factor can lead to more efficient use of storage. When blocks are larger, fewer blocks are required to hold a file, so there is less space consumed by the 300 bytes of overhead that accompany each block.

Can we conclude from this example that larger blocking factors always lead to more efficient storage? Not necessarily. Since we can put only an integral number of blocks on a track and since tracks are fixed in length, we almost always lose some space at the end of a track. Here we have the internal fragmentation problem again, but this time it applies to fragmentation within a *track*. The greater the block size, the greater potential amount of internal track fragmentation. What would have happened if we had chosen a blocking factor of 98 in the preceding example? What about 97?

The flexibility introduced by the use of blocks, rather than sectors, can save time, since it lets the programmer determine to a large extent how data is to be organized physically on a disk. On the negative side, blocking schemes *require* the programmer and/or operating system to do the extra work of determining the data organization. Also, the very flexibility introduced by the use of blocking schemes precludes the synchronization of I/O operations with the physical movement of the disk, which sectoring permits. This means that strategies such as sector interleaving cannot be used to improve performance.

3.1.6 The Cost of a Disk Access

To give you a feel for the factors contributing to the total amount of time needed to access a file on a fixed disk, we calculate some access times. A disk access can be divided into three distinct physical operations, each with its own cost: *seek time, rotational delay,* and *transfer time.*

Seek Time

Seek time is the time required to move the access arm to the correct cylinder. The amount of time spent seeking during a disk access depends, of course, on how far the arm has to move. If we are accessing a file sequentially and the file is packed into several consecutive cylinders, seeking needs to be done only after all the tracks on a cylinder have been processed, and then the read/write head needs to move the width of only one track. At the other extreme, if we are alternately accessing sectors from two files that are stored at opposite extremes on a disk (one at the innermost cylinder, one at the outermost cylinder), seeking is very expensive.

Seeking is likely to be more costly in a multiuser environment, where several processes are contending for use of the disk at one time, than in a single-user environment, where disk usage is dedicated to one process.

Since seeking can be very costly, system designers often go to great extremes to minimize seeking. In an application that merges three files, for example, it is not unusual to see the three input files stored on three different drives and the output file stored on a fourth drive, so no seeking need be done as I/O operations jump from file to file.

Since it is usually impossible to know exactly how many tracks will be traversed in every seek, we usually try to determine the *average seek time* required for a particular file operation. If the starting and ending positions for each access are random, it turns out that the average seek traverses one-third of the total number of cylinders that the read/write head ranges over.[3] Manufacturers' specifications for disk drives often list this figure as the average seek time for the drives. Most hard disks available today have average seek times of less than 10 milliseconds (msec), and high-performance disks have average seek times as low as 7.5 msec.

Rotational Delay

Rotational delay refers to the time it takes for the disk to rotate so the sector we want is under the read/write head. Hard disks usually rotate at about 5000 rpm, which is one revolution per 12 msec. On average, the rotational delay is half a revolution, or about 6 msec. On floppy disks, which often rotate at only 360 rpm, average rotational delay is a sluggish 83.3 msec.

---

3. Derivations of this result, as well as more detailed and refined models, can be found in Wiederhold (1983), Knuth (1998), Teory and Fry (1982), and Salzberg (1988).

As in the case of seeking, these averages apply only when the read/write head moves from some random place on the disk surface to the target track. In many circumstances, rotational delay can be much less than the average. For example, suppose that you have a file that requires two or more tracks, that there are plenty of available tracks on one cylinder, and that you write the file to disk sequentially, with one write call. When the first track is filled, the disk can immediately begin writing to the second track, without any rotational delay. The "beginning" of the second track is effectively staggered by just the amount of time it takes to switch from the read/write head on the first track to the read/write head on the second. Rotational delay, as it were, is virtually nonexistent. Furthermore, when you read the file back, the position of data on the second track ensures that there is no rotational delay in switching from one track to another. Figure 3.10 illustrates this staggered arrangement.

Transfer Time

Once the data we want is under the read/write head, it can be transferred. The transfer time is given by the formula

$$\text{Transfer time} = \frac{\text{number of bytes transferred}}{\text{number of bytes on a track}} \times \text{rotation time}$$

If a drive is sectored, the transfer time for one sector depends on the number of sectors on a track. For example, if there are sixty-three sectors per track, the time required to transfer one sector would be 1/63 of a revo-

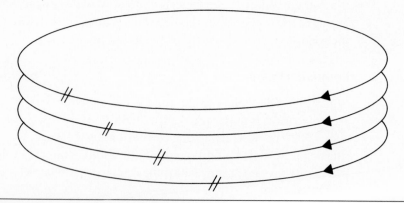

Figure 3.10 When a single file can span several tracks on a cylinder, we can stagger the beginnings of the tracks to avoid rotational delay when moving from track to track during sequential access.

lution, or 0.19 msec. The Seagate Cheetah rotates at 10 000 rpm. The transfer time for a single sector (170 sectors per track) is 0.036 msec. This results in a peak transfer rate of more than 14 megabytes per second.

Some Timing Computations

Let's look at two different file processing situations that show how different types of file access can affect access times. We will compare the time it takes to access a file *in sequence* with the time it takes to access all of the records in the file *randomly*. In the former case, we use as much of the file as we can whenever we access it. In the random-access case, we are able to use only one record on each access.

The basis for our calculations is the high performance Seagate Cheetah 9-gigabyte fixed disk described in Table 3.1. Although it is typical only of a certain class of fixed disk, the observations we draw as we perform these calculations are quite general. The disks used with personal computers are smaller and slower than this disk, but the nature and relative costs of the factors contributing to total access times are essentially the same.

The highest performance for data transfer is achieved when files are in one-track units. Sectors are interleaved with an interleave factor of 1, so data on a given track can be transferred at the stated transfer rate.

Let's suppose that we wish to know how long it will take, using this drive, to read an 8 704 000-byte file that is divided into thirty-four thousand 256-byte records. First we need to know how the file is distributed on the disk. Since the 4096-byte cluster holds sixteen records, the file will be stored as a sequence of 2125 4096-byte sectors occupying one hundred tracks.

This means that the disk needs one hundred tracks to hold the entire 8704 kilobytes that we want to read. We assume a situation in which the one hundred tracks are randomly dispersed over the surface of the disk. (This is an extreme situation chosen to dramatize the point we want to make. Still, it is not so extreme that it could not easily occur on a typical overloaded disk that has a large number of small files.)

Now we are ready to calculate the time it would take to read the 8704-kilobyte file from the disk. We first estimate the time it takes to read the file sector by sector *in sequence*. This process involves the following operations for each track:

Average seek	8 msec
Rotational delay	3 msec
Read one track	6 msec
Total	17 msec

We want to find and read one hundred tracks, so

$$\text{Total time} = 100 \times 17 \text{ msec} = 1700 \text{ msec} = 1.7 \text{ seconds}$$

Now let's calculate the time it would take to read in the same thirty-four thousand records using *random access* instead of sequential access. In other words, rather than being able to read one sector right after another, we assume that we have to access the records in an order that requires jumping from track to track every time we read a new sector. This process involves the following operations for each record:

Average seek	8 msec
Rotational delay	3 msec
Read one cluster $(1/21.5 \times 6 \text{ msec})$	0.28 msec
Total	11.28 msec

Total time = 34 000 $\times$ 11.28 msec = 9250 msec = 9.25 seconds

This difference in performance between sequential access and random access is very important. If we can get to the right location on the disk and read a lot of information sequentially, we are clearly much better off than if we have to jump around, *seeking* every time we need a new record. Remember that seek time is very expensive; when we are performing disk operations, we should try to minimize seeking.

3.1.7 Effect of Block Size on Performance: A Unix Example

In deciding how best to organize disk storage allocation for several versions of BSD Unix, the Computer Systems Research Group (CSRG) in Berkeley investigated the trade-offs between block size and performance in a Unix environment (Leffler et al., 1989). The results of the research provide an interesting case study involving trade-offs between block size, fragmentation, and access time.

The CSRG research indicated that a minimum block size of 512 bytes, standard at the time on Unix systems, was not very efficient in a typical Unix environment. Files that were several blocks long often were scattered over many cylinders, resulting in frequent seeks and thereby significantly decreasing throughput. The researchers found that doubling the block size to 1024 bytes improved performance by more than a factor of 2. But even with 1024-byte blocks, they found that throughput was only about 4 percent of the theoretical maximum. Eventually, they found that 4096-byte blocks provided the fastest throughput, but this led to large amounts of wasted space due to internal fragmentation. These results are summarized in Table 3.2.

Table 3.2 The amount of wasted space as a function of block size.

Space Used (MB)	Percent Waste	Organization
775.2	0.0	Data only, no separation between files
807.8	4.2	Data only, each file starts on 512-byte boundary
828.7	6.9	Data + inodes, 512-byte block Unix file system
866.5	11.8	Data + inodes, 1024-byte block Unix file system
948.5	22.4	Data + inodes, 2048-byte block Unix file system
1128.3	45.6	Data + inodes, 4096-byte block Unix file system

From *The Design and Implementation of the 4.3BSD Unix Operating System,* Leffler et al., p. 198.

To gain the advantages of both the 4096-byte and the 512-byte systems, the Berkeley group implemented a variation of the cluster concept (see Section 3.1.3). In the new implementation, the researchers allocate 4096-byte blocks for files that are big enough to need them; but for smaller files, they allow the large blocks to be divided into one or more fragments. With a fragment size of 512 bytes, as many as eight small files can be stored in one block, greatly reducing internal fragmentation. With the 4096/512 system, wasted space was found to decline to about 12 percent.

3.1.8 Disk as Bottleneck

Disk performance is increasing steadily, even dramatically, but disk speeds still lag far behind local network speeds. A high-performance disk drive with 50 kilobytes per track can transmit at a peak rate of about 5 megabytes per second, and only a fraction of that under normal conditions. High-performance networks, in contrast, can transmit at rates of as much as 100 megabytes per second. The result can often mean that a process is *disk bound*—the network and the computer's central processing unit (CPU) have to wait inordinate lengths of time for the disk to transmit data.

A number of techniques are used to solve this problem. One is multi-programming, in which the CPU works on other jobs while waiting for the data to arrive. But if multiprogramming is not available or if the process simply cannot afford to lose so much time waiting for the disk, methods must be found to speed up disk I/O.

One technique now offered on many high-performance systems is called *striping*. Disk striping involves splitting the parts of a file on several different drives, then letting the separate drives deliver parts of the file to the network simultaneously. Disk striping can be used to put different blocks of the file on different drives or to spread individual blocks onto different drives.

Disk striping exemplifies an important concept that we see more and more in system configurations—*parallelism.* Whenever there is a bottleneck at some point in the system, consider duplicating the source of the bottleneck and configure the system so several of them operate in parallel.

If we put different blocks on different drives, independent processes accessing the same file will not necessarily interfere with each other. This improves the throughput of the system by improving the speed of multiple jobs, but it does not necessarily improve the speed of a single drive. There is a significant possibility of a reduction in seek time, but there is no guarantee.

The speed of single jobs that do large amounts of I/O can be significantly improved by spreading each block onto many drives. This is commonly implemented in *RAID* (redundant array of independent disks) systems which are commercially available for most computer systems. For an eight-drive RAID, for example, the controller receives a single block to write and breaks it into eight pieces, each with enough data for a full track. The first piece is written to a particular track of the first disk, the second piece to the same track of the second disk, and so on. The write occurs at a sustained rate of eight times the rate of a single drive. The read operation is similar, the same track is read from each drive, the block in reassembled in cache, and the cache contents are transmitted back through the I/O channel. RAID systems are supported by a large memory cache on the disk controller to support very large blocks.

Another approach to solving the disk bottleneck is to avoid accessing the disk at all. As the cost of memory steadily decreases, more and more programmers are using memory to hold data that a few years ago had to be kept on a disk. Two effective ways in which memory can be used to replace secondary storage are memory disks and disk caches.

A *RAM disk* is a large part of memory configured to simulate the behavior of a mechanical disk in every respect except speed and volatility. Since data can be located in memory without a seek or rotational delay, RAM disks can provide much faster access than mechanical disks. Since memory is normally volatile, the contents of a RAM disk are lost when the computer is turned off. RAM disks are often used in place of floppy disks because they are much faster than floppies and because relatively little memory is needed to simulate a typical floppy disk.

A *disk cache*[4] is a large block of memory configured to contain *pages* of data from a disk. A typical disk-caching scheme might use a 256-kilo-byte cache with a disk. When data is requested from secondary memory, the file manager first looks into the disk cache to see if it contains the page with the requested data. If it does, the data can be processed immediately. Otherwise, the file manager reads the page containing the data from disk, replacing some page already in the disk cache.

Cache memory can provide substantial improvements in performance, especially when a program's data access patterns exhibit a high degree of *locality*. Locality exists in a file when blocks that are accessed in close temporal sequence are stored close to one another on the disk. When a disk cache is used, blocks that are close to one another on the disk are much more likely to belong to the page or pages that are read in with a single read, diminishing the likelihood that extra reads are needed for extra accesses.

RAM disks and cache memory are examples of *buffering,* a very important and frequently used family of I/O techniques. We take a closer look at buffering in Section 3.9.

In these three techniques we see once again examples of the need to make trade-offs in file processing. With RAM disks and disk caches, there is tension between the cost/capacity advantages of disk over memory on the one hand, and the speed of memory on the other. Striping provides opportunities to increase throughput enormously, but at the cost of a more complex and sophisticated disk management system. Good file design balances these tensions and costs creatively.

3.2 Magnetic Tape

Magnetic tape units belong to a class of devices that provide no direct accessing facility but can provide very rapid sequential access to data. Tapes are compact, stand up well under different environmental conditions, are easy to store and transport, and are less expensive than disks. Many years ago tape systems were widely used to store application data. An application that needed data from a specific tape would issue a request

---

4. The term *cache* (as opposed to *disk cache*) generally refers to a very high-speed block of primary memory that performs the same types of performance-enhancing operations with respect to memory that a disk cache does with respect to secondary memory.

for the tape, which would be mounted by an operator onto a tape drive. The application could then directly read and write on the tape. The tremendous reduction in the cost of disk systems has changed the way tapes are used. At present, tapes are primarily used as archival storage. That is, data is written to tape to provide low cost storage and then copied to disk whenever it is needed. Tapes are very common as backup devices for PC systems. In high performance and high volume applications, tapes are commonly stored in racks and supported by a robot system that is capable of moving tapes between storage racks and tape drives.

3.2.1 Types of Tape Systems

There has been tremendous improvement in tape technology in the past few years. There are now a variety of tape formats with prices ranging from $150 to $150,000 per tape drive. For $150, a PC owner can add a tape backup system, with sophisticated backup software, that is capable of storing 4 gigabytes of data on a single $30 tape. For larger systems, a high performance tape system could easily store hundreds of terabytes in a tape robot system costing millions of dollars. Table 3.3 shows a comparison of some current tape systems.

In the past, most computer installations had a number of reel-to-reel tape drives and large numbers of racks or cabinets holding tapes. The primary media was one-half inch magnetic tape on 10.5-inch reels with 3600 feet of tape. In the next section we look at the format and data transfer capabilities of these tape systems which use nine linear tracks and are usually referred to as *nine-track tapes*.

Table 3.3 Comparison of some current tape systems

Tape Model	Media Format	Loading	Capacity	Tracks	Transfer Rate
9-track	one-half inch reel	autoload	200 MB	9 linear	1 MB/sec
Digital linear tape	DLT cartridge	robot	35 GB	36 linear	5 MB/sec
HP Colorado T3000	one-quarter inch cartridge	manual	1.6 GB	helical	0.5 MB/sec
StorageTek Redwood	one-half inch cartridge	robot silo	50 GB	helical	10 MB/sec

Newer tape systems are usually based on a *tape cartridge* medium where the tape and its reels are contained in a box. The tape media formats that are available include 4 mm, 8 mm, VHS, 1/2 inch, and 1/4 inch.

3.2.2 An Example of a High-Performance Tape System

The StorageTek Redwood SD3 is one of the highest-performance tape systems available in 1997. It is usually configured in a *silo* that contains storage racks, a tape robot, and multiple tape drives. The tapes are 4-by-4-inch cartridges with one-half inch tape. The tapes are formatted with helical tracks. That is, the tracks are at an angle to the linear direction of the tape. The number of individual tracks is related to the length of the tape rather than the width of the tape as in linear tapes. The expected reliable storage time is more than twenty years, and average durability is 1 million head passes.

The performance of the SD3 is achieved with tape capacities of up to 50 gigabytes and a sustained transfer rate of 11 megabytes per second. This transfer rate is necessary to store and retrieve data produced by the newest generation of scientific experimental equipment, including the Hubbell telescope, the Earth Observing System (a collection of weather satellites), seismographic instruments, and a variety of particle accelerators.

An important characteristic of a tape silo system is the speed of seeking, rewinding, and loading tapes. The SD3 silo using 50-gigabyte tapes has an average seek time of 53 seconds and can rewind in a maximum of 89 seconds. The load time is only 17 seconds. The time to read or write a full tape is about 75 minutes. Hence, the overhead to rewind, unload, and load is only 3 percent. Another way to look at this is that any tape in the silo can be mounted in under 2 minutes with no operator intervention.

3.2.3 Organization of Data on Nine-Track Tapes

Since tapes are accessed sequentially, there is no need for addresses to identify the locations of data on a tape. On a tape, the logical position of a byte within a file corresponds directly to its physical position relative to the start of the file. We may envision the surface of a typical tape as a set of parallel tracks, each of which is a sequence of bits. If there are nine tracks (see Fig. 3.11), the nine bits that are at corresponding positions in the nine respective tracks are taken to constitute 1 byte, plus a *parity bit*. So a byte can be thought of as a one-bit-wide slice of tape. Such a slice is called a *frame*.

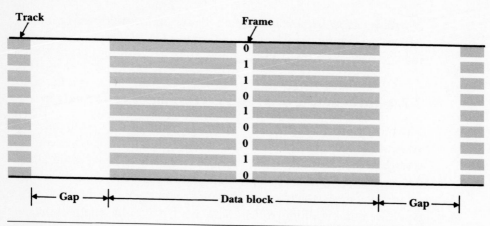

Figure 3.11 Nine-track tape.

The parity bit is not part of the data but is used to check the validity of the data. If *odd parity* is in effect, this bit is set to make the number of 1 bits in the frame *odd.* Even parity works similarly but is rarely used with tapes.

Frames (bytes) are grouped into data blocks whose size can vary from a few bytes to many kilobytes, depending on the needs of the user. Since tapes are often read one block at a time and since tapes cannot stop or start instantaneously, blocks are separated by *interblock gaps,* which contain no information and are long enough to permit stopping and starting. When tapes use odd parity, no valid frame can contain all 0 bits, so a large number of consecutive 0 frames is used to fill the interrecord gap.

Tape drives come in many shapes, sizes, and speeds. Performance differences among drives can usually be measured in terms of three quantities:

Tape density—commonly 800, 1600, or 6250 bits per inch (bpi) per track, but recently as much as 30 000 bpi;

Tape speed—commonly 30 to 200 inches per second (ips); and

Size of interblock gap—commonly between 0.3 inch and 0.75 inch.

Note that a 6250-bpi nine-track tape contains 6250 bits per inch per track, and 6250 *bytes* per inch when the full nine tracks are taken together. Thus in the computations that follow, 6250 bpi is usually taken to mean 6250 bytes of data per inch.

3.2.4 Estimating Tape Length Requirements

Suppose we want to store a backup copy of a large mailing-list file with one million 100-byte records. If we want to store the file on a 6250-bpi tape that has an interblock gap of 0.3 inches, how much tape is needed?

To answer this question we first need to determine what takes up space on the tape. There are two primary contributors: interblock gaps and data blocks. For every data block there is an interblock gap. If we let

b = the physical length of a data block,
g = the length of an interblock gap, and
n = the number of data blocks

then the space requirement s for storing the file is

$$s = n \times (b + g)$$

We know that g is 0.3 inch, but we do not know what b and n are. In fact, b is whatever we want it to be, and n depends on our choice of b. Suppose we choose each data block to contain one 100-byte record. Then b, the length of each block, is given by

$$b = \frac{\text{block size (bytes per block)}}{\text{tape density (bytes per inch)}} \quad \frac{100}{6250} = 0.016 \text{ inch}$$

and n, the number of blocks, is 1 million (one per record).

The number of records stored in a physical block is called the *blocking factor*. It has the same meaning it had when it was applied to the use of blocks for disk storage. The blocking factor we have chosen here is 1 because each block has only one record. Hence, the space requirement for the file is

$$s = 1\,000\,000 \times (0.016 + 0.3) \text{ inch}$$
$$= 1\,000\,000 \times 0.316 \text{ inch}$$
$$= 316\,000 \text{ inches}$$
$$= 26\,333 \text{ feet}$$

Magnetic tapes range in length from 300 feet to 3600 feet, with 2400 feet being the most common length. Clearly, we need quite a few 2400-foot tapes to store the file. Or do we? You may have noticed that our choice of block size was not a very smart one from the standpoint of space usage. The interblock gaps in the physical representation of the file take up about *nineteen times* as much space as the data blocks do. If we were to take a snapshot of our tape, it would look something like this:

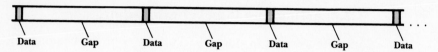

Most of the space on the tape is not used!

Clearly, we should consider increasing the relative amount of space used for actual data if we want to try to squeeze the file onto one 2400-foot tape. If we increase the blocking factor, we can *decrease* the number of blocks, which decreases the number of interblock gaps, which in turn decreases the amount of space consumed by interblock gaps. For example, if we increase the blocking factor from 1 to 50, the number of blocks becomes

$$n = \frac{1\ 000\ 000}{50} = 20\ 000$$

and the space requirement for interblock gaps decreases from 300 000 inches to 6000 inches. The space requirement for the data is of course the same as was previously. What has changed is the *relative* amount of space occupied by the gaps, as compared to the data. Now a snapshot of the tape would look much different:

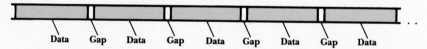

We leave it to you to show that the file can fit easily on one 2400-foot tape when a blocking factor of 50 is used.

When we compute the space requirements for our file, we produce numbers that are quite specific to our file. A more general measure of the effect of choosing different block sizes is *effective recording density*. The effective recording density is supposed to reflect the amount of actual data that can be stored per inch of tape. Since this depends exclusively on the relative sizes of the interblock gap and the data block, it can be defined as

$$\frac{\text{number of bytes per block}}{\text{number of inches required to store a block}}$$

When a blocking factor of 1 is used in our example, the number of bytes per block is 100, and the number of inches required to store a block is 0.316. Hence, the effective recording density is

$$\frac{100\ \text{bytes}}{0.316\ \text{inches}} = 316.4\ \text{bpi}$$

which is a far cry from the *nominal* recording density of 6250 bpi.

Either way you look at it, space utilization is sensitive to the relative sizes of data blocks and interblock gaps. Let us now see how they affect the amount of *time* it takes to transmit tape data.

3.2.5 Estimating Data Transmission Times

If you understand the role of interblock gaps and data block sizes in determining effective recording density, you can probably see immediately that these two factors also affect the rate of data transmission. Two other factors that affect the rate of data transmission to or from tape are the nominal recording density and the speed with which the tape passes the read/write head. If we know these two values, we can compute the *nominal data transmission rate:*

$$\text{Nominal rate} = \text{tape density (bpi)} \times \text{tape speed (ips)}$$

Hence, our 6250-bpi, 200-ips tape has a nominal transmission rate of

$$
\begin{aligned}
6250 \times 200 &= 1\,250\,000 \text{ bytes/sec} \\
&= 1250 \text{ kilobytes/sec}
\end{aligned}
$$

This rate is competitive with most disk drives.

But what about those interblock gaps? Once our data gets dispersed by interblock gaps, the *effective transmission rate* certainly suffers. Suppose, for example, that we use our blocking factor of 1 with the same file and tape drive discussed in the preceding section (one million 100-byte records, 0.3-inch gap). We saw that the effective recording density for this tape organization is 316.4 bpi. If the tape is moving at a rate of 200 ips, then its effective transmission rate is

$$
\begin{aligned}
316.4 \times 200 &= 63\,280 \text{ bytes/sec} \\
&= 63.3 \text{ kilobytes/sec}
\end{aligned}
$$

a rate that is about *one-twentieth* the nominal rate!

It should be clear that a blocking factor larger than 1 improves on this result and that a substantially larger blocking factor improves on it substantially.

Although there are other factors that can influence performance, block size is generally considered to be the one variable with the greatest influence on space utilization and data transmission rate. The other factors we have included—gap size, tape speed, and recording density—are often beyond the control of the user. Another factor that can sometimes be important is the time it takes to start and stop the tape. We consider start/stop time in the exercises at the end of this chapter.

3.3   Disk versus Tape

In the past, magnetic tape and magnetic disk accounted for the lion's share of all secondary storage applications. Disk was excellent for random access and storage of files for which immediate access was desired; tape was ideal for processing data sequentially and for long-term storage of files. Over time, these roles have changed somewhat in favor of disk.

The major reason that tape was preferable to disk for sequential processing is that tapes are dedicated to one process, while disk generally serves several processes. This means that between accesses a disk read/write head tends to move away from the location where the next sequential access will occur, resulting in an expensive seek; the tape drive, being dedicated to one process, pays no such price in seek time.

This problem of excessive seeking has gradually diminished, and disk has taken over much of the secondary storage niche previously occupied by tape. This change is largely because of the continued dramatic decreases in the cost of disk and memory storage. To understand this change fully, we need to understand the role of memory buffer space in performing I/O.[5] Briefly, it is that performance depends largely on how big a chunk of file we can transmit at any time; as more memory space becomes available for I/O buffers, the number of accesses decreases correspondingly, which means that the number of seeks required goes down as well. Most systems now available, even small systems, have enough memory to decrease the number of accesses required to process most files that disk becomes quite competitive with tape for sequential processing. This change, along with the superior versatility and decreasing costs of disks, has resulted in use of disk for most sequential processing, which in the past was primarily the domain of tape.

This is not to say that tapes should not be used for sequential processing. If a file is kept on tape and there are enough drives available to use them for sequential processing, it may be more efficient to process the file directly from tape than to stream it to disk and process it sequentially.

Although it has lost ground to disk in sequential processing applications, tape remains important as a medium for long-term archival storage. Tape is still far less expensive than magnetic disk, and it is very easy and fast to stream large files or sets of files between tape and disk. In this context, tape has emerged as one of our most important media (along with CD-ROM) for *tertiary* storage.

---

5. Techniques for memory buffering are covered in Section 3.9.

3.4   Introduction to CD-ROM

CD-ROM is an acronym for Compact Disc, Read-Only Memory.[6] It is a CD audio disc that contains digital data rather than digital sound. CD-ROM is commercially interesting because it can hold a lot of data and can be reproduced cheaply. A single disc can hold more than 600 megabytes of data. That is approximately two hundred thousand printed pages, enough storage to hold almost four hundred books the size of this one. Replicates can be stamped from a master disc for about only a dollar a copy.

CD-ROM is read-only (or write-once) in the same sense as a CD audio disc: once it has been recorded, it cannot be changed. It is a publishing medium, used for distributing information to many users, rather than a data storage and retrieval medium like magnetic disks. CD-ROM has become the preferred medium for distribution of all types of software and for publication of database information such as telephone directories, zip codes, and demographic information. There are also many CD-ROM products that deliver textual data, such as bibliographic indexes, abstracts, dictionaries, and encyclopedias, often in association with digitized images stored on the disc. They are also used to publish video information and, of course, digital audio.

3.4.1 A Short History of CD-ROM

CD-ROM is the offspring of videodisc technology developed in the late 1960s and early 1970s, before the advent of the home VCR. The goal was to store movies on disc. Different companies developed a number of methods for storing video signals, including the use of a needle to respond mechanically to grooves in a disc, much like a vinyl LP record does. The consumer products industry spent a great deal of money developing the different technologies, including several approaches to optical storage, then spent years fighting over which approach should become standard. The surviving format is one called LaserVision. By the time LaserVision emerged as the winner, the competing developers had not only spent enormous sums of money but had also lost important market opportunities. These hard lessons were put to use in the subsequent development of CD audio and CD-ROM.

---

6. Usually we spell disk with a *k*, but the convention among optical disc manufacturers is to spell it with a *c*.

From the outset, there was an interest in using LaserVision discs to do more than just record movies. The LaserVision format supports recording in both a constant linear velocity (CLV) format that maximizes storage capacity and a constant angular velocity (CAV) format that enables fast seek performance. By using the CAV format to access individual video frames quickly, a number of organizations, including the MIT Media Lab, produced prototype interactive video discs that could be used to teach and entertain.

In the early 1980s, a number of firms began looking at the possibility of storing digital, textual information on LaserVision discs. LaserVision stores data in an analog form; it is, after all, storing an analog video signal. Different firms came up with different ways of encoding digital information in analog form so it could be stored on the disc. The capabilities demonstrated in the prototypes and early, narrowly distributed products were impressive. The videodisc has a number of performance characteristics that make it a technically more desirable medium than the CD-ROM; in particular, one can build drives that seek quickly and deliver information from the disc at a high rate of speed. But, reminiscent of the earlier disputes over the physical format of the videodisc, each of these pioneers in the use of LaserVision discs as computer peripherals had incompatible encoding schemes and error correction techniques. There was no standard format, and none of the firms was large enough to impose its format over the others through sheer marketing muscle. Potential buyers were frightened by the lack of a standard; consequently, the market never grew.

During this same period Philips and Sony began work on a way to store music on optical discs. Rather than storing the music in the kind of analog form used on videodiscs, they developed a digital data format. Philips and Sony had learned hard lessons from the expensive standards battles over videodiscs. This time they worked with other players in the consumer products industry to develop a licensing system that resulted in the emergence of CD audio as a broadly accepted, standard format as soon as the first discs and players were introduced. CD audio appeared in the United States in early 1984. CD-ROM, which is a digital data format built on top of the CD audio standard, emerged shortly thereafter. The first commercially available CD-ROM drives appeared in 1985.

Not surprisingly, the firms that were delivering digital data on LaserVision discs saw CD-ROM as a threat to their existence. They also recognized, however, that CD-ROM promised to provide what had always eluded them in the past: a standard physical format. Anyone with a CD-ROM drive was guaranteed that he or she could find and read a sector off of any disc manufactured by any firm. For a storage medium to be used in publishing, standardization at such a fundamental level is essential.

What happened next is remarkable considering the history of standards and cooperation within an industry. The firms that had been working on products to deliver computer data from videodiscs recognized that a standard physical format, such as that provided by CD-ROM, was not enough. A standard physical format meant that everyone would be able to read sectors off of any disc. But computer applications do not work in terms of sectors; they store data in files. Having an agreement about finding sectors, without further agreement about how to organize the sectors into files, is like everyone agreeing on an alphabet without having settled on how letters are to be organized into words on a page. In late 1985 the firms emerging from the videodisc/digital data industry, all of which were relatively small, called together many of the much larger firms moving into the CD-ROM industry to begin work on a standard file system that would be built on top of the CD-ROM format. In a rare display of cooperation, the different firms, large and small, worked out the main features of a file system standard by early summer of 1986; that work has become an official international standard for organizing files on CD-ROM.

The CD-ROM industry is still young, though in the past years it has begun to show signs of maturity: it is moving away from concentration on such matters as disc formats to a concern with CD-ROM applications. Rather than focusing on the new medium in isolation, vendors are seeing it as an enabling mechanism for new systems. As it finds more uses in a broader array of applications, CD-ROM looks like an optical publishing technology that will be with us over the long term.

Recordable CD drives make it possible for users to store information on CD. The price of the drives and the price of the blank recordable CDs make this technology very appealing for backup. Unfortunately, while the speed of CD readers has increased substantially, with 12X (twelve times CD audio speed) as the current standard, CD recorders work no faster than 2X, or about 300 kilobytes per second.

The latest new technology for CDs is the DVD, which stands for Digital Video Disc, or Digital Versatile Disk. The Sony Corporation has developed DVD for the video market, especially for the new high definition TVs, but DVD is also available for storing files. The density of both tracks and bits has been increased to yield a sevenfold increase in storage capacity. DVD is also available in a two-sided medium that yields 10 gigabytes per disc.

3.4.2 CD-ROM as a File Structure Problem

CD-ROM presents interesting file structure problems because it is a medium with great strengths and weaknesses. The strengths of CD-ROM include its high storage capacity, its inexpensive price, and its durability. The key weakness is that seek performance on a CD-ROM is very slow, often taking from a half second to a second per seek. In the introduction to this textbook we compared memory access and magnetic disk access and showed that if memory access is analogous to your taking twenty seconds to look up something in the index to this textbook, the equivalent disk access would take fifty-eight days, or almost 2 months. With a CD-ROM the analogy stretches the disc access to more than *two and a half years!* This kind of performance, or lack of it, makes intelligent file structure design a critical concern for CD-ROM applications. CD-ROM provides an excellent test of our ability to integrate and adapt the principles we have developed in the preceding chapters of this book.

3.5   Physical Organization of CD-ROM

CD-ROM is the child of CD audio. In this instance, the impact of heredity is strong, with both positive and negative aspects. Commercially, the CD audio parentage is probably wholly responsible for CD-ROM's viability. It is because of the enormous CD audio market that it is possible to make these discs so inexpensively. Similarly, advances in the design and decreases in the costs of making CD audio players affect the performance and price of CD-ROM drives. Other optical disc media without the benefits of this parentage have not experienced the commercial success of CD-ROM.

On the other hand, making use of the manufacturing capacity associated with CD audio means adhering to the fundamental physical organization of the CD audio disc. Audio discs are designed to play music, not to provide fast, random access to data. This biases CD toward having high storage capacity and moderate data transfer rates and against decent seek performance. If an application requires good random-access performance, that performance has to emerge from our file structure design efforts; it won't come from anything inherent in the medium.

3.5.1 Reading Pits and Lands

CD-ROMs are stamped from a master disc. The master is formed by using the digital data we want to encode to turn a powerful laser on and off very quickly. The master disc, which is made of glass, has a coating that is changed by the laser beam. When the coating is developed, the areas hit by the laser beam turn into pits along the track followed by the beam. The smooth, unchanged areas between the pits are called *lands*. The copies formed from the master retain this pattern of pits and lands.

When we read the stamped copy of the disc, we focus a beam of laser light on the track as it moves under the optical pickup. The pits scatter the light, but the lands reflect most of it back to the pickup. This alternating pattern of high- and low-intensity reflected light is the signal used to reconstruct the original digital information. The encoding scheme used for this signal is not simply a matter of calling a pit a 1 and a land a 0. Instead, the 1s are represented by the transitions from pit to land and back again. Every time the light intensity changes, we get a 1. The 0s are represented by the amount of time between transitions; the longer between transitions, the more 0s we have.

If you think about this encoding scheme, you realize that it is not possible to have two adjacent 1s—1s are always separated by 0s. In fact, due to the limits of the resolution of the optical pickup, there must be at least two 0s between any pair of 1s. This means that the raw pattern of 1s and 0s has to be translated to get the 8-bit patterns of 1s and 0s that form the bytes of the original data. This translation scheme, which is done through a lookup table, turns the original 8 bits of data into 14 expanded bits that can be represented in the pits and lands on the disc; the reading process reverses this translation. Figure 3.12 shows a portion of the lookup table values. Readers who have looked closely at the specifications for CD players may have encountered the term *EFM* encoding. *EFM* stands for "eight to fourteen modulation" and refers to this translation scheme.

Figure 3.12 A portion of the EFM encoding table.

Decimal value	Original bits	Translated bits
0	00000000	01001000100000
1	00000001	10000100000000
2	00000010	10010000100000
3	00000011	10001000100000
4	00000100	01000100000000
5	00000101	00000100010000
6	00000110	00010000100000
7	00000111	00100100000000
8	00001000	01001001000000

It is important to realize that since we represent the 0s in the EFM-encoded data by the *length of time* between transitions, our ability to read the data is dependent on moving the pits and lands under the optical pickup at a precise and constant speed. As we will see, this affects the CD-ROM drive's ability to seek quickly.

3.5.2 CLV Instead of CAV

Data on a CD-ROM is stored in a single, spiral track that winds for almost 3 miles from the center to the outer edge of the disc. This spiral pattern is part of the CD-ROM's heritage from CD audio. For audio data, which requires a lot of storage space, we want to pack the data on the disc as tightly as possible. Since we "play" audio data, often from start to finish without interruption, seeking is not important. As Fig. 3.13 shows, a spiral pattern serves these needs well. A sector toward the outer edge of the disc takes the same amount of space as a sector toward the center of the disc. This means that we can write all of the sectors at the maximum density permitted by the storage medium. Since reading the data requires that it pass under the optical pickup device at a constant rate, the constant data density implies that the disc has to spin more slowly when we are reading at the outer edges than when we are reading toward the center. This is why the spiral is a Constant Linear Velocity (CLV) format: as we seek from the center to the edge, we change the rate of rotation of the disc so the linear speed of the spiral past the pickup device stays the same.

By contrast, the familiar Constant Angular Velocity (CAV) arrangement shown in Fig. 3.13, with its concentric tracks and pie-shaped sectors, writes data less densely in the outer tracks than in the tracks toward the center. We are wasting storage capacity in the outer tracks but have the advantage of being able to spin the disc at the same speed for all positions of the read head. Given the sector arrangement shown in the figure, one rotation reads eight sectors, no matter where we are on the disc. Furthermore, a timing mark placed on the disk makes it easy to find the start of a sector.

The CLV format is responsible, in large part, for the poor seeking performance of CD-ROM drives. The CAV format provides definite track boundaries and a timing mark to find the start of a sector. But the CLV format provides no straightforward way to jump to a specific location. Part of the problem is associated with the need to change rotational speed as we seek across the disc. To read the address information that is stored on the disc along with the user's data, we need to be moving the data under

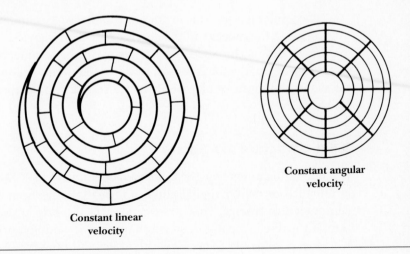

Constant angular
velocity

Constant linear
velocity

Figure 3.13 CLV and CAV recording.

the optical pickup at the correct speed. But to know how to adjust the speed, we need to be able to read the address information so we know where we are. How does the drive's control mechanism break out of this loop? In practice, the answer often involves making guesses and finding the correct speed through trial and error. This takes time and slows down seek performance.

On the positive side, the CLV sector arrangement contributes to the CD-ROM's large storage capacity. Given a CAV arrangement, the CD-ROM would have only a little better than half its present capacity.

3.5.3 Addressing

The use of the CLV organization means that the familiar cylinder, track, sector method of identifying a sector address will not work on a CD-ROM. Instead, we use a sector-addressing scheme that is related to the CD-ROM's roots as an audio playback device. Each second of playing time on a CD is divided into seventy-five sectors, each of which holds 2 kilobytes of data. According to the original Philips/Sony standard, a CD, whether used for audio or CD-ROM, contains at least one hour of playing time. That means that the disc is capable of holding at least 540 000 kilobytes of data:

60 minutes × 60 seconds/minute × 75 sectors/second = 270 000 sectors

In fact, since it is possible to put more than seventy minutes of playing time on a CD, the capacity of the disk is over 600 megabytes.

We address a given sector by referring to the minute, second, and sector of play. So, the thirty-fourth sector in the twenty-second second in the sixteenth minute of play would be addressed with the three numbers 16:22:34.

3.5.4 Structure of a Sector

It is interesting to see how the fundamental design of the CD disc, initially intended to deliver digital audio information, has been adapted for computer data storage. This investigation will also help answer the question: If the disc is capable of storing a quarter of a million printed pages, why does it hold only an hour's worth of Roy Orbison?

When we want to store sound, we need to convert a wave pattern into digital form. Figure 3.14 shows a wave. At any given point in time, the wave has a specific amplitude. We digitize the wave by measuring the amplitude at very frequent intervals and storing the measurements. So, the question of how much storage space we need to represent a wave digitally turns into two other questions: How much space does it take to store each amplitude sample? How often do we take samples?

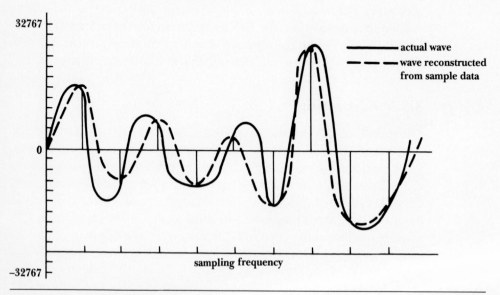

Figure 3.14 Digital sampling of a wave.

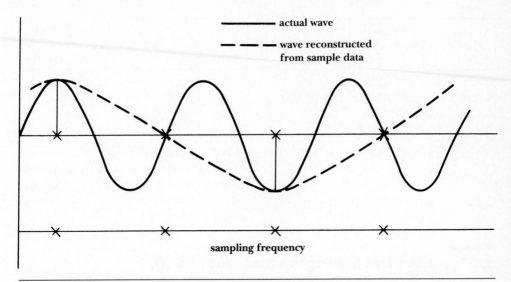

Figure 3.15 The effect of sampling at less than twice the frequency of the wave.

CD audio uses 16 bits to store each amplitude measurement; that means that the "ruler" we use to measure the height of the wave has 65 536 different gradations. To approximate a wave accurately through digital sampling, we need to take the samples at a rate that is more than twice as frequent as the highest frequency we want to capture. This makes sense if you look at the wave in Fig. 3.15. You can see that if we sample at less than twice the frequency of the wave, we lose information about the variation in the wave pattern. The designers of CD audio selected a sampling frequency of 44.1 kilohertz, or 44 100 times per second, so they could record sounds with frequencies ranging up to 20 kilohertz (20 000 cycles per second), which is toward the upper bound of what people can hear.

So, if we are taking a 16-bit, or 2-byte, sample 44 100 times per second, we need to store 88 200 bytes per second. Since we want to store stereo sound, we need double this and store 176 400 bytes per second. You can see why storing an hour of Roy Orbison takes so much space.

If you divide the 176 400-byte-per-second storage capacity of the CD into seventy-five sectors per second, you have 2352 bytes per sector. CD-ROM divides up this "raw" sector storage as shown in Fig. 3.16 to provide 2 kilobytes of user data storage, along with addressing information, error detection, and error correction information. The error correction information is necessary because, although CD audio contains redundancy for error correction, it is not adequate to meet computer data storage needs.

12 bytes synch	4 bytes sector ID	2,048 bytes user data	4 bytes error detection	8 bytes null	276 bytes error correction

Figure 3.16 Structure of a CD-ROM sector.

The audio error correction would result in an average of one incorrect byte for every two discs. The additional error correction information stored within the 2352-byte sector decreases this error rate to 1 uncorrectable byte in every twenty thousand discs.

3.6 CD-ROM Strengths and Weaknesses

As we say throughout this book, good file design is responsive to the nature of the medium, making use of strengths and minimizing weaknesses. We begin, then, by cataloging the strengths and weaknesses of CD-ROM.

3.6.1 Seek Performance

The chief weakness of CD-ROM is the random-access performance. Current magnetic disk technology is such that the average time for a random data access, combining seek time and rotational delay, is about 30 msec. On a CD-ROM, this average access takes 500 msec and can take up to a second or more. Clearly, our file design strategies must avoid seeks to an even greater extent than on magnetic disks.

3.6.2 Data Transfer Rate

A CD-ROM drive reads seventy sectors, or 150 kilobytes of data per second. This data transfer rate is part of the fundamental definition of CD-ROM; it can't be changed without leaving behind the commercial advantages of adhering to the CD audio standard. It is a modest transfer rate, about five times faster than the transfer rate for floppy disks, and an order of magnitude slower than the rate for good Winchester disks. The inadequacy of the transfer rate makes itself felt when we are loading large files, such as those associated with digitized images. On the other hand, the transfer rate is fast enough relative to the CD-ROM's seek performance that we have a design incentive to organize data into blocks, reading more data with each seek in the hope that we can avoid as much seeking as possible.

3.6.3 Storage Capacity

A CD-ROM holds more than 600 megabytes of data. Although it is possible to use up this storage area very quickly, particularly if you are storing raster images, 600 megabytes is big when it comes to text applications. If you decide to download 600 megabytes of text with a 2400-baud modem, it will take about three days of constant data transmission, assuming errorless transmission conditions. Many typical text databases and document collections published on CD-ROM use only a fraction of the disc's capacity.

The design benefit arising from such large capacity is that it enables us to build indexes and other support structures that can help overcome some of the limitations associated with CD-ROM's poor seek performance.

3.6.4 Read-Only Access

From a design standpoint, the fact that CD-ROM is a publishing medium, a storage device that cannot be changed after manufacture, provides significant advantages. We never have to worry about updating. This not only simplifies some of the file structures but also means that it is worthwhile to optimize our index structures and other aspects of file organization. We know that our efforts to optimize access will not be lost through later additions or deletions.

3.6.5 Asymmetric Writing and Reading

For most media, files are written and read using the same computer system. Often, reading and writing are both interactive and are therefore constrained by the need to provide quick response to the user. CD-ROM is different. We create the files to be placed on the disc once; then we distribute the disc, and it is accessed thousands, even millions, of times. We are in a position to bring substantial computing power to the task of file organization and creation, even when the disc will be used on systems with much less capability. In fact, we can use extensive batch-mode processing on large computers to try to provide systems that will perform well on small machines. We make the investment in intelligent, carefully designed file structures only once; users can enjoy the benefits of this investment again and again.

3.7   Storage as a Hierarchy

Although the best mixture of devices for a computing system depends on the needs of the system's users, we can imagine any computing system as a hierarchy of storage devices of different speed, capacity, and cost. Figure 3.17 summarizes the different types of storage found at different levels in such hierarchies and shows approximately how they compare in terms of access time, capacity, and cost.

Types of memory	Devices and media	Access times (sec)	Capacities (bytes)	Cost (Cents/bit)
Primary				
Registers	Semiconductors	$10^{-9} - 10^{-5}$	$10^{0} - 10^{9}$	$10^{0} - 10^{-3}$
Memory				
RAM disk and disk cache				
Secondary				
Direct-access	Magnetic disks	$10^{-3} - 10^{-1}$	$10^{4} - 10^{9}$	$10^{-2} - 10^{-5}$
Serial	Tape and mass storage	$10^{1} - 10^{2}$	$10^{0} - 10^{11}$	$10^{-5} - 10^{-7}$
Offline				
Archival and backup	Removable magnetic disks, optical discs, and tapes	$10^{0} - 10^{2}$	$10^{4} - 10^{12}$	$10^{-5} - 10^{-7}$

Figure 3.17 Approximate comparisons of types of storage.

3.8 A Journey of a Byte

What happens when a program writes a byte to a file on a disk? We know what the program does (it makes a call to a write function), and we now know something about how the byte is stored on a disk. But we haven't looked at what happens *between* the program and the disk. The whole story of what happens to data between program and disk is not one we can tell here, but we can give you an idea of the many different pieces of hardware and software involved and the many jobs that have to be done by looking at an example of a journey of 1 byte.

Suppose we want to append a byte representing the character *P* stored in a character variable `ch` to a file named in the variable `textfile` stored somewhere on a disk. From the program's point of view, the entire journey that the byte will take might be represented by the statement

```
write(textfile, ch, 1)
```

but the journey is much longer than this simple statement suggests.

The `write` statement results in a call to the computer's operating system, which has the task of seeing that the rest of the journey is completed successfully (Fig. 3.18). Often our program can provide the operating system with information that helps it carry out this task more effectively, but once the operating system has taken over, the job of overseeing the rest of the journey is largely beyond our program's control.

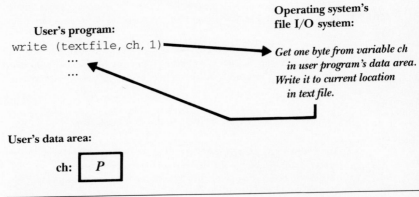

Figure 3.18 The write statement tells the operating system to send one character to disk and gives the operating system the location of the character. The operating system takes over the job of writing, and then returns control to the calling program.

3.8.1 The File Manager

An operating system is not a single program but a collection of programs, each one designed to manage a different part of the computer's resources. Among these programs are ones that deal with file-related matters and I/O devices. We call this subset of programs the operating system's *file manager*. The file manager may be thought of as several layers of procedures (Fig. 3.19), with the upper layers dealing mostly with symbolic, or *logical*, aspects of file management, and the lower layers dealing more with the

Logical

1. The program asks the operating system to write the contents of the variable *c* to the next available position in TEXT.

2. The operating system passes the job on to the file manager.

3. The file manager looks up TEXT in a table containing information about it, such as whether the file is open and available for use, what types of access are allowed, if any, and what physical file the logical name TEXT corresponds to.

4. The file manager searches a file allocation table for the physical location of the sector that is to contain the byte.

5. The file manager makes sure that the last sector in the file has been stored in a system I/O buffer in RAM, then deposits the '*P*' into its proper position in the buffer.

6. The file manager gives instructions to the I/O processor about where the byte is stored in RAM and where it needs to be sent on the disk.

7. The I/O processor finds a time when the drive is available to receive the data and puts the data in proper format for the disk. It may also buffer the data to send it out in chunks of the proper size for the disk.

8. The I/O processor sends the data to the disk controller.

9. The controller instructs the drive to move the read/write head to the proper track, waits for the desired sector to come under the read/write head, then sends the byte to the drive to be deposited, bit-by-bit, on the surface of the disk.

Physical

Figure 3.19 Layers of procedures involved in transmitting a byte from a program's data area to a file called *textfile* on disk.

physical aspects. Each layer calls the one below it, until, at the lowest level, the byte is written to the disk.

The file manager begins by finding out whether the logical characteristics of the file are consistent with what we are asking it to do with the file. It may look up the requested file in a table, where it finds out such things as whether the file has been opened, what type of file the byte is being sent to (a binary file, a text file, or some other organization), who the file's owner is, and whether write access is allowed for this particular user of the file.

The file manager must also determine where in the file `textfile` the *P* is to be deposited. Since the *P* is to be appended to the file, the file manager needs to know where the end of the file is—the physical location of the last sector in the file. This information is obtained from the file allocation table (FAT) described earlier. From the FAT, the file manager locates the drive, cylinder, track, and sector where the byte is to be stored.

3.8.2 The I/O Buffer

Next, the file manager determines whether the sector that is to contain the *P* is already in memory or needs to be loaded into memory. If the sector needs to be loaded, the file manager must find an available *system I/O buffer* space for it and then read it from the disk. Once it has the sector in a buffer in memory, the file manager can deposit the *P* into its proper position in the buffer (Fig. 3.20). The system I/O buffer allows the file manager to read and write data in sector-sized or block-sized units. In other words, it enables the file manager to ensure that the organization of data in memory conforms to the organization it will have on the disk.

Instead of sending the sector immediately to the disk, the file manager usually waits to see if it can accumulate more bytes going to the same sector before transmitting anything. Even though the statement `write(textfile,ch,1)` seems to imply that our character is being sent immediately to the disk, it may in fact be kept in memory for some time before it is sent. (There are many situations in which the file manager cannot wait until a buffer is filled before transmitting it. For instance, if `textfile` were closed, it would have to flush all output buffers holding data waiting to be written to `textfile` so the data would not be lost.)

3.8.3 The Byte Leaves Memory: The I/O Processor and Disk Controller

So far, all of our byte's activities have occurred within the computer's primary memory and have probably been carried out by the computer's

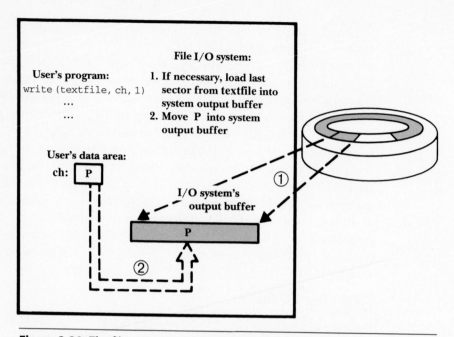

Figure 3.20 The file manager moves *P* from the program's data area to a system output buffer where it may join other bytes headed for the same place on the disk. If necessary, the file manager may have to load the corresponding sector from the disk into the system output buffer.

central processing unit. The byte has traveled along data paths that are designed to be very fast and are relatively expensive. Now it is time for the byte to travel along a data path that is likely to be slower and narrower than the one in primary memory. (A typical computer might have an internal data-path width of 4 bytes, whereas the width of the path leading to the disk might be only 2 bytes.)

Because of bottlenecks created by these differences in speed and data-path widths, our byte and its companions might have to wait for an external data path to become available. This also means that the CPU has extra time on its hands as it deals out information in small enough chunks and at slow enough speeds that the world outside can handle them. In fact, the differences between the internal and external speeds for transmitting data are often so great that the CPU can transmit to several external devices simultaneously.

The processes of disassembling and assembling groups of bytes for transmission to and from external devices are so specialized that it is unreasonable to ask an expensive, general-purpose CPU to spend its valuable time doing I/O when a simpler device could do the job and free the CPU to do the work that it is most suited for. Such a special-purpose device is called an *I/O processor*.

An I/O processor may be anything from a simple chip capable of taking a byte and passing it along one cue, to a powerful, small computer capable of executing very sophisticated programs and communicating with many devices simultaneously. The I/O processor takes its instructions from the operating system, but once it begins processing I/O, it runs independently, relieving the operating system (and the CPU) of the task of communicating with secondary storage devices. This allows I/O processes and internal computing to overlap.[7]

In a typical computer, the file manager might now tell the I/O processor that there is data in the buffer to be transmitted to the disk, how much data there is, and where it is to go on the disk. This information might come in the form of a little program that the operating system constructs and the I/O processor executes (Fig. 3.21).

The job of controlling the operation of the disk is done by a device called a *disk controller*. The I/O processor asks the disk controller if the disk drive is available for writing. If there is much I/O processing, there is a good chance that the drive will not be available and that our byte will have to wait in its buffer until the drive becomes available.

What happens next often makes the time spent so far seem insignificant in comparison: the disk drive is instructed to move its read/write head to the track and sector on the drive where our byte and its companions are to be stored. For the first time, a device is being asked to do something mechanical! The read/write head must seek to the proper track (unless it is already there) and then wait until the disk has spun around so the desired sector is under the head. Once the track and sector are located, the I/O processor (or perhaps the controller) can send out bytes, one at a time, to the drive. Our byte waits until its turn comes; then it travels alone to the drive, where it probably is stored in a little 1-byte buffer while it waits to be deposited on the disk.

Finally, as the disk spins under the read/write head, the 8 bits of our byte are deposited, one at a time, on the surface of the disk (Fig. 3.21). There the *P* remains, at the end of its journey, spinning at a leisurely 50 to 100 miles per hour.

---

7. On many systems the I/O processor can take data directly from memory, without further involvement from the CPU. This process is called *direct memory access* (DMA). On other systems, the CPU must place the data in special I/O registers before the I/O processor can have access to it.

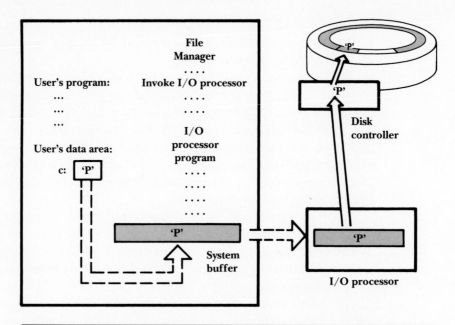

Figure 3.21 The file manager sends the I/O processor instructions in the form of an I/O processor program. The I/O processor gets the data from the system buffer, prepares it for storing on the disk, then sends it to the disk controller, which deposits it on the surface of the disk.

3.9 Buffer Management

Any user of files can benefit from some knowledge of what happens to data traveling between a program's data area and secondary storage. One aspect of this process that is particularly important is the use of buffers. Buffering involves working with large chunks of data in memory so the number of accesses to secondary storage can be reduced. We concentrate on the operation of *system* I/O buffers; but be aware that the use of buffers within programs can also substantially affect performance.

3.9.1 Buffer Bottlenecks

We know that a file manager allocates I/O buffers that are big enough to hold incoming data, but we have said nothing so far about *how many* buffers are used. In fact, it is common for file managers to allocate several buffers for performing I/O.

To understand the need for several system buffers, consider what happens if a program is performing both input and output on one character at a time and only one I/O buffer is available. When the program asks for its first character, the I/O buffer is loaded with the sector containing the character, and the character is transmitted to the program. If the program then decides to output a character, the I/O buffer is filled with the sector into which the output character needs to go, destroying its original contents. Then when the next input character is needed, the buffer contents have to be written to disk to make room for the (original) sector containing the second input character, and so on.

Fortunately, there is a simple and generally effective solution to this ridiculous state of affairs, and that is to use more than one system buffer. For this reason, I/O systems almost always use at least two buffers—one for input and one for output.

Even if a program transmits data in only one direction, the use of a single system I/O buffer can slow it down considerably. We know, for instance, that the operation of reading a sector from a disk is extremely slow compared with the amount of time it takes to move data in memory, so we can guess that a program that reads many sectors from a file might have to spend much of its time waiting for the I/O system to fill its buffer every time a read operation is performed before it can begin processing. When this happens, the program that is running is said to be *I/O bound*—the CPU spends much of its time just waiting for I/O to be performed. The solution to this problem is to use more than one buffer and to have the I/O system filling the next sector or block of data while the CPU is processing the current one.

3.9.2 Buffering Strategies

Multiple Buffering

Suppose that a program is only writing to a disk and that it is I/O bound. The CPU wants to be filling a buffer at the same time that I/O is being performed. If *two* buffers are used and I/O-CPU overlapping is permitted, the CPU can be filling one buffer while the contents of the other are being transmitted to disk. When both tasks are finished, the roles of the buffers can be exchanged. This method of swapping the roles of two buffers after each output (or input) operation is called *double buffering*. Double buffering allows the operating system to operate on one buffer while the other buffer is being loaded or emptied (Fig. 3.22).

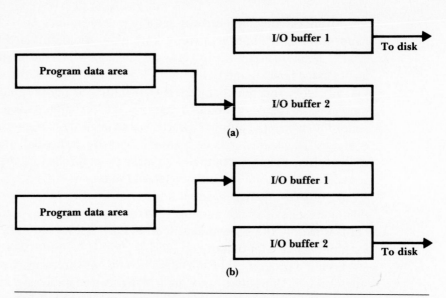

Figure 3.22 Double buffering: (a) the contents of system I/O buffer 1 are sent to disk while I/O buffer 2 is being filled; and (b) the contents of buffer 2 are sent to disk while I/O buffer 1 is being filled.

This technique of swapping system buffers to allow processing and I/O to overlap need not be restricted to two buffers. In theory, any number of buffers can be used, and they can be organized in a variety of ways. The actual management of system buffers is usually done by the operating system and can rarely be controlled by programmers who do not work at the systems level. It is common, however, for programmers to be able to control the *number* of system buffers assigned to jobs.

Some file systems use a buffering scheme called *buffer pooling:* when a system buffer is needed, it is taken from a pool of available buffers and used. When the system receives a request to read a certain sector or block, it looks to see if one of its buffers already contains that sector or block. If no buffer contains it, the system finds from its pool of buffers one that is not currently in use and loads the sector or block into it.

Several different schemes are used to decide which buffer to take from a buffer pool. One generally effective strategy is to take the buffer that is *least recently used.* When a buffer is accessed, it is put on a least-recently-used queue so it is allowed to retain its data until all other less-recently-used buffers have been accessed. The least-recently-used (LRU) strategy for replacing old data with new data has many applications in computing.

It is based on the assumption that a block of data that has been used recently is more likely to be needed in the near future than one that has been used less recently. (We encounter LRU again in later chapters.)

It is difficult to predict the point at which the addition of extra buffers ceases to contribute to improved performance. As the cost of memory continues to decrease, so does the cost of using more and bigger buffers. On the other hand, the more buffers there are, the more time it takes for the file system to manage them. When in doubt, consider experimenting with different numbers of buffers.

Move Mode and Locate Mode

Sometimes it is not necessary to distinguish between a program's data area and system buffers. When data must always be copied from a system buffer to a program buffer (or vice versa), the amount of time taken to perform the move can be substantial. This way of handling buffered data is called *move mode*, as it involves moving chunks of data from one place in memory to another before they can be accessed.

There are two ways that move mode can be avoided. If the file manager can perform I/O directly between secondary storage and the program's data area, no extra move is necessary. Alternatively, the file manager could use system buffers to handle all I/O but provide the program with the *locations*, using pointer variables, of the system buffers. Both techniques are examples of a general approach to buffering called *locate mode*. When locate mode is used, a program is able to operate directly on data in the I/O buffer, eliminating the need to transfer data between an I/O buffer and a program buffer.

Scatter/Gather I/O

Suppose you are reading in a file with many blocks, and each block consists of a header followed by data. You would like to put the headers in one buffer and the data in a different buffer so the data can be processed as a single entity. The obvious way to do this is to read the whole block into a single big buffer; then move the different parts to their own buffers. Sometimes we can avoid this two-step process using a technique called *scatter input*. With scatter input, a single read call identifies not one, but a collection of buffers into which data from a single block is to be scattered.

The converse of scatter input is *gather output*. With gather output, several buffers can be gathered and written with a single write call; this avoids the need to copy them to a single output buffer. When the cost of copying several buffers into a single output buffer is high, scatter/gather can have a significant effect on the running time of a program.

It is not always obvious when features like scatter/gather, locate mode, and buffer pooling are available in an operating system. You often have to go looking for them. Sometimes you can invoke them by communicating with your operating system, and sometimes you can cause them to be invoked by organizing your program in ways that are compatible with the way the operating system does I/O. Throughout this text we return many times to the issue of how to enhance performance by thinking about how buffers work and adapting programs and file structures accordingly.

3.10 I/O in Unix

We see in the journey of a byte that we can view I/O as proceeding through several layers. Unix provides a good example of how these layers occur in a real operating system, so we conclude this chapter with a look at Unix. It is of course beyond the scope of this text to describe the Unix I/O layers in detail. Rather, our objective here is just to pick a few features of Unix that illustrate points made in the text. A secondary objective is to familiarize you with some of the important terminology used in describing Unix systems. For a comprehensive, detailed look at how Unix works, plus a thorough discussion of the design decisions involved in creating and improving Unix, see Leffler et al. (1989).

3.10.1 The Kernel

In Figure 3.19 we see how the process of transmitting data from a program to an external device can be described as proceeding through a series of layers. The topmost layer deals with data in *logical*, structural terms. We store in a file a name, a body of text, an image, an array of numbers, or some other logical entity. This reflects the view that an application has of what goes into a file. The layers that follow collectively carry out the task of turning the logical object into a collection of bits on a *physical* device.

Likewise, the topmost I/O layer in Unix deals with data primarily in logical terms. This layer in Unix consists of *processes* that impose certain logical views on files. Processes are associated with solving some problem, such as counting the words in the file or searching for somebody's address. Processes include *shell routines* like `cat` and `tail`, *user programs* that

operate on files, and *library routines* like `scanf` and `fread` that are
called from programs to read strings, numbers, and so on.

Below this layer is the Unix *kernel,* which incorporates all the rest of
the layers.[8] The components of the kernel that do I/O are illustrated in
Figure 3.23. The kernel views all I/O as operating on a sequence of bytes,
so once we pass control to the kernel all assumptions about the logical
view of a file are gone. The decision to design Unix this way—to make all
operations below the top layer independent of an application's logical view
of a file—is unusual. It is also one of the main attractions in choosing Unix
as a focus for this text, for Unix lets us make all of the decisions about the
logical structure of a file, imposing no restrictions on how we think about
the file beyond the fact that it must be built from a sequence of bytes.

---

8. It is beyond the scope of this text to describe the Unix kernel in detail. For a full description of the
   Unix kernel, including the I/O system, see Leffler et al. (1989).

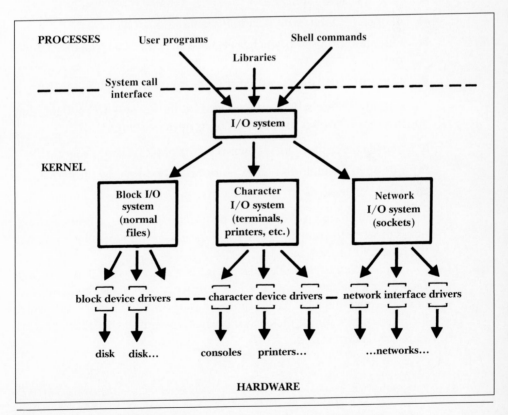

Figure 3.23 Kernel I/O structure.

Let's illustrate the journey of a byte through the kernel, as we did earlier in this chapter by tracing the results of an I/O statement. We assume in this example that we are writing a character to disk. This corresponds to the left branch of the I/O system in Fig. 3.23.

When your program executes a system call such as

```
write (fd, &ch, 1);
```

the kernel is invoked immediately.[9] The routines that let processes communicate directly with the kernel make up the *system call interface*. In this case, the system call instructs the kernel to write a character to a file.

The kernel I/O system begins by connecting the file descriptor (fd) in your program to some file or device in the file system. It does this by proceeding through a series of four tables that enable the kernel to find its way from a process to the places on the disk that will hold the file they refer to. The four tables are

- a file descriptor table;
- an open file table, with information about open files;
- a file allocation table, which is part of a structure called an index node; and
- a table of index nodes, with one entry for each file in use.

Although these tables are managed by the kernel's I/O system, they are, in a sense, "owned" by different parts of the system:

- The file descriptor table is owned by the process (your program).
- The open file table and index node table are owned by the kernel.
- The index node is part of the file system.

The four tables are invoked in turn by the kernel to get the information it needs to write to your file on disk. Let's see how this works by looking at the functions of the tables.

The *file descriptor table* (Fig. 3.24a) is a simple table that associates each of the file descriptors used by a process with an entry in another table, the open file table. Every process has its own descriptor table, which includes entries for all files it has opened, including the "files" stdin, stdout, and stderr.

---

9. This should not be confused with a *library* call, such as *fprintf*, which invokes the standard library to perform some additional operations on the data, such as converting it to an ASCII format, and *then* makes a corresponding system call.

(a) *descriptor* table

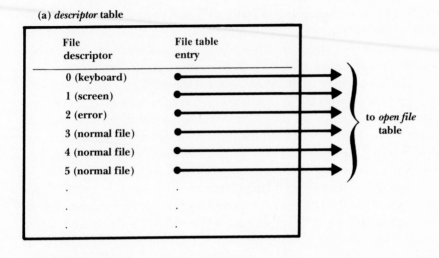

(b) *open file* table

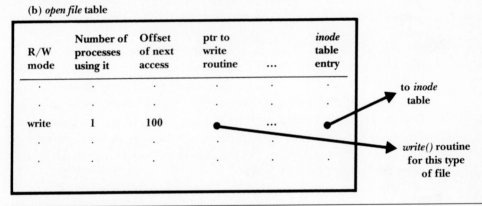

Figure 3.24 Descriptor table and open file table.

The *open file* table (Fig. 3.24b) contains entries for every open file. Every time a file is opened or created, a new entry is added to the open file table. These entries are called *file structures,* and they contain important information about how the corresponding file is to be used, such as the read/write mode used when it was opened, the number of processes currently using it, and the offset within the file to be used for the next read or write. The open file table also contains an array of pointers to generic functions that can be used to operate on the file. These functions will differ depending on the type of file.

It is possible for several different processes to refer to the same open file table entry so one process could read part of a file, another process could read the next part, and so forth, with each process taking over where the previous one stopped. On the other hand, if the same file is opened by two separate open statements, two separate entries are made in the table, and the two processes operate on the file quite independently.[10]

The information in the open file table is transitory. It tells the kernel what it can do with a file that has been opened in a certain way and provides information on how it can operate on the file. The kernel still needs more information about the file, such as where the file is stored on disk, how big the file is, and who owns it. This information is found in an *index node,* more commonly referred to as an *inode* (Fig. 3.25).

An inode is a more permanent structure than an open file table's file structure. A file structure exists only while a file is open for access, but an inode exists as long as its corresponding file exists. For this reason, a file's inode is kept on disk *with* the file (though not physically adjacent to the file). When a file is opened, a copy of its inode is usually loaded into memory where it is added to the aforementioned *inode table* for rapid access.

For the purposes of our discussion, the most important component of the inode is a list (index) of the disk blocks that make up the file. This list is the Unix counterpart to the file allocation table that we described earlier in this chapter.[11] Once the kernel's I/O system has the inode information, it knows all it needs to know about the file. It then invokes an I/O processor program that is appropriate for the type of data, the type of operation, and the type of device that is to be written. In Unix, this program is called a *device driver.*

The device driver sees that your data is moved from its buffer to its proper place on disk. Before we look at the role of device drivers in Unix, it is instructive to look at how the kernel distinguishes among the different kinds of file data it must deal with.

3.10.2 Linking File Names to Files

It is instructive to look a little more closely at how a file name is linked to the corresponding file. All references to files begin with a directory, for it is

---

10. Of course, there are risks in letting this happen. If you are writing to a file with one process at the same time that you are independently reading from the file with another, the meaning of these may be difficult to determine.

11. This might not be a simple linear array. To accommodate both large and small files, this table often has a dynamic, tree-like structure.

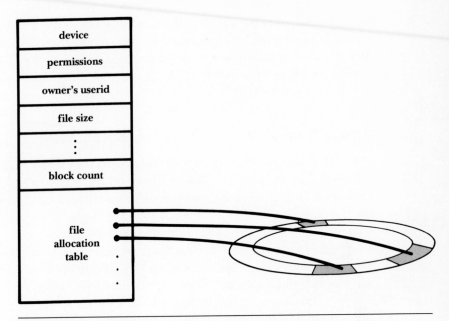

Figure 3.25 An inode. The inode is the data structure used by Unix to describe the file. It includes the device containing the file, permissions, owner and group IDs, and file allocation table, among other things.

in directories that file names are kept. In fact, a directory is just a small file that contains, for each file, a file name together with a pointer to the file's inode on disk.[12] This pointer from a directory to the inode of a file is called a *hard link*. It provides a direct reference from the file name to all other information about the file. When a file is opened, this hard link is used to bring the inode into memory and to set up the corresponding entry in the open file table.

It is possible for several file names to point to the same inode, so one file can have several different names. A field in the inode tells how many hard links there are to the inode. This means that if a file name is deleted and there are other file names for the same file, the file itself is not deleted; its inode's hard-link count is just decremented by one.

There is another kind of link, called a *soft link*, or *symbolic link*. A symbolic link links a file name to another file name rather than to an actu-

---

12. The actual structure of a directory is a little more complex than this, but these are the essential parts. See Leffler, et al. (1989) for details.

al file. Instead of being a pointer to an inode, a soft link is a pathname of some file. Since a symbolic link does not point to an actual file, it can refer to a directory or even to a file in a different file system. Symbolic links are not supported on all Unix systems. Unix System 4.3BSD supports symbolic links, but System V does not.

3.10.3 Normal Files, Special Files, and Sockets

The "everything is a file" concept in Unix works only when we recognize that some files are quite a bit different from others. We see in Fig. 3.23 that the kernel distinguishes among three different types of files. *Normal files* are the files that this text is about. *Special files* almost always represent a stream of characters and control signals that drive some device, such as a line printer or a graphics device. The first three file descriptors in the descriptor table (Fig. 3.24a) are special files. *Sockets* are abstractions that serve as endpoints for interprocess communication.

At a certain conceptual level, these three different types of Unix files are very similar, and many of the same routines can be used to access any of them. For instance, you can establish access to all three types by opening them, and you can write to them with the write system call.

3.10.4 Block I/O

In Fig. 3.23, we see that the three different types of files access their respective devices via three different I/O systems: the *block I/O system,* the *character I/O system,* and the *network I/O system.* Henceforth we ignore the second and third categories, since it is normal file I/O that we are most concerned with in this text.[13]

The block I/O system is the Unix counterpart of the file manager in the journey of a byte. It concerns itself with how to transmit normal file data, viewed by the user as a sequence of bytes, onto a block-oriented device like a disk or tape. Given a byte to store on a disk, for example, it arranges to read in the sector containing the byte to be replaced, to replace the byte, and to write the sector back to the disk.

The Unix view of a block device most closely resembles that of a disk. It is a randomly addressable array of fixed blocks. Originally, all blocks

---

13. This is not entirely true. Sockets, for example, can be used to move normal files from place to place. In fact, high-performance network systems bypass the normal file system in favor of sockets to squeeze every bit of performance out of the network.

were 512 bytes, which was the common sector size on most disks. No other organization (such as clusters) was imposed on the placement of files on disk. (In Section 3.1.7 we saw how the design of later Unix systems dealt with this convention.)

3.10.5 Device Drivers

For each peripheral device there is a separate set of routines, called a *device driver,* that performs the I/O between the I/O buffer and the device. A device driver is roughly equivalent to the I/O processor program described in the journey of a byte.

Since the block I/O system views a peripheral device as an array of physical blocks, addressed as block 0, block 1, and so on, a block I/O device driver's job is to take a block from a buffer, destined for one of these physical blocks, and see that it gets deposited in the proper physical place on the device. This saves the block I/O part of the kernel from having to know anything about the specific device it is writing to, other than its identity and that it is a block device. A thorough discussion of device drivers for block, character, and network I/O can be found in Leffler et al. (1989).

3.10.6 The Kernel and File Systems

In Chapter 2 we described the Unix concept of a *file system.* A Unix file system is a collection of files, together with secondary information about the files in the system. A file system includes the directory structure, the directories, ordinary files, and the inodes that describe the files.

In our discussions we talk about the file system as if it is part of the kernel's I/O system, which it is, but it is also in a sense separate from it. All parts of a file system reside on disk, rather than in memory where the kernel does its work. These parts are brought into memory by the kernel as needed. This separation of the file system from the kernel has many advantages. One important advantage is that we can tune a file system to a particular device or usage pattern independently of how the kernel views files. The discussions of BSD Unix block organization in Section 3.1.7 are file-system concerns, for example, and need not have any effect on how the kernel works.

Another advantage of keeping the file system and I/O system distinct is that we can have separate file systems that are organized differently, perhaps on different devices, but are accessible by the same kernel. In Appendix A, for instance, we describe the design of a file system on CD-ROM that is organized quite differently from a typical disk-based file system yet looks just like any other file system to the user and to the I/O system.

3.10.7 Magnetic Tape and Unix

Important as it is to computing, magnetic tape is somewhat of an orphan in the Unix view of I/O. A magnetic tape unit has characteristics similar to both block I/O devices (block oriented) and character devices (primarily used for sequential access) but does not fit nicely into either category. Character devices read and write streams of data, not blocks, and block devices in general access blocks randomly, not sequentially.

Since block I/O is generally the less inappropriate of the two inappropriate paradigms for tape, a tape device is normally considered in Unix to be a block I/O device and hence is accessed through the block I/O interface. But because the block I/O interface is most often used to write to random-access devices, disks, it does not require blocks to be written in sequence, as they must be written to a tape. This problem is solved by allowing only one write request at a time per tape drive. When high-performance I/O is required, the character device interface can be used in a raw mode to stream data to tapes, bypassing the stage that requires the data to be collected into relatively small blocks before or after transmission.

SUMMARY

In this chapter we look at the software environment in which file processing programs must operate and at some of the hardware devices on which files are commonly stored, hoping to understand how they influence the ways we design and process files. We begin by looking at the two most common storage media: magnetic disks and tapes.

A disk drive consists of a set of read/write heads that are interspersed among one or more platters. Each platter contributes one or two surfaces, each surface contains a set of concentric tracks, and each track is divided into sectors or blocks. The set of tracks that can be read without moving the read/write heads is called a cylinder.

There are two basic ways to address data on disks: by sector and by block. Used in this context, the term *block* refers to a group of records that are stored together on a disk and treated as a unit for I/O purposes. When blocks are used, the user is better able to make the physical organization of data correspond to its logical organization, and hence can sometimes improve performance. Block-organized drives also sometimes make it possible for the disk drive to search among blocks on a track for a record with a certain key without first having to transmit the unwanted blocks into memory.

Three possible disadvantages of block-organized devices are the danger of internal track fragmentation, the burden of dealing with the extra complexity that the user has to bear, and the loss of opportunities to do some of the kinds of synchronization (such as sector interleaving) that sector-addressing devices provide.

The cost of a disk access can be measured in terms of the time it takes for seeking, rotational delay, and transfer time. If sector interleaving is used, it is possible to access logically adjacent sectors by separating them physically by one or more sectors. Although it takes much less time to access a single record directly than sequentially, the extra seek time required for doing direct accesses makes it much slower than sequential access when a series of records is to be accessed.

Despite increasing disk performance, network speeds have improved to the point that disk access is often a significant bottleneck in an overall I/O system. A number of techniques are available to address this problem, including striping, the use of RAM disks, and disk caching.

Research done in connection with BSD Unix shows that block size can have a major effect on performance. By increasing the default block size from 512 bytes to 4096 bytes, throughput was improved enormously, especially for large files, because eight times as much data could be transferred in a single access. A negative consequence of this reorganization was that wasted storage increased from 6.9 percent for 512-byte blocks to 45.6 percent for 4096-byte blocks. It turned out that this problem of wasted space could be dealt with by treating the 4096-byte blocks as clusters of 512-byte blocks, which could be allocated to different files.

Though not as important as disks, magnetic tape has an important niche in file processing. Tapes are inexpensive, reasonably fast for sequential processing, compact, robust, and easy to store and transport. Data is usually organized on tapes in 1-bit-wide parallel tracks, with a bit-wide cross section of tracks interpreted as 1 or more bytes. When estimating processing speed and space utilization, it is important to recognize the role played by the interblock gap. Effective recording density and effective transmission rate are useful measurements of the performance one can expect to achieve for a given physical file organization.

In comparing disk and tape as secondary storage media, we see that disks are replacing tape in more and more cases. This is largely because memory is becoming less expensive relative to secondary storage, which means that one of the earlier advantages of tape over disk, the ability to do sequential access without seeking, has diminished significantly.

CD-ROM is an electronic publishing medium that allows us to replicate and distribute large amounts of information very inexpensively. The primary disadvantage of CD-ROM is that seek performance is relatively slow. This is not a problem that can be solved simply by building better drives; the limits in seek performance grow directly from the fact that CD-ROM is built on top of the CD audio standard. Adherence to this standard, even given its limitations, is the basis for CD-ROM's success as a publishing medium. Consequently, CD-ROM application developers must look to careful file structure design to build fast, responsive retrieval software.

This chapter follows a journey of a byte as it is sent from memory to disk. The journey involves the participation of many different programs and devices, including

- a user's program, which makes the initial call to the operating system;
- the operating system's file manager, which maintains tables of information that it uses to translate between the program's logical view of the file and the physical file where the byte is to be stored;
- an I/O processor and its software, which transmit the byte, synchronizing the transmission of the byte between an I/O buffer in memory and the disk;
- the disk controller and its software, which instruct the drive about how to find the proper track and sector and then send the byte; and
- the disk drive, which accepts the byte and deposits it on the disk surface.

Next, we take a closer look at buffering, focusing mainly on techniques for managing buffers to improve performance. Some techniques include double buffering, buffer pooling, locate-mode buffering, and scatter/gather buffering.

We conclude with a second look at I/O layers, this time concentrating on Unix. We see that every I/O system call begins with a call to the Unix kernel, which knows nothing about the logical structure of a file, treating all data essentially the same—as a sequence of bytes to be transmitted to some external device. In doing its work the I/O system in the kernel invokes four tables: a file descriptor table, an open file table, an inode table, and a file access table in the file's inode. Once the kernel has determined which device to use and how to access it, it calls on a device driver to carry out the accessing.

Although it treats every file as a sequence of bytes, the kernel I/O system deals differently with three different types of I/O: block I/O, character I/O, and network I/O. In this text we concentrate on block I/O. We look briefly at the special role of the file system within the kernel, describing how it uses links to connect file names in directories to their corresponding inodes. Finally, we remark on the reasons that magnetic tape does not fit well into the Unix paradigm for I/O.

KEY TERMS

Block. Unit of data organization corresponding to the amount of data transferred in a single access. *Block* often refers to a collection of records, but it may be a collection of sectors (see *cluster*) whose size has no correspondence to the organization of the data. A block is sometimes called a physical record; a sector is sometimes called a block.

Block device. In Unix, a device such as a disk drive that is organized in blocks and accessed accordingly.

Block I/O. I/O between a computer and a block device.

Block organization. Disk drive organization that allows the user to define the size and organization of blocks and then access a block by giving its block address or the key of one of its records. (See *sector organization*.)

Blocking factor. The number of records stored in one block.

bpi. Bits per inch per track. On a disk, data is recorded serially on tracks. On a tape, data is recorded in parallel on several tracks, so a 6250-bpi nine-track tape contains 6250 bytes per inch, when all nine tracks are taken into account (one track used for parity).

Cartridge tape. Tape systems in which the media are stored in a container, rather than on independent tape reels.

Character device. In Unix, a device such as a keyboard or printer (or tape drive when stream I/O is used) that sends or receives data in the form of a stream of characters.

Character I/O. I/O between a computer and a character device.

Cluster. Minimum unit of space allocation on a sectored disk, consisting of one or more contiguous sectors. The use of large clusters can improve sequential access times by guaranteeing the ability to read longer spans of data without seeking. Small clusters tend to decrease internal fragmentation.

Controller. Device that directly controls the operation of one or more secondary storage devices, such as disk drives and magnetic tape units.

Count subblock. On block-organized drives, a small block that precedes each data block and contains information about the data block, such as its byte count and its address.

Cylinder. The set of tracks on a disk that are directly above and below each other. All of the tracks in a given cylinder can be accessed without having to move the access arm—they can be accessed without the expense of seek time.

Descriptor table. In Unix, a table associated with a single process that links all of the file descriptors generated by that process to corresponding entries in an open file table.

Device driver. In Unix, an I/O processor program invoked by the kernel that performs I/O for a particular device.

Direct access storage device (DASD). Disk or other secondary storage device that permits access to a specific sector or block of data without first requiring the reading of the blocks that precede it.

Direct memory access (DMA). Transfer of data directly between memory and peripheral devices, without significant involvement by the CPU.

Disk cache. A segment of memory configured to contain pages of data from a disk. Disk caches can lead to substantial improvements in access time when access requests exhibit a high degree of locality.

Disk drive. An assemblage of magnetic disks mounted on the same vertical shaft. A disk drive is treated as a single unit consisting of a number of cylinders equivalent to the number of tracks per surface.

Disk striping. Storing information on multiple disk drives by splitting up the information and accessing all of the drives in parallel.

Effective recording density. Recording density after taking into account the space used by interblock gaps, nondata subblocks, and other space-consuming items that accompany data.

Effective transmission rate. Transmission rate after taking into account the time used to locate and transmit the block of data in which a desired record occurs.

Extent. One or more adjacent clusters allocated as part (or all) of a file. The number of extents in a file reflects how dispersed the file is over the disk. The more dispersed a file, the more seeking must be done in moving from one part of the file to another.

File allocation table (FAT). A table that contains mappings to the physical locations of all the clusters in all files on disk storage.

File manager. The part of an operating system that is responsible for managing files, including a collection of programs whose responsibilities range from keeping track of files to invoking I/O processes that transmit information between primary and secondary storage.

File structure. In connection with the open file table in a Unix kernel, the term *file structure* refers to a structure that holds information the kernel needs about an open file. File structure information includes such things as the file's read/write mode, the number of processes currently using it, and the offset within the file to be used for the next read or write.

File system. In Unix, a hierarchical collection of files, usually kept on a single secondary device, such as a hard disk or CD-ROM.

Fixed disk. A disk drive with platters that may not be removed.

Formatting. The process of preparing a disk for data storage, involving such things as laying out sectors, setting up the disk's file allocation table, and checking for damage to the recording medium.

Fragmentation. Space that goes unused within a cluster, block, track, or other unit of physical storage. For instance, track fragmentation occurs when space on a track goes unused because there is not enough space left to accommodate a complete block.

Frame. A 1-bit-wide slice of tape, usually representing a single byte.

Hard link. In Unix, an entry in a directory that connects a file name to the inode of the corresponding file. There can be several hard links to a single file; hence a file can have several names. A file is not deleted until all hard links to the file are deleted.

Index node. In Unix, a data structure associated with a file that describes the file. An index node includes such information as a file's type, its owner and group IDs, and a list of the disk blocks that comprise the file. A more common name for index node is *inode*.

Inode. *See* index node.

Interblock gap. An interval of blank space that separates sectors, blocks, or subblocks on tape or disk. In the case of tape, the gap provides sufficient space for the tape to accelerate or decelerate when starting or stopping. On both tapes and disks the gaps enable the read/write heads to tell accurately when one sector (or block or subblock) ends and another begins.

Interleaving factor. Since it is often not possible to read physically adjacent sectors of a disk, logically adjacent sectors are sometimes arranged so they are not physically adjacent. This is called interleaving. The interleaving factor refers to the number of physical sectors the next logically adjacent sector is located from the current sector being read or written.

I/O processor. A device that carries out I/O tasks, allowing the CPU to work on non-I/O tasks.

Kernel. The central part of the Unix operating system.

Key subblock. On block-addressable drives, a block that contains the key of the last record in the data block that follows it, allowing the drive to search among the blocks on a track for a block containing a certain key, without having to load the blocks into primary memory.

Mass storage system. General term applied to storage units with large capacity. Also applied to very high-capacity secondary storage systems that are capable of transmitting data between a disk and any of several thousand tape cartridges within a few seconds.

Nominal recording density. Recording density on a disk track or magnetic tape without taking into account the effects of gaps or nondata subblocks.

Nominal transmission rate. Transmission rate of a disk or tape unit without taking into account the effects of such extra operations as seek time for disks and interblock gap traversal time for tapes.

Open file table. In Unix, a table owned by the kernel with an entry, called a file structure, for each open file. See *file structure*.

Parity. An error-checking technique in which an extra parity bit accompanies each byte and is set in such a way that the total number of 1 bits is even (even parity) or odd (odd parity).

Platter. One disk in the stack of disks on a disk drive.

Process. An executing program. In Unix, several instances of the same program can be executing at the same time, as separate processes. The kernel keeps a separate file descriptor table for each process.

RAID disk system. An array of disk drives that provide access to the disks in parallel. Storage of files on RAID systems often involves disk striping.

RAM disk. Block of memory configured to simulate a disk.

Rotational delay. The time it takes for the disk to rotate so the desired sector is under the read/write head.

Scatter/gather I/O. Buffering techniques that involve, on input, scattering incoming data into more than one buffer and, on output, gathering data from several buffers to be output as a single chunk of data.

Sector. The fixed-sized data blocks that together make up the tracks on certain disk drives. Sectors are the smallest addressable unit on a disk whose tracks are made up of sectors.

Sector organization. Disk drive organization that uses sectors.

Seek time. The time required to move the access arm to the correct cylinder on a disk drive.

Sequential access device. A device, such as a magnetic tape unit or card reader, in which the medium (for example, tape) must be accessed from the beginning. Sometimes called a serial device.

Socket. In Unix, a socket is an abstraction that serves as an endpoint of communication within some domain. For example, a socket can be used to provide direct communication between two computers. Although in some ways the kernel treats sockets like files, we do not deal with sockets in this text.

Soft link. See *symbolic link*.

Special file. In Unix, the term *special file* refers to a stream of characters and control signals that drive some device, such as a line printer or a graphics device.

Streaming tape drive. A tape drive whose primary purpose is to dump large amounts of data from disk to tape or from tape to disk.

Subblock. When blocking is used, there are often separate groupings of information concerned with each individual block. For example, a count subblock, a key subblock, and a data subblock might all be present.

Symbolic link. In Unix, an entry in a directory that gives the pathname of a file. Since a symbolic link is an indirect pointer to a file, it is not as closely associated with the file as a hard link. Symbolic links can point to directories or even to files in other file systems.

Track. The set of bytes on a single surface of a disk that can be accessed without seeking (without moving the access arm). The surface of a disk can be thought of as a series of concentric circles with each circle corresponding to a particular position of the access arm and read/write heads. Each of these circles is a track.

Transfer time. Once the data we want is under the read/write head, we have to wait for it to pass under the head as we read it. The amount of time required for this motion and reading is the transfer time.

FURTHER READINGS

Many textbooks contain more detailed information on the material covered in this chapter. In the area of operating systems and file management systems, we have found the operating system texts by Deitel (1989), Silberschatz and Galvin (1998), and Tannenbaum, et al. (1997) useful. Hanson (1982) has a great deal of material on blocking and buffering, secondary storage devices, and performance.

Ritchie and Thompson (1974), Kernighan and Ritchie (1978), and McKusick et al. (1984) provide information on how file I/O is handled in the Unix operating system. The latter provides a good case study of ways in which a file system can be altered to provide substantially faster throughput for certain applications. A comprehensive coverage of Unix I/O from the design perspective can be found in Leffler et al. (1989). Information about I/O devices and file system services for Windows 95 and Windows NT is covered in Hart (1997).

Information on specific systems and devices can often be found in manuals and documentation published by manufacturers and in web sites. Information on specific disks, tapes, and CDs that is presented in this chapter comes from web sites for Seagate, Western Digital, StorageTek, and Sony, among others.

EXERCISES

1. Determine as well as you can what the journey of a byte would be like on your system. You may have to consult technical reference manuals that describe your computer's file management system, operating system, and peripheral devices. You may also want to talk to local gurus who have experience using your system.

2. Suppose you are writing a list of names to a text file, one name per write statement. Why is it not a good idea to close the file after every write and then reopen it before the next write?

3. Find out what utility routines for monitoring I/O performance and disk utilization are available on your computer system. If you have a large computing system, there are different routines available for different kinds of users, depending on what privileges and responsibilities they have.

4. When you create or open a file in C++, you must provide certain information to your computer's file manager so it can handle your file properly. Compared to certain languages, such as Cobol, the amount of information you must provide in C++ is very small. Find a text or manual on PL/I or Cobol and look up the ENVIRONMENT file description attribute, which can be used to tell the file manager a great deal about how you expect a file to be organized and used. Compare PL/I or Cobol with C++ in terms of the types of file specifications available to the programmer.

5. Much is said in section 3.1 about how disk space is organized physically to store files. Assume that no such complex organization is used and that every file must occupy a single contiguous piece of a disk, somewhat the way a file is stored on tape. How does this simplify disk storage? What problems does it create?

6. A disk drive uses 512-byte sectors. If a program requests that a 128-byte record be written to disk, the file manager may have to read a sector from the disk before it can write the record. Why? What could you do to decrease the number of times such an extra read is likely to occur?

7. Use the Internet to determine the detailed characteristics of current disk drives. Reproduce the information in Table 3.1 for three new disk drives.

8. In early Unix systems, inodes were kept together on one part of a disk, while the corresponding data was scattered elsewhere on the disk. Later editions divided disk drives into groups of adjacent cylinders called cylinder groups, in which each cylinder group contains inodes and their corresponding data. How does this new organization improve performance?

9. In early Unix systems, the minimum block size was 512 bytes, with a cluster size of one. The block size was increased to 1024 bytes in 4.0BSD, more than doubling its throughput. Explain how this could occur.

10. Draw pictures that illustrate the role of fragmentation in determining the numbers in Table 3.2, section 3.1.7.

11. The IBM 3350 disk drive uses block addressing. The two subblock organizations described in the text are available:

    Count-data, where the extra space used by count subblock and interblock gaps is equivalent to 185 bytes; and

    Count-key-data, where the extra space used by the count and key subblocks and accompanying gaps is equivalent to 267 bytes, plus the key size.

    An IBM 3350 has 19 069 usable bytes available per track, 30 tracks per cylinder, and 555 cylinders per drive. Suppose you have a file with 350 000 80-byte records that you want to store on a 3350 drive. Answer the following questions. Unless otherwise directed, assume that the blocking factor is 10 and that the count-data subblock organization is used.

    a. How many blocks can be stored on one track? How many records?
    b. How many blocks can be stored on one track if the count-key-data subblock organization is used and key size is 13 bytes?
    c. Make a graph that shows the effect of block size on storage utilization, assuming count-data subblocks. Use the graph to help predict the best and worst possible blocking factor in terms of storage utilization.
    d. Assuming that access to the file is always sequential, use the graph from 11c to predict the best and worst blocking factor. Justify your answer in terms of efficiency of storage utilization and processing time.
    e. How many cylinders are required to hold the file (blocking factor 10 and count-data format)? How much space will go unused due to internal track fragmentation?
    f. If the file were stored on contiguous cylinders and if there were no interference from other processes using the disk drive, the average seek time for a random access of the file would be about 12 msec. Use this rate to compute the average time needed to access one record randomly.
    g. Explain how retrieval time for random accesses of records is affected by increasing block size. Discuss trade-offs between storage efficiency and retrieval when different block sizes are used. Make a table with different block sizes to illustrate your explanations.
    h. Suppose the file is to be sorted, and a shell sort is to be used to sort the file. Since the file is too large to read into memory, it will be

sorted in place, on the disk. It is estimated (Knuth, 1973b, p. 380) that this requires about 15 $N^{1.25}$ moves of records, where N represents the total number of records in the file. Each move requires a random access. If all of the preceding is true, how long does it take to sort the file? (As you will see, this is not a very good solution. We provide much better ones in Chapter 7, which deals with cosequential processing.)

12. A sectored disk drive differs from one with a block organization in that there is less of a correspondence between the logical and physical organization of data records or blocks.

    For example, consider the Seagate Cheetah 9 disk drive, described in Table 3.1. From the drive's (and drive controller's) point of view, a file is just a vector of bytes divided into 512-byte sectors. Since the drive knows nothing about where one record ends and another begins, a record can span two or more sectors, tracks, or cylinders.

    One common way that records are formatted is to place a two-byte field at the beginning of each block, giving the number of bytes of data, followed by the data itself. There is no extra gap and no other overhead. Assuming that this organization is used, and that you want to store a file with 350 000 80-byte records, answer the following questions:

    a. How many records can be stored on one track if one record is stored per block?
    b. How many cylinders are required to hold the file?
    c. How might you block records so each physical record access results in 10 actual records being accessed? What are the benefits of doing this?

13. Suppose you have a collection of 500 large images stored in files, one image per file, and you wish to "animate" these images by displaying them in sequence on a workstation at a rate of at least 15 images per second over a high-speed network. Your secondary storage consists of a disk farm with 30 disk drives, and your disk manager permits striping over as many as 30 drives, if you request it. Your drives are guaranteed to perform I/O at a steady rate of 2 megabytes per second. Each image is 3 megabytes in size. Network transmission speeds are not a problem.

    a. Describe in broad terms the steps involved in doing such an animation in real time from disk.
    b. Describe the performance issues that you have to consider in implementing the animation. Use numbers.

c. How might you configure your I/O system to achieve the desired performance?

14. Consider the 1 000 000-record mailing-list file discussed in the text. The file is to be backed up on 2400-foot reels of 6250-bpi tape with 0.3-inch interblock gaps. Tape speed is 200 inches per second.

    a. Show that only one tape would be required to back up the file if a blocking factor of 50 is used.

    b. If a blocking factor of 50 is used, how many extra records could be accommodated on a 2400-foot tape?

    c. What is the effective recording density when a blocking factor of 50 is used?

    d. How large does the blocking factor have to be to achieve the maximum effective recording density? What negative results can result from increasing the blocking factor? (*Note:* An I/O buffer large enough to hold a block must be allocated.)

    e. What would be the minimum blocking factor required to fit the file onto the tape?

    f. If a blocking factor of 50 is used, how long would it take to read one block, including the gap? What would the effective transmission rate be? How long would it take to read the entire file?

    g. How long would it take to perform a binary search for one record in the file, assuming that it is not possible to read backwards on the tape? (Assume that it takes 60 seconds to rewind the tape.) Compare this with the expected average time it would take for a sequential search for one record.

    h. We implicitly assume in our discussions of tape performance that the tape drive is always reading or writing at full speed, so no time is lost by starting and stopping. This is not necessarily the case. For example, some drives automatically stop after writing each block.

       Suppose that the extra time it takes to start before reading a block and to stop after reading the block totals 1 msec and that the drive must start before and stop after reading each block. How much will the effective transmission rate be decreased due to starting and stopping if the blocking factor is 1? What if it is 50?

15. Why are there interblock gaps on linear tapes? In other words, why do we not just jam all records into one block?

16. The use of large blocks can lead to severe internal fragmentation of tracks on disks. Does this occur when tapes are used? Explain.

17. Each MS-DOS file system (or drive) uses a FAT with 64K entries. For each disk in Table 3.1, give the minimum sector size if the disk is configured as a single MS-DOS drive. Each file uses a minimum of one sector.

18. Use the Internet to determine the characteristics of the second generation of Digital Versatile Disc (DVD). What are the plans to put four independent surfaces on a single disc? What are the density, sector size, and transfer rate for these new disc systems?

4

Fundamental File Structure Concepts

❖ Introduce file structure concepts dealing with
- Stream files,
- Reading and writing fields and records,
- Field and record boundaries,
- Fixed-length and variable-length fields and records, and
- Packing and unpacking records and buffers.
❖ Present an object-oriented approach to file structures
- Methods of encapsulating object value and behavior in classes,
- Classes for buffer manipulation,
- Class hierarchy for buffer and file objects and operations,
- Inheritance and virtual functions, and
- Template classes.

4.1 Field and Record Organization

When we build file structures, we are making it possible to make data *persistent*. That is, one program can create data in memory and store it in a file and another program can read the file and re-create the data in its memory. The basic unit of data is the *field*, which contains a single data value. Fields are organized into aggregates, either as many copies of a single field (an *array*) or as a list of different fields (a *record*). Programming language type definitions allows us to define the structure of records. When a record is stored in memory, we refer to it as an *object* and refer to its fields as *members*. When that object is stored in a file, we call it simply a record.

In this chapter we investigate the many ways that objects can be represented as records in files. We begin by considering how to represent fields and continue with representations of aggregates. The simplest representation is with a file organized as a stream of bytes.

4.1.1 A Stream File

Suppose the objects we wish to store contain name and address information about a collection of people. We will use objects of class `Person`, from Section 1.5, "Using Objects in C++," to store information about individuals. Figure 4.1 (and file `writestr.cpp`) gives a C++ function (`operator <<`) to write the fields of a `Person` to a file as a stream of bytes.

File `writstrm.cpp` in Appendix D includes this output function, together with a function to accept names and addresses from the keyboard and a main program. You should compile and run this program. We use it as the basis for a number of experiments, and you can get a better feel for the differences between the file structures we are discussing if you perform the experiments yourself.

The following names and addresses are used as input to the program:

Mary Ames	Alan Mason
123 Maple	90 Eastgate
Stillwater, OK 74075	Ada, OK 74820

When we list the output file on our terminal screen, here is what we see:

```
AmesMary123 MapleStillwaterOK74075MasonAlan90 EastgateAdaOK74820
```

The program writes the information out to the file precisely as specified, as a stream of bytes containing no added information. But in meeting our specifications, the program creates a kind of reverse Humpty-Dumpty problem. Once we put all that information together as a single byte stream, there is no way to get it apart again.

```
ostream & operator << (ostream & outputFile, Person & p)
{ // insert (write) fields into stream
   outputFile << p.LastName
     << p.FirstName
     << p.Address
     << p.City
     << p.State
     << p.ZipCode;
   return outputFile;
}
```

Figure 4.1 Function to write (<<) a `Person` as a stream of bytes.

We have lost the integrity of the fundamental organizational units of our input data; these fundamental units are not the individual characters but meaningful aggregates of characters, such as "Ames" or "123 Maple." When we are working with files, we call these fundamental aggregates *fields*. A field is *the smallest logically meaningful unit of information in a file.*[1]

A field is a logical notion; it is a *conceptual tool*. A field does not necessarily exist in any physical sense, yet it is important to the file's structure. When we write out our name and address information as a stream of undifferentiated bytes, we lose track of the fields that make the information meaningful. We need to organize the file in some way that lets us keep the information divided into fields.

4.1.2 Field Structures

There are many ways of adding structure to files to maintain the identity of fields. Four of the most common methods follow:

- Force the fields into a predictable length.
- Begin each field with a length indicator.
- Place a *delimiter* at the end of each field to separate it from the next field.
- Use a "keyword = value" expression to identify each field and its contents.

Method 1: Fix the Length of Fields

The fields in our sample file vary in length. If we force the fields into predictable lengths, we can pull them back out of the file simply by counting our way to the end of the field. We can define a `struct` in C or a `class` in C++ to hold these fixed-length fields, as shown in Fig. 4.2. As you can see, the only difference between the C and C++ versions is the use of the keyword `struct` or `class` and the designation of the fields of class `Person` as `public` in C++.

---

1. Readers should not confuse the terms *field* and *record* with the meanings given to them by some programming languages, including Ada. In Ada, a record is an aggregate data structure that can contain members of different types, where each member is referred to as a field. As we shall see, there is often a direct correspondence between these definitions of the terms and the fields and records that are used in files. However, the terms *field* and *record* as we use them have much more general meanings than they do in Ada.

In C:	In C++:
```struct Person{```	```class Person { public:```
``` char last [11];```	``` char last [11];```
``` char first [11];```	``` char first [11];```
``` char address [16];```	``` char address [16];```
``` char city [16];```	``` char city [16];```
``` char state [3];```	``` char state [3];```
``` char zip [10];```	``` char zip [10];```
```};```	```};```

Figure 4.2 Definition of record to hold person information.

In this example, each field is a character array that can hold a string value of some maximum size. The size of the array is one larger than the longest string it can hold. This is because strings in C and C++ are stored with a terminating 0 byte. The string "Mary" requires five characters to store. The functions in `string.h` assume that each string is stored this way. A fixed-size field in a file does not need to add this extra character. Hence, an object of class `Person` can be stored in 61 bytes: 10+10+15+15+2+9.

Using this kind of fixed-field length structure changes our output so it looks like that shown in Fig. 4.3(a). Simple arithmetic is sufficient to let us recover the data from the original fields.

One obvious disadvantage of this approach is that adding all the padding required to bring the fields up to a fixed length makes the file much larger. Rather than using 4 bytes to store the last name "Ames," we use 10. We can also encounter problems with data that is too long to fit into the allocated amount of space. We could solve this second problem by fixing all the fields at lengths that are large enough to cover all cases, but this would make the first problem of wasted space in the file even worse.

Because of these difficulties, the fixed-field approach to structuring data is often inappropriate for data that inherently contains a large amount of variability in the length of fields, such as names and addresses. But there are kinds of data for which fixed-length fields are highly appropriate. If every field is already fixed in length or if there is very little variation in field lengths, using a file structure consisting of a continuous stream of bytes organized into fixed-length fields is often a very good solution.

```
Ames      Mary      123 Maple      Stillwater      OK74075
Mason     Alan      90 Eastgate    Ada             OK74820
```

(a)

```
04Ames04Mary09123 Maple10Stillwater02OK0574075
05Mason04Alan1190 Eastgate03Ada02OK0574820
```

(b)

```
Ames|Mary|123 Maple|Stillwater|OK|74075|
Mason|Alan|90 Eastgate|Ada|OK|74820|
```

(c)

```
last=Ames|first=Mary|address=123 Maple|city=Stillwater|
state=OK|zip=74075|
```

(d)

Figure 4.3 Four methods for organizing fields within records. (a) Each field is of fixed length. (b) Each field begins with a length indicator. (c) Each field ends with a delimiter |. (d) Each field is identified by a key word.

Method 2: Begin Each Field with a Length Indicator

Another way to make it possible to count to the end of a field is to store the field length just ahead of the field, as illustrated in Fig. 4.3(b). If the fields are not too long (less than 256 bytes), it is possible to store the length in a single byte at the start of each field. We refer to these fields as *length-based*.

Method 3: Separate the Fields with Delimiters

We can also preserve the identity of fields by separating them with delimiters. All we need to do is choose some special character or sequence of characters that will not appear within a field and then *insert* that delimiter into the file after writing each field.

The choice of a delimiter character can be very important as it must be a character that does not get in the way of processing. In many instances *white-space characters* (blank, new line, tab) make excellent delimiters because they provide a clean separation between fields when we list them on the console. Also, most programming languages include I/O statements which, by default, assume that fields are separated by white space.

Unfortunately, white space would be a poor choice for our file since blanks often occur as legitimate characters within an address field. Therefore, instead of white space we use the vertical bar character as our delimiter, so our file appears as in Fig. 4.3(c). Readers should modify the original stream-of-bytes program, `writstrm.cpp`, so that it places a delimiter after each field. We use this delimited field format in the next few sample programs.

Method 4: Use a "Keyword = Value" Expression to Identify Fields

This option, illustrated in Fig. 4.3(d), has an advantage that the others do not: it is the first structure in which a field provides information about itself. Such *self-describing* structures can be very useful tools for organizing files in many applications. It is easy to tell which fields are contained in a file, even if we don't know ahead of time which fields the file is supposed to contain. It is also a good format for dealing with missing fields. If a field is missing, this format makes it obvious, because the keyword is simply not there.

You may have noticed in Fig. 4.3(d) that this format is used in combination with another format, a delimiter to separate fields. While this may not always be necessary, in this case it is helpful because it shows the division between each value and the keyword for the following field.

Unfortunately, for the address file this format also wastes a lot of space: 50 percent or more of the file's space could be taken up by the keywords. But there are applications in which this format does not demand so much overhead. We discuss some of these applications in Section 5.6: "Portability and Standardization."

4.1.3 Reading a Stream of Fields

Given a modified version of `operator <<` that uses delimiters to separate fields, we can write a function that overloads the extraction operator (operator >>) that reads the stream of bytes back in, breaking the stream into fields and storing it as a `Person` object. Figure 4.4 contains the implementation of the extraction operation. Extensive use is made of the `istream` method `getline`. The arguments to `getline` are a character array to hold the string, a maximum length, and a delimiter. `Getline` reads up to the first occurrence of the delimiter, or the end-of-line,

```
istream & operator >> (istream & stream, Person & p)
{ // read delimited fields from file
   char delim;
   stream.getline(p.LastName, 30,'|');
   if (strlen(p.LastName)==0) return stream;
   stream.getline(p.FirstName,30,'|');
   stream.getline(p.Address,30,'|');
   stream.getline(p.City, 30,'|');
   stream.getline(p.State,15,'|');
   stream.getline(p.ZipCode,10,'|');
   return stream;
}
```

Figure 4.4 Extraction operator for reading delimited fields into a `Person` object.

whichever comes first. A full implementation of the program to read a stream of delimited `Person` objects in C++, `readdel.cpp`, is included in Appendix D.

When this program is run using our delimited-field version of the file containing data for Mary Ames and Alan Mason, the output looks like this:

```
Last Name   'Ames'
First Name  'Mary'
Address     '123 Maple'
City        'Stillwater'
State       'OK'
Zip Code    '74075'
Last Name   'Mason'
First Name  'Alan'
Address     '90 Eastgate'
City        'Ada'
State       'OK'
Zip Code    '74820'
```

Clearly, we now preserve the notion of a field as we store and retrieve this data. But something is still missing. We do not really think of this file as a stream of fields. In fact, the fields are grouped into records. The first six fields form a record associated with Mary Ames. The next six are a record associated with Alan Mason.

4.1.4 Record Structures

A *record* can be defined as *a set of fields that belong together when the file is viewed in terms of a higher level of organization.* Like the notion of a field, a record is another conceptual tool. It is another level of organization that we impose on the data to preserve meaning. Records do not necessarily exist in the file in any physical sense, yet they are an important logical notion included in the file's structure.

Most often, as in the example above, a record in a file represents a structured data object. Writing a record into a file can be thought of as saving the state (or value) of an object that is stored in memory. Reading a record from a file into a memory resident object restores the state of the object. It is our goal in designing file structures to facilitate this transfer of information between memory and files. We will use the term *object* to refer to data residing in memory and the term *record* to refer to data residing in a file.

In C++ we use *class* declarations to describe objects that reside in memory. The members, or attributes, of an object of a particular class correspond to the fields that need to be stored in a file record. The C++ programming examples are focused on adding methods to classes to support using files to preserve the state of objects.

Following are some of the most often used methods for organizing the records of a file:

■ Require that the records be a predictable number of bytes in length.

■ Require that the records be a predictable number of fields in length.

■ Begin each record with a length indicator consisting of a count of the number of bytes that the record contains.

■ Use a second file to keep track of the beginning byte address for each record.

■ Place a delimiter at the end of each record to separate it from the next record.

Method 1: Make Records a Predictable Number of Bytes (Fixed-Length Records)

A *fixed-length record file* is one in which each record contains the same number of bytes. This method of recognizing records is analogous to the first method we discussed for making fields recognizable. As we will see in the chapters that follow, fixed-length record structures are among the most commonly used methods for organizing files.

The C structure `Person` (or the C++ class of the same name) that we define in our discussion of fixed-length fields is actually an example of a fixed-length *record* as well as an example of fixed-length fields. We have a fixed number of fields, each with a predetermined length, that combine to make a fixed-length record. This kind of field and record structure is illustrated in Fig. 4.5(a).

It is important to realize, however, that fixing the number of bytes in a record does not imply that the size or number of fields in the record must be fixed. Fixed-length records are frequently used as containers to hold variable numbers of variable-length fields. It is also possible to mix fixed- and variable-length fields within a record. Figure 4.5(b) illustrates how variable-length fields might be placed in a fixed-length record.

Method 2: Make Records a Predictable Number of Fields

Rather than specify that each record in a file contain some fixed number of bytes, we can specify that it will contain a fixed number of fields. This is a good way to organize the records in the name and address file we have been looking at. The program in `writstrm.cpp` asks for six pieces of information for every person, so there are six contiguous fields in the file for each record (Fig. 4.5c). We could modify `readdel` to recognize fields simply by counting the fields *modulo* six, outputting record boundary information to the screen every time the count starts over.

Method 3: Begin Each Record with a Length Indicator

We can communicate the length of records by beginning each record with a field containing an integer that indicates how many bytes there are in the rest of the record (Fig. 4.6a on page 128). This is a commonly used method for handling variable-length records. We will look at it more closely in the next section.

Method 4: Use an Index to Keep Track of Addresses

We can use an *index* to keep a byte offset for each record in the original file. The byte offsets allow us to find the beginning of each successive record and compute the length of each record. We look up the position of a record in the index then seek to the record in the data file. Figure 4.6(b) illustrates this two-file mechanism.

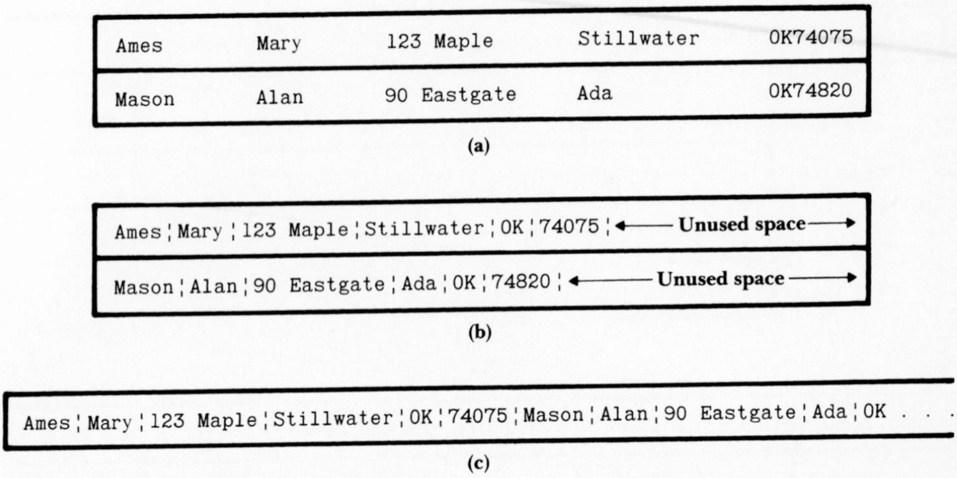

Ames	Mary	123 Maple	Stillwater	OK74075
Mason	Alan	90 Eastgate	Ada	OK74820

(a)

```
Ames ┆ Mary ┆ 123 Maple ┆ Stillwater ┆ OK ┆ 74075 ┆ ◄─── Unused space ───►
```
```
Mason ┆ Alan ┆ 90 Eastgate ┆ Ada ┆ OK ┆ 74820 ┆ ◄──── Unused space ───►
```

(b)

```
Ames ┆ Mary ┆ 123 Maple ┆ Stillwater ┆ OK ┆ 74075 ┆ Mason ┆ Alan ┆ 90 Eastgate ┆ Ada ┆ OK  . . .
```

(c)

Figure 4.5 Three ways of making the lengths of records constant and predictable. (a) Counting bytes: fixed-length records with fixed-length fields. (b) Counting bytes: fixed-length records with variable-length fields. (c) Counting fields: six fields per record.

Method 5: Place a Delimiter at the End of Each Record

This option, at a record level, is exactly analogous to the solution we used to keep the *fields* distinct in the sample program we developed. As with fields, the delimiter character must not get in the way of processing. Because we often want to read files directly at our console, a common choice of a record delimiter for files that contain readable text is the end-of-line character (carriage return/new-line pair or, on Unix systems, just a new-line character: \n). In Fig 4.6(c) we use a # character as the record delimiter.

4.1.5 A Record Structure That Uses a Length Indicator

None of these approaches to preserving the idea of a *record* in a file is appropriate for all situations. Selection of a method for record organization depends on the nature of the data and on what you need to do with it. We begin by looking at a record structure that uses a record-length field at the beginning of the record. This approach lets us preserve the *variability* in the length of records that is inherent in our initial stream file.

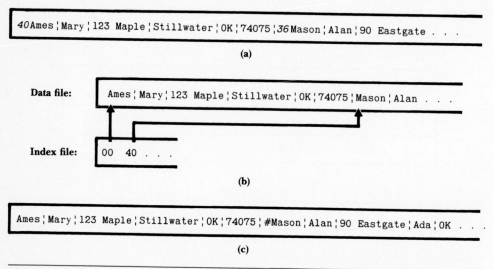

Figure 4.6 Record structures for variable-length records. (a) Beginning each record with a length indicator. (b) Using an index file to keep track of record addresses. (c) Placing the delimiter # at the end of each record.

Writing the Variable-Length Records to the File

Implementing variable-length records is partially a matter of building on the program in `writstrm.cpp` that we created earlier in this chapter, but it also involves addressing some new problems:

- If we want to put a length indicator at the *beginning* of every record (before any other fields), we must know the sum of the lengths of the fields in each record before we can begin writing the record to the file. We need to accumulate the entire contents of a record in a *buffer* before writing it out.

- In what form should we write the record-length field to the file? As a binary integer? As a series of ASCII characters?

The concept of buffering is one we run into again and again as we work with files. In this case, the buffer can simply be a character array into which we place the fields and field delimiters as we collect them. A C++ function `WritePerson`, written using the C string functions, is found in Figure 4.7. This function creates a buffer; fills it with the delimited field values using `strcat`, the string concatenation function; calculates the length of the of the buffer using `strlen`; then writes the buffer length and the buffer to the output stream.

```
const int MaxBufferSize = 200;
int WritePerson (ostream & stream, Person & p)
{   char buffer [MaxBufferSize]; // create buffer of fixed size
    strcpy(buffer, p.LastName); strcat(buffer,"|");
    strcat(buffer, p.FirstName); strcat(buffer,"|");
    strcat(buffer, p.Address);  strcat(buffer,"|");
    strcat(buffer, p.City);  strcat(buffer,"|");
    strcat(buffer, p.State);  strcat(buffer,"|");
    strcat(buffer, p.ZipCode);  strcat(buffer,"|");
    short length=strlen(buffer);
    stream.write (&length, sizeof(length)); // write length
    stream.write (&buffer, length);
}
```

Figure 4.7 Function `WritePerson` writes a variable-length, delimited buffer to a file.

Representing the Record Length

The question of how to represent the record length is a little more difficult. One option would be to write the length in the form of a 2-byte binary integer before each record. This is a natural solution in C, since it does not require us to go to the trouble of converting the record length into character form. Furthermore, we can represent much bigger numbers with an integer than we can with the same number of ASCII bytes (for example, 32 767 versus 99). It is also conceptually interesting, since it illustrates the use of a fixed-length binary field in combination with variable-length character fields.

Another option is to convert the length into a character string using formatted output. With C streams, we use `fprintf`; with C++ stream classes, we use the overloaded insertion operator (<<):

```
fprintf (file, "%d ", length); // with C streams
stream << length << ' '; // with C++ stream classes
```

Each of these lines inserts the length as a decimal string followed by a single blank that functions as a delimiter.

In short, it is easy to store the integers in the file as fixed-length, 2-byte fields containing integers. It is just as easy to make use of the automatic conversion of integers into characters for text files. File structure design is always an exercise in flexibility. Neither of these approaches is correct; good design consists of choosing the approach that is most *appropriate* for a given language and computing environment. In the functions included

```
40 Ames|Mary|123 Maple|Stillwater|OK|74075|36
Mason|Alan|90 Eastgate|Ada|OK|74820
```

Figure 4.8 Records preceded by record-length fields in character form.

in program `readvar.cpp` in Appendix D, we have implemented our record structure using binary field to hold the length. The output from an implementation with a text length field is shown in Fig. 4.8. Each record now has a record length field preceding the data fields. This field is delimited by a blank. For example, the first record (for Mary Ames) contains 40 characters, counting from the first *A* in "Ames" to the final delimiter after "74075," so the characters *4* and *0* are placed before the record, followed by a blank.

Since the implementation of variable-length records presented in Section 4.2 uses binary integers for the record length, we cannot simply print it to a console screen. We need a way to interpret the noncharacter portion of the file. In the next section, we introduce the file dump, a valuable tool for viewing the contents of files. But first, let's look at how to read in any file written with variable-length records.

Reading the Variable-Length Records from the File

Given our file structure of variable-length records preceded by record-length fields, it is easy to write a program that reads through the file, record by record, displaying the fields from each of the records on the screen. The program must read the length of a record, move the characters of the record into a buffer, then break the record into fields. The code to read and break up the record is included in function `ReadVariablePerson` in Fig. 4.9. The function is quite simple because it takes advantage of the extraction operator that was previously defined for reading directly from a file. The implementation of `ReadVariablePerson` may be hard to understand because it uses features of C++ that we haven't yet covered. In particular, class `istrstream` (input string stream) is a type of input stream that uses the same operators as other input streams but has its value stored in a character string instead of in a file. The extraction operation of Figure 4.4 works just as well on a string stream as it does on a file stream. This is a wonderful result of the use of inheritance in C++ classes. We use inheritance extensively in later C++ classes, but that will have to wait for Section 4.3.

```
int ReadVariablePerson (istream & stream, Person & p)
{ // read a variable sized record from stream and store it in p
   short length;
   stream . read (&length, sizeof(length));
   char * buffer = new char[length+1];// create buffer space
   stream . read (buffer, length);
   buffer [length] = 0; // terminate buffer with null
   istrstream strbuff (buffer); // create a string stream
   strbuff >> p; // use the istream extraction operator
   return 1;
}
```

Figure 4.9 Function `ReadVariablePerson` that reads a variable-sized `Person` record.

4.1.6 Mixing Numbers and Characters: Use of a File Dump

File dumps give us the ability to look inside a file at the actual bytes that are stored there. Consider, for instance, the record-length information in the text file that we were examining a moment ago. The length of the Ames record, the first one in the file, is 40 characters, including delimiters. The actual bytes stored *in the file* look like the representation in Fig. 4.10(a). In the mixed binary and text implementation, where we choose to represent the length field as a 2-byte integer, the bytes look like the representation in Fig. 4.10(b).

As you can see, the *number* 40 is not the same as the set of characters *4* and *0*. The 1-byte hex value of the *binary integer* 40 is 0x28; the hex values of the *characters 4* and *0* are 0x34 and 0x30. (We are using the C language convention of identifying hexadecimal numbers through the use of the prefix 0x.) So, when we are storing a number in ASCII form, it is the hex values of the *ASCII characters* that go into the file, not the hex value of the number itself.

Figure 4.10(b) shows the byte representation of the number 40 stored as an integer (this is called storing the number in *binary* form, even though we usually view the output as a hexadecimal number). Now the hexadecimal value stored in the file is that of the number itself. The ASCII characters that happen to be associated with the number's hexadecimal value have no obvious relationship to the number. Here is what the version of the file that uses binary integers for record lengths looks like if we simply print it on a terminal screen:

```
(Ames | Mary | 123 Maple | Stillwater | OK | 74075 | $Mason|Alan|…
```

— 0x28 is ASCII code for '('
— Blank, since '\0' is unprintable.

— 0x28 is ASCII code for '('
— Blank; '\0' is unprintable.

The ASCII representations of characters and numbers in the actual record come out nicely enough, but the binary representations of the length fields are displayed cryptically. Let's take a different look at the file, this time using the Unix dump utility od. Entering the Unix command

```
od -xc filename
```

produces the following:

```
Offset       Values
0000000   \0   (   A   m   e   s   |   M   a   r   y   |   1   2   3
            0028    416d    6573    7c4d    6172    797c    3132    3320
0000020    M   a   p   l   e   |   S   t   i   l   l   w   a   t   e   r
            4d61    706c    657c    5374    696c    6c77    6174    6572
0000040    |   O   K   |   7   4   0   7   5   |  \0   $   M   a   s   o
            7c4f    4b7c    3734    3037    357c    0024    4d61    736f
0000060    n   |   A   l   a   n   |   9   0       E   a   s   t   g   a
            6e7c    416c    616e    7c39    3020    4561    7374    6761
0000100    t   e   |   A   d   a   |   O   K   |   7   4   8   2   0   |
            7465    7c41    6461    7c4f    4b7c    3734    3832    307c
```

As you can see, the display is divided into three different kinds of data. The column on the left labeled Offset gives the offset of the first byte of the row that is being displayed. The byte offsets are given in octal form; since each line contains 16 (decimal) bytes, moving from one line to the next adds 020 to the range. Every pair of lines in the printout contains inter-

	Decimal value of number	Hex value stored in bytes		ASCII character form
(a) 40 stored as ASCII chars:	40	34	30	4 0
(b) 40 stored as a 2-byte integer:	40	00	28	'\0' '('

Figure 4.10 The number 40, stored as ASCII characters and as a short integer.

pretations of the bytes in the file in ASCII and hexadecimal. These representations were requested on the command line with the -xc flag (x = hex; c = character).

Let's look at the first row of ASCII values. As you would expect, the data placed in the file in ASCII form appears in this row in a readable way. But there are hexadecimal values for which there is no printable ASCII representation. The only such value appearing in this file is 0 x 00. But there could be many others. For example, the hexadecimal value of the number 500 000 000 is 0x1DCD6500. If you write this value out to a file, an od of the file with the option -xc looks like this:

```
0000000 \035\315  e  \0
         1dcd  6500
```

The only printable byte in this file is the one with the value 0x65 (e). Od handles all of the others by listing their equivalent octal values in the ASCII representation.

The hex dump of this output from writrec shows how this file structure represents an interesting mix of a number of the organizational tools we have encountered. In a single record we have both binary and ASCII data. Each record consists of a fixed-length field (the byte count) and several delimited, variable-length fields. This kind of mixing of different data types and organizational methods is common in real-world file structures.

A Note about Byte Order

If your computer is a PC or a computer from DEC, such as a VAX, your octal dump for this file will probably be different from the one we see here. These machines store the individual bytes of numeric values in a reverse order. For example, if this dump were executed on a PC, using the MS-DOS debug command, the hex representation of the first 2-byte value in the file would be 0x2800 rather than 0x0028.

This reverse order also applies to long, 4-byte integers on these machines. This is an aspect of files that you need to be aware of if you expect to make sense out of dumps like this one. A more serious consequence of the byte-order differences among machines occurs when we move files from a machine with one type of byte ordering to one with a different byte ordering. We discuss this problem and ways to deal with it in Section 5.6, "Portability and Standardization."

4.2 Using Classes to Manipulate Buffers

Now that we understand how to use buffers to read and write information, we can use C++ classes to encapsulate the pack, unpack, read, and write operations of buffer objects. An object of one of these buffer classes can be used for output as follows: start with an empty buffer object, pack field values into the object one by one, then write the buffer contents to an output stream. For input, initialize a buffer object by reading a record from an input stream, then extract the object's field values, one by one. Buffer objects support only this behavior. A buffer is not intended to allow modification of packed values nor to allow pack and unpack operations to be mixed. As the classes are described, you will see that no direct access is allowed to the data members that hold the contents of the buffer. A considerable amount of extra error checking has been included in these classes.

There are three classes defined in this section: one for delimited fields, one for length-based fields, and one for fixed-length fields. The first two field types use variable-length records for input and output. The fixed-length fields are stored in fixed-length records.

4.2.1 Buffer Class for Delimited Text Fields

The first buffer class, `DelimTextBuffer`, supports variable-length buffers whose fields are represented as delimited text. A part of the class definition is given as Fig. 4.11. The full definition is in file `deltext.h` in Appendix E. The full implementations of the class methods are in `deltext.cpp`. Operations on buffers include constructors, read and write, and field pack and unpack. Data members are used to store the delimiter used in pack and unpack operations, the actual and maximum number of bytes in the buffer, and the byte (or character) array that contains the value of the buffer. We have also included an extension of the class `Person` from Fig. 4.2 to illustrate the use of buffer objects.

The following code segment declares objects of class `Person` and class `DelimTextBuffer`, packs the person into the buffer, and writes the buffer to a file:

```
Person MaryAmes;
DelimTextBuffer buffer;
buffer . Pack (MaryAmes . LastName);
buffer . Pack (MaryAmes . FirstName);
```

```
class DelimTextBuffer
{  public:
      DelimTextBuffer (char Delim = '|', int maxBytes = 1000);
      int Read (istream & file);
      int Write (ostream & file) const;
      int Pack (const char * str, int size = -1);
      int Unpack (char * str);
private:
      char Delim; // delimiter character
      char * Buffer; // character array to hold field values
      int BufferSize; // current size of packed fields
      int MaxBytes; // maximum number of characters in the
buffer
      int NextByte; // packing/unpacking position in buffer
};
```

Figure 4.11 Main methods and members of class `DelimTextBuffer`.

```
            . . .
      buffer . Pack (MaryAmes . ZipCode);
      buffer . Write (stream);
```

This code illustrates how default values are used in C++. The declaration of object `buffer` has no arguments, but the only constructor for `DelimTextBuffer` has two parameters. There is no error here, since the constructor declaration has default values for both parameters. A call that omits the arguments has the defaults substituted. The following two declarations are completely equivalent:

```
DelimTextBuffer buffer; // default arguments used
DelimTextBuffer buffer ('|', 1000); // arguments given explicitly
```

Similarly, the calls on the `Pack` method have only a single argument, so the second argument (`size`) takes on the default value -1.

The `Pack` method copies the characters of its argument `str` to the buffer and then adds the delimiter character. If the `size` argument is not -1, it specifies the number of characters to be written. If `size` is -1, the C function `strlen` is used to determine the number of characters to write. The `Unpack` function does not need a size, since the field that is being unpacked consists of all of the characters up to the next instance of the delimiter. The implementation of `Pack` and `Unpack` utilize the private member `NextByte` to keep track of the current position in the buffer. The `Unpack` method is implemented as follows:

```
int DelimTextBuffer :: Unpack (char * str)
// extract the value of the next field of the buffer
{
    int len = -1; // length of packed string
    int start = NextByte; // first character to be unpacked
    for (int i = start; i < BufferSize; i++)
      if (Buffer[i] == Delim)
        {len = i - start; break;}
    if (len == -1) return FALSE; // delimeter not found
    NextByte += len + 1;
    if (NextByte > BufferSize) return FALSE;
    strncpy (str, &Buffer[start], len);
    str [len] = 0; // zero termination for string
    return TRUE;
}
```

The Read and Write methods use the variable-length strategy as described in Section 4.1.6. A binary value is used to represent the length of the record. Write inserts the current buffer size, then the characters of the buffer. Read clears the current buffer contents, extracts the record size, reads the proper number of bytes into the buffer, and sets the buffer size:

```
int DelimTextBuffer :: Read (istream & stream)
{
    Clear ();
    stream . read ((char *)&BufferSize, sizeof(BufferSize));
    if (stream.fail()) return FALSE;
    if (BufferSize > MaxBytes) return FALSE; // buffer overflow
    stream . read (Buffer, BufferSize);
    return stream . good ();
}
```

4.2.2 Extending Class Person with Buffer Operations

The buffer classes have the capability of packing any number and type of values, but they do not record how these values are combined to make objects. In order to pack and unpack a buffer for a Person object, for instance, we have to specify the order in which the members of Person are packed and unpacked. Section 4.1 and the code in Appendix D included operations for packing and unpacking the members of Person objects in insertion (<<) and extraction (>>) operators. In this section and Appendix E, we add those operations as methods of class Person. The definition of the class has the following method for packing delimited text buffers. The unpack operation is equally simple:

```
int Person::Pack (DelimTextBuffer & Buffer) const
{// pack the fields into a DelimTextBuffer
    int result;
    result = Buffer . Pack (LastName);
    result = result && Buffer . Pack (FirstName);
    result = result && Buffer . Pack (Address);
    result = result && Buffer . Pack (City);
    result = result && Buffer . Pack (State);
    result = result && Buffer . Pack (ZipCode);
    return result;
}
```

4.2.3 Buffer Classes for Length-Based and Fixed-length Fields

Representing records of length-based fields and records of fixed-length fields requires a change in the implementations of the Pack and Unpack methods of the delimited field class, but the class definitions are almost exactly the same. The main members and methods of class LengthTextBuffer are given in Fig. 4.12. The full class definition and method implementation are given in lentext.h and lentext.cpp

```
class LengthTextBuffer
{  public:
    LengthTextBuffer (int maxBytes = 1000);
    int Read (istream & file);
    int Write (ostream & file) const;
    int Pack (const char * field, int size = -1);
    int Unpack (char * field);
private:
    char * Buffer; // character array to hold field values
    int BufferSize; // size of packed fields
    int MaxBytes; // maximum number of characters in the buffer
    int NextByte; // packing/unpacking position in buffer
};
```

Figure 4.12 Main methods and members of class LengthTextBuffer.

in Appendix E. The only changes that are apparent from this figure are the name of the class and the elimination of the `delim` parameter on the constructor. The code for the `Pack` and `Unpack` methods is substantially different, but the `Read` and `Write` methods are exactly the same.

Class `FixedTextBuffer`, whose main members and methods are in Fig. 4.13 (full class in `fixtext.h` and `fixtext.cpp`), is different in two ways from the other two classes. First, it uses a fixed collection of fixed-length fields. Every buffer value has the same collection of fields, and the `Pack` method needs no size parameter. The second difference is that it uses fixed-length records. Hence, the `Read` and `Write` methods do not use a length indicator for buffer size. They simply use the fixed size of the buffer to determine how many bytes to read or write.

The method `AddField` is included to support the specification of the fields and their sizes. A buffer for objects of class `Person` is initialized by the new method `InitBuffer` of class `Person`:

```
int Person::InitBuffer (FixedTextBuffer & Buffer)
// initialize a FixedTextBuffer to be used for Person objects
{
    Buffer . Init (6, 61);//6 fields, 61 bytes total
    Buffer . AddField (10); // LastName [11];
    Buffer . AddField (10); // FirstName [11];
    Buffer . AddField (15); // Address [16];
```

```
class FixedTextBuffer
{  public:
    FixedTextBuffer (int maxBytes = 1000);
    int AddField (int fieldSize);
    int Read (istream & file);
    int Write (ostream & file) const;
    int Pack (const char * field);
    int Unpack (char * field);
private:
    char * Buffer; // character array to hold field values
    int BufferSize; // size of packed fields
    int MaxBytes; // maximum number of characters in the buffer
    int NextByte; // packing/unpacking position in buffer
    int * FieldSizes; // array of field sizes
};
```

Figure 4.13 Main methods and members of class `FixedTextBuffer`.

```
Buffer . AddField (15); // City [16];
Buffer . AddField (2);  // State [3];
Buffer . AddField (9);  // ZipCode [10];
return 1;
}
```

4.3   Using Inheritance for Record Buffer Classes

A reading of the cpp files for the three classes above shows a striking similarity: a large percentage of the code is duplicated. In this section, we eliminate almost all of the duplication through the use of the inheritance capabilities of C++.

4.3.1 Inheritance in the C++ Stream Classes

C++ incorporates *inheritance* to allow multiple classes to share members and methods. One or more base classes define members and methods, which are then used by subclasses. The stream classes are defined in such a hierarchy. So far, our discussion has focused on class fstream, as though it stands alone. In fact, fstream is embedded in a class hierarchy that contains many other classes. The read operations, including the extraction operators are defined in class istream. The write operations are defined in class ostream. Class fstream inherits these operations from its parent class iostream, which in turn inherits from istream and ostream. The following definitions are included in iostream.h and fstream.h:

```
class istream: virtual public ios { . . .
class ostream: virtual public ios { . . .
class iostream: public istream, public ostream { . . .
class ifstream: public fstreambase, public istream { . . .
class ofstream: public fstreambase, public ostream { . . .
class fstream: public fstreambase, public iostream { . . .
```

We can see that this is a complex collection of classes. There are two base classes, ios and fstreambase, that provide common declarations and basic stream operations (ios) and access to operating system file operations (fstreambase). There are uses of *multiple inheritance* in these classes; that is, classes have more than one base class. The keyword *virtual* is used to ensure that class `ios` is included only once in the ancestry of any of these classes.

Objects of a class are also objects of their base classes, and generally, include members and methods of the base classes. An object of class `fstream`, for example, is also an object of classes `fstreambase`, `iostream`, `istream`, `ostream`, and `ios` and includes all of the members and methods of those base classes. Hence, the read method and extraction (>>) operations defined in `istream` are also available in `iostream`, `ifstream`, and `fstream`. The open and close operations of class `fstreambase` are also members of class `fstream`.

An important benefit of inheritance is that operations that work on base class objects also work on derived class objects. We had an example of this benefit in the function `ReadVariablePerson` in Section 4.1.5 that used an `istrstream` object `strbuff` to contain a string buffer. The code of that function passed `strbuff` as an argument to the person extraction function that expected an `istream` argument. Since `istrstream` is derived from `istream`, `strbuff` *is* an `istream` object and hence can be manipulated by this `istream` operation.

4.3.2 A Class Hierarchy for Record Buffer Objects

The characteristics of the three buffer classes of Section 4.2 can be combined into a single class hierarchy, as shown in Fig. 4.14. Appendix F has the full implementation of these classes. The members and methods that are common to all of the three buffer classes are included in the base class `IOBuffer`. Other methods are in classes `VariableLengthBuffer` and `FixedLengthBuffer`, which support the read and write operations for different types of records. Finally the classes `LengthFieldBuffer`, `DelimFieldBuffer`, and `FixedFieldBuffer` have the pack and unpack methods for the specific field representations.

The main members and methods of class `IOBuffer` are given in Fig. 4.15. The full class definition is in file `iobuffer.h`, and the implementation of the methods is in file `iobuffer.cpp`. The common members of all of the buffer classes, `BufferSize`, `MaxBytes`, `NextByte`, and `Buffer`, are declared in class `IOBuffer`. These members are in the `protected` Section of `IOBuffer`.

This is our first use of protected access, which falls between private (no access outside the class) and public (no access restrictions). Protected members of a class can be used by methods of the class and by methods of

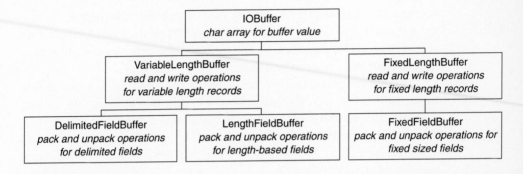

Figure 4.14 Buffer class hierarchy

classes derived from the class. The protected members of `IOBuffer` can be used by methods in all of the classes in this hierarchy. Protected members of `VariableLengthBuffer` can be used in its subclasses but not in classes `IOBuffer` and `FixedLengthBuffer`.

The constructor for class `IOBuffer` has a single parameter that specifies the maximum size of the buffer. Methods are declared for reading, writing, packing, and unpacking. Since the implementation of these methods depends on the exact nature of the record and its fields, `IOBuffer` must leave its implementation to the subclasses.

Class `IOBuffer` defines these methods as *virtual* to allow each subclass to define its own implementation. The = 0 declares a *pure virtual*

```
class IOBuffer
{public:
    IOBuffer (int maxBytes = 1000); // a maximum of maxBytes
    virtual int Read (istream &) = 0; // read a buffer
    virtual int Write (ostream &) const = 0; // write a buffer
    virtual int Pack (const void * field, int size = -1) = 0;
    virtual int Unpack (void * field, int maxbytes = -1) = 0;
 protected:
    char * Buffer; // character array to hold field values
    int BufferSize; // sum of the sizes of packed fields
    int MaxBytes; // maximum number of characters in the buffer
};
```

Figure 4.15 Main members and methods of class `IOBuffer`.

method. This means that the class `IOBuffer` does not include an implementation of the method. A class with pure virtual methods is an *abstract*
class. No objects of such a class can be created, but pointers and references
to objects of this class can be declared.

The full implementation of read, write, pack, and unpack operations
for delimited text records is supported by two more classes. The reading
and writing of variable-length records are included in the class
`VariableLengthBuffer`, as given in Figure 4.16 and files `varlen.h`
and `varlen.cpp`. Packing and unpacking delimited fields is in class
`DelimitedFieldBuffer` and in files `delim.h` and `delim.cpp`.
The code to implement these operations follows the same structure as in
Section 4.2 but incorporates additional error checking. The `Write`
method of `VariableLengthBuffer` is implemented as follows:

```
int VariableLengthBuffer :: Write (ostream & stream) const
// read the length and buffer from the stream
{
   int recaddr = stream . tellp ();
   unsigned short bufferSize = BufferSize;
   stream . write ((char *)&bufferSize, sizeof(bufferSize));
   if (!stream) return -1;
   stream . write (Buffer, BufferSize);
   if (!stream.good ()) return -1;
   return recaddr;
}
```

The method is implemented to test for all possible errors and to return
information to the calling routine via the return value. We test for failure in the write operations using the expressions `!stream` and
`!stream.good()`, which are equivalent. These are two different ways
to test if the stream has experienced an error. The `Write` method returns
the address in the stream where the record was written. The address is
determined by calling `stream.tellg()` at the beginning of the function. `Tellg` is a method of `ostream` that returns the current location of
the put pointer of the stream. If either of the write operations fails, the
value −1 is returned.

An effective strategy for making objects persistent must make it easy
for an application to move objects from memory to files and back correctly. One of the crucial aspects is ensuring that the fields are packed and
unpacked in the same order. The class `Person` has been extended to
include pack and unpack operations. The main purpose of these operations is to specify an ordering on the fields and to encapsulate error testing. The unpack operation is:

```
class VariableLengthBuffer: public IOBuffer
{  public:
   VariableLengthBuffer (int MaxBytes = 1000);
   int Read (istream &);
   int Write (ostream &) const;
   int SizeOfBuffer () const; // return current size of buffer
};

class DelimFieldBuffer: public VariableLengthBuffer
{  public:
   DelimFieldBuffer (char Delim = -1, int maxBytes = 1000;
   int Pack (const void*, int size = -1);
   int Unpack (void * field, int maxBytes = -1);
 protected:
   char Delim;
};
```

Figure 4.16 Classes VariableLengthBuffer and DelimFieldBuffer.

```
int Person::Unpack (IOBuffer & Buffer)
{
    Clear ();
    int numBytes;
    numBytes = Buffer . Unpack (LastName);
    if (numBytes == -1) return FALSE;
    LastName[numBytes] = 0;
    numBytes = Buffer . Unpack (FirstName);
    if (numBytes == -1) return FALSE;
    . . . // unpack the other fields
    return TRUE;
}
```

This method illustrates the power of virtual functions. The parameter of Person::Unpack is an object of type IOBuffer, but a call to Unpack supplies an argument that can be an object of any subclass of IOBuffer. The calls to Buffer.Unpack in the method Person::Unpack are virtual function calls. In calls of this type, the determination of exactly which Unpack method to call is not made during compilation as it is with nonvirtual calls. Instead, the actual type of the object Buffer is used to determine which function to call. In the following example of calling Unpack, the calls to Buffer.Unpack use the method DelimFieldBuffer::Unpack.

```
Person MaryAmes;
DelimFieldBuffer Buffer;
MaryAmes . Unpack (Buffer);
```

The full implementation of the I/O buffer classes includes class `LengthFieldBuffer`, which supports field packing with length plus value representation. This class is like `DelimFieldBuffer` in that it is implemented by specifying only the pack and unpack methods. The read and write operations are supported by its base class, `VariableLengthBuffer`.

4.4 Managing Fixed-Length, Fixed-Field Buffers

Class `FixedLengthBuffer` is the subclass of `IOBuffer` that supports read and write of fixed-length records. For this class, each record is of the same size. Instead of storing the record size explicitly in the file along with the record, the write method just writes the fixed-size record. The read method must know the size in order to read the record correctly. Each `FixedLengthBuffer` object has a protected field that records the record size.

Class `FixedFieldBuffer`, as shown in Fig. 4.17 and files `fixfld.h` and `fixfld.cpp`, supports a fixed set of fixed-length fields. One difficulty with this strategy is that the unpack method has to know the length of all of the fields. To make it convenient to keep track of the

```
class FixedFieldBuffer: public FixedLengthBuffer
public:
   FixedFieldBuffer (int maxFields, int RecordSize = 1000);
   FixedFieldBuffer (int maxFields, int * fieldSize);
   int AddField (int fieldSize); // define the next field
   int Pack (const void * field, int size = -1);
   int Unpack (void * field, int maxBytes = -1);
   int NumberOfFields () const; // return number of defined fields
protected:
   int * FieldSize; // array to hold field sizes
   int MaxFields; // maximum number of fields
   int NumFields; // actual number of defined fields
};
```

Figure 4.17 Class `FixedFieldBuffer`.

field lengths, class `FixedFieldBuffer` keeps track of the field sizes. The protected member `FieldSize` holds the field sizes in an integer array. The `AddField` method is used to specify field sizes. In the case of using a `FixedFieldBuffer` to hold objects of class `Person`, the `InitBuffer` method can be used to fully initialize the buffer:

```
int Person::InitBuffer (FixedFieldBuffer & Buffer)
// initialize a FixedFieldBuffer to be used for Persons
{
   int result;
   result = Buffer . AddField (10); // LastName [11];
   result = result && Buffer . AddField (10); // FirstName [11];
   result = result && Buffer . AddField (15); // Address [16];
   result = result && Buffer . AddField (15); // City [16];
   result = result && Buffer . AddField (2);  // State [3];
   result = result && Buffer . AddField (9); // ZipCode [10];
   return result;
}
```

Starting with a buffer with no fields, `InitBuffer` adds the fields one at a time, each with its own size. The following code prepares a buffer for use in reading and writing objects of class `Person`:

```
FixedFieldBuffer Buffer(6, 61); // 6 fields, 61 bytes total
MaryAmes.InitBuffer (Buffer);
```

Unpacking `FixedFieldBuffer` objects has to be done carefully. The object has to include information about the state of the unpacking. The member `NextByte` records the next character of the buffer to be unpacked, just as in all of the `IOBuffer` classes. `FixedFieldBuffer` has additional member `NextField` to record the next field to be unpacked. The method `FixedFieldBuffer::Unpack` is implemented as follows:

```
int FixedFieldBuffer :: Unpack (void * field, int maxBytes)
{
   if (NextField == NumFields || Packing)
     // buffer is full or not in unpacking mode
     return -1;
   int start = NextByte; // first byte to be unpacked
   int packSize = FieldSize[NextField]; // bytes to be unpacked
   memcpy (field, &Buffer[start], packSize); //move the bytes
   NextByte += packSize; // advance NextByte to following char
   NextField ++; // advance NextField
   if (NextField == NumFields) Clear (); // all fields unpacked
     return packSize;
}
```

4.5   An Object-Oriented Class for Record Files

Now that we know how to transfer objects to and from files, it is appropriate to encapsulate that knowledge in a class that supports all of our file operations. Class BufferFile (in files buffile.h and buffile.cpp of Appendix F) supports manipulation of files that are tied to specific buffer types. An object of class BufferFile is created from a specific buffer object and can be used to open and create files and to read and write records. Figure 4.18 has the main data methods and members of BufferFile.

Once a BufferFile object has been created and attached to an operating system file, each read or write is performed using the same buffer. Hence, each record is guaranteed to be of the same basic type. The following code sample shows how a file can be created and used with a DelimFieldBuffer:

```
DelimFieldBuffer buffer;
BufferFile file (buffer);
file . Open (myfile);
file . Read ();
buffer . Unpack (myobject);
```

```
class BufferFile
{public:
   BufferFile (IOBuffer &); // create with a buffer
   int Open (char * filename, int MODE); // open an existing file
   int Create (char * filename, int MODE); // create a new file
   int Close ();
   int Rewind (); // reset to the first data record
   // Input and Output operations
   int Read (int recaddr = -1);
   int Write (int recaddr = -1);
   int Append (); // write the current buffer at the end of file
protected:
   IOBuffer & Buffer; // reference to the file's buffer
   fstream File; // the C++ stream of the file
};
```

Figure 4.18 Main data members and methods of class BufferFile.

A buffer is created, and the `BufferFile` object `file` is attached to it. Then `Open` and `Read` methods are called for `file`. After the `Read`, `buffer` contains the packed record, and `buffer.Unpack` puts the record into `myobject`.

When `BufferFile` is combined with a fixed-length buffer, the result is a file that is guaranteed to have every record the same size. The full implementation of `BufferFile`, which is described in Section 5.2, "More about Record Structures," puts a `header` record on the beginning of each file. For fixed-length record files, the header includes the record size. `BufferFile::Open` reads the record size from the file header and compares it with the record size of the corresponding buffer. If the two are not the same, the `Open` fails and the file cannot be used.

This illustrates another important aspect of object-oriented design. Classes can be used to guarantee that operations on objects are performed correctly. It's easy to see that using the wrong buffer to read a file record is disastrous to an application. It is the encapsulation of classes like `BufferFile` that add safety to our file operations.

SUMMARY

The lowest level of organization that we normally impose on a file is a *stream of bytes*. Unfortunately, by storing data in a file merely as a stream of bytes, we lose the ability to distinguish among the fundamental informational units of our data. We call these fundamental pieces of information *fields*. Fields are grouped together to form *records*. Recognizing fields and records requires that we impose structure on the data in the file.

There are many ways to separate one field from the next and one record from the next:

- Fix the length of each field or record.
- Begin each field or record with a count of the number of bytes that it contains.
- Use delimiters to mark the divisions between entities.

In the case of fields, another useful technique is to use a "keyword = value" form to identify fields.

In this chapter we use the record structure with a length indicator at the beginning of each record to develop programs for writing and reading a simple file of variable-length records containing names and addresses of individuals. We use buffering to accumulate the data in an individual record before we know its length to write it to the file. Buffers are also useful in allowing us to read in a complete record at one time. We represent the length field of each record as a binary number or as a sequence of ASCII digits. In the former case, it is useful to use a *file dump* to examine the contents of our file.

The field packing and unpacking operations, in their various forms, can be encapsulated into C++ classes. The three different field representation strategies—delimited, length-based, and fixed-length—are implemented in separate classes. Almost all of the members and methods of these classes are identical. The only differences are in the exact packing and unpacking and in the minor differences in read and write between the variable-length and fixed-length record structures.

A better strategy for representing these objects lies in the use of a class hierarchy. Inheritance allows related classes to share members. For example, the two field packing strategies of delimited and length based can share the same variable-length record read and write methods. Virtual methods make the class hierarchy work.

The class `BufferFile` encapsulates the file operations of open, create, close, read, write, and seek in a single object. Each `BufferFile` object is attached to a buffer. The read and write operations move data between file and buffer. The use of `BufferFile` adds a level of protection to our file operations. Once a disk file is connected to a `BufferFile` object, it can be manipulated only with the related buffer.

KEY TERMS

Byte count field. A field at the beginning of a variable-length record that gives the number of bytes used to store the record. The use of a byte count field allows a program to transmit (or skip over) a variable-length record without having to deal with the record's internal structure.

Delimiter. One or more characters used to separate fields and records in a file.

Field. The smallest logically meaningful unit of information in a file. A record in a file is usually made up of several fields.

Fixed-length record. A file organization in which all records have the same length. Records are padded with blanks, nulls, or other characters so they extend to the fixed length. Since all the records have the same length, it is possible to calculate the beginning position of any record, making *direct access* possible.

Inheritance. A strategy for allowing classes to share data members and methods. A derived class inherits the members of its base class and may add additional members or modify the members it inherits.

Record. A collection of related fields. For example, the name, address, and so on of an individual in a mailing-list file would make up one record.

Stream of bytes. Term describing the lowest-level view of a file. If we begin with the basic *stream-of-bytes* view of a file, we can then impose our own higher levels of order on the file, including field, record, and block structures.

Variable-length record. A file organization in which the records have no predetermined length. They are just as long as they need to be and therefore make better use of space than fixed-length records do. Unfortunately, we cannot calculate the byte offset of a variable-length record by knowing only its relative record number.

Virtual method. A member function that can have different versions for different derived classes. A virtual function call dynamically selects the appropriate version for an object.

FURTHER READINGS

Object-oriented design is quite well covered in many books and articles. They range from a basic introduction, as in Irvine (1996), to the presentation of examples of solving business problems with object-oriented methods in Yourdon and Argila (1996). Booch (1991) is a comprehensive study of the use of object-oriented design methods. The use of files to store information is included in many database books, including Elmasri and Navathe (1994) and Silberschatz, Korth, and Sudarshan (1997).

EXERCISES

1. Find situations for which each of the four field structures described in the text might be appropriate. Do the same for each of the record structures described.

2. Discuss the appropriateness of using the following characters to delimit fields or records: carriage return, linefeed, space, comma, period, colon, escape. Can you think of situations in which you might want to use different delimiters for different fields?

3. Suppose you want to change class `Person` and the programs in section 4.1 to include a phone number field. What changes need to be made?

4. Suppose you need to keep a file in which every record has both fixed- and variable-length fields. For example, suppose you want to create a file of employee records, using fixed-length fields for each employee's ID (primary key), sex, birth date, and department, and using variable-length fields for each name and address. What advantages might there be to using such a structure? Should we put the variable-length portion first or last? Either approach is possible; how can each be implemented?

5. One record structure not described in this chapter is called *labeled*. In a labeled record structure each field that is represented is preceded by a label describing its contents. For example, if the labels *LN, FN, AD, CT, ST,* and *ZP* are used to describe the six fixed-length fields for a name and address record, it might appear as follows:

```
LNAmes     FNMary     AD123 Maple     CTStillwaterSTOKZP74075
```

Under what conditions might this be a reasonable, even desirable, record structure?

6. Define the terms *stream of bytes, stream of fields,* and *stream of records.*

7. Investigate the implementation of virtual functions in an implementation of C++. What data structure is used to represent the binding of function calls to function bodies? What is the interaction between the implementation of virtual functions and the constructors for classes?

8. Report on the basic field and record structures available in Ada or Cobol.

9. Compare the use of ASCII characters to represent *everything* in a file with the use of binary and ASCII data mixed together.

10. If you list the contents of a file containing both binary and ASCII characters on your terminal screen, what results can you expect? What happens when you list a completely binary file on your screen? (*Warning:* If you actually try this, do so with a very small file. You could lock up or reconfigure your terminal or even log yourself off!)

11. The following is a hex dump of the first few bytes from a file which uses variable-length records, a two-byte length, and delimited text fields. How long is the first record? What are its contents?

```
00244475   6D707C46   7265647C   38323120
4B6C7567   657C4861   636B6572   7C50417C
36353533   357C2E2E   48657861   64656369
```

12. The `Write` methods of the `IOBuffer` classes let the user change records but not delete records. How must the file structure and access procedures be modified to allow for deletion if we do not care about reusing the space from deleted records? How do the file structures and procedures change if we do want to reuse the space? Programming Exercises 21–26 of Chapter 6 ask you to implement various types of deletion.

13. What happens when method `VariableLengthBuffer::Write` is used to replace (or update) a record in a file, and the previous record had a different size? Describe possible solutions to this problem. Programming Exercise 25 of Chapter 6 asks you to implement a correct `Update` method.

PROGRAMMING EXERCISES

14. Rewrite the insertion (<<) operator of file `writestr.cpp` so that it uses the following field representations:

    a. Method 1, fixed length fields.
    b. Method 2, fields with length indicators.
    c. Method 3, fields delimited by "|".
    d. Method 4, fields with keyword tags.

15. Rewrite the extraction (>>) operator of file `readstr.cpp` so that it uses the following field representations:

    a. Method 1, fixed length fields.
    b. Method 2, fields with length indicators.
    c. Method 4, fields with keyword tags.

16. Write a program `writevar.cpp` that produces a file of `Person` objects that is formatted to be input to `readvar.cpp`.

17. Design and implement a class `KeywordBuffer` that pack buffers with keyword tags.

18. Modify class `FixedLengthBuffer` to support multiple field types within a single buffer. Make sure that the buffer does not overflow. You will need to add methods `PackFixed`, `PackLength`, and `PackDelim` and the corresponding unpack methods. You will also need to modify class `Person` or to create a new class, whose `Pack` and `Unpack` operations take advantage of these new capabilities.

19. Repeat Programming Exercise 16 for class `VariableLengthBuffer`.

20. Redesign the IOBuffer classes to allow arbitrary field packing as in the previous two exercises but this time via virtual pack and unpack methods. One purpose of this exercise is to allow class BufferFile to support these new capabilities.

21. Implement direct read by RRN for buffer class FixedLengthBuffer. Add a new implementation for the virtual methods DRead and DWrite in class FixedLengthBuffer.

PROGRAMMING PROJECT

This is the third part of the programming project. We add methods to store objects as records in files and load objects from files, using the IOBuffer classes of this chapter.

22. Add Pack and Unpack methods to class Student. Use class BufferFile to create a file of student records. Test these methods using the types of buffers supported by the IOBuffer classes.

23. Add Pack and Unpack methods to class CourseRegistration. Use class BufferFile to create a file of course registrations. Test these methods using the types of buffers supported by the IOBuffer classes.

The next part of the programming project is in Chapter 6.

5

Managing Files of Records

❖ Extend the file structure concepts of Chapter 4:
  – Search keys and canonical forms,
  – Sequential search,
  – Direct access, and
  – File access and file organization.
❖ Examine other kinds of file structures in terms of
  – Abstract data models,
  – Metadata,
  – Object-oriented file access, and
  – Extensibility.
❖ Examine issues of portability and standardization.

5.1   Record Access

5.1.1 Record Keys

Since our new file structure so clearly focuses on a record as the quantity of information that is being read or written, it makes sense to think in terms of retrieving just one specific record rather than reading all the way through the file, displaying everything. When looking for an individual record, it is convenient to identify the record with a *key* based on the record's contents. For example, in our name and address file we might want to access the "Ames record" or the "Mason record" rather than thinking in terms of the "first record" or "second record." (Can you remember which record comes first?) This notion of a *key* is another fundamental conceptual tool. We need to develop a more exact idea of what a key is.

When we are looking for a record containing the last name Ames, we want to recognize it even if the user enters the key in the form "AMES," "ames," or "Ames." To do this, we must define a standard form for keys, along with associated rules and procedures for converting keys into this standard form. A standard form of this kind is often called a *canonical form* for the key. One meaning of the word *canon* is rule, and the word *canonical* means conforming to the rule. A canonical form for a search key is the *single* representation for that key that conforms to the rule.

As a simple example, we could state that the canonical form for a key requires that the key consist solely of uppercase letters and have no extra blanks at the end. So, if someone enters "Ames," we would convert the key to the canonical form "AMES" before searching for it.

It is often desirable to have *distinct keys,* or keys that uniquely identify a single record. If there is not a one-to-one relationship between the key and a single record, the program has to provide additional mechanisms to allow the user to resolve the confusion that can result when more than one record fits a particular key. Suppose, for example, that we are looking for Mary Ames's address. If there are several records in the file for several different people named Mary Ames, how should the program respond? Certainly it should not just give the address of the first Mary Ames it finds. Should it give all the addresses at once? Should it provide a way of scrolling through the records?

The simplest solution is to *prevent* such confusion. The prevention takes place as new records are added to the file. When the user enters a new record, we form a unique canonical key for that record and then search the file for that key. This concern about uniqueness applies only to *primary keys*. A primary key is, by definition, the key that is used to identify a record uniquely.

It is also possible, as we see later, to search on *secondary keys*. An example of a secondary key might be the city field in our name and address file. If we wanted to find all the records in the file for people who live in towns named Stillwater, we would use some canonical form of "Stillwater" as a secondary key. Typically, secondary keys do not uniquely identify a record.

Although a person's name might at first seem to be a good choice for a primary key, a person's name runs a high risk of failing the test for uniqueness. A name is a perfectly fine secondary key and in fact is often an important secondary key in a retrieval system, but there is too great a likelihood that two names in the same file will be identical.

The reason a name is a risky choice for a primary key is that it contains a real data value. In general, *primary keys should be dataless*. Even when we think we are choosing a unique key, if it contains data, there is a danger that unforeseen identical values could occur. Sweet (1985) cites an example of a file system that used a person's social security number as a primary key for personnel records. It turned out that, in the particular population that was represented in the file, there was a large number of people who were not United States citizens, and in a different part of the organization, all of these people had been assigned the social security number 999-99-9999!

Another reason, other than uniqueness, that a primary key should be dataless is that a primary key should be *unchanging*. If information that corresponds to a certain record changes and that information is contained in a primary key, what do you do about the primary key? You probably cannot change the primary key, in most cases, because there are likely to be reports, memos, indexes, or other sources of information that refer to the record by its primary key. As soon as you change the key, those references become useless.

A good rule of thumb is to avoid putting data into primary keys. If we want to access records according to data content, we should assign this content to secondary keys. We give a more detailed look at record access by primary and secondary keys in Chapter 6. For the rest of this chapter, we suspend our concern about whether a key is primary or secondary and concentrate on finding things by key.

5.1.2 A Sequential Search

Now that you know about keys, you should be able to write a program that reads through the file, record by record, looking for a record with a particular key. Such *sequential searching* is just a simple extension of our `read-var` program—adding a comparison operation to the main loop to see if the key for the record matches the key we are seeking. We leave the program as an exercise.

Evaluating Performance of Sequential Search

In the chapters that follow, we find ways to search for records that are faster than the sequential search mechanism. We can use sequential searching as a kind of baseline against which to measure the improvements we make. It is important, therefore, to find some way of expressing the amount of time and work expended in a sequential search.

Developing a performance measure requires that we decide on a unit of work that usefully represents the constraints on the performance of the whole process. When we describe the performance of searches that take place in electronic memory, where comparison operations are more expensive than fetch operations to bring data in from memory, we usually use the *number of comparisons* required for the search as the measure of work. But, given that the cost of a comparison in memory is so small compared with the cost of a disk access, comparisons do not fairly represent the performance constraints for a search through a file on secondary storage. Instead, we count low-level `Read` calls. We assume that each `Read` call requires a seek and that any one `Read` call is as costly as any other. We know from the discussions of matters, such as system buffering in Chapter 3, that these assumptions are not strictly accurate. But in a multiuser environment where many processes are using the disk at once, they are close enough to correct to be useful.

Suppose we have a file with a thousand records, and we want to use a sequential search to find Al Smith's record. How many `Read` calls are required? If Al Smith's record is the first one in the file, the program has to read in only a single record. If it is the last record in the file, the program makes a thousand `Read` calls before concluding the search. For an average search, 500 calls are needed.

If we double the number of records in a file, we also double both the average and the maximum number of `Read` calls required. Using a sequential search to find Al Smith's record in a file of two thousand records requires, on the average, a thousand calls. In other words, the amount of work required for a sequential search is directly proportional to the number of records in the file.

In general, the work required to search sequentially for a record in a file with n records is proportional to n: it takes at most n comparisons; on average it takes approximately $n/2$ comparisons. A sequential search is said to be of the order $O(n)$ because the time it takes is proportional to n.[1]

Improving Sequential Search Performance with Record Blocking

It is interesting and useful to apply some of the information from Chapter 3 about disk performance to the problem of improving sequential search performance. We learned in Chapter 3 that the major cost associated with a disk access is the time required to perform a seek to the right location on

---

1. If you are not familiar with this "big-oh" notation, you should look it up. Knuth (1997) is a good source.

the disk. Once data transfer begins, it is relatively fast, although still much slower than a data transfer within memory. Consequently, the cost of seeking and reading a record, then seeking and reading another record, is greater than the cost of seeking just once then reading two successive records. (Once again, we are assuming a multiuser environment in which a seek is required for each separate Read call.) It follows that we should be able to improve the performance of sequential searching by reading in a *block* of several records all at once and then processing that block of records in memory.

We began the previous chapter with a stream of bytes. We grouped the bytes into fields, then grouped the fields into records. Now we are considering a yet higher level of organization—grouping records into blocks. This new level of grouping, however, differs from the others. Whereas fields and records are ways of maintaining the logical organization within the file, blocking is done strictly as a performance measure. As such, the block size is usually related more to the physical properties of the disk drive than to the content of the data. For instance, on sector-oriented disks, the block size is almost always some multiple of the sector size.

Suppose that we have a file of four thousand records and that the average length of a record is 512 bytes. If our operating system uses sector-sized buffers of 512 bytes, then an unblocked sequential search requires, on the average, 2,000 Read calls before it can retrieve a particular record. By blocking the records in groups of sixteen per block so each Read call brings in 8 kilobytes worth of records, the number of reads required for an average search comes down to 125. Each Read requires slightly more time, since more data is transferred from the disk, but this is a cost that is usually well worth paying for such a large reduction in the number of reads.

There are several things to note from this analysis and discussion of record blocking:

- Although blocking can result in substantial performance improvements, it does not change the order of the sequential search operation. The cost of searching is still $O(n)$, increasing in direct proportion to increases in the size of the file.

- Blocking clearly reflects the differences between memory access speed and the cost of accessing secondary storage.

- Blocking does not change the number of comparisons that must be done in memory, and it probably increases the amount of data transferred between disk and memory. (We always read a whole block, even if the record we are seeking is the first one in the block.)

■ Blocking saves time because it decreases the amount of seeking. We find, again and again, that this differential between the cost of seeking and the cost of other operations, such as data transfer or memory access, is the force that drives file structure design.

When Sequential Searching Is Good

Much of the remainder of this text is devoted to identifying better ways to access individual records; sequential searching is just too expensive for most serious retrieval situations. This is unfortunate because sequential access has two major practical advantages over other types of access: it is extremely easy to program, and it requires the simplest of file structures.

Whether sequential searching is advisable depends largely on how the file is to be used, how fast the computer system is that is performing the search, and how the file is structured. There are many situations in which a sequential search is reasonable. Here are some examples:

■ ASCII files in which you are searching for some pattern (see `grep` in the next section);

■ Files with few records (for example, ten records);

■ Files that hardly ever need to be searched (for example, tape files usually used for other kinds of processing); and

■ Files in which you want all records with a certain secondary key value, where a large number of matches is expected.

Fortunately, these sorts of applications do occur often in day-to-day computing—so often, in fact, that operating systems provide many utilities for performing sequential processing. Unix is one of the best examples of this, as we see in the next section.

5.1.3 Unix Tools for Sequential Processing

Recognizing the importance of having a standard file structure that is simple and easy to program, the most common file structure that occurs in Unix is *an ASCII file with the new-line character as the record delimiter and, when possible, white space as the field delimiter.* Practically all files that we create with Unix editors use this structure. And since most of the built-in C and C++ functions that perform I/O write to this kind of file, it is common to see data files that consist of fields of numbers or words separated by blanks or tabs and records separated by new-line characters. Such files are simple and easy to process. We can, for instance, generate an ASCII file with a simple program and then use an editor to browse through it or alter it.

Unix provides a rich array of tools for working with files in this form. Since this kind of file structure is inherently sequential (records are variable in length, so we have to pass from record to record to find any particular field or record), many of these tools process files sequentially.

Suppose, for instance, that we choose the white-space/new-line structure for our address file, ending every field with a tab and ending every record with a new line. While this causes some problems in distinguishing fields (a blank is white space, but it doesn't separate a field) and in that sense is not an ideal structure, it buys us something very valuable: the full use of those Unix tools that are built around the white-space/new-line structure. For example, we can print the file on our console using any of a number of utilities, some of which follow.

cat

```
% cat myfile
Ames Mary 123 Maple Stillwater OK    74075
MasonAlan 90 Eastgate    Ada   OK    74820
```

Or we can use tools like wc and grep for processing the files.

wc

The command wc (word count) reads through an ASCII file sequentially and counts the number of lines (delimited by new lines), words (delimited by white space), and characters in a file:

```
% wc myfile
    2    14    76
```

grep

It is common to want to know if a text file has a certain word or character string in it. For ASCII files that can reasonably be searched sequentially, Unix provides an excellent filter for doing this called grep (and its variants egrep and fgrep). The word grep stands for *generalized regular expression*, which describes the type of pattern that grep is able to recognize. In its simplest form, grep searches sequentially through a file for a pattern. It then returns to standard output (the console) all the lines in the file that contain the pattern.

```
% grep Ada myfile
MasonAlan 90 Eastgate    Ada   OK    74820
```

We can also combine tools to create, on the fly, some very powerful file processing software. For example, to find the number of lines containing the word *Ada* and the number of words and bytes in those lines we use

```
% grep Ada myfile | wc
      1      7     36
```

As we move through the text, we will encounter a number of other powerful Unix commands that sequentially process files with the basic white-space/new-line structure.

5.1.4 Direct Access

The most radical alternative to searching sequentially through a file for a record is a retrieval mechanism known as *direct access.* We have direct access to a record when we can seek directly to the beginning of the record and read it in. Whereas sequential searching is an $O(n)$ operation, direct access is $O(1)$. No matter how large the file is, we can still get to the record we want with a single seek. Class IOBuffer includes direct read (DRead) and write (DWrite) operations using the byte address of the record as the record reference:

```
int IOBuffer::DRead (istream & stream, int recref)
// read specified record
{
  stream . seekg (recref, ios::beg);
  if (stream . tellg () != recref) return -1;
  return Read (stream);
}
```

The DRead function begins by seeking to the requested spot. If this does not work, the function fails. Typically this happens when the request is beyond the end-of-file. After the seek succeeds, the regular, sequential Read method of the buffer object is called. Because Read is virtual, the system selects the correct one.

Here we are able to write the direct read and write methods for the base class IOBuffer, even though that class does not have sequential read and write functions. In fact, even when we add new derived classes with their own different Read and Write methods, we still do not have to change Dread. Score another one for inheritance and object-oriented design!

The major problem with direct access is knowing where the beginning of the required record is. Sometimes this information about record location is carried in a separate index file. But, for the moment, we assume that we do not have an index. We assume that we know the *relative record number* (RRN) of the record we want. RRN is an important concept that emerges from viewing a file as a collection of records rather than as a collection of bytes. If a file is a sequence of records, the RRN of a record gives its position relative to the beginning of the file. The first record in a file has RRN 0, the next has RRN 1, and so forth.[2]

In our name and address file, we might tie a record to its RRN by assigning membership numbers that are related to the order in which we enter the records in the file. The person with the first record might have a membership number of 1001, the second a number of 1002, and so on. Given a membership number, we can subtract 1001 to get the RRN of the record.

What can we do with this RRN? Not much, given the file structures we have been using so far, which consist of variable-length records. The RRN tells us the relative position of the record we want in the sequence of records, but we still have to read sequentially through the file, counting records as we go, to get to the record we want. An exercise at the end of this chapter explores a method of moving through the file called *skip sequential* processing, which can improve performance somewhat, but looking for a particular RRN is still an $O(n)$ process.

To support direct access by RRN, we need to work with records of fixed, known length. If the records are all the same length, we can use a record's RRN to calculate the *byte offset* of the start of the record relative to the start of the file. For instance, if we are interested in the record with an RRN of 546 and our file has a fixed-length record size of 128 bytes per record, we can calculate the byte offset as

$$\text{Byte offset} = 546 \times 128 = 69\,888$$

In general, given a fixed-length record file where the record size is r, the byte offset of a record with an RRN of n is

$$\text{Byte offset} = n \times r$$

Programming languages and operating systems differ regarding where this byte offset calculation is done and even whether byte offsets are used for addressing within files. In C++ (and the Unix and MS-DOS operating systems), where a file is treated as just a sequence of bytes, the application program does the calculation and uses the seekg and seekp methods to

---

2. In keeping with the conventions of C and C++, we assume that the RRN is a *zero-based* count. In some file systems, the count starts at 1 rather than 0.

jump to the byte that begins the record. All movement within a file is in terms of bytes. This is a very low-level view of files; the responsibility for translating an RRN into a byte offset belongs wholly to the application program and not at all to the programming language or operating system.

Class `FixedLengthBuffer` can be extended with its own methods `DRead` and `DWrite` that interpret the `recref` argument as RRN instead of byte address. The methods are defined as virtual in class `IOBuffer` to allow this. The code in Appendix F does not include this extension; it is left as an exercise.

The Cobol language and the operating environments in which Cobol is often used (OS/MVS, VMS) are examples of a much different, higher-level view of files. The notion of a sequence of bytes is simply not present when you are working with record-oriented files in this environment. Instead, files are viewed as collections of records that are accessed by keys. The operating system takes care of the translation between a key and a record's location. In the simplest case, the key isjust the record's RRN, but the determination of location within the file is still not the programmer's concern.

5.2 More about Record Structures

5.2.1 Choosing a Record Structure and Record Length

Once we decide to fix the length of our records so we can use the RRN to give us direct access to a record, we have to decide on a record length. Clearly, this decision is related to the size of the fields we want to store in the record. Sometimes the decision is easy. Suppose we are building a file of sales transactions that contain the following information about each transaction:

- A six-digit account number of the purchaser,
- Six digits for the date field,
- A five-character stock number for the item purchased,
- A three-digit field for quantity, and
- A ten-position field for total cost.

These are all fixed-length fields; the sum of the field lengths is 30 bytes. Normally we would stick with this record size, but if performance is so important that we need to squeeze every bit of speed out of our retrieval system, we might try to fit the record size to the block organization of our disk. For instance, if we intend to store the records on a typical sectored disk (see Chapter 3) with a sector size of 512 bytes or some other power of 2, we might decide to pad the record out to 32 bytes so we can place an integral number of records in a sector. That way, records will never span sectors.

The choice of a record length is more complicated when the lengths of the fields can vary, as in our name and address file. If we choose a record length that is the sum of our estimates of the largest possible values for all the fields, we can be reasonably sure that we have enough space for everything, but we also waste a lot of space. If, on the other hand, we are conservative in our use of space and fix the lengths of fields at smaller values, we may have to leave information out of a field. Fortunately, we can avoid this problem to some degree by appropriate design of the field structure *within* a record.

In our earlier discussion of record structures, we saw that there are two general approaches we can take toward organizing fields within a fixed-length record. The first, illustrated in Fig. 5.1(a) and implemented in class `FixedFieldBuffer`, uses fixed-length fields inside the fixed-length record. This is the approach we took for the sales transaction file previously described. The second approach, illustrated in Fig. 5.1(b), uses the fixed-length record as a kind of standard-sized container for holding something that looks like a variable-length record.

The first approach has the virtue of simplicity: it is very easy to "break out" the fixed-length fields from within a fixed-length record. The second approach lets us take advantage of an averaging-out effect that usually occurs: the longest names are not likely to appear in the same record as the longest address field. By letting the field boundaries vary, we can make

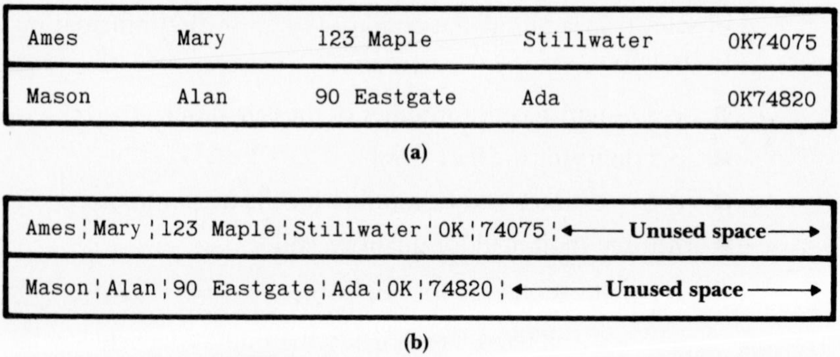

(a)

(b)

Figure 5.1 Two fundamental approaches to field structure within a fixed-length record. (a) Fixed-length records with fixed-length fields. (b) Fixed-length records with variable-length fields.

more efficient use of a fixed amount of space. Also, note that the two approaches are not mutually exclusive. Given a record that contains a number of truly fixed-length fields and some fields that have variable-length information, we might design a record structure that combines these two approaches.

One interesting question that must be resolved in the design of this kind of structure is that of distinguishing the real-data portion of the record from the unused-space portion. The range of possible solutions parallels that of the solutions for recognizing variable-length records in any other context: we can place a record-length count at the beginning of the record, we can use a special delimiter at the end of the record, we can count fields, and so on. As usual, there is no single right way to implement this file structure; instead we seek the solution that is most appropriate for our needs and situation.

Figure 5.2 shows the hex dump output from the two styles of representing variable-length fields in a fixed-length record. Each file has a *header record* that contains three 2-byte values: the size of the header, the number of records, and the size of each record. A full discussion of headers is deferred to the next section. For now, however, just look at the structure of the data records. We have italicized the length fields at the start of the records in the file dump. Although we filled out the records in Fig. 5.2b with blanks to make the output more readable, this blank fill is unnecessary. The length field at the start of the record guarantees that we do not read past the end of the data in the record.

5.2.2 Header Records

It is often necessary or useful to keep track of some general information about a file to assist in future use of the file. A *header record* is often placed at the beginning of the file to hold this kind of information. For example, in some languages there is no easy way to jump to the end of a file, even though the implementation supports direct access. One simple solution is to keep a count of the number of records in the file and to store that count somewhere. We might also find it useful to include information such as the length of the data records, the date and time of the file's most recent update, the name of the file, and so on. Header records can help make a file a self-describing object, freeing the software that accesses the file from having to know *a priori* everything about its structure, hence making the file-access software able to deal with more variation in file structures.

The header record usually has a different structure than the data records in the file. The file of Fig. 5.2a, for instance, uses a 32-byte header

```
0000000   0020 0002 0040 0000 0000 0000 0000 0000   ..........   Header: header size (32),
0000020   0000 0000 0000 0000 0000 0000 0000 0000                record count (2), record size (64)
0000040   416d 6573 7c4d 6172 797c 3132 3320 4d61   Ames|Mary|123 Ma   First record
0000060   706c 657c 5374 696c 6c77 6174 6572 7c4f   ple|Stillwater|O
0000100   4b7c 3734 3037 357c 0000 0000 0000 0000   K|74075|.....
0000120   0000 0000 0000 0000 0000 0000 0000 0000
0000140   4d61 736f 6e7c 416c 616e 7c39 3020 4561   Mason|Alan|90 Ea   Second record
0000160   7374 6761 7465 7c41 6461 7c4f 4b7c 3734   stgate|Ada|OK|74
0000200   3832 307c 0000 0000 0000 0000 0000 0000   820|...
0000220   0000 0000 0000 0000 0000
```

(a)

```
0000000   0042 0002 0044 0000 0000 0000 0000 0000   ..........   Header: header size (66),
0000020   0000 0000 0000 0000 0000 0000 0000 0000                record count (2), record size (68)
0000040   0000 0000 0000 0000 0000 0000 0000 0000
0000060   0000 0000 0000 0000 0000 0000 0000
0000100   0000 0000
0000102   0028 416d 6573 7c4d 6172 797c 3132   (.Ames|Mary|12   First record
0000120   3320 4d61 706c 657c 5374 696c 6c77   3 Maple|Stillw   Integer in first
0000140   6174 6572 7c4f 4b7c 3734 3037 357c   ater|OK|74075|   two bytes contains
0000160   2020 2020 2020 2020 2020 2020         the number of
0000200   2020 2020                             bytes of data in the record
0000204   0024 4d61 736f 6e7c 416c 616e   $.Mason|Alan        Second record
0000220   7c39 3020 4561 7374 6761 7465 7c41   |90 Eastgate|A
0000240   6461 7c4f 4b7c 3734 3832 307c   da|OK|74820|
0000260   2020 2020 2020 2020 2020 2020
0000300   2020 2020 2020 2020
```

(b)

Figure 5.2 Two different record structures that carry variable-length fields in a fixed-length record. (a) File containing a 32- (20₁₆) byte header and two fixed-length records (64 bytes each) containing variable-length fields that are terminated by a null character. (b) File containing a 66- (42₁₆) byte header and fixed-length records (68 bytes each) beginning with a fixed-length (2-byte) field that indicates the number of usable bytes in the record's variable-length fields.

record, whereas the data records each contain 64 bytes. Furthermore, the data records of this file contain only character data, whereas the header record contains integer fields that record the header record size, the number of data records, and the data record size.

Header records are a widely used, important file design tool. For example, when we reach the point at which we are discussing the construction of tree-structured indexes for files, we will see that header records are often placed at the beginning of the index to keep track of such matters as the RRN of the record that is the root of the index.

5.2.3 Adding Headers to C++ Buffer Classes

This section is an example of how to add header processing to the `IOBuffer` class hierarchy. It is not intended to show an optimal strategy for headers. However, these headers are used in all further examples in the book. The `Open` methods of new classes take advantage of this header strategy to verify that the file being opened is appropriate for its use. The important principle is that each file contains a header that incorporates information about the type of objects stored in the file.

The full definition of our buffer class hierarchy, as given in Appendix F, has been extended to include methods that support header records. Class `IOBuffer` includes the following methods:

```
virtual int ReadHeader ();
virtual int WriteHeader ();
```

Most of the classes in the hierarchy include their own versions of these methods. The write methods add a header to a file and return the number of bytes in the header. The read methods read the header and check for consistency. If the header at the beginning of a file is not the proper header for the buffer object, a `FALSE` value is returned; if it is the correct header, `TRUE` is returned.

To illustrate the use of headers, we look at fixed-length record files as defined in classes `IOBuffer` and `FixedLengthBuffer`. These classes were introduced in Chapter 4 and now include methods `ReadHeader` and `WriteHeader`. Appendix F contains the implementation of these methods of all of the buffer classes. The `WriteHeader` method for `IOBuffer` writes the string `IOBuffer` at the beginning of the file. The header for `FixedLengthBuffer` adds the string `Fixed` and the record size.

The `ReadHeader` method of `FixedLengthBuffer` reads the record size from the header and checks that its value is the same as that of the `BufferSize` member of the buffer object. That is, `ReadHeader` verifies that the file was created using fixed-size records that are the right size for using the buffer object for reading and writing.

Another aspect of using headers in these classes is that the header can be used to initialize the buffer. At the end of `FixedLengthBuffer::ReadHeader` (see Appendix F), after the buffer has been found to be uninitialized, the record size of the buffer is set to the record size that was read from the header.

You will recall that in Section 4.5, "An Object-Oriented Class for Record Files," we introduced class `BufferFile` as a way to guarantee the proper interaction between buffers and files. Now that the buffer classes support headers, `BufferFile::Create` puts the correct header in every file, and `Buffer::Open` either checks for consistency or initializes the buffer, as appropriate. `BufferFile::ReadHeader` is called by `Open` and does all of its work in a single virtual function call. Appendix F has the details of the implementation of these methods.

`BufferFile::Rewind` repositions the get and put file pointers to the beginning of the first data record—that is, after the header record. This method is required because the `HeaderSize` member is protected. Without this method, it would be impossible to initiate a sequential read of the file.

5.3   Encapsulating Record I/O Operations in a Single Class

A good object-oriented design for making objects persistent should provide operations to read and write objects directly. So far, the write operation requires two separate operations: pack into a buffer and write the buffer to a file. In this section, we introduce class `RecordFile` which supports a read operation that takes an object of some class and writes it to a file. The use of buffers is hidden inside the class.

The major problem with defining class `RecordFile` is how to make it possible to support files for different object types without needing different versions of the class. Consider the following code that appears to read a `Person` from one file and a `Recording` (a class defined in Chapter 7) from another file:

```
Person p; RecordFile pFile;  pFile . Read (p);
Recording r;    RecordFile rFile;  rFile . Read (r);
```

Is it possible that class `RecordFile` can support read and unpack for a `Person` and a `Recording` without change? Certainly the objects are different—they have different unpacking methods. Virtual function calls do not help because `Person` and `Recording` do not have a common base type. It is the C++ *template* feature that solves our problem by supporting parameterized function and class definitions. Figure 5.3 gives the definition of the template class `RecordFile`.

```
#include "buffile.h"
#include "iobuffer.h"
// template class to support direct read and write of records
// The template parameter RecType must support the following
//     int Pack (BufferType &); pack record into buffer
//     int Unpack (BufferType &); unpack record from buffer

template <class RecType>
class RecordFile: public BufferFile
{public:
        int Read (RecType & record, int recaddr = -1);
        int Write (const RecType & record, int recaddr = -1);
        RecordFile (IOBuffer & buffer): BufferFile (buffer) {}
};

// template method bodies
template <class RecType>
int RecordFile<RecType>::Read (RecType & record, int recaddr = -1)
{
        int writeAddr, result;
        writeAddr = BufferFile::Read (recaddr);
        if (!writeAddr) return -1;
        result = record . Unpack (Buffer);
        if (!result) return -1;
        return writeAddr;
}

template <class RecType>
int RecordFile<RecType>::Write (const RecType & record, int recad-
dr = -1)
{
        int result;
        result = record . Pack (Buffer);
        if (!result) return -1;
        return BufferFile::Write (recaddr);
}
```

Figure 5.3 Template class `RecordFile`.

The definition of class `RecordFile` is a template in the usual sense of the word: a pattern that is used as a guide to make something accurately. The definition does not define a specific class but rather shows how particular record file classes can be constructed. When a template class is supplied with values for its parameters, it becomes a real class. For instance, the following defines an object called `PersonFile`:

```
RecordFile<Person> PersonFile (Buffer);
```

The object `Personfile` is a `RecordFile` that operates on Person objects. All of the operations of `RecordFile<Person>` are available, including those from the parent class `BufferFile`. The following code includes legitimate uses of `PersonFile`:

```
Person person;
PersonFile.Create("person.dat", ios::in); // create a file
PersonFile.Read(person); // read a record into person
PersonFile.Append(person); // write person at end of file
PersonFile.Open("person.dat", ios::in); // open and check header
```

Template definitions in C++ support the reuse of code. We can write a single class and use it in multiple contexts. The same `RecordFile` class declared here and used for files of `Person` objects will be used in subsequent chapters for quite different objects. No changes need be made to `RecordFile` to support these different uses.

Program `testfile.cpp`, in Appendix F, uses `RecordFile` to test all of the buffer I/O classes. It also includes a template function, `TestBuffer`, which is used for all of the buffer tests.

5.4   File Access and File Organization

In the course of our discussions in this and the previous chapter, we have looked at

- Variable-length records,
- Fixed-length records,
- Sequential access, and
- Direct access.

The first two of these relate to aspects of *file organization;* the last two have to do with *file access.* The interaction between file organization and file access is a useful one; we need to look at it more closely before continuing.

Most of what we have considered so far falls into the category of file organization:

- Can the file be divided into fields?
- Is there a higher level of organization to the file that combines the fields into records?
- Do all the records have the same number of bytes or fields?
- How do we distinguish one record from another?
- How do we organize the internal structure of a fixed-length record so we can distinguish between data and extra space?

We have seen that there are many possible answers to these questions and that the choice of a particular file organization depends on many things, including the file-handling facilities of the language you are using and the *use you want to make of the file.*

Using a file implies access. We looked first at sequential access, ultimately developing a *sequential search.* As long as we did not know where individual records began, sequential access was the only option open to us. When we wanted *direct access,* we fixed the length of our records, and this allowed us to calculate precisely where each record began and to seek directly to it.

In other words, our desire for direct *access* caused us to choose a fixed-length record file *organization.* Does this mean that we can equate fixed-length records with direct access? Definitely not. There is nothing about our having fixed the length of the records in a file that precludes sequential access; we certainly could write a program that reads sequentially through a fixed-length record file.

Not only can we elect to read through the fixed-length records sequentially but we can also provide direct access to *variable-length* records simply by keeping a list of the byte offsets from the start of the file for the placement of each record. We chose a fixed-length record structure for the files of Fig. 5.2 because it is simple and adequate for the data we wanted to store. Although the lengths of our names and addresses vary, the variation is not so great that we cannot accommodate it in a fixed-length record.

Consider, however, the effects of using a fixed-length record organization to provide direct access to documents ranging in length from a few hundred bytes to more than a hundred kilobytes. Using fixed-length records to store these documents would be disastrously wasteful of space, so some form of variable-length record structure would have to be found. Developing file structures to handle such situations requires that you clearly distinguish between the matter of *access* and your options regarding *organization*.

The restrictions imposed by the language and file system used to develop your applications impose limits on your ability to take advantage of this distinction between access method and organization. For example, the C++ language provides the programmer with the ability to implement direct access to variable-length records, since it allows access to any byte in the file. On the other hand, Pascal, even when seeking is supported, imposes limitations related to the language's definition of a file as a collection of elements that are all of the same *type* and, consequently, size. Since the elements must all be of the same size, direct access to variable-length records is difficult, at best, in Pascal.

5.5   Beyond Record Structures

Now that we have a grip on the concepts of organization and access, we look at some interesting new file organizations and more complex ways of accessing files. We want to extend the notion of a file beyond the simple idea of records and fields.

We begin with the idea of abstract data models. Our purpose here is to put some distance between the physical and logical organization of files to allow us to focus more on the information content of files and less on physical format.

5.5.1 Abstract Data Models for File Access

The history of file structures and file processing parallels that of computer hardware and software. When file processing first became common on computers, magnetic tape and punched cards were the primary means used to store files. Memory space was dear, and programming languages were primitive. Programmers as well as users were compelled to view file data exactly as it might appear on a tape or cards—as a sequence of fields and records. Even after the data was loaded into memory, the tools for manipulating and viewing the data were unsophisticated and reflected the magnetic tape metaphor. Data processing meant processing fields and records in the traditional sense.

Gradually, computer users began to recognize that computers could process more than just fields and records. Computers could, for instance, process and transmit sound, and they could process and display images and documents (Fig. 5.4). These kinds of applications deal with information that does not fit the metaphor of data stored as sequences of records that are divided into fields, even if, ultimately, the data might be stored physically in the form of fields and records. It is easier, in the mind's eye, to envision data objects such as documents, images, and sound as objects we manipulate in ways that are specific to the objects, rather than simply as fields and records on a disk.

The notion that we need not view data only as it appears on a particular medium is captured in the phrase *abstract data model*, a term that encourages an application-oriented view of data rather than a medium-oriented one. The organization and access methods of abstract data models are described in terms of how an application views the data rather than how the data might physically be stored.

One way we save a user from having to know about objects in a file is to keep information in the file that file-access software can use to "understand" those objects. A good example of how this might be done is to put file structure information in a header.

5.5.2 Headers and Self-Describing Files

We have seen how a header record can be used to keep track of how many records there are in a file. If our programming language permits it, we can put much more elaborate information about a file's structure in the header. When a file's header contains this sort of information, we say the file is *self-describing*. Suppose, for instance, that we store in a file the following information:

Figure 5.4 Data such as sound, images, and documents do not fit the traditional metaphor of data stored as sequences of records that are divided into fields.

- A name for each field,
- The width of each field, and
- The number of fields per record.

We can now write a program that can read and print a meaningful display of files with any number of fields per record and any variety of fixed-length field widths. In general, the more file structure information we put into a file's header, the less our software needs to know about the specific structure of an individual file.

As usual, there is a trade-off: if we do not hard-code the field and record structures of files in the programs that read and write them, the programs must be more sophisticated. They must be flexible enough to interpret the self-descriptions they find in the file headers.

Consider the class `FixedFieldBuffer`, which keeps track of the sizes of all fields. We can extend the header to be more self-describing by including the number of fields and their sizes. The final piece of the header is created by the `FixedFieldBuffer::WriteHeader` method. For this header, we want to record the number of fields and the size of each field. This information is stored in the members `NumFields` and `FieldSize`. This requires a variable-sized header, since the number of fields, hence the number of sizes in the header, are different for different record types. We choose to store this information in the file header by writing it directly into the file as a sequence of fixed-size binary fields. This strategy is very compact and is easy to implement. Now `FixedFieldBuffer::ReadHeader` can check for full consistency of file and buffer and can also fully initialize a buffer when opening a file.

The resulting file with its header for our two `Person` objects is given in Fig. 5.5. The value after "Fixed" in italics (*00 0000 3d*) is the record size, 61. The value after "Field" in italics (*0000 0006*) is the number of fields. The field sizes follow, 4 bytes each.

One advantage of putting this header in the file is that the `FixedFieldBuffer` object can be initialized from the header. The `ReadHeader` method of `FixedFieldBuffer`, after reading the header, checks whether the buffer object has been initialized. If not, the information from the header is used to initialize the object. The body of `ReadHeader` is given in Appendix F.

5.5.3 Metadata

Suppose you are an astronomer interested in studying images generated by telescopes that scan the sky, and you want to design a file structure for the

0000000	I	O	B	u	f	f	e	r	F	i	x	e	d	\0	\0	\0
	494f		4275		6666		6572		4669		7865		6400		0000	
0000020	=	F	i	e	l	d	\0	\0	\0 006	\0	\0	\0	\n	\0	\0
	3d46		6965		6c64		0000		0006		0000		000a		0000	
0000040	\0	\n	\0	\0	\0 017	\0	\0	\0 017	\0	\0	\0 002	\0	\0			
	000a		0000		000f		0000		000f		0000		0002		0000	
0000060	\0	\t	A	m	e	s	\0	\0	\0	\0	\0	\0	M	a	r	y
	0009		416d		6573		0000		0000		0000		4d61		7279	
0000100	\0	\0	\0	\0	\0	\0	1	2	3		M	a	p	l	e	\0
	0000		0000		0000		3132		3320		4d61		706c		6500	
0000120	\0	\0	\0	\0	\0	S	t	i	l	l	w	a	t	e	r	\0
	0000		0000		0053		7469		6c6c		7761		7465		7200	
0000140	\0	\0	\0	\0	O	K	7	4	0	7	5	\0	\0	\0	\0	M
	0000		0000		4f4b		3734		3037		3500		0000		004d	
0000160	a	s	o	n	\0	\0	\0	\0	\0	A	l	a	n	\0	\0	\0
	6173		6f6e		0000		0000		0041		6c61		6e00		0000	
0000200	\0	\0	\0	9	0		E	a	s	t	g	a	t	e	\0	\0
	0000		0039		3020		4561		7374		6761		7465		0000	
0000220	\0	\0	A	d	a	\0	\0	\0	\0	\0	\0	\0	\0	\0	\0	\0
	0000		4164		6100		0000		0000		0000		0000		0000	
0000240	\0	O	K	7	4	8	2	0	\0	\0	\0	\0				
	004f		4b37		3438		3230		0000		0000					

Figure 5.5 File dump of a fixed-field file with descriptive header.

digital representations of these images (Fig. 5.6). You expect to have many images, perhaps thousands, that you want to study, and you want to store one image per file. While you are primarily interested in studying the images, you will certainly need information *about* each image: where in the sky the image is from, when it was made, what telescope was used, what other images are related, and so forth.

This kind of information is called *metadata*—data that describes the primary data in a file. Metadata can be incorporated into any file whose primary data requires supporting information. If a file is going to be shared by many users, some of whom might not otherwise have easy access to its metadata, it may be most convenient to store the metadata in the file. A common place to store metadata in a file is the header record.

Typically, a community of users of a particular kind of data agrees on a standard format for holding metadata. For example, a standard format called FITS (Flexible Image Transport System) has been developed by the International Astronomers' Union for storing the kind of astronomical

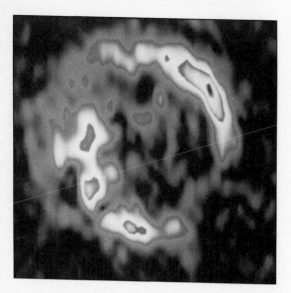

Figure 5.6 To make sense of this 2-megabyte image, an astronomer needs such metadata as the kind of image it is, the part of the sky it is from, and the telescope that was used to view it. Astronomical metadata is often stored in the same file as the data itself. (This image shows polarized radio emission from the southern spiral galaxy NGC 5236 [M83] as observed with the Very Large Array radio telescope in New Mexico.)

data just described in a file's header.[3] A FITS header is a collection of 2880-byte blocks of 80-byte ASCII records, in which each record contains a single piece of metadata. Figure 5.7 shows part of a FITS header. In a FITS file, the header is followed by the numbers that describe the image, one binary number per observed point of the image.

Note that the designers of the FITS format chose to use ASCII in the header but binary values for the image. ASCII headers are easy to read and process and, since they occur only once, take up relatively little space. Because the numbers that make a FITS image are rarely read by humans but are first processed into a picture and then displayed, binary format is the preferred choice for them.

A FITS image is a good example of an abstract data model. The data is meaningless without the interpretive information contained in the header, and FITS-specific methods must be employed to convert FITS data into an understandable image. Another example is the raster image, which we will look at next.

5.5.4 Color Raster Images

From a user's point of view, a modern computer is as much a graphical device as it is a data processor. Whether we are working with documents,

---

3. For more details on FITS, see the references listed at the end of this chapter in "Further Readings."

```
SIMPLE   =                        T /CONFORMS TO BASIC FORMAT
BITPIX   =                       16 / BITS PER PIXEL
NAXIS    =                        2 / NUMBER OF AXES
NAXIS1   =                      256 / RA AXIS DIMENSION
NAXIS2   =                      256 / DEC AXIS DIMENSION
EXTEND   =                        F / T MEANS STANDARD EXTENSIONS EXIST
BSCALE   =          0.000100000 / TRUE = [TAPE*BSCALE]<pl>BZERO
BZERO    =          0.000000000 / OFFSET TO TRUE PIXEL VALUES
MAP_TYPE= 'REL EXPOSURE'         / INTENSITY OR RELATIVE EXPOSURE MAP
BUNIT    = '                '    / DIMENSIONLESS PEAK EXPOSURE FRACTION
CRVAL1   =               0.625 / RA   REF POINT VALUE (DEGREES)
CRPIX1   =             128.500 / RA   REF POINT PIXEL LOCATION
CDELT1   =         -0.006666700 / RA   INCREMENT ALONG AXIS (DEGREES)
CTYPE1   = 'RA--TAN'            / RA   TYPE
CROTA1   =               0.000 / RA   ROTATION
CRVAL2   =              71.967 / DEC  REF POINT VALUE (DEGREES)
CRPIX2   =             128.500 / DEC  REF POINT PIXEL LOCATION
CDELT2   =          0.006666700 / DEC  INCREMENT ALONG AXIS (DEGREES)
CTYPE2   = 'DEC--TAN'           / DEC  TYPE
CROTA2   =               0.000 / DEC  ROTATION
EPOCH    =              1950.0 / EPOCH OF COORDINATE SYSTEM
ARR TYPE=                    4 / 1=DP, 3=FP, 4=I
DATAMAX =               1.000 / PEAK INTENSITY (TRUE)
DATAMIN =               0.000 / MINIMUM INTENSITY (TRUE)
ROLL ANG=            -22.450 / ROLL ANGLE (DEGREES)
BAD ASP =                   0 / 0=good, 1=bad(Do not use roll angle)
TIME LIV=              5649.6 / LIVE TIME (SECONDS)
OBJECT   = 'REM6791            ' / SEQUENCE NUMBER
AVGOFFY =               1.899 / AVG Y OFFSET IN PIXELS, 8 ARCSEC/PIXEL
AVGOFFZ =               2.578 / AVG Z OFFSET IN PIXELS, 8 ARCSEC/PIXEL
RMSOFFY =               0.083 / ASPECT SOLN RMS Y PIXELS, 8 ARCSC/PIX
RMSOFFZ =               0.204 / ASPECT SOLN RMS Z PIXELS, 8 ARCSC/PIX
TELESCOP= 'EINSTEIN           ' / TELESCOPE
INSTRUME= 'IPC                ' / FOCAL PLANE DETECTOR
OBSERVER= '2                  ' / OBSERVER #: 0=CFA; 1=CAL; 2=MIT; 3=GSFC
GALL     =             119.370 / GALACTIC LONGITUDE OF FIELD CENTER
GALB     =               9.690 / GALACTIC LATITUDE OF FIELD CENTER
DATE OBS= '80/238             ' / YEAR & DAY NUMBER FOR OBSERVATION START
DATE STP= '80/238             ' / YEAR & DAY NUMBER FOR OBSERVATION STOP
TITLE    = 'SNR SURVEY: CTA1                                         '
ORIGIN   = 'HARVARD-SMITHSONIAN CENTER FOR ASTROPHYSICS              '
DATE     = '22/09/1989         ' / DATE FILE WRITTEN
TIME     = '05:26:53           ' / TIME FILE WRITTEN
END
```

Figure 5.7 Sample FITS header. On each line, the data to the left of the / is the actual metadata (data about the raw data that follows in the file). For example, the second line (BITPIX = 16) indicates that the raw data in the file will be stored in 16-bit integer format. Everything to the right of a / is a comment, describing for the reader the meaning of the metadata that precedes it. Even a person uninformed about the FITS format can learn a great deal about this file just by reading through the header.

spreadsheets, or numbers, we are likely to be viewing and storing pictures in addition to whatever other information we work with. Let's examine one type of image, the color raster image, as a means to filling in our conceptual understanding of data objects.

A color raster image is a rectangular array of colored dots, or *pixels*,[4] that are displayed on a screen. A FITS image is a raster image in the sense that the numbers that make up a FITS image can be converted to colors, and then displayed on a screen. There are many different kinds of metadata that can go with a raster image, including

- The dimensions of the image—the number or pixels per row and the number of rows.

- The number of bits used to describe each pixel. This determines how many colors can be associated with each pixel. A 1-bit image can display only two colors, usually black and white. A 2-bit image can display four colors (2^2), an 8-bit image can display 256 colors (2^8), and so forth.

- A *color lookup table*, or *palette*, indicating which color is to be assigned to each pixel value in the image. A 2-bit image uses a color lookup table with 4 colors, an 8-bit image uses a table with 256 colors, and so forth.

If we think of an image as an abstract data type, what are some methods that we might associate with images? There are the usual ones associated with getting things in and out of a computer: a *read image* routine and a *store image* routine. Then there are those that deal with images as special objects:

- Display an image in a window on a console screen,
- Associate an image with a particular color lookup table,
- Overlay one image onto another to produce a composite image, and
- Display several images in succession, producing an animation.

The color raster image is an example of a type of data object that requires more than the traditional field/record file structure. This is particularly true when more than one image might be stored in a single file or when we want to store a document or other complex object together with images in a file. Let's look at some ways to mix object types in one file.

---

4. *Pixel* stands for "picture element."

5.5.5 Mixing Object Types in One File

Keywords

The FITS header (Fig. 5.7) illustrates an important technique, described earlier, for identifying fields and records: the use of *keywords*. In the case of FITS headers, we do not know which fields are going to be contained in any given header, so we identify each field using a *keyword = value* format.

Why does this format work for FITS files, whereas it was inappropriate for our address file? For the address file we saw that the use of keywords demanded a high price in terms of space, possibly even doubling the size of the file. In FITS files the amount of overhead introduced by keywords is quite small. When the image is included, the FITS file in the example contains approximately 2 megabytes. The keywords in the header occupy a total of about 400 bytes, or about 0.02 percent of the total file space.

Tags

With the addition via keywords of file structure information and metadata to a header, we see that a file can be more than just a collection of repeated fields and records. Can we extend this notion beyond the header to other, more elaborate objects? For example, suppose an astronomer would like to store *several* FITS images of different sizes in a file, together with the usual metadata, plus perhaps lab notes describing what the scientist learned from the image (Fig. 5.8). Now we can think of our file as a mixture of objects that may be very different in content—a view that our previous file structures do not handle well. Maybe we need a new kind of file structure.

There are many ways to address this new file design problem. One would be simply to put each type of object into a variable-length record and write our file processing programs so they know what each record looks like: the first record is a header for the first image, the second record

Figure 5.8 Information that an astronomer wants to include in a file.

is the image, the third record is a document, the fourth is a header for the second image, and so forth. This solution is workable and simple, but it has some familiar drawbacks:

■ Objects must be accessed sequentially, making access to individual images in large files time-consuming.

■ The file must contain exactly the objects that are described, in exactly the order indicated. We could not, for instance, leave out the notebook for some of the images (or in some cases leave out the notebook altogether) without rewriting all programs that access the file to reflect the changes in the file's structure.

A solution to these problems is hinted at in the FITS header: each line begins with a keyword that identifies the metadata field that follows in the line. Why not use keywords to identify *all* objects in the file—not just the fields in the headers but the headers themselves as well as the images and any other objects we might need to store? Unfortunately, the "keyword = data" format makes sense in a FITS header—it is short and fits easily in an 80-byte line—but it doesn't work at all for objects that vary enormously in size and content. Fortunately, we can generalize the keyword idea to address these problems by making two changes:

■ Lift the restriction that each record be 80 bytes, and let it be big enough to hold the object that is referenced by the keyword.

■ Place the keywords in an index table, together with the byte offset of the actual metadata (or data) and a length indicator that indicates how many bytes the metadata (or data) occupies in the file.

The term *tag* is commonly used in place of *keyword* in connection with this type of file structure. The resulting structure is illustrated in Fig. 5.9. In it we encounter two important conceptual tools for file design: (1) the use of an *index table* to hold descriptive information about the primary data, and (2) the use of *tags* to distinguish different types of objects. These tools allow us to store in one file a mixture of objects—objects that can vary from one another in structure and content.

Tag structures are common among standard file formats in use today. For example, a structure called TIFF (Tagged Image File Format) is a very popular tagged file format used for storing images. HDF (Hierarchical Data Format) is a standard tagged structure used for storing many different kinds of scientific data, including images. In the world of document storage and retrieval, SGML (Standard General Markup Language) is a *language* for describing document structures and for defining tags used to mark up that structure. Like FITS, each of these provides an interesting

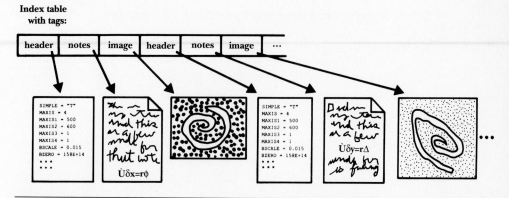

Figure 5.9 Same as Fig. 5.8, except with tags identifying the objects.

study in file design and standardization. References to further information on each are provided at the end of this chapter, in "Further Readings."

Accessing Files with Mixtures of Data Objects

The idea of allowing files to contain widely varying objects is compelling, especially for applications that require large amounts of metadata or unpredictable mixes of different kinds of data, for it frees us of the requirement that all records be fundamentally the same. As usual, we must ask what this freedom costs us. To gain some insight into the costs, imagine that you want to write a program to access objects in such a file. You now have to read and write tags as well as data, and the structure and format for different data types are likely to be different. Here are some questions you will have to answer almost immediately:

- When we want to read an object of a particular type, how do we search for the object?
- When we want to store an object in the file, how and where do we store its tag, and where exactly do we put the object?
- Given that different objects will have very different appearances within a file, how do we determine the correct method for storing or retrieving the object?

The first two questions have to do with accessing the table that contains the tags and pointers to the objects. Solutions to this problem are dealt with in detail in Chapter 6, so we defer their discussion until then. The third question, how to determine the correct methods for accessing objects, has implications that we briefly touch on here.

5.5.6 Representation-Independent File Access

We have used the term *abstract data model* to describe the view that an application has of a data object. This is essentially an in-memory, application-oriented view of an object, one that ignores the physical format of objects as they are stored in files. Taking this view of objects buys our software two things:

■ It delegates to separate modules the responsibility of translating to and from the physical format of the object, letting the application modules concentrate on the task at hand. (For example, an image processing program that can operate in memory on 8-bit images should not have to worry about the fact that a particular image comes from a file that uses the 32-bit FITS format.)

■ It opens up the possibility of working with objects that at some level fit the same abstract data model, even though they are stored in different formats. The in-memory representations of the images could be identical, even though they come from files with quite different formats.)

As an example that illustrates both points, suppose you have an image processing application program (we'll call it `find_star`) that operates in memory on 8-bit images, and you need to process a collection of images. Some are stored in FITS files in a FITS format, and some in TIFF files in a different format. A representation-independent approach (Fig. 5.10) would provide the application program with a routine (let's call it `read_image`) for reading images into memory in the expected 8-bit form, letting the application concentrate on the image processing task. For its part, the routine `read_image`, given a file to get an image from, determines the format of the image within the file, invokes the proper procedure to read the image in that format, and converts it from that format into the 8-bit memory format that the application needs.

Tagged file formats are one way to implement this conceptual view of file organization and file access. The specification of a tag can be accompanied by a specification of methods for reading, writing, and otherwise manipulating the corresponding data object according to the needs of an application. Indeed, any specification that separates the definition of the abstract data model from that of the corresponding file format lends itself to the representation-independent approach.

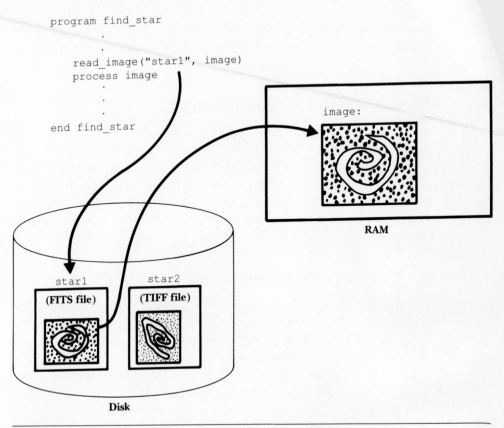

Figure 5.10 Example of object-oriented access. The program `find_star` knows nothing about the file format of the image that it wants to read. The routine `read_image` has methods to convert the image from whatever format it is stored in on disk into the 8-bit in-memory format required by `find_star`.

5.5.7 Extensibility

One of the advantages of using tags to identify objects within files is that we do not have to know *a priori* what all of the objects that our software may eventually have to deal with will look like. We have just seen that if our program is to be able to access a mixture of objects in a file, it must have methods for reading and writing each object. Once we build into our software a mechanism for choosing the appropriate methods for a given type of object, it is easy to imagine extending, at some future time, the types of objects that our software can support. Every time we encounter a new type of object that we would like to accommodate in our files, we can implement methods for reading and writing that object and add those methods to the repertoire of methods available to our file processing software.

5.6   Portability and Standardization

A recurring theme in several of the examples we have just seen is that people often want to share files. Sharing files means making sure that they are accessible on all of the different computers that they might turn up on and that they are somehow compatible with all of the different programs that will access them. In this final section, we look at two complementary topics that affect the sharability of files: portability and standardization.

5.6.1 Factors Affecting Portability

Imagine that you work for a company that wishes to share simple data files such as our address file with some other business. You get together with the other business to agree on a common field and record format, and you discover that your business does all of its programming and computing in C on a Sun computer and the other business uses Turbo Pascal on a PC. What sorts of issues would you expect to arise?

Differences among Operating Systems

In Chapter 2 in the section "Special Characters in Files," we saw that MS-DOS adds an extra line-feed character every time it encounters a carriage return character, whereas on most other file systems this is not the case. This means that every time our address file has a byte with hex value 0x0d, even if that byte is not meant to be a carriage return, the file is not extended by an extra 0x0a byte.

This example illustrates the fact that *the ultimate physical format of the same logical file can vary depending on differences among operating systems.*

Differences among Languages

Earlier in this chapter, when discussing header records, we chose to make header records and data records different sizes, but a Pascal programmer must use the same size for every record in the file. C++ allows us to mix and match fixed record lengths according to our needs, but Pascal requires that all records in a nontext file be the same size.

This illustrates a second factor impeding portability among files: *the physical layout of files produced with different languages may be constrained by the way the languages let you define structures within a file.*

Differences in Machine Architectures

Consider the hex dump in Fig. 5.2 which shows a file generated by a C program running on a Sun Ultra. The first line of the hex dump contains part of the header record:

```
0000000   0020 0002 0040 0000 0000 0000 0000 0000
```

The first pair of bytes contains the size of the header record, in this case 20_{16}—or 32_{10}. The next two pairs of bytes also contain integer values. If the same program is compiled and executed on a PC or a VAX, the hex dump of the first line will look like this:

```
0000000   2000 0200 4000 0000 0000 0000 0000 0000
```

Why are the bytes reversed in this version of the program? The answer is that in both cases the numbers were written to the file exactly as they appeared in memory, and the two different machines represent 2-byte integers differently—the Sun stores the high-order byte, followed by the low-order byte; the PC and VAX store the low-order byte, followed by the high-order byte.

This reverse order also applies to 4-byte integers on these machines. For example, in our discussion of file dumps we saw that the hexadecimal value of $500\,000\,000_{10}$ is $1dcd6500_{16}$. If you write this value out to a file on a PC, or some other reverse-order machine, a hex dump of the file created looks like this:

```
0000000   0065 cd1d
```

The problem of data representation is not restricted only to byte order of binary numbers. The way structures are laid out in memory can vary from machine to machine and compiler to compiler. For example, suppose you have a C program containing the following lines of code:

```
struct {
   int  cost;
   char ident[4];
} item;
...
write (fd, &item, sizeof(item));
```

and you want to write files using this code on two different machines, a Cray T90 and a Sun Ultra. Because it likes to operate on 64-bit words, Cray's C compiler allocates a minimum of 8 bytes for any element in a `struct`, so it allocates 16 bytes for the `struct item`. When it executes the `write` statement, then, the Cray writes 16 bytes to the file. The same program compiled on a Sun Ultra writes only 8 bytes, as you probably would expect, and on most PCs it writes 6 bytes: same exact program; same language; three different results.

Text is also encoded differently on different platforms. In this case the differences are primarily restricted to two different types of systems: those that use EBCDIC[5] and those that use ASCII. EBCDIC is a standard created by IBM, so machines that need to maintain compatibility with IBM must support EBCDIC. Most others support ASCII. A few support both. Hence, text written to a file from an EBCDIC-based machine may well not be readable by an ASCII-based machine.

Equally serious, when we go beyond simple English text, is the problem of representing different character sets from different national languages. This is an enormous problem for developers of text databases.

5.6.2 Achieving Portability

Differences among languages, operating systems, and machine architectures represent three major problems when we need to generate portable files. Achieving portability means determining how to deal with these differences. And the differences are often not just differences between two platforms, for many different platforms could be involved.

The most important requirement for achieving portability is to recognize that it is not a trivial matter and to take steps ahead of time to insure it. Following are some guidelines.

Agree on a Standard Physical Record Format and Stay with It

A physical standard is one that is represented the same physically, no matter what language, machine, or operating system is used. FITS is a good example of a physical standard, for it specifies exactly the physical format of each header record, the keywords that are allowed, the order in which keywords may appear, and the bit pattern that must be used to represent the binary numbers that describe the image.

---

5. EBCDIC stands for Extended Binary Coded Decimal Interchange Code.

Unfortunately, once a standard is established, it is very tempting to improve on it by changing it in some way, thereby rendering it no longer a standard. If the standard is sufficiently extensible, this temptation can sometimes be avoided. FITS, for example, has been extended a few times over its lifetime to support data objects that were not anticipated in its original design, yet all additions have remained compatible with the original format.

One way to make sure that a standard has staying power is to make it simple enough that files can be written in the standard format from a wide range of machines, languages, and operating systems. FITS again exemplifies such a standard. FITS headers are ASCII 80-byte records in blocks of thirty-six records each, and FITS images are stored as one contiguous block of numbers, both very simple structures that are easy to read and write in most modern operating systems and languages.

Agree on a Standard Binary Encoding for Data Elements

The two most common types of basic data elements are text and numbers. In the case of text, ASCII and EBCDIC represent the most common encoding schemes, with ASCII standard on virtually all machines except IBM mainframes. Depending on the anticipated environment, one of these should be used to represent all text.[6]

The situation for binary numbers is a little cloudier. Although the number of different encoding schemes is not large, the likelihood of having to share data among machines that use different binary encodings can be quite high, especially when the same data is processed both on large mainframes and on smaller computers. Two standards efforts have helped diminish the problem, however: IEEE Standard formats and External Data Representation (XDR).

IEEE has established standard format specifications for 32-bit, 64-bit, and 128-bit floating point numbers, and for 8-bit, 16-bit, and 32-bit integers. With a few notable exceptions (for example, IBM mainframes, Cray, and Digital), most computer manufacturers have followdd these guidelines in designing their machines. This effort goes a long way toward providing portable number encoding schemes.

XDR is an effort to go the rest of the way. XDR not only specifies a set of standard encodings for all files (the IEEE encodings) but provides for a

---

6. Actually, there are different versions of both ASCII and EBCDIC. However, for most applications and for the purposes of this text, it is sufficient to consider each as a single character set.

set of routines for each machine for converting from its binary encoding when writing to a file and vice versa (Fig. 5.11). Hence, when we want to store numbers in XDR, we can read or write them by replacing read and write routines in our program with XDR routines. The XDR routines take care of the conversions.[7]

Once again, FITS provides us with an excellent example: the binary numbers that constitute a FITS image must conform to the IEEE Standard. Any program written on a machine with XDR support can thus read and write portable FITS files.

Number and Text Conversion

Sometimes the use of standard data encodings is not feasible. For example, suppose you are working primarily on IBM mainframes with software that deals with floating point numbers and text. If you choose to store your data in IEEE Standard formats, every time your program reads or writes a

---

7. XDR is used for more than just number conversions. It allows a C programmer to describe arbitrary data structures in a machine-independent fashion. XDR originated as a Sun protocol for transmitting data that is accessed by more than one type of machine. For further information, see Sun (1986 or later).

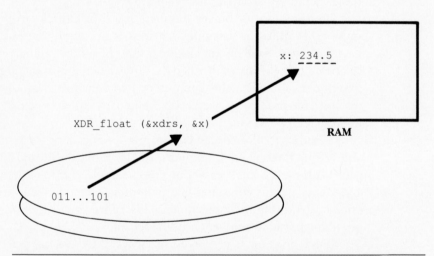

Figure 5.11 XDR specifies a standard external data representation for numbers stored in a file. XDR routines are provided for converting to and from the XDR representation to the encoding scheme used on the host machine. Here a routine called XDR_float translates a 32-bit floating point number from its XDR representation on disk to that of the host machine.

number or character, it must translate the number from the IBM format to the corresponding IEEE format. This is not only time-consuming but can result in loss of accuracy. It is probably better in this case to store your data in native IBM format in your files.

What happens, then, when you want to move your files back and forth between your IBM and a VAX, which uses a different native format for numbers and generally uses ASCII for text? You need a way to convert from the IBM format to the VAX format and back. One solution is to write (or borrow) a program that translates IBM numbers and text to their VAX equivalents, and vice versa. This simple solution is illustrated in Fig. 5.12(a).

But what if, in addition to IBM and VAX computers, you find that your data is likely to be shared among many different platforms that use different numeric encodings? One way to solve this problem is to write a program to convert from each of the representations to every other representation. This solution, illustrated in Fig. 5.12(b), can get rather complicated. In general, if you have n different encoding schemes, you will need $n(n-1)$ different translators. If n is large, this can be very messy. Not only do you need many translators, but you need to keep track, for each file, of where the file came from and/or where it is going in order to know which translator to use.

In this case, a better solution would probably be to agree on a standard intermediate format, such as XDR, and translate files into XDR whenever they are to be exported to a different platform. This solution is illustrated in Fig. 5.12(c). Not only does it reduce the number of translators from $n(n-1)$ to $2n$, but it should be easy to find translators to convert from most platforms to and from XDR. One negative aspect of this solution is that it requires *two* conversions to go from any one platform to another, a cost that has to be weighed against the complexity of providing $n(n-1)$ translators.

File Structure Conversion

Suppose you are a doctor and you have X-ray raster images of a particular organ taken periodically over several minutes. You want to look at a certain image in the collection using a program that lets you zoom in and out and detect special features in the image. You have another program that lets you animate the collection of images, showing how it changes over several minutes. Finally, you want to annotate the images and store them in a special X-ray archive—and you have another program for doing that. What do you do if each of these three programs requires that your image be in a different format?

(a) Converting between IBM and Vax native format
requires two conversion routines.

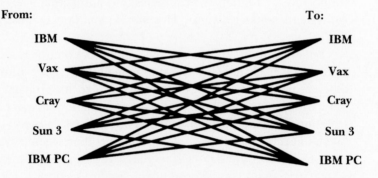

(b) Converting directly between five different native formats
requires 20 conversion routines.

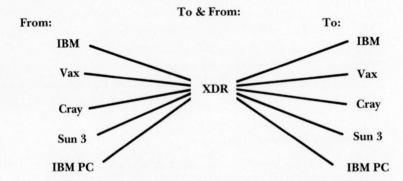

(c) Converting between five different native formats via an
intermediate standard format requires 10 conversion routines.

Figure 5.12 Direct conversion between n native machines formats requires
$n(n-1)$ conversion routines, as illustrated in (a) and (b). Conversion via an
intermediate standard format requires $2n$ conversion routines, as illustrated
in (c).

The conversion problems that apply to atomic data encoding also apply to file structures for more complex objects, like images, but at a different level. Whereas character and number encoding are tied closely to specific platforms, more complex objects and their representations just as often are tied to specific *applications*.

For example, there are many software packages that deal with images and very little agreement about a file format for storing them. When we look at this software, we find different solutions to this problem.

- Require that the user supply images in a format that is compatible with the one used by the package. This places the responsibility on the user to convert from one format to another. For such situations, it may be preferable to provide utility programs that translate from one format to another and that are invoked whenever translating.

- Process only images that adhere to some predefined standard format. This places the responsibility on a community of users and software developers for agreeing on and enforcing a standard. FITS is a good example of this approach.

- Include different sets of I/O methods capable of converting an image from several different formats into a standard memory structure that the package can work with. This places the burden on the software developer to develop I/O methods for file object types that may be stored differently but for the purposes of an application are conceptually the same. You may recognize this approach as a variation on the concept of *object-oriented access* that we discussed earlier.

File System Differences

Finally, if you move files from one file system to another, chances are you will find differences in the way files are organized physically. For example, Unix systems write files to tapes in 512-byte blocks, but non-Unix systems often use different block sizes, such as 2880-bytes—thirty-six 80-byte records. (Guess where the FITS blocking format comes from?) When transferring files between systems, you may need to deal with this problem.

Unix and Portability

Recognizing problems such as the block-size problem just described, Unix provides a utility called dd. Although dd is intended primarily for copying tape data to and from Unix systems, it can be used to convert data from any physical source. The dd utility provides the following options, among others:

- Convert from one block size to another,
- Convert fixed-length records to variable-length, or vice versa,
- Convert ASCII to EBCDIC, or vice versa,
- Convert all characters to lowercase (or to uppercase), and
- Swap every pair of bytes.

Of course, the greatest contribution Unix makes to the problems discussed here is Unix itself. By its simplicity and ubiquity, Unix encourages the use of the same operating system, the same file system, the same views of devices, and the same general views of file organization, no matter what particular hardware platform you happen to be using.

For example, one of the authors works in an organization with a nationwide constituency that operates many different computers, including two Crays, a Connection Machine, and many Sun, Apple, IBM, Silicon Graphics, and Digital workstations. Because each runs some flavor of Unix, they all incorporate precisely the same view of all external storage devices, they all use ASCII, and they all provide the same basic programming environment and file management utilities. Files are not perfectly portable within this environment, for reasons that we have covered in this chapter; but the availability of Unix goes a long way toward facilitating the rapid and easy transfer of files among the applications, programming environments, and hardware systems that the organization supports.

SUMMARY

One higher level of organization, in which records are grouped into *blocks*, is also often imposed on files. This level is imposed to improve I/O performance rather than our logical view of the file.

Sometimes we identify individual records by their *relative record numbers* (RRNs) in a file. It is also common, however, to identify a record by a *key* whose value is based on some of the record's content. Key values must occur in, or be converted to, some predetermined *canonical form* if they are to be recognized accurately and unambiguously by programs. If every record's key value is distinct from all others, the key can be used to identify and locate the unique record in the file. Keys that are used in this way are called *primary keys*.

In this chapter we look at the technique of searching sequentially through a file looking for a record with a particular key. Sequential search can perform poorly for long files, but there are times when sequential searching is reasonable. Record blocking can be used to improve the I/O time for a sequential search substantially. Two useful Unix utilities that process files sequentially are `wc` and `grep`.

In our discussion of ways to separate records, it is clear that some of the methods provide a mechanism for looking up or calculating the *byte offset* of the beginning of a record. This, in turn, opens up the possibility of accessing the record *directly*, by RRN, rather than sequentially.

The simplest record formats for permitting direct access by RRN involve the use of fixed-length records. When the data comes in fixed-size quantities (for example, zip codes), fixed-length records can provide good performance and good space utilization. If there is a lot of variation in the amount and size of data in records, however, the use of fixed-length records can result in expensive waste of space. In such cases the designer should look carefully at the possibility of using variable-length records.

Sometimes it is helpful to keep track of general information about files, such as the number of records they contain. A *header record,* stored at the beginning of the file it pertains to, is a useful tool for storing this kind of information. Header records have been added to the I/O buffer class and class `BufferFile`. These headers support a guarantee of consistent access to records in files.

It is important to be aware of the difference between *file access* and *file organization.* We try to organize files in such a way that they give us the types of access we need for a particular application. For example, one of the advantages of a fixed-length record organization is that it allows access that is either sequential or direct.

In addition to the traditional view of a file as a more or less regular collection of fields and records, we present a more purely logical view of the contents of files in terms of *abstract data models,* a view that lets applications ignore the physical structure of files altogether.

Defining a single class to support file operations for arbitrary data objects requires the use of C++ *templates.* Class `RecordFile` implements this abstract data model approach as a template class with a single parameter. The application programmer need only define `Pack` and `Unpack` methods, using the buffer classes defined in Chapter 4, and `RecordFile` does the rest. The application can create, open, and close files, and read and write records with no additional concern about file structures.

This abstract data model view is often more appropriate to data objects such as sound, images, and documents. We call files *self-describing* when they do not require an application to reveal their structure but provide that information themselves. Another concept that deviates from the traditional view is *metadata,* in which the file contains data that describes the primary data in the file. FITS files, used for storing astronomical images, contain extensive headers with metadata.

The use of abstract data models, self-describing files, and metadata makes it possible to mix a variety of different types of data objects in one file. When this is the case, file access is more object oriented. Abstract data models also facilitate *extensible* files—files whose structures can be extended to accommodate new kinds of objects.

Portability becomes increasingly important as files are used in more heterogeneous computing environments. Differences among operating systems, languages, and machine architectures all lead to the need for portability. One important way to foster portability is *standardization,* which means agreeing on physical formats, encodings for data elements, and file structures.

If a standard does not exist and it becomes necessary to convert from one format to another, it is still often much simpler to have one standard format that all converters convert into and out of. Unix provides a utility called dd that facilitates data conversion. The Unix environment supports portability simply by being commonly available on a large number of platforms.

KEY TERMS

Block. A collection of records stored as a physically contiguous unit on secondary storage. In this chapter, we use record blocking to improve I/O performance during sequential searching.

Canonical form. A standard form for a key that can be derived, by the application of well-defined rules, from the particular, nonstandard form of the data found in a record's key field(s) or provided in a search request supplied by a user.

Direct access. A file accessing mode that involves jumping to the exact location of a record. Direct access to a fixed-length record is usually accomplished by using its *relative record number* (RRN), computing its byte offset, and then seeking to the first byte of the record.

Extensibility. A characteristic of some file organizations that makes it possible to extend the types of objects that the format can accommodate without having to redesign the format. For example, tagged file formats lend themselves to extensibility, for they allow the addition of new tags for new data objects and associated new methods for accessing the objects.

File-access method. The approach used to locate information in a file. In general, the two alternatives are *sequential access* and *direct access.*

File organization method. The combination of conceptual and physical structures used to distinguish one record from another and one field from another. An example of a kind of file organization is fixed-length records containing variable numbers of variable-length delimited fields.

Header record. A record placed at the beginning of a file that is used to store information about the file contents and the file organization.

Key. An expression derived from one or more of the fields within a record that can be used to locate that record. The fields used to build the key are sometimes called the *key fields.* Keyed access provides a way of performing content-based retrieval of records, rather than retrieval based merely on a record's position.

Metadata. Data in a file that is not the primary data but describes the primary data in a file. Metadata can be incorporated into any file whose primary data requires supporting information. If a file is going to be shared by many users, some of whom might not otherwise have easy access to its metadata, it may be most convenient to store the metadata in the file itself. A common place to store metadata in a file is the header record.

Portability. That characteristic of files that describes how amenable they are to access on a variety of different machines, via a variety of different operating systems, languages, and applications.

Primary key. A key that uniquely identifies each record and is used as the primary method of accessing the records.

Record. A collection of related fields. For example, the name, address, and so forth of an individual in a mailing list file would probably make up one record.

Relative record number (RRN). An index giving the position of a record relative to the beginning of its file. If a file has fixed-length records, the RRN can be used to calculate the *byte offset* of a record so the record can be accessed directly.

Representation-independent file access. A form of file access in which applications access data objects in terms of the applications' in-memory view of the objects. Separate methods associated with the objects are responsible for translating to and from the physical format of the object, letting the application concentrate on the task at hand.

Self-describing files. Files that contain information such as the number of records in the file and formal descriptions of the file's record structure, which can be used by software in determining how to access the file. A file's header is a good place for this information.

Sequential access. Sequential access to a file means reading the file from the beginning and continuing until you have read in everything that you need. The alternative is direct access.

Sequential search. A method of searching a file by reading the file from the beginning and continuing until the desired record has been found.

Template class. A parameterized class definition. Multiple classes can share the same definition and code through the use of template classes and template functions in C++.

FURTHER READINGS

Sweet (1985) is a short but stimulating article on key field design. A number of interesting algorithms for improving performance in sequential searches are described in Gonnet (1984) and, of course, in Knuth (1973b).

Self-describing file formats like FITS—see Wells, Greisen, and Harten (1981)—for scientific files have had significant development over the past years. Two of the most prominent format strategies are the Hierarchical Data Format (HDF), available from the HDF Web site at http://hdf.ncsa.uiuc.edu, and the Common Data Format (CDF) which has a web site at http://nssdc.gsfc.nasa.gov/cdf/cdf_home.html.

EXERCISES

1. If a key in a record is already in canonical form and the key is the first field of the record, it is possible to search for a record by key without ever separating out the key field from the rest of the fields. Explain.

2. It has been suggested (Sweet, 1985) that primary keys should be "data-less, unchanging, unambiguous, and unique." These concepts are

interrelated since, for example, a key that contains data runs a greater risk of changing than a dataless key. Discuss the importance of each of these concepts, and show by example how their absence can cause problems. The primary key used in our example file violates at least one of the criteria. How might you redesign the file (and possibly its corresponding information content) so primary keys satisfy these criteria?

3. How many comparisons would be required on the average to find a record using sequential search in a 100 000-record disk file? If the record is not in the file, how many comparisons are required? If the file is blocked so that 50 records are stored per block, how many disk accesses are required on average? What if only one record is stored per block?

4. In our evaluation of performance for sequential search, we assume that every read results in a seek. How do the assumptions change on a single-user machine with access to a magnetic disk? How do these changed assumptions affect the analysis of sequential searching?

5. Design a header structure for a `Person` file of fixed-sized records that stores the names of the fields in addition to the sizes of the fields. How would you have to modify class `FixedFieldBuffer` to support the use of such a header?

6. Separate code must be generated for each instantiation of a template class, but there is no standard for controlling this code generation. What is the mechanism in your C++ compiler that is used to describe when to generate code for template instances?

7. In our discussion of the uses of relative record numbers (RRNs), we suggest that you can create a file in which there is a direct correspondence between a primary key, such as membership number, and RRN, so we can find a person's record by knowing just the name or membership number. What kinds of difficulties can you envision with this simple correspondence between membership number and RRN? What happens if we want to delete a name? What happens if we change the information in a record in a variable-length record file and the new record is longer?

8. Assume that we have a variable-length record file with long records (greater than 1000 bytes each, on the average). Assume that we are looking for a record with a particular RRN. Describe the benefits of using the contents of a byte count field to skip sequentially from

record to record to find the one we want. This is called *skip sequential* processing. Use your knowledge of system buffering to describe why this is useful only for long records. If the records are sorted in order by key and blocked, what information do you have to place at the start of each block to permit even faster skip sequential processing?

9. Suppose you have a fixed-length record with fixed-length fields, and the sum of the field lengths is 30 bytes. A record with a length of 30 bytes would hold them all. If we intend to store the records on a sectored disk with 512-byte sectors (see Chapter 3), we might decide to pad the record out to 32 bytes so we can place an integral number of records in a sector. Why would we want to do this?

10. Why is it important to distinguish between file access and file organization?

11. What is an abstract data model? Why did the early file processing programs not deal with abstract data models? What are the advantages of using abstract data models in applications? In what way does the Unix concept of standard input and standard output conform to the notion of an abstract data model? (See "Physical Files and Logical Files in Unix" in Chapter 2.)

12. What is metadata?

13. In the FITS header in Fig. 5.7, some metadata provides information about the file's structure, and some provides information about the scientific context in which the corresponding image was recorded. Give three examples of each.

14. In the FITS header in Fig. 5.7, there is enough information for a program to determine how to read the entire file. Assuming that the size of the block containing the header must be a multiple of 2,880 bytes, how large is the file? What proportion of the file contains header information?

15. In the discussion of field organization, we list the "keyword = value" construct as one possible type of field organization. How is this notion applied in tagged file structures? How does a tagged file structure support object-oriented file access? How do tagged file formats support extensibility?

16. List three factors that affect portability in files.

17. List three ways that portability can be achieved in files.

18. What is XDR? XDR is actually much more extensive than what we described in this chapter. If you have access to XDR documentation

(see "Further Readings" at the end of this chapter), look up XDR and list the ways that it supports portability.

19. What is the IEEE standard format for 32-bit, 64-bit, and 128-bit floating point values? Does your computer implement floating point values in the IEEE format?

PROGRAMMING EXERCISES

20. Implement methods such as `findByLastName(char*)`, `findByFirstName(char*)`, and so on, that search through a `BufferFile<Person>` for a record that has the appropriate field that matches the argument.

21. Write a `ReadByRRN` method for variable-length record files that finds a record on the basis of its position in the file. For example, if requested to find the 547th record in a file, it would read through the first 546 records and then print the contents of the 547th record. Implement skip sequential search (see Exercise 8) to avoid reading the contents of unwanted records.

22. Write a driver for `findByLastName` that reads names from a separate transaction file that contains only the keys of the records to be extracted. Write the selected records to a separate output file. First, assume that the records are in no particular order. Then assume that both the main file and the transaction file are sorted by key. In the latter case, how can you make your program more efficient?

23. Implement an update operation for class `BufferFile` that works for fixed-length record file. Write a driver program that allows a user to select a record-by-record number and enter new values for all of the fields.

24. Make any or all of the following alterations to the update function from Exercise 23.

    a. Let the user identify the record to be changed by name, rather than RRN.

    b. Let the user change individual fields without having to change an entire record.

    c. Let the user choose to view the entire file.

25. Write a program that reads a file and outputs the file contents as a file dump. The file dump should have a format similar to the one used in the examples in this chapter. The program should accept the name of

the input file on the command line. Output should be to standard output (terminal screen).

26. Develop a set of rules for translating the dates August 7, 1949, Aug. 7, 1949, 8-7-49, 08-07-49, 8/7/49, and other, similar variations into a common canonical form. Write a function that accepts a string containing a date in one of these forms and returns the canonical form, according to your rules. Be sure to document the limitations of your rules and function.

Organizing Files for Performance

6

❖ Look at several approaches to *data compression*.

❖ Look at *storage compaction* as a simple way of reusing space in a file.

❖ Develop a procedure for deleting fixed-length records that allows vacated file space to be reused dynamically.

❖ Illustrate the use of *linked lists* and *stacks* to manage an *avail list*.

❖ Consider several approaches to the problem of deleting variable-length records.

❖ Introduce the concepts associated with the terms *internal fragmentation* and *external fragmentation*.

❖ Outline some *placement strategies* associated with the reuse of space in a variable-length record file.

❖ Provide an introduction to the idea of a *binary search*.

❖ Examine the limitations of binary searching.

❖ Develop a *keysort* procedure for sorting larger files; investigate the costs associated with keysort.

❖ Introduce the concept of a *pinned record*.

CHAPTER OUTLINE

6.1 Data Compression
    6.1.1 Using a Different Notation
    6.1.2 Suppressing Repeating Sequences
    6.1.3 Assigning Variable-Length Codes
    6.1.4 Irreversible Compression Techniques
    6.1.5 Compression in Unix
6.2 Reclaiming Space in Files
    6.2.1 Record Deletion and Storage Compaction
    6.2.2 Deleting Fixed-Length Records for Reclaiming Space
         Dynamically
    6.2.3 Deleting Variable-Length Records
    6.2.4 Storage Fragmentation
    6.2.5 Placement Strategies
6.3 Finding Things Quickly: An Introduction to Internal Sorting and Binary Searching
    6.3.1 Finding Things in Simple Field and Record Files
    6.3.2 Search by Guessing: Binary Search
    6.3.3 Binary Search versus Sequential Search
    6.3.4 Sorting a Disk File in Memory
    6.3.5 The Limitations of Binary Searching and Internal Sorting
6.4 Keysorting
    6.4.1 Description of the Method
    6.4.2 Limitations of the Keysort Method
    6.4.3 Another Solution: Why Bother to Write the File Back?
    6.4.4 Pinned Records

We have already seen how important it is for the file system designer to consider how a file is to be accessed when deciding on how to create fields, records, and other file structures. In this chapter we continue to focus on file organization, but the motivation is different. We look at ways to organize or reorganize files in order to improve performance.

In the first section we look at how we organize files to make them smaller. Compression techniques let us make files smaller by encoding the basic information in the file.

Next we look at ways to reclaim unused space in files to improve performance. Compaction is a batch process that we can use to purge holes of unused space from a file that has undergone many deletions and updates. Then we investigate dynamic ways to maintain performance by reclaiming space made available by deletions and updates of records during the life of a file.

In the third section we examine the problem of reorganizing files by sorting them to support simple binary searching. Then, in an effort to find a better sorting method, we begin a conceptual line of thought that will continue throughout the rest of this text: we find a way to improve file performance by creating an external structure through which we can access the file.

6.1   Data Compression

In this section we look at some ways to make files smaller. There are many reasons for making files smaller. Smaller files

- Use less storage, resulting in cost savings;
- Can be transmitted faster, decreasing access time or, alternatively, allowing the same access time with a lower and cheaper bandwidth; and
- Can be processed faster sequentially.

Data compression involves encoding the information in a file in such a way that it takes up less space. Many different techniques are available for compressing data. Some are very general, and some are designed for specific kinds of data, such as speech, pictures, text, or instrument data. The variety of data compression techniques is so large that we can only touch on the topic here, with a few examples.

6.1.1   Using a Different Notation

Remember our `Person` file from Chapter 4? It had several fixed-length fields, including `LastName`, `State`, and `ZipCode`. Fixed-length fields such as these are good candidates for compression. For instance, the `State` field in the `Person` file required 2 ASCII bytes, 16 bits. How many bits are *really* needed for this field? Since there are only fifty states, we could represent all possible states with only 6 bits. Thus, we could encode all state names in a single 1-byte field, resulting in a space savings of 1 byte, or 50 percent, per occurrence of the state field.

This type of compression technique, in which we decrease the number of bits by finding a more *compact notation,*[1] is one of many compression

---

1. Note that the original two-letter notation we used for "state" is itself a more compact notation for the full state name.

techniques classified as *redundancy reduction*. The 10 bits that we were able to throw away were redundant in the sense that having 16 bits instead of 6 provided no extra information.

What are the costs of this compression scheme? In this case, there are many:

■ By using a pure binary encoding, we have made the file unreadable by humans.

■ We incur some cost in encoding time whenever we add a new state-name field to our file and a similar cost for decoding when we need to get a readable version of state name from the file.

■ We must also now incorporate the encoding and/or decoding modules in all software that will process our address file, increasing the complexity of the software.

With so many costs, is this kind of compression worth it? We can answer this only in the context of a particular application. If the file is already fairly small, if the file is often accessed by many different pieces of software, and if some of the software that will access the file cannot deal with binary data (for example, an editor), then this form of compression is a bad idea. On the other hand, if the file contains several million records and is generally processed by one program, compression is probably a very good idea. Because the encoding and decoding algorithms for this kind of compression are extremely simple, the savings in access time is likely to exceed any processing time required for encoding or decoding.

6.1.2 Suppressing Repeating Sequences

Imagine an 8-bit image of the sky that has been processed so only objects above a certain brightness are identified and all other regions of the image are set to some background color represented by the pixel value 0. (See Fig. 6.1.)

Sparse arrays of this sort are very good candidates for a kind of compression called *run-length encoding*, which in this example works as follows. First, we choose one special, unused byte value to indicate that a run-length code follows. Then, the run-length encoding algorithm goes like this:

■ Read through the pixels that make up the image, copying the pixel values to the file in sequence, except where the same pixel value occurs more than once in succession.

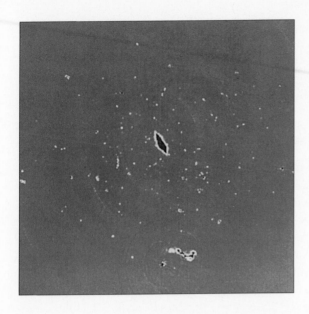

Figure 6.1 The empty space in this astronomical image is represented by repeated sequences of the same value and is thus a good candidate for compression. (This FITS image shows a radio continuum structure around the spiral galaxy NGC 891 as observed with the Westerbork Synthesis radio telescope in The Netherlands.)

■ Where the same value occurs more than once in succession, substitute the following 3 bytes, in order:

- The special run-length code indicator;
- The pixel value that is repeated; and
- The number of times that the value is repeated (up to 256 times).

For example, suppose we wish to compress an image using run-length encoding, and we find that we can omit the byte 0xff from the representation of the image. We choose the byte 0xff as our run-length code indicator. How would we encode the following sequence of hexadecimal byte values?

22 23 24 24 24 24 24 24 24 25 26 26 26 26 26 26 25 24

The first three pixels are to be copied in sequence. The runs of 24 and 26 are both run-length encoded. The remaining pixels are copied in sequence. The resulting sequence is

22 23 ff 24 07 25 ff 26 06 25 24

Run-length encoding is another example of redundancy reduction. It can be applied to many kinds of data, including text, instrument data, and sparse matrices. Like the compact notation approach, the run-length encoding algorithm is a simple one whose associated costs rarely affect performance appreciably.

Unlike compact notation, run-length encoding does not guarantee any particular amount of space savings. A "busy" image with a lot of variation will not benefit appreciably from run-length encoding. Indeed, under some circumstances, the aforementioned algorithm could result in a "compressed" image that is larger than the original image.

6.1.3 Assigning Variable-Length Codes

Suppose you have two different symbols to use in an encoding scheme: a dot (·) and a dash (-). You have to assign combinations of dots and dashes to letters of the alphabet. If you are very clever, you might determine the most frequently occurring letters of the alphabet (*e* and *t*) and use a single dot for one and a single dash for the other. Other letters of the alphabet will be assigned two or more symbols, with the more frequently occurring letters getting fewer symbols.

Sound familiar? You may recognize this scheme as the oldest and most common of the *variable-length codes,* the Morse code. Variable-length codes, in general, are based on the principle that some values occur more frequently than others, so the codes for those values should take the least amount of space. Variable-length codes are another form of redundancy reduction.

A variation on the compact notation technique, the Morse code can be implemented using a table lookup, where the table never changes. In contrast, since many sets of data values do not exhibit a predictable frequency distribution, more modern variable-length coding techniques dynamically build the tables that describe the encoding scheme. One of the most successful of these is the *Huffman code,* which determines the probabilities of each value occurring in the data set and then builds a binary tree in which the search path for each value represents the code for that value. More frequently occurring values are given shorter search paths in the tree. This tree is then turned into a table, much like a Morse code table, that can be used to encode and decode the data.

For example, suppose we have a data set containing only the seven letters shown in Fig. 6.2, and each letter occurs with the probability indicated. The third row in the figure shows the Huffman codes that would be assigned to the letters. Based on Fig. 6.2, the string "abde" would be encoded as "101000000001."

In the example, the letter *a* occurs much more often than any of the others, so it is assigned the 1-bit code 1. Notice that the minimum number of bits needed to represent these seven letters is 3, yet in this case as many as 4 bits are required. This is a necessary trade-off to ensure that the

```
Letter:       a   b   c   d    e    f    g
Probability: 0.4 0.1 0.1 0.1  0.1  0.1  0.1
Code          1   010 011 0000 0001 0010 0011
```

Figure 6.2 Example showing the Huffman encoding for a set of seven letters, assuming certain probabilities (from Lynch, 1985).

distinct codes can be stored together, without delimiters between them, and still be recognized.

6.1.4 Irreversible Compression Techniques

The techniques we have discussed so far preserve all information in the original data. In effect, they take advantage of the fact that the data, in its original form, contains redundant information that can be removed and then reinserted at a later time. Another type of compression, *irreversible compression*, is based on the assumption that some information can be sacrificed.[2]

An example of irreversible compression would be shrinking a raster image from, say, 400-by-400 pixels to 100-by-100 pixels. The new image contains 1 pixel for every 16 pixels in the original image, and there is no way, in general, to determine what the original pixels were from the one new pixel.

Irreversible compression is less common in data files than reversible compression, but there are times when the information that is lost is of little or no value. For example, speech compression is often done by *voice coding*, a technique that transmits a paramaterized description of speech, which can be synthesized at the receiving end with varying amounts of distortion.

6.1.5 Compression in Unix

Both Berkeley and System V Unix provide compression routines that are heavily used and quite effective. System V has routines called `pack` and `unpack`, which use Huffman codes on a byte-by-byte basis. Typically, `pack` achieves 25 to 40 percent reduction on text files, but appreciably less on binary files that have a more uniform distribution of byte values. When

---

2. Irreversible compression is sometimes called "entropy reduction" to emphasize that the average information (entropy) is reduced.

`pack` compresses a file, it automatically appends a .z to the end of the packed file, signaling to any future user that the file has been compressed using the standard compression algorithm.

Berkeley Unix has routines called `compress` and `uncompress`, which use an effective dynamic method called Lempel-Ziv (Welch, 1984). Except for using different compression schemes, `compress` and `uncompress` behave almost the same as `pack` and `unpack`.[3] Compress appends a .Z to the end of files it has compressed.

Because these routines are readily available on Unix systems and are very effective general-purpose routines, it is wise to use them whenever there are no compelling reasons to use other techniques.

6.2 Reclaiming Space in Files

Suppose a record in a variable-length record file is modified in such a way that the new record is longer than the original record. What do you do with the extra data? You could append it to the end of the file and put a pointer from the original record space to the extension of the record. Or you could rewrite the whole record at the end of the file (unless the file needs to be sorted), leaving a hole at the original location of the record. Each solution has a drawback: in the former case, the job of processing the record is more awkward and slower than it was originally; in the latter case, the file contains wasted space.

In this section we take a close look at the way file organization deteriorates as a file is modified. In general, modifications can take any one of three forms:

- Record addition,
- Record updating, and
- Record deletion.

If the only kind of change to a file is record addition, there is no deterioration of the kind we cover in this chapter. It is only when variable-length records are updated, or when either fixed- or variable-length records are deleted, that maintenance issues become complicated and interesting. Since record updating can always be treated as a record dele-

---

3. Many implementations of System V Unix also support `compress` and `uncompress` as Berkeley extensions.

tion followed by a record addition, our focus is on the effects of record deletion. When a record has been deleted, we want to reuse the space.

6.2.1 Record Deletion and Storage Compaction

Storage compaction makes files smaller by looking for places in a file where there is no data at all and recovering this space. Since empty spaces occur in files when we delete records, we begin our discussion of compaction with a look at record deletion.

Any record-deletion strategy must provide some way for us to recognize records as deleted. A simple and usually workable approach is to place a special mark in each deleted record. For example, in the file of `Person` objects with delimited fields developed in Chapter 4, we might place an asterisk as the first field in a deleted record. Figures 6.3(a) and 6.3(b) show a name and address file similar to the one in Chapter 4 before and after the second record is marked as deleted. (The dots at the ends of records 0 and 2 represent padding between the last field and the end of each record.)

Once we are able to recognize a record as deleted, the next question is how to reuse the space from the record. Approaches to this problem that rely on storage compaction do not reuse the space for a while. The records are simply marked as deleted and left in the file for a period of time. Programs using the file must include logic that causes them to ignore records that are marked as deleted. One benefit to this approach is that it is usually possible to allow the user to undelete a record with very little

```
Ames|Mary|123 Maple|Stillwater|OK|74075|........................
Morrison|Sebastian|9035 South Hillcrest|Forest Village|OK|74820|
Brown|Martha|625 Kimbark|Des Moines|IA|50311|...................
```
(a)

```
Ames|Mary|123 Maple|Stillwater|OK|74075|........................
*|rrison|Sebastian|9035 South Hillcrest|Forest Village|OK|74820|
Brown|Martha|625 Kimbark|Des Moines|IA|50311|...................
```
(b)

```
Ames|Mary|123 Maple|Stillwater|OK|74075|........................
Brown|Martha|625 Kimbark|Des Moines|IA|50311|...................
```
(c)

Figure 6.3 Storage requirements of sample file using 64-byte fixed-length records. (a) Before deleting the second record. (b) After deleting the second record. (c) After compaction—the second record is gone.

effort. This is particularly easy if you keep the deleted mark in a special field rather than destroy some of the original data, as in our example.

The reclamation of space from the deleted records happens all at once. After deleted records have accumulated for some time, a special program is used to reconstruct the file with all the deleted records squeezed out as shown in Fig. 6.3(c). If there is enough space, the simplest way to do this compaction is through a file copy program that skips over the deleted records. It is also possible, though more complicated and time-consuming, to do the compaction in place. Either of these approaches can be used with both fixed- and variable-length records.

The decision about how often to run the storage compaction program can be based on either the number of deleted records or the calendar. In accounting programs, for example, it often makes sense to run a compaction procedure on certain files at the end of the fiscal year or at some other point associated with closing the books.

6.2.2 Deleting Fixed-Length Records for Reclaiming Space Dynamically

Storage compaction is the simplest and most widely used of the storage reclamation methods we discuss. There are some applications, however, that are too volatile and interactive for storage compaction to be useful. In these situations we want to reuse the space from deleted records as soon as possible. We begin our discussion of such dynamic storage reclamation with a second look at fixed-length record deletion, since fixed-length records make the reclamation problem much simpler.

In general, to provide a mechanism for record deletion with subsequent reutilization of the freed space, we need to be able to guarantee two things:

■ That deleted records are marked in some special way, and

■ That we can find the space that deleted records once occupied so we can reuse that space when we add records.

We have already identified a method of meeting the first requirement: we mark records as deleted by putting a field containing an asterisk at the beginning of deleted records.

If you are working with fixed-length records and are willing to search sequentially through a file before adding a record, you can always provide the second guarantee if you have provided the first. Space reutilization can take the form of looking through the file, record by record, until a deleted record is found. If the program reaches the end of the file without finding a deleted record, the new record can be appended at the end.

Unfortunately, this approach makes adding records an intolerably slow process, if the program is an interactive one and the user has to sit at the terminal and wait as the record addition takes place. To make record reuse happen more quickly, we need

■   A way to know immediately if there are empty slots in the file, and

■   A way to jump directly to one of those slots if they exist.

Linked Lists

The use of a *linked list* for stringing together all of the available records can meet both of these needs. A linked list is a data structure in which each element or *node* contains some kind of reference to its successor in the list. (See Fig. 6.4.)

If you have a head reference to the first node in the list, you can move through the list by looking at each node and then at the node's pointer field, so you know where the next node is located. When you finally encounter a pointer field with some special, predetermined end-of-list value, you stop the traversal of the list. In Fig. 6.4 we use a -1 in the pointer field to mark the end of the list.

When a list is made up of deleted records that have become *available space* within the file, the list is usually called an *avail list*. When inserting a new record into a fixed-length record file, any one available record is just as good as any other. There is no reason to prefer one open slot over another since all the slots are the same size. It follows that there is no reason to order the avail list in any particular way. (As we see later, this situation changes for variable-length records.)

Stacks

The simplest way to handle a list is as a stack. A stack is a list in which all insertions and removals of nodes take place at one end of the list. So, if we

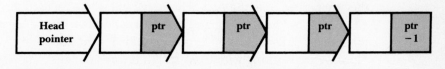

Figure 6.4 A linked list.

have an avail list managed as a stack that contains relative record numbers (RRN) 5 and 2, and then add RRN 3, it looks like this before and after the addition of the new node:

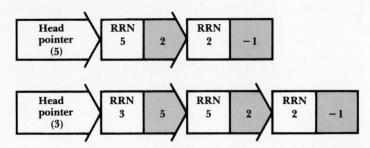

When a new node is added to the top or front of a stack, we say that it is pushed onto the stack. If the next thing that happens is a request for some available space, the request is filled by taking RRN 3 from the avail list. This is called popping the stack. The list returns to a state in which it contains only records 5 and 2.

Linking and Stacking Deleted Records

Now we can meet the two criteria for rapid access to reusable space from deleted records. We need

- A way to know immediately if there are empty slots in the file, and
- A way to jump directly to one of those slots if it exists.

Placing the deleted records on a stack meets both criteria. If the pointer to the top of the stack contains the end-of-list value, then we know that there are no empty slots and that we have to add new records by appending them to the end of the file. If the pointer to the stack top contains a valid node reference, then we know not only that a reusable slot is available, but also exactly where to find it.

Where do we keep the stack? Is it a separate list, perhaps maintained in a separate file, or is it somehow embedded within the data file? Once again, we need to be careful to distinguish between *physical* and *conceptual* structures. The deleted, available records are not moved anywhere when they are pushed onto the stack. They stay right where we need them, located in the file. The stacking and linking are done by arranging and rearranging the links used to make one available record slot point to the next. Since we are working with fixed-length records in a disk file rather than with memory addresses, the pointing is not done with *pointer* variables in the formal sense but through relative record numbers (RRNs).

Suppose we are working with a fixed-length record file that once contained seven records (RRNs 0–6). Furthermore, suppose that records 3 and 5 have been deleted, *in that order,* and that deleted records are marked by replacing the first field with an asterisk. We can then use the second field of a deleted record to hold the link to the next record on the avail list. Leaving out the details of the valid, in-use records, Fig. 6.5(a) shows how the file might look.

Record 5 is the first record on the avail list (top of the stack) as it is the record that is most recently deleted. Following the linked list, we see that record 5 points to record 3. Since the *link field* for record 3 contains -1, which is our end-of-list marker, we know that record 3 is the last slot available for reuse.

Figure 6.5(b) shows the same file after record 1 is also deleted. Note that the contents of all the other records on the avail list remain unchanged. Treating the list as a stack results in a minimal amount of list reorganization when we push and pop records to and from the list.

If we now add a new name to the file, it is placed in record 1, since RRN 1 is the first available record. The avail list would return to the

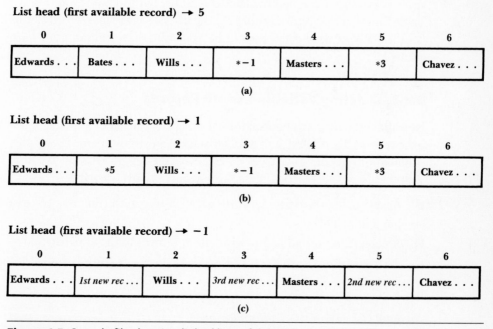

Figure 6.5 Sample file showing linked lists of deleted records. (a) After deletion of records 3 and 5, in that order. (b) After deletion of records 3, 5, and 1, in that order. (c) After insertion of three new records.

configuration shown in Fig. 6.5(a). Since there are still two record slots on the avail list, we could add two more names to the file without increasing the size of the file. After that, however, the avail list would be empty as shown in Fig. 6.5(c). If yet another name is added to the file, the program knows that the avail list is empty and that the name requires the addition of a new record at the end of the file.

Implementing Fixed-Length Record Deletion

Implementing mechanisms that place deleted records on a linked avail list and that treat the avail list as a stack is relatively straightforward. We need a suitable place to keep the RRN of the first available record on the avail list. Since this is information that is specific to the data file, it can be carried in a header record at the start of the file.

When we delete a record, we must be able to mark the record as deleted and then place it on the avail list. A simple way to do this is to place an * (or some other special mark) at the beginning of the record as a deletion mark, followed by the RRN of the next record on the avail list.

Once we have a list of available records within a file, we can reuse the space previously occupied by deleted records. For this we would write a single function that returns either (1) the RRN of a reusable record slot or (2) the RRN of the next record to be appended if no reusable slots are available.

6.2.3 Deleting Variable-Length Records

Now that we have a mechanism for handling an avail list of available space once records are deleted, let's apply this mechanism to the more complex problem of reusing space from deleted variable-length records. We have seen that to support record reuse through an avail list, we need

- A way to link the deleted records together into a list (that is, a place to put a link field);
- An algorithm for adding newly deleted records to the avail list; and
- An algorithm for finding and removing records from the avail list when we are ready to use them.

An Avail List of Variable-Length Records

What kind of file structure do we need to support an avail list of variable-length records? Since we will want to delete whole records and then place records on an avail list, we need a structure in which the record is a clearly defined entity. The file structure of `VariableLengthBuffer`, in which we define the length of each record by placing a byte count at the beginning of each record, will serve us well in this regard.

We can handle the contents of a deleted variable-length record just as we did with fixed-length records. That is, we can place a single asterisk in the first field, followed by a binary link field pointing to the next deleted record on the avail list. The avail list can be organized just as it was with fixed-length records, but with one difference: we cannot use relative record numbers for *links.* Since we cannot compute the byte offset of variable-length records from their RRNs, the links must contain the byte offsets themselves.

To illustrate, suppose we begin with a variable-length record file containing the three records for Ames, Morrison, and Brown introduced earlier. Figure 6.6(a) shows what the file looks like (minus the header) before any deletions, and Fig. 6.6(b) shows what it looks like after the deletion of the second record. The periods in the deleted record signify discarded characters.

Adding and Removing Records

Let's address the questions of adding and removing records to and from the list together, since they are clearly related. With fixed-length records we

HEAD.FIRST_AVAIL: −1

```
40 Ames¦Mary¦123 Maple¦Stillwater¦OK¦74075¦64 Morrison¦Sebastian
¦9035 South Hillcrest¦Forest Village¦OK¦74820¦45 Brown¦Martha¦62
5 Kimbark¦Des Moines¦IA¦50311¦
```
                                   (a)

HEAD.FIRST_AVAIL: 43 ────────────────────────┐
                                                 ↓
```
40 Ames¦Mary¦123 Maple¦Stillwater¦OK¦74075¦64 *¦ −1............
.........................................45 Brown¦Martha¦62
5 Kimbark¦Des Moines¦IA 50311¦
```
                                   (b)

Figure 6.6 A sample file for illustrating variable-length record deletion. (a) Original sample file stored in variable-length format with byte count (header record not included). (b) Sample file after deletion of the second record (periods show discarded characters).

could access the avail list as a stack because one member of the avail list is just as usable as any other. That is not true when the record slots on the avail list differ in size, as they do in a variable-length record file. We now have an extra condition that must be met before we can reuse a record: the record must be the right size. For the moment we define *right size* as "big enough." Later we find that it is sometimes useful to be more particular about the meaning of *right size*.

It is possible, even likely, that we need to *search through* the avail list for a record slot that is the right size. We can't just pop the stack and expect the first available record to be big enough. Finding a proper slot on the avail list now means traversing the list until a record slot that is big enough to hold the new record is found.

For example, suppose the avail list contains the deleted record slots shown in Fig. 6.7(a), and a record that requires 55 bytes is to be added. Since the avail list is not empty, we traverse the records whose sizes are 47 (too small), 38 (too small), and 72 (big enough). Having found a slot big enough to hold our record, we remove it from the avail list by creating a new link that jumps over the record as shown in Fig. 6.7(b). If we had reached the end of the avail list before finding a record that was large enough, we would have appended the new record at the end of the file.

Because this procedure for finding a reusable record looks through the entire avail list if necessary, we do not need a sophisticated method for putting newly deleted records onto the list. If a record of the right size is

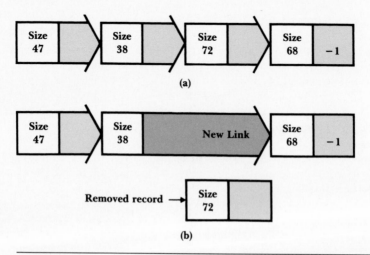

Figure 6.7 Removal of a record from an avail list with variable-length records. (a) Before removal. (b) After removal.

somewhere on this list, our get-available-record procedure eventually finds it. It follows that we can continue to push new members onto the front of the list, just as we do with fixed-length records.

Development of algorithms for adding and removing avail list records is left to you as part of the exercises found at the end of this chapter.

6.2.4 Storage Fragmentation

Let's look again at the fixed-length record version of our three-record file (Fig. 6.8). The dots at the ends of the records represent characters we use as padding between the last field and the end of the records. The padding is wasted space; it is part of the cost of using fixed-length records. Wasted space *within* a record is called *internal fragmentation.*

Clearly, we want to minimize internal fragmentation. If we are working with fixed-length records, we attempt this by choosing a record length that is as close as possible to what we need for each record. But unless the actual data is fixed in length, we have to put up with a certain amount of internal fragmentation in a fixed-length record file.

One of the attractions of variable-length records is that they minimize wasted space by doing away with internal fragmentation. The space set aside for each record is exactly as long as it needs to be. Compare the fixed-length example with the one in Fig. 6.9, which uses the variable-length record structure—a byte count followed by delimited data fields. The only space (other than the delimiters) that is not used for holding data in each record is the count field. If we assume that this field uses 2 bytes, this amounts to only 6 bytes for the three-record file. The fixed-length record file wastes 24 bytes in the very first record.

```
Ames¦Mary¦123 Maple¦Stillwater¦OK¦74075¦........................
Morrison¦Sebastian¦9035 South Hillcrest¦Forest Village¦OK¦74820¦
Brown¦Martha¦625 Kimbark¦Des Moines¦IA¦50311¦...................
```

Figure 6.8 Storage requirements of sample file using 64-byte fixed-length records.

```
40 Ames¦Mary¦123 Maple¦Stillwater¦OK¦74075¦64 Morrison¦Sebastian
¦9035 South Hillcrest¦Forest Village¦OK¦74820¦45 Brown¦Martha¦62
5 Kimbark¦Des Moines¦IA¦50311¦
```

Figure 6.9 Storage requirements of sample file using variable-length records with a count field.

But before we start congratulating ourselves for solving the problem of wasted space due to internal fragmentation, we should consider what happens in a variable-length record file after a record is deleted and replaced with a shorter record. If the shorter record takes less space than the original record, internal fragmentation results. Figure 6.10 shows how the problem could occur with our sample file when the second record in the file is deleted and the following record is added:

`Ham|Al|28 Elm|Ada|OK|70332|`

It appears that escaping internal fragmentation is not so easy. The slot vacated by the deleted record is 37 bytes larger than is needed for the new record. Since we treat the extra 37 bytes as part of the new record, they are not on the avail list and are therefore unusable. But instead of keeping the 64-byte record slot intact, suppose we break it into two parts: one part to hold the new Ham record, and the other to be placed back on the avail list. Since we would take only as much space as necessary for the Ham record, there would be no internal fragmentation.

Figure 6.11 shows what our file looks like if we use this approach to insert the record for Al Ham. We steal the space for the Ham record *from the end* of the 64-byte slot and leave the first 35 bytes of the slot on the avail list. (The available space is 35 rather than 37 bytes because we need 2 bytes to form a new size field for the Ham record.) The 35 bytes still on the avail list can be used to hold yet another record. Figure 6.12 shows the effect of inserting the following 25-byte record:

`Lee|Ed|Rt 2|Ada|OK|74820|`

```
HEAD.FIRST_AVAIL: 43  ─────────────────────────────┐
                                                    ▼
40 Ames ¦Mary¦ 123 Maple ¦Stillwater ¦OK ¦74075 ¦64 * ¦  -1.............
..................................................45 Brown ¦Martha ¦62
5 Kimbark¦Des Moines¦IA¦50311¦
```
(a)

```
HEAD.FIRST_AVAIL: -1

40 Ames ¦Mary¦123 Maple ¦Stillwater ¦OK¦74075 ¦64 Ham¦Al¦28 Elm¦Ada¦
OK¦70332¦......................................45 Brown ¦Martha ¦62
5 Kimbark¦Des Moines¦IA¦50311¦
```
(b)

Figure 6.10 Illustration of fragmentation with variable-length records. (a) After deletion of the second record (unused characters in the deleted record are replaced by periods). (b) After the subsequent addition of the record for Al Ham.

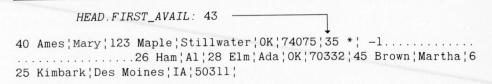

HEAD.FIRST_AVAIL: 43

```
40 Ames¦Mary¦123 Maple¦Stillwater¦OK¦74075¦35 *¦ -1.............
...............26 Ham¦Al¦28 Elm¦Ada¦OK¦70332¦45 Brown¦Martha¦6
25 Kimbark¦Des Moines¦IA¦50311¦
```

Figure 6.11 Combating internal fragmentation by putting the unused part of the deleted slot back on the avail list.

As we would expect, the new record is carved out of the 35-byte record that is on the avail list. The data portion of the new record requires 25 bytes, and we need 2 more bytes for another size field. This leaves 8 bytes in the record still on the avail list.

What are the chances of finding a record that can make use of these 8 bytes? Our guess would be that the probability is close to zero. These 8 bytes are not usable, even though they are not trapped inside any other record. This is an example of *external fragmentation*. The space is actually on the avail list rather than being locked inside some other record but is too fragmented to be reused.

There are some interesting ways to combat external fragmentation. One way, which we discussed at the beginning of this chapter, is *storage compaction*. We could simply regenerate the file when external fragmentation becomes intolerable. Two other approaches are as follows:

■ If two record slots on the avail list are physically adjacent, combine them to make a single, larger record slot. This is called *coalescing the holes* in the storage space.

■ Try to minimize fragmentation before it happens by adopting a placement strategy that the program can use as it selects a record slot from the avail list.

HEAD, FIRST_AVAIL: 43

```
40¦Ames¦Mary¦123 Maple¦Stillwater¦OK¦74075¦8 *¦ -1...25 Lee¦Ed¦
Rt 2¦Ada¦OK¦74820¦26 Ham¦Al¦28 Elm¦Ada¦OK¦70332¦45 Brown¦Martha¦6
25 Kimbark¦ Des Moines¦IA¦50311¦
```

Figure 6.12 Addition of the second record into the slot originally occupied by a single deleted record.

Coalescing holes presents some interesting problems. The avail list is not kept in *physical* record order; if there are two deleted records that are physically adjacent, there is no reason to presume that they are linked adjacent to each other on the avail list. Exercise 15 at the end of this chapter provides a discussion of this problem along with a framework for developing a solution.

The development of better *placement strategies,* however, is a different matter. It is a topic that warrants a separate discussion, since the choice among alternative strategies is not as obvious as it might seem at first glance.

6.2.5 Placement Strategies

Earlier we discussed ways to add and remove variable-length records from an avail list. We add records by treating the avail list as a stack and putting deleted records at the front. When we need to remove a record slot from the avail list (to add a record to the file), we look through the list, starting at the beginning, until we either find a record slot that is big enough or reach the end of the list.

This is called a *first-fit* placement strategy. The least possible amount of work is expended when we place newly available space on the list, and we are not very particular about the closeness of fit as we look for a record slot to hold a new record. We accept the first available record slot that will do the job, regardless of whether the slot is ten times bigger than what is needed or whether it is a perfect fit.

We could, of course, develop a more orderly approach for placing records on the avail list by keeping them in either ascending or descending sequence by size. Rather than always putting the newly deleted records at the front of the list, these approaches involve moving through the list, looking for the place to insert the record to maintain the desired sequence.

If we order the avail list in *ascending* order by size, what is the effect on the closeness of fit of the records that are retrieved from the list? Since the retrieval procedure searches sequentially through the avail list until it encounters a record that is big enough to hold the new record, the first record encountered is the *smallest* record that will do the job. The fit between the available slot and the new record's needs would be as close as we can make it. This is called a *best-fit* placement strategy.

A best-fit strategy is intuitively appealing. There is, of course, a price to be paid for obtaining this fit. We end up having to search through at least a part of the list—not only when we get records from the list, but also when we put newly deleted records on the list. In a real-time environment, the extra processing time could be significant.

A less obvious disadvantage of the best-fit strategy is related to the idea of finding the best possible fit and ensuring that the free area left over after inserting a new record into a slot is as small as possible. Often this remaining space is too small to be useful, resulting in external fragmentation. Furthermore, the slots that are least likely to be useful are the ones that will be placed toward the beginning of the list, making first-fit searches longer as time goes on.

These problems suggest an alternative strategy. What if we arrange the avail list so it is in *descending* order by size? Then the largest record slot on the avail list would always be at the head of the list. Since the procedure that retrieves records starts its search at the beginning of the avail list, it always returns the largest available record slot if it returns any slot at all. This is known as a *worst-fit* placement strategy. The amount of space in the record slot, beyond what is actually needed, is as large as possible.

A *worst-fit* strategy does not, at least initially, sound very appealing. But consider the following:

■ The procedure for removing records can be simplified so it looks only at the first element of the avail list. If the first record slot is not large enough to do the job, none of the others will be.

■ By extracting the space we need from the *largest* available slot, we are assured that the unused portion of the slot is as large as possible, decreasing the likelihood of external fragmentation.

What can you conclude from all of this? It should be clear that no one placement strategy is superior under all circumstances. The best you can do is formulate a series of general observations and then, given a particular design situation, try to select the strategy that seems most appropriate. Here are some suggestions. The judgment will have to be yours.

■ Placement strategies make sense only with regard to volatile, variable-length record files. With fixed-length records, placement is simply not an issue.

■ If space is lost due to *internal fragmentation,* the choice is between first fit and best fit. A worst-fit strategy truly makes internal fragmentation worse.

■ If the space is lost due to *external fragmentation,* one should give careful consideration to a worst-fit strategy.

6.3 Finding Things Quickly: An Introduction to Internal Sorting and Binary Searching

This text begins with a discussion of the cost of accessing secondary storage. You may remember that the magnitude of the difference between accessing memory and seeking information on a fixed disk is such that, if we magnify the time for a memory access to twenty seconds, a similarly magnified disk access would take fifty-eight days.

So far we have not had to pay much attention to this cost. This section, then, marks a kind of turning point. Once we move from fundamental organizational issues to the matter of searching a file for a particular piece of information, the cost of a seek becomes a major factor in determining our approach. And what is true for searching is all the more true for sorting. If you have studied sorting algorithms, you know that even a good sort involves making many comparisons. If each of these comparisons involves a seek, the sort is agonizingly slow.

Our discussion of sorting and searching, then, goes beyond simply getting the job done. We develop approaches that minimize the number of disk accesses and therefore minimize the amount of time expended. This concern with minimizing the number of seeks continues to be a major focus throughout the rest of this text. This is just the beginning of a quest for ways to order and find things quickly.

6.3.1 Finding Things in Simple Field and Record Files

All of the programs we have written up to this point, despite any other strengths they offer, share a major failing: the only way to retrieve or find a record with any degree of rapidity is to look for it by relative record number. If the file has fixed-length records, knowing the RRN lets us compute the record's byte offset and jump to it using direct access.

But what if we do not know the byte offset or RRN of the record we want? How likely is it that a question about this file would take the form, "What is the record stored in RRN 23?" Not very likely, of course. We are much more likely to know the identity of a record by its key, and the question is more likely to take the form, "What is the record for Jane Kelly?"

Given the methods of organization developed so far, access by key implies a sequential search. What if there is no record containing the requested key? Then we would have to look through the entire file. What if we suspect that there might be more than one record that contains the key, and we want to find them all? Once again, we would be doomed to looking at every record in the file. Clearly, we need to find a better way to handle keyed access. Fortunately, there are many better ways.

6.3.2 Search by Guessing: Binary Search

Suppose we are looking for a record for Jane Kelly in a file of one thousand fixed-length records, and suppose the file is sorted so the records appear in ascending order by key. We start by comparing KELLY JANE (the canonical form of the search key) with the middle key in the file, which is the key whose RRN is 500. The result of the comparison tells us which half of the file contains Jane Kelly's record. Next, we compare KELLY JANE with the middle key among records in the selected half of the file to find out which quarter of the file Jane Kelly's record is in. This process is repeated until either Jane Kelly's record is found or we have narrowed the number of potential records to zero.

This kind of searching is called binary searching. An algorithm for binary searching on a file of fixed-sized records is shown in Fig. 6.13. Binary searching takes at most ten comparisons—to find Jane Kelly's record if it is in the file, or to determine that it is not in the file. Compare this with a sequential search for the record. If there are one thousand records, then it takes at most one thousand comparisons to find a given record (or establish that it is not present); on the average, five hundred comparisons are needed.

We refer to the code in Fig. 6.13 as an algorithm, not a function, even though it is given in the form of a C++ function. This is because this is not a full implementation of binary search. Details of the implementation of the method are not given. From the code, we can infer that there must be a class `FixedRecordFile` that has methods `NumRecs` and `ReadByRRN` and that those methods have certain specific meaning. In particular, `NumRecs` must return the number of records in the `FixedRecordFile`, and `ReadByRRN` must read the record at a specific RRN and unpack it into a `RecType` object.

It is reasonable to suppose that a full implementation of binary search would be a template function with parameters for the type of the data record and the type of the key. It might also be a method of a fixed-record file class. Changing these details will not affect the algorithm and might not even require changes in the code. We do know, however, that in order to perform binary search, we must be able to read the file by relative record number, we must have assignment and key extraction methods on the data record type, and we must have relational operations on the key type.

```
int BinarySearch
   (FixedRecordFile & file, RecType & obj, KeyType & key)
// binary search for key
// if key found, obj contains corresponding record, 1 returned
// if key not found, 0 returned
{
   int low = 0; int high = file.NumRecs()-1;
   while (low <= high)
   {
      int guess = (high - low) / 2;
      file.ReadByRRN (obj, guess);
      if (obj.Key() == key) return 1; // record found
      if (obj.Key() < key) high = guess - 1;// search before guess
      else low = guess + 1;// search after guess
   }
   return 0; // loop ended without finding key
}
```

Figure 6.13 A binary search algorithm.

Figure 6.14 gives the minimum definitions that must be present to allow a successful compilation of BinarySearch. This includes a class RecType with a Key method that returns the key value of an object and class KeyType with equality and less-than operators. No further details of any of these classes need be given.

```
class KeyType
{public:
   int operator == (KeyType &); // equality operator
   int operator < (KeyType &); // less than operator
};

class RecType {public: KeyType Key();};

class FixedRecordFile
{public:
   int NumRecs();
   int ReadByRRN (RecType & record, int RRN);
};
```

Figure 6.14 Classes and methods that must be implemented to support the binary search algorithm.

This style of algorithm presentation is the object-oriented replacement for the pseudocode approach, which has been widely used to describe algorithms. Pseudocode is typically used to describe an algorithm without including all of the details of implementation. In Fig. 6.13, we have been able to present the algorithm without all of the details but in a form that can be passed through a compiler to verify that it is syntactically correct and conforms in its use of its related objects. The contrast between object-oriented design and pseudocode is that the object-oriented approach uses a specific syntax and a specific interface. The object-oriented approach is no harder to write but has significantly more detail.

6.3.3 Binary Search versus Sequential Search

In general, a binary search of a file with n records takes at most

$$\lfloor \log_2 n \rfloor + 1 \text{ comparisons}$$

and on average approximately

$$\lfloor \log_2 n \rfloor + 1/2 \text{ comparisons.}$$

A binary search is therefore said to be $O(\log_2 n)$. In contrast, you may recall that a sequential search of the same file requires at most n comparisons, and on average ?(tk?) n, which is to say that a sequential search is $O(n)$.

The difference between a binary search and a sequential search becomes even more dramatic as we increase the size of the file to be searched. If we double the number of records in the file, we double the number of comparisons required for sequential search; when binary search is used, doubling the file size adds only one more guess to our worst case. This makes sense, since we know that each guess eliminates half of the possible choices. So, if we tried to find Jane Kelly's record in a file of two thousand records, it would take at most

$$1 + \lfloor \log_2 2000 \rfloor = 11 \text{ comparisons}$$

whereas a sequential search would average

$$1/2 \, n = 1000 \text{ comparisons}$$

and could take up to two thousand comparisons.

Binary searching is clearly a more attractive way to find things than sequential searching. But, as you might expect, there is a price to be paid before we can use binary searching: it works only when the list of records is ordered in terms of the key we are using in the search. So, to make use of binary searching, we have to be able to sort a list on the basis of a key.

Sorting is a very important part of file processing. Next, we will look at some simple approaches to sorting files in memory, at the same time introducing some important new concepts in file structure design. We take a second look at sorting in Chapter 8, when we deal with some tough problems that occur when files are too large to sort in memory.

6.3.4 Sorting a Disk File in Memory

Consider the operation of any internal sorting algorithm with which you are familiar. The algorithm requires multiple passes over the list that is to be sorted, comparing and reorganizing the elements. Some of the items in the list are moved a long distance from their original positions in the list. If such an algorithm were applied directly to data stored on a disk, it is clear that there would be a lot of jumping around, seeking, and rereading of data. This would be a very slow operation—unthinkably slow.

If the entire contents of the file can be held in memory, a very attractive alternative is to read the entire file from the disk into memory and then do the sorting there, using an *internal sort*. We still have to access the data on the disk, but this way we can access it sequentially, sector after sector, without having to incur the costs of a lot of seeking and of multiple passes over the disk.

This is one instance of a general class of solutions to the problem of minimizing disk usage: force your disk access into a sequential mode, performing the more complex, direct accesses in memory.

Unfortunately, it is often not possible to use this simple kind of solution, but when you can, you should take advantage of it. In the case of sorting, internal sorts are increasingly viable as the amount of memory space grows. A good illustration of an internal sort is the Unix `sort` utility, which sorts files in memory if it can find enough space. This utility is described in Chapter 8.

6.3.5 The Limitations of Binary Searching and Internal Sorting

Let's look at three problems associated with our "sort, then binary search" approach to finding things.

Problem 1: Binary Searching Requires More Than One or Two Accesses

In the average case, a binary search requires approximately $\lfloor \log_2 n \rfloor + 1/2$ comparisons. If each comparison requires a disk access, a series of binary searches on a list of one thousand items requires, on the average, 9.5 accesses per request. If the list is expanded to one hundred thousand items, the average search length extends to 16.5 accesses. Although this is a tremendous improvement over the cost of a sequential search for the key, it is also true that 16 accesses, or even 9 or 10 accesses, is not a negligible cost. The cost of this searching is particularly noticeable and objectionable, if we are doing a large enough number of repeated accesses by key.

When we access records by relative record number rather than by key, we are able to retrieve a record with a single access. That is an order of magnitude of improvement over the ten or more accesses that binary searching requires with even a moderately large file. Ideally, we would like to approach RRN retrieval performance while still maintaining the advantages of access by key. In the following chapter, on the use of index structures, we begin to look at ways to move toward this ideal.

Problem 2: Keeping a File Sorted Is Very Expensive

Our ability to use a binary search has a price attached to it: we must keep the file in sorted order by key. Suppose we are working with a file to which we add records as often as we search for existing records. If we leave the file in unsorted order, conducting sequential searches for records, then on average each search requires reading through half the file. Each record addition, however, is very fast, since it involves nothing more than jumping to the end of the file and writing a record.

If, as an alternative, we keep the file in sorted order, we can cut down substantially on the cost of searching, reducing it to a handful of accesses. But we encounter difficulty when we add a record, since we want to keep all the records in sorted order. Inserting a new record into the file requires, on average, that we not only read through half the records, but that we also shift the records to open up the space required for the insertion. We are actually doing more work than if we simply do sequential searches on an unsorted file.

The costs of maintaining a file that can be accessed through binary searching are not always as large as in this example involving frequent record addition. For example, it is often the case that searching is required much more frequently than record addition. In such a circumstance, the benefits of faster retrieval can more than offset the costs of keeping the file sorted. As another example, there are many applications in which record additions can be accumulated in a transaction file and made in a batch mode. By sorting the list of new records before adding them to the main file, it is possible to merge them with the existing records. As we see in

Chapter 8, such merging is a sequential process, passing only once over each record in the file. This can be an efficient, attractive approach to maintaining the file.

So, despite its problems, there are situations in which binary searching appears to be a useful strategy. However, knowing the costs of binary searching also lets us see better solutions to the problem of finding things by key. Better solutions will have to meet at least one of the following conditions:

- They will not involve reordering of the records in the file when a new record is added, and

- They will be associated with data structures that allow for substantially more rapid, efficient reordering of the file.

In the chapters that follow we develop approaches that fall into each of these categories. Solutions of the first type can involve the use of simple indexes. They can also involve hashing. Solutions of the second type can involve the use of tree structures, such as a B-tree, to keep the file in order.

Problem 3: An Internal Sort Works Only on Small Files

Our ability to use binary searching is limited by our ability to sort the file. An internal sort works only if we can read the entire contents of a file into the computer's electronic memory. If the file is so large that we cannot do that, we need a different kind of sort.

In the following section we develop a variation on internal sorting called a *keysort*. Like internal sorting, keysort is limited in terms of how large a file it can sort, but its limit is larger. More important, our work on keysort begins to illuminate a new approach to the problem of finding things that will allow us to avoid the sorting of records in a file.

6.4   Keysorting

Keysort, sometimes referred to as *tag sort,* is based on the idea that when we sort a file in memory the only things that we really need to sort are the record keys; therefore, we do not need to read the whole file into memory during the sorting process. Instead, we read the keys from the file into memory, sort them, and then rearrange the records in the file according to the new ordering of the keys.

Since keysort never reads the complete set of records into memory, it can sort larger files than a regular internal sort, given the same amount of memory.

6.4.1 Description of the Method

To keep things simple, we assume that we are dealing with a fixed-length record file of the kind developed in Chapter 4, with a count of the number of records stored in a header record.

We present the algorithm in an object-oriented pseudocode. As in Section 6.3.3, we need to identify the supporting object classes. The file class (FixedRecordFile) must support methods NumRecs and ReadByRRN. In order to store the key RRN pairs from the file, we need a class KeyRRN that has two data members, KEY and RRN. Figure 6.15 gives the minimal functionality required by these classes.

The algorithm begins by reading the key RRN pairs into an array of KeyRRN objects. We call this array KEYNODES[]. Figure 6.16 illustrates the relationship between the array KEYNODES[] and the actual file at the

```
class FixedRecordFile
{public:
    int NumRecs ();
    int ReadByRRN (RecType & record, int RRN);
    // additional methods required for keysort
    int Create (char * fileName);
    int Append (RecType & record);
};

class KeyRRN
// contains a pair (KEY, RRN)
{public:
    KeyType KEY; int RRN;
    KeyRRN();
    KeyRRN (KeyType key, int rrn);
};

int Sort (KeyRRN [], int numKeys); // sort array by key
```

Figure 6.15 Minimal functionality required for classes used by the keysort algorithm.

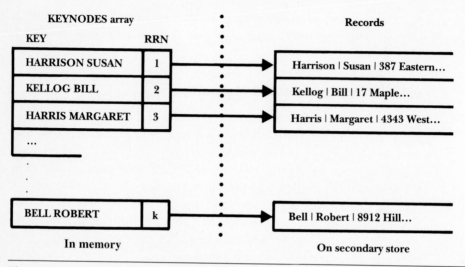

Figure 6.16 Conceptual view of KEYNODES array to be used in memory by internal sort routine and record array on secondary store.

time the keysort procedure begins. The RRN field of each array element contains the RRN of the record associated with the corresponding key.

The actual sorting process simply sorts the KEYNODES[] array according to the KEYfield. This produces an arrangement like that shown in Fig. 6.17. The elements of KEYNODES[] are now sequenced in such a way that the first element has the RRN of the record that should be moved to the first position in the file, the second element identifies the record that should be second, and so forth.

Once KEYNODES[] is sorted, we are ready to reorganize the file according to this new ordering by reading the records from the input file and writing to a new file in the order of the KEYNODES[] array.

Figure 6.18 gives an algorithm for keysort. This algorithm works much the same way that a normal internal sort would work, but with two important differences:

■   Rather than read an entire record into a memory array, we simply read each record into a temporary buffer, extract the key, then discard it; and

■   When we are writing the records out in sorted order, we have to read them in a second time, since they are not all stored in memory.

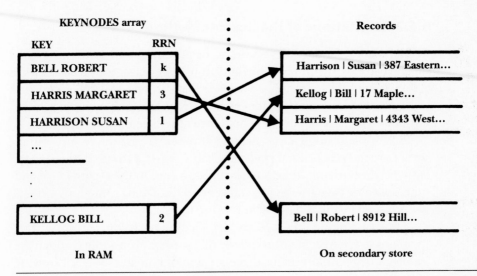

Figure 6.17 Conceptual view of KEYNODES array and file after sorting keys in memory.

```
int KeySort (FixedRecordFile & inFile, char * outFileName)
{
  RecType obj;
  KeyRRN * KEYNODES = new KeyRRN [inFile . NumRecs()];
  // read file and load Keys
  for (int i = 0; i < inFile . NumRecs(); i++)
  {
    inFile . ReadByRRN (obj, i);// read record i
    KEYNODES[i] = KeyRRN(obj.Key(),i);//put key and RRN into Keys
  }
  Sort (KEYNODES, inFile . NumRecs());// sort Keys
  FixedRecordFile outFile;// file to hold records in key order
  outFile . Create (outFileName);// create a new file
  // write new file in key order
  for (int j = 0; j < inFile . NumRecs(); j++)
  {
    inFile . ReadByRRN (obj, KEYNODES[j].RRN);//read in key order
    outFile . Append (obj);// write in key order
  }
  return 1;
}
```

Figure 6.18 Algorithm for keysort

6.4.2 Limitations of the Keysort Method

At first glance, keysorting appears to be an obvious improvement over sorting performed entirely in memory; it might even appear to be a case of getting something for nothing. We know that sorting is an expensive operation and that we want to do it in memory. Keysorting allows us to achieve this objective without having to hold the entire file in memory at once.

But, while reading about the operation of writing the records out in sorted order, even a casual reader probably senses a cloud on this apparently bright horizon. In keysort we need to read in the records a second time before we can write out the new sorted file. Doing something twice is never desirable. But the problem is worse than that.

Look carefully at the `for` loop that reads in the records before writing them out to the new file. You can see that we are not reading through the input file sequentially. Instead, we are working in sorted order, moving from the sorted KEYNODES[] to the RRNs of the records. Since we have to seek to each record and read it in before writing it back out, creating the sorted file requires as many random seeks into the input file as there are records. As we have noted a number of times, there is an enormous difference between the time required to read all the records in a file sequentially and the time required to read those same records if we must seek to each record separately. What is worse, we are performing all of these accesses in alternation with write statements to the output file. So, even the writing of the output file, which would otherwise appear to be sequential, involves seeking in most cases. The disk drive must move the head back and forth between the two files as it reads and writes.

The getting-something-for-nothing aspect of keysort has suddenly evaporated. Even though keysort does the hard work of sorting in memory, it turns out that creating a sorted version of the file from the map supplied by the KEYNODES[] array is not at all a trivial matter when the only copies of the records are kept on secondary store.

6.4.3 Another Solution: Why Bother to Write the File Back?

The idea behind keysort is an attractive one: why work with an entire record when the only parts of interest, as far as sorting and searching are concerned, are the fields used to form the key? There is a compelling parsimony behind this idea, and it makes keysorting look promising. The promise fades only when we run into the problem of rearranging all the records in the file so they reflect the new, sorted order.

It is interesting to ask whether we can avoid this problem by simply not bothering with the task that is giving us trouble. What if we just skip the time-consuming business of writing out a sorted version of the file? What if, instead, we simply write out a copy of the array of canonical key nodes? If we do without writing the records back in sorted order, writing out the contents of our KEYNODES[] array instead, we will have written a program that outputs an *index* to the original file. The relationship between the two files is illustrated in Fig. 6.19.

This is an instance of one of our favorite categories of solutions to computer science problems: if some part of a process begins to look like a bottleneck, consider skipping it altogether. Ask if you can do without it. Instead of creating a new, sorted copy of the file to use for searching, we have created a second kind of file, an index file, that is to be used in conjunction with the original file. If we are looking for a particular record, we do our binary search on the index file and then use the RRN stored in the index file record to find the corresponding record in the original file.

There is much to say about the use of index files, enough to fill several chapters. The next chapter is about the various ways we can use a simple index, which is the kind of index we illustrate here. In later chapters we talk about different ways of organizing the index to provide more flexible access and easier maintenance.

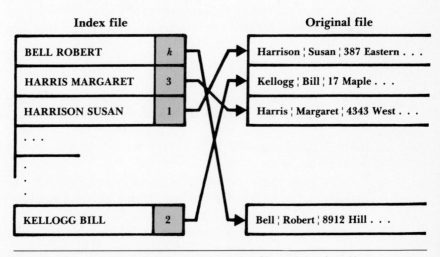

Figure 6.19 Relationship between the index file and the data file.

6.4.4 Pinned Records

In section 6.2 we discussed the problem of updating and maintaining files. Much of that discussion revolved around the problems of deleting records and keeping track of the space vacated by deleted records so it can be reused. An avail list of deleted record slots is created by linking all of the available slots together. This linking is done by writing a link field into each deleted record that points to the next deleted record. This link field gives very specific information about the exact physical location of the next available record.

When a file contains such references to the physical locations of records, we say that these records are *pinned*. You can gain an appreciation for this particular choice of terminology if you consider the effects of sorting one of these files containing an avail list of deleted records. A pinned record is one that cannot be moved. Other records in the same file or in some other file (such as an index file) contain references to the physical location of the record. If the record is moved, these references no longer lead to the record; they become *dangling pointers,* pointers leading to incorrect, meaningless locations in the file.

Clearly, the use of pinned records in a file can make sorting more difficult and sometimes impossible. But what if we want to support rapid access by key while still reusing the space made available by record deletion? One solution is to use an index file to keep the sorted order of the records while keeping the data file in its original order. Once again, the problem of finding things leads to the suggestion that we need to take a close look at the use of indexes, which, in turn, leads us to the next chapter.

SUMMARY

In this chapter we look at ways to organize or reorganize files to improve performance in some way.

Data compression methods are used to make files smaller by re-encoding data that goes into a file. Smaller files use less storage, take less time to transmit, and can often be processed faster sequentially.

The notation used for representing information can often be made more compact. For instance, if a 2-byte field in a record can take on only fifty values, the field can be encoded using 6 bits instead of 16. Another form of compression called *run-length encoding* encodes sequences of repeating values rather than writing all of the values in the file.

A third form of compression assigns variable-length codes to values depending on how frequently the values occur. Values that occur often are given shorter codes, so they take up less space. *Huffman codes* are an example of variable-length codes.

Some compression techniques are *irreversible* in that they lose information in the encoding process. The Unix utilities compress, uncompress, pack, and unpack provide good compression in Unix.

A second way to save space in a file is to recover space in the file after it has undergone changes. A volatile file, one that undergoes many changes, can deteriorate very rapidly unless measures are taken to adjust the file organization to the changes. One result of making changes to files is storage fragmentation.

Internal fragmentation occurs when there is wasted space within a record. In a fixed-length record file, internal fragmentation can result when variable-length records are stored in fixed slots. It can also occur in a variable-length record file when one record is replaced by another record of a smaller size. *External fragmentation* occurs when holes of unused space between records are created, normally because of record deletions.

There are a number of ways to combat fragmentation. The simplest is *storage compaction,* which squeezes out the unused space caused from external fragmentation by sliding all of the undeleted records together. Compaction is generally done in a batch mode.

Fragmentation can be dealt with *dynamically* by reclaiming deleted space when records are added. The need to keep track of the space to be reused makes this approach more complex than compaction.

We begin with the problem of deleting fixed-length records. Since finding the first field of a fixed-length record is very easy, deleting a record can be accomplished by placing a special mark in the first field.

Since all records in a fixed-length record file are the same size, the reuse of deleted records need not be complicated. The solution we adopt consists of collecting all the available record slots into an *avail list.* The avail list is created by stringing together all the deleted records to form a *linked list* of deleted record spaces.

In a fixed-length record file, any one record slot is just as usable as any other slot; they are interchangeable. Consequently, the simplest way to maintain the linked avail list is to treat it as a *stack.* Newly available records are added to the avail list by *pushing* them onto the front of the list; record slots are removed from the avail list by *popping* them from the front of the list.

Next, we consider the matter of deleting variable-length records. We still form a linked list of available record slots, but with variable-length records we need to be sure that a record slot is the right size to hold the new record. Our initial definition of *right size* is simply in terms of being big enough. Consequently, we need a procedure that can search through the avail list until it finds a record slot that is big enough to hold the new record. Given such a function and a complementary function that places newly deleted records on the avail list, we can implement a system that deletes and reuses variable-length records.

We then consider the amount and nature of fragmentation that develops inside a file due to record deletion and reuse. Fragmentation can happen *internally* if the space is lost because it is locked up inside a record. We develop a procedure that breaks a single, large, variable-length record slot into two or more smaller ones, using exactly as much space as is needed for a new record and leaving the remainder on the avail list. We see that, although this could decrease the amount of wasted space, eventually the remaining fragments are too small to be useful. When this happens, space is lost to *external fragmentation.*

There are a number of things that one can do to minimize external fragmentation. These include (1) *compacting* the file in a batch mode when the level of fragmentation becomes excessive; (2) *coalescing* adjacent record slots on the avail list to make larger, more generally useful slots; and (3) adopting a *placement strategy* to select slots for reuse in a way that minimizes fragmentation. Development of algorithms for coalescing holes is left as part of the exercises at the end of this chapter. Placement strategies need more careful discussion.

The placement strategy used up to this point by the variable-length record deletion and reuse procedures is a *first-fit* strategy. This strategy is simple: If the record slot is big enough, use it. By keeping the avail list in sorted order, it is easy to implement either of two other placement strategies:

- *Best fit,* in which a new record is placed in the smallest slot that is still big enough to hold it. This is an attractive strategy for variable-length record files in which the fragmentation is *internal.* It involves more overhead than other placement strategies.

- *Worst fit,* in which a new record is placed in the largest record slot available. The idea is to have the leftover portion of the slot be as large as possible.

There is no firm rule for selecting a placement strategy; the best one can do is use informed judgment based on a number of guidelines.

In the third major section of this chapter, we look at ways to find things quickly in a file through the use of a key. In preceding chapters it was not possible to access a record rapidly without knowing its physical location or relative record number. Now we explore some of the problems and opportunities associated with keyed direct access.

This chapter develops only one method of finding records by key—binary searching. Binary searching requires $O(\log_2 n)$ comparisons to find a record in a file with n records and hence is far superior to sequential searching. Since binary searching works only on a sorted file, a sorting procedure is an absolute necessity. The problem of sorting is complicated by the fact that we are sorting files on secondary storage rather than vectors in memory. We need to develop a sorting procedure that does not require seeking back and forth over the file.

Three disadvantages are associated with sorting and binary searching as developed up to this point:

- Binary searching is an enormous improvement over sequential searching, but it still usually requires more than one or two accesses per record. The need for fewer disk accesses becomes especially acute in applications where a large number of records are to be accessed by key.

- The requirement that the file be kept in sorted order can be expensive. For active files to which records are added frequently, the cost of keeping the file in sorted order can outweigh the benefits of binary searching.

- A memory sort can be used only on relatively small files. This limits the size of the files that we could organize for binary searching, given our sorting tools.

The third problem can be solved partially by developing more powerful sorting procedures, such as a keysort. This approach to sorting resembles a memory sort in most respects, but does not use memory to hold the entire file. Instead, it reads in only the keys from the records, sorts the keys, and then uses the sorted list of keys to rearrange the records on secondary storage so they are in sorted order.

The disadvantage to a keysort is that rearranging a file of n records requires n random seeks out to the original file, which can take much more time than a sequential reading of the same number of records. The inquiry into keysorting is not wasted, however. Keysorting naturally leads to the suggestion that we merely write the sorted list of keys off to secondary storage, setting aside the expensive matter of rearranging the file. This list of keys, coupled with RRN tags pointing back to the original records, is an example of an index. We look at indexing more closely in Chapter 7.

This chapter closes with a discussion of another, potentially hidden, cost of sorting and searching. Pinned records are records that are referenced elsewhere (in the same file or in some other file) according to their physical position in the file. Sorting and binary searching cannot be applied to a file containing pinned records, since the sorting, by definition, is likely to change the physical position of the record. Such a change causes other references to this record to become inaccurate, creating the problem of dangling pointers.

KEY TERMS

Avail list. A list of the space, freed through record deletion, that is available for holding new records. In the examples considered in this chapter, this list of space took the form of a linked list of deleted records.

Best fit. A placement strategy for selecting the space on the avail list used to hold a new record. Best-fit placement finds the available record slot that is closest in size to what is needed to hold the new record.

Binary search. A binary search algorithm locates a key in a sorted list by repeatedly selecting the middle element of the list, dividing the list in half, and forming a new, smaller list from the half that contains the key. This process is continued until the selected element is the key that is sought.

Coalescence. If two deleted, available records are physically adjacent, they can be combined to form a single, larger available record space. This process of combining smaller available spaces into a larger one is known as *coalescing holes*. Coalescence is a way to counteract the problem of external fragmentation.

Compaction. A way of getting rid of all *external fragmentation* by sliding all the records together so there is no space lost between them.

Data compression. Encoding information in a file in such a way as to take up less space.

External fragmentation. A form of fragmentation that occurs in a file when there is unused space outside or between individual records.

First fit. A placement strategy for selecting a space from the avail list. First-fit placement selects the first available record slot large enough to hold the new record.

Fragmentation. The unused space within a file. The space can be locked within individual records *(internal fragmentation)* or between individual records *(external fragmentation)*.

Huffman code. A variable-length code in which the lengths of the codes are based on their probability of occurrence.

Internal fragmentation. A form of fragmentation that occurs when space is wasted in a file because it is locked up, unused, inside of records. Fixed-length record structures often result in internal fragmentation.

Irreversible compression. Compression in which information is lost.

Keysort. A method of sorting a file that does not require holding the entire file in memory. Only the keys are held in memory, along with pointers that tie these keys to the records in the file from which they are extracted. The keys are sorted, and the sorted list of keys is used to construct a new version of the file that has the records in sorted order. The primary advantage of a keysort is that it requires less memory than a memory sort. The disadvantage is that the process of constructing a new file requires a lot of seeking for records.

Linked list. A collection of nodes that have been organized into a specific sequence by means of references placed in each node that point to a single successor node. The *logical* order of a linked list is often different from the physical order of the nodes in the computer's memory.

Pinned record. A record is pinned when there are other records or file structures that refer to it by its physical location. It is pinned in the sense that we are not free to alter the physical location of the record: doing so destroys the validity of the physical references to the record. These references become useless dangling pointers.

Placement strategy. As used in this chapter, a placement strategy is a mechanism for selecting the space on the avail list that is to be used to hold a new record added to the file.

Redundancy reduction. Any form of compression that does not lose information.

Run-length encoding. A compression method in which runs of repeated codes are replaced by a count of the number of repetitions of the code, followed by the code that is repeated.

Stack. A kind of list in which all additions and deletions take place at the same end.

Variable-length encoding. Any encoding scheme in which the codes are of different lengths. More frequently occurring codes are given shorter lengths than frequently occurring codes. Huffman encoding is an example of variable-length encoding.

Worst fit. A placement strategy for selecting a space from the avail list. Worst-fit placement selects the largest record slot, regardless of how small the new record is. Insofar as this leaves the largest possible record slot for reuse, worst fit can sometimes help minimize *external fragmentation*.

FURTHER READINGS

A thorough treatment of data compression techniques can be found in Lynch (1985). The Lempel-Ziv method is described in Welch (1984). Huffman encoding is covered in many data structures texts and also in Knuth (1997).

Somewhat surprising, the literature concerning storage fragmentation and reuse often does not consider these issues from the standpoint of secondary storage. Typically, storage fragmentation, placement strategies, coalescing of holes, and garbage collection are considered in the context of reusing space within electronic random access memory. As you read this literature with the idea of applying the concepts to secondary storage, it is necessary to evaluate each strategy in light of the cost of accessing secondary storage. Some strategies that are attractive when used in electronic memory are too expensive on secondary storage.

Discussions about space management in memory are usually found under the heading "Dynamic Storage Allocation." Knuth (1997) provides a good, though technical, overview of the fundamental concerns associated with dynamic storage allocation, including placement strategies. Standish (1989) provides a more complete overview of the entire subject, reviewing much of the important literature on the subject.

This chapter only touches the surface of issues relating to searching and sorting files. A large part of the remainder of this text is devoted to exploring the issues in more detail, so one source for further reading is the present text. But there is much more that has been written about even the relatively simple issues raised in this chapter. The classic reference on sorting and searching is Knuth (1998). Knuth provides an excellent discussion of the limitations of keysort methods. He also develops a very complete discussion of binary searching, clearly bringing out the analogy between binary searching and the use of binary trees.

EXERCISES

1. In our discussion of compression, we show how we can compress the "state name" field from 16 bits to 6 bits, yet we say that this gives us a space savings of 50 percent, rather than 62.5 percent, as we would expect. Why is this so? What other measures might we take to achieve the full 62.5 percent savings?

2. What is redundancy reduction? Why is run-length encoding an example of redundancy reduction?

3. What is the maximum run length that can be handled in the run-length encoding described in the text? If much longer runs were common, how might you handle them?

4. Encode each of the following using run-length encoding. Discuss the results, and indicate how you might improve the algorithm.

   a. 01 01 01 01 01 01 01 01 01 04 04 02 02 02 03 03 03 03 04 05 06 06 07

   b. 07 07 02 02 03 03 05 05 06 06 05 05 04 04

5. From Fig. 6.2, determine the Huffman code for the sequence "cdffe."

6. What is the difference between internal and external fragmentation? How can compaction affect the amount of internal fragmentation in a file? What about external fragmentation?

7. In-place compaction purges deleted records from a file without creating a separate new file. What are the advantages and disadvantages of in-place compaction compared withto compaction in which a separate compacted file is created?

8. Why is a best-fit placement strategy a bad choice if there is significant loss of space due to external fragmentation?

9. Conceive of an inexpensive way to keep a continuous record of the amount of fragmentation in a file. This fragmentation measure could be used to trigger the batch processes used to reduce fragmentation.

10. Suppose a file must remain sorted. How does this affect the range of placement strategies available?

11. Develop an algorithm in the style of Fig. 6.13 for performing in-place compaction in a variable-length record file that contains size fields at the start of each record. What operations must be added to class `RecordFile` to support this compaction algorithm?

12. Consider the process of updating rather than deleting a variable-length record. Outline a procedure for handling such updating, accounting for the update possibly resulting in either a longer or shorter record.

13. In Section 6.3, we raised the question of where to keep the stack containing the list of available records. Should it be a separate list, perhaps maintained in a separate file, or should it be embedded within the data file? We chose the latter organization for our implementation. What advantages and disadvantages are there to the second approach? What other kinds of file structures can you think of to facilitate various kinds of record deletion?

14. In some files, each record has a delete bit that is set to 1 to indicate that the record is deleted. This bit can also be used to indicate that a record is inactive rather than deleted. What is required to reactivate an inactive record? Could reactivation be done with the deletion procedures we have used?

15. In this chapter we outlined three general approaches to the problem of minimizing storage fragmentation: (a) implementation of a placement strategy, (b) coalescing of holes, and (c) compaction. Assuming an interactive programming environment, which of these strategies would be used on the fly, as records are added and deleted? Which strategies would be used as batch processes that could be run periodically?

16. Why do placement strategies make sense only with variable-length record files?

17. Compare the average case performance of binary search with sequential search for records, assuming
    a. That the records being sought are guaranteed to be in the file,
    b. That half of the time the records being sought are not in the file, and
    c. That half of the time the records being sought are not in the file and that missing records must be inserted.

    Make a table showing your performance comparisons for files of 5000, 10 000, 20 000, 50 000, and 100 000 records.

18. If the records in Exercise 17 are blocked with 30 records per block, how does this affect the performance of the binary and sequential searches?

19. An internal sort works only with files small enough to fit in memory. Some computing systems provide users who have an almost unlimited amount of memory with a memory management technique called *virtual memory.* Discuss the use of internal sorting to sort large files on systems that use virtual memory. Be sure to consider the disk activity that is required to support virtual memory.

20. Our discussion of keysorting covers the considerable expense associated with the process of actually creating the sorted output file, given the sorted vector of pointers to the canonical key nodes. The expense revolves around two primary areas of difficulty:

    a. Having to jump around in the input file, performing many seeks to retrieve the records in their new, sorted order; and
    b. Writing the output file at the same time we are reading the input file—jumping back and forth between the files can involve seeking.

    Design an approach to this problem usingthat uses buffers to hold a number of records and, therefore mitigating these difficulties. If your solution is to be viable, obviously the buffers must use less memory than a sort taking place entirely within electronic memory.

PROGRAMMING EXERCISES

Exercises 21–22 and 23–26 investigate the problem of implementing record deletion and update. It is very appropriate to combine them into one or two design and implementation projects.

21. Add method `Delete` to class `BufferFile` to support deletion of fixed-length records. Add a field to the beginning of each record to mark whether the record is active or deleted. Modify the Read and Append methods to react to this field. In particular, Read should either fail to read, if the current record is deleted, or read the next active record. You may need to modify classes `IOBuffer` and `FixedLengthRecord`.

22. Extend the implementation of Exercise 21 to keep a list of deleted records so that deleted records can be reused by the `Append` method. Modify the `Append` method to place a new record into a deleted

record, if one is available. You may consider adding a field to the file header to store the address of the head of the deleted list and using space in each deleted record to store the address of the next deleted record.

23. Repeat Exercise 21 for variable-length records.

24. Repeat Exercise 22 for variable-length records.

25. Add an `Update` method (or modify `Write`) to class `BufferFile` to support the correct replacement of the record in the current file position with a new record. Your implementation of these methods must properly handle the case in which where the size of the new record is different from that of the record it replaces. In the case where the new size is smaller, you may choose to make the necessary changes to allow the new record to occupy the space of the old record, even though not all bytes are used. Note that in this case, the record size in the file, and the buffer size may be different.

26. Improve the variable-length record deletion procedure from Exercise 24 so that it checks to see if the newly deleted record is contiguous with any other deleted records. If there is contiguity, coalesce the records to make a single, larger available record slot. Some things to consider as you address this problem are as follows:

    a. The avail list does not keep records arranged in physical order; the next record on the avail list is not necessarily the next deleted record in the physical file. Is it possible to merge these two views of the avail list, the physical order and the logical order, into a single list? If you do this, what placement strategy will you use?

    b. Physical adjacency can include records that precede as well as follow the newly deleted record. How will you look for a deleted record that precedes the newly deleted record?

    c. Maintaining two views of the list of deleted records implies that as you discover physically adjacent records you have to rearrange links to update the nonphysical avail list. What additional complications would we encounter if we were combining the coalescing of holes with a best-fit or worst-fit strategy?

27. Implement the `BinarySearch` function of Fig. 6.13 for class `Person` using the canonical form of the combination of last name and first name as the key. Write a driver program to test the function. Assume that the files are created with using class `RecordFile<Person>` using a fixed-length buffer.

28. Modify the `BinarySearch` function so that if the key is not in the file, it returns the relative record number that the key would occupy were it in the file. The function should also continue to indicate whether the key was found or not.

29. Write a driver that uses the new `BinarySearch` function developed in Exercise 28. If the sought-after key is in the file, the program should display the record contents. If the key is not found, the program should display a list of the keys that surround the position that the key would have occupied. You should be able to move backward or forward through this list at will. Given this modification, you do not have to remember an entire key to retrieve it. If, for example, you know that you are looking for someone named Smith, but cannot remember the person's first name, this new program lets you jump to the area where all the Smith records are stored. You can then scroll back and forth through the keys until you recognize the right first name.

30. Write an internal sort that can sort a variable-length record file created with class `BufferFile`.

PROGRAMMING PROJECT

This is the fourth part of the programming project. We add methods to delete records from files and update objects in files. This depends on the solution to Exercises 21–25. This part of the programming project is optional. Further projects do not depend on this part.

31. Use the `Delete` and `Update` operations described in Exercises 21–25 to produce files of student records that support delete and update.

32. Use the `Delete` and `Update` operations described in Exercises 21–25 to produce files of student records that support delete and update.

The next part of the programming project is in Chapter 7.

7

Indexing

❖ Introduce concepts of *indexing* that have broad applications in the design of file systems.

❖ Introduce the use of a *simple linear index* to provide rapid access to records in an entry-sequenced, variable-length record file.

❖ Investigate the implications of the use of indexes for file maintenance.

❖ Introduce the template features of C++.

❖ Discuss the object-oriented approach to indexed sequential files.

❖ Describe the use of indexes to provide access to records by more than one key.

❖ Introduce the idea of an *inverted list,* illustrating *Boolean operations* on lists.

❖ Discuss the issue of *when to bind* an index key to an address in the data file.

❖ Introduce and investigate the implications of *self-indexing* files.

7.1   What Is an Index?

The last few pages of many books contain an index. Such an index is a table containing a list of topics (keys) and numbers of pages where the topics can be found (reference fields).

All indexes are based on the same basic concept—keys and reference fields. The types of indexes we examine in this chapter are called *simple indexes* because they are represented using *simple arrays* of structures that contain the keys and reference fields. In later chapters we look at indexing schemes that use more complex data structures, especially trees. In this chapter, however, we want to emphasize that indexes can be very simple and still provide powerful tools for file processing.

The index to a book provides a way to find a topic quickly. If you have ever had to use a book that doesn't have a good index, you already know that an index is a desirable alternative to scanning through the book sequentially to find a topic. In general, indexing is another way to handle the problem we explored in Chapter 6: an index is a way to find things.

Consider what would happen if we tried to apply the previous chapter's methods, sorting and binary searching, to the problem of finding things in a book. Rearranging all the words in the book so they were in alphabetical order certainly would make finding any particular term easier but would obviously have disastrous effects on the meaning of the book. In a sense, the terms in the book are pinned records. This is an absurd example, but it clearly underscores the power and importance of the index as a conceptual tool. Since it works by indirection, *an index lets you impose order on a file without rearranging the file.* This not only keeps us from disturbing pinned records, but also makes matters such as record addition much less expensive than they are with a sorted file.

Take, as another example, the problem of finding books in a library. We want to be able to locate books by a specific author, title, or subject area. One way of achieving this is to have three copies of each book and three separate library buildings. All of the books in one building would be sorted by author's name, another building would contain books arranged by title, and the third would have them ordered by subject. Again, this is an absurd example, but one that underscores another important advantage of indexing. Instead of using multiple arrangements, a library uses a card catalog. The card catalog is actually a set of three indexes, each using a different *key field,* and all of them using the same catalog number as a *reference field.* Another use of indexing, then, is to provide *multiple access paths* to a file.

We also find that indexing gives us *keyed access to variable-length record files.* Let's begin our discussion of indexing by exploring this problem of access to variable-length records and the simple solution that indexing provides.

One final note: the example data objects used in the following sections are musical recordings. This may cause some confusion as we use the term *record* to refer to an object in a file, and *recording* to refer to a data object. We will see how to get information about recordings by finding records in files. We've tried hard to make a distinction between these two terms. The distinction is between the file system view of the elements that make up files (records), and the user's or application's view of the objects that are being manipulated (recordings).

7.2 A Simple Index for Entry-Sequenced Files

Suppose we own an extensive collection of musical recordings, and we want to keep track of the collection through the use of computer files. For each recording, we keep the information shown in Fig. 7.1. Appendix G includes files `recordng.h` and `recordng.cpp` that define class

Identification number
Title
Composer or composers
Artist or artists
Label (publisher)

Figure 7.1 Contents of a data record.

Recording. Program makerec.cpp in Appendix G uses classes DelimFieldBuffer and BufferFile to create the file of Recording objects displayed in Fig. 7.2. The first column of the table contains the record addresses associated with each record in the file.

Suppose we formed a *primary key* for these recordings consisting of the initials for the company label combined with the recording's ID number. This will make a good primary key as it should provide a *unique* key for each entry in the file. We call this key the *Label ID*. The canonical form for the *Label ID* consists of the uppercase form of the Label field followed immediately by the ASCII representation of the ID number. For example,

LON2312

Record address	Label	ID number	Title	Composer(s)	Artist(s)
17	LON	2312	Romeo and Juliet	Prokofiev	Maazel
62	RCA	2626	Quartet in C Sharp Minor	Beethoven	Julliard
117	WAR	23699	Touchstone	Corea	Corea
152	ANG	3795	Symphony No. 9	Beethoven	Giulini
196	COL	38358	Nebraska	Springsteen	Springsteen
241	DG	18807	Symphony No. 9	Beethoven	Karajan
285	MER	75016	Coq d'Or Suite	Rimsky-Korsakov	Leinsdorf
338	COL	31809	Symphony No. 9	Dvorak	Bernstein
382	DG	139201	Violin Concerto	Beethoven	Ferras
427	FF	245	Good News	Sweet Honey in the Rock	Sweet Honey in the Rock

Figure 7.2 Contents of sample recording file.

How could we organize the file to provide rapid keyed access to individual records? Could we sort the file and then use binary searching? Unfortunately, binary searching depends on being able to jump to the middle record in the file. This is not possible in a variable-length record file because direct access by relative record number is not possible; there is no way to know where the middle record is in any group of records.

An alternative to sorting is to construct an index for the file. Figure 7.3 illustrates such an index. On the right is the data file containing information about our collection of recordings, with one variable-length data record per recording. Only four fields are shown (Label, ID number, Title, and Composer), but it is easy to imagine the other information filling out each record.

On the left is the index, each entry of which contains a *key* corresponding to a certain Label ID in the data file. Each key is associated with a *reference field* giving the address of the first byte of the corresponding data record. ANG3795, for example, corresponds to the reference field containing the number 152, meaning that the record containing full information on the recording with Label ID ANG3795 can be found starting at byte number 152 in the record file.

Index			**Recording file**
Key	Reference field	Address of record	Actual data record
ANG3795	152	17	LON I 2312 I Romeo and Juliet I Prokofiev I ...
COL31809	338	62	RCA I 2626I Quartet in C Sharp Minor I Beethoven I ...
COL38358	196	117	WAR I 23699 I Touchstone I Corea I ...
DG139201	382	152	ANG I 3795 I Symphony No. 9 I Beethoven I ...
DG18807	241	196	COL I 38358 I Nebraska I Springsteen I ...
FF245	427	241	DG I 18807 I Symphony No. 9 I Beethoven I ...
LON2312	17	285	MER I 75016 I Coq d'Or Suite I Rimsky-Korsakov I ...
MER75016	285	338	COL I 31809 I Symphony No. 9 I Dvorak I ...
RCA2626	62	382	DG I 139201 I Violin Concerto I Beethoven I ...
WAR23699	117	427	FF I 245 I Good News ISweet Honey in the Rock I ...

Figure 7.3 Index of the sample recording file.

The structure of the index object is very simple. It is a list of pairs of fields: a key field and a byte-offset field. There is one entry in the index for each record in the data file. Class TextIndex of Fig. 7.4 encapsulates the index data and index operations. The full implementation of class TextIndex is given in files textind.h and textind.cpp of Appendix G. An index is implemented with arrays to hold the keys and record references. Each object is declared with a maximum number of entries and can be used for unique keys (no duplicates) and for nonunique keys (duplicates allowed). The methods Insert and Search do most of the work of indexing. The protected method Find locates the element key and returns its index. If the key is not in the index, Find returns -1. This method is used by Insert, Remove, and Search.

A C++ feature used in this class is the *destructor*, method ~TextIndex. This method is automatically called whenever a TextIndex object is deleted, either because of the return from a function that includes the declaration of a TextIndex object or because of explicit deletion of an object created dynamically with new. The role of the destructor is to clean up the object, especially when it has dynamically created data members. In the case of class TextIndex, the protected members Keys and RecAddrs are created dynamically by the constructor and should be deleted by the destructor to avoid an obvious memory leak:

TextIndex::~TextIndex (){delete Keys; delete RecAddrs;}

```
class TextIndex
{public:
    TextIndex (int maxKeys = 100, int unique = 1);
    int Insert (const char * key, int recAddr); // add to index
    int Remove (const char * key); // remove key from index
    int Search (const char * key) const;
        // search for key, return recaddr
    void Print (ostream &) const;
protected:
    int MaxKeys; // maximum number of entries
    int NumKeys; // actual number of entries
    char * * Keys; // array of key values
    int * RecAddrs; // array of record references
    int Find (const char * key) const;
    int Init (int maxKeys, int unique);
    int Unique; // if true, each key must be unique in the index
};
```

Figure 7.4 Class TextIndex.

Note also that the index is sorted, whereas the data file is not. Consequently, although Label ID ANG3795 is the first entry in the index, it is not necessarily the first entry in the data file. In fact, the data file is *entry sequenced,* which means that the records occur in the order they are entered into the file. As we will see, the use of an entry-sequenced file can make record addition and file maintenance much simpler than the case with a data file that is kept sorted by some key.

Using the index to provide access to the data file by Label ID is a simple matter. The code to use our classes to retrieve a single record by key from a recording file is shown in the function `RetrieveRecording`:

```
int RetrieveRecording (Recording & recording, char * key,
        TextIndex & RecordingIndex, BufferFile & RecordingFile)
// read and unpack the recording, return TRUE if succeeds
{ int result;
  result = RecordingFile . Read (RecordingIndex.Search(key));
  if (result == -1) return FALSE;
  result = recording.Unpack (RecordingFile.GetBuffer());
  return result;
}
```

With an open file and an index to the file in memory, `RetrieveRecording` puts together the index search, file read, and buffer unpack operations into a single function.

Keeping the index in memory as the program runs also lets us find records by key more quickly with an indexed file than with a sorted one since the binary searching can be performed entirely in memory. Once the byte offset for the data record is found, a single seek is all that is required to retrieve the record. The use of a sorted data file, on the other hand, requires a seek for each step of the binary search.

7.3   Using Template Classes in C++ for Object I/O

A good object-oriented design for a file of objects should provide operations to read and write data objects without having to go through the intermediate step of packing and unpacking buffers. In Chapter 4, we supported I/O for data with the buffer classes and class `BufferFile`. In order to provide I/O for objects, we added `Pack` and `Unpack` methods to our `Person` object class. This approach gives us the required functionality but stops short of providing a read operation whose arguments are a file and a data object. We want a class `RecordFile` that makes the following code possible:

```
Person p; RecordFile pFile;    pFile . Read (p);
Recording r;    RecordFile rFile;    rFile . Read (r);
```

The major difficulty with defining class `RecordFile` is making it possible to support files for different record types without having to modify the class. Is it possible that class `RecordFile` can support read and unpack for a `Person` and a `Recording` without change? Certainly the objects are different; they have different unpacking methods. Virtual function calls do not help because `Person` and `Recording` do not have a common base type. It seems that class `RecordFile` needs to be parameterized so different versions of the class can be constructed for different types of data objects.

It is the C++ *template* feature that supports parameterized function and class definitions, and `RecordFile` is a template class. As shown in Fig. 7.5, class `RecordFile` includes the parameter `RecType`, which is used as the argument type for the read and write methods of the class. Class `RecordFile` is derived from `BufferFile`, which provides most of the functionality. The constructor for `RecordFile` is given inline and simply calls the `BufferFile` constructor.

The definitions of `pFile` and `rFile` just given are not consistent with use of a template class. The actual declarations and calls are:

```
RecordFile <Person> pFile;       pFile . Read (p);
RecordFile <Recording> rFile;    rFile . Read (p);
```

```
template <class RecType>
class RecordFile: public BufferFile
{public:
    int Read (RecType & record, int recaddr = -1);
    int Write (const RecType & record, int recaddr = -1);
    int Append (const RecType & record);
    RecordFile (IOBuffer & buffer): BufferFile (buffer) {}
};
// The template parameter RecType must have the following methods
// int Pack (IOBuffer &); pack record into buffer
// int Unpack (IOBuffer &); unpack record from buffer
```

Figure 7.5 Template Class RecordFile.

Object `rFile` is of type `RecordFile<Recording>`, which is an *instance* of class `RecordFile`. The call to `rFile.Read` looks the same as the call to `pFile.Read`, and the two methods share the same source code, but the implementations of the classes are somewhat different. In particular, the `Pack` and `Unpack` methods of class `Recording` are used for methods of object `rFile`, but `Person` methods are used for `pFile`.

The implementation of method `Read` of class `RecordFile` is given in Fig. 7.6; the implementation of all the methods are in file `recfile.h` in Appendix G. The method makes use of the `Read` method of `BufferFile` and the `Unpack` method of the parameter `RecType`. A new version of `RecordFile::Read` is created by the C++ compiler for each instance of `RecordFile`. The call `rFile.Read(r)` calls `Recording::Unpack`, and the call `pFile.Read(p)` calls `Person::Unpack`.

Class `RecordFile` accomplishes the goal of providing object-oriented I/O for data. Adding I/O to an existing class (class `Recording`, for example) requires three steps:

1. Add methods `Pack` and `Unpack` to class `Recording`.
2. Create a buffer object to use in the I/O:

   `DelimFieldBuffer Buffer;`
3. Declare an object of type `RecordFile<Recording>`:

   `RecordFile<Recording> rFile (Buffer);`

Now we can directly open a file and read and write objects of class `Recording`:

```
Recording r1, r2;
rFile . Open ("myfile");
rFile . Read (r1);
rFile . Write (r2);
```

7.4   Object-Oriented Support for Indexed, Entry-Sequenced Files of Data Objects

Continuing with our object-oriented approach to I/O, we will add indexed access to the sequential access provided by class `RecordFile`. A new class, `IndexedFile`, extends `RecordFile` with `Update` and

```
template <class RecType>
int RecordFile<RecType>::Read (RecType & record, int recaddr)
{
   int writeAddr, result;
   writeAddr = BufferFile::Read (recaddr);
   if (!writeAddr) return -1;
   result = record . Unpack (Buffer); //RecType::Unpack
   if (!result) return -1;
   return writeAddr;
}
```

Figure 7.6   Implementation of RecordFile::Read.

`Append` methods that maintain a primary key index of the data file and a `Read` method that supports access to object by key.

So far, we have classes `TextIndex`, which supports maintenance and search by primary key, and `RecordFile`, which supports create, open, and close for files as well as read and write for data objects. We have already seen how to create a primary key index for a data file as a memory object. There are still two issues to address:

■ How to make a persistent index of a file. That is, how to store the index in a file when it is not in memory.

■ How to guarantee that the index is an accurate reflection of the contents of the data file.

7.4.1 Operations Required to Maintain an Indexed File

The support and maintenance of an entry-sequenced file coupled with a simple index requires the operations to handle a number of different tasks. Besides the `RetrieveRecording` function described previously, other operations used to find things by means of the index include the following:

■ Create the original empty index and data files,

■ Load the index file into memory before using it,

■ Rewrite the index file from memory after using it,

■ Add data records to the data file,

■ Delete records from the data file,

■ Update records in the data file, and

■ Update the index to reflect changes in the data file.

A great benefit of our object-oriented approach is that everything we need to implement these operations is already available in the methods of our classes. We just need to glue them together. We begin by identifying the methods required for each of these operations. We continue to use class `Recording` as our example data class.

Creating the Files

Two files must be created: a data file to hold the data objects and an index file to hold the primary key index. Both the index file and the data file are created as empty files, with header records and nothing else. This can be accomplished quite easily using the `Create` method implemented in class `BufferFile`. The data file is represented by an object of class `RecordFile<Recording>`. The index file is a `BufferFile` of fixed-size records, as described below. As an example of the manipulation of index files, program `makeind.cpp` of Appendix G creates an index file from a file of recordings.

Loading the Index into Memory

Both loading (reading) and storing (writing) objects is supported in the `IOBuffer` classes. With these buffers, we can make files of index objects. For this example, we are storing the full index in a single object, so our index file needs only one record. As our use of indexes develops in the rest of the book, we will make extensive use of multiple record index files.

We need to choose a particular buffer class to use for our index file. We define class `TextIndexBuffer` as a derived class of `FixedFieldBuffer` to support reading and writing of index objects. `TextIndexBuffer` includes pack and unpack methods for index objects. This style is an alternative to adding these methods to the data class, which in this case is `TextIndexBuffer`. The full implementation of class `TextIndexBuffer` is in files `tindbuff.h` and `tindbuff.cpp` in Appendix G.

Rewriting the Index File from Memory

As part of the `Close` operation on an `IndexedFile`, the index in memory needs to be written to the index file. This is accomplished using the `Rewind` and `Write` operations of class `BufferFile`.

It is important to consider what happens if this rewriting of the index does not take place or if it takes place incompletely. Programs do not always run to completion. A program designer needs to guard against power failures, the operator turning the machine off at the wrong time, and other such disasters. One of the dangers associated with reading an index into memory and then writing it out when the program is over is that the copy of the index on disk will be out of date and incorrect if the program is interrupted. It is imperative that a program contain at least the following two safeguards to protect against this kind of error:

- There should be a mechanism that permits the program to know when the index is out of date. One possibility involves setting a status flag as soon as the copy of the index in memory is changed. This status flag could be written into the header record of the index file on disk as soon as the index is read into memory and subsequently cleared when the index is rewritten. All programs could check the status flag before using an index. If the flag is found to be set, the program would know that the index is out of date.

- If a program detects that an index is out of date, the program must have access to a procedure that reconstructs the index from the data file. This should happen automatically and take place before any attempt is made to use the index.

Record Addition

Adding a new record to the data file requires that we also add an entry to the index. Adding to the data file itself uses `RecordFile<Recording>::Write`. The record key and the resulting record reference are then inserted into the index record using `TextIndex.Insert`.

Since the index is kept in sorted order by key, insertion of the new index entry probably requires some rearrangement of the index. In a way, the situation is similar to the one we face as we add records to a sorted data file. We have to shift or slide all the entries with keys that come in order after the key of the record we are inserting. The shifting opens up a space for the new entry. The big difference between the work we have to do on the index entries and the work required for a sorted data file is that the index is contained *wholly in memory*. All of the index rearrangement can be done without any file access. The implementation of `TextIndex::Insert` is given in file `textind.cpp` of Appendix G.

Record Deletion

In Chapter 6 we described a number of approaches to deleting records in variable-length record files that allow for the reuse of the space occupied by these records. These approaches are completely viable for our data file because, unlike a sorted data file, the records in this file need not be moved around to maintain an ordering on the file. This is one of the great advantages of an indexed file organization: we have rapid access to individual records by key without disturbing pinned records. In fact, the indexing itself pins all the records. The implementation of data record deletion is not included in this text but has been left as exercises.

Of course, when we delete a record from the data file, we must also delete the corresponding entry from our index, using `TextIndex::Delete`. Since the index is in memory during program execution, deleting the index entry and shifting the other entries to close up the space may not be an overly expensive operation. Alternatively, we could simply mark the index entry as deleted, just as we might mark the corresponding data record. Again, see `textind.cpp` for the implementation of `TextIndex::Delete`.

Record Updating

Record updating falls into two categories:

■ *The update changes the value of the key field.* This kind of update can bring about a reordering of the index file as well as the data file. Conceptually, the easiest way to think of this kind of change is as a deletion followed by an insertion. This delete/insert approach can be implemented while still providing the program user with the view that he or she is merely changing a record.

■ *The update does not affect the key field.* This second kind of update does not require rearrangement of the index file but may well involve reordering of the data file. If the record size is unchanged or decreased by the update, the record can be written directly into its old space. But if the record size is increased by the update, a new slot for the record will have to be found. In the latter case the starting address of the rewritten record must replace the old address in the corresponding `RecAddrs` element. Again, the delete/insert approach to maintaining the index can be used. It is also possible to implement an operation simply to change the `RecAddrs` member.

7.4.2 Class TextIndexedFile

Class TextIndexedFile is defined in Fig. 7.7 and in file indfile.h
in Appendix G. It supports files of data objects with primary keys that are
strings. As expected, there are methods: Create, Open, Close, Read
(sequential and indexed), Append, and Update. In order to ensure the
correlation between the index and the data file, the members that represent the index in memory (Index), the index file (IndexFile), and the
data file (DataFile) are protected members. The only access to these
members for the user is through the methods. TextIndexedFile is a
template class so that data objects of arbitrary classes can be used.

```
template <class RecType>
class TextIndexedFile
{public:
    int Read (RecType & record); // read next record
    int Read (char * key, RecType & record); // read by key
    int Append (const RecType & record);
    int Update (char * oldKey, const RecType & record);
    int Create (char * name, int mode=ios::in|ios::out);
    int Open (char * name, int mode=ios::in|ios::out);
    int Close ();
    TextIndexedFile (IOBuffer & buffer,
        int keySize, int maxKeys = 100);
    ~TextIndexedFile (); // close and delete
protected:
    TextIndex Index;
    BufferFile IndexFile;
    TextIndexBuffer IndexBuffer;
    RecordFile<RecType> DataFile;
    char * FileName; // base file name for file
    int SetFileName(char * fileName,
        char *& dataFileName, char *& indexFileName);
};
// The template parameter RecType must have the following method
//    char * Key()
```

Figure 7.7 Class TextIndexedFile

As an example, consider `TextIndexedFile::Append`:

```
template <class RecType>
int TextIndexedFile<RecType>::Append (const RecType &
record)
{
   char * key = record.Key();
   int ref = Index.Search(key);
   if (ref != -1) // key already in file
      return -1;
   ref = DataFile . Append(record);
   int result = Index . Insert (key, ref);
   return ref;
}
```

The `Key` method is used to extract the key value from the record. A search of the index is used to determine if the key is already in the file. If not, the record is appended to the data file, and the resulting address is inserted into the index along with the key.

7.4.3 Enhancements to Class TextIndexedFile

Other Types of Keys

Even though class `TextIndexedFile` is parameterized to support a variety of data object classes, it restricts the key type to string (`char *`). It is not hard to produce a template class `SimpleIndex` with a parameter for the key type. Often, changing a class to a template class requires adding a template parameter and then simply replacing a class name with the parameter name—in this case, replacing `char *` by `keytype`. However, the peculiar way that strings are implemented in C and C++ makes this impossible. Any array in C and C++ is represented by a pointer, and equality and assignment operators are defined accordingly. Since a string is an array, string assignment is merely pointer assignment. If you review the methods of class `TextIndex`, you will see that `strcmp` is used to test for key equality, and `strcpy` is used for key assignment. In order to produce a template index class, the dependencies on `char *` must be removed. The template class `SimpleIndex` is included in files `simpind.h` and `simpind.tc` in Appendix G. It is used as the basis for the advanced indexing strategies of Chapter 9.

In C++, assignment and other operators can be overloaded only for class objects, not for predefined types like `int` and `char *`. In order to use a template index class for string keys, a class `String` is needed. Files `strclass.h` and `strclass.cpp` of Appendix G have the definition and implementation of this class, which was first mentioned in Chapter 1. Included in this class are a copy constructor, a constructor with a `char *` parameter, overloaded assignment and comparison operators, and a conversion operator to `char *` (`operator char*`). The following code shows how `String` objects and C strings become interchangeable:

```
String strObj(10); char * strArray[11]; // strings of <=10 chars
strObj = strArray; // uses String::String(char *)
strArray = strObj; // uses String::operator char * ();
```

The first assignment is implemented by constructing a temporary `String` object using the `char *` constructor and then doing `String` assignment. In this way the constructor acts like a conversion operator to class `String`. The second assignment uses the conversion operator from class `String` to convert the `String` object to a simple C string.

Data Object Class Hierarchies

So far, we have required that every object stored in a `RecordFile` must be of the same type. Can the I/O classes support objects that are of a variety of types but all from the same type hierarchy? If the type hierarchy supports virtual pack methods, the `Append` and `Update` will correctly add records to indexed files. That is, if `BaseClass` supports `Pack`, `Unpack`, and `Key`, the class `TextIndexedFile<BaseClass>` will correctly output objects derived from `BaseClass`, each with its appropriate `Pack` method.

What about `Read`? The problem here is that in a virtual function call, it is the type of the calling object that determines which method to call. For example, in this code it is the type of the object referenced by `Obj` (`*Obj`) that determines which `Pack` and `Unpack` are called:

```
BaseClass * Obj = new Subclass1;
Obj->Pack(Buffer); Obj->Unpack(Buffer); // virtual function calls
```

In the case of the `Pack`, this is correct. Information from `*Obj`, of type `Subclass1`, is transferred to `Buffer`. However, in the case of `Unpack`, it is a transfer of information from `Buffer` to `*Obj`. If `Buffer` has been filled from an object of class `Subclass2` or `BaseClass`, the unpacking cannot be done correctly. In essence, it is the source of information (contents of the buffer) that determines the type of the object in the `Unpack`, not the memory object. The virtual function call does not work in this case. An object from a file can be read only into a memory object of the correct type.

A reliable solution to the read problem—that is, one that does not attempt to read a record into an object of the wrong type—is not easy to implement in C++. It is not difficult to add a type identifier to each data record. We can add record headers in much the same fashion as file headers. However, the read operation must be able to determine reliably the type of the target object. There is no support in C++ for guaranteeing accurate type identification of memory objects.

Multirecord Index Files

Class `TextIndexedFile` requires that the entire index fit in a single record. The maximum number of records in the file is fixed when the file is created. This is obviously an oversimplification of the index structure and a restriction on its utility. Is it worth the effort to extend the class so that this restriction is eliminated?

It would be easy to modify class `TextIndexedFile` to allow the index to be an array of `TextIndex` objects. We could add protected methods `Insert`, `Delete`, and `Search` to manipulate the arrays of index objects. None of this is much trouble. However, as we will see in the following section and in Chapter 9, a sorted array of index objects, each with keys less than the next, does not provide a very satisfactory index for large files. For files that are restricted to a small number of records, class `TextIndexedFile` will work quite well as it is.

Optimization of Operations

The most obvious optimization is to use binary search in the `Find` method, which is used by `Search`, `Insert`, and `Remove`. This is very reasonable and is left as an exercise.

Another source of some improvement is to avoid writing the index record back to the index file when it has not been changed. The standard way to do this is to add a flag to the index object to signal when it has been changed. This flag is set to *false* when the record is initially loaded into memory and set to *true* whenever the index record is modified, that is, by the `Insert` and `Remove` methods. The `Close` method can check this flag and write the record only when necessary. This optimization gains importance when manipulating multirecord index files.

7.5 Indexes That Are Too Large to Hold in Memory

The methods we have been discussing—and, unfortunately, many of the advantages associated with them—are tied to the assumption that the index is small enough to be loaded into memory in its entirety. If the index is too large for this approach to be practical, then index access and maintenance must be done on secondary storage. With simple indexes of the kind we have been discussing, accessing the index on a disk has the following disadvantages:

- Binary searching of the index requires several seeks instead of taking place at memory speeds. Binary searching of an index on secondary storage is not substantially faster than the binary searching of a sorted file.

- Index rearrangement due to record addition or deletion requires shifting or sorting records on secondary storage. This is literally millions of times more expensive than performing these same operations in memory.

Although these problems are no worse than those associated with any file that is sorted by key, they are severe enough to warrant the consideration of alternatives. Any time a simple index is too large to hold in memory, you should consider using

- A *hashed* organization if access speed is a top priority; or
- A *tree-structured*, or multilevel, index, such as a *B-tree*, if you need the flexibility of both keyed access and ordered, sequential access.

These alternative file organizations are discussed at length in the chapters that follow. But, before writing off the use of simple indexes on secondary storage altogether, we should note that they provide some important advantages over the use of a data file sorted by key even if the index cannot be held in memory:

- A simple index makes it possible to use a binary search to obtain keyed access to a record in a variable-length record file. The index provides the service of associating a fixed-length and therefore binary-searchable record with each variable-length data record.

- If the index entries are substantially smaller than the data file records, sorting and maintaining the index can be less expensive than sorting and maintaining the data file. There is simply less information to move around in the index file.

■ If there are pinned records in the data file, the use of an index lets us rearrange the keys without moving the data records.

There is another advantage associated with the use of simple indexes, one that we have not yet discussed. By itself, it can be reason enough to use simple indexes even if they do not fit into memory. Remember the analogy between an index and a library card catalog? The card catalog provides multiple views or arrangements of the library's collection, even though there is only one set of books arranged in a single order. Similarly, we can use multiple indexes to provide multiple views of a data file.

7.6   Indexing to Provide Access by Multiple Keys

One question that might reasonably arise at this point is: All this indexing business is pretty interesting, but who would ever want to find a recording using a key such as DG18807? What I want is a recording of Beethoven's Symphony No. 9.

Let's return to our analogy of our index as a library card catalog. Suppose we think of our primary key, the Label ID, as a kind of catalog number. Like the catalog number assigned to a book, we have taken care to make our Label ID unique. Now in a library it is very unusual to begin by looking for a book with a particular catalog number (for example, "I am looking for a book with a catalog number QA331T5 1959."). Instead, one generally begins by looking for a book on a particular subject, with a particular title, or by a particular author (for example, "I am looking for a book on functions," or "I am looking for *The Theory of Functions* by Titchmarsh."). Given the subject, author, or title, one looks in the card catalog to find the *primary key*, the catalog number.

Similarly, we could build a catalog for our record collection consisting of entries for album title, composer, and artist. These fields are *secondary key fields*. Just as the library catalog relates an author entry (secondary key) to a card catalog number (primary key), so can we build an index file that relates Composer to Label ID, as illustrated in Fig. 7.8.

Along with the similarities, there is an important difference between this kind of secondary key index and the card catalog in a library. In a library, once you have the catalog number you can usually go directly to the stacks to find the book since the books are arranged in order by catalog number. In other words, the books are sorted by primary key. The actual data records in our file, on the other hand, are *entry sequenced*.

Composer index

Secondary key	Primary key
BEETHOVEN	ANG3795
BEETHOVEN	DG139201
BEETHOVEN	DG18807
BEETHOVEN	RCA2626
COREA	WAR23699
DVORAK	COL31809
PROKOFIEV	LON2312
RIMSKY-KORSAKOV	MER75016
SPRINGSTEEN	COL38358
SWEET HONEY IN THE R	FF245

Figure 7.8
Secondary key index
organized by composer.

Consequently, after consulting the composer index to find the Label ID, you must consult one additional index, our primary key index, to find the actual byte offset of the record that has this particular Label ID. Figure 7.9 shows part of the class definition for a secondary key index and a read function that searches a secondary key index for the primary key. It then uses the primary key to read an `IndexedFile`.

Clearly it is possible to relate secondary key references (for example, Beethoven) directly to a byte offset (241) rather than to a primary key (DG18807). However, there are excellent reasons for postponing this binding of a secondary key to a specific address for as long as possible. These reasons become clear as we discuss the way that fundamental file operations such as record deletion and updating are affected by the use of secondary indexes.

Record Addition

When a secondary index is present, adding a record to the file means adding an entry to the secondary index. The cost of doing this is very simi-

```
class SecondaryIndex
// An index in which the record reference is a string
{public:
    int Insert (char * secondaryKey, char * primaryKey);
    char * Search (char * secondaryKey); // return primary key
        ...
};
template <class RecType>
int SearchOnSecondary (char * composer, SecondaryIndex index,
        IndexedFile<RecType> dataFile, RecType & rec)
{
    char * Key = index.Search (composer);
    // use primary key index to read file
    return dataFile . Read (Key, rec);
}
```

Figure 7.9 SearchOnSecondary: an algorithm to retrieve a single record from a recording file through a secondary key index.

lar to the cost of adding an entry to the primary index: either records must be shifted, or a vector of pointers to structures needs to be rearranged. As with primary indexes, the cost of doing this decreases greatly if the secondary index can be read into memory and changed there.

Note that the key field in the secondary index file is stored in canonical form (all of the composers' names are capitalized), since this is the form we want to use when we are consulting the secondary index. If we want to print out the name in normal, mixed upper- and lowercase form, we can pick up that form from the original data file. Also note that the secondary keys are held to a fixed length, which means that sometimes they are truncated. The definition of the canonical form should take this length restriction into account if searching the index is to work properly.

One important difference between a secondary index and a primary index is that a secondary index can contain duplicate keys. In the sample index illustrated in Fig. 7.10, there are four records with the key BEETHOVEN. Duplicate keys are, of course, grouped together. Within this group, they should be ordered according to the values of the reference fields. In this example, that means placing them in order by Label ID. The reasons for this second level of ordering become clear a little later, as we discuss retrieval based on combinations of two or more secondary keys.

Title index

Secondary key	Primary key
COQ D'OR SUITE	MER75016
GOOD NEWS	FF245
NEBRASKA	COL38358
QUARTET IN C SHARP M	RCA2626
ROMEO AND JULIET	LON2312
SYMPHONY NO. 9	ANG3795
SYMPHONY NO. 9	COL31809
SYMPHONY NO. 9	DG18807
TOUCHSTONE	WAR23699
VIOLIN CONCERTO	DG139201

Figure 7.10

Secondary key index organized by recording title.

Record Deletion

Deleting a record usually implies removing all references to that record in the file system. So removing a record from the data file would mean removing not only the corresponding entry in the primary index but also all of the entries in the secondary indexes that refer to this primary index entry. The problem with this is that secondary indexes, like the primary index, are maintained in sorted order by key. Consequently, deleting an entry would involve rearranging the remaining entries to close up the space left open by deletion.

This delete-all-references approach would indeed be advisable if the secondary index referenced the data file directly. If we did not delete the secondary key references and if the secondary keys were associated with actual byte offsets in the data file, it could be difficult to tell when these references were no longer valid. This is another instance of the pinned-record problem. The reference fields associated with the secondary keys would be pointing to byte offsets that could, after deletion and subsequent space reuse in the data file, be associated with different data records.

But we have carefully avoided referencing actual addresses in the secondary key index. After we search to find the secondary key, we do another search, this time on primary key. Since the primary index *does* reflect changes due to record deletion, a search for the primary key of a record that has been deleted will fail, returning a record-not-found condition. In a sense, the updated primary key index acts as a kind of final check, protecting us from trying to retrieve records that no longer exist.

Consequently, one option that is open to us when we delete a record from the data file is to modify and rearrange only the primary key index. We could safely leave intact the references to the deleted record that exist in the secondary key indexes. Searches starting from a secondary key index that lead to a deleted record are caught when we consult the primary key index.

If there are a number of secondary key indexes, the savings that results from not having to rearrange all of these indexes when a record is deleted can be substantial. This is especially important when the secondary key indexes are kept on secondary storage. It is also important with an interactive system in which the user is waiting at a terminal for the deletion operation to complete.

There is, of course, a cost associated with this shortcut: deleted records take up space in the secondary index files. In a file system that undergoes few deletions, this is not usually a problem. In a somewhat more volatile file structure, it is possible to address the problem by periodically removing from the secondary index files all entries that contain references that are no longer in the primary index. If a file system is so volatile that even periodic purging is not adequate, it is probably time to consider another index structure, such as a B-tree, that allows for deletion without having to rearrange a lot of records.

Record Updating

In our discussion of record deletion, we find that the primary key index serves as a kind of protective buffer, insulating the secondary indexes from changes in the data file. This insulation extends to record updating as well. If our secondary indexes contain references directly to byte offsets in the data file, then updates to the data file that result in changing a record's physical location in the file also require updating the secondary indexes. But, since we are confining such detailed information to the primary index, data file updates affect the secondary index only when they change either the primary or the secondary key. There are three possible situations:

■ *Update changes the secondary key:* if the secondary key is changed, we may have to rearrange the secondary key index so it stays in sorted order. This can be a relatively expensive operation.

■ *Update changes the primary key:* this kind of change has a large impact on the primary key index but often requires that we update only the affected reference field (*Label ID* in our example) in all the secondary indexes. This involves searching the secondary indexes (on the unchanged secondary keys) and rewriting the affected fixed-length field. It does not require reordering of the secondary indexes unless the corresponding secondary key occurs more than once in the index. If a secondary key does occur more than once, there may be some local reordering, since records having the same secondary key are ordered by the reference field (primary key).

■ *Update confined to other fields:* all updates that do not affect either the primary or secondary key fields do not affect the secondary key index, even if the update is substantial. Note that if there are several secondary key indexes associated with a file, updates to records often affect only a subset of the secondary indexes.

7.7 Retrieval Using Combinations of Secondary Keys

One of the most important applications of secondary keys involves using two or more of them in combination to retrieve special subsets of records from the data file. To provide an example of how this can be done, we will extract another secondary key index from our file of recordings. This one uses the recording's *title* as the key, as illustrated in Fig. 7.10. Now we can respond to requests such as

■ Find the recording with Label ID COL38358 (primary key access);

■ Find all the recordings of Beethoven's work (secondary keyñcomposer); and

■ Find all the recordings titled "Violin Concerto" (secondary keyñtitle).

What is more interesting, however, is that we can also respond to a request that *combines* retrieval on the composer index with retrieval on the title index, such as: Find all recordings of Beethoven's Symphony No. 9. Without the use of secondary indexes, this kind of request requires a sequential search through the entire file. Given a file containing thousands, or even hundreds, of records, this is a very expensive process. But, with the aid of secondary indexes, responding to this request is simple and quick.

We begin by recognizing that this request can be rephrased as a Boolean *and* operation, specifying the intersection of two subsets of the data file:

```
Find all data records with:
    composer = 'BEETHOVEN' and title = 'SYMPHONY NO. 9'
```

We begin our response to this request by searching the composer index for the list of Label IDs that identify recordings with Beethoven as the composer. This yields the following list of Label IDs:

```
ANG3795
DG139201
DG18807
RCA2626
```

Next we search the title index for the Label IDs associated with records that have SYMPHONY NO. 9 as the title key:

```
ANG3795
COL31809
DG18807
```

Now we perform the Boolean *and*, which is a match operation, combining the lists so only the members that appear in *both* lists are placed in the output list.

```
Composers          Titles              Matched list
ANG3795 ———————————— ANG3795 ———————————— ANG3795
DG139201           COL31809          ┌── DG18807
DG18807 ———————————— DG18807 ————————┘
RCA2626
```

We give careful attention to algorithms for performing this kind of match operation in Chapter 8. Note that this kind of matching is much easier if the lists that are being combined are in sorted order. That is the reason that, when we have more than one entry for a given secondary key, the records are ordered by the primary key reference fields.

Finally, once we have the list of primary keys occurring in both lists, we can proceed to the primary key index to look up the addresses of the data file records. Then we can retrieve the records:

```
ANG | 3795  | Symphony No. 9 | Beethoven | Guilini
DG  | 18807 | Symphony No. 9 | Beethoven | Karajan
```

This is the kind of operation that makes computer-indexed file systems useful in a way that far exceeds the capabilities of manual systems. We have only one copy of each data file record, and yet, working through the secondary indexes, we have multiple views of these records: we can look at them in order by title, by composer, or by any other field that interests us. Using the computer's ability to combine sorted lists rapidly, we can even combine different views, retrieving *intersections* (Beethoven *and* Symphony No. 9) or *unions* (Beethoven *or* Prokofiev *or* Symphony No. 9) of these views. And since our data file is entry sequenced, we can do all of this without having to sort data file records and can confine our sorting to the smaller index records that can often be held in memory.

Now that we have a general idea of the design and uses of secondary indexes, we can look at ways to improve these indexes so they take less space and require less sorting.

7.8 Improving the Secondary Index Structure: Inverted Lists

The secondary index structures that we have developed so far result in two distinct difficulties:

- We have to rearrange the index file *every time* a new record is added to the file, even if the new record is for an existing secondary key. For example, if we add another recording of Beethoven's Symphony No. 9 to our collection, both the composer and title indexes would have to be rearranged, even though both indexes already contain entries for secondary keys (but not the Label IDs) that are being added.

- If there are duplicate secondary keys, the secondary key field is repeated for each entry. This wastes space because it makes the files larger than necessary. Larger index files are less likely to fit in memory.

7.8.1 A First Attempt at a Solution

One simple response to these difficulties is to change the secondary index structure so it associates an *array* of references with each secondary key.

For example, we might use a record structure that allows us to associate up to four Label ID reference fields with a single secondary key, as in

BEETHOVEN	ANG3795	DG139201	DG18807	RCA2626

Figure 7.11 provides a schematic example of how such an index would look if used with our sample data file.

The major contribution of this revised index structure is its help in solving our first difficulty: the need to rearrange the secondary index file every time a new record is added to the data file. Looking at Fig. 7.11, we can see that the addition of another recording of a work by Prokofiev does not require the addition of another record to the index. For example, if we add the recording

```
ANG  36193 Piano Concertos 3 and 5  Prokofiev Francois
```

we need to modify only the corresponding secondary index record by inserting a second Label ID:

PROKOFIEV	ANG36193	LON2312

Since we are not adding another record to the secondary index, there is no need to rearrange any records. All that is required is a rearrangement of the fields in the existing record for Prokofiev.

Although this new structure helps avoid the need to rearrange the secondary index file so often, it does have some problems. For one thing, it provides space for only four Label IDs to be associated with a given key. In the very likely case that more than four Label IDs will go with some key, we need a mechanism for keeping track of the extra Label IDs.

A second problem has to do with space usage. Although the structure does help avoid the waste of space due to the repetition of identical keys, this space savings comes at a potentially high cost. By extending the fixed length of each of the secondary index records to hold more reference fields, we might easily lose more space to internal fragmentation than we gained by not repeating identical keys.

Since we don't want to waste any more space than we have to, we need to ask whether we can improve on this record structure. Ideally, what we would like to do is develop a new design, a revision of our revision, that

Revised composer index

Secondary key	Set of primary key references			
BEETHOVEN	ANG3795	DG139201	DG18807	RCA2626
COREA	WAR23699			
DVORAK	COL31809			
PROKOFIEV	LON2312			
RIMSKY-KORSAKOV	MER75016			
SPRINGSTEEN	COL38358			
SWEET HONEY IN THE R	FF245			

Figure 7.11 Secondary key index containing space for multiple references for each secondary key.

- Retains the attractive feature of not requiring reorganization of the secondary indexes for every new entry to the data file;
- Allows more than four Label IDs to be associated with each secondary key; and
- Eliminates the waste of space due to internal fragmentation.

7.8.2 A Better Solution: Linking the List of References

Files such as our secondary indexes, in which a secondary key leads to a set of one or more primary keys, are called *inverted lists.* The sense in which the list is inverted should be clear if you consider that we are working our way backward from a secondary key to the primary key to the record itself.

The second word in the term "inverted list" also tells us something important: we are, in fact, dealing with a *list* of primary key references. Our revised secondary index, which collects a number of Label IDs for each secondary key, reflects this list aspect of the data more directly than our initial secondary index. Another way of conceiving of this list aspect of our inverted list is illustrated in Fig. 7.12.

As Fig. 7.12 shows, an ideal situation would be to have each secondary key point to a different list of primary key references. Each of these lists

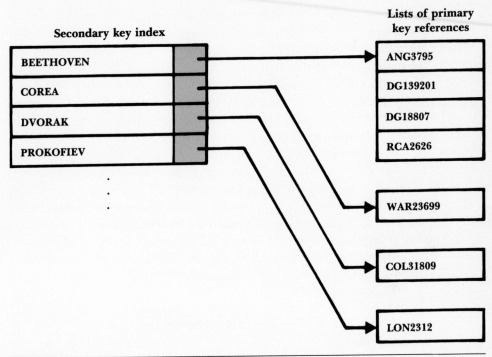

Figure 7.12 Conceptual view of the primary key reference fields as a series of lists.

could grow to be just as long as it needs to be. If we add the new Prokofiev record, the list of Prokofiev references becomes

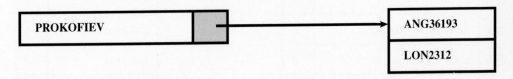

Similarly, adding two new Beethoven recordings adds just two additional elements to the list of references associated with the Beethoven key. Unlike our record structure which allocates enough space for four Label IDs for each secondary key, the lists could contain hundreds of references, if needed, while still requiring only one instance of a secondary key. On the other hand, if a list requires only one element, then no space is lost to internal fragmentation. Most important, we need to rearrange only the file of secondary keys if a new composer is added to the file.

How can we set up an unbounded number of different lists, each of varying length, without creating a large number of small files? The simplest way is through the use of linked lists. We could redefine our secondary index so it consists of records with two fields—a secondary key field and a field containing the relative record number of the first corresponding primary key reference (Label ID) in the inverted list. The actual primary key references associated with each secondary key would be stored in a separate, entry-sequenced file.

Given the sample data we have been working with, this new design would result in a secondary key file for composers and an associated Label ID file that are organized as illustrated in Fig. 7.13. Following the links for the list of references associated with Beethoven helps us see how the Label ID List file is organized. We begin, of course, by searching the secondary key index of composers for Beethoven. The record that we find points us to relative record number (RRN) 3 in the Label ID List file. Since this is a fixed-length file, it is easy to jump to RRN 3 and read in its Label ID

Improved revision of the composer index

	Secondary Index file				Label ID List file	
0	BEETHOVEN	3		0	LON2312	−1
1	COREA	2		1	RCA2626	−1
2	DVORAK	7		2	WAR23699	−1
3	PROKOFIEV	10		3	ANG3795	8
4	RIMSKY-KORSAKOV	6		4	COL38358	−1
5	SPRINGSTEEN	4		5	DG18807	1
6	SWEET HONEY IN THE R	9		6	MER75016	−1
				7	COL31809	−1
				8	DG139201	5
				9	FF245	−1
				10	ANG36193	0

Figure 7.13 Secondary key index referencing linked lists of primary key references.

(ANG3795). Associated with this Label ID is a link to a record with RRN 8. We read in the Label ID for that record, adding it to our list (ANG379 DG139201). We continue following links and collecting Label IDs until the list looks like this:

```
ANG3795    DG139201    DG18807    RCA2626
```

The link field in the last record read from the Label ID List file contains a value of -1. As in our earlier programs, this indicates end-of-list, so we know that we now have all the Label ID references for Beethoven records.

To illustrate how record addition affects the Secondary Index and Label ID List files, we add the Prokofiev recording mentioned earlier:

```
ANG  36193 Piano Concertos 3 and 5  Prokofiev Francois
```

You can see (Fig. 7.13) that the Label ID for this new recording is the last one in the Label ID List file, since this file is entry sequenced. Before this record is added, there is only one Prokofiev recording. It has a Label ID of LON2312. Since we want to keep the Label ID Lists in order by ASCII character values, the new recording is inserted in the list for Prokofiev so it logically precedes the LON2312 recording.

Associating the Secondary Index file with a new file containing linked lists of references provides some advantages over any of the structures considered up to this point:

- The only time we need to rearrange the Secondary Index file is when a new composer's name is added or an existing composer's name is changed (for example, it was misspelled on input). Deleting or adding recordings for a composer who is already in the index involves changing only the Label ID List file. Deleting *all* the recordings for a composer could be handled by modifying the Label ID List file while leaving the entry in the Secondary Index file in place, using a value of -1 in its reference field to indicate that the list of entries for this composer is empty.

- In the event that we need to rearrange the Secondary Index file, the task is quicker now since there are fewer records and each record is smaller.

- Because there is less need for sorting, it follows that there is less of a penalty associated with keeping the Secondary Index files off on secondary storage, leaving more room in memory for other data structures.

- The Label ID List file is entry sequenced. That means that it *never* needs to be sorted.

- Since the Label ID List file is a fixed-length record file, it would be very easy to implement a mechanism for reusing the space from deleted records, as described in Chapter 6.

There is also at least one potentially significant disadvantage to this kind of file organization: the Label IDs associated with a given composer are no longer guaranteed to be grouped together physically. The technical term for such "togetherness" is *locality*. With a linked, entry-sequenced structure such as this, it is less likely that there will be locality associated with the logical groupings of reference fields for a given secondary key. Note, for example, that our list of Label IDs for Prokofiev consists of the very last and the very first records in the file. This lack of locality means that picking up the references for a composer with a long list of references could involve a large amount of *seeking* back and forth on the disk. Note that this kind of seeking would not be required for our original Secondary Index file structure.

One obvious antidote to this seeking problem is to keep the Label ID List file in memory. This could be expensive and impractical, given many secondary indexes, except for the interesting possibility of using the same Label ID List file to hold the lists for a number of Secondary Index files. Even if the file of reference lists were too large to hold in memory, it might be possible to obtain a performance improvement by holding only a part of the file in memory at a time, paging sections of the file in and out of memory as they are needed.

Several exercises at the end of the chapter explore these possibilities more thoroughly. These are very important problems, as the notion of dividing the index into pages is fundamental to the design of B-trees and other methods for handling large indexes on secondary storage.

7.9   Selective Indexes

Another interesting feature of secondary indexes is that they can be used to divide a file into parts and provide a selective view. For example, it is possible to build a *selective index* that contains only the titles of classical recordings in the record collection. If we have additional information about the recordings in the data file, such as the date the recording was released, we could build selective indexes such as "recordings released prior to 1970" and "recordings since 1970." Such selective index information could be combined into Boolean *and* operations to respond to requests such as "List all the recordings of Beethoven's Ninth Symphony released since 1970." Selective indexes are sometimes useful when the contents of a file fall naturally and logically into several broad categories.

7.10   Binding

A recurrent and very important question that emerges in the design of file systems that use indexes is: *At what point is the key bound to the physical address of its associated record?*

In the file system we are designing in the course of this chapter, the *binding* of our primary keys to an address takes place *at the time the files are constructed.* The secondary keys, on the other hand, are bound to an address *at the time that they are used.*

Binding at the time of the file construction results in faster access. Once you have found the right index record, you have in hand the byte offset of the data record you are seeking. If we elected to bind our secondary keys to their associated records at the time of file construction so when we find the DVORAK record in the composer index we would know immediately that the data record begins at byte 338 in the data file, secondary key retrieval would be simpler and faster. The improvement in performance is particularly noticeable if both the primary and secondary index files are used on secondary storage rather than in memory. Given the arrangement we designed, we would have to perform a binary search of the composer index and then a binary search of the primary key index before being able to jump to the data record. Binding early, at file construction time, eliminates the need to search on the primary key.

The disadvantage of binding directly in the file, of *binding tightly,* is that reorganizations of the data file must result in modifications to all bound index files. This reorganization cost can be very expensive, particularly with simple index files in which modification would often mean shifting records. By postponing binding until execution time, when the records are being used, we are able to develop a secondary key system that involves a minimal amount of reorganization when records are added or deleted.

Another important advantage to postponing binding until a record is retrieved is that this approach is safer. As we see in the system that we set up, associating the secondary keys with reference fields consisting of primary keys allows the primary key index to act as a kind of final check of whether a record is really in the file. The secondary indexes can afford to be wrong. This situation is very different if the secondary index keys contain addresses. We would then be jumping directly from the secondary key into the data file; the address would need to be right.

This brings up a related safety aspect: it is always more desirable to make important changes in one place rather than in many places. With a bind-at-retrieval-time scheme such as we developed, we need to remember to make a change in only one place, the primary key index, if we move a data record. With a more tightly bound system, we have to make many changes successfully to keep the system internally consistent, braving power failures, user interruptions, and so on.

When designing a new file system, it is better to deal with this question of binding *intentionally* and *early* in the design process rather than letting the binding just happen. In general, tight, in-the-data binding is most attractive when

- The data file is static or nearly so, requiring little or no adding, deleting, or updating of records; and

- Rapid performance during actual retrieval is a high priority.

For example, tight binding is desirable for file organization on a mass-produced, read-only optical disk. The addresses will never change because no new records can ever be added; consequently, there is no reason not to obtain the extra performance associated with tight binding.

For file applications in which record addition, deletion, and updating do occur, however, binding at retrieval time is usually the more desirable option. Postponing binding as long as possible usually makes these operations simpler and safer. If the file structures are carefully designed, and, in particular, if the indexes use more sophisticated organizations such as B-trees, retrieval performance is usually quite acceptable, even given the additional work required by a bind-at-retrieval system.

SUMMARY

We began this chapter with the assertion that indexing as a way of structuring a file is an alternative to sorting because records can be found *by key*. Unlike sorting, indexing permits us to perform *binary searches* for keys in variable-length record files. If the index can be held in memory, record addition, deletion, and retrieval can be done much more quickly with an indexed, entry-sequenced file than with a sorted file.

Template classes in C++ provide support for sharing class definitions and code among a number of unrelated classes. Template classes are used in this chapter for class `RecordFile`, which supports I/O of data records without explicit packing and unpacking of buffers, and for general purpose index records in class `SimpleIndex`.

Support for sequential and indexed access to a data file is provided by the template class `TextIndexedFile`. It extends the capabilities of class `RecordFile` by adding indexed read, update, and append operations. Each modification of the data file is accompanied by the proper changes to the index. Each `TextIndexedFile` object is represented by an index record object in memory and two files, a data file and an index file. The `TextIndexedFile::Close` method writes the contents of the index record object into the index file and closes both files.

Indexes can do much more than merely improve on access time: they can provide us with new capabilities that are inconceivable with access methods based on sorted data records. The most exciting new capability involves the use of multiple secondary indexes. Just as a library card catalog allows us to regard a collection of books in author order, title order, or subject order, so index files allow us to maintain different views of the records in a data file. We find that not only can we use secondary indexes to obtain different views of the file but we can also combine the associated lists of primary key references and thereby combine particular views.

In this chapter we address the problem of how to rid our secondary indexes of two liabilities:

- The need to repeat duplicate secondary keys, and
- The need to rearrange the secondary indexes every time a record is added to the data file.

A first solution to these problems involves associating a fixed-size *vector* of reference fields with each secondary key. This solution results in an overly large amount of internal fragmentation but illustrates the attractiveness of handling the reference fields associated with a particular secondary key as a group, or *list*.

Our next iteration of solutions to our secondary index problems is more successful and much more interesting. We can treat the primary key references as an entry-sequenced file, forming the necessary lists through the use of *link fields* associated with each primary record entry. This allows us to create a secondary index file that, in the case of the composer index, needs rearrangement only when we add new composers to the data file.

The entry-sequenced file of linked reference lists never requires sorting. We call this kind of secondary index structure an *inverted list.*

There are also, of course, disadvantages associated with our new solution. The most serious disadvantage is that our file demonstrates less locality: lists of associated records are less likely to be physically adjacent. A good antidote to this problem is to hold the file of linked lists in memory. We note that this is made more plausible because a single file of primary references can link the lists for a number of secondary indexes.

As indicated by the length and breadth of our consideration of secondary indexing, multiple keys, and inverted lists, these topics are among the most interesting aspects of indexed access to files. The concepts of secondary indexes and inverted lists become even more powerful later, as we develop index structures that are themselves more powerful than the simple indexes we consider here. But, even so, we already see that for small files consisting of no more than a few thousand records, approaches to inverted lists that rely merely on simple indexes can provide a user with a great deal of capability and flexibility.

KEY TERMS

Binding. Binding takes place when a key is associated with a particular physical record in the data file. In general, binding can take place either during the preparation of the data file and indexes or during program execution. In the former case, called *tight binding,* the indexes contain explicit references to the associated physical data record. In the latter case, the connection between a key and a particular physical record is postponed until the record is retrieved in the course of program execution.

Entry-sequenced file. A file in which the records occur in the order that they are entered into the file.

Index. An index is a tool for finding records in a file. It consists of a *key field* on which the index is searched and a *reference field* that tells where to find the data file record associated with a particular key.

Inverted list. The term *inverted list* refers to indexes in which a key may be associated with a *list* of reference fields pointing to documents that contain the key. The secondary indexes developed toward the end of this chapter are examples of inverted lists.

Key field. The key field is the portion of an index record that contains the canonical form of the key that is being sought.

Locality. Locality exists in a file when records that will be accessed in a given temporal sequence are found in physical proximity to each other on the disk. Increased locality usually results in better performance, as records that are in the same physical area can often be brought into memory with a single *read* request to the disk.

Reference field. The reference field is the portion of an index record that contains information about where to find the data record containing the information listed in the associated key field of the index.

Selective index. A selective index contains keys for only a portion of the records in the data file. Such an index provides the user with a view of a specific subset of the file's records.

Simple index. All the index structures discussed in this chapter are simple indexes insofar as they are all built around the idea of an ordered, linear sequence of index records. All these simple indexes share a common weakness: adding records to the index is expensive. As we see later, tree-structured indexes provide an alternate, more efficient solution to this problem.

Template class. A C++ class that is parameterized, typically with class (or type) parameters. Templates allow a single class definition to be used to construct a family of different classes, each with different arguments for the parameters.

FURTHER READINGS

We have much more to say about indexing in later chapters, where we take up the subjects of tree-structured indexes and indexed sequential file organizations. The topics developed in the current chapter, particularly those relating to secondary indexes and inverted files, are also covered by many other file and data structure texts. The few texts that we list here are of interest because they either develop certain topics in more detail or present the material from a different viewpoint.

Wiederhold (1983) provides a survey of many of the index structures we discuss, along with a number of others. His treatment is more mathematical than that provided in our text. Tremblay and Sorenson (1984) provide a comparison of inverted list structures with an alternative organization called *multilist* files. M. E. S. Loomis (1989) provides a similar discussion, along with some examples oriented toward COBOL users. Kroenke (1998) discuss inverted lists in the context of their application in information retrieval systems.

EXERCISES

1. Until now, it was not possible to perform a binary search on a variable-length record file. Why does indexing make binary search possible? With a fixed-length record file it *is* possible to perform a binary search. Does this mean that indexing need not be used with fixed-length record files?

2. Why is `Title` not used as a primary key in the `Recording` file described in this chapter? If it were used as a secondary key, what problems would have to be considered in deciding on a canonical form for titles?

3. What is the purpose of keeping an out-of-date-status flag in the header record of an index? In a multiprogramming environment, this flag might be found to be set by one program because another program is in the process of reorganizing the index. How should the first program respond to this situation?

4. Consult a reference book on C++ to determine how template classes like `RecordFile` are implemented. How does the compiler process the method bodies of a template class? How does the compiler process template instantiations?

5. Explain how the use of an index pins the data records in a file.

6. When a record in a data file is updated, corresponding primary and secondary key indexes may or may not have to be altered, depending on whether the file has fixed- or variable-length records, and depending on the type of change made to the data record. Make a list of the different updating situations that can occur, and explain how each affects the indexes.

7. Discuss the problem that occurs when you add the following recording to the recordings file, assuming that the composer index shown in Fig. 7.11 is used. How might you solve the problem without substantially changing the secondary key index structure?

   ```
   LON    1259    Fidelio     Beethoven    Maazel
   ```

8. How are the structures in Fig. 7.13 changed by the addition of the recording

   ```
   LON    1259    Fidelio     Beethoven    Maazel
   ```

9. Suppose you have the data file described in this chapter, but it's greatly expanded, with a primary key index and secondary key indexes

organized by composer, artist, and title. Suppose that an inverted list structure is used to organize the secondary key indexes. Give step-by-step descriptions of how a program might answer the following queries:

a. List all recordings of Bach or Beethoven, and

b. List all recordings by Perleman of pieces by Mozart or Joplin.

10. Using the program `makerec.cpp`, create a file of recordings. Make a file dump of the file and find the size and contents of the header as well asand the starting address and the size for each record.

11. Use the program `makeind.cpp` to create an index file for the recording file created by program `makerec.cpp`. Using a file dump, find the size and contents of the header, the address and size of the record, and the contents of the record.

12. The method and timing of binding affect two important attributes of a file system—speed and flexibility. Discuss the relevance of these attributes, and the effect of binding time on them, for a hospital patient datainformation system designed to provide information about current patients by patient name, patient ID, location, medication, doctor or doctors, and illness.

PROGRAMMING AND DESIGN EXERCISES

13. Add method(s) to class `TextIndex` to support iterating through the index in key order. One possible strategy is to define two methods:

```
int FirstRecAddr (); // return reference for the smallest key
int NextRecAddr (); // return reference for the next key
```

Implementation of these methods can be supported by adding members to the class.

14. Write a program to print the records of a `Recording` file in key order. One way to implement this program is to read all the records of the file and create an index record in memory and then iterate through the index in key order and read and print the records. Test the program on the file produced by `makerec.cpp`.

15. Write a program to print the records of a file of type `RecordFile<Recording>` in key order. Test the program on the file produced by `makeind.cpp`.

16. Modify the method `TextIndex::Search` to perform a binary search on the key array.

17. Implement the Remove methods of class `TextIndexedFile`.

18. Extend class `TextIndexedFile` to support the creation of an indexed file from a simple data file. That is, add a method that initializes a `TextIndexedFile` object by opening and reading the existing data file and creating an index from the records in the file.

19. As a major programming project, create a class hierarchy based on `Recording` that has different information for different types of recordings. Develop a class to support input and output of records of these types. The class should be consistent with the style described in the part of Section 7.4.3 about data object class hierarchies. The `Unpack` methods must be sensitive to the type of object that is being initialized by the call.

20. Define and implement a class `SecondaryIndex` to support secondary indexes, as described in Section 7.6. Use this class to create a class `RecordingFile` that uses `RecordFile` as its base class to manage the primary index and the data file and has secondary indexes for the Composer and Artist fields.

21. When searching secondary indexes that contain multiple records for some of the keys, we do not want to find just *any* record for a given secondary key; we want to find the *first* record containing that key. Finding the first record allows us to read ahead, sequentially, extracting all of the records for the given key. Write a variation of a search method that returns the relative record number of the *first* record containing the given key.

22. Identify and eliminate memory leaks in the code of Appendix F.

PROGRAMMING PROJECT

This is the fifth part of the programming project. We add indexes to the data files created by the third part of the project in Chapter 4.

23. Use class `IndexedFile` (or `TextIndexedFile`) to create an index of a file of student objects, using student identifier as key. Write a driver program to create an index file from the student record file created by the program of part three of the programming project in Chapter 4.

24. Use class `IndexedFile` (or `TextIndexedFile`) to create an index of a file of course registration objects, using student identifier as key. Note that the student identifier is not unique in course registration files. Write a driver program to create an index file from the course registration record file created by the program of part three of the programming project in Chapter 4.

25. Write a program that opens an indexed student file and an indexed course registration file and retrieves information on demand. Prompt a user for a student identifier and print all objects that match it.

26. Develop a class that supports indexed access to course registration files by student identifier and by course identifier (secondary key). See Exercise 20 for an implementation of secondary indexes. Extend the program of Exercise 25 to allow retrieval of information about specific courses.

27. Extend the above projects to support update and deletion of student records and course registration records.

The next part of the programming project is in Chapter 8.

8

Cosequential Processing and the Sorting of Large Files

❖ Describe a class of frequently used processing activities known as *cosequential processes.*

❖ Provide a general object-oriented model for implementing all varieties of cosequential processes.

❖ Illustrate the use of the model to solve a number of different kinds of cosequential processing problems, including problems other than simple merges and matches.

❖ Introduce *heapsort* as an approach to overlapping I/O with sorting in memory.

❖ Show how merging provides the basis for sorting very large files.

❖ Examine the costs of *K*-way merges on disk and find ways to reduce those costs.

❖ Introduce the notion of *replacement selection.*

❖ Examine some of the fundamental concerns associated with sorting large files using tapes rather than disks.

❖ Introduce Unix utilities for sorting, merging, and cosequential processing.

CHAPTER OUTLINE

Cosequential operations involve *the coordinated processing of two or more sequential lists to produce a single output list.* Sometimes the processing results in a *merging,* or *union,* of the items in the input lists; sometimes the goal is a *matching,* or *intersection,* of the items in the lists; and other times the operation is a combination of matching and merging. These kinds of operations on sequential lists are the basis of a great deal of file processing.

In the first half of this chapter we develop a general object-oriented model for performing cosequential operations, illustrate its use for simple matching and merging operations, then apply it to the development of a more complex general ledger program. Next we apply the model to multi-way merging, which is an essential component of external sort-merge operations. We conclude the chapter with a discussion of external sort-merge procedures, strategies, and trade-offs, paying special attention to performance considerations.

8.1   An Object-Oriented Model for Implementing Cosequential Processes

Cosequential operations usually appear to be simple to construct; given the information that we provide in this chapter, this appearance of simplicity can be turned into reality. However, it is also true that approaches to cosequential processing are often confused, poorly organized, and incorrect. These examples of bad practice are by no means limited to student programs: the problems also arise in commercial programs and textbooks. The difficulty with these incorrect programs is usually that they are not organized around a single, clear model for cosequential processing. Instead, they seem to deal with the various exception conditions and problems of a cosequential process in an *ad hoc* rather than systematic way.

This section addresses such lack of organization head on. We present a single, simple model that can be the basis for the construction of any kind of cosequential process. By understanding and adhering to the design principles inherent in the model, you will be able to write cosequential procedures that are simple, short, and robust.

We present this model by defining a class `CosequentialProcess` that supports processing of any type of list, in the same way that class `IOBuffer` supports buffer operations on any type of buffer. Class `CosequentialProcess` includes operations to match and merge lists. It defines the list processing operations required for cosequential processing as virtual methods. We will then define new subclasses that include the methods for accessing the elements of particular types of lists.

8.1.1 Matching Names in Two Lists

Suppose we want to output the names common to the two lists shown in Fig. 8.1. This operation is usually called a *match operation,* or an *intersection.* We assume, for the moment, that we will not allow duplicate names within a list and that the lists are sorted in ascending order.

We begin by reading in the initial item from each list, and we find that they match. We output this first item as a member of the *match set,* or *intersection set.* We then read in the next item from each list. This time the

List 1	List 2
ADAMS	ADAMS
CARTER	ANDERSON
CHIN	ANDREWS
DAVIS	BECH
FOSTER	BURNS
GARWICK	CARTER
JAMES	DAVIS
JOHNSON	DEMPSEY
KARNS	GRAY
LAMBERT	JAMES
MILLER	JOHNSON
PETERS	KATZ
RESTON	PETERS
ROSEWALD	ROSEWALD
TURNER	SCHMIDT
	THAYER
	WALKER
	WILLIS

Figure 8.1 Sample input lists for cosequential operations.

item in List 2 is less than the item in List 1. When we are processing these lists visually as we are now, we remember that we are trying to match the item CARTER from List 1 and scan down List 2 until we either find it or jump beyond it. In this case, we eventually find a match for CARTER, so we output it, read in the next item from each list, and continue the process. Eventually we come to the end of one of the lists. Since we are looking for items common to both lists, we know we can stop at this point.

Although the match procedure appears to be quite simple, there are a number of matters that have to be dealt with to make it work reasonably well.

- *Initializing:* we need to arrange things in such a way that the procedure gets going properly.

- *Getting and accessing the next list item:* we need simple methods that support getting the next list element and accessing it.

- *Synchronizing:* we have to make sure that the current item from one list is never so far ahead of the current item on the other list that a match will be missed. Sometimes this means getting the next item from List 1, sometimes from List 2, sometimes from both lists.

- *Handling end-of-file conditions:* when we get to the end of either List 1 or List 2, we need to halt the program.

- *Recognizing errors:* when an error occurs in the data (for example, duplicate items or items out of sequence), we want to detect it and take some action.

Finally, we would like our algorithm to be reasonably efficient, simple, and easy to alter to accommodate different kinds of data. The key to accomplishing these objectives in the model we are about to present lies in the way we deal with the third item in our list—synchronizing.

At each step in the processing of the two lists, we can assume that we have two items to compare: a current item from List 1 and a current item from List 2. Let's call these two current items `Item(1)` and `Item(2)`. We can compare the two items to determine whether `Item(1)` is less than, equal to, or greater than `Item(2)`:

- If `Item(1)` is *less than* `Item(2)`, we get the next item from List 1;

- If `Item(1)` is *greater than* `Item(2)`, we get the next item from List 2; and

- If the items are the same, we output the item and get the next items from the two lists.

It turns out that this can be handled very cleanly with a single loop containing one three-way conditional statement, as illustrated in the algorithm of Fig. 8.2. The key feature of this algorithm is that *control always returns to the head of the main loop after every step of the operation.* This means that no extra logic is required within the loop to handle the case when List 1 gets ahead of List 2, or List 2 gets ahead of List 1, or the end-of-file condition is reached on one list before it is on the other. Since each pass through the main loop looks at the next pair of items, the fact that one list may be longer than the other does not require any special logic. Nor does the end-of-file condition—each operation to get a new item resets the MoreNames flag that records whether items are available in both lists. The while statement simply checks the value of the flag MoreNames on every cycle.

```
int Match (char * List1Name, char * List2Name,
     char * OutputListName)
{
   int MoreItems;// true if items remain in both of the lists

   // initialize input and output lists
   InitializeList (1, List1Name);// initialize List 1
   InitializeList (2, List2Name);// initialize List 2
   InitializeOutput(OutputListName);

   // get first item from both lists
   MoreItems = NextItemInList(1) && NextItemInList(2);

   while (MoreItems){// loop until no items in one of the lists
     if (Item(1) < Item(2))
       MoreItems = NextItemInList(1);
     else if (Item(1) == Item(2)) // Item1 == Item2
     {
       ProcessItem (1); // match found
       MoreItems = NextItemInList(1) && NextItemInList(2);
     }
     else // Item(1) > Item(2)
       MoreItems = NextItemInList(2);
   }
   FinishUp();
   return 1;
}
```

Figure 8.2 Cosequential match function based on a single loop.

The logic inside the loop is equally simple. Only three possible conditions can exist after reading an item: the *if-then-else* logic handles all of them. Because we are implementing a match process here, output occurs only when the items are the same.

Note that the main program does not concern itself with such matters as getting the next item, sequence checking, and end-of-file detection. Since their presence in the main loop would only obscure the main synchronization logic, they have been relegated to supporting methods. It is also the case that these methods are specific to the particular type of lists being used and must be different for different applications.

Method `NextItemInList` has a single parameter that identifies which list is to be manipulated. Its responsibility is to read the next name from the file, store it somewhere, and return *true* if it was able to read another name and *false* otherwise. It can also check the condition that the list must be in ascending order with no duplicate entries.

Method `Match` must be supported by defining methods `InitializeList`, `InitializeOutput`, `NextItemInList`, `Item`, `ProcessItem`, and `FinishUp`. The `Match` method is perfectly general and is not dependent on the type of the items nor on the way the lists are represented. These details are provided by the supporting methods that need to be defined for the specific needs of particular applications. What follows is a description of a class `CosequentialProcessing` that supports method `Match` and a class `StringListProcess` that defines the supporting operations for the lists like those of Figure 8.1.

Class `CosequentialProcessing`, as given in Fig. 8.3 and in file `coseq.h` and `coseq.cpp` of Appendix H, encapsulates the ideas of cosequential processing that were described in the earlier example of list matching. Note that this is an abstract class, since it does not contain definitions of the supporting methods. This is a template class so the operations that compare list items can be different for different applications. The code of method `Match` in Fig. 8.2 is exactly that of method `Match2Lists` of this class, as you can see in file `coseq.cpp`.

In order to use class `CosequentialProcess` for the application described earlier, we need to create a subclass `StringListProcess` that defines the specific supporting methods. Figure 8.4 (and file `strlist.h` of Appendix H) shows the definition of class `StringListProcess`. The implementations of the methods are given in file `strlist.cpp` of Appendix H. The class definition allows any number of input lists. Protected members are included for the input and

```
template <class ItemType>
class CosequentialProcess
// base class for cosequential processing
{public:
   // The following methods provide basic list processing
   // These must be defined in subclasses
   virtual int InitializeList (int ListNumber, char * ListName)=0;
   virtual int InitializeOutput (char * OutputListName)=0;
   virtual int NextItemInList (int ListNumber)=0;
      //advance to next item in this list
   virtual ItemType Item (int ListNumber) = 0;
      // return current item from this list
   virtual int ProcessItem (int ListNumber)=0;
      // process the item in this list
   virtual int FinishUp()=0; // complete the processing

   // 2-way cosequential match method
   virtual int Match2Lists
      (char * List1Name, char * List2Name, char * OutputListName);
};
```

Figure 8.3 Main members and methods of a general class for cosequential processing.

output files and for the values of the current item of each list. Member
LowValue is a value that is smaller than any value that can appear in a
list—in this case, the null string (" "). LowValue is used so that method
NextItemInList does not have to get the first item in any special way.
Member HighValue has a similar use, as we will see in the next section.

Given these classes, you should be able to work through the two lists
provided in Fig. 8.1, following the code, and demonstrate to yourself that
these simple procedures can handle the various resynchronization problems that these sample lists present. A main program (file match.cpp)
to process the lists stored in files list1.txt and list2.txt is

```
#include "coseq.h"
int main ()
{
   StringListProcess ListProcess(2);// process with 2 lists
   ListProcess.Match2Lists ("list1.txt","list2.txt","match.txt");
}
```

```
class StringListProcess: public CosequentialProcess<String&>
// Class to process lists that are files of strings, one per line
{
public:
   StringListProcess (int NumberOfLists); // constructor

   // Basic list processing methods
   int InitializeList (int ListNumber, char * List1Name);
   int InitializeOutput (char * OutputListName);
   int NextItemInList (int ListNumber); //get next
   String& Item (int ListNumber);//return current
   int ProcessItem (int ListNumber); // process the item
   int FinishUp(); // complete the processing
protected:
   ifstream * Lists; // array of list files
   String * Items; // array of current Item from each list
   ofstream OutputList;
   static const char * LowValue;
   static const char * HighValue;
};
```

Figure 8.4 A subclass to support lists that are files of strings, one per line.

8.1.2 Merging Two Lists

The three-way-test, single-loop model for cosequential processing can easily be modified to handle *merging* of lists simply by producing output for every case of the *if-then-else* construction since a merge is a *union* of the list contents.

   An important difference between matching and merging is that with merging we must read *completely* through each of the lists. This necessitates a change in how MoreNames is set. We need to keep this flag set to TRUE as long as there are records in *either* list. At the same time, we must recognize that one of the lists has been read completely, and we should avoid trying to read from it again. Both of these goals can be achieved if we introduce two MoreNames variables, one for each list, and set the stored Item value for the completed list to some value (we call it HighValue) that

■ Cannot possibly occur as a legal input value, and

■ Has a *higher* collating sequence value than any possible legal input value. In other words, this special value would come *after* all legal input values in the file's ordered sequence.

For HighValue, we use the string "\xFF" which is a string of only one character and that character has the hex value FF, which is the largest character value.

Method Merge2Lists is given in Fig. 8.5 and in file coseq.cpp of Appendix H. This method has been added to class CosequentialProcess. No modifications are required to class StringListProcess.

```
template <class ItemType>
int CosequentialProcess<ItemType>::Merge2Lists
    (char * List1Name, char * List2Name, char * OutputListName)
{
    int MoreItems1, MoreItems2; // true if more items in list
    InitializeList (1, List1Name);
    InitializeList (2, List2Name);
    InitializeOutput (OutputListName);
    MoreItems1 = NextItemInList(1);
    MoreItems2 = NextItemInList(2);

    while (MoreItems1 || MoreItems2){// if either file has more
        if (Item(1) < Item(2))
        {// list 1 has next item to be processed
            ProcessItem (1);
            MoreItems1 = NextItemInList(1);
        }
        else if (Item(1) == Item(2))
        {// lists have the same item, process from list 1
            ProcessItem (1);
            MoreItems1 = NextItemInList(1);
            MoreItems2 = NextItemInList(2);
        }
        else // Item(1) > Item(2)
        {// list 2 has next item to be processed
            ProcessItem (2);
            MoreItems2 = NextItemInList(2);
        }
    }
    FinishUp();
    return 1;
}
```

Figure 8.5 Cosequential merge procedure based on a single loop.

Once again, you should use this logic to work, step by step, through the lists provided in Fig. 8.1 to see how the resynchronization is handled and how the use of the `HighValue` forces the procedure to finish both lists before terminating.

With these two examples, we have covered all of the pieces of our model. Now let us summarize the model before adapting it to a more complex problem.

8.1.3 Summary of the Cosequential Processing Model

Generally speaking, the model can be applied to problems that involve the performance of set operations (union, intersection, and more complex processes) on two or more sorted input files to produce one or more output files. In this summary of the cosequential processing model, we assume that there are only two input files and one output file. It is important to understand that the model makes certain general assumptions about the nature of the data and type of problem to be solved. Following is a list of the assumptions, together with clarifying comments.

Assumptions	*Comments*
Two or more input files are to be processed in a parallel fashion to produce one or more output files.	In some cases an output file may be the same file as one of the input files.
Each file is sorted on one or more key fields, and all files are ordered in the same ways on the same fields.	It is not necessary that all files have the same record structures.
In some cases, there must exist a high-key value that is greater than any legitimate record key and a low-key value that is less than any legitimate record key.	The use of a high-key value and a low-key value is not absolutely necessary, but it can help avoid the need to deal with beginning-of-file and end-of-file conditions as special cases, hence decreasing complexity.
Records are to be processed in logical sorted order.	The physical ordering of records is irrelevant to the model, but in practice it may be important to the way the model is implemented. Physical ordering can have a large impact on processing efficiency

Assumptions (*cont.*)

For each file there is only one current record. This is the record whose key is accessible within the main synchronization loop.

Records can be manipulated only in internal memory.

Comments (*cont.*)

The model does not prohibit looking ahead or looking back at records, but such operations should be restricted to subclasses and should not be allowed to affect the structure of the main synchronization loop.

A program cannot alter a record in place on secondary storage.

Given these assumptions, the essential components of the model are:

1. Initialization. Previous item values for all files are set to the low value; then current records for all files are read from the first logical records in the respective files.
2. One main synchronization loop is used, and the loop continues as long as relevant records remain.
3. Within the body of the main synchronization loop is a selection based on comparison of the record keys from respective input file records. If there are two input files, the selection takes the form given in function `Match` of Fig. 8.2.
4. Input files and output files are sequence checked by comparing the previous item value with the new item value when a record is read. After a successful sequence check, the previous item value is set to the new item value to prepare for the next input operation on the corresponding file.
5. High values are substituted for actual key values when end-of-file occurs. The main processing loop terminates when high values have occurred for all relevant input files. The use of high values eliminates the need to add special code to deal with each end-of-file condition. (This step is not needed in a pure match procedure because a match procedure halts when the first end-of-file condition is encountered.)
6. All possible I/O and error detection activities are to be relegated to supporting methods so the details of these activities do not obscure the principal processing logic.

This three-way-test, single-loop model for creating cosequential processes is both simple and robust. You will find very few applications requiring the coordinated sequential processing of two files that cannot be handled neatly and efficiently with the model. We now look at a problem that is much more complex than a simple match or merge but that nevertheless lends itself nicely to solution by means of the model.

8.2   Application of the Model to a General Ledger Program

8.2.1   The Problem

Suppose we are given the problem of designing a general ledger posting program as part of an accounting system. The system includes a journal file and a ledger file. The ledger contains month-by-month summaries of the values associated with each of the bookkeeping accounts. A sample portion of the ledger, containing only checking and expense accounts, is illustrated in Fig. 8.6.

The journal file contains the monthly transactions that are ultimately to be posted to the ledger file. Figure 8.7 shows these journal transactions. Note that the entries in the journal file are paired. This is because every check involves both subtracting an amount from the checking account balance and adding an amount to at least one expense account. The accounting-program package needs procedures for creating this journal file interactively, probably outputting records to the file as checks are keyed in and then printed.

Acct. No.	Account title	Jan	Feb	Mar	Apr
101	Checking account #1	1032.57	2114.56	5219.23	
102	Checking account #2	543.78	3094.17	1321.20	
505	Advertising expense	25.00	25.00	25.00	
510	Auto expenses	195.40	307.92	501.12	
515	Bank charges	0.00	0.00	0.00	
520	Books and publications	27.95	27.95	87.40	
525	Interest expense	103.50	255.20	380.27	
535	Miscellaneous expense	12.45	17.87	23.87	
540	Office expense	57.50	105.25	138.37	
545	Postage and shipping	21.00	27.63	57.45	
550	Rent	500.00	1000.00	1500.00	
555	Supplies	112.00	167.50	2441.80	

Figure 8.6 Sample ledger fragment containing checking and expense accounts.

Acct. No	Check No.	Date	Description	Debit/ credit
101	1271	04/02/86	Auto expense	-78.70
510	1271	04/02/97	Tune-up and minor repair	78.70
101	1272	04/02/97	Rent	-500.00
550	1272	04/02/97	Rent for April	500.00
101	1273	04/04/97	Advertising	-87.50
505	1273	04/04/97	Newspaper ad re: new product	87.50
102	670	04/02/97	Office expense	-32.78
540	670	04/02/97	Printer cartridge	32.78
101	1274	04/02/97	Auto expense	-31.83
510	1274	04/09/97	Oil change	31.83

Figure 8.7 Sample journal entries.

Once the journal file is complete for a given month, meaning that it contains all of the transactions for that month, the journal must be posted to the ledger. *Posting* involves associating each transaction with its account in the ledger. For example, the printed output produced for accounts 101, 102, 505, and 510 during the posting operation, given the journal entries in Fig. 8.7, might look like the output illustrated in Fig. 8.8.

```
101     Checking account #1
        1271  04/02/86     Auto expense                       -78.70
        1272  04/02/97     Rent                              -500.00
        1273  04/04/97     Advertising                        -87.50
        1274  04/02/97     Auto expense                       -31.83
                           Prev. bal: 5219.23   New bal:        4521.20
102     Checking account #2
         670  04/02/97     Office expense                     -32.78
                           Prev. bal: 1321.20   New bal:        1288.42
505     Advertising expense
        1273  04/04/97     Newspaper ad re: new product        87.50
                           Prev. bal: 25.00     New bal:         112.50
510     Auto expenses
        1271  04/02/97     Tune-up and minor repair            78.70
        1274  04/09/97     Oil change                          31.83
                           Prev. bal: 501.12    New bal:         611.65
```

Figure 8.8 Sample ledger printout showing the effect of posting from the journal.

How is the posting process implemented? Clearly, it uses the account number as a *key* to relate the journal transactions to the ledger records. One possible solution involves building an index for the ledger so we can work through the journal transactions using the account number in each journal entry to look up the correct ledger record. But this solution involves seeking back and forth across the ledger file as we work through the journal. Moreover, this solution does not really address the issue of creating the output list, in which all the journal entries relating to an account are collected together. Before we could print the ledger balances and collect journal entries for even the first account, 101, we would have to proceed all the way through the journal list. Where would we save the transactions for account 101 as we collect them during this complete pass through the journal?

A much better solution is to begin by collecting all the journal transactions that relate to a given account. This involves sorting the journal transactions by account number, producing a list ordered as in Fig. 8.9.

Now we can create our output list by working through both the ledger and the sorted journal *cosequentially*, meaning that we process the two lists sequentially and in parallel. This concept is illustrated in Fig. 8.10. As we start working through the two lists, we note that we have an initial match on account number. We know that multiple entries are possible in the journal file but not in the ledger, so we move ahead to the next entry in the

Acct. No	Check No.	Date	Description	Debit/ credit
101	1271	04/02/86	Auto expense	-78.70
101	1272	04/02/97	Rent	-500.00
101	1273	04/04/97	Advertising	-87.50
101	1274	04/02/97	Auto expense	-31.83
102	670	04/02/97	Office expense	-32.78
505	1273	04/04/97	Newspaper ad re: new product	87.50
510	1271	04/02/97	Tune-up and minor repair	78.70
510	1274	04/09/97	Oil change	31.83
540	670	04/02/97	Printer cartridge	32.78
550	1272	04/02/97	Rent for April	500.00

Figure 8.9 List of journal transactions sorted by account number.

journal. The account numbers still match. We continue doing this until the account numbers no longer match. We then *resynchronize* the cosequential action by moving ahead in the ledger list. This process is often referred to as a *master-transaction process*. In this case the ledger entry is the master record and the journal entry is the transaction entry.

This matching process seems simple, as in fact it is, as long as every account in one file also appears in another. But there will be ledger accounts for which there is no journal entry, and there can be typographical errors that create journal account numbers that do not exist in the ledger. Such situations can make resynchronization more complicated and can result in erroneous output or infinite loops if the programming is done in an ad hoc way. By using the cosequential processing model, we can guard against these problems. Let us now apply the model to our ledger problem.

8.2.2 Application of the Model to the Ledger Program

The monthly ledger posting program must perform two tasks:

- It needs to update the ledger file with the correct balance for each account for the current month.

- It must produce a printed version of the ledger that not only shows the beginning and current balance for each account but also lists all the journal transactions for the month.

Ledger List		Journal List		
101	Checking account #1	101	1271	Auto expense
		101	1272	Rent
		101	1273	Advertising
		101	1274	Auto expense
102	Checking account #2	102	670	Office expense
505	Advertising expense	505	1273	Newspaper ad re: new product
510	Auto expenses	510	1271	Tune-up and minor repair
		510	1274	Oil change

Figure 8.10 Conceptual view of cosequential matching of the ledger and journal files.

We focus on the second task as it is the more difficult. Let's look again at the form of the printed output, this time extending the output to include a few more accounts as shown in Fig. 8.11. As you can see, the printed output from the monthly ledger posting program shows the balances of all ledger accounts, whether or not there were transactions for the account. From the point of view of the ledger accounts, the process is a *merge*, since even unmatched ledger accounts appear in the output.

What about unmatched journal accounts? The ledger accounts and journal accounts are not equal in authority. The ledger file *defines* the set of legal accounts; the journal file contains entries that are to be *posted* to the accounts listed in the ledger. The existence of a journal account that does not match a ledger account indicates an error. From the point of view of the journal accounts, the posting process is strictly one of *matching*. Our post method needs to implement a kind of combined merging/ matching algorithm while simultaneously handling the chores of printing account title lines, individual transactions, and summary balances.

```
101    Checking account #1
       1271    04/02/86      Auto expense                            -78.70
       1272    04/02/97      Rent                                   -500.00
       1274    04/02/97      Auto expense                            -31.83
       1273    04/04/97      Advertising                             -87.50
               Prev. bal:   5219.23  New bal:     4521.20
102    Checking account #2
        670    04/02/97      Office expense                          -32.78
               Prev. bal:   1321.20  New bal:     1288.42
505    Advertising expense
       1273    04/04/97      Newspaper ad re: new product             87.50
               Prev. bal:     25.00  New bal:      112.50
510    Auto expenses
       1271    04/02/97      Tune-up and minor repair                 78.70
       1274    04/09/97      Oil change                               31.83
               Prev. bal:    501.12  New bal:      611.65
515    Bank charges
               Prev. bal:      0.00  New bal:        0.00
520    Books and publications
               Prev. bal:     87.40  New bal:       87.40
```

Figure 8.11 Sample ledger printout for the first six accounts.

In summary, there are three different steps in processing the ledger entries:

1. Immediately after reading a new ledger object, we need to print the header line and initialize the balance for the next month from the previous month's balance.

2. For each transaction object that matches, we need to update the account balance.

3. After the last transaction for the account, the balance line should be printed. This is the place where a new ledger record could be written to create a new ledger file.

This posting operation is encapsulated by defining subclass `MasterTransactionProcess` of `CosequentialProcess` and defining three new pure virtual methods, one for each of the steps in processing ledger entries. Then we can give the full implementation of the posting operation as a method of this class. Figure 8.12 shows the definition of this class. Figure 8.13 has the code for the three-way-test loop of method `PostTransactions`. The new methods of the class are used for processing the master records (in this case the ledger entries). The transaction records (journal entries) can be processed by the `ProcessItem` method that is in the base class.

The reasoning behind the three-way test is as follows:

1. If the ledger (master) account number (`Item[1]`) is less than the journal (transaction) account number (`Item[2]`), then there are no more transactions to add to the ledger account this month (perhaps there were none at all), so we print the ledger account balances (`ProcessEndMaster`) and read in the next ledger account (`NextItemInList(1)`). If the account exists (`MoreMasters` is true), we print the title line for the new account (`ProcessNewMaster`).

2. If the account numbers match, then we have a journal transaction that is to be posted to the current ledger account. We add the transaction amount to the account balance for the new month (`ProcessCurrentMaster`), print the description of the transaction (`ProcessItem(2)`), then read the next journal entry (`NextItemInList(1)`). Note that unlike the match case in either the matching or merging algorithms, we do not read a new entry from both accounts. This is a reflection of our acceptance of more than one journal entry for a single ledger account.

```
template <class ItemType>
class MasterTransactionProcess:
   public CosequentialProcess<ItemType>
// a cosequential process that supports
// master/transaction processing
{public:
   MasterTransactionProcess ();//constructor
   virtual int ProcessNewMaster ()=0;
      // processing when new master read
   virtual int ProcessCurrentMaster ()=0;
      // processing for each transaction for a master
   virtual int ProcessEndMaster ()=0;
      // processing after all transactions for a master
   virtual int ProcessTransactionError ()=0;
      // no master for transaction

   // cosequential processing of master and transaction records
   int PostTransactions (char * MasterFileName,
      char * TransactionFileName, char * OutputListName);
};
```

Figure 8.12 Class MasterTransactionProcess.

```
   while (MoreMasters || MoreTransactions)
      if (Item(1) < Item(2)){// finish this master record
         ProcessEndMaster();
         MoreMasters = NextItemInList(1);
         if (MoreMasters) ProcessNewMaster();
      }
      else if (Item(1) == Item(2)){ // transaction matches master
         ProcessCurrentMaster(); // another transaction for master
         ProcessItem (2);// output transaction record
         MoreTransactions = NextItemInList(2);
      }
      else { // Item(1) > Item(2) transaction with no master
         ProcessTransactionError();
         MoreTransactions = NextItemInList(2);
      }
```

Figure 8.13 Three-way-test loop for method PostTransactions of class
MasterTransactionProcess.

3. If the journal account is less than the ledger account, then it is an unmatched journal account, perhaps due to an input error. We print an error message (`ProcessTransactionError`) and continue with the next transaction.

In order to complete our implementation of the ledger posting application, we need to create a subclass `LedgerProcess` that includes implementation of the `NextItemInList`, `Item`, and `ProcessItem` methods and the methods for the three steps of master record processing. This new class is given in files `ledgpost.h` and `ledgpost.cpp` of Appendix H. The master processing methods are all very simple, as shown in Fig. 8.14.

The remainder of the code for the ledger posting program, including the simple main program, is given in files `ledger.h`, `ledger.cpp`, and `post.cpp` in Appendix H. This includes the `ostream` formatting that produced Figs. 8.8 and 8.11. The classes `Ledger` and `Journal` make extensive use of the `IOBuffer` and `RecordFile` classes for their file operations.

The development of this ledger posting procedure from our basic cosequential processing model illustrates how the simplicity of the model contributes to its adaptability. We can also generalize the model in an entirely different direction, extending it to enable cosequential processing

```
int LedgerProcess::ProcessNewMaster ()
{// print the header and setup last month's balance
   ledger.PrintHeader(OutputList);
   ledger.Balances[MonthNumber] = ledger.Balances[MonthNumber-1];
}


int LedgerProcess::ProcessCurrentMaster ()
{// add the transaction amount to the balance for this month
   ledger.Balances[MonthNumber] += journal.Amount;
}

int LedgerProcess::ProcessEndMaster ()
{// print the balances line to output
   PrintBalances(OutputList,
      ledger.Balances[MonthNumber-1],ledger.Balances[MonthNumber]);
}
```

Figure 8.14 Master record processing for ledger objects.

of more than two input files at once. To illustrate this, we now extend the model to include multiway merging.

8.3 Extension of the Model to Include Multiway Merging

The most common application of cosequential processes requiring more than two input files is a *K-way merge,* in which we want to merge *K* input lists to create a single, sequentially ordered output list. *K* is often referred to as the *order* of a *K*-way merge.

8.3.1 A *K*-way Merge Algorithm

Recall the synchronizing loop we use to handle a two-way merge of two lists of names. This merging operation can be viewed as a process of deciding which of two input items has the *minimum* value, outputting that item, then moving ahead in the list from which that item is taken. In the event of duplicate input items, we move ahead in each list.

Suppose we keep an array of lists and array of the items (or keys) that are being used from each list in the cosequential process:

```
list[0], list[1], list[2],... list[k-1]
Item[0], Item[1], Item[3],... Item[k-1]
```

The main loop for the merge processing requires a call to a *MinIndex* function to find the index of item with the minimum collating sequence value and an inner loop that finds all lists that are using that item:

```
int minItem = MinIndex(Item,k); // find an index of minimum item
ProcessItem(minItem); // Item(minItem) is the next output
for (i = 0; i<k; i++) // look at each list
   if (Item(minItem) == Item(i)) // advance list i
      MoreItems[i] = NextItemInList(i);
```

Clearly, the expensive parts of this procedure are finding the minimum and testing to see in which lists the item occurs and which files therefore need to be read. Note that because the item can occur in several lists, every one of these *if* tests must be executed on every cycle through the loop. However, it is often possible to guarantee that a single item, or key, occurs in only one list. In this case, the procedure becomes simpler and more efficient.

```
int minI = minIndex(Item,k); // find index of minimum item
ProcessItem(minI); // Item[minI] is the next output
MoreItems[minI]=NextItemInList(minI);
```

The resulting merge procedure clearly differs in many ways from our initial three-way-test, single-loop merge for two lists. But, even so, the single-loop parentage is still evident: there is no looping within a list. We determine which lists have the key with the lowest value, output that key, move ahead one key in each of those lists, and loop again. The procedure is as simple as it is powerful.

8.3.2 A Selection Tree for Merging Large Numbers of Lists

The K-way merge described earlier works nicely if K is no larger than 8 or so. When we begin merging a larger number of lists, the set of sequential comparisons to find the key with the minimum value becomes noticeably expensive. We see later that for practical reasons it is rare to want to merge more than eight files at one time, so the use of sequential comparisons is normally a good strategy. If there is a need to merge considerably more than eight lists, we could replace the loop of comparisons with a *selection tree.*

The use of a selection tree is an example of the classic time-versus-space trade-off we so often encounter in computer science. We reduce the time required to find the key with the lowest value by using a data structure to save information about the relative key values across cycles of the procedure's main loop. The concept underlying a selection tree can be readily communicated through a diagram such as that in Fig. 8.15. Here we have used lists in which the keys are numbers rather than strings.

The selection tree is a kind of *tournament* tree in which each higher-level node represents the "winner" (in this case the *minimum* key value) of the comparison between the two descendent keys. The minimum value is always at the root node of the tree. If each key has an associated reference to the list from which it came, it is a simple matter to take the key at the root, read the next element from the associated list, then run the tournament again. Since the tournament tree is a binary tree, its depth is

$$\lceil \log_2 K \rceil$$

for a merge of K lists. The number of comparisons required to establish a new tournament winner is, of course, related to this depth rather than being a linear function of K.

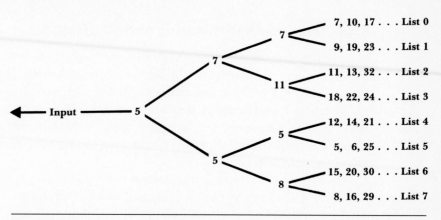

Figure 8.15 Use of a selection tree to assist in the selection of a key with minimum value in a *K*-way merge.

8.4   A Second Look at Sorting in Memory

In Chapter 6 we considered the problem of sorting a disk file that is small enough to fit in memory. The operation we described involves three separate steps:

1.   Read the entire file from disk into memory.
2.   Sort the records using a standard sorting procedure, such as shellsort.
3.   Write the file back to disk.

The total time taken to sort the file is the sum of the times for the three steps. We see that this procedure is much faster than sorting the file in place, on the disk, because both reading and writing are sequential and each record is read once and written once.

Can we improve on the time that it takes for this memory sort? If we assume that we are reading and writing the file as efficiently as possible and we have chosen the best internal sorting routine available, it would seem not. Fortunately, there is one way that we might speed up an algorithm that has several parts, and that is to perform some of those parts in parallel.

Of the three operations involved in sorting a file that is small enough to fit into memory, is there any way to perform some of them in parallel? If we have only one disk drive, clearly we cannot overlap the reading and writing operations, but how about doing either the reading or writing (or both) at the same time that we sort the file?

8.4.1 Overlapping Processing and I/O: Heapsort

Most of the time when we use an internal sort, we have to wait until we have the whole file in memory before we can start sorting. Is there an internal sorting algorithm that is reasonably fast and that can begin sorting numbers immediately as they are read rather than waiting for the whole file to be in memory? In fact there is, and we have already seen part of it in this chapter. It is called *heapsort,* and it is loosely based on the same principle as the selection tree.

Recall that the selection tree compares keys as it encounters them. Each time a new key arrives, it is compared with the others; and if it is the smallest key, it goes to the root of the tree. This is very useful for our purposes because it means that we can begin sorting keys as they arrive in memory rather than waiting until the entire file is loaded before we start sorting. That is, sorting can occur in parallel with reading.

Unfortunately, in the case of the selection tree, each time a new smallest key is found, it is output to the file. We cannot allow this to happen if we want to sort the whole file because we cannot begin outputting records until we know which one comes first, second, and so on, and we won't know this until we have seen all of the keys.

Heapsort solves this problem by keeping all of the keys in a structure called a *heap.* A heap is a binary tree with the following properties:

1. Each node has a single key, and that key is greater than or equal to the key at its parent node.

2. It is a *complete* binary tree, which means that all of its leaves are on no more than two levels and that all of the keys on the lower level are in the leftmost position.

3. Because of properties 1 and 2, storage for the tree can be allocated sequentially as an array in such a way that the root node is index 1 and the indexes of the left and right children of node i are 2i and 2i + 1, respectively. Conversely, the index of the parent of node j is $\lfloor j/2 \rfloor$.

Figure 8.16 shows a heap in both its tree form and as it would be stored in an array. Note that this is only one of many possible heaps for the given set of keys. In practice, each key has an associated record that is either stored in the array with the key or pointed to by a pointer stored with the key.

Property 3 is very useful for our purposes because it means that a heap is just an array of keys in which the positions of the keys in the array are sufficient to impose an ordering on the entire set of keys. There is no need

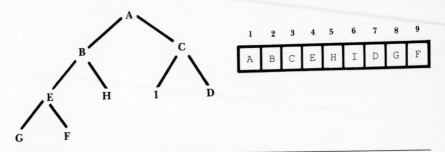

Figure 8.16 A heap in both its tree form and as it would be stored in an array.

for pointers or other dynamic data structuring overhead to create and maintain the heap. (As we pointed out earlier, there may be pointers associating each key with its corresponding record, but this has nothing to do with maintaining the heap.)

8.4.2 Building the Heap While Reading the File

The algorithm for heapsort has two parts. First we build the heap; then we output the keys in sorted order. The first stage can occur at virtually the same time that we read the data, so in terms of elapsed time it comes essentially free. The main members of a simple class `Heap` and its `Insert` method that adds a string to the heap is shown in Fig. 8.17. A full implementation of this class and a test program are in file `heapsort.cpp` in Appendix H. Figure 8.18 contains a sample application of this algorithm.

This shows how to build the heap, but it doesn't tell how to make the input overlap with the heap-building procedure. To solve that problem, we need to look at how we perform the read operation. For starters, we are not going to do a seek every time we want a new record. Instead, we read a block of records at a time into an input buffer and then operate on all of the records in the block before going on to the next block. In terms of memory storage, the input buffer for each new block of keys can be part of the memory area that is set up for the heap. Each time we read a new block, we just append it to the end of the heap (that is, the input buffer "moves" as the heap gets larger). The first new record is then at the end of the heap array, as required by the `Insert` function (Fig. 8.17). Once that record is absorbed into the heap, the next new record is at the end of the heap array, ready to be absorbed into the heap, and so forth.

```
class Heap
{public:
   Heap(int maxElements);
   int Insert (char * newKey);
   char * Remove();
protected:
   int MaxElements; int NumElements;
   char ** HeapArray;
   void Exchange(int i, int j); // exchange element i and j
   int Compare (int i, int j) // compare element i and j
      {return strcmp(HeapArray[i],HeapArray[j]);}
};
int Heap::Insert(char * newKey)
{
   if (NumElements == MaxElements) return FALSE;
   NumElements++; // add the new key at the last position
   HeapArray[NumElements] = newKey;
   // re-order the heap
   int k = NumElements; int parent;
   while (k > 1) // k has a parent
   {
      parent = k / 2;
      if (Compare(k, parent) >= 0) break;
         // HeapArray[k] is in the right place
      // else exchange k and parent
      Exchange(k, parent);
      k = parent;
   }
   return TRUE;
}
```

Figure 8.17 Class Heap and method Insert.

Use of an input buffer avoids an excessive number of seeks, but it still doesn't let input occur at the same time that we build the heap. We saw in Chapter 3 that the way to make processing overlap with I/O is to use more than one buffer. With multiple buffering, as we process the keys in one block from the file, we can simultaneously read later blocks from the file. If we use multiple buffers, how many should we use, and where should we put them? We already answered these questions when we decided to put each new block at the end of the array. Each time we

FDCGHIBEA

New key to be inserted	Heap, after insertion of the new key	Selected heaps in tree form
F	1 2 3 4 5 6 7 8 9 F	
D	1 2 3 4 5 6 7 8 9 D F	
C	1 2 3 4 5 6 7 8 9 C F D	
G	1 2 3 4 5 6 7 8 9 C F D G	
H	1 2 3 4 5 6 7 8 9 C F D G H	
I	1 2 3 4 5 6 7 8 9 C F D G H I	
B	1 2 3 4 5 6 7 8 9 B F C G H I D	
E	1 2 3 4 5 6 7 8 9 B E C F H I D G	
A	1 2 3 4 5 6 7 8 9 A B C E H I D G F	

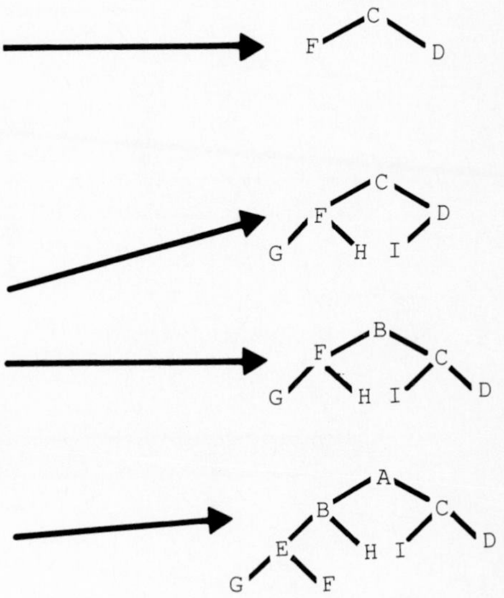

Figure 8.18 Sample application of the heap-building algorithm. The keys F, D, C, G, H, I, B, E, and A are added to the heap in the order shown.

add a new block, the array gets bigger by the size of that block, in effect creating a new input buffer for each block in the file. So the number of buffers is the number of blocks in the file, and they are located in sequence in the array.

Figure 8.19 illustrates the technique that we have just described, in which we append each new block of records to the end of the heap, thereby employing a memory-sized set of input buffers. Now we read new blocks as fast as we can, never having to wait for processing before reading a new block. On the other hand, processing (heap building) cannot occur on a given block until the block to be processed is read, so there *may* be some delay in processing if processing speeds are faster than reading speeds.

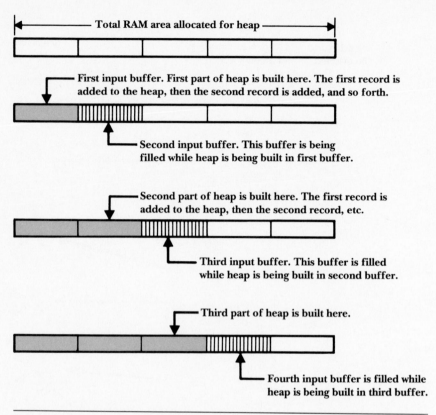

Figure 8.19 Illustration of the technique described in the text for overlapping input with heap building in memory. First read in a block into the first part of memory. The first record is the first record in the heap. Then extend the heap to include the second record, and incorporate that record into the heap, and so forth. While the first block is being processed, read in the second block. When the first block is a heap, extend it to include the first record in the second block, incorporate that record into the heap, and go on to the next record. Continue until all blocks are read in and the heap is completed.

8.4.3 Sorting While Writing to the File

The second and final step involves writing the heap in sorted order. Again, it is possible to overlap I/O (in this case writing) with processing. First, let's look at how to output the sorted keys. Retrieving the keys in order is simply a repetition of the following steps:

1. Determine the value of the key in the first position of the heap. This is the smallest value in the heap.

2. Move the largest value in the heap into the first position, and decrease the number of elements by one. The heap is now out of order at its root.

3. Reorder the heap by exchanging the largest element with the smaller of its children and moving down the tree to the new position of the largest element until the heap is back in order.

Each time these three steps are executed, the smallest value is retrieved and removed from the heap. Figure 8.20 contains the code for method `Remove` that implements these steps. Method `Compare` simply compares two heap elements and returns −1 if the left element is smaller.

Again, there is nothing inherent in this algorithm that lets it overlap with I/O, but we can take advantage of certain features of the algorithm to

```
char * Heap::Remove()
{// remove the smallest element, reorder the heap,
 // and return the smallest element
    // put the smallest value into 'val' for use in return
    char * val = HeapArray[1];

    // put largest value into root
    HeapArray[1] = HeapArray[NumElements];
    // decrease the number of elements
    NumElements−;

    // reorder the heap by exchanging and moving down
        int k = 1; // node of heap that contains the largest value
        int newK; // node to exchange with largest value
        while (2*k <= NumElements)// k has at least one child
        {    // set newK to the index of smallest child of k
            if (Compare(2*k, 2*k+1)<0) newK = 2*k;
            else newK = 2*k+1;
            // done if k and newK are in order
            if (Compare(k, newK) < 0) break; //in order
            Exchange(k, newK); // k and newK out of order
            k = newK; // continue down the tree
        }
        return val;
}
```

Figure 8.20 MethodRemove of class Heap removes the smallest element and reorders the heap.

make overlapping happen. First, we see that we know immediately which record will be written first in the sorted file; next, we know what will come second; and so forth. So as soon as we have identified a block of records, we can write that block, and while we are writing that block, we can identify the next block, and so forth.

Furthermore, each time we identify a block to write, we make the heap smaller by exactly the size of a block, freeing that space for a new output buffer. So just as was the case when building the heap, we can have as many output buffers as there are blocks in the file. Again, a little coordination is required between processing and output, but the conditions exist for the two to overlap almost completely.

A final point worth making about this algorithm is that all I/O it performs is essentially sequential. All records are read in the order in which they occur in the file to be sorted, and all records are written in sorted order. The technique could work equally well if the file were kept on tape or disk. More important, since all I/O is sequential, we know that it can be done with a minimum amount of seeking.

8.5 Merging as a Way of Sorting Large Files on Disk

In Chapter 6 we ran into problems when we needed to sort files that were too large to be wholly contained in memory. The chapter offered a partial, but ultimately unsatisfactory, solution to this problem in the form of a *keysort*, in which we needed to hold only the keys in memory, along with pointers to each key's corresponding record. Keysort had two shortcomings:

1. Once the keys were sorted, we then had to bear the substantial cost of seeking to each record in sorted order, reading each record in and then writing it into the new, sorted file.

2. With keysorting, the size of the file that can be sorted is limited by the number of key/pointer pairs that can be contained in memory. Consequently, we still cannot sort really large files.

As an example of the kind of file we cannot sort with either a memory sort or a keysort, suppose we have a file with 8 000 000 records, each of which is 100 bytes long and contains a key field that is 10 bytes long. The total length of this file is about 800 megabytes. Let us further suppose that we have 10 megabytes of memory available as a work area, not counting memory used to hold the program, operating system, I/O buffers, and so forth. Clearly, we cannot sort the whole file in memory. We cannot even sort all the keys in memory, because it would require 80 megabytes.

The multiway merge algorithm discussed in Section 8.3 provides the beginning of an attractive solution to the problem of sorting large files such as this one. Since memory-sorting algorithms such as heapsort can work in place, using only a small amount of overhead for maintaining pointers and some temporary variables, we can create a sorted subset of our full file by reading records into memory until the memory work area is almost full, sorting the records in this work area, then writing the sorted records back to disk as a sorted subfile. We call such a sorted subfile a *run*. Given the memory constraints and record size in our example, a run could contain approximately

$$\frac{10\ 000\ 000\ \text{bytes of memory}}{100\ \text{bytes per record}} = 100\ 000\ \text{records}$$

Once we create the first run, we then read a new set of records, once again filling memory, and create another run of 100 000 records. In our example, we repeat this process until we have created eighty runs, with each run containing 100 000 sorted records.

Once we have the eighty runs in eighty separate files on disk, we can perform an eighty-way merge of these runs, using the multiway merge logic outlined in Section 8.3, to create a completely sorted file containing all the original records. A schematic view of this run creation and merging process is provided in Fig. 8.21.

This solution to our sorting problem has the following features:

- It can, in fact, sort large files and can be extended to files of any size.

- Reading of the input file during the run-creation step is sequential and hence is much faster than input that requires seeking for every record individually (as in a keysort).

- Reading through each run during merging and writing the sorted records is also sequential. Random accesses are required only as we switch from run to run during the merge operation.

- If a heapsort is used for the in-memory part of the merge, as described in Section 8.4, we can overlap these operations with I/O so the in-memory part does not add appreciably to the total time for the merge.

- Since I/O is largely sequential, tapes can be used if necessary for both input and output operations.

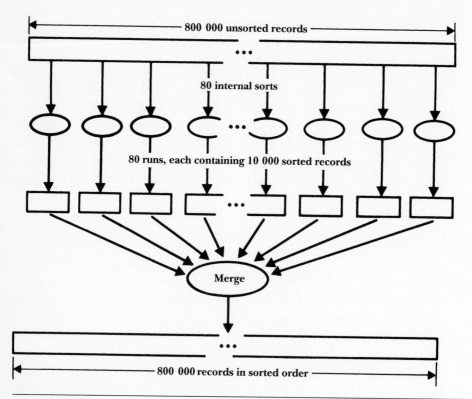

Figure 8.21 Sorting through the creation of runs (sorted subfiles) and subsequent merging of runs.

8.5.1 How Much Time Does a Merge Sort Take?

This general approach to the problem of sorting large files looks promising. To compare this approach with others, we now look at how much time it takes. We do this by taking our 8 million record files and seeing how long it takes to do a merge sort on the Seagate Cheetah 9 disk drive whose specifications are listed in Table 3.1. You might recall that this was the fastest disk available for PCs in early 1997. Please note that our intention here is not to derive time estimates that mean anything in any environment other than the hypothetical environment we have posited. Nor do we want to overwhelm you with numbers or provide you with magic formulas for determining how long a particular sort on a real system will *really* take. Rather, our goal in this section is to derive some benchmarks that we can use to compare several variations on the basic merge sort approach to sorting external files.

We can simplify matters by making the following simplifying assumptions about the computing environment:

■ Entire files are always stored in contiguous areas on disk (extents), and a single cylinder-to-cylinder seek takes no time. Hence, *only one seek is required for any single sequential access.*

■ Extents that span more than one track are physically staggered in such a way that *only one rotational delay is required per access.*

We see in Fig. 8.21 that there are four times when I/O is performed. During the sort phase:

■ Reading all records into memory for sorting and forming runs, and
■ Writing sorted runs to disk.

During the merge phase:

■ Reading sorted runs into memory for merging, and
■ Writing sorted file to disk.

Let's look at each of these in order.

Step 1: Reading Records into Memory for Sorting and Forming Runs

Since we sort the file in 10-megabyte chunks, we read 10 megabytes at a time from the file. In a sense, memory is a 10-megabyte input buffer that we fill up eighty times to form the eighty runs. In computing the total time to input each run, we need to include the amount of time it takes to *access* each block (seek time + rotational delay), plus the amount of time it takes to *transfer* each block. We keep these two times separate because, as we see later in our calculations, the role that each plays can vary significantly depending on the approach used.

From Table 3.1 we see that seek and rotational delay times are 8 msec[1] and 3 msec, respectively, so total time per seek is 11 msec.[2] The transmission rate is approximately 14 500 bytes per msec. Total input time for the sort phase consists of the time required for 80 seeks, plus the time required to transfer 800 megabytes:

---

1. Unless the computing environment has many active users pulling the read/write head to other parts of the disk, seek time is likely to be less than the average, since many of the blocks that make up the file are probably going to be physically adjacent to one another on the disk. Many will be on the same cylinder, requiring no seeks at all. However, for simplicity we assume the average seek time.

2. For simplicity, we use the term *seek* even though we really mean *seek and rotational delay*. Hence, the time we give for a seek is the time that it takes to perform an average seek followed by an average rotational delay.

$$\begin{array}{llr}
\text{Access}: & 80 \text{ seeks} \times 11 \text{ msec} = & 1 \text{ sec} \\
\text{Transfer}: & 800 \text{ megabytes @ } 14\,500 \text{ bytes/msec} = & 60 \text{ sec} \\
\hline
\text{Total}: & & 61 \text{ sec}
\end{array}$$

Step 2: Writing Sorted Runs to Disk

In this case, writing is just the reverse of reading—the same number of seeks and the same amount of data to transfer. So it takes another 61 seconds to write the 80 sorted runs.

Step 3: Reading Sorted Runs into Memory for Merging

Since we have 10 megabytes of memory for storing runs, we divide 10 megabytes into 80 parts for buffering the 80 runs. In a sense, we are real-locating our 10 megabytes of memory as 80 input buffers. Each of the 80 buffers then holds 1/80th of a run (125 000 bytes), so we have to access *each* run 80 times to read all of it. Because there are 80 runs, in order to complete the merge operation (Fig. 8.22) we end up making

$$80 \text{ runs} \times 80 \text{ seeks} = 6400 \text{ seeks}.$$

Total seek and rotation time is then 6400×11 msec = 70 seconds. Since 800 megabytes is still transferred, transfer time is still 60 seconds.

Step 4: Writing Sorted File to Disk

To compute the time for writing the file, we need to know how big our output buffers are. Unlike steps 1 and 2, where our big memory sorting

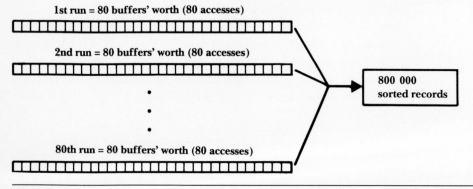

Figure 8.22 Effect of buffering on the number of seeks required, where each run is as large as the available work area in memory.

space doubled as our I/O buffer, we are now using that memory space for storing the data from the runs *before* it is merged. To keep matters simple, let us assume that we can allocate two 200 000-byte output buffers.[3] With 200 000-byte buffers, we need to make

$$\frac{800\ 000\ 000}{200\ 000\ \text{bytes per seek}} = 4000\ \text{seeks.}$$

Total seek and rotation time is then 4000×11 msec $= 44$ seconds. Transfer time is still 60 seconds.

The time estimates for the four steps are summarized in the first row in Table 8.1. The total time for this merge sort is 356 seconds, or 5 minutes, 56 seconds. The sort phase takes 122 seconds, and the merge phase takes 234 seconds.

To gain an appreciation of the improvement that this merge sort approach provides us, we need only look at how long it would take us to do one part of a nonmerging method like the keysort method described in Chapter 6. The last part of the keysort algorithm (Fig. 6.16) consists of this for loop:

```
// write new file in key order
for (int j = 0; j < inFile . NumRecs(); j++)
{
   inFile . ReadByRRN (obj, Keys[j] . RRN);// read in key order
   outFile . Append (obj);// write in key order
}
```

---

3. We use two buffers to allow double buffering; we use 20 000 bytes per buffer because that is approximately the size of a track on our hypothetical disk drive.

Table 8.1 Time estimates for merge sort of 80-megabyte file, assuming use of the Seagate Cheetah 9 disk drive described in Table 3.1. The total time for the sort phase (steps 1 and 2) is 14 seconds, and the total time for the merge phase is 126 seconds.

	Number of seeks	Amount transferred (megabytes)	Seek + rotation time (seconds)	Transfer time (seconds)	Total time (seconds)
Sort: reading	800	800	1	60	61
Sort: writing	800	800	1	60	61
Merge: reading	6400	800	70	60	130
Merge: writing	4000	800	44	60	104
Totals	10 560	3200	116	240	356

This *for* loop requires us to do a separate seek for every record in the file. That is 8 000 000 seeks. At 11 msec per seek, the total time required to perform that one operation works out to 88 000 seconds, or 24 hours, 26 minutes, 40 seconds!

Clearly, for large files the merge sort approach in general is the best option of any that we have seen. Does this mean that we have found the best technique for sorting large files? If sorting is a relatively rare event and files are not too large, the particular approach to merge sorting that we have just looked at produces acceptable results. Let's see how those results stand up as we change some of the parameters of our sorting example.

8.5.2 Sorting a File That Is Ten Times Larger

The first question that comes to mind when we ask about the general applicability of a computing technique is: What happens when we make the problem bigger? In this instance, we need to ask how this approach stands up as we scale up the size of the file.

Before we look at how a bigger file affects the performance of our merge sort, it will help to examine the *kinds* of I/O that are being done in the two different phases—the sort phase and the merge phase. We will see that for the purposes of finding ways to improve on our original approach, we need pay attention only to one of the two phases.

A major difference between the sort phase and the merge phase is in the amount of sequential (versus random) access that each performs. By using heapsort to create runs during the sort phase, we guarantee that all I/O is, in a sense, sequential.[4] Since sequential access implies minimal seeking, we cannot *algorithmically* speed up I/O during the sort phase. No matter what we do with the records in the file, we have to read them and write them all at least once. Since we cannot improve on this phase by changing the way we do the sort or merge, we ignore the sort phase in the analysis that follows.

The merge phase is a different matter. In particular, the *reading step* of the merge phase is different. Since there is a memory buffer for each run, and these buffers get loaded and reloaded at unpredictable times, the read step of the merge phase is, to a large extent, one in which random accesses

---

4. It is *not* sequential in the sense that in a multiuser environment there will be other users pulling the read/write head to other parts of the disk between reads and writes, possibly forcing the disk to do a seek each time it reads or writes a block.

are the norm. Furthermore, the number and size of the memory buffers that we read the run data into determine the number of times we have to do random accesses. If we can somehow reconfigure these buffers in ways that reduce the number of random accesses, we can speed up I/O correspondingly. So, if we are going to look for ways to improve performance in a merge sort algorithm, *our best hope is to look for ways to cut down on the number of random accesses that occur while reading runs during the merge phase.*

What about the write step of the merge phase? Like the steps of the sort phase, this step is not influenced by differences in the way we organize runs. Improvements in the way we organize the merge sort do not affect this step. On the other hand, we will see later that it is helpful to include this phase when we measure the results of changes in the organization of the merge sort.

To sum up, since the merge phase is the only one in which we can improve performance by improving the method, we concentrate on it from now on. Now let's get back to the question that we started this section with: What happens when we make the problem bigger? How, for instance, is the time for the merge phase affected if our file is 80 million records rather than 8 million?

If we increase the size of our file by a factor of 10 without increasing the memory space, we clearly need to create more runs. Instead of 80 initial 100 000-record runs, we now have 800 runs. This means we have to do an 800-way merge in our 10 megabytes of memory space. This, in turn, means that during the merge phase we must divide memory into 800 buffers. Each of the 800 buffers holds 1/800th of a run, so we would end up making 800 seeks per run, and

$$800 \text{ runs} \times 800 \text{ seeks/run} = 640\,000 \text{ seeks altogether}$$

The times for the merge phase are summarized in Table 8.2. Note that the total time is more than 2 hours and 24 minutes, almost 25 times greater than for the 800-megabyte file. By increasing the size of our file, we have gotten ourselves back into the situation we had with keysort, in which we can't do the job we need to do without doing a huge amount of seeking. In this instance, by increasing the order of the merge from 80 to 800, we made it necessary to divide our 10-megabyte memory area into 800 tiny buffers for doing I/O; and because the buffers are tiny, each requires many seeks to process its corresponding run.

If we want to improve performance, clearly we need to look for ways to improve on the amount of time spent getting to the data during the merge phase. We will do this shortly, but first let us generalize what we have just observed.

Table 8.2 Time estimates for merge sort of 8000-megabyte file, assuming use of the Seagate Cheetah 9 disk drive described in Table 3.1. The total time for the merge phase is 7600 seconds, or 2 hours, 6 minutes, 40 seconds.

	Number of seeks	Amount transferred (megabytes)	Seek + rotation time (seconds)	Transfer time (seconds)	Total time (seconds)
Merge: reading	640 000	8000	7040	600	7640
Merge: writing	40 000	8000	440	600	1040
Totals	680 000	16 000	7480	1200	8680

8.5.3 The Cost of Increasing the File Size

Obviously, the big difference between the time it took to merge the 800-megabyte file and the 8000-megabyte file was due to the difference in total seek and rotational delay times. You probably noticed that the number of seeks for the larger file is 100 times the number of seeks for the first file, and 100 is the square of the difference in size between the two files. We can formalize this relationship as follows: in general, for a K-way merge of K runs where each run is as large as the memory space available, the buffer size for each of the runs is

$$\left(\frac{1}{K}\right) \times \text{size of memory space} = \left(\frac{1}{K}\right) \times \text{size of each run}$$

so K seeks are required to read all of the records in each individual run. Since there are K runs altogether, the merge operation requires K^2 seeks. Hence, measured in terms of seeks, our sort merge is an $O(K^2)$ operation. Because K is directly proportional to N (if we increase the number of records from 8 000 000 to 80 000 000, K increases from 80 to 800) it also follows that our sort merge is an $O(N^2)$ operation, measured in terms of seeks.

This brief, formal look establishes the principle that as files grow large, we can expect the time required for our merge sort to increase rapidly. It would be very nice if we could find some ways to reduce this time. Fortunately, there are several ways:

■ Allocate more hardware, such as disk drives, memory, and I/O channels;

- Perform the merge in more than one step, reducing the order of each merge and increasing the buffer size for each run;
- Algorithmically increase the lengths of the initial sorted runs; and
- Find ways to overlap I/O operations.

In the following sections we look at each of these ways in detail, beginning with the first: invest in more hardware.

8.5.4 Hardware-Based Improvements

We have seen that changes in our sorting algorithm can improve performance. Likewise, we can make changes in our hardware that will also improve performance. In this section we look at three possible changes to a system configuration that could lead to substantial decreases in sort time:

- Increasing the amount of memory,
- Increasing the number of disk drives, and
- Increasing the number of I/O channels.

Increasing the Amount of Memory

It should be clear now that when we have to divide limited buffer space into many small buffers, we increase seek and rotation times to the point where they overwhelm all other sorting operations. Roughly speaking, the increase in the number of seeks is proportional to the square of the increase in file size, given a fixed amount of total buffer space.

It stands to reason, then, that increasing memory space ought to have a substantial effect on total sorting time. A larger memory size means longer and fewer initial runs during the sort phase, and it means fewer seeks per run during the merge phase. The product of fewer runs and fewer seeks per run means a substantial reduction in total seeks.

Let's test this conclusion with our 80 000 000-record file, which took about 2 hours, 6 minutes using 10 megabytes of memory. Suppose we are able to obtain 40 megabytes of memory buffer space for our sort. Each of the initial runs would increase from 100 000 records to 400 000 records, resulting in two hundred 400 000-record runs. For the merge phase, the internal buffer space would be divided into 200 buffers, each capable of holding 1/200th of a run, meaning that there would be $200 \times 200 = 40\ 000$ seeks. Using the same time estimates that we used for the previous two cases, the total time for this merge is 16 minutes, 40 seconds, nearly a sevenfold improvement.

Increasing the Number of Dedicated Disk Drives

If we could have a separate read/write head for every run and no other users contending for use of the same read/write heads, there would be no delay due to seek time after the original runs are generated. The primary source of delay would now be rotational delays and transfers, which would occur every time a new block had to be read.

For example, if each run is on a separate, dedicated drive, our 800-way merge calls for only 800 seeks (one seek per run), down from 640 000, cutting the total seek and rotation times from 7040 seconds to 1 second. Of course, we can't configure 800 separate disk drives every time we want to do a sort, but perhaps something short of this is possible. For instance, if we had two disk drives to dedicate to the merge, we could assign one to input and the other to output, so reading and writing could overlap whenever they occurred simultaneously. (This approach takes some clever buffer management, however. We discuss this later in this chapter.)

Increasing the Number of I/O Channels

If there is only one I/O channel, no two transmissions can occur at the same time, and the total transmission time is the one we have computed. But if there is a separate I/O channel for each disk drive, I/O can overlap completely.

For example, if for our 800-way merge there are 800 channels from 800 disk drives, then transmissions can overlap completely. Practically speaking, it is unlikely that 800 channels and 800 disk drives are available, and even if they were, it is unlikely that all transmissions would overlap because all buffers would not need to be refilled at one time. Nevertheless, increasing the number of I/O channels could improve transmission time substantially.

So we see that there are ways to improve performance if we have some control over how our hardware is configured. In those environments in which external sorting occupies a large percentage of computing time, we are likely to have at least some such control. On the other hand, many times we are not able to expand a system specifically to meet sorting needs that we might have. When this is the case, we need to look for algorithmic ways to improve performance, and this is what we do now.

8.5.5 Decreasing the Number of Seeks Using Multiple-Step Merges

One of the hallmarks of a solution to a file structure problem, as opposed to the solution of a mere data structure problem, is the attention given to the enormous difference in cost between accessing information on disk and accessing information in memory. If our merging problem involved only memory operations, the relevant measure of work, or expense, would be the number of *comparisons* required to complete the merge. The *merge pattern* that would minimize the number of comparisons for our sample problem, in which we want to merge 800 runs, would be the 800-way merge considered. Looked at from a point of view that ignores the cost of seeking, this K-way merge has the following desirable characteristics:

- Each record is read only once.

- If a selection tree is used for the comparisons performed in the merging operation, as described in Section 8.3, then the number of comparisons required for a K-way merge of N records (total) is a function of $N \times \log_2 K$.

- Since K is directly proportional to N, this is an $O(N \times \log_2 N)$ operation (measured in numbers of comparisons), which is to say that it is reasonably efficient even as N grows large.

This would all be very good news were we working exclusively in memory, but the very purpose of this *merge sort* procedure is to be able to sort files that are too large to fit into memory. Given the task at hand, the costs associated with disk seeks are orders of magnitude greater than the costs of operations in memory. Consequently, if we can sacrifice the advantages of an 800-way merge and trade them for savings in access time, we may be able to obtain a net gain in performance.

We have seen that one of the keys to reducing seeks is to reduce the number of runs that we have to merge, thereby giving each run a bigger share of available buffer space. In the previous section we accomplished this by adding more memory. Multiple-step merging provides a way for us to apply the same principle without having to buy more memory.

In multiple-step merging, we do not try to merge all runs at one time. Instead, we break the original set of runs into small groups and merge the runs in these groups separately. On each of these smaller merges, more buffer space is available for each run; hence, fewer seeks are required per run. When all of the smaller merges are completed, a second pass merges the new set of merged runs.

It should be clear that this approach will lead to fewer seeks on the first pass, but now there is a second pass. Not only are a number of seeks required for reading and writing on the second pass, but extra transmission time is used in reading and writing all records in the file. Do the advantages of the two-pass approach outweigh these extra costs? Let's revisit the merge step of our 80 million record sort to find out.

Recall that we began with 800 runs of 100 000 records each. Rather than merging all 800 runs at once, we could merge them as, say, 25 sets of 32 runs each, followed by a 25-way merge of the intermediate runs. This scheme is illustrated in Fig. 8.23.

When compared with our original 800-way merge, this approach has the disadvantage of requiring that we read every record twice: once to form the intermediate runs and again to form the final sorted file. But, since each step of the merge is reading from 25 input files at a time, we are able to use larger buffers and avoid a large number of disk seeks. When we analyzed the seeking required for the 800-way merge, disregarding seeking for the output file, we calculated that the 800-way merge involved 640 000 seeks between the input files. Let's perform similar calculations for our multistep merge.

First Merge Step

For each of the 32-way merges of the initial runs, each input buffer can hold 1/32 run, so we end up making $32 \times 32 = 1024$ seeks. For all 25 of the

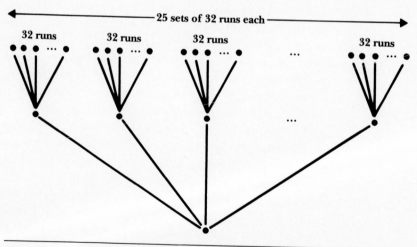

Figure 8.23 Two-step merge of 800 runs.

32-way merges, we make $25 \times 1024 = 25\ 600$ seeks. Each of the resulting runs is 3 200 000 records, or 320 megabytes.

Second Merge Step

For each of the 25 final runs, 1/25 of the total buffer space is allocated, so each input buffer can hold 4000 records, or 1/800 run. Hence, in this step there are 800 seeks per run, so we end up making $25 \times 800 = 20\ 000$ seeks, and

The total number of seeks for the two steps $= 25\ 600 + 20\ 000 = 45\ 600$

So, by accepting the cost of processing each record twice, we reduce the number of seeks for reading from 640 000 to 45 600, and we haven't spent a penny for extra memory.

But what about the *total* time for the merge? We save on access times for inputting data, but there are costs. We now have to transmit all of the records four times instead of two, so transmission time increases by 1200 seconds. Also, we write the records twice, rather than once, requiring an extra 40 000 seeks. When we add these extra operations, the total time for the merge is 3782 seconds, or about 1 hour, 3 minutes, compared with 2 hours, 25 minutes for the single-step merge. These results are summarized in Table 8.3.

Once more, note that the essence of what we have done is to find a way to increase the available buffer space for each run. We trade extra passes over the data for a dramatic decrease in random accesses. In this case the trade is certainly a profitable one.

Table 8.3 Time estimates for two-step merge sort of 8000-megabyte file, assuming use of the Seagate Cheetah 9 disk drive described in Table 3.1. The total time is 27 minutes.

	Number of seeks	Amount transferred (megabytes)	Seek + rotation time (seconds)	Transfer time (seconds)	Total time (seconds)
1st Merge: reading	25 600	8000	282	600	882
1st Merge: writing	40 000	8000	440	600	1040
2nd Merge: reading	20 000	8000	220	600	820
2nd Merge: writing	40 000	8000	440	600	1040
Totals	125 600	32 000	1382	2400	3782

If we can achieve such an improvement with a two-step merge, can we do even better with three steps? Perhaps, but it is important to note in Table 8.3 that we have reduced total seek and rotation times to the point where transmission times are more expensive. Since a three-step merge would require yet another pass over the file, we have reached a point of diminishing returns.

We also could have chosen to distribute our initial runs differently. How would the merge perform if we did 400 two-way merges, followed by one 400-way merge, for instance? A rigorous analysis of the trade-offs between seek and rotation time and transmission time, accounting for different buffer sizes, is beyond the scope of our treatment of the subject.[5] Our goal is simply to establish the importance of the interacting roles of the major costs in performing merge sorts: seek and rotation time, transmission time, buffer size, and number of runs. In the next section we focus on the pivotal role of the last of these—the number of runs.

8.5.6 Increasing Run Lengths Using Replacement Selection

What would happen if we could somehow increase the size of the initial runs? Consider, for example, our earlier sort of 80 000 000 records in which each record was 100 bytes. Our initial runs were limited to approximately 100 000 records because the memory work area was limited to 10 megabytes. Suppose we are somehow able to create runs of twice this length, containing 200 000 records each. Then, rather than needing to perform an 800-way merge, we need to do only a 400-way merge. The available memory is divided into 400 buffers, each holding 1/800th of a run. Hence, the number of seeks required per run is 800, and the total number of seeks is

$$800 \text{ seeks/run} \times 400 \text{ runs} = 320\,000 \text{ seeks},$$

half the number required for the 800-way merge of 100 000-byte runs.

In general, if we can somehow increase the size of the initial runs, we decrease the amount of work required during the merge step of the sorting process. A longer initial run means fewer total runs, which means a lower-order merge, which means bigger buffers, which means fewer seeks. But how, short of buying twice as much memory for the computer, can we create initial runs that are twice as large as the number of records that we

---

5. For more rigorous and detailed analyses of these issues, consult the references cited at the end of this chapter, especially Knuth (1998) and Salzberg (1988, 1990).

can hold in memory? The answer, once again, involves sacrificing some efficiency in our in-memory operations in return for decreasing the amount of work to be done on disk. In particular, the answer involves the use of an algorithm known as *replacement selection*.

Replacement selection is based on the idea of always *selecting* the key from memory that has the lowest value, outputting that key, and then *replacing* it with a new key from the input list. Replacement selection can be implemented as follows:

1. Read a collection of records and sort them using heapsort. This creates a heap of sorted values. Call this heap the *primary heap*.

2. Instead of writing the entire primary heap in sorted order (as we do in a normal heapsort), write only the record whose key has the lowest value.

3. Bring in a new record and compare the value of its key with that of the key that has just been output.

   a. If the new key value is higher, insert the new record into its proper place in the primary heap along with the other records that are being selected for output. (This makes the new record part of the run that is being created, which means that the run being formed will be larger than the number of keys that can be held in memory at one time.)

   b. If the new record's key value is lower, place the record in a *secondary heap* of records with key values lower than those already written. (It cannot be put into the primary heap because it cannot be included in the run that is being created.)

4. Repeat step 3 as long as there are records left in the primary heap and there are records to be read. When the primary heap is empty, make the secondary heap into the primary heap, and repeat steps 2 and 3.

To see how this works, let's begin with a simple example, using an input list of only six keys and a memory work area that can hold only three keys. As Fig. 8.24 illustrates, we begin by reading into memory the three keys that fit there and use heapsort to sort them. We select the key with the minimum value, which happens to be 5 in this example, and output that key. We now have room in the heap for another key, so we read one from the input list. The new key, which has a value of 12, now becomes a member of the set of keys to be sorted into the output run. In fact, because it is smaller than the other keys in memory, 12 is the next key that is output. A new key is read into its place, and the process continues. When

Input:
21, 67, 12, 5, 47, 16

└─ Front of input string

Remaining input	Memory ($P = 3$)			Output run					
21, 67, 12	5	47	16						–
21, 67	12	47	16						5
21	67	47	16					12,	5
–	67	47	21				16,	12,	5
–	67	47	–			21,	16,	12,	5
–	67	–	–		47,	21,	16,	12,	5
–	–	–	–	67,	47,	21,	16,	12,	5

Figure 8.24 Example of the principle underlying replacement selection.

the process is complete, it produces a sorted list of six keys while using only three memory locations.

In this example the entire file is created using only one heap, but what happens if the fourth key in the input list is 2 rather than 12? This key arrives in memory too late to be output into its proper position relative to the other keys: the 5 has already been written to the output list. Step 3b in the algorithm handles this case by placing such values in a second heap, to be included in the next run. Figure 8.25 illustrates how this process works. During the first run, when keys that are too small to be included in the primary heap are brought in, we mark them with parentheses, indicating that they have to be held for the second run.

It is interesting to use this example to compare the action of replacement selection to the procedure we have been using up to this point, namely that of reading keys into memory, sorting them, and outputting a run that is the size of the memory space. In this example our input list contains thirteen keys. A series of successive memory sorts, given only three memory locations, results in five runs. The replacement selection procedure results in only two runs. Since the disk accesses during a multiway merge can be a major expense, replacement selection's ability to create longer, and therefore fewer, runs can be an important advantage.

Two questions emerge at this point:

1. Given P locations in memory, how long a run can we expect replacement selection to produce, on the average?

2. What are the costs of using replacement selection?

Input:

33, 18, 24, 58, 14, 17, 7, 21, 67, 12, 5, 47, 16

└── **Front of input string**

Remaining input	Memory (P = 3)			Output run
33, 18, 24, 58, 14, 17, 7, 21, 67, 12	5	47	16	—
33, 18, 24, 58, 14, 17, 7, 21, 67	12	47	16	5
33, 18, 24, 58, 14, 17, 7, 21	67	47	16	12, 5
33, 18, 24, 58, 14, 17, 7	67	47	21	16, 12, 5
33, 18, 24, 58, 14, 17	67	47	(7)	21, 16, 12, 5
33, 18, 24, 58, 14	67	(17)	(7)	47, 21, 16, 12, 5
33, 18, 24, 58	(14)	(17)	(7)	67, 47, 21, 16, 12, 5

First run complete; start building the second

33, 18, 24, 58	14	17	7	—
33, 18, 24	14	17	58	7
33, 18	24	17	58	14, 7
33	24	18	58	17, 14, 7
—	24	33	58	18, 17, 14, 7
—	—	33	58	24, 18, 17, 14, 7
—	—	—	58	33, 24, 18, 17, 14, 7
—			—	58, 33, 24, 18, 17, 14, 7

Figure 8.25 Step-by-step operation of replacement selection working to form two sorted runs.

Average Run Length for Replacement Selection

The answer to the first question is that, on the average, we can expect a run length of $2P$, given P memory locations. Knuth[6] provides an excellent description of an intuitive argument for why this is so:

A clever way to show that $2P$ is indeed the expected run length was discovered by E. F. Moore, who compared the situation to a snowplow on a circular track [U.S. Patent 2983904 (1961), Cols. 3–4]. Consider the situation shown [page 336]; flakes of snow are falling uniformly on a circular road, and a lone snowplow is continually clearing the snow. Once the snow has been plowed off the road, it disappears from the system. Points on the road may be designated by real numbers x, $0 \le x < 1$; a flake of snow falling at position x represents an input record whose key is x,

---

6. From Donald Knuth, *The Art of Computer Programming*, vol. 3 1973, Addison-Wesley, Reading, Mass. Pages 254–55 and Figs. 64 and 65. Reprinted with permission.

and the snowplow represents the output of replacement selection. The ground speed of the snowplow is inversely proportional to the height of the snow that it encounters, and the situation is perfectly balanced so that the total amount of snow on the road at all times is exactly P. A new run is formed in the output whenever the plow passes point 0.

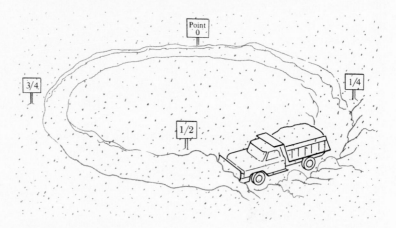

After this system has been in operation for a while, it is intuitively clear that it will approach a stable situation in which the snowplow runs at constant speed (because of the circular symmetry of the track). This means that the snow is at constant height when it meets the plow, and the height drops off linearly in front of the plow as shown [below]. It follows that the volume of snow removed in one revolution (namely the run length) is twice the amount present at any one time (namely P).

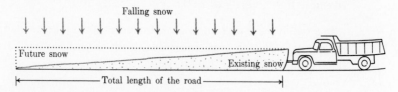

So, given a random ordering of keys, we can expect replacement selection to form runs that contain about twice as many records as we can hold in memory at one time. It follows that replacement selection creates half as many runs as a series of memory sorts of memory contents, assuming that the replacement selection and the memory sort have access to the same amount of memory. (As we see in a moment, the replacement selection does, in fact, have to make do with less memory than the memory sort.)

It is often possible to create runs that are substantially longer than $2P$. In many applications, the order of the records is *not* wholly random; the keys are often already partially in ascending order. In these cases replacement selection can produce runs that, on the average, exceed $2P$. (Consider what would happen if the input list is already sorted.) Replacement selection becomes an especially valuable tool for such partially ordered input files.

The Costs of Using Replacement Selection

Unfortunately, the no-free-lunch rule applies to replacement selection, as it does to so many other areas of file structure design. In the worked-by-hand examples we have looked at up to this point, we have been inputting records into memory one at a time. We know, in fact, that the cost of seeking for every single input record is prohibitive. Instead, we want to buffer the input, which means, in turn, that we are not able to use *all* of the memory for the operation of replacement selection. Some of it has to be used for input and output buffering. This cost, and the affect it has on available space for sorting, is illustrated in Fig. 8.26.

To see the effects of this need for buffering during the replacement selection step, let's return to our example in which we sort 80 000 000 records, given a memory area that can hold 100 000 records.

For the memory sorting methods such as heapsort, which simply read records into memory until it is full, we can perform sequential reads of 100 000 records at a time, until 800 runs have been created. This means that the sort step requires 1600 seeks: 800 for reading and 800 for writing.

For replacement selection we might use an input/output buffer that can hold, for example, 25 000 records, leaving enough space to hold 75 000 records for the replacement selection process. If the I/O buffer holds 2500 records, we can perform sequential reads of 25 000 records at a time, so it

```
                    heapsort area
```

(a) In-RAM sort: all available space used for the sort.

```
  i/o buffer  |         heapsort area
```

(b) Replacement selection: some of available space is used for I/O.

Figure 8.26 In-memory sort versus replacement selection, in terms of their use of available memory for sorting operation.

takes 80 000 000/25 000 = 3200 seeks to access all records in the file. This means that the sort step for replacement selection requires 6400 seeks: 3200 for reading and 3200 for writing.

If the records occur in a random key sequence, the average run length using replacement selection will be $2 \times 75\,000 = 150\,000$ records, and there will be about 80 000 000/150 000 = 534 such runs produced. For the merge step we divide the 10 megabytes of memory into 534 buffers, which hold an average of 187.3 records, so we end up making 150 000/187.3 = 801 seeks per run, and

$$801 \text{ seeks per run} \times 534 \text{ runs} = 427\,734 \text{ seeks altogether}$$

Table 8.4 compares the access times required to sort the 80 million records using both a memory sort and replacement selection. The table includes our initial 800-way merge and two replacement selection examples. The second replacement selection example, which produces runs of 400 000 records while using only 75 000 record storage locations in memory, assumes that there is already a good deal of sequential ordering within the input records.

It is clear that, given randomly distributed input data, replacement selection can substantially reduce the number of runs formed. Even though replacement selection requires four times as many seeks to form the runs, the reduction in the amount of seeking effort required to merge the runs more than offsets the extra amount of seeking that is required to form the runs. And when the original data is assumed to possess enough order to make the runs 400 000 records long, replacement selection produces less than one-third as many seeks as memory sorting.

8.5.7 Replacement Selection Plus Multistep Merging

While these comparisons highlight the advantages of replacement selection over memory sorting, we would probably not in reality choose the one-step merge patterns shown in Table 8.4. We have seen that two-step merges can result in much better performance than one-step merges. Table 8.5 shows how these same three sorting schemes compare when two-step merges are used. From Table 8.5 (page 340) we see that the total number of seeks is dramatically less in every case than it was for the one-step merges. Clearly, the method used to form runs is not nearly as important as the use of multistep, rather than one-step, merges.

Furthermore, because the number of seeks required for the merge steps is much smaller in all cases, while the number of seeks required to

Table 8.4 Comparison of access times required to sort 80 million records using both memory sort and replacement selection. Merge order is equal to the number of runs formed.

Approach	Number of records per seek to form runs	Size of runs formed	Number of runs formed	Number of seeks required to form runs	Merge order used	Total number of seeks	Total seek and rotational delay time	
							(hr)	(min)
800 memory sorts followed by an 800-way merge	100 000	100 000	800	1600	800	681 600	2	5
Replacement selection followed by 534-way merge (records in random order)	25 000	150 000	534	6400	534	521 134	1	36
Replacement selection followed by 200-way merge (records partially ordered)	25 000	400 000	200	6400	200	206 400	00	38

Table 8.5 Comparison of access times required to sort 80 million records using both memory sort and replacement selection, each followed by a two-step merge.

Approach	Number of records per seek to form runs	Size of runs formed	Number of runs formed	Merge pattern used	Number of seeks in merge phases	Total number of seeks	Total seek and rotational delay time	
							(hr)	*(min)*
800 memory sorts	100 000	100 000	800	25 × 32-way then 25-way	25 600/20 000	127 200	0	24
Replacement selection (records in random order)	25 000	150 000	534	19 × 28-way then 19-way	22 876/15 162	124 438	0	23
Replacement selection (records partially ordered)	25 000	400 000	200	20 × 10-way then 20-way	8 000/16 000	110 400	0	20

form runs remains the same, the latter have a bigger effect *proportionally* on the final total, and the differences between the memory-sort based method and replacement selection are diminished.

The differences between the one-step and two-step merges are exaggerated by the results in Table 8.5 because they don't take into account the amount of time spent transmitting the data. The two-step merges require that we transfer the data between memory and disk two more times than the one-step merges. Table 8.6 shows the results after adding transmission time to our results. The two-step merges are still better, and replacement selection still wins, but the results are less dramatic.

8.5.8 Using Two Disk Drives with Replacement Selection

Interestingly, and fortunately, replacement selection offers an opportunity to save on both transmission and seek times in ways that memory sort methods do not. As usual, this is at a cost, but if sorting time is expensive, it could well be worth the cost.

Suppose we have two disk drives to which we can assign the separate dedicated tasks of reading and writing during replacement selection. One drive, which contains the original file, does only input, and the other does only output. This has two very nice results: (1) it means that input and output can overlap, reducing transmission time by as much as 50 percent; and (2) seeking is virtually eliminated.

If we have two disks at our disposal, we should also configure memory to take advantage of them. We configure memory as follows: we allocate two buffers each for input and output, permitting double buffering, and allocate the rest of memory for forming the selection tree. This arrangement is illustrated in Fig. 8.27.

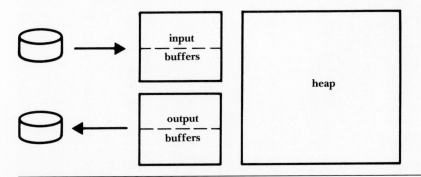

Figure 8.27 Memory organization for replacement selection.

Table 8.6 Comparison of sort merges illustrated in Tables 8.4 and 8.5, taking transmission times into account.

Approach	Number of records per seek to form runs	Merge pattern used	Number of seeks for sorts and merges	Seek + rotational delay time (*min*)	Total passes over the file	Total transmission time (*min*)	Total of seek, rotation, and transmission time (*min*)
800 memory sorts followed by an 800-way merge	100 000	800-way	681/700	125	4	40	165
Replacement selection followed by a 534-way merge (records in random order)	25 000	534-way	521/134	96	4	40	136
Replacement selection followed by a 200-way merge (records partially ordered)	25 000	200-way	206/400	38	4	40	78
800 memory sorts followed by a two-step merge	100 000	25 × 32-way one 25-way	127/200	23	6	60	83
Replacement selection followed by a two-step merge (records in random order)	25 000	19 × 28-way one 19-way	124 /438	23	6	60	83
Replacement selection followed by a two-step merge (records partially ordered)	25 000	20 × 10-way one 20-way	110/400	20	6	60	80

Let's see how the merge sort process might proceed to take advantage of this configuration.

First, the sort phase. We begin by reading enough records to fill up the heap-sized part of memory and form the heap. Next, as we move records from the heap into one of the output buffers, we replace those records with records from one of the input buffers, adjusting the tree in the usual manner. While we empty one input buffer into the tree, we can be filling the other one from the input disk. This permits processing and input to overlap. Similarly, at the same time that we are filling one of the output buffers from the tree, we can transmit the contents of the other to the output disk. In this way, run selection and output can overlap.

During the merge phase, the output disk becomes the input disk, and vice versa. Since the runs are all on the same disk, seeking will occur on the input disk. But output is still sequential, since it goes to a dedicated drive.

Because of the overlapping of so many parts of this procedure, it is difficult to estimate the amount of time the procedure is likely to take. But it should be clear that by substantially reducing seeking and transmission time, we are attacking those parts of the sort merge that are the most costly.

8.5.9 More Drives? More Processors?

If two drives can improve performance, why not three, or four, or more? Isn't it true that the more drives we have to hold runs during the merge phase, the faster we can perform I/O? Up to a point this is true, but of course the number and speed of I/O processors must be sufficient to keep up with the data streaming in and out. And there will also be a point at which I/O becomes so fast that processing can't keep up with it.

But who is to say that we can use only one processor? A decade ago, it would have been farfetched to imagine doing sorting with more than one processor, but now it is very common to be able to dedicate more than one processor to a single job. Possibilities include the following:

- Mainframe computers, many of which spend a great deal of their time sorting, commonly come with two or more processors that can simultaneously work on different parts of the same problem.

- Vector and array processors can be programmed to execute certain kinds of algorithm orders of magnitude faster than scalar processors.

- Massively parallel machines provide thousands, even millions, of processors that can operate independently and at the same time communicate in complex ways with one another.

■ Very fast local area networks and communication software make it relatively easy to parcel out different parts of the same process to several different machines.

It is not appropriate, in this text, to cover in detail the implications of these newer architectures for external sorting. But just as the changes over the past decade in the availability and performance of memory and disk storage have altered the way we look at external sorting, we can expect it to change many more times as the current generation of new architectures becomes commonplace.

8.5.10 Effects of Multiprogramming

In our discussions of external sorting on disk we are, of course, making tacit assumptions about the computing environment in which this merging is taking place. We are assuming, for example, that the merge job is running in a dedicated environment (no multiprogramming). If, in fact, the operating system is multiprogrammed, as it normally is, the total time for the I/O might be longer, as our job waits for other jobs to perform their I/O.

On the other hand, one of the reasons for multiprogramming is to allow the operating system to find ways to increase the efficiency of the overall system by overlapping processing and I/O among different jobs. So the system could be performing I/O for our job while it is doing CPU processing on others, and vice versa, diminishing any delays caused by overlap of I/O and CPU processing within our job.

Effects such as these are hard to predict, even when you have much information about your system. Only experimentation can determine what real performance will be like on a busy, multiuser system.

8.5.11 A Conceptual Toolkit for External Sorting

We can now list many tools that can improve external sorting performance. It should be our goal to add these various tools to our conceptual toolkit for designing external sorts and to pull them out and use them whenever they are appropriate. A full listing of our new set of tools would include the following:

■ For in-memory sorting, use heapsort for forming the original list of sorted elements in a run. With it and double buffering, we can overlap input and output with internal processing.

■ Use as much memory as possible. It makes the runs longer and provides bigger and/or more buffers during the merge phase.

■ If the number of initial runs is so large that total seek and rotation time is much greater than total transmission time, use a multistep merge. It increases the amount of transmission time but can decrease the number of seeks enormously.

■ Consider using replacement selection for initial run formation, especially if there is a possibility that the runs will be partially ordered.

■ Use more than one disk drive and I/O channel so reading and writing can overlap. This is especially true if there are no other users on the system.

■ Keep in mind the fundamental elements of external sorting and their relative costs, and look for ways to take advantage of new architectures and systems, such as parallel processing and high-speed local area networks.

8.6   Sorting Files on Tape

There was a time when it was usually faster to perform large external sorts on tape than on disk, but this is much less the case now. Nevertheless, tape is still used in external sorting, and we would be remiss if we did not consider sort merge algorithms designed for tape.

There are a large number of approaches to sorting files on tape. After approximately one hundred pages of closely reasoned discussion of different alternatives for tape sorting, Knuth (1998) summarizes his analysis in the following way:

> **Theorem A.** It is difficult to decide which merge pattern is best in a given situation.

Because of the complexity and number of alternative approaches and because of the way that these alternatives depend so closely on the specific characteristics of the hardware at a particular computer installation, our objective here is merely to communicate some of the fundamental issues associated with tape sorting and merging. For a more comprehensive discussion of specific alternatives, we recommend the work of Knuth (1998) as a starting point.

From a general perspective, the steps involved in sorting on tape resemble those we discussed with regard to sorting on disk:

1. Distribute the unsorted file into sorted *runs,* and
2. Merge the runs into a single sorted file.

Replacement selection is almost always a good choice as a method for creating the initial runs during a tape sort. You will remember that the problem with replacement selection when we are working on disk is that the amount of seeking required during run creation more than offsets the advantage of creating longer runs. This seeking problem disappears when the input is from tape. So, for a tape-to-tape sort, it is almost always advisable to take advantage of the longer runs created by replacement selection.

8.6.1 The Balanced Merge

Given that the question of how to create the initial runs has such a straightforward answer, it is clear that it is in the merging process that we encounter all of the choices and complexities implied by Knuth's tongue-in-cheek theorem. These choices include the question of how to *distribute* the initial runs on tape and questions about the process of merging from this initial distribution. Let's look at some examples to show what we mean.

Suppose we have a file that, after the sort phase, has been divided into ten runs. We look at a number of different methods for merging these runs on tape, assuming that our computer system has four tape drives. Since the initial, unsorted file is read from one of the drives, we have the choice of initially distributing the ten runs on two or three of the other drives. We begin with a method called *two-way balanced merging,* which requires that the initial distribution be on two drives and that at each step of the merge except the last, the output be distributed on two drives. Balanced merging is the simplest tape merging algorithm that we look at; it is also, as you will see, the slowest.

The balanced merge proceeds according to the pattern illustrated in Fig. 8.28.

This balanced merge process is expressed in an alternate, more compact form in Fig. 8.29 (page 348). The numbers inside the table are the run lengths measured in terms of the number of initial runs included in each merged run. For example, in step 1, all the input runs consist of a single initial run. By step 2, the input runs each consist of a pair of initial runs. At the start of step 3, tape drive T1 contains one run consisting of four initial runs followed by a run consisting of two initial runs. This method of illustration more clearly shows the way some of the intermedi-

	Tape	Contains runs				
	T1	R1	R3	R5	R7	R9
Step 1	T2	R2	R4	R6	R8	R10
	T3	—				
	T4	—				
	T1	—				
Step 2	T2	—				
	T3	R1–R2	R5–R6	R9–R10		
	T4	R3–R4	R7–R8			
	T1	R1–R4	R9–R10			
Step 3	T2	R5–R8				
	T3	—				
	T4	—				
	T1	—				
Step 4	T2	—				
	T3	R1–R8				
	T4	R9–R10				
	T1	R1–R10				
Step 5	T2	—				
	T3	—				
	T4	—				

Figure 8.28 Balanced four-tape merge of ten runs.

ate runs combine and grow into runs of lengths 2, 4, and 8, whereas the one run that is copied again and again stays at length 2 until the end. The form used in this illustration is used throughout the following discussions on tape merging.

Since there is no seeking, the cost associated with balanced merging on tape is measured in terms of how much time is spent transmitting the data. In the example, we passed over all of the data four times during the merge phase. In general, given some number of initial runs, how many passes over the data will a two-way balanced merge take? That is, if we start with N runs, how many passes are required to reduce the number of runs to 1? Since each step combines two runs, the number of runs after each

	T1	**T2**	**T3**	**T4**
Step 1	1 1 1 1 1	1 1 1 1 1	—	—
				Merge ten runs
Step 2	—	—	2 2 2	2 2
				Merge ten runs
Step 3	4 2	4	—	—
				Merge ten runs
Step 4	—	—	8	2
				Merge ten runs
Step 5	10	—	—	—

Figure 8.29 Balanced four-tape merge of ten runs expressed in a more compact table notation.

step is half the number for the previous step. If p is the number of passes, then we can express this relationship as

$$(\tfrac{1}{2})^p \cdot N \leq 1$$

from which it can be shown that

$$p = \lceil \log_2 N \rceil$$

In our simple example, $N = 10$, so four passes over the data were required. Recall that for our partially sorted 800-megabyte file there were 200 runs, so $\lceil \log_2 200 \rceil = 8$ passes are required for a balanced merge. If reading and writing overlap perfectly, each pass takes about 11 minutes,[7] so the total time is 1 hour, 28 minutes. This time is not competitive with our disk-based merges, even when a single disk drive is used. The transmission times far outweigh the savings in seek times.

8.6.2 The *K*-way Balanced Merge

If we want to improve on this approach, it is clear that we must find ways to reduce the number of passes over the data. A quick look at the formula tells us that we can reduce the number of passes by increasing the order of each merge. Suppose, for instance, that we have 20 tape drives, 10 for input

---

7. This assumes the 6250 bpi tape used in the examples in Chapter 3. If the transport speed is 200 inches per second, the transmission rate is 1250 kilobytes per second, assuming no blocking. At this rate an 800-megabyte file takes 640 seconds, or 10 minutes 40 seconds to read.

and 10 for output, at each step. Since each step combines 10 runs, the number of runs after each step is one-tenth the number for the previous step. Hence, we have

$$(\tfrac{1}{10})^p \cdot N \le 1$$

and

$$p = \lceil \log_{10} N \rceil$$

In general, a k-*way balanced merge* is one in which the order of the merge at each step (except possibly the last) is k. Hence, the number of passes required for a k-way balanced merge with N initial runs is

$$p = \lceil \log_k N \rceil$$

For a 10-way balanced merge of our 800-megabyte file with 200 runs, $\log_{10} 200 = 3$, so three passes are required. The best estimated time now is reduced to a more respectable 42 minutes. Of course, the cost is quite high: we must keep 20 working tape drives on hand for the merge.

8.6.3 Multiphase Merges

The balanced merging algorithm has the advantage of being very simple; it is easy to write a program to perform this algorithm. Unfortunately, one reason it is simple is that it is "dumb" and cannot take advantage of opportunities to save work. Let's see how we can improve on it.

We can begin by noting that when we merge the extra run with empty runs in steps 3 and 4, we don't really accomplish anything. Figure 8.30 shows how we can dramatically reduce the amount of work that has to be done by simply not copying the extra run during step 3. Instead of merging this run with a dummy run, we simply stop tape T3 where it is. Tapes T1 and T2 now each contain a single run made up of four of the initial runs. We rewind all the tapes but T3 and then perform a three-way merge of the runs on tapes T1, T2, and T3, writing the final result on T4. Adding this intelligence to the merging procedure reduces the number of initial runs that must be read and written from forty down to twenty-eight.

The example in Fig. 8.30 clearly indicates that there are ways to improve on the performance of balanced merging. It is important to be able to state, in general terms, what it is about this second merging pattern that saves work:

■   We use a higher-order merge. In place of two two-way merges, we use one three-way merge.

	T1	**T2**	**T3**	**T4**	
Step 1	1 1 1 1 1	1 1 1 1 1	—	—	
					Merge ten runs
Step 2	—	—	2 2 2	2 2	
					Merge eight runs
Step 3	4	4	. . 2	—	
					Merge ten runs
Step 4	—	—	—	10	

Figure 8.30 Modification of balanced four-tape merge that does not rewind between steps 2 and 3 to avoid copying runs.

■ We extend the merging of runs from one tape over several steps. Specifically, we merge some of the runs from T3 in step 3 and some in step 4. We could say that we merge the runs from T3 in two *phases*.

These ideas, the use of higher-order merge patterns and the merging of runs from a tape in *phases,* are the basis for two well-known approaches to merging called *polyphase merging* and *cascade merging*. In general, these merges share the following characteristics:

■ The initial distribution of runs is such that at least the initial merge is a *J*-1-way merge, where *J* is the number of available tape drives.

■ The distribution of the runs across the tapes is such that the tapes often contain different numbers of runs.

Figure 8.31 illustrates how a polyphase merge can be used to merge ten runs distributed on four tape drives. This merge pattern reduces the number of initial runs that must be read and written from forty (for a balanced two-way merge) to twenty-five. It is easy to see that this reduction is a consequence of the use of several three-way merges in place of two-way merges. It should also be clear that the ability to do these operations as three-way merges is related to the uneven nature of the initial distribution. Consider, for example, what happens if the initial distribution of runs is 4–3–3 rather than 5–3–2. We can perform three three-way merges to open up space on T3, but this also clears all the runs off of T2 and leaves only a single run on T1. Obviously, we are not able to perform another three-way merge as a second step.

Several questions arise at this point:

1. How does one choose an initial distribution that leads readily to an efficient merge pattern?

	T1	T2	T3	T4
Step 1	1 1 1 1 1	1 1 1	1 1	—
Step 2	. . 1 1 1	. . 1	—	3 3
Step 3	. . . 1 1	—	5	. 3
Step 4	 1	4	5	—
Step 5	—	—	—	10

Merge six runs

Merge five runs

Merge four runs

Merge ten runs

Figure 8.31 Polyphase four-tape merge of ten runs.

2. Are there algorithmic descriptions of the merge patterns, given an initial distribution?

3. Given *N* runs and *J* tape drives, is there some way to compute the *optimal* merging performance so we have a yardstick against which to compare the performance of any specific algorithm?

Precise answers to these questions are beyond the scope of this text; in particular, the answer to the last question requires a more mathematical approach to the problem than the one we have taken here. Readers wanting more than an intuitive understanding of how to set up initial distributions should consult Knuth (1998).

8.6.4 Tapes versus Disks for External Sorting

A decade ago 1 megabyte of memory was considered a substantial amount of memory to allocate to any single job, and extra disk drives were very costly. This meant that many of the disk sorting techniques to decrease seeking that we have seen were not available to us or were very limited.

Suppose, for instance, that we want to sort our 8000-megabyte file and there is only 1 megabyte of memory available instead of 10 megabytes. The approach that we used for allocating memory for replacement selection would provide 250 kilobytes for buffering and 750 kilobytes for our selection tree. From this we can expect 5334 runs of 15 000 records each, versus 534 when there is a megabyte of memory. For a one-step merge, this tenfold increase in the number of runs results in a hundredfold increase in the number of seeks. What took three hours with 10 megabytes of memory now takes three hundred hours, just for the seeks! No wonder tapes, which are basically sequential and require no seeking, were preferred.

But now memory is much more readily available. Runs can be longer and fewer, and seeks are much less of a problem. Transmission time is now more important. The best way to decrease transmission time is to reduce the number of passes over the data, and we can do this by increasing the order of the merge. Since disks are random-access devices, very large-order merges can be performed, even if there is only one drive. Tapes, however, are not random-access devices; we need an extra tape drive for every extra run we want to merge. Unless a large number of drives is available, we can perform only low-order merges, and that means large numbers of passes over the data. Disks are better.

8.7 Sort-Merge Packages

Many good utility programs are available for users who need to sort large files. Often the programs have enough intelligence to choose from one of several strategies, depending on the nature of the data to be sorted and the available system configuration. They also often allow users to exert some control (if they want it) over the organization of data and strategies used. Consequently, even if you are using a commercial sort package rather than designing your own sorting procedure, it helps to be familiar with the variety of different ways to design merge sorts. It is especially important to have a good general understanding of the most important factors and trade-offs influencing performance.

8.8 Sorting and Cosequential Processing in Unix

Unix has a number of utilities for performing cosequential processing. It also has sorting routines, but nothing at the level of sophistication that you find in production sort-merge packages. In the following discussion we introduce some of these utilities. For full details, consult the Unix documentation.

8.8.1 Sorting and Merging in Unix

Because Unix is not an environment in which one expects to do frequent sorting of large files of the type we discuss in this chapter, sophisticated sort-merge packages are not generally available on Unix systems. Still, the sort routines you find in Unix are quick and flexible and quite adequate for the types of applications that are common in a Unix environment. We can divide Unix sorting into two categories: (1) the `sort` command, and (2) callable sorting routines.

The Unix `sort` Command

The `sort` command has many different options, but the simplest one is to sort the lines in an ASCII file in ascending lexical order. (A line is any sequence of characters ending with the new-line character ,.) By default, the `sort` utility takes its input file name from the command line and writes the sorted file to standard output. If the file to be sorted is too large to fit in memory, `sort` performs a merge sort. If more than one file is named on the input line, `sort` sorts and merges the files.

As a simple example, suppose we have an ASCII file called `team` with names of members of a basketball team, together with their classes and their scoring averages:

```
Jean Smith Senior 8.8
Chris Mason Junior 9.6
Pat Jones Junior 3.2
Leslie Brown Sophomore 18.2
Pat Jones Freshman 11.4
```

To sort the file, enter

```
$ sort team
Chris Mason Junior 9.6
Jean Smith Senior 8.8
Leslie Brown Sophomore 18.2
Pat Jones Freshman 11.4
Pat Jones Junior 3.2
```

Notice that by default `sort` considers an entire line as the sort key. Hence, of the two players named Pat Jones, the freshman occurs first in the output because "Freshman" is lexically smaller than "Junior." The assumption that the key is an entire line can be overridden by sorting on specified key fields. For `sort` a key field is assumed to be any sequence of characters delimited by spaces or tabs. You can indicate which key fields to use for sorting by giving their positions:

```
+pos1 [-pos2]
```

where `pos1` tells how many fields to skip before starting the key, and `pos2` tells which field to end with. If `pos2` is omitted, the key extends to the end of the line. Hence, entering

```
$ sort +1 -2 team
```

causes the file *team* to be sorted according to last names. (There is also a form of `pos1` and `pos2` that allows you to specify the character within a field to start a key with.)

The following options, among others, allow you to override the default ASCII ordering used by `sort`:

-d Use "dictionary" ordering: only letters, digits, and blanks are significant in comparisons.

-f "Fold" lowercase letters into uppercase. (This is the canonical form that we defined in Chapter 4.)

-r "Reverse" the sense of comparison: sort in descending ASCII order.

Notice that `sort` sorts lines, and within lines it compares groups of characters delimited by white space. In the language of Chapter 4, records are lines, and fields are groups of characters delimited by white space. This is consistent with the most common Unix view of fields and records within Unix text files.

The `qsort` *Library Routine*

The Unix library routine `qsort` is a general sorting routine. Given a table of data, `qsort` sorts the elements in the table in place. A table could be the contents of a file, loaded into memory, where the elements of the table are its records. In C, `qsort` is defined as follows:

```
qsort(char *base, int nel, int width, int (*compar()) )
```

The argument `base` is a pointer to the base of the data, `nel` is the number of elements in the table, and `width` is the size of each element. The last argument, `compar()`, is the name of a user-supplied comparison function that `qsort` uses to compare keys. `compar` must have two parameters that are pointers to elements that are to be compared. When `qsort` needs to compare two elements, it passes to `compar` pointers to these elements, and `compar` compares them, returning an integer that is less than, equal to, or greater than zero, depending on whether the first argument is considered less than, equal to, or greater than the second argument. A full explanation of how to use `qsort` is beyond the scope of this text. Consult the Unix documentation for details.

8.8.2 Cosequential Processing Utilities in Unix

Unix provides a number of utilities for cosequential processing. The `sort` utility, when used to merge files, is one example. In this section we introduce three others: `diff`, `cmp`, and `comm`.

cmp

Suppose you find in your computer that you have two team files, one called `team` and the other called `myteam`. You think that the two files are the same, but you are not sure. You can use the command `cmp` to find out.

`cmp` compares two files. If they differ, it prints the byte and line number where they differ; otherwise it does nothing. If all of one file is identical to the first part of another, it reports that end-of-file was reached on the shorter file before any differences were found.

For example, suppose the file `team` and `myteam` have the following contents:

team

```
Jean Smith Senior 8.8
Chris Mason Junior 9.6
Pat Jones Junior 3.2
Leslie Brown Sophomore 18.2
Pat Jones Freshman 11.4
```

myteam

```
Jean Smith Senior 8.8
Stacy Fox Senior 1.6
Chris Mason Junior 9.6
Pat Jones Junior 5.2
Leslie Brown Sophomore 18.2
Pat Jones Freshman 11.4
```

`cmp` tells you where they differ:

```
$ cmp team myteam
team myteam differ: char 23 line 2
```

Since `cmp` simply compares files on a byte-by-byte basis until it finds a difference, it makes no assumptions about fields or records. It works with both text and nontext files.

diff

`cmp` is useful if you want to know if two files are different, but it doesn't tell you much about how they differ. The command `diff` gives fuller information. `diff` tells which lines must be changed in two files to bring them into agreement. For example:

```
$ diff team myteam
1a2
> Stacy Fox Senior 1.6
3c4
< Pat Jones Junior 3.2
---
> Pat Jones Junior 5.2
```

The 1a2 indicates that after line 1 in the first file, we need to *add* line 2 from the second file to make them agree. This is followed by the line from the second file that would need to be added. The 3c4 indicates that we need to *change* line 3 in the first file to make it look like line 4 in the second file. This is followed by a listing of the two differing lines, where the leading <indicates that the line is from the first file, and the >indicates that it is from the second file.

One other indicator that could appear in `diff` output is d, meaning that a line in the first file has been *deleted* in the second file. For example, 12d15 means that line 12 in the first file appears to have been deleted from being right after line 15 in the second file. Notice that `diff`, like `sort`, is designed to work with lines of text. It would not work well with non-ASCII text files.

comm

Whereas `diff` tells what is different about two files, `comm` compares two files, which must be ordered in ASCII collating sequence, to see what they have in common. The syntax for `comm` is the following:

```
comm [-123] file1 file2
```

`comm` produces three columns of output. Column 1 lists the lines that are in `file1` only; column 2 lists lines in `file2` only, and column 3 lists lines that are in both files. For example,

```
$ sort team > ts
$ sort myteam > ms
$ comm ts ms
                Chris Mason Junior 9.6
                Jean Smith Senior 8.8
                Leslie Brown Sophomore 18.2
                Pat Jones Freshman 11.4
```

```
          Pat Jones Junior 3.2
     Pat Jones Junior 5.2
     Stacy Fox Senior 1.6
```

Selecting any of the flags 1, 2, or 3 allows you to print only those columns you are interested in.

The `sort`, `diff`, `comm`, and `cmp` commands (and the `qsort` function) are representative of what is available in Unix for sorting and cosequential processing. As we have said, they have many useful options that we don't cover that you will be interested in reading about.

SUMMARY

In the first half of this chapter, we develop a cosequential processing model and apply it to two common problems—updating a general ledger and merge sorting. The model is presented as a class hierarchy, using virtual methods to tailor the model to particular types of lists. In the second half of the chapter we identify the most important factors influencing performance in merge-sorting operations and suggest some strategies for achieving good performance.

The cosequential processing model can be applied to problems that involve operations such as matching and merging (and combinations of these) on two or more sorted input files. We begin the chapter by illustrating the use of the model to perform a simple match of the elements common to two lists and a merge of two lists. The procedures we develop to perform these two operations embody all the basic elements of the model.

In its most complete form, the model depends on certain assumptions about the data in the input files. We enumerate these assumptions in our formal description of the model. Given these assumptions, we can describe the processing components of the model and define pure virtual functions that represent those components.

The real value of the cosequential model is that it can be adapted to more substantial problems than simple matches or merges by extending the class hierarchy. We illustrate this by using the model to design a general ledger accounting program.

All of our early sample applications of the model involve only two input files. We next adapt the model to a multiway merge to show how the model might be extended to deal with more than two input lists. The problem of finding the minimum key value during each pass through the main loop becomes more complex as the number of input files increases. Its solution involves replacing the three-way selection statement with either a multiway selection or a procedure that keeps current keys in a list structure that can be processed more conveniently.

We see that the application of the model to k-way merging performs well for small values of k, but that for values of k greater than 8 or so, it is more efficient to find the minimum key value by means of a selection tree.

After discussing multiway merging, we shift our attention to a problem that we encountered in a previous chapter—how to sort large files. We begin with files that are small enough to fit into memory and introduce an efficient sorting algorithm, *heapsort,* which makes it possible to overlap I/O with the sorting process.

The generally accepted solution when a file is too large for in-memory sorts is some form of *merge sort.* A merge sort involves two steps:

1. Break the file into two or more sorted subfiles, or runs, using internal sorting methods; and

2. Merge the runs.

Ideally, we would like to keep every run in a separate file so we can perform the merge step with one pass through the runs. Unfortunately, practical considerations sometimes make it difficult to do this effectively.

The critical elements when merging many files on disk are seek and rotational delay times and transmission times. These times depend largely on two interrelated factors: the number of different runs being merged and the amount of internal buffer space available to hold parts of the runs. We can reduce seek and rotational delay times in two ways:

- By performing the merge in more than one step; and/or
- By increasing the sizes of the initial sorted runs.

In both cases, the order of each merge step can be reduced, increasing the sizes of the internal buffers and allowing more data to be processed per seek.

Looking at the first alternative, we see how performing the merge in several steps can decrease the number of seeks dramatically, though it also means that we need to read through the data more than once (increasing total data transmission time).

The second alternative is realized through use of an algorithm called *replacement selection.* Replacement selection, which can be implemented using the selection tree mentioned earlier, involves selecting from memory the key that has the lowest value, outputting that key, and replacing it with a new key from the input list.

With randomly organized files, replacement selection can be expected to produce runs twice as long as the number of internal storage locations available for performing the algorithms. Although this represents a major step toward decreasing the number of runs that need to be merged, it carries an additional cost. The need for a large buffer for performing the replacement selection operation leaves relatively little space for the I/O buffer, which means that many more seeks are involved in forming the runs than are needed when the sort step uses an in-memory sort. If we compare the total number of seeks required by the two different approaches, we find that replacement selection can require more seeks; it performs substantially better only when there is a great deal of order in the initial file.

Next we turn our attention to file sorting on tapes. Since file I/O with tapes does not involve seeking, the problems and solutions associated with tape sorting can differ from those associated with disk sorting, although the fundamental goal of working with fewer, longer runs remains. With tape sorting, the primary measure of performance is the number of times each record must be transmitted. (Other factors, such as tape rewind time, can also be important, but we do not consider them here.)

Since tapes do not require seeking, replacement selection is almost always a good choice for creating initial runs. As the number of drives available to hold run files is limited, the next question is how to distribute the files on the tapes. In most cases, it is necessary to put several runs on each of several tapes, reserving one or more other tapes for the results. This generally leads to merges of several steps, with the total number of runs being decreased after each merge step. Two approaches to doing this are *balanced merges* and *multiphase merges.* In a *k*-way balanced merge, all input tapes contain approximately the same number of runs, there are the same number of output tapes as there are input tapes, and the input tapes are read through entirely during each step. The number of runs is decreased by a factor of *k* after each step.

A multiphase merge (such as a *polyphase merge* or a *cascade merge*) requires that the runs initially be distributed unevenly among all but one of the available tapes. This increases the order of the merge and as a result can decrease the number of times each record has to be read. It turns out that the initial distribution of runs among the first set of input tapes has a major effect on the number of times each record has to be read.

Next, we discuss briefly the existence of sort-merge utilities, which are available on most large systems and can be very flexible and effective. We conclude the chapter with a listing of Unix utilities used for sorting and cosequential processing.

KEY TERMS

Balanced merge. A multistep merging technique that uses the same number of input devices as output devices. A two-way balanced merge uses two input tapes, each with approximately the same number of runs on it, and produces two output tapes, each with approximately half as many runs as the input tapes. A balanced merge is suitable for merge sorting with tapes, though it is not generally the best method (see *multiphase merging*).

cmp. A Unix utility for determining whether two files are identical. Given two files, it reports the first byte where the two files differ, if they differ.

comm. A Unix utility for determining which lines two files have in common. Given two files, it reports the lines they have in common, the lines that are in the first file and not in the second, and the lines that are in the second file and not in the first.

Cosequential operations. Operations applied to problems that involve the performance of union, intersection, and more complex set operations on two or more sorted input files to produce one or more output files built from some combination of the elements of the input files. Cosequential operations commonly occur in matching, merging, and file-updating problems.

diff. A Unix utility for determining all the lines that differ between two files. It reports the lines that need to be added to the first file to make it like the second, the lines that need to be deleted from the second file to make it like the first, and the lines that need to be changed in the first file to make it like the second.

Heapsort. A sorting algorithm especially well suited for sorting large files that fit in memory because its execution can overlap with I/O. A variation of heapsort is used to obtain longer runs in the replacement selection algorithm.

HighValue. A value used in the cosequential model that is greater than any possible key value. By assigning HighValue as the current key value for files for which an end-of-file condition has been encountered, extra logic for dealing with end-of-file conditions can be simplified.

***k*-way merge.** A merge in which *k* input files are merged to produce one output file.

LowValue. A value used in the cosequential model that is less than any possible key value. By assigning LowValue as the previous key value during initialization, the need for certain other special start-up code is eliminated.

Match. The process of forming a sorted output file consisting of all the elements common to two or more sorted input files.

Merge. The process of forming a sorted output file that consists of the union of the elements from two or more sorted input files.

Multiphase merge. A multistep tape merge in which the initial distribution of runs is such that at least the initial merge is a J-1-way merge (J is the number of available tape drives) and in which the distribution of runs across the tapes is such that the merge performs efficiently at every step. (See *polyphase merge*.)

Multistep merge. A merge in which not all runs are merged in one step. Rather, several sets of runs are merged separately, each set producing one long run consisting of the records from all of its runs. These new, longer sets are then merged, either all together or in several sets. After each step, the number of runs is decreased and the length of the runs is increased. The output of the final step is a single run consisting of the entire file. (Be careful not to confuse our use of the term *multistep merge* with *multiphase merge*.) Although a multistep merge is theoretically more time-consuming than a single-step merge, it can involve much less seeking when performed on a disk, and it may be the only reasonable way to perform a merge on tape if the number of tape drives is limited.

Order of a merge. The number of different files, or runs, being merged. For example, 100 is the order of a 100-way merge.

Polyphase merge. A multiphase merge in which, ideally, the merge order is maximized at every step.

qsort. A general-purpose Unix library routine for sorting files that employs a user-defined comparison function.

Replacement selection. A method of creating initial runs based on the idea of always *selecting* from memory the record whose key has the lowest value, outputting that record, and then *replacing* it in memory with a new record from the input list. When new records are brought in with keys that are greater than those of the most recently output records, they eventually become part of the run being created. When new records have keys that are less than those of the most recently output records, they are held over for the next run. Replacement selection generally produces runs that are substantially longer than runs that can be created by in-memory sorts and hence can help improve performance in merge sorting. When using replacement selection with merge sorts on disk, however, one must be careful that the extra seeking required for replacement selection does not outweigh the benefits of having longer runs to merge.

Run. A sorted subset of a file resulting from the sort step of a sort merge or one of the steps of a multistep merge.

Selection tree. A binary tree in which each higher-level node represents the winner of the comparison between the two descendent keys. The minimum (or maximum) value in a selection tree is always at the root node, making the selection tree a good data structure for merging several lists. It is also a key structure in replacement selection algorithms, which can be used for producing long runs for merge sorts. (*Tournament sort,* an internal sort, is also based on the use of a selection tree.)

Sequence checking. Checking that records in a file are in the expected order. It is recommended that all files used in a cosequential operation be sequence checked.

sort. A Unix utility for sorting and merging files.

Synchronization loop. The main loop in the cosequential processing model. A primary feature of the model is to do all synchronization within a single loop rather than in multiple nested loops. A second objective is to keep the main synchronization loop as simple as possible. This is done by restricting the operations that occur within the loop to those that involve current keys and by relegating as much special logic as possible (such as error checking and end-of-file checking) to subprocedures.

Theorem A (Knuth). It is difficult to decide which merge pattern is best in a given situation.

FURTHER READINGS

The subject matter treated in this chapter can be divided into two separate topics: the presentation of a model for cosequential processing and discussion of external merging procedures on tape and disk. Although most file processing texts discuss cosequential processing, they usually do it in the context of specific applications, rather than presenting a general model that can be adapted to a variety of applications. We found this useful and flexible model through Dr. James VanDoren who developed this form of the model himself for presentation in the file structures course that he teaches. We are not aware of any discussion of the cosequential model elsewhere in the literature.

Quite a bit of work has been done toward developing simple and effective algorithms to do sequential file updating, which is an important instance of cosequential processing. The results deal with some of the same problems the cosequential model deals with, and some of the solutions are similar. See Levy (1982) and Dwyer (1981) for more.

Unlike cosequential processing, external sorting is a topic that is covered widely in the literature. The most complete discussion of the subject, by far, is in Knuth (1998). Students interested in the topic of external sorting must, at some point, familiarize themselves with Knuth's definitive summary of the subject. Knuth also describes replacement selection, as evidenced by our quoting from his book in this chapter.

Salzberg (1990) describes an approach to external sorting that takes advantage of replacement selection, parallelism, distributed computing, and large amounts of memory. Cormen, Leiserson, and Rivest (1990) and Loomis (1989) also have chapters on external sorting.

EXERCISES

1. Consider the cosequential `Merge2Lists` method of Fig. 8.5 and the supporting methods of class `CosequentialProcess` in Appendix H. Comment on how they handle the following initial conditions. If they do not correctly handle a situation, indicate how they might be altered to do so.

   a. List 1 empty and List 2 not empty

   b. List 1 not empty and List 2 empty

   c. List 1 empty and List 2 empty

2. Section 8.3.1 includes the body of a loop for doing a k-way merge, assuming that there are no duplicate names. If duplicate names are allowed, one could add to the procedure a facility for keeping a list of subscripts of duplicate lowest names. Modify the body of the loop to implement this. Describe the changes required to the supporting methods.

3. In Section 8.3, two methods are presented for choosing the lowest of K keys at each step in a K-way merge: a linear search and use of a selection tree. Compare the performances of the two approaches in terms of numbers of comparisons for $K = 2$, 4, 8, 16, 32, and 100. Why do you think the linear approach is recommended for values of K less than 8?

4. Suppose you have 80 megabytes of memory available for sorting the 8 000 000-record file described in Section 8.5.

    a. How long does it take to sort the file using the merge-sort algorithm described in Section 8.5.1?

    b. How long does it take to sort the file using the keysort algorithm described in Chapter 6?

    c. Why will keysort not work if there are ten megabytes of memory available for the sorting phase?

5. How much seek time is required to perform a one-step merge such as the one described in Section 8.5 if the time for an average seek is 10 msec and the amount of available internal buffer space is 5000 K? 1000 K?

6. Performance in sorting is often measured in terms of the number of comparisons. Explain why the number of comparisons is not adequate for measuring performance in sorting large files.

7. In our computations involving the merge sorts, we made the simplifying assumption that only one seek and one rotational delay are required for any single sequential access. If this were not the case, a great deal more time would be required to perform I/O. For example, for the 800-megabyte file used in the example in Section 8.5.1, for the input step of the sort phase ("reading all records into memory for sorting and forming runs"), each individual run could require many accesses. Now let's assume that the extent size for our hypothetical drive is 80 000 bytes (approximately one track) and that all files are stored in track-sized blocks that must be accessed separately (one seek and one rotational delay per block).

    a. How many seeks does step 1 now require?

    b. How long do steps 1, 2, 3, and 4 now take?

    c. How does increasing the file size by a factor of 10 now affect the total time required for the merge sort?

8. Derive two formulas for the number of seeks required to perform the merge step of a one-step k-way sort merge of a file with r records

divided into k runs, where the amount of available memory is equivalent to M records. If an internal sort is used for the sort phase, you can assume that the length of each run is M, but if replacement selection is used, you can assume that the length of each run is about $2M$. Why?

9. Assume a quiet system with four separately addressable disk drives, each of which is able to hold several gigabytes. Assume that the 800-megabyte file described in Section 8.5 is already on one of the drives. Design a sorting procedure for this sample file that uses the separate drives to minimize the amount of seeking required. Assume that the final sorted file is written off to tape and that buffering for this tape output is handled invisibly by the operating system. Is there any advantage to be gained by using replacement selection?

10. Use replacement selection to produce runs from the following files, assuming $P = 4$.

   a. 2329517955413513318241147
   b. 3591117182324293341475155
   c. 5551474133292423181711953

11. Suppose you have a disk drive that has 10 read/write heads per surface, so 10 cylinders may be accessed at any one time without having to move the actuator arm. If you could control the physical organization of runs stored on disk, how might you be able to exploit this arrangement in performing a sort merge?

12. Assume we need to merge 14 runs on four tape drives. Develop merge patterns starting from each of these initial distributions:

   a. 8—4—2
   b. 7—4—3
   c. 6—5—3
   d. 5—5—4.

13. A four-tape polyphase merge is to be performed to sort the list 24 36 13 25 16 45 29 38 23 50 22 19 43 30 11 27 48. The original list is on tape 4. Initial runs are of length 1. After initial sorting, tapes 1, 2, and 3 contain the following runs (a slash separates runs):

   Tape 1: 24 / 36 / 13 / 25

   Tape 2: 16 / 45 / 29 / 38 / 23 / 50   Tape 3: 22 / 19 / 43 / 30 / 11 / 27 / 47

   a. Show the contents of tape 4 after one merge phase.
   b. Show the contents of all four tapes after the second and fourth phases.

c. Comment on the appropriateness of the original 4—6—7 distribution for performing a polyphase merge.

14. Obtain a copy of the manual for one or more commercially available sort-merge packages. Identify the different kinds of choices available to users of the packages. Relate the options to the performance issues discussed in this chapter.

15. A join operation matches two files by matching field values in the two files. In the ledger example, a join could be used to match master and transaction records that have the same account numbers. The ledger posting operation could be implemented with a sorted ledger file and an indexed, entry-sequenced transaction file by reading a master record and then using the index to find all corresponding transaction records.

    Compare the speed of this join operation with the cosequential processing method of this chapter. Don't forget to include the cost of sorting the transaction file.

PROGRAMMING EXERCISES

16. Modify method `LedgerProcess::ProcessEndMaster` so it updates the ledger file with the new account balances for the month.

17. Implement the *k*-way merge in class `CosequentialProcessing` using an object of class Heap to perform the merge selection.

18. Implement a *k*-way match in class `CosequentialProcessing`.

19. Implement the sort merge operation using class Heap to perform replacement selection to create the initial sorted runs and class CosequentialProcessing to perform the merge phases.

PROGRAMMING PROJECT

This is the sixth part of the programming project. We develop applications that produce student transcripts and student grade reports from information contained in files produced by the programming project of Chapter 4.

20. Use class `CosequentialProcesses` and `MasterTransactionProcess` to develop an application that produces student transcripts. For each student record (master) print the student information and a list of all courses (transaction) taken by the student. As input, use a file of student records sorted by student identifier and a file of course registration records sorted by student identifiers.

21. Use class `CosequentialProcesses` and `MasterTransactionProcess` to develop an application that produces student grade reports. As input, use a file of student records sorted by student identifier and a file of course registrations with grades for a single semester.

The next part of the programming project is in Chapter 9.

9

Multilevel Indexing and B-Trees

❖ Place the development of B-trees in the historical context of the problems they were designed to solve.

❖ Look briefly at other tree structures that might be used on secondary storage, such as paged AVL trees.

❖ Introduce multirecord and multilevel indexes and evaluate the speed of the search operation.

❖ Provide an understanding of the important properties possessed by B-trees and show how these properties are especially well suited to secondary storage applications.

❖ Present the object-oriented design of B-trees

  – Define class BTreeNode, the in-memory representation of the nodes of B-trees.

  – Define class BTree, the full representation of B-trees including all operations.

❖ Explain the implementation of the fundamental operations on B-trees.

❖ Introduce the notion of page buffering and virtual B-trees.

❖ Describe variations of the fundamental B-tree algorithms, such as those used to build B* trees and B-trees with variable-length records.

9.1   Introduction: The Invention of the B-Tree

Computer science is a young discipline. As evidence of this youth, consider that at the start of 1970, after astronauts had twice traveled to the moon, B-trees did not yet exist. Today, twenty-seven years later, it is hard to think of a major, general-purpose file system that is not built around a B-tree design.

Douglas Comer, in his excellent survey article, "The Ubiquitous B-Tree" (1979), recounts the competition among computer manufacturers and independent research groups in the late 1960s. The goal was the discovery of a general method for storing and retrieving data in large file systems that would provide rapid access to the data with minimal overhead cost. Among the competitors were R. Bayer and E. McCreight, who were working for Boeing Corporation. In 1972 they published an article, "Organization and Maintenance of Large Ordered Indexes," which announced B-trees to the world. By 1979, when Comer published his survey article, B-trees had already become so widely used that Comer was able to state that "the B-tree is, *de facto,* the standard organization for indexes in a database system."

We have reprinted the first few paragraphs of the 1972 Bayer and McCreight article[1] because it so concisely describes the facets of the problem that B-trees were designed to solve: how to access and efficiently maintain an index that is too large to hold in memory. You will remember that this is the same problem that is left unresolved in Chapter 7, on simple index structures. It will be clear as you read Bayer and McCreight's introduction that their work goes straight to the heart of the issues we raised in the indexing chapter.

In this paper we consider the problem of organizing and maintaining an index for a dynamically changing random access file. By an *index* we mean a collection of index elements which are pairs *(x, a)* of fixed size physically adjacent data items, namely a key *x* and some associated information *a*. The key *x* identifies a unique element in the index, the associated information is typically a pointer to a record or a collection of records in a random access file. For this paper the associated information is of no further interest.

We assume that the index itself is so voluminous that only rather small parts of it can be kept in main store at one time. Thus the bulk of the index must be kept on some backup store. The class of backup stores considered are *pseudo random access devices* which have rather long access or wait time—as opposed to a true random access device like core store—and a rather high data rate once the transmission of physically sequential data has been initiated. Typical pseudo random access devices are: fixed and moving head disks, drums, and data cells.

Since the data file itself changes, it must be possible not only to search the index and to retrieve elements, but also to delete and to insert

---

1. From Acta-Informatica, 1:173–189, ©1972, Springer Verlag, New York. Reprinted with permission.

keys—more accurately index elements—economically. The index organization described in this paper allows retrieval, insertion, and deletion of keys in time proportional to $\log_k I$ or better, where I is the size of the index, and k is a device dependent natural number which describes the page size such that the performance of the maintenance and retrieval scheme becomes near optimal.

Bayer and McCreight's statement that they have developed a scheme with retrieval time proportional to $\log_k I$, where k is related to the page size, is very significant. As we will see, the use of a B-tree with a page size of sixty-four to index an file with 1 million records results in being able to find the key for any record in no more than three seeks to the disk. A binary search on the same file can require as many as twenty seeks. Moreover, we are talking about getting this kind of performance from a system that requires only minimal overhead as keys are inserted and deleted.

Before looking in detail at Bayer and McCreight's solution, let's first return to a more careful look at the problem, picking up where we left off in Chapter 7. We will also look at some of the data and file structures that were routinely used to attack the problem before the invention of B-trees. Given this background, it will be easier to appreciate the contribution made by Bayer and McCreight's work.

One last matter before we begin: why the name *B-tree?* Comer (1979) provides this footnote:

> The origin of "B-tree" has never been explained by [Bayer and McCreight]. As we shall see, "balanced," "broad," or "bushy" might apply. Others suggest that the "B" stands for Boeing. Because of his contributions, however, it seems appropriate to think of B-trees as "Bayer"-trees.

9.2 Statement of the Problem

The fundamental problem with keeping an index on secondary storage is, of course, that accessing secondary storage is slow. This can be broken down into two more specific problems:

- *Searching the index must be faster than binary searching.* Searching for a key on a disk often involves seeking to different disk tracks. Since seeks are expensive, a search that has to look in more than three or four locations before finding the key often requires more time than is desirable. If we are using a binary search, four seeks is enough only to differentiate among fifteen items. An average of about 9.5 seeks is required to find a key in an index of one thousand items using a binary search. We need to find a way to home in on a key using fewer seeks.

■ *Insertion and deletion must be as fast as search.* As we saw in Chapter 7, if inserting a key into an index involves moving a large number of the other keys in the index, index maintenance is very nearly impractical on secondary storage for indexes consisting of only a few hundred keys, much less thousands of keys. We need to find a way to make insertions and deletions that have only local effects in the index rather than requiring massive reorganization.

These were the two critical problems that confronted Bayer and McCreight in 1970. They serve as guideposts for steering our discussion of the use of tree structures and multilevel indexes for secondary storage retrieval.

9.3 Indexing with Binary Search Trees

Let's begin by addressing the second of these two problems: looking at the cost of keeping a list in sorted order so we can perform binary searches. Given the sorted list in Fig. 9.1, we can express a binary search of this list as a *binary search tree,* as shown in Fig. 9.2.

Using elementary data structure techniques, it is a simple matter to create nodes that contain right and left link fields so the binary search tree can be constructed as a linked structure. Figure 9.3 illustrates a linked representation of the first two levels of the binary search tree shown in Fig. 9.2. In each node, the left and right links point to the left and right *children* of the node.

What is wrong with binary search trees? We have already said that binary search is not fast enough for disk resident indexing. Hence, a binary search tree cannot solve our problem as stated earlier. However, this is not the only problem with binary search trees. Chief among these is the lack of an effective strategy of balancing the tree. That is, making sure that the height of the leaves of the tree is uniform: no leaf is much farther from the root than any other leaf. Historically, a number of attempts were made to solve these problems, and we will look at two of them: AVL trees and paged binary trees.

AX CL DE FB FT HN JD KF NR PA RF SD TK WS YJ

Figure 9.1 Sorted list of keys.

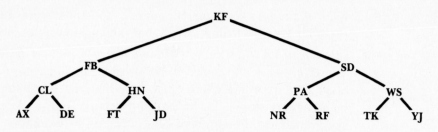

Figure 9.2 Binary search tree representation of the list of keys.

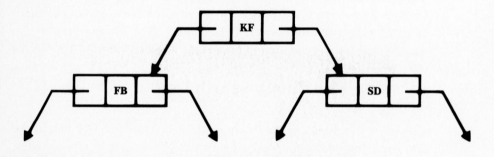

Figure 9.3 Linked representation of part of a binary search tree.

However, to focus on the costs and not the advantages is to miss the important new capability that this tree structure gives us: we no longer have to sort the file to perform a binary search. Note that the records in the file illustrated in Fig. 9.4 appear in random rather than sorted order. The sequence of the records in the file has no necessary relation to the structure of the tree; all the information about the logical structure is carried in the link fields. The very positive consequence that follows from this is that if we add a new key to the file, such as LV, we need only link it to the appropriate leaf node to create a tree that provides search performance that is as good as we would get with a binary search on a sorted list. The tree with LV added is illustrated in Fig. 9.5 (page 376).

Search performance on this tree is still good because the tree is in a *balanced* state. By balanced we mean that the height of the shortest path to a leaf does not differ from the height of the longest path by more than one level. For the tree in Fig. 9.5, this difference of one is as close as we can get to *complete balance,* in which all the paths from root to leaf are exactly the same length.

Figure 9.4
Record contents for a
linked representation
of the binary tree in
Figure 9.2.

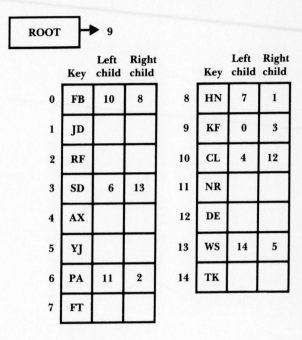

	Key	Left child	Right child		Key	Left child	Right child
0	FB	10	8	8	HN	7	1
1	JD			9	KF	0	3
2	RF			10	CL	4	12
3	SD	6	13	11	NR		
4	AX			12	DE		
5	YJ			13	WS	14	5
6	PA	11	2	14	TK		
7	FT						

Consider what happens if we go on to enter the following eight keys to the tree in the sequence in which they appear:

```
NP MB TM LA UF ND TS NK
```

Just searching down through the tree and adding each key at its correct position in the search tree results in the tree shown in Fig. 9.6.

The tree is now out of balance. This is a typical result for trees that are built by placing keys into the tree as they occur without rearrangement. The resulting disparity between the length of various search paths is undesirable in any binary search tree, but it is especially troublesome if the nodes of the tree are being kept on secondary storage. There are now keys that require seven, eight, or nine seeks for retrieval. A binary search on a sorted list of these twenty-four keys requires only five seeks in the worst case. Although the use of a tree lets us avoid sorting, we are paying for this convenience in terms of extra seeks at retrieval time. For trees with hundreds of keys, in which an out-of-balance search path might extend to thirty, forty, or more seeks, this price is too high.

If each node is treated as a fixed-length record in which the link fields contain relative record numbers (RRNs) pointing to other nodes, then it is possible to place such a tree structure on secondary storage. Figure 9.4

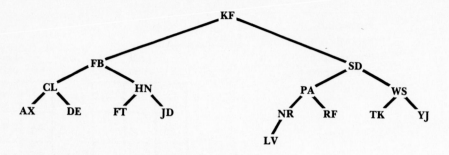

Figure 9.5 Binary search tree with LV added.

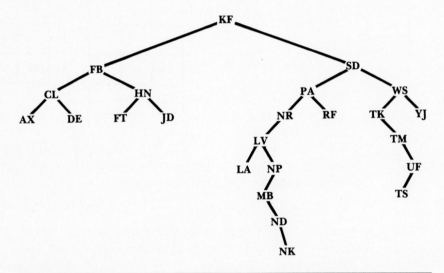

Figure 9.6 Binary search tree showing the effect of added keys.

illustrates the contents of the fifteen records that would be required to form the binary tree depicted in Fig. 9.2.

Note that more than half of the link fields in the file are empty because they are leaf nodes with no children. In practice, leaf nodes need to contain some special character, such as -1, to indicate that the search through the tree has reached the leaf level and that there are no more nodes on the search path. We leave the fields blank in this figure to make them more noticeable, illustrating the potentially substantial cost in terms of space utilization incurred by this kind of linked representation of a tree.

9.3.1 AVL Trees

Earlier we said that there is no *necessary* relationship between the order in which keys are entered and the structure of the tree. We stress the word *necessary* because it is clear that order of entry is, in fact, important in determining the structure of the sample tree illustrated in Fig. 9.6. The reason for this sensitivity to the order of entry is that, so far, we have just been linking the newest nodes at the leaf levels of the tree. This approach can result in some very undesirable tree organizations. Suppose, for example, that our keys consist of the letters A–G and that we receive these keys in alphabetical order. Linking the nodes as we receive them produces a degenerate tree that is, in fact, nothing more than a linked list, as illustrated in Fig. 9.7.

The solution to this problem is somehow to reorganize the nodes of the tree as we receive new keys, maintaining a near optimal tree structure. One elegant method for handling such reorganization results in a class of trees known as *AVL trees,* in honor of the pair of Russian mathematicians, G. M. Adel'son-Vel'skii and E. M. Landis, who first defined them. An AVL tree is a *height-balanced* tree. This means that there is a limit placed on the amount of difference allowed between the heights of any two subtrees sharing a common root. In an AVL tree the maximum allowable difference is one. An AVL tree is therefore called a *height-balanced 1-tree* or *HB(1) tree.* It is a member of a more general class of height-balanced trees known as *HB(k)* trees, which are permitted to be *k* levels out of balance.

The trees illustrated in Fig. 9.8 have the AVL, or HB(1) property. Note that no two subtrees of any root differ by more than one level. The trees in Fig. 9.9 are *not* AVL trees. In each of these trees, the root of the subtree that is not in balance is marked with an *X*.

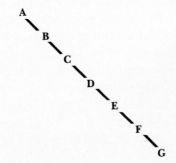

Figure 9.7
A degenerate tree.

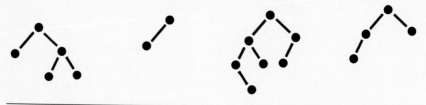

Figure 9.8 AVL trees.

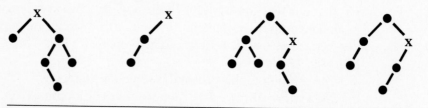

Figure 9.9 Trees that are not AVL trees.

The two features that make AVL trees important are

■ By setting a maximum allowable difference in the height of any two subtrees, AVL trees guarantee a minimum level of performance in searching; and

■ Maintaining a tree in AVL form as new nodes are inserted involves the use of one of a set of four possible rotations. Each of the rotations is confined to a single, local area of the tree. The most complex of the rotations requires only five pointer reassignments.

AVL trees are an important class of data structure. The operations used to build and maintain AVL trees are described in Knuth (1998), Standish (1980), and elsewhere. AVL trees are not themselves directly applicable to most file structure problems because, like all strictly *binary* trees, they have too many levels—they are too *deep*. However, in the context of our general discussion of the problem of accessing and maintaining indexes that are too large to fit in memory, AVL trees are interesting because they suggest that it is possible to define procedures that maintain height balance.

The fact that an AVL tree is height-balanced guarantees that search performance approximates that of a *completely balanced* tree. For example, the completely balanced form of a tree made up from the input keys

B C G E F D A

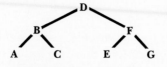

Figure 9.10
A completely balanced
search tree.

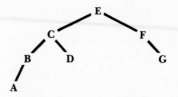

Figure 9.11 A search tree
constructed using AVL procedures.

is illustrated in Fig. 9.10, and the AVL tree resulting from the same input keys, arriving in the same sequence, is illustrated in Fig. 9.11.

For a completely balanced tree, the worst-case search to find a key, given N possible keys, looks at

$$\log_2 (N + 1)$$

levels of the tree. For an AVL tree, the worst-case search could look at

$$1.44 \log_2 (N + 2)$$

levels. So, given 1 000 000 keys, a completely balanced tree requires seeking to 20 levels for some of the keys, but never to 21 levels. If the tree is an AVL tree, the maximum number of levels increases to only 29. This is a very interesting result, given that the AVL procedures guarantee that a single reorganization requires no more than five pointer reassignments. Empirical studies by VanDoren and Gray (1974), among others, have shown that such local reorganizations are required for approximately every other insertion into the tree and for approximately every fourth deletion. So height balancing using AVL methods guarantees that we will obtain a reasonable approximation of optimal binary tree performance at a cost that is acceptable in most applications using primary, random-access memory.

When we are using secondary storage, a procedure that requires more than five or six seeks to find a key is less than desirable; twenty or twenty-eight seeks is unacceptable. Returning to the two problems that we identified earlier in this chapter,

■ Binary searching requires too many seeks, and

■ Keeping an index in sorted order is expensive,

we can see that height-balanced trees provide an acceptable solution to the second problem. Now we need to turn our attention to the first problem.

9.3.2 Paged Binary Trees

Disk utilization of a binary search tree is extremely inefficient. That is, when we read a node of a binary search tree, there are only three useful pieces of information—the key value and the addresses of the left and right subtrees. Each disk read produces a minimum of a single page—at least 512 bytes. Reading a binary node wastes most of the data read from the disk. Since this disk read is the critical factor in the cost of searching, we cannot afford to waste the reads. It is imperative that we choose an index record that uses all of the space read from the disk.

The paged binary tree attempts to address the problem by locating multiple binary nodes on the same disk page. In a paged system, you do not incur the cost of a disk seek just to get a few bytes. Instead, once you have taken the time to seek to an area of the disk, you read in an entire page from the file. This page might consist of a great many individual records. If the next bit of information you need from the disk is in the page that was just read in, you have saved the cost of a disk access.

Paging, then, is a potential solution to the inefficient disk utilization of binary search trees. By dividing a binary tree into pages and then storing each page in a block of contiguous locations on disk, we should be able to reduce the number of seeks associated with any search. Figure 9.12 illustrates such a paged tree. In this tree we are able to locate any one

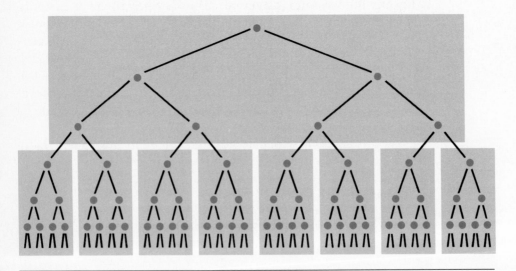

Figure 9.12 Paged binary tree.

of the 63 nodes in the tree with no more than two disk accesses. Note that every page holds 7 nodes and can branch to eight new pages. If we extend the tree to one additional level of paging, we add sixty-four new pages; we can then find any one of 511 nodes in only three seeks. Adding yet another level of paging lets us find any one of 4095 nodes in only four seeks. A binary search of a list of 4095 items can take as many as twelve seeks.

Clearly, breaking the tree into pages has the potential to result in faster searching on secondary storage, providing us with much faster retrieval than any other form of keyed access that we have considered up to this point. Moreover, our use of a page size of seven in Fig. 9.12 is dictated more by the constraints of the printed page than by anything having to do with secondary storage devices. A more typical example of a page size might be 8 kilobytes, capable of holding 511 key/reference field pairs. Given this page size and assuming that each page contains a completely balanced full tree and that the pages are organized as a completely balanced full tree, it is then possible to find any one of 134 217 727 keys with only three seeks. That is the kind of performance we are looking for. Note that, while the number of seeks required for a worst-case search of a completely full, balanced binary tree is

$$\log_2 (N + 1)$$

where N is the number of keys in the tree, the number of seeks required for the *paged* versions of a completely full, balanced tree is

$$\log_{k+1} (N + 1)$$

where N is, once again, the number of keys. The new variable, k, is the number of keys held in a single page. The second formula is actually a generalization of the first, since the number of keys in a page of a purely binary tree is 1. It is the logarithmic effect of the page size that makes the impact of paging so dramatic:

$$\log_2 (134\ 217\ 727 + 1) = 27 \text{ seeks}$$
$$\log_{511+1} (134\ 217\ 727 + 1) = 3 \text{ seeks}$$

The use of large pages does not come free. Every access to a page requires the transmission of a large amount of data, most of which is not used. This extra transmission time is well worth the cost, however, because it saves so many seeks, which are far more time-consuming than the extra transmissions. A much more serious problem, which we look at next, has to do with keeping the paged tree organized.

9.3.3 Problems with Paged Trees

The major problem with paged trees is still inefficient disk usage. In the example in Fig. 9.12, there are seven tree nodes per page. Of the fourteen reference fields in a single page, six of them are reference nodes within the page. That is, we are using fourteen reference fields to distinguish between eight subtrees. We could represent the same information with seven key fields and eight subtree references. A significant amount of the space in the node is still being wasted.

Is there any advantage to storing a binary search tree within the page? It's true that in doing so we can perform binary search. However, if the keys are stored in an array, we can still do our binary search. The only problem here is that insertion requires a linear number of operations. We have to remember, however, that the factor that determines the cost of search is the number of disk accesses. We can do almost anything in memory in the time it takes to read a page. The bottom line is that there is no compelling reason to produce a tree inside the page.

The second problem, if we decide to implement a paged tree, is how to build it. If we have the entire set of keys in hand before the tree is built, the solution to the problem is relatively straightforward: we can sort the list of keys and build the tree from this sorted list. Most important, if we plan to start building the tree from the root, we know that the middle key in the sorted list of keys should be the *root key* within the *root page* of the tree. In short, we know where to begin and are assured that this beginning point will divide the set of keys in a balanced manner.

Unfortunately, the problem is much more complicated if we are receiving keys in random order and inserting them as soon as we receive them. Assume that we must build a paged tree as we receive the following sequence of single-letter keys:

```
C S D T A M P I B W N G U R K E H O L J Y Q Z F X V
```

We will build a paged binary tree that contains a maximum of three keys per page. As we insert the keys, we rotate them within a page as necessary to keep each page as balanced as possible. The resulting tree is illustrated in Fig. 9.13. Evaluated in terms of the depth of the tree (measured in pages), this tree does not turn out too badly. (Consider, for example, what happens if the keys arrive in alphabetical order.)

Even though this tree is not dramatically misshapen, it clearly illustrates the difficulties inherent in building a paged binary tree from the top down. When you start from the root, the initial keys must, of necessity, go into the root. In this example at least two of these keys, C and D, are not keys that we want there. They are adjacent in sequence and tend toward the beginning of the total set of keys. Consequently, they force the tree out of balance.

Once the wrong keys are placed in the root of the tree (or in the root of any subtree farther down the tree), what can you do about it? Unfortunately, there is no easy answer to this. We cannot simply rotate entire pages of the tree in the same way that we would rotate individual keys in an unpaged tree. If we rotate the tree so the initial root page moves down to the left, moving the C and D keys into a better position, then the S key is out of place. So we must break up the pages. This opens up a whole world of possibilities and difficulties. Breaking up the pages implies rearranging them to create new pages that are both internally balanced and well arranged relative to other pages. Try creating a page rearrangement algorithm for the simple, three-keys-per-page tree from Fig. 9.13. You will find it very difficult to create an algorithm that has only local effects, rearranging just a few pages. The tendency is for rearrangements and adjustments to spread out through a large part of the tree. This situation grows even more complex with larger page sizes.

So, although we have determined that collecting keys into pages is a very good idea from the standpoint of reducing seeks to the disk, we have

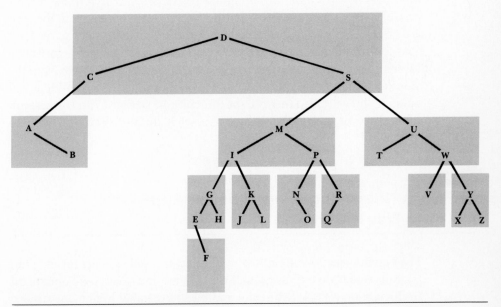

Figure 9.13 Paged tree constructed from keys arriving in random input sequence.

not yet found a way to collect the right keys. We are still confronting at least two unresolved questions:

- How do we ensure that the keys in the root page turn out to be good *separator* keys, dividing up the set of other keys more or less evenly?

- How do we avoid grouping keys, such as C, D, and S in our example, that should not share a page?

There is, in addition, a third question that we have not yet had to confront because of the small page size of our sample tree:

- How can we guarantee that each of the pages contains at least some minimum number of keys? If we are working with a larger page size, such as 8191 keys per page, we want to avoid situations in which a large number of pages each contains only a few dozen keys.

Bayer and McCreight's 1972 B-tree article provides a solution directed precisely at these questions.

A number of the elegant, powerful ideas used in computer science have grown out of looking at a problem from a different viewpoint. B-trees are an example of this viewpoint-shift phenomenon.

The key insight required to make the leap from the kinds of trees we have been considering to a new solution, B-trees, is that we can choose to *build trees upward from the bottom instead of downward from the top.* So far, we have assumed the necessity of starting construction from the root as a given. Then, as we found that we had the wrong keys in the root, we tried to find ways to repair the problem with rearrangement algorithms. Bayer and McCreight recognized that the decision to work down from the root was, of itself, the problem. Rather than finding ways to undo a bad situation, they decided to avoid the difficulty altogether. With B-trees, you allow the root to *emerge*, rather than set it up and then find ways to change it.

9.4 Multilevel Indexing: A Better Approach to Tree Indexes

The previous section attempted to develop an ideal strategy for indexing large files based on building search trees, but serious flaws were uncovered. In this section we take a different approach. Instead of basing our strategy on binary tree searches, we start with the single record indexing strategy of

Chapter 7. We extend this to multirecord indexes and then multilevel indexes. Ultimately, this approach, too, is flawed, but it is the source of the primary efficiency of searching and leads us directly to B-trees.

In Chapter 7, we noted that a single record index puts a limit on the number of keys allowed and that large files need multirecord indexes. A multirecord index consists of a sequence of simple index records. The keys in one record in the list are all smaller than the keys of the next record. A binary search is possible on a file that consists of an ordered sequence of index records, but we already know that binary search is too expensive.

To illustrate the benefits of an indexed approach, we use the large example file of Chapter 8, an 80-megabyte file of 8 000 000 records, 100 bytes each, with 10-byte keys. An index of this file has 8 000 000 key-reference pairs divided among a sequence of index records. Let's suppose that we can put 100 key-reference pairs in a single index record. Hence there are 80 000 records in the index. In order to build the index, we need to read the original file, extract the key from each record, and sort the keys. The strategies outlined in Chapter 8 can be used for this sorting. The 100 largest keys are inserted into an index record, and that record is written to the index file. The next largest 100 keys go into the next record of the file, and so on. This continues until we have 80 000 index records in the index file. Although we have reduced the number of records to be searched by a factor of 100, we still must find a way to speed up the search of this 80 000-record file.

Can we build an index of the index file, and how big will it be? Since the index records form a sorted list of keys, we can choose one of the keys (for example, the largest) in each index record as the key of that whole record. These *second-level* keys can be used to build a second-level index with 80 000 keys, or 800 index records. In searching the second-level index for a key k, we choose the smallest second-level key that is greater than or equal to k. If k is in the first-level index, it must be in the block referenced by that second-level key.

Continuing to a third level, we need just 8 index records to index the largest keys in the 800 second-level records. Finally, the fourth level consists of a single index record with only 8 keys. These four levels together form an index tree with a fan-out of 100 and can be stored in a single index file. Each node of the tree is an index record with 100 children. Each of the children of a node is itself an index node, except at the leaves. The children of the leaf nodes are data records.

A single index file containing the full four-level index of 8 000 000 records requires 80 809 index records, each with 100 key-reference pairs. The lowest level index is an index to the data file, and its reference fields are record addresses in the data file. The other indexes use their reference fields for index record addresses, that is, addresses within the index file.

The costs associated with this multilevel index file are the space overhead of maintaining the extra levels, the search time, and the time to insert and delete elements. The space overhead is 809 more records than the 80 000 minimum for an index of the data file. This is just 1 percent. Certainly this is not a burden.

The search time is simple to calculate—it's three disk reads! An analysis of search time always has multiple parts: the minimum search time, the maximum search time, and the average search time for keys that are in the index and for keys that are not in the index. For this multilevel index, all of these cases require searching four index records. That is, each level of the index must be searched. For a key that is in the index, we need to search all the way to the bottom level to get the data record address. For a key not in the index, we need to search all the way to the bottom to determine that it is missing. The average, minimum, and maximum number of index blocks to search are all four, that is, the number of levels in the index. Since there is only one block at the top level, we can keep that block in memory. Hence, a maximum of three disk accesses are required for any key search. It might require fewer disk reads if any of the other index records are already in memory.

Look how far we've come: an arbitrary record in an 80-megabyte file can be read with just four disk accesses—three to search the index and one to read the data record. The total space overhead, including the primary index, is well below 10 percent of the data file size. This tree is not full, since the root node has only eight children and can accommodate one hundred. This four-level tree will accommodate twelve times this many data records, or a total of 100 million records in a file of 10 gigabytes. Any one of these records can be found with only three disk accesses. This is what we need to produce efficient indexed access!

The final factor in the cost of multilevel indexes is the hardest one. How can we insert keys into the index? Recall that the first-level index is an ordered sequence of records. Does this imply that the index file must be sorted? The search strategy relies on indexes and record addresses, not on record placement in the file. As with the simple indexes of Chapter 7, this indexed search supports entry-sequenced records. As long as the location of the highest level index record is known, the other records can be anywhere in the file.

Having an entry-sequenced index file does not eliminate the possibility of linear insertion time. For instance, suppose a new key is added that will be the smallest key in the index. This key must be inserted into the first record of the first-level index. Since that record is already full with one hundred elements, its largest key must be inserted into the second record, and so on. Every record in the first-level index must be changed. This requires 80 000 reads and writes. This is truly a fatal flaw in simple multilevel indexing.

9.5   B-Trees: Working up from the Bottom

B-trees are multilevel indexes that solve the problem of linear cost of insertion and deletion. This is what makes B-trees so good, and why they are now the standard way to represent indexes. The solution is twofold. First, don't require that the index records be full. Second, don't shift the overfull keys to the next record; instead split an overfull record into two records, each half full. Deletion takes a similar strategy of merging two records into a single record when necessary.

Each node of a B-tree is an index record. Each of these records has the same maximum number of key-reference pairs, called the *order* of the B-tree. The records also have a minimum number of key-reference pairs, typically half of the order. A B-tree of order one hundred has a minimum of fifty keys and a maximum of one hundred keys per record. The only exception is the single root node, which can have a minimum of two keys.

An attempt to insert a new key into an index record that is not full is cheap. Simply update the index record. If the new key is the new largest key in the index record, it is the new higher-level key of that record, and the next higher level of the index must be updated. The cost is bounded by the height of the tree.

When insertion into an index record causes it to be overfull, it is split into two records, each with half of the keys. Since a new index node has been created at this level, the largest key in this new node must be inserted into the next higher level node. We call this the *promotion* of the key. This promotion may cause an overflow at that level. This in turn causes that node to be split, and a key promoted to the next level. This continues as far as necessary. If the index record at the highest level overflows, it must be split. This causes another level to be added to the multilevel index. In this way, a B-tree grows up from the leaves. Again the cost of insertion is bounded by the height of the tree.

The rest of the secrets of B-trees are just working out the details. How to split nodes, how to promote keys, how to increase the height of the tree, and how to delete keys.

9.6   Example of Creating a B-Tree

Let's see how a B-tree grows given the key sequence that produces the paged binary tree illustrated in Fig. 9.13. The sequence is

C S D T A M P I B W N G U R K E H O L J Y Q Z F X V

We use an order four B-tree (maximum of four key-reference pairs per node). Using such a small node size has the advantage of causing pages to split more frequently, providing us with more examples of splitting. We omit explicit indication of the reference fields so we can fit a larger tree on the printed page.

Figure 9.14 illustrates the growth of the tree up to the point where it is about to split the root for the second time. The tree starts with a single empty record. In Fig. 9.14(a), the first four keys are inserted into that record. When the fifth key, A, is added in Fig. 9.14(b), the original node is split and the tree grows by one level as a new root is created. The keys in the root are the largest key in the left leaf, D, and the largest key in the right leaf, T.

The keys M, P, and I all belong in the rightmost leaf node, since they are larger than the largest key in the right node. However, inserting I makes the rightmost leaf node overfull, and it must be split, as shown in Fig. 9.14(c). The largest key in the new node, P, is inserted into the root. This process continues in Figs. 9.14(d) and (e), where B, W, N, G, and U are inserted.

In the tree of Fig. 9.14(e), the next key in the list, R, should be put into the rightmost leaf node, since it is greater than the largest key in the previous node, P, and less than or equal to the largest key in that node, W. However, the rightmost leaf node is full, and so is the root. Splitting that leaf node will overfill the root node. At this point a new root must be created, and the height of the tree increased to three.

Figure 9.15 shows the tree as it grows to height three. The figure also shows how the tree continues to grow as the remaining keys in the sequence are added. Figure 9.15(b) stops after Z is added. The next key in the sequence, F, requires splitting the second-leaf node, as shown in Fig. 9.15(c). Although the leaf level of the tree is not shown in a single line, it is still a single level. Insertions of X and V causes the rightmost leaf to be

a) Insertions of C, S, D, T
into the initial node.

b) Insertion of A causes node to split
and the largest key in each leaf node
(D and T) to be placed in the root
node.

c) M and P are inserted into the
rightmost leaf node, then insertion
of I causes it to split.

d) Insertions of B, W, N, and G into
leaf nodes causes another split and
the root is now full.

e) Insertion of U proceeds without
incident, but R would have to be
inserted into the rightmost leaf,
which is full.

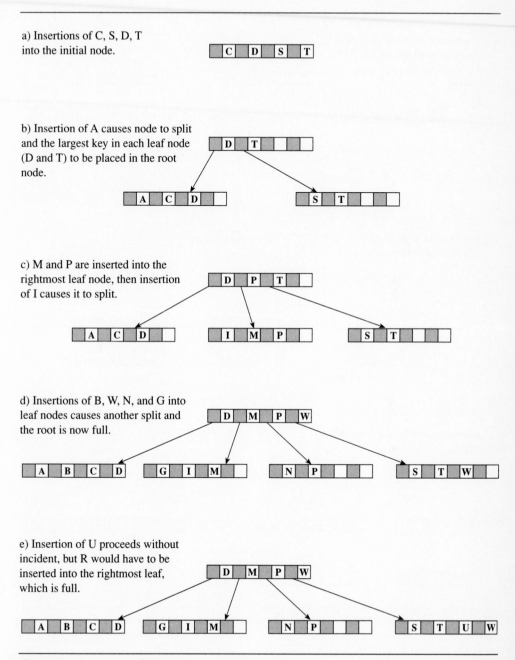

Figure 9.14 Growth of a B-tree, part 1. The tree grows to a point at which the root needs
to be split the second time.

a) Insertion of R causes the rightmost leaf node to split, insertion into the root to split and the tree grows to level three.

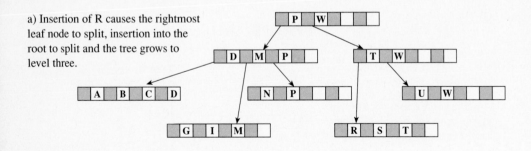

b) Insertions of K, E, H, O, L, J, Y, Q, and Z, continue with another node split.

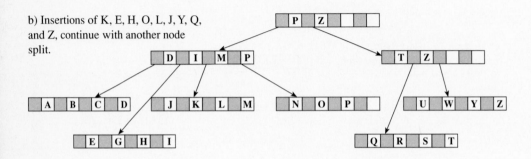

c) Insertions of F, X, and V finish the insertion of the alphabet.

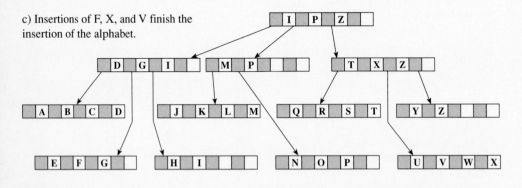

Figure 9.15 Growth of a B-tree, part 2. The root splits to level three; remaining keys are inserted.

overfull and split. The rightmost leaf of the middle level is also overfull and is split. All twenty-six letters are inserted into a tree of height three and order four.

Note that the number of nodes affected by any insertion is never more than two nodes per level (one changed and a new one created by a split), so the insertion cost is strictly linear in the height of the tree.

9.7   An Object-Oriented Representation of B-Trees

9.7.1 Class BTreeNode: Representing B-Tree Nodes in Memory

As we have seen, a B-tree is an index file associated with a data file. Most of the operations on B-trees, including insertion and deletion, are applied to the B-tree nodes in memory. The B-tree file simply stores the nodes when they are not in memory. Hence, we need a class to represent the memory resident B-tree nodes. Class BTreeNode, given in Fig. 9.16 and in file btnode.h of Appendix I, is a template class based on the SimpleIndex template class that was described in Section 7.4.3. Note that a BTreeNode object has methods to insert and remove a key and to split and merge nodes. There are also protected members that store the file address of the node and the minimum and maximum number of keys. You may notice that there is no search method defined in the class. The search method of the base class SimpleIndex works perfectly well.

It is important to note that not every data member of a BTreeNode has to be stored when the object is not in memory. The difference between the memory and the disk representations of BTreeNode objects is managed by the pack and unpack operations.

Class BTreeNode is designed to support some optimizations of the in-memory operations. For example, the number of keys is actually one more than the order of the tree, as shown in the constructor. The call to the SimpleIndex constructor creates an index record with maxKeys+1 elements:

```
template <class keyType>
BTreeNode<keyType>::BTreeNode(int maxKeys, int unique)
    :SimpleIndex<keyType>(maxKeys+1, unique)
{   Init ();}
```

```
template <class keyType>
class BTreeNode: public SimpleIndex <keyType>
// this is the in-memory version of the BTreeNode
{public:
    BTreeNode(int maxKeys, int unique = 1);
    int Insert (const keyType key, int recAddr);
    int Remove (const keyType key, int recAddr = -1);
    int LargestKey (); // returns value of Largest key
    int Split (BTreeNode<keyType>*newNode);//move into newNode
    int Pack (IOBuffer& buffer) const;
    int Unpack (IOBuffer& buffer);
protected:
    int MaxBKeys; // maximum number of keys in a node
    int Init ();
    friend class BTree<keyType>;
};
```

Figure 9.16 The main members and methods of class BTreeNode: template class for B-tree node in memory.

For this class, the order of the B-tree node (member `MaxBKeys`) is one less than the value of `MaxKeys`, which is a member of the base class `SimpleIndex`. Making the index record larger allows the `Insert` method to create an overfull node. The caller of `BTreeNode::Insert` needs to respond to the overflow in an appropriate fashion. Similarly, the `Remove` method can create an underfull node.

Method `Insert` simply calls `SimpleIndex::Insert` and then checks for overflow. The value returned is 1 for success, 0 for failure, and −1 for overflow:

```
template <class keyType>
int BTreeNode<keyType>::Insert (const keyType key, int recAddr)
{
    int result = SimpleIndex<keyType>::Insert (key, recAddr);
    if (!result) return 0; // insert failed
    if (NumKeys > MaxBKeys) return -1; // node overflow
    return 1;
}
```

9.7.2 Class BTree: Supporting Files of B-Tree Nodes

We now look at class BTree which uses in-memory BTreeNode objects, adds the file access portion, and enforces the consistent size of the nodes. Figure 9.17 and file btree.h of Appendix I contain the definition of class BTree. Here are methods to create, open, and close a B-tree and to search, insert, and remove key-reference pairs. In the protected area of the class, we find methods to transfer nodes from disk to memory (Fetch) and back to disk (Store). There are members that hold the root node in memory and represent the height of the tree and the file of index records. Member Nodes is used to keep a collection of tree nodes in memory and reduce disk accesses, as will be explained later.

```
template <class keyType>
class BTree
{public:
    BTree(int order, int keySize=sizeof(keyType), int unique=1);
    int Open (char * name, int mode);
    int Create (char * name, int mode);
    int Close ();
    int Insert (const keyType key, const int recAddr);
    int Remove (const keyType key, const int recAddr = -1);
    int Search (const keyType key, const int recAddr = -1);
protected:
    typedef BTreeNode<keyType> BTNode; // necessary shorthand
    BTNode * FindLeaf (const keyType key);
        // load a branch into memory down to the leaf with key
    BTNode * Fetch(const int recaddr);//load node into memory
    int Store (BTNode *);// store node into file
    BTNode Root;
    int Height; // height of tree
    int Order; // order of tree
    BTNode ** Nodes; // storage for a branch
    // Nodes[1] is level 1, etc. (see FindLeaf)
    // Nodes[Height-1] is leaf
    RecordFile<BTNode> BTreeFile;
};
```

Figure 9.17 Main members and methods of class BTree: whole B-tree implementation—including methods Create, Open, Search, Insert, and Remove.

9.8 B-Tree Methods Search, Insert, and Others

Now that we have seen the principles of B-tree operations and we have the class definitions and the single node operations, we are ready to consider the details of the B-tree methods.

9.8.1 Searching

The first B-tree method we examine is a tree-searching procedure. Searching is a good place to begin because it is relatively simple, yet it still illustrates the characteristic aspects of most B-tree algorithms:

■ They are iterative, and

■ They work in two stages, operating alternatively on entire pages (class BTree) and then *within* pages (class BTreeNode).

The searching procedure is iterative, loading a page into memory and then searching through the page, looking for the key at successively lower levels of the tree until it reaches the leaf level. Figure 9.18 contains the code for method Search and the protected method FindLeaf that does almost all of the work. Let's work through the methods by hand, searching for the key L in the tree illustrated in Fig. 9.15(a). For an object btree of type BTree<char> and an integer recAddr, the following code finds that there is no data file record with key L:

```
recAddr = btree.Search ('L');
```

Method Search calls method FindLeaf, which searches down a branch of the tree, beginning at the root, which is referenced by the pointer value Nodes[0]. In the first iteration, with level = 1, the line

```
recAddr = Nodes[level-1]->Search(key,-1,0);
```

is an inexact search and finds that L is less than P, the first key in the record. Hence, recAddr is set to the first reference in the root node, which is the index file address of the first node in the second level of the tree of Fig. 9.15(a). The line

```
Nodes[level]=Fetch(recAddr);
```

reads that second-level node into a new BTreeNode object and makes Nodes[1] point to this new object. The second iteration, with level = 2, searches for L in this node. Since L is less than M, the second key in the

```
template <class keyType>
int BTree<keyType>::Search (const keyType key, const int recAddr)
{
    BTreeNode<keyType> * leafNode;
    leafNode = FindLeaf (key);
    return leafNode -> Search (key, recAddr);
}

template <class keyType>
BTreeNode<keyType> * BTree<keyType>::FindLeaf (const keyType key)
// load a branch into memory down to the leaf with key
{
    int recAddr, level;
    for (level = 1; level < Height; level++)
    {
        recAddr = Nodes[level-1]->Search(key,-1,0);//inexact search
        Nodes[level]=Fetch(recAddr);
    }
    return Nodes[level-1];
}
```

Figure 9.18 Method BTree::Search and BTree::FindLeaf.

record, the second reference is selected, and the second node in the leaf level of the tree is loaded into Nodes[2]. After the for loop increments level, the iteration stops, and FindLeaf returns the address of this leaf node. At the end of this method, the array Nodes contains pointers to the complete branch of the tree.

After FindLeaf returns, method Search uses an exact search of the leaf node to find that there is no data record that has key L. The value returned is − 1.

Now let's use method Search to look for G, which *is* in the tree of Fig. 9.15(a). It follows the same downward path that it did for L, but this time the exact search in method Search finds G in position 1 of the second-leaf node. It returns the first reference field in the node, which is the data file address of the record with key G.

9.8.2 Insertion

There are two important observations we can make about the insertion, splitting, and promotion process:

■ It begins with a search that proceeds all the way down to the leaf level, and

■ After finding the insertion location at the leaf level, the work of insertion, overflow detection, and splitting proceeds upward from the bottom.

Consequently, we can conceive of our iterative procedure as having three phases:

1. Search to the leaf level, using method `FindLeaf`, before the iteration;
2. Insertion, overflow detection, and splitting on the upward path;
3. Creation of a new root node, if the current root was split.

Let's use the example of inserting R and its data record address (called `recAddr`) into the tree of Fig. 9.14(e) so we can watch the insertion procedure work through these phases. The result of this insertion is shown in Fig. 9.15(a). Method `Insert` is the most complicated of the methods included in file `btree.tc` in Appendix I. We will look at some of its code here.

The first operation in method `Insert` is to search to the root for key R using `FindLeaf`:

```
thisNode = FindLeaf (key);
```

As described above, `FindLeaf` loads a complete branch into memory. In this case, `Nodes[0]` is the root node, and `Nodes[1]` is the rightmost leaf node (containing S, T, U, and W).

The next step is to insert *R* into the leaf node

```
result = thisNode -> Insert (key, recAddr);
```

The result here is that an overflow is detected. The object `thisNode` now has five keys. The node must be split into two nodes, using the following code:

```
newNode = NewNode();
thisNode -> Split (newNode);
Store(thisNode);  Store(newNode);
```

Now the two nodes, one with keys R, S, and T, and one with U and W, have been stored back in the file. We are done with the leaf level and are ready to move up the tree.

The next step is to update the parent node. Since the largest key in `thisNode` has changed, method `UpdateKey` is used to record the change (`largestKey` has been set to the previous largest key in `thisNode`):

```
parentNode->UpdateKey(largestKey, thisNode->LargestKey());
```

Hence the value W in the root is changed to T. Then the largest value in the new node is inserted into the root of the tree:

```
parentNode->Insert(newNode->LargestKey(), newNode->RecAddr);
```

The value W is inserted into the root. This is often called *promoting* the key W. This causes the root to overflow with five keys. Again, the node is split, resulting in a node with keys D, M, and P, and one with T and W.

There is no higher level of the tree, so a new root node is created, and the keys P and W are inserted into it. This is accomplished by the following code:

```
int newAddr = BTreeFile.Append(Root);//put previous root into file
// insert 2 keys in new root node
Root.Keys[0]=thisNode->LargestKey();
Root.RecAddrs[0]=newAddr;
Root.Keys[1]=newNode->LargestKey();
Root.RecAddrs[1]=newNode->RecAddr;
Root.NumKeys=2;
Height++;
```

It begins by appending the old root node into the B-tree file. The very first index record in the file is always the root node, so the old root node, which is no longer the root, must be put somewhere else. Then the insertions are performed. Finally the height of the tree is increased by one.

`Insert` uses a number of support functions. The most obvious one is method `BTreeNode::Split` which distributes the keys between the original page and the new page. Figure 9.19 contains an implementation of this method. Some additional error checking is included in the full implementation in Appendix I. Method `Split` simply removes some of the keys and references from the overfull node and puts them into the new node.

The full implementation of `BTree::Insert` in Appendix I includes code to handle the special case of the insertion of a new largest key in the tree. This is the only case where an insertion adds a new largest key to a node. This can be verified by looking at method `FindLeaf`, which is used to determine the leaf node to be used in insertion. `FindLeaf` always chooses a node whose largest key is greater than or equal to the search key. Hence, the only case where `FindLeaf` returns a leaf node in which the search key is greater than the largest key is where that leaf node is the rightmost node in the tree and the search key is greater than any key in the tree. In this case, the insertion of the new key

```
template <class keyType>
int BTreeNode<keyType>::Split (BTreeNode<keyType> * newNode)
{
    // find the first Key to be moved into the new node
    int midpt = (NumKeys+1)/2;
    int numNewKeys = NumKeys - midpt;
    // move the keys and recaddrs from this to newNode
    for (int i = midpt; i< NumKeys; i++)
    {
        newNode->Keys[i-midpt] = Keys[i];
        newNode->RecAddrs[i-midpt] = RecAddrs[i];
    }
    // set number of keys in the two Nodes
    newNode->NumKeys = numNewKeys;
    NumKeys = midpt;
    return 1;
}
```

Figure 9.19 Method `Split` of class `BTreeNode`.

requires changing the largest key in the rightmost node in every level of the index. The code to handle this special case is included in `BTree::Insert`.

9.8.3 Create, Open, and Close

We need methods to create, open, and close B-tree files. Our object-oriented design and the use of objects from previous classes have made these methods quite simple, as you can see in file `btree.tc` of Appendix I. Method `Create` has to write the empty root node into the file `BTreeFile` so that its first record is reserved for that root node. Method `Open` has to open `BTreeFile` and load the root node into memory from the first record in the file. Method `Close` simply stores the root node into `BTreeFile` and closes it.

9.8.4 Testing the B-Tree

The file `tstbtree.cpp` in Appendix I has the full code of a program to test creation and insertion of a B-tree. Figure 9.20 contains most of the code. As you can see, this program uses a single character key (class

```
const char * keys="CSDTAMPIBWNGURKEHOLJYQZFXV";
const int BTreeSize = 4;
main (int argc, char * argv)
{
    int result, i;
    BTree <char> bt (BTreeSize);
    result = bt.Create ("testbt.dat",ios::in|ios::out);
    for (i = 0; i<26; i++)
    {
        cout<<"Inserting "<<keys[i]<<endl;
        result = bt.Insert(keys[i],i);
        bt.Print(cout); // print after each insert
    }
    return 1;
}
```

Figure 9.20 Program tstbtree.cpp.

BTree<char>) and inserts the alphabet in the same order as in Fig. 9.14 and 9.15. The tree that is created is identical in form to those pictured in the figures.

9.9 B-Tree Nomenclature

Before moving on to discuss B-tree performance and variations on the basic B-tree algorithms, we need to formalize our B-tree terminology. Providing careful definitions of terms such as *order* and *leaf* enables us to state precisely the properties that must be present for a data structure to qualify as a B-tree.

This definition of B-tree properties, in turn, informs our discussion of matters such as the procedure for deleting keys from a B-tree.

Unfortunately, the literature on B-trees is not uniform in its use of terms. Reading that literature and keeping up with new developments therefore require some flexibility and some background: the reader needs to be aware of the different uses of some of the fundamental terms.

For example, Bayer and McCreight (1972), Comer (1979), and a few others refer to the *order* of a B-tree as the *minimum* number of *keys* that can be in a page of a tree. So, our initial sample B-tree (Fig. 9.14), which can hold a *maximum* of four keys per page, has an *order* of two, using Bayer and McCreight's terminology. The problem with this definition of order is that it becomes clumsy when you try to account for pages that hold an *odd*, maximum number of keys. For example, consider the following question: Within the Bayer and McCreight framework, is the page of an order three B-tree full when it contains six keys or when it contains seven keys?

Knuth (1998) and others have addressed the odd/even confusion by defining the *order* of a B-tree to be the *maximum* number of *descendants* that a page can have. This is the definition of *order* that we use in this text. Note that this definition differs from Bayer and McCreight's in two ways: it references a *maximum,* not a *minimum,* and it counts *descendants* rather than *keys.*

When you split the page of a B-tree, the descendants are divided as evenly as possible between the new page and the old page. Consequently, every page except the root and the leaves has at *least m/2* descendants. Expressed in terms of a ceiling function, we can say that the minimum number of descendants is $\lceil m/2 \rceil$.

Another term that is used differently by different authors is *leaf.* Bayer and McCreight refer to the lowest level of keys in a B-tree as the leaf level. This is consistent with the nomenclature we have used in this text. Other authors, including Knuth, consider the leaves of a B-tree to be one level *below* the lowest level of keys. In other words, they consider the leaves to be the actual data records that might be pointed to by the lowest level of keys in the tree. We do *not* use this definition; instead we stick with the notion of leaf as the lowest level of B-tree nodes.

Finally, many authors call our definition of B-tree a *B+ tree.* The term *B-tree* is often used for a version of the B-tree that has data record references in all of the nodes, instead of only in the leaf nodes. A major difference is that our version has the full index in the leaf nodes and uses the interior nodes as higher level indexes. This results in a duplication of keys, since each key in an interior node is duplicated at each lower level. The other version eliminates this duplication of key values, and instead includes data record references in interior nodes. While it seems that this will save space and reduce search times, in fact it often does neither. The major deficiency of this version is that the size of the interior nodes is much larger for the same order B-tree. Another way to look at the difference is that for the same amount of space in the interior nodes, by eliminating the data references, we could significantly increase the order of the tree, resulting in shallower trees. Of course, the shallower the tree, the shorter the search.

In this book, we use the term *B⁺ tree* to refer to a somewhat more complex situation in which the data file is not entry sequenced but is organized into a linked list of sorted blocks of records. The data file is organized in much the same way as the leaf nodes of a B-tree. The great advantage of the B⁺ tree organization is that both indexed access and sequential access are optimized. This technique is explained in detail in the next chapter.

You may have recognized that the largest key in each interior B-tree node is not needed in the searching. That is, in method `FindLeaf`, whenever the search key is bigger than any key in the node, the search proceeds to the rightmost child. It is possible and common to implement B-trees with one less key than reference in each interior node. However, the insertion method is made more complicated by this optimization, so it has been omitted in the B-tree classes and is included as a programming exercise.

9.10 Formal Definition of B-Tree Properties

Given these definitions of order and leaf, we can formulate a precise statement of the properties of a B-tree of order *m:*

- Every page has a maximum of *m* descendants.
- Every page, except for the root and the leaves, has at least $\lceil m/2 \rceil$ descendants.
- The root has at least two descendants (unless it is a leaf).
- All the leaves appear on the same level.
- The leaf level forms a complete, ordered index of the associated data file.

9.11 Worst-Case Search Depth

It is important to have a quantitative understanding of the relationship between the page size of a B-tree, the number of keys to be stored in the tree, and the number of levels that the tree can extend. For example, you might know that you need to store 1 000 000 keys and that, given the nature of your storage hardware and the size of your keys, it is reasonable to consider using a B-tree of order 512 (maximum of 511 keys per page). Given these two facts, you need to be able to answer the question: In the worst case, what will be the maximum number of disk accesses required to locate a key in the tree? This is the same as asking how deep the tree will be.

We can answer this question by noting that every key appears in the leaf level. Hence, we need to calculate the maximum height of a tree with 1 000 000 keys in the leaves.

Next we need to observe that we can use the formal definition of B-tree properties to calculate the *minimum* number of descendants that can extend from any level of a B-tree of some given order. This is of interest because we are interested in the *worst-case* depth of the tree. The worst case occurs when every page of the tree has only the minimum number of descendants. In such a case the keys are spread over a *maximal height* for the tree and a *minimal breadth*.

For a B-tree of order m, the minimum number of descendants from the root page is 2, so the second level of the tree contains only 2 pages. Each of these pages, in turn, has at least $\lceil m/2 \rceil$ descendants. The third level, then, contains

$$2 \times \lceil m/2 \rceil$$

pages. Since each of these pages, once again, has a minimum of $\lceil m/2 \rceil$ descendants, the general pattern of the relation between depth and the minimum number of descendants takes the following form:

Level	Minimum number of descendants
1 (root)	2
2	$2 \times \lceil m/2 \rceil$
3	$2 \times \lceil m/2 \rceil \times \lceil m/2 \rceil$ or $2 \times \lceil m/2 \rceil^2$
4	$2 \times \lceil m/2 \rceil^3$
...	...
d	$2 \times \lceil n/2 \rceil^{d-1}$

So, in general, for any level d of a B-tree, the *minimum* number of descendants extending from that level is

$$2 \times \lceil m/2 \rceil^{d-1}$$

For a tree with N keys in its leaves, we can express the relationship between keys and the minimum height d as

$$N \geq 2 \times \lceil m/2 \rceil^{d-1}$$

Solving for d, we arrive at the following expression:

$$d \le 1 + \log_{\lceil m/2 \rceil}(N/2).$$

This expression gives us an *upper bound* for the depth of a B-tree with N keys. Let's find the upper bound for the hypothetical tree that we describe at the start of this section: a tree of order 512 that contains 1 000 000 keys. Substituting these specific numbers into the expression, we find that

$$d \le 1 + \log_{256} 500\ 000$$

or

$$d \le 3.37$$

So we can say that given 1 000 000 keys, a B-tree of order 512 has a depth of no more than three levels.

9.12   Deletion, Merging, and Redistribution

Indexing 1 000 000 keys in no more than three levels of a tree is precisely the kind of performance we are looking for. As we have just seen, this performance is predicated on the B-tree properties we described earlier. In particular, the ability to guarantee that B-trees are broad and shallow rather than narrow and deep is coupled with the rules that state the following:

- Every page except for the root and the leaves has at least $\lceil m/2 \rceil$ descendants.

- A page contains at least $\lceil m/2 \rceil$ keys and no more than m keys.

We have already seen that the process of page splitting guarantees that these properties are maintained when new keys are inserted into the tree. We need to develop some kind of equally reliable guarantee that these properties are maintained when keys are *deleted* from the tree.

Working through some simple deletion situations by hand helps us demonstrate that the deletion of a key can result in several different situations. We start with the B-tree of Fig. 9.15(c) that contains all the letters of the alphabet. Consider what happens when we try to delete some of its keys.

The simplest situation is illustrated in the result of deleting key C in Fig. 9.21(a). Deleting the key from the first leaf node does not cause an

a) Removal of key C from Fig. 9.15c.
Change occurs only in leaf node

b) Result of deleting P from Fig.
9.15c. P changes to O in the second
level and the root.

c) Result of deleting H from Fig.
9.15c. Removal of H caused an
underflow, and two leaf nodes were
merged.

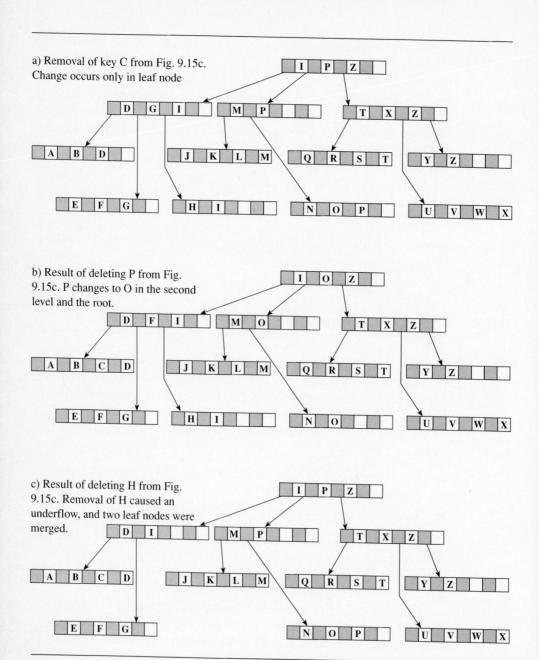

Figure 9.21 Three situations that can occur during deletions.

underflow in the node and does not change its largest value. Consequently, deletion involves nothing more than removing the key from the node.

Deleting the P in Fig. 9.21(b) is more complicated. Removal of P from the second leaf node does not cause underflow, but it does change the largest key in the node. Hence, the second-level node must be modified to reflect this change. The key to the second leaf node becomes O, and the second-level node must be modified so that it contains O instead of P. Since P was the largest key in the second node in the second level, the root node must also have key P replaced by O.

Deleting the H in Fig 9.21(c) causes an underflow in the third leaf node. After H is deleted, the last remaining key in the node, I, is inserted into the neighbor node, and the third leaf node is deleted. Since the second leaf node has only three keys, there is room for the key I in that node. This illustrates a more general *merge* operation. After the merge, the second-level node is modified to reflect the current status of the leaf nodes.

Merging and other modifications can propagate to the root of the B-tree. If the root ends up with only one key and one child, it can be eliminated. Its sole child node becomes the new root of the tree and the tree gets shorter by one level.

The rules for deleting a key k from a node n in a B-tree are as follows:

1. If n has more than the minimum number of keys and the k is not the largest in n, simply delete k from n.

2. If n has more than the minimum number of keys and the k is the largest in n, delete k and modify the higher level indexes to reflect the new largest key in n.

3. If n has exactly the minimum number of keys and one of the siblings of n has few enough keys, merge n with its sibling and delete a key from the parent node.

4. If n has exactly the minimum number of keys and one of the siblings of n has extra keys, redistribute by moving some keys from a sibling to n, and modify the higher level indexes to reflect the new largest keys in the affected nodes.

Rules 3 and 4 include references to "few enough keys" to allow merging and "extra keys" to allow redistribution. These are not exclusive rules, and the implementation of delete is allowed to choose which rule to use when they are both applicable. Look at the example of an order five tree in Fig. 9.22, and consider deleting keys C, M, and W. Since three is the minimum number of keys, deleting any of these keys requires some adjustment of the leaf nodes. In the case of deleting *C*, the only sibling node has three

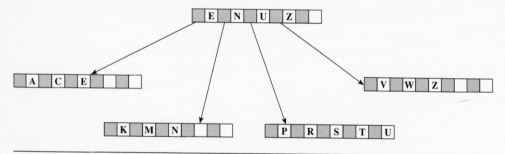

Figure 9.22 Example of order five B-tree. Consider delete of keys C, M, and W.

keys. After deleting C, there are five keys in the two sibling nodes, so a merge is allowed. No redistribution is possible because the sibling node has the minimum number of keys. In the case of deleting W, the only sibling has five keys, so one or two of the keys can be moved to the under-full node. No merge is possible here, since there are seven keys remaining in the two sibling nodes—too many for a single node. In the case of delet-ing M, there are two options: merge with the left sibling or redistribute keys in the right sibling.

9.12.1 Redistribution

Unlike merge, which is a kind of reverse split, redistribution is a new idea. Our insertion algorithm does not require operations analogous to redis-tribution.

Redistribution differs from both splitting and merging in that it never causes the collection of nodes in the tree to change. It is guaranteed to have strictly local effects. Note that the term *sibling* implies that the pages have the same parent page. If there are two nodes at the leaf level that are logi-cally adjacent but do not have the same parent—for example, HI and JKLM in the tree of Fig. 9.22(a)—these nodes are not siblings. Redistribution algorithms are generally written so they do not consider moving keys between nodes that are not siblings, even when they are logi-cally adjacent. Can you see the reasoning behind this restriction?

Another difference between redistribution on the one hand and merg-ing and splitting on the other is that there is no necessary, fixed prescrip-tion for how the keys should be rearranged. A single deletion in a properly formed B-tree cannot cause an underflow of more than one key. Therefore, redistribution can restore the B-tree properties by moving only one key from a sibling into the page that has underflowed, even if the distribution of the keys between the pages is very uneven. Suppose, for example, that we are managing a B-tree of order 101. The minimum number of keys that can be in a page is 50; the maximum is 100. Suppose we have one page that contains the minimum and a sibling that contains the maximum. If a key is deleted from the page containing 50 keys, an underflow condition occurs. We can correct the condition through redistribution by moving one key, 50 keys, or any number of keys between 1 and 50. The usual strategy is to divide the keys as evenly as possible between the pages. In this instance that means moving 25 keys.

9.13   Redistribution During Insertion: A Way to Improve Storage Utilization

As you may recall, B-tree insertion does not require an operation analogous to redistribution; splitting is able to account for all instances of overflow. This does not mean, however, that it is not *desirable* to use redistribution during insertion as an option, particularly since a set of B-tree maintenance algorithms must already include a redistribution procedure to support deletion. Given that a redistribution procedure is already present, what advantage might we gain by using it as an alternative to node splitting?

Redistribution during insertion is a way of avoiding, or at least postponing, the creation of new pages. Rather than splitting a full page and creating two approximately half-full pages, redistribution lets us place some of the overflowing keys into another page. The use of redistribution in place of splitting should therefore tend to make a B-tree more efficient in its utilization of space.

It is possible to quantify this efficiency of space usage by viewing the amount of space used to store information as a percentage of the total amount of space required to hold the B-tree. After a node splits, each of the two resulting pages is about half full. So, in the worst case, space utilization in a B-tree using two-way splitting is around 50 percent. Of course, the actual degree of space utilization is better than this worst-case figure. Yao (1978) has shown that, for large trees of relatively large order, space utilization approaches a theoretical average of about 69 percent if insertion is handled through two-way splitting.

The idea of using redistribution as an alternative to splitting when possible, splitting a page only when both of its siblings are full, is introduced in Bayer and McCreight's original paper (1972). The paper includes some experimental results that show that two-way splitting results in a space utilization of 67 percent for a tree of order 121 after five thousand random insertions. When the experiment was repeated, using redistribution when possible, space utilization increased to over 86 percent. Subsequent empirical testing by students at Oklahoma State University using B-trees of order 49 and 303 also resulted in space utilization exceeding 85 percent when redistribution was used. These findings and others suggest that any serious application of B-trees to even moderately large files should implement insertion procedures that handle overflow through redistribution when possible.

9.14   B* Trees

In his review and amplification of work on B-trees in 1973, Knuth (1998) extends the notion of redistribution during insertion to include new rules for splitting. He calls the resulting variation on the fundamental B-tree form a *B** tree.

Consider a system in which we are postponing splitting through redistribution, as outlined in the preceding section. If we are considering any page other than the root, we know that when it is finally time to split, the page has at least one sibling that is also full. This opens up the possibility of a two-to-three split rather than the usual one-to-two or two-way split.

The important aspect of this two-to-three split is that it results in pages that are each about two-thirds full rather than just half full. This makes it possible to define a new kind of B-tree, called a B* tree, which has the following properties:

1. Every page has a maximum of m descendants.
2. Every page except for the root has at least $\lceil (2m - 1)/3 \rceil$ descendants.
3. The root has at least two descendants (unless it is a leaf).
4. All the leaves appear on the same level.

The critical changes between this set of properties and the set we define for a conventional B-tree are in rule 2: a B* tree has pages that contain a minimum $\lceil (2m - 1)/3 \rceil$ keys. This new property, of course, affects procedures for deletion and redistribution.

To implement B* tree procedures, one must also deal with the question of splitting the root, which, by definition, never has a sibling. If there is no sibling, no two-to-three split is possible. Knuth suggests allowing the root to grow to a size larger than the other pages so, when it does split, it can produce two pages that are each about two-thirds full. This has the advantage of ensuring that all pages below the root level adhere to B* tree characteristics. However, it has the disadvantage of requiring that the procedures be able to handle a page that is larger than all the others. Another solution is to handle the splitting of the root as a conventional one-to-two split. This second solution avoids any special page-handling logic. On the other hand, it complicates deletion, redistribution, and other procedures that must be sensitive to the minimum number of keys allowed in a page. Such procedures would have to be able to recognize that pages descending from the root might legally be only half full.

9.15   Buffering of Pages: Virtual B-Trees

We have seen that the B-tree can be a very efficient, flexible storage structure that maintains its balanced properties after repeated deletions and insertions and that provides access to any key with just a few disk accesses. However, focusing on just the structural aspects, as we have so far, can cause us inadvertently to overlook ways of using this structure to full advantage. For example, the fact that a B-tree has a depth of three levels does not at all mean that we need to do three disk accesses to retrieve keys from pages at the leaf level. We can do much better than that.

Obtaining better performance from B-trees involves looking in a precise way at our original problem. We needed to find a way to make efficient use of indexes that are too large to be held *entirely* in memory. Up to this point we have approached this problem in an all-or-nothing way: an index has been held entirely in memory, organized as a list or binary tree, or accessed entirely on secondary store, using a B-tree structure. But, stating that we cannot hold *all* of an index in memory does not imply that we cannot hold *some* of it there. In fact, our implementation of class BTree is already keeping the root in memory at all times and keeping a full branch in memory during insertion and deletion.

For example, assume that we have an index containing 1 megabyte of records and that we cannot reasonably use more than 256 kilobytes of memory for index storage at any given time. Given a page size of 4 kilo-bytes, holding around 64 keys per page, our B-tree can be contained in three levels. We can reach any one of our keys in no more than two disk accesses. That is certainly acceptable, but why should we settle for this kind of performance? Why not try to find a way to bring the average number of disk accesses per search down to one disk access or less?

If we're thinking of the problem strictly in terms of physical storage structures, retrieval averaging one disk access or less sounds impossible. But remember, our objective was to find a way to manage our megabyte of index within 256 kilobytes of memory, not within the 4 kilobytes required to hold a single page of our tree.

The simple, keep-the-root strategy we have been using suggests an important, more general approach: rather than just holding the root page in memory, we can create a *page buffer* to hold some number of B-tree pages, perhaps five, ten, or more. As we read pages in from the disk in response to user requests, we fill up the buffer. Then, when a page is requested, we access it from memory if we can, thereby avoiding a disk access. If the page is not in memory, then we read it into the buffer from secondary storage, replacing one of the pages that was previously there. A B-tree that uses a memory buffer in this way is sometimes referred to as a *virtual B-tree*.

For our implementation, we can use the `Nodes` member and the `Fetch` and `Store` methods to manage this page buffer. `Fetch` and `Store` can keep track of which nodes are in memory and avoid the disk read or write whenever possible. This modification is included as an exercise.

9.15.1 LRU Replacement

Clearly, such a buffering scheme works only if we are more likely to request a page that is in the buffer than one that is not. The process of accessing the disk to bring in a page that is *not* already in the buffer is called a *page fault*. There are two causes of page faults:

1. We have never used the page.
2. It was once in the buffer but has since been replaced with a new page.

The first cause of page faults is unavoidable: if we have not yet read in and used a page, there is no way it can already be in the buffer. But the second cause is one we can try to minimize through buffer management. The critical management decision arises when we need to read a new page into a buffer that is already full: which page do we decide to replace?

One common approach is to replace the page that was least recently used; this is called *LRU* replacement. Note that this is different from replacing the page that was *read into* the buffer least recently. Instead, the LRU method keeps track of the *requests* for pages. The page to be replaced is the one that has gone the longest time without a request for use.

Some research by Webster (1980) shows the effect of increasing the number of pages that can be held in the buffer area under an LRU replacement strategy. Table 9.1 summarizes a small but representative portion of Webster's results. It lists the average number of disk accesses per search given different numbers of page buffers. These results are obtained using a simple LRU replacement strategy without accounting for page height. Keeping less than 15 percent of the tree in memory (20 pages out of the total 140) reduces the average number of accesses per search to less than one.

Note that the decision to use LRU replacement is based on the assumption that we are more likely to need a page that we have used recently than we are to need a page that we have never used or one that we used some time ago. If this assumption is not valid, then there is absolutely no reason to retain preferentially pages that were used recently. The term for this kind of assumption is *temporal locality*. We are assuming that there is a kind of *clustering* of the use of certain pages over time. The hierarchical nature of a B-tree makes this kind of assumption reasonable.

For example, during redistribution after overflow or underflow, we access a page and then access its sibling. Because B-trees are hierarchical, accessing a set of sibling pages involves repeated access to the parent page in rapid succession. This is an instance of temporal locality; it is easy to see how it is related to the tree's hierarchy.

9.15.2 Replacement Based on Page Height

There is another, more direct way to use the hierarchical nature of the B-tree to guide decisions about page replacement in the buffers. Our simple, keep-the-root strategy exemplifies this alternative: always retain the pages that occur at the highest levels of the tree. Given a larger amount of buffer

Table 9.1 Effect of using more buffers with a simple LRU replacement strategy.

Buffer Count	1	5	10	20
Average Accesses per Search	3.00	1.71	1.42	0.97

Number of keys = 2400
Total pages = 140
Tree height = 3 levels

space, it might be possible to retain not only the root, but also all of the pages at the second level of a tree.

Let's explore this notion by returning to a previous example in which we have access to 256 kilobytes of memory and a 1-megabyte index. Since our page size is 4 kilobytes, we could build a buffer area that holds 64 pages within the memory area. Assume that our 1 megabyte worth of index requires around 1.2 megabytes of storage on disk (storage utilization = 83 percent). Given the 4-kilobyte page size, this 1.2 megabytes requires slightly more than 300 pages. We assume that, on the average, each of our pages has around 30 descendants. It follows that our three-level tree has, of course, a single page at the root level, followed by 9 or 10 pages at the second level, with all the remaining pages at the leaf level. Using a page replacement strategy that always retains the higher-level pages, it is clear that our 64-page buffer eventually contains the root page and all the pages at the second level. The approximately 50 remaining buffer slots are used to hold leaf-level pages. Decisions about which of these pages to replace can be handled through an LRU strategy. It is easy to see how, given a sizable buffer, it is possible to bring the average number of disk accesses per search down to a number that is less than one.

Webster's research (1980) also investigates the effect of taking page height into account, giving preference to pages that are higher in the tree when it comes time to decide which pages to keep in the buffers. Augmenting the LRU strategy with a weighting factor that accounts for page height reduces the average number of accesses, given a 10-page buffer, from 1.42 accesses per search down to 1.12 accesses per search.

9.15.3 Importance of Virtual B-Trees

It is difficult to overemphasize the importance of including a page buffering scheme with any implementation of a B-tree index structure. Because the B-tree structure is so interesting and powerful, it is easy to fall into the trap of thinking that the B-tree organization is itself a sufficient solution to the problem of accessing large indexes that must be maintained on secondary storage. As we have emphasized, to fall into that trap is to lose sight of the original problem: to find a way to *reduce* the amount of memory required to handle large indexes. We did not, however, need to reduce the amount of memory to the amount required for a single index page. It is usually possible to find enough memory to hold a number of pages. Doing so can dramatically increase system performance.

9.16   Variable-Length Records and Keys

In many applications the information associated with a key varies in length. Secondary indexes that reference inverted lists are an excellent example of this. One way to handle this variability is to place the associated information in a separate, variable-length record file; the B-tree would contain a reference to the information in this other file. Another approach is to allow a variable number of keys and records in a B-tree page.

Up to this point we have regarded B-trees as being of some order *m*. Each page has a fixed maximum and minimum number of keys that it can legally hold. The notion of a variable-length record and, therefore, a variable number of keys per page is a significant departure from the point of view we have developed so far. A B-tree with a variable number of keys per page clearly has no single, fixed order.

The variability in length can also extend to the keys as well as to entire records. For example, in a file in which people's names are the keys, we might choose to use only as much space as required for a name rather than allocate a fixed-size field for each key. As we saw in earlier chapters, implementing a structure with variable-length fields can allow us to put many more names in a given amount of space since it eliminates internal fragmentation. If we can put more keys in a page, then we have a larger number of descendants from a page and very probably a tree with fewer levels.

Accommodating this variability in length means using a different kind of page structure. We look at page structures appropriate for use with variable-length keys in detail in the next chapter. We also need a different criterion for deciding when a page is full and when it is in an underflow condition. Rather than use a maximum and minimum number of keys per page, we need to use a maximum and minimum number of bytes.

Once the fundamental mechanisms for handling variable-length keys or records are in place, interesting new possibilities emerge. For example, we might consider the notion of biasing the splitting and redistribution methods so that the shortest variable-length keys are promoted upward in preference to longer keys. The idea is that we want to have pages with the largest numbers of descendants up high in the tree, rather than at the leaf level. Branching out as broadly as possible as high as possible in the tree tends to reduce the overall height of the tree. McCreight (1977) explores this notion in the article, "Pagination of B* Trees with Variable-Length Records."

The principal point we want to make with these examples of variations on B-tree structures is that this chapter introduces only the most basic forms of this very useful, flexible file structure. Implementations of B-trees do not slavishly follow the textbook form of B-trees. Instead, they use many of the other organizational techniques we study in this book, such as variable-length record structures in combination with the fundamental B-tree organization to make new, special-purpose file structures uniquely suited to the problems at hand.

SUMMARY

We begin this chapter by picking up the problem we left unsolved at the end of Chapter 7: simple, linear indexes work well if they are held in memory, but they are expensive to maintain and search if they are so big that they must be held on secondary storage. The expense of using secondary storage is most evident in two areas:

- Sorting of the index; and
- Searching, since even binary searching requires more than two or three disk accesses.

We first address the question of structuring an index so it can be kept in order without sorting. We use tree structures to do this, discovering that we need a *balanced* tree to ensure that the tree does not become overly deep after repeated random insertions. We see that AVL trees provide a way of balancing a binary tree with only a small amount of overhead.

Next we turn to the problem of reducing the number of disk accesses required to search a tree. The solution to this problem involves dividing the tree into pages so a substantial portion of the tree can be retrieved with a single disk access. Paged indexes let us search through very large numbers of keys with only a few disk accesses.

Unfortunately, we find that it is difficult to combine the idea of *paging* of tree structures with the *balancing* of these trees by AVL methods. The most obvious evidence of this difficulty is associated with the problem of selecting the members of the root page of a tree or subtree when the tree is built in the conventional top-down manner. This sets the stage for introducing Bayer and McCreight's work on B-trees, which solves the paging and balancing dilemma by starting from the leaf level, promoting keys upward as the tree grows.

Our discussion of B-trees begins by emphasizing the multilevel index approach. We include a full implementation of insertion and searching and examples of searching, insertion, overflow detection, and splitting to show how B-trees grow while maintaining balance in a paged structure. Next we formalize our description of B-trees. This formal definition permits us to develop a formula for estimating worst-case B-tree depth. The formal description also motivates our work on developing deletion procedures that maintain the B-tree properties when keys are removed from a tree.

Once the fundamental structure and procedures for B-trees are in place, we begin refining and improving on these ideas. The first set of improvements involves increasing the storage utilization within B-trees. Of course, increasing storage utilization can also result in a decrease in the height of the tree and therefore in improvements in performance. We sometimes find that by redistributing keys during insertion rather than splitting pages, we can improve storage utilization in B-trees so it averages around 85 percent. Carrying our search for increased storage efficiency even further, we find that we can combine redistribution during insertion with a different kind of splitting to ensure that the pages are about two-thirds full rather than only half full after the split. Trees using this combination of redistribution and two-to-three splitting are called *B** trees.

Next we turn to the matter of buffering pages, creating a *virtual B-tree.* We note that the use of memory is not an all-or-nothing choice: indexes that are too large to fit into memory do not have to be accessed *entirely* from secondary storage. If we hold pages that are likely to be reused in memory, then we can save the expense of reading these pages in from the disk again. We develop two methods of guessing which pages are to be reused. One method uses the height of the page in the tree to decide which pages to keep. Keeping the root has the highest priority, the root's descendants have the next priority, and so on. The second method for selecting pages to keep in memory is based on recentness of use: we always replace the least recently used (LRU) page and retain the pages used most recently. We see that it is possible to combine these methods and that doing so can result in the ability to find keys while using an average of less than one disk access per search.

We close the chapter with a brief look at the use of variable-length records within the pages of a B-tree, noting that significant savings in space and consequent reduction in the height of the tree can result from the use of variable-length records. The modification of the basic textbook B-tree definition to include the use of variable-length records is just one example of the many variations on B-trees that are used in real-world implementations.

KEY TERMS

AVL tree. A height-balanced (HB(1)) binary tree in which insertions and deletions can be performed with minimal accesses to local nodes. AVL trees are interesting because they keep branches from getting overly long after many random insertions.

B-tree of order *m*. A multilevel index tree with these properties:

0   Every node has a maximum of *m* descendants.
1   Every node except the root has at least $\lceil m/2 \rceil$ descendants.
2   The root has at least two descendants (unless it is a leaf).
3   All of the leaves appear on the same level.

B-trees are built upward from the leaf level, so creation of new pages always starts at the leaf level.

   The power of B-trees lies in the facts that they are balanced (no overly long branches); they are shallow (requiring few seeks); they accommodate random deletions and insertions at a relatively low cost while remaining in balance; and they guarantee at least 50 percent storage utilization.

B* tree. A special B-tree in which each node is at least two-thirds full. B* trees generally provide better storage utilization than B-trees.

Height-balanced tree. A tree structure with a special property: for each node there is a limit to the amount of difference that is allowed among the heights of any of the node's subtrees. An *HB(k)* tree allows subtrees to be *k* levels out of balance. (See *AVL tree.*)

Leaf of a B-tree. A page at the lowest level in a B-tree. All leaves in a B-tree occur at the same level.

Merging. When a B-tree node underflows (becomes less than 50 percent full), it sometimes becomes necessary to combine the node with an adjacent node, thus decreasing the total number of nodes in the tree. Since merging involves a change in the number of nodes in the tree, its effects can require reorganization at many levels of the tree.

Order of a B-tree. The maximum number of descendants that a node in the B-tree can have.

Paged index. An index that is divided into blocks, or pages, each of which can hold many keys. The use of paged indexes allows us to search through very large numbers of keys with only a few disk accesses.

Redistribution. When a B-tree node underflows (becomes less than 50 percent full), it may be possible to move keys into the node from an adjacent node with the same parent. This helps ensure that the 50 percent-full property is maintained. When keys are redistributed, it becomes necessary to alter the contents of the parent as well. Redistribution, as opposed to *merging,* does not involve creation or deletion of nodes—its effects are entirely local. Often redistribution can also be used as an alternative to splitting.

Splitting. Creation of two nodes out of one when the original node becomes overfull. Splitting results in the need to promote a key to a higher-level node to provide an index separating the two new nodes.

Virtual B-tree. A B-tree index in which several pages are kept in memory in anticipation of the possibility that one or more of them will be needed by a later access. Many different strategies can be applied to replacing pages in memory when virtual B-trees are used, including the least-recently-used strategy and height-weighted strategies.

FURTHER READINGS

Currently available textbooks on file and data structures contain surprisingly brief discussions on B-trees. These discussions do not, in general, add substantially to the information presented in this chapter and the following chapter. Consequently, readers interested in more information about B-trees must turn to the articles that have appeared in journals over the past 15 years.

The article that introduced B-trees to the world is Bayer and McCreight's "Organization and Maintenance of Large Ordered Indexes" (1972). It describes the theoretical properties of B-trees and includes empirical results concerning, among other things, the effect of using redistribution in addition to splitting during insertion. Readers should be aware that the notation and terminology used in this article differ from those used in this text in a number of important respects.

Comer's (1979) survey article, "The Ubiquitous B-tree," provides an excellent overview of some important variations on the basic B-tree form. Knuth's (1998) discussion of B-trees, although brief, is an important resource in part because many of the variant forms such as B* trees were first collected together in Knuth's discussion. McCreight (1977) looks specifically at operations on trees that use variable-length records and that are therefore of variable order. Although this article speaks specifically about B* trees, the consideration of variable-length records can be applied to many other B-tree forms. In "Time and Space Optimality on B-trees," Rosenberg and Snyder (1981) analyze the effects of initializing B-trees with the minimum number of nodes. In "Analysis of Design Alternatives for Virtual Memory Indexes," Murayama and Smith (1977) look at three factors that affect the cost of retrieval: choice of search strategy, whether pages in the index are structured, and whether keys are compressed. Gray and Reuter (1993) provide an analysis of issues in B-tree implementation. Zoellick (1986) discusses the use of B-tree—like structures on optical discs.

Since B-trees in various forms have become a standard file organization for databases, a good deal of interesting material on applications of B-trees can be found in the database literature. Held and Stonebraker (1978), Snyder (1978), Kroenke (1998), and Elmasri and Navathe (1994) discuss the use of B-trees in database systems generally. Ullman (1986) covers the problem of dealing with applications in which several programs have access to the same database concurrently and identifies literature concerned with concurrent access to B-tree.

Uses of B-trees for secondary key access are covered in many of the previously cited references. There is also a growing literature on multidimensional dynamic indexes, including variants of the B-tree, *k-d* B-tree and R trees. *K-d* B-trees are described in papers by Ouskel and Scheuermann (1981) and Robinson (1981). R trees support multidimensional queries, so-called *range queries*, and were first described in Guttman (1984) and further extended in Sellis et al (1987), Beckmann et al (1990), and Kamel and Floutsos (1992). Shaffer (1997) and Standish (1995) include extensive coverage of a variety of tree structures. Other approaches to secondary indexing include the use of *tries* and *grid files*. Tries are covered in many texts on files and data structures, including Knuth (1998) and Loomis (1989). Grid files are covered thoroughly in Nievergelt et al. (1984).

An interesting early paper on the use of dynamic tree structures for processing files is "The Use of Tree Structures for Processing Files," by Sussenguth (1963). Wagner (1973) and Keehn and Lacy (1974) examine the index design considerations that led to the development of VSAM. VSAM uses an index structure very similar to a B-tree but appears to have been developed independently of Bayer and McCreight's work. Readers interested in learning more about AVL trees should read Knuth (1998), who takes a more rigorous, mathematical look at AVL tree operations and properties.

EXERCISES

1. Balanced binary trees can be effective index structures for memory-based indexing, but they have several drawbacks when they become so large that part or all of them must be kept on secondary storage. The following questions should help bring these drawbacks into focus and thus reinforce the need for an alternative structure such as the B-tree.

   a. There are two major problems with using binary search to search a simple sorted index on secondary storage: the number of disk accesses is larger than we would like, and the time it takes to keep the index sorted is substantial. Which of the problems does a binary search tree alleviate?

   b. Why is it important to keep search trees balanced?

   c. In what way is an AVL tree better than a simple binary search tree?

   d. Suppose you have a file with 1 000 000 keys stored on disk in a completely full, balanced binary search tree. If the tree is not paged, what is the maximum number of accesses required to find a key? If the tree is paged in the manner illustrated in Fig. 9.12, but with each page able to hold 15 keys and to branch to 16 new pages, what is the maximum number of accesses required to find a key? If the page size is increased to hold 511 keys with branches to 512 nodes, how does the maximum number of accesses change?

   e. Consider the problem of balancing the three-key-per-page tree in Fig. 9.13 by rearranging the pages. Why is it difficult to create a tree-balancing algorithm that has only local effects? When the page size increases to a more likely size (such as 512 keys), why does it become difficult to guarantee that each of the pages contains at least some minimum number of keys?

   f. Explain the following statement: B-trees are built upward from the bottom, whereas binary trees are built downward from the top.

   g. Although B-trees are generally considered superior to binary search trees for external searching, binary trees are still commonly used for internal searching. Why is this so?

2. Show the B-trees of order four that result from loading the following sets of keys in order:

   a. C G J X

   b. C G J X N S U O A E B H I

   c. C G J X N S U O A E B H I F

   d. C G J X N S U O A E B H I F K L Q R T V U W Z

3. Given a B-tree of order 256,

   a. What is the maximum number of descendants from a page?

   b. What is the minimum number of descendants from a page (excluding the root and leaves)?

   c. What is the minimum number of descendants from the root?

   d. What is the maximum depth of the tree if it contains 100 000 keys?

4. Using a method similar to that used to derive the formula for worst-case depth, derive a formula for best-case, or minimum, depth for an order m B-tree with N keys. What is the minimum depth of the tree described in the preceding question?

5. Suppose you have a B-tree index for an unsorted file containing N data records, where each key has stored with it the RRN of the corresponding record. The depth of the B-tree is d. What are the maximum and minimum numbers of disk accesses required to

   a. Retrieve a record?

   b. Add a record?

   c. Delete a record?

   d. Retrieve all records from the file in sorted order?

   Assume that page buffering is *not* used. In each case, indicate how you arrived at your answer.

6. Show the trees that result after each of the keys N, P, Q, and Y is deleted from the B-tree of Figure 9.15(c).

7. A common belief about B-trees is that a B-tree cannot grow deeper unless it is 100 percent full. Discuss this.

8. Suppose you want to delete a key from a node in a B-tree. You look at the right sibling and find that redistribution does not work; merging would be necessary. You look to the left and see that redistribution is an option here. Do you choose to merge or redistribute?

9. What is the difference between a B* tree and a B-tree? What improvement does a B* tree offer over a B-tree, and what complications does it introduce? How does the minimum depth of an order m B* tree compare with that of an order m B-tree?

10. What is a virtual B-tree? How can it be possible to average fewer than one access per key when retrieving keys from a three-level virtual B-tree? Write a description for an LRU replacement scheme for a ten-page buffer used in implementing a virtual B-tree.

11. Discuss the trade-offs between storing the information indexed by the keys in a B-tree with the key and storing the information in a separate file.

12. We noted that, given variable-length keys, it is possible to optimize a tree by building in a bias toward promoting shorter keys. With fixed-order trees we promote the middle key. In a variable-order, variable-length key tree, what is the meaning of "middle key"? What are the trade-offs associated with building in a bias toward shorter keys in this selection of a key for promotion? Outline an implementation for this selection and promotion process.

PROGRAMMING EXERCISES

13. Implement the `Delete` method of class `BTree`.

14. Modify classes `BTreeNode` and `BTree` to have one more reference than key in each interior mode.

15. Write an interactive program that allows a user to find, insert, and delete keys from a B-tree.

16. Write a B-tree program that uses keys that are strings rather than single characters.

17. Write a program that builds a B-tree index for a data file in which records contain more information than just a key. Use the `Person`, `Recording`, `Ledger`, or `Transaction` files from previous chapters.

18. Implement B* trees by modifying class `BTree`.

PROGRAMMING PROJECT

This is the seventh part of the programming project. We add B-tree indexes to the data files created by the third part of the project in Chapter 4.

19. Use class `BTree` to create a B-tree index of a student record file with the student identifier as key. Write a driver program to create a B-tree file from an existing student record file.

20. Use class `BTree` to create a B-tree index of a course registration record file with the student identifier as key. Write a driver program to create a B-tree file from an existing course registration record file.

21. Write a program that opens a B-tree indexed student file and a B-tree indexed course registration file and retrieves information on demand. Prompt a user for a student identifier, and print all objects that match it.

The next part of the programming project is in Chapter 10.

10

Indexed Sequential File Access and Prefix B+ Trees

❖ Introduce *indexed sequential* files.

❖ Describe operations on a *sequence set* of blocks that maintains records in order by key.

❖ Show how an *index set* can be built on top of the sequence set to produce an indexed sequential file structure.

❖ Introduce the use of a B-tree to maintain the index set, thereby introducing *B+ trees* and *simple prefix B+ trees*.

❖ Illustrate how the B-tree index set in a simple prefix B+ tree can be of variable order, holding a variable number of separators.

❖ Compare the strengths and weaknesses of B+ trees, simple prefix B+ trees, and B-trees.

10.1   Indexed Sequential Access

Indexed sequential file structures provide a choice between two alternative views of a file:

- *Indexed:* the file can be seen as a set of records that is *indexed* by key; or

- *Sequential:* the file can be accessed sequentially (physically contiguous records—no seeking), returning records in order by key.

The idea of having a single organizational method that provides both of these views is a new one. Up to this point we have had to choose between them. As a somewhat extreme, though instructive, example of the potential divergence of these two choices, consider the file structure of Chapter 9 that consists of a file of entry-sequenced records indexed by a separate B-tree. This structure provides excellent *indexed* access to any individual record by key, even as records are added and deleted. Now let's suppose that we also want to use this file as part of a cosequential merge. In cosequential processing we want to retrieve all the records in order by key. Since the records in this file system are *entry sequenced*, the only way to retrieve them in order by key without sorting is through the index. For a file of *N* records, following the *N* pointers from the index into the entry-sequenced set requires N essentially random seeks into the record file. This is a *much* less efficient process than the sequential reading of physically adjacent records—so much so that it is unacceptable for any situation in which cosequential processing is a frequent occurrence.

On the other hand, our discussions of indexing show us that a file consisting of a set of records sorted by key, though ideal for cosequential processing, is an unacceptable structure when we want to access, insert, and delete records by key in random order.

What if an application involves both interactive random access and cosequential batch processing? There are many examples of such dual-mode applications. Student record systems at universities, for example, require keyed access to individual records while also requiring a large amount of batch processing, as when grades are posted or when fees are paid during registration. Similarly, credit card systems require both batch processing of charge slips and interactive checks of account status. Indexed sequential access methods were developed in response to these kinds of needs.

10.2   Maintaining a Sequence Set

We set aside, for the moment, the indexed part of indexed sequential access, focusing on the problem of keeping a set of records in physical order by key as records are added and deleted. We refer to this ordered set of records as a *sequence set*. We will assume that once we have a good way of maintaining a sequence set, we will find some way to index it as well. You will notice a strong parallel between these sequence set methods and the methods presented in Chapter 9 for creating and maintaining B-trees.

10.2.1   The Use of Blocks

We can immediately rule out sorting and resorting the entire sequence set as records are added and deleted, since we know that sorting an entire file is an expensive process. We need instead to find a way to *localize* the changes. One of the best ways to restrict the effects of an insertion or deletion to just a part of the sequence set involves a tool we first encountered in Chapters 3 and 4: we can collect the records into *blocks*.

When we block records, the block becomes the basic unit of input and output. We read and write entire blocks at once. Consequently, the size of the buffers we use in a program is such that they can hold an entire block.

After reading in a block, all the records in a block are in memory, where we can work on them or rearrange them much more rapidly.

An example illustrates how the use of blocks can help us keep a sequence set in order. Suppose we have records that are keyed on last name and collected together so there are four records in a block. We also include *link fields* in each block that point to the preceding block and the following block. We need these fields because, as you will see, consecutive blocks are not necessarily physically adjacent.

As with B-trees, the insertion of new records into a block can cause the block to *overflow*. The overflow condition can be handled by a block-splitting process that is analogous to, but not the same as, the block-splitting process used in a B-tree. For example, Fig. 10.1(a) shows what our blocked sequence set looks like before any insertions or deletions take place. We show only the forward links. In Fig. 10.1(b) we have inserted a new record with the key CARTER. This insertion causes block 2 to split. The second half of what was originally block 2 is found in block 4 after the split. Note that this block-splitting process operates differently from the splitting we encountered in B-trees. In a B-tree a split results in the *promotion* of a key. Here things are simpler: we just divide the records between two blocks and rearrange the links so we can still move through the file in order by key, block after block.

Deletion of records can cause a block to be less than half full and therefore to *underflow*. Once again, this problem and its solutions are analogous to what we encounter when working with B-trees. Underflow in a B-tree can lead to either of two solutions:

- If a neighboring node is also half full, we can *merge* the two nodes, freeing one up for reuse.

- If the neighboring nodes are more than half full, we can *redistribute* records between the nodes to make the distribution more nearly even.

Underflow within a block of our sequence set can be handled through the same kinds of processes. As with insertion, the process for the sequence set is simpler than the process for B-trees since the sequence set is *not* a tree and there are, therefore, no keys and records in a parent node. In Fig. 10.1(c) we show the effects of deleting the record for DAVIS. Block 4 underflows and is then merged with its successor in *logical* sequence, which is block 3. The merging process frees up block 3 for reuse. We do not show an example in which underflow leads to redistribution rather than merging, because it is easy to see how the redistribution process works. Records are simply moved between logically adjacent blocks.

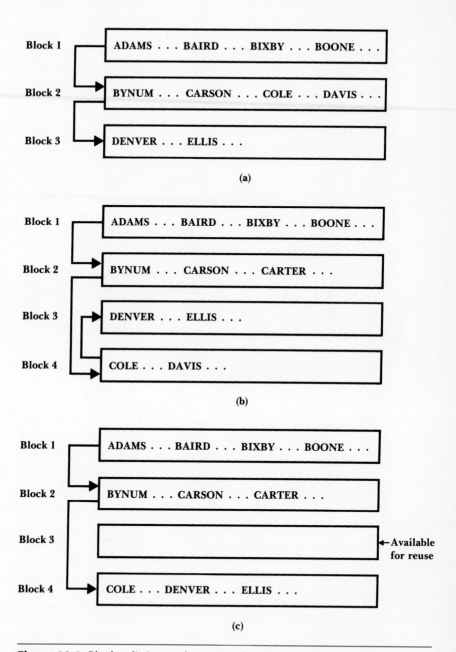

Figure 10.1 Block splitting and merging due to insertions and deletions in the sequence set. (a) Initial blocked sequence set. (b) Sequence set after insertion of CARTER record—block 2 splits, and the contents are divided between blocks 2 and 4. (c) Sequence set after deletion of DAVIS record—block 4 is less than half full, so it is concatenated with block 3.

Given the separation of records into blocks, along with these fundamental block-splitting, merging, and redistribution operations, we can keep a sequence set in order by key without ever having to sort the entire set of records. As always, nothing comes free; consequently, there are costs associated with this avoidance of sorting:

- Once insertions are made, our file takes up more space than an unblocked file of sorted records because of internal fragmentation within a block. However, we can apply the same kinds of strategies used to increase space utilization in a B-tree (for example, the use of redistribution in place of splitting during insertion, two-to-three splitting, and so on). Once again, the implementation of any of these strategies must account for the fact that the sequence set *is not a tree* and therefore there is no promotion of keys.

- The order of the records is not necessarily *physically* sequential throughout the file. The maximum guaranteed extent of physical sequentiality is within a block.

This last point leads us to the important question of selecting a block size.

10.2.2 Choice of Block Size

As we work with our sequence set, a block is the basic unit for our I/O operations. When we read data from the disk, we never read less than a block; when we write data, we always write at least one block. A block is also, as we have said, the maximum *guaranteed* extent of physical sequentiality. It follows that we should think in terms of *large* blocks, with each block holding many records. So the question of block size becomes one of identifying the *limits* on block size: why not make the block size so big we can fit the entire file in a single block?

One answer to this is the same as the reason we cannot always use a memory sort on a file: we usually do not have enough memory available. So our first consideration regarding an upper bound for block size is as follows:

Consideration 1: The block size should be such that we can hold several blocks in memory at once. For example, in performing a block split or merging, we want to be able to hold at least two blocks in memory at a time. If we are implementing two-to-three splitting to conserve disk space, we need to hold at least three blocks in memory at a time.

Although we are presently focusing on the ability to access our sequence set *sequentially,* we eventually want to consider the problem of randomly accessing a single record from our sequence set. We have to read in an entire block to get at any one record within that block. We can therefore state a second consideration:

Consideration 2: Reading in or writing out a block should not take very long. Even if we had an unlimited amount of memory, we would want to place an upper limit on the block size so we would not end up reading in the entire file just to get at a single record.

This second consideration is more than a little imprecise. How long is very long? We can refine this consideration by factoring in some of our knowledge of the performance characteristics of disk drives:

Consideration 2 (redefined): The block size should be such that we can access a block without having to bear the cost of a disk seek within the block read or block write operation.

This is not a *mandatory* limitation, but it is a sensible one: we are interested in a block because it contains records that are physically adjacent, so let's not extend blocks beyond the point at which we can guarantee such adjacency. And where is that?

When we discussed sector formatted disks back in Chapter 3, we introduced the term *cluster.* A cluster is the minimum number of sectors allocated at a time. If a cluster consists of eight sectors, then a file containing only 1 byte still uses up eight sectors on the disk. The reason for clustering is that it guarantees a minimum amount of physical sequentiality. As we move from cluster to cluster in reading a file, we may incur a disk seek, but within a cluster the data can be accessed without seeking.

One reasonable suggestion for deciding on a block size, then, is to make each block equal to the size of a cluster. Often the cluster size on a disk system has already been determined by the system administrator. But what if you are configuring a disk system for a particular application and can therefore choose your own cluster size? You need to consider the issues relating to cluster size raised in Chapter 3, along with the constraints imposed by the amount of memory available and the number of blocks you want to hold in memory at once. As is so often the case, the final decision will probably be a compromise between a number of divergent considerations. The important thing is that the compromise be a truly *informed* decision, based on knowledge of how I/O devices and file structures work rather than just a guess.

If you are working with a disk system that is not sector oriented but allows you to choose the block size for a particular file, a good starting point is to think of a block as an entire track of the disk. You may want to revise this downward, to half a track, for instance, depending on memory constraints, record size, and other factors.

10.3   Adding a Simple Index to the Sequence Set

We have created a mechanism for maintaining a set of records so we can access them sequentially in order by key. It is based on the idea of grouping the records into blocks then maintaining the blocks, as records are added and deleted, through splitting, merging, and redistribution. Now let's see whether we can find an efficient way to locate some specific block containing a particular record, given the record's key.

We can view each of our blocks as containing a *range* of records, as illustrated in Fig. 10.2. This is an outside view of the blocks (we have not actually read any blocks and so do not know *exactly* what they contain), but it is sufficiently informative to allow us to choose which block *might* have the record we are seeking. We can see, for example, that if we are looking for a record with the key BURNS, we want to retrieve and inspect the second block.

It is easy to see how we could construct a simple, single-level index for these blocks. We might choose, for example, to build an index of fixed-length records that contain the key for the last record in each block, as shown in Fig. 10.3. Note that we are using the largest key in the block as the key of the whole block. In Chapter 9, we used the smallest key in a B-tree node as the key of the whole block, again because it is a little simpler. Yet another programming exercise is included in Chapter 9 to make the revisions required to use largest keys.

The combination of this kind of index with the sequence set of blocks provides complete indexed sequential access. If we need to retrieve a

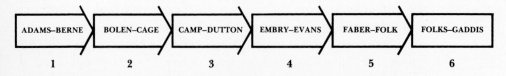

Figure 10.2 Sequence of blocks showing the range of keys in each block.

Key	Block number
BERNE	1
CAGE	2
DUTTON	3
EVANS	4
FOLK	5
GADDIS	6

Figure 10.3 Simple index for the sequence set illustrated in Fig. 10.2.

specific record, we consult the index and then retrieve the correct block; if we need sequential access we start at the first block and read through the linked list of blocks until we have read them all. As simple as this approach is, it is a very workable one as long as the entire index can be held in memory. The requirement that the index be held in memory is important for two reasons:

■ Since this is a simple index of the kind we discussed in Chapter 7, we find specific records by means of a binary search of the index. Binary searching works well if the searching takes place in memory, but, as we saw in the previous chapter on B-trees, it requires too many seeks if the file is on a secondary storage device.

■ As the blocks in the sequence set are changed through splitting, merging, and redistribution, the index has to be updated. Updating a simple, fixed-length record index of this kind works well if the index is relatively small and contained in memory. If, however, the updating requires seeking to individual index records on disk, the process can become very expensive. Once again, this is a point we discussed more completely in earlier chapters.

What do we do, then, if the file contains so many blocks that the block index does not conveniently fit into memory? In the preceding chapter we found that we could divide the index structure into *pages,* much like the *blocks* we are discussing here, handling several pages, or blocks, of the index in memory at a time. More specifically, we found that B-trees are an excellent file structure for handling indexes that are too large to fit entirely in memory. This suggests that we might organize the index to our sequence set as a B-tree.

The use of a B-tree index for our sequence set of blocks is a very powerful notion. The resulting hybrid structure is known as a *B+ tree,* which is appropriate since it is a B-tree index *plus* a sequence set that holds the records. Before we can fully develop the notion of a B⁺ tree, we need to think more carefully about what it is we need to keep in the index.

10.4 The Content of the Index: Separators Instead of Keys

The purpose of the index we are building is to assist us when we are searching for a record with a specific key. The index must guide us to the block in the sequence set that contains the record, if it exists in the sequence set at all. The index serves as a kind of road map for the sequence set. We are interested in the content of the index only insofar as it can assist us in getting to the correct block in the sequence set; the index set does not itself contain answers, only information about where to go to get answers.

Given this view of the index set as a road map, we can take the very important step of recognizing that *we do not need to have keys in the index set.* Our real need is for *separators.* Figure 10.4 shows one possible set of separators for the sequence set in Fig. 10.2.

Note that there are many potential separators capable of distinguishing between two blocks. For example, all of the strings shown between blocks 3 and 4 in Fig. 10.5 are capable of guiding us in our choice between the blocks as we search for a particular key. If a string comparison between the key and any of these separators shows that the key precedes the separator, we look for the key in block 3. If the key follows the separator, we look in block 4.

If we are willing to treat the separators as variable-length entities within our index structure (we talk about how to do this later), we can save space by placing the *shortest separator* in the index structure. Consequently, we use E as the separator to guide our choice between blocks 3 and 4. Note that there is not always a unique shortest separator. For exam-

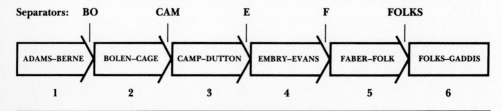

Figure 10.4 Separators between blocks in the sequence set.

DUTU
DVXGHESJF
DZ
E
EBQX
ELEEMOSYNARY

CAMP–DUTTON

EMBRY–EVANS

3

4

Figure 10.5 A list of potential separators.

ple, BK, BN, and BO are separators that are all the same length and are equally effective as separators between blocks 1 and 2 in Fig. 10.4. We choose BO and all of the other separators contained in Fig. 10.4 by using the logic embodied in the C++ function shown in Fig. 10.6.

Note that these functions can produce a separator that is the same as the second key. This situation is illustrated in Fig. 10.4 by the separator between blocks 5 and 6, which is the same as the first key contained in block 6. It follows that, as we use the separators as a road map to the sequence set, we must decide to retrieve the block to the right of the separator or the one to the left of the separator according to the following rule:

Relation of search key and separator	Decision
Key < separator	Go left
Key = separator	Go right
Key > separator	Go right

```
void FindSeparator (char * key1, char * key2, char * sep)
{// key1, key2, and sep point to the beginning of char arrays
   while (1) // loop until break
   {
      *sep = *key2; sep ++; //move the current character into sep
      if (*key2 != *key1) break; // stop when a difference is found
      if (*key2 == 0) break; // stop at end of key2
      key1 ++; key2 ++; // move to the next character of keys
   }
   *sep = 0; // null terminate the separator string
}
```

Figure 10.6 C++ function to find a shortest separator.

10.5   The Simple Prefix B⁺ Tree

Figure 10.7 shows how we can form the separators identified in Fig. 10.4 into a B-tree index of the sequence set blocks. The B-tree index is called the *index set*. Taken together with the sequence set, it forms a file structure called a *simple prefix B⁺ tree*. The modifier *simple prefix* indicates that the index set contains shortest separators, or *prefixes* of the keys rather than copies of the actual keys. Our separators are simple because they are, simply, prefixes. They are just the initial letters within the keys. More complicated (not simple) methods of creating separators from key prefixes remove unnecessary characters from the front of the separator as well as from the rear. (See Bayer and Unterauer, 1977, for a more complete discussion of prefix B⁺ trees.)[1]

As was noted previously, the implementation of B-trees in Chapter 9 has the same number of keys and references in all nodes, even though for interior nodes, the last key is not needed. We drop the extra key in the following examples and discussion. If we had as many separators as we

---

1. The literature on B⁺ trees and simple prefix B⁺ trees is remarkably inconsistent in the nomenclature used for these structures. B⁺ trees are sometimes called B* trees; simple prefix B⁺ trees are sometimes called simple prefix B-trees. Comer's important article in *Computing Surveys* in 1979 has reduced some of the confusion by providing a consistent, standard nomenclature which we use here.

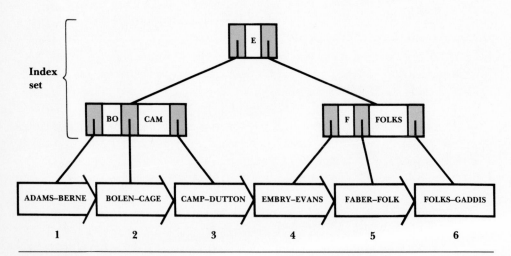

Figure 10.7 A B-tree index set for the sequence set, forming a simple prefix B⁺ tree.

have children (references), the last separator would be larger than the largest key in the subtree. In essence, it separates keys in the subtree from those that are larger than the largest key in the subtree. This last separator is truly not needed in a prefix tree.

Note that the index set is a B-tree, and a node containing N separators branches to $N + 1$ children. If we are searching for the record with the key EMBRY, we start at the root of the index set, comparing EMBRY with the separator E. Since EMBRY comes after E, we branch to the right, retrieving the node containing the separators F and FOLKS. Since EMBRY comes before even the first of these separators, we follow the branch that is to the left of the F separator, which leads us to block 4, the correct block in the sequence set.

10.6   Simple Prefix B⁺ Tree Maintenance

10.6.1 Changes Localized to Single Blocks in the Sequence Set

Let's suppose that we want to delete the records for EMBRY and FOLKS and that neither of these deletions results in any merging or redistribution within the sequence set. Since there is no merging or redistribution, the effect of these deletions on the *sequence set* is limited to changes *within* blocks 4 and 6. The record that was formerly the second record in block 4 (let's say that its key is ERVIN) is now the first record. Similarly, the former second record in block 6 (we assume it has a key of FROST) now starts that block. These changes can be seen in Fig. 10.8.

The more interesting question is what effect, if any, these deletions have on the *index set*. The answer is that since the number of sequence set blocks is unchanged and since no records are moved between blocks, the index set can also remain unchanged. This is easy to see in the case of the EMBRY deletion: E is still a perfectly good separator for sequence set blocks 3 and 4, so there is no reason to change it in the index set. The case of the FOLKS deletion is a little more confusing because the string FOLKS appears both as a key in the deleted record and as a separator within the index set. To avoid confusion, remember to distinguish clearly between these two uses of the string FOLKS: FOLKS can continue to serve as a separator between blocks 5 and 6 even though the FOLKS record is deleted. (One could argue that although we do not *need* to replace the FOLKS

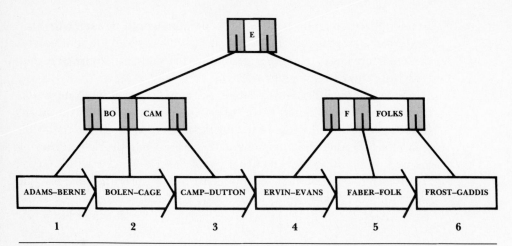

Figure 10.8 The deletion of the EMBRY and FOLKS records from the sequence set leaves the index set unchanged.

separator, we should do so anyway because it is now possible to construct a *shorter* separator. However, the cost of making such a change in the index set usually outweighs the benefits associated with saving a few bytes of space.)

The effect of inserting into the sequence set new records that do not cause block splitting is much the same as the effect of these deletions that do not result in merging: the index set remains unchanged. Suppose, for example, that we insert a record for EATON. Following the path indicated by the separators in the index set, we find that we will insert the new record into block 4 of the sequence set. We assume, for the moment, that there is room for the record in the block. The new record becomes the first record in block 4, but no change in the index set is necessary. This is not surprising: we decided to insert the record into block 4 on the basis of the existing information in the index set. It follows that the existing information in the index set is sufficient to allow us to find the record again.

10.6.2 Changes Involving Multiple Blocks in the Sequence Set

What happens when the addition and deletion of records to and from the sequence set *does* change the number of blocks in the sequence set? Clearly, if we have more blocks, we need additional separators in the index set, and if we have fewer blocks, we need fewer separators. Changing the number of separators certainly has an effect on the index set, where the separators are stored.

Since the index set for a simple prefix B+ tree is just a normal B-tree, the changes to the index set are handled according to the familiar rules for B-tree insertion and deletion.[2] In the following examples, we assume that the index set is a B-tree of order three, which means that the maximum number of separators we can store in a node is two. We use this small node size for the index set to illustrate node splitting and merging while using only a few separators. As you will see later, implementations of simple prefix B+ trees place a much larger number of separators in a node of the index set.

We begin with an insertion into the sequence set shown in Fig. 10.8. Specifically, let's assume that there is an insertion into the first block and that this insertion causes the block to split. A new block (block 7) is brought in to hold the second half of what was originally the first block. This new block is linked into the correct position in the sequence set, following block 1 and preceding block 2 (these are the *physical* block numbers). These changes to the sequence set are illustrated in Fig. 10.9.

---

2. As you study the material here, you may find it helpful to refer back to Chapter 9, where we discuss B-tree operations in much more detail.

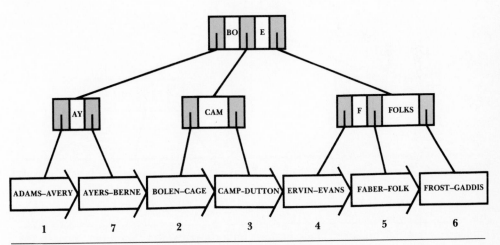

Figure 10.9 An insertion into block 1 causes a split and the consequent addition of block 7. The addition of a block in the sequence set requires a new separator in the index set. Insertion of the AY separator into the node containing BO and CAM causes a node split in the index set B-tree and consequent promotion of BO to the root.

Note that the separator that formerly distinguished between blocks 1 and 2, the string BO, is now the separator for blocks 7 and 2. We need a new separator, with a value of AY, to distinguish between blocks 1 and 7. As we start to place this separator into the index set, we find that the node into which we want to insert it, containing BO and CAM, is already full. Consequently, insertion of the new separator causes a split and promotion, according to the usual rules for B-trees. The promoted separator, BO, is placed in the root of the index set.

Now let's suppose we delete a record from block 2 of the sequence set and that this causes an underflow condition and consequent merging of blocks 2 and 3. Once the merging is complete, block 3 is no longer needed in the sequence set, and the separator that once distinguished between blocks 2 and 3 must be removed from the index set. Removing this separator, CAM, causes an underflow in an index set node. Consequently, there is another merging, this time in the index set, that results in the demotion of the BO separator from the root, bringing it back down into a node with the AY separator. Once these changes are complete, the simple prefix B⁺ tree has the structure illustrated in Fig. 10.10.

Although in these examples a block split in the sequence set results in a node split in the index set and a merging in the sequence set results in a

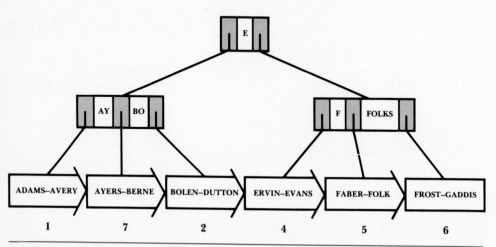

Figure 10.10 A deletion from block 2 causes underflow and the consequent merging of blocks 2 and 3. After the merging, block 3 is no longer needed and can be placed on an avail list. Consequently, the separator CAM is no longer needed. Removing CAM from its node in the index set forces a merging of index set nodes, bringing BO back down from the root.

merging in the index set, there is not always this correspondence of action. Insertions and deletions in the index set are handled as standard B-tree operations; whether there is splitting or a simple insertion, merging or a simple deletion, depends entirely on how full the index set node is.

Writing procedures to handle these kinds of operations is a straight-forward task if you remember that the changes take place *from the bottom up*. Record insertion and deletion *always* take place in the sequence set, since that is where the records are. If splitting, merging, or redistribution is necessary, perform the operation just as you would *if there were no index set at all*. Then, after the record operations in the sequence set are complete, make changes as necessary in the index set:

■ If blocks are split in the sequence set, a new separator must be inserted into the index set;

■ If blocks are merged in the sequence set, a separator must be removed from the index set; and

■ If records are redistributed between blocks in the sequence set, the value of a separator in the index set must be changed.

Index set operations are performed according to the rules for B-trees. This means that node splitting and merging *propagate* up through the higher levels of the index set. We see this in our examples as the BO separator moves in and out of the root. Note that the operations on the sequence set do not involve this kind of propagation. That is because the sequence set is a linear, linked list, whereas the index set is a tree. It is easy to lose sight of this distinction and to think of an insertion or deletion in terms of a *single* operation on the *entire* simple prefix B+ tree. This is a good way to become confused. Remember: insertions and deletions happen in the *sequence set* because that is where the records are. Changes to the index set are secondary; they are a byproduct of the fundamental operations on the sequence set.

10.7 Index Set Block Size

Up to this point we have ignored the important issues of size and structure of the index set nodes. Our examples have used extremely small index set nodes and have treated them as fixed-order B-tree nodes, even though the separators are variable in length. We need to develop more realistic, useful ideas about the size and structure of index set nodes.

The physical size of a node for the index set is usually the same as the physical size of a block in the sequence set. When this is the case, we speak of index set *blocks,* rather than *nodes,* just as we speak of sequence set blocks. There are a number of reasons for using a common block size for the index and sequence sets:

- The block size for the sequence set is usually chosen because there is a good fit among this block size, the characteristics of the disk drive, and the amount of memory available. The choice of an index set block size is governed by consideration of the same factors; therefore, the block size that is best for the sequence set is usually best for the index set.

- A common block size makes it easier to implement a buffering scheme to create a *virtual* simple prefix B$^+$ tree, similar to the virtual B-trees discussed in the preceding chapter.

- The index set blocks and sequence set blocks are often mingled within the same file to avoid seeking between two separate files while accessing the simple prefix B$^+$ tree. Use of one file for both kinds of blocks is simpler if the block sizes are the same.

10.8 Internal Structure of Index Set Blocks: A Variable-Order B-Tree

Given a large, fixed-size block for the index set, how do we store the separators within it? In the examples considered so far, the block structure is such that it can contain only a fixed number of separators. The entire motivation behind the use of *shortest* separators is the possibility of packing more of them into a node. This motivation disappears completely if the index set uses a fixed-order B-tree in which there is a fixed number of separators per node.

We want each index set block to hold a variable number of variable-length separators. How should we go about searching through these separators? Since the blocks are probably large, any single block can hold a large number of separators. Once we read a block into memory for use, we want to be able to do a binary rather than sequential search on its list of separators. We therefore need to structure the block so it can support a binary search, despite the fact that the separators are of variable length.

In Chapter 7, which covers indexing, we see that the use of a separate index can provide a means of performing binary searches lists of variable-

AsBaBroCChCraDeleEdiErrFaFle		00 02 04 07 08 10 13 17 20 23 25
◀——— Concatenated ———▶ separators		◀—— Index to separators ——▶

Figure 10.11 Variable-length separators and corresponding index.

length entities. If the index consists of fixed-length references, we can use binary searching on the index, retrieving the variable-length records or fields through indirection. For example, suppose we are going to place the following set of separators into an index block:

`As, Ba, Bro, C, Ch, Cra, Dele, Edi, Err, Fa, Fle`

(We are using lowercase letters rather than all uppercase letters so you can find the separators more easily when we merge them.) We could merge these separators and build an index for them, as shown in Fig. 10.11.

If we are using this block of the index set as a road map to help us find the record in the sequence set for "Beck," we perform a binary search on the index to the separators, retrieving first the middle separator, "Cra," which starts in position 10. Note that we can find the length of this separator by looking at the starting position of the separator that follows. Our binary search eventually tells us that "Beck" falls between the separators "Ba" and "Bro." Then what do we do?

The purpose of the index set road map is to guide us downward through the levels of the simple prefix B$^+$ tree, leading us to the sequence set block we want to retrieve. Consequently, the index set block needs some way to store references to its children, to the blocks descending from it in the next lower level of the tree. We assume that the references are made in terms of a relative block number (RBN), which is analogous to a relative record number except that it references a fixed-length block rather than a record. If there are N separators within a block, the block has $N + 1$ children and therefore needs space to store $N + 1$ RBNs in addition to the separators and the index to the separators.

There are many ways to combine the list of separators, the index to separators, and the list of RBNs into a single index set block. One possible approach is illustrated in Fig. 10.12. In addition to the vector of separators, the index to these separators, and the list of associated block numbers, this block structure includes:

■ *Separator count:* we need this to help us find the middle element in the index to the separators so we can begin our binary search.

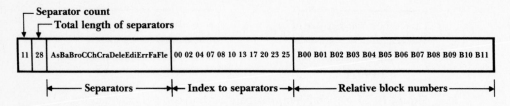

Figure 10.12 Structure of an index set block.

■ *Total length of separators:* the list of merged separators varies in length from block to block. Since the index to the separators begins at the end of this variable-length list, we need to know how long the list is so we can find the beginning of our index.

Let's suppose, once again, that we are looking for a record with the key "Beck" and that the search has brought us to the index set block pictured in Fig. 10.12. The total length of the separators and the separator count allow us to find the beginning, the end, and consequently the middle of the index to the separators. As in the preceding example, we perform a binary search of the separators through this index, finally concluding that the key "Beck" falls between the separators "Ba" and "Bro." *Conceptually,* the relation between the keys and the RBNs is illustrated in Fig. 10.13.

As Fig. 10.13 makes clear, discovering that the key falls between "Ba" and "Bro" allows us to decide that the *next* block we need to retrieve has the RBN stored in the B02 position of the RBN vector. This next block could be another index set block and thus another block of the road map, or it could be the sequence set block that we are looking for. In either case, the quantity and arrangement of information in the current index set block is sufficient to let us conduct our binary search *within* the index block and proceed to the next block in the simple prefix B⁺ tree.

There are many alternate ways to arrange the fundamental components of this index block. (For example, would it be easier to build the block if the vector of keys were placed at the end of the block? How would you handle the fact that the block consists of both *character* and *integer*

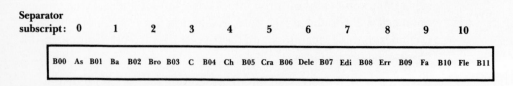

Figure 10.13 Conceptual relationship of separators and relative block numbers.

entities with no constant, fixed dividing point between them?) For our purposes here, the specific implementation details for this particular index block structure are not nearly as important as the block's *conceptual structure*. This kind of index block structure illustrates two important points.

The first point is that a block is not just an arbitrary chunk cut out of a homogeneous file; it can be more than just a set of records. A block can have a sophisticated internal structure all its own, including its own internal index, a collection of variable-length records, separate sets of fixed-length records, and so forth. This idea of building more sophisticated data structures inside of each block becomes increasingly attractive as the block size increases. With very large blocks it becomes imperative that we have an efficient way of processing all of the data within a block once it has been read into memory. This point applies not only to simple prefix B+ trees but to any file structure using a large block size.

The second point is that a node within the B-tree index set of our simple prefix B+ tree is of variable order, since each index set block contains a variable number of separators. This variability has interesting implications:

- The number of separators in a block is directly limited by block size rather than by some predetermined *order* (as in an *order m* B-tree). The index set will have the maximum *order*, and therefore the minimum depth, that is possible given the degree of compression used to form the separators.

- Since the tree is of *variable order*, operations such as determining when a block is full, or half full, are no longer a simple matter of comparing a separator count against some fixed maximum or minimum. Decisions about when to split, merge, or redistribute become more complicated.

The exercises at the end of this chapter provide opportunities for exploring variable-order trees more thoroughly.

10.9   Loading a Simple Prefix B+ Tree

In the previous description of the simple prefix B+ tree, we focus first on building a sequence set and subsequently present the index set as something that is added or built on top of the sequence set. It is not only possible to *conceive* of simple prefix B+ trees this way, as a sequence set with an added index, but one can also *build* them this way.

One way of building a simple prefix B⁺ tree, of course, is through a series of successive insertions. We would use the procedures outlined in section 10.6, where we discuss the maintenance of simple prefix B⁺ trees, to split or redistribute blocks in the sequence set and in the index set as we added blocks to the sequence set. The difficulty with this approach is that splitting and redistribution are relatively expensive. They involve searching down through the tree for each insertion then reorganizing the tree as necessary on the way back up. These operations are fine for tree *mainte-nance* as the tree is updated, but when we are loading the tree we do not have to contend with a *random-order* insertion and therefore do not need procedures that are so powerful, flexible, and expensive. Instead, we can begin by sorting the records that are to be loaded. Then we can guarantee that the next record we encounter is the next record we need to load.

Working from a sorted file, we can place the records into sequence set blocks, one by one, starting a new block when the one we are working with fills up. As we make the transition between two sequence set blocks, we can determine the shortest separator for the blocks. We can collect these separators into an index set block that we build and hold in memory until it is full.

To develop an example of how this works, let's assume that we have sets of records associated with terms that are being compiled for a book index. The records might consist of a list of the occurrences of each term. In Fig. 10.14 we show four sequence set blocks that have been written out to the disk and one index set block that has been built in memory from the shortest separators derived from the sequence set block keys. As you can see, the next sequence set block consists of a set of terms ranging from CATCH through CHECK, and therefore the next separator is CAT. Let's suppose that the index set block is now full. We write it out to disk. Now what do we do with the separator CAT?

Clearly, we need to start a new index block. However, we cannot place CAT into another index block at the same level as the one containing the

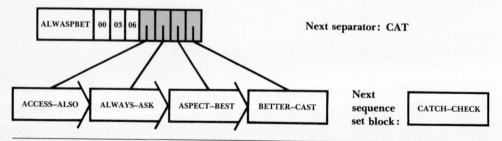

Figure 10.14 Formation of the first index set block as the sequence set is loaded.

separators ALW, ASP, and BET because we cannot have two blocks at the same level without having a parent block. Instead, we promote the CAT separator to a higher-level block. However, the higher-level block cannot point directly to the sequence set; it must point to the lower-level index blocks. This means that we will now be building *two* levels of the index set in memory as we build the sequence set. Figure 10.15 illustrates this working-on-two-levels phenomenon: the addition of the CAT separator requires us to start a new, root-level index block as well as a lower-level index block. (Actually, we are working on *three* levels at once since we are also constructing the sequence set blocks in memory.) Figure 10.16 shows what the index looks like after even more sequence set blocks are added. As you can see, the lower-level index block that contained no separators when we added CAT to the root has now filled up. To establish that the tree works, do a search for the term CATCH. Then search for the two terms CASUAL and CATALOG. How can you tell that these terms are not in the sequence set?

It is instructive to ask what would happen if the last record were CHECK, so the construction of the sequence sets and index sets would stop with the configuration shown in Fig. 10.15. The resulting simple prefix B⁺ tree would contain an index set node that holds no separators. This is not an isolated possibility. If we use this sequential loading method to build the tree, there will be many points during the loading process at which there is an empty or nearly empty index set node. If the index set grows to more than two levels, this empty node problem can occur at even higher levels of the tree, creating a potentially severe out-of-

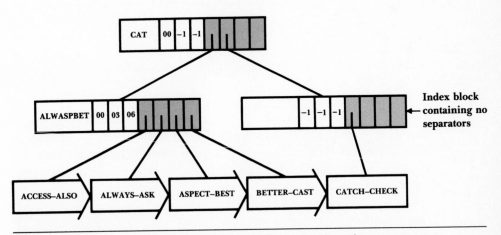

Figure 10.15 Simultaneous building of two index set levels as the sequence set continues to grow.

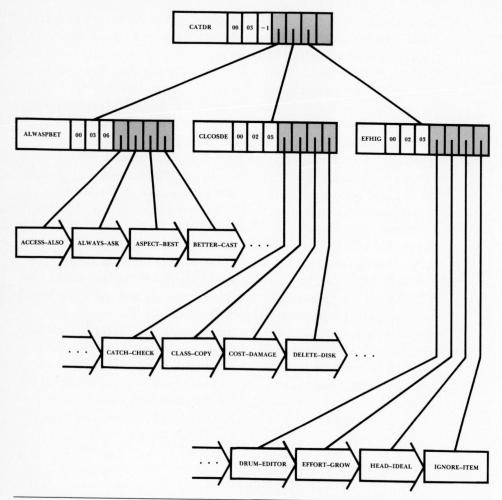

Figure 10.16 Continued growth of index set built up from the sequence set.

balance problem. Clearly, these empty node and nearly empty node conditions violate the B-tree rules that apply to the index set. However, once a tree is loaded and goes into regular use, the fact that a node is violating B-tree conditions can be used to guarantee that the node will be corrected through the action of normal B-tree maintenance operations. It is easy to write the procedures for insertion and deletion so a redistribution procedure is invoked when an underfull node is encountered.

The advantages of loading a simple prefix B$^+$ tree in this way, as a sequential operation following a sort of the records, almost always outweigh the disadvantages associated with the possibility of creating blocks that contain too few records or too few separators. The principal advantage is that the loading process goes more quickly because

■ The output can be written sequentially;

■ We make only one pass over the data, rather than the many passes associated with random order insertions; and

■ No blocks need to be reorganized as we proceed.

There are two additional advantages to using a separate loading process such as the one we have described. These advantages are related to performance after the tree is loaded rather than performance during loading:

■ Random insertion produces blocks that are, on the average, between 67 percent and 80 percent full. In the preceding chapter, when we were discussing B-trees, we increased this number by using such mechanisms as redistribution during insertion rather than just block splitting. But, still, we never had the option of filling the blocks completely so we had 100 percent utilization. The sequential loading process changes this. If we want, we can load the tree so it starts out with 100 percent utilization. This is an attractive option if we do not expect to add very many records to the tree. On the other hand, if we anticipate many insertions, sequential loading allows us to select any other degree of utilization that we want. Sequential loading gives us much more control over the amount and placement of empty space in the newly loaded tree.

■ In the loading example presented in Fig. 10.15, we write out the first four sequence set blocks and then write out the index set block containing the separators for these sequence set blocks. If we use the same file for both sequence set and index set blocks, this process guarantees that an index set block starts out in *physical proximity* to the sequence set blocks that are its descendants. In other words, our sequential loading process is creating a degree of *spatial locality* within our file. This locality can minimize seeking as we search down through the tree.

10.10 B⁺ Trees

Our discussions up to this point have focused primarily on simple prefix B⁺ trees. These structures are actually a variant of an approach to file organization known simply as a *B⁺ tree*. The difference between a simple prefix

B$^+$ tree and a plain B$^+$ tree is that the latter structure does not involve the use of prefixes as separators. Instead, the separators in the index set are simply copies of the actual keys. Contrast the index set block shown in Fig. 10.17, which illustrates the initial loading steps for a B$^+$ tree, with the index block that is illustrated in Fig. 10.14, where we are building a simple prefix B$^+$ tree.

The operations performed on B$^+$ trees are essentially the same as those discussed for simple prefix B$^+$ trees. Both B$^+$ trees and simple prefix B$^+$ trees consist of a set of records arranged in key order in a sequence set, coupled with an index set that provides rapid access to the block containing any particular key/record combination. The only difference is that in the simple prefix B$^+$ tree we build an index set of shortest separators formed from key prefixes.

One of the reasons behind our decision to focus first on simple prefix B$^+$ trees, rather than on the more general notion of a B$^+$ tree, is that we want to distinguish between the role of the *separators* in the index set and *keys* in the sequence set. It is much more difficult to make this distinction when the separators are exact copies of the keys. By beginning with simple prefix B$^+$ trees, we have the pedagogical advantage of working with separators that are clearly different from the keys in the sequence set.

But another reason for starting with simple prefix B$^+$ trees is that they are quite often a more desirable alternative than the plain B$^+$ tree. We want the index set to be as shallow as possible, which implies that we want to place as many separators into an index set block as we can. Why use anything longer than the simple prefix in the index set? In general, the answer to this question is that we do not, in fact, want to use anything longer than a simple prefix as a separator; consequently, simple prefix B$^+$ trees are often a good solution. There are, however, at least two factors that might give favor to using a B$^+$ tree that uses full copies of keys as separators.

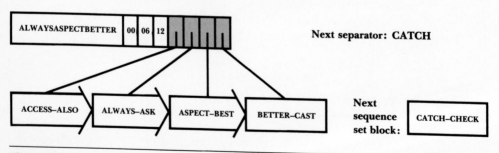

Figure 10.17 Formation of the first index set block in a B$^+$ tree without the use of shortest separators.

- The reason for using shortest separators is to pack more of them into an index set block. As we have already said, this implies, ineluctably, the use of variable-length fields within the index set blocks. For some applications the cost of the extra overhead required to maintain and use this variable-length structure outweighs the benefits of shorter separators. In these cases one might choose to build a straightforward B⁺ tree using fixed-length copies of the keys from the sequence set as separators.

- Some key sets do not show much compression when the simple prefix method is used to produce separators. For example, suppose the keys consist of large, consecutive alphanumeric sequences such as 34C18K756, 34C18K757, 34C18K758, and so on. In this case, to enjoy appreciable compression, we need to use compression techniques that remove redundancy from the *front* of the key. Bayer and Unterauer (1977) describe such compression methods. Unfortunately, they are more expensive and complicated than simple prefix compression. If we calculate that tree height remains acceptable with the use of full copies of the keys as separators, we might elect to use the no-compression option.

10.11 B-Trees, B⁺ Trees, and Simple Prefix B⁺ Trees in Perspective

In this chapter and the preceding chapter we have looked at a number of tools used in building file structures. These tools—B-trees, B⁺ trees, and simple prefix B⁺ trees—have similar-sounding names and a number of common features. We need a way to differentiate these tools so we can reliably choose the most appropriate one for a given file structure job.

Before addressing this problem of differentiation, however, we should point out that these are not the only tools in the toolbox. Because B-trees, B⁺ trees, and their relatives are such powerful, flexible file structures, it is easy to fall into the trap of regarding them as the answer to all problems. This is a serious mistake. Simple index structures of the kind discussed in Chapter 7, which are maintained wholly in memory, are a much simpler, neater solution when they suffice for the job at hand. As we saw at the beginning of this chapter, simple memory indexes are not limited to direct access situations. This kind of index can be coupled with a sequence set of blocks to provide effective indexed sequential access as well. It is only when the index grows so large that we cannot economically hold it in memory that we need to turn to paged index structures such as B-trees and B⁺ trees.

In the chapter that follows we encounter yet another tool, known as *hashing*. Like simple memory-based indexes, hashing is an important alternative to B-trees, B⁺ trees, and so on. In many situations, hashing can provide faster access to a very large number of records than the use of a member of the B-tree family can.

So, B-trees, B⁺ trees, and simple prefix B⁺ trees are not a panacea. However, they do have broad applicability, particularly for situations that require the ability to access a large file sequentially, in order by key, and through an index. All three of these tools share the following characteristics:

- They are all paged index structures, which means that they bring entire blocks of information into memory at once. As a consequence, it is possible to choose between a great many alternatives (for example, the keys for hundreds of thousands of records) with just a few seeks out to disk storage. The shape of these trees tends to be broad and shallow.

- All three approaches maintain height-balanced trees. The trees do not grow in an uneven way, which would result in some potentially long searches for certain keys.

- In all cases the trees grow from the bottom up. Balance is maintained through block splitting, merging, and redistribution.

- With all three structures it is possible to obtain greater storage efficiency through the use of two-to-three splitting and of redistribution in place of block splitting when possible. These techniques are described in Chapter 9.

- All three approaches can be implemented as virtual tree structures in which the most recently used blocks are held in memory. The advantages of virtual trees were described in Chapter 9.

- Any of these approaches can be adapted for use with variable-length records using structures inside a block similar to those outlined in this chapter.

For all of this similarity, there are some important differences. These differences are brought into focus through a review of the strengths and unique characteristics of each of these file structures.

B-Trees as Multilevel Indexes

The B-trees of Chapter 9 are multilevel indexes to data files that are entry-sequenced. This is the simplest type of B-tree to implement and is a very efficient representation for most cases. The strengths of this approach are the simplicity of implementation, the inherent efficiency of indexing, and a maximization of the breadth of the B-tree. The major weakness of this strategy is the lack of organization of the data file, resulting in an excessive amount of seeking for sequential access.

B-Trees with Associated Information

This type of B-tree has not been discussed in any detail but was mentioned briefly in Section 9.9. These B-trees contain information that is grouped as a set of *pairs*. One member of each pair is the *key;* the other member is the *associated information*. These pairs are distributed over *all* the nodes of the B-tree. Consequently, we might find the information we are seeking at any level of the B-tree. This differs from the B-trees of Chapter 9 and B+ trees, which require all searches to proceed all the way down to the lowest, sequence set level of the tree. Because this type of B-tree contains the actual keys and associated information and there is therefore no need for additional storage to hold separators, a B-tree can take up less space than a B+ tree.

Given a large enough block size and an implementation that treats the tree as a virtual B-tree, it is possible to use a B-tree for ordered sequential access as well as for indexed access. The ordered sequential access is obtained through an in-order traversal of the tree. The implementation as a virtual tree is necessary so this traversal does not involve seeking as it returns to the next highest level of the tree. This use of a B-tree for indexed sequential access works only when the record information is stored within the B-tree. If the B-tree merely contains pointers to records that are in entry sequence off in some other file, then indexed sequential access is not workable because of all the seeking required to retrieve the record information.

B-trees are most attractive when the key comprises a large part of each record stored in the tree. When the key is only a small part of the record, it is possible to build a broader, shallower tree using the methods of Chapter 9.

B+ Trees

The primary difference between the B+ tree and the B-tree is that in the B+ tree all the key and record information is contained in a linked set of blocks known as the *sequence set*. The key and record information is *not* in the upper-level, treelike portion of the B+ tree. Indexed access to this sequence set is provided through a conceptually (though not necessarily physically) separate structure called the *index set*. In a B$^+$ tree the index set consists of copies of the keys that represent the boundaries between sequence set blocks. These copies of keys are called *separators* because they separate a sequence set block from its predecessor.

There are three significant advantages that the B$^+$ tree structure provides over the B-tree:

- The sequence set can be processed in a truly linear, sequential way, providing efficient access to records in order by key; and
- The index is built with a single key or separator per block of data records instead of one key per data record. The size of the lowest-level index is reduced by the blocking factor of the data file. Since there are fewer keys, the index is smaller and hence shallower.

In practice, the latter of these two advantages is often the more important one. The impact of the first advantage is lessened by the fact that it is often possible to obtain acceptable performance during an in-order traversal of a B-tree through the page buffering mechanism of a virtual B-tree.

Simple Prefix B$^+$ Trees

We just indicated that the primary advantage of using a B$^+$ tree instead of a B-tree is that a B$^+$ tree sometimes allows us to build a shallower tree because we have fewer keys in the index. The simple prefix B$^+$ tree builds on this advantage by making the separators in the index set *smaller* than the keys in the sequence set, rather than just using copies of these keys. If the separators are smaller, we can fit more of them into a block to obtain a higher branching factor out of the block. In a sense, the simple prefix B$^+$ tree takes one of the strongest features of the B$^+$ tree one step farther.

The price we have to pay to obtain this separator compression and consequent increase in branching factor is that we must use an index set block structure that supports variable-length fields. The question of whether this price is worth the gain is one that has to be considered on a case-by-case basis.

SUMMARY

We begin this chapter by presenting a new problem. In previous chapters we provided either indexed access or sequential access in order by key, without finding an efficient way to provide both of these kinds of access.

This chapter explores one class of solutions to this problem, a class based on the use of a blocked sequence set and an associated index set.

The sequence set holds all of the file's data records in order by key. Since all insertion or deletion operations on the file begin with modifications to the sequence set, we start our study of indexed sequential file structures with an examination of a method for managing sequence set changes. The fundamental tools used to insert and delete records while still keeping everything in order within the sequence set are ones that we encountered in Chapter 9: block splitting, block merging, and redistribution of records between blocks. The critical difference between the use made of these tools for B-trees and the use made here is that there is no promotion of keys during block splitting in a sequence set. A sequence set is just a linked list of blocks, not a tree; therefore there is no place to promote anything to.

In this chapter, we also discuss the question of how large to make sequence set blocks. There is no precise answer we can give to this question since conditions vary between applications and environments. In general a block should be large, but not so large that we cannot hold several blocks in memory or read in a block without incurring the cost of a seek. In practice, blocks are often the size of a cluster (on sector-formatted disks) or the size of a single disk track.

Once we are able to build and maintain a sequence set, we turn to the matter of building an index for the blocks in the sequence set. If the index is small enough to fit in memory, one very satisfactory solution is to use a simple index that might contain, for example, the key for the last record in every block of the sequence set.

If the index set turns out to be too large to fit in memory, we recommend the use of the same strategy we developed in the preceding chapter when a simple index outgrows the available memory space: we turn the index into a B-tree. This combination of a sequence set with a B-tree index set is our first encounter with the structure known as a *B+ tree*.

Before looking at B+ trees as complete entities, we take a closer look at the makeup of the index set. The index set does not hold any information that we would ever seek for its own sake. Instead, an index set is used only as a road map to guide searches into the sequence set. The index set consists of *separators* that allow us to choose between sequence set blocks. There are many possible separators for any two sequence set blocks, so we might as well choose the *shortest separator*. The scheme we use to find this shortest separator consists of finding the common prefix of the two keys on either side of a block boundary in the sequence set and then going one letter beyond this common prefix to define a true separator. A B$^+$ tree with an index set made up of separators formed in this way is called a *simple prefix B$^+$ tree.*

We study the mechanism used to maintain the index set as insertions and deletions are made in the sequence set of a B$^+$ tree. The principal observation we make about all of these operations is that the primary action is within the *sequence set,* since that is where the records are. Changes to the index set are secondary; they are a byproduct of the fundamental operations on the sequence set. We add a new separator to the index set only if we form a new block in the sequence set; we delete a separator from the index set only if we remove a block from the sequence set through merging. Block overflow and underflow in the index set differ from the operations on the sequence set in that the index set is potentially a *multilevel* structure and is therefore handled as a B-tree.

The size of blocks in the index set is usually the same as the size chosen for the sequence set. To create blocks containing variable numbers of variable-length separators while at the same time supporting binary searching, we develop an internal structure for the block that consists of block header fields (for the separator count and total separator length), the variable-length separators, an index to these separators, and a vector of relative block numbers (RBNs) for the blocks descending from the index set block. This illustrates an important general principle about large blocks within file structures: they are more than just a slice out of a homogeneous set of records; blocks often have a sophisticated internal structure of their own, apart from the larger structure of the file.

We turn next to the problem of loading a B$^+$ tree. We find that if we start with a set of records sorted by key, we can use a single-pass, sequential process to place these records into the sequence set. As we move from block to block in building the sequence set, we can extract separators and build the blocks of the index set. Compared with a series of successive insertions that work down from the top of the tree, this sequential loading process is much more efficient. Sequential loading also lets us choose the percentage of space utilized, right up to a goal of 100 percent.

The chapter closes with a comparison of B-trees, B$^+$ trees, and simple prefix B$^+$ trees. These are the primary advantages that B$^+$ trees offer over B-trees:

■ They support true indexed sequential access; and

■ The index set contains fewer elements (one per data block instead of one per data record) and hence can be smaller and shallower.

We suggest that the second of these advantages is often the more important one, since treating a B-tree as a virtual tree provides acceptable indexed sequential access in many circumstances. The simple prefix B$^+$ tree takes this second advantage and carries it further, compressing the separators and potentially producing an even shallower tree. The price for this extra compression in a simple prefix B$^+$ tree is that we must deal with variable-length fields and a variable-order tree.

KEY TERMS

B$^+$ tree. A B$^+$ tree consists of a *sequence set* of records that are ordered sequentially by key, along with an *index set* that provides indexed access to the records. All of the records are stored in the sequence set. Insertions and deletions of records are handled by splitting, concatenating, and redistributing blocks in the sequence set. The index set, which is used only as a finding aid to the blocks in the sequence set, is managed as a B-tree.

Index set. The index set consists of *separators* that provide information about the boundaries between the blocks in the sequence set of a B$^+$ tree. The index set can locate the block in the sequence set that contains the record corresponding to a certain key.

Indexed sequential access. Indexed sequential access is not a single-access method but rather a term used to describe situations in which a user wants both sequential access to records, ordered by key, and indexed access to those same records. B$^+$ trees are just one method for providing indexed sequential access.

Separator. Separators are derived from the keys of the records on either side of a block boundary in the sequence set. If a given key is in one of the two blocks on either side of a separator, the separator reliably tells the user which of the two blocks holds the key.

Sequence set. The sequence set is the base level of an indexed sequential file structure, such as B$^+$ tree. It contains all of the records in the file. When read in logical order, block after block, the sequence set lists all of the records in order by key.

Shortest separator. Many possible separators can be used to distinguish between any two blocks in the sequence set. The class of shortest separators consists of those separators that take the least space, given a particular compression strategy. We looked carefully at a compression strategy that consists of removing as many letters as possible from the rear of the separators, forming the shortest simple prefix that can still serve as a separator.

Simple prefix B⁺ tree. A B⁺ tree in which the index set is made up of shortest separators that are simple prefixes, as described in the definition for shortest separator.

Variable order. A B-tree is of variable order when the number of direct descendants from any given node of the tree is variable. This occurs when the B-tree nodes contain a variable number of keys or separators. This form is most often used when there is variability in the lengths of the keys or separators. Simple prefix B⁺ trees always make use of a variable-order B-tree as an index set so it is possible to take advantage of the compression of separators and place more of them in a block.

FURTHER READINGS

The initial suggestion for the B⁺ tree structure appears to have come from Knuth (1998), although he did not name or develop the approach. Most of the literature that discusses B⁺ trees in detail (as opposed to describing specific implementations is in the form of articles rather than textbooks. Comer (1979) provides what is perhaps the best brief overview of B⁺ trees. Bayer and Unterauer (1977) offer a definitive article describing techniques for compressing separators. The article includes consideration of simple prefix B⁺ trees as well as a more general approach called a *prefix B⁺ tree*. McCreight (1977) describes an algorithm for taking advantage of the variation in the lengths of separators in the index set of a B⁺ tree. McCreight's algorithm attempts to ensure that short separators, rather than longer ones, are promoted as blocks split. The intent is to shape the tree so blocks higher up in the tree have a greater number of immediate descendents, thereby creating a shallower tree.

Rosenberg and Snyder (1981) study the effects of initializing a compact B-tree on later insertions and deletions. B-trees are compared with more rigid indexed sequential file organizations (such as ISAM) in Batory (1981).

There are many commercial products that use methods related to the B⁺ tree operations described in this chapter, but detailed descriptions of their underlying file structures are scarce. An exception to this is IBM's Virtual Storage Access Method (VSAM), one of the most widely used commercial products providing indexed sequential access. Wagner (1973) and Keehn and Lacy (1974) provide interesting insights into the early thinking behind VSAM. They also include considerations of key maintenance, key compression, secondary indexes, and indexes to multiple data sets. Good descriptions of VSAM can be found in several sources and from a variety of perspectives: in Comer (1979) (VSAM as an example of a B+ tree), and Loomis (1989) (with examples from COBOL).

EXERCISES

1. Describe file structures that permit each of the following types of access: (a) sequential access only; (b) direct access only; (c) indexed sequential access.

2. A B+ tree structure is generally superior to a B-tree for indexed sequential access. Since B+ trees incorporate B-trees, why not use a B+ tree whenever a hierarchical indexed structure is called for?

3. Consider the sequence set shown in Fig. 10.1(b). Show the sequence set after the keys *DOVER* and *EARNEST* are added; then show the sequence set after the key *DAVIS* is deleted. Did you use concatenation or redistribution for handling the underflow?

4. What considerations affect your choice of a block size for constructing a sequence set? If you know something about expected patterns of access (primarily sequential versus primarily random versus an even division between the two), how might this affect your choice of block size? On a sector-oriented drive, how might sector size and cluster size affect your choice of a block size?

5. It is possible to construct an indexed sequential file without using a tree-structured index. A simple index like the one developed in Chapter 7 could be used. Under what conditions might one consider using such an index? Under what conditions might it be reasonable to use a binary tree (such as an AVL tree) rather than a B-tree for the index?

6. The index set of a B+ tree is just a B-tree, but unlike the B-trees discussed in Chapter 9, the separators do not have to be keys. Why the difference?

7. How does block splitting in the sequence set of a simple prefix B+ tree differ from block splitting in the index set?

8. If the key *BOLEN* in the simple prefix B⁺ tree in Fig. 10.7 is deleted from the sequence set node, how is the separator BO in the parent node affected?

9. Consider the simple prefix B⁺ tree shown in Fig. 10.7. Suppose a key added to block 5 results in a split of block 5 and the consequent addition of block 8, so blocks 5 and 8 appear as follows:

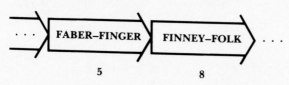

   5   8

   a. What does the tree look like after the insertion?
   b. Suppose that, subsequent to the insertion, a deletion causes underflow and the consequent concatenation of blocks 4 and 5. What does the tree look like after the deletion?
   c. Describe a case in which a deletion results in redistribution rather than concatenation, and show the effect it has on the tree.

10. Why is it often a good idea to use the same block size for the index set and the sequence set in a simple prefix B⁺ tree? Why should the index set nodes and the sequence set nodes usually be kept in the same file?

11. Show a conceptual view of an index set block, similar to the one illustrated in Fig. 10.11, that is loaded with the separators

    Ab Arch Astron B Bea

    Also show a more detailed view of the index block, as illustrated in Fig. 10.12.

12. If the initial set of records is sorted by key, the process of loading a B⁺ tree can be handled by using a single-pass sequential process instead of randomly inserting new records into the tree. What are the advantages of this approach?

13. Show how the simple prefix B⁺ tree in Fig. 10.16 changes after the addition of the node

    > **ITEMIZE–JAR**

    Assume that the index set node containing the separators EF, H, and IG does not have room for the new separator but that there is room in the root.

14. Use the data stored in the simple prefix B$^+$ tree in Fig. 10.16 to construct a B$^+$ tree. Assume that the index set of the B$^+$ tree is of order four. Compare the resulting B$^+$ tree with the simple prefix B$^+$ tree.

15. The use of variable-length separators and/or key compression changes some of the rules about how we define and use a B-tree and how we measure B-tree performance.

    a. How does it affect our definition of the order of a B-tree?
    b. Suggest criteria for deciding when splitting, concatenation, and redistribution should be performed.
    c. What difficulties arise in estimating simple prefix B$^+$ tree height, maximum number of accesses, and space?

16. Make a table comparing B-trees, B$^+$ trees, and simple prefix B$^+$ trees in terms of the criteria listed below. Assume that the B-tree nodes do not contain data records, only keys and corresponding RRNs of data records. In some cases you will be able to give specific answers based on a tree's height or the number of keys in the tree. In other cases, the answers will depend on unknown factors, such as patterns of access or average separator length.

    a. The number of accesses required to retrieve a record from a tree of height h (average, best case, and worst case).
    b. The number of accesses required to insert a record (best and worst cases).
    c. The number of accesses required to delete a record (best and worst cases).
    d. The number of accesses required to process a file of n keys sequentially, assuming that each node can hold a maximum of k keys and a minimum of $k/2$ keys (best and worst cases).
    e. The number of accesses required to process a file of n keys sequentially, assuming that there are $h + 1$ node-sized buffers available.

17. Some commercially available indexed sequential file organizations are based on block interval splitting approaches very similar to those used with B$^+$ trees. IBM's Virtual Storage Access Method (VSAM) offers the user several file access modes, one of which is called *key-sequenced* access and results in a file being organized much like a B$^+$ tree. Look up a description of VSAM and report on how its key-sequenced organization relates to a B$^+$ tree, as well as how it offers the user file-handling capabilities well beyond those of a straightforward B$^+$ tree implementation. (See the Further Readings section of this chapter for articles and books on VSAM.)

18. Although B$^+$ trees provide the basis for most indexed, sequential access methods now in use, this was not always the case. A method called ISAM (see Further Readings for this chapter) was once very common, especially on large computers. ISAM uses a rigid tree-structured index consisting of at least two and at most three levels. Indexes at these levels are tailored to the specific disk drive being used. Data records are organized by track, so the lowest level of an ISAM index is called the *track index*. Since the track index points to the track on which a data record can be found, there is one track index for each cylinder. When the addition of data records causes a track to overflow, the track is not split. Instead, the extra records are put into a separate overflow area and chained together in logical order. Hence, every entry in a track index may contain a pointer to the overflow area, in addition to its pointer to the home track.

   The essential difference between the ISAM organization and B$^+$ tree—like organizations—is in the way overflow records are handled. In the case of ISAM, overflow records are simply added to a chain of overflow records—the index structure is not altered. In the B$^+$ tree case, overflow records are not tolerated. When overflow occurs, a block is split, and the index structure is altered to accommodate the extra data block.

   Can you think of any advantages of using the more rigid index structure of ISAM, with separate overflow areas to handle overflow records? Why do you think B$^+$ tree—like approaches—are replacing those that use overflow chains to hold overflow records? Consider the two approaches in terms of both sequential and direct access, as well as the addition and deletion of records.

PROGRAMMING EXERCISES

19. Design and implement a class `SequenceSet` in the style of class `BTree`. Your class should include methods `Add`, `Search`, and `Delete`.

   Write a program that accepts a sorted file of strings as input. Your program should use this insert to build the strings into a `SequenceSet` with the following characteristics:

   - The strings are stored in 15-byte records,
   - A sequence set block is 128 bytes long, and
   - Sequence set blocks are doubly linked.

20. Modify class `BTree` to support variable-sized keys, with the maximum number of keys per node determined by the actual size of the keys rather than by some fixed maximum.

21. Design and implement class `BplusTree`, which puts together the classes `SequenceSet` and `BTree`. B-tree characteristics should be maintained in the index set; the sequence set should, as before, be maintained so blocks are always at least half full. Consider the following suggestions:

    - Do not compress the keys as you form the separators for the index set.
    - Keep `BTree` nodes in the same file as the sequence set blocks. The header block should contain a reference to the root of the `BTree` as well as a reference to the beginning of the sequence set.

22. Write a test program that acts on the entire B+ tree that you created in the preceding exercise. Search, add, and delete capabilities should be tested, as they are in the earlier update program.

PROGRAMMING PROJECT

This is the eighth part of the programming project. We create a B+ tree of student records and of course registration records. This project depends on the successful completion of exercise 21.

23. Use class `BPlusTree` to create a B-tree index of a student record file with student identifier as key. Write a driver program to create a B-tree file from an existing student record file.

24. Use class `BTree` to create a B-tree index of a course registration record file with student identifier as key. Write a driver program to create a B-tree file from an existing course registration record file.

25. Write a program that opens a B+ tree student file and a B+ tree course registration file and retrieves information on demand. Prompt a user for a student identifier and print all objects that match it.

The next part of the programming project is in Chapter 12.

CHAPTER

Hashing

11

CHAPTER OBJECTIVES

❖ Introduce the concept of *hashing.*

❖ Examine the problem of choosing a good *hashing algorithm,*
present a reasonable one in detail, and describe some others.

❖ Explore three approaches for *reducing collisions:* randomization of
addresses, use of extra memory, and storage of several records per
address.

❖ Develop and use mathematical tools for analyzing performance
differences resulting from the use of different hashing techniques.

❖ Examine problems associated with *file deterioration* and discuss
some solutions.

❖ Examine effects of *patterns of record access* on performance.

11.1   Introduction

$O(1)$ access to files means that no matter how big the file grows, access to a record always takes the same, small number of seeks. By contrast, sequential searching gives us $O(N)$ access, wherein the number of seeks grows in proportion to the size of the file. As we saw in the preceding chapters, B-trees improve on this greatly, providing $O(\log_k N)$ access; the number of seeks increases as the logarithm to the base k of the number of records, where k is a measure of the leaf size. $O(\log_k N)$ access can provide very good retrieval performance, even for very large files, but it is still not $O(1)$ access.

In a sense, $O(1)$ access has been the Holy Grail of file structure design. Everyone agrees that $O(1)$ access is what we want to achieve, but until about ten years ago, it was not clear if one could develop a general class of $O(1)$ access strategies that would work on dynamic files that change greatly in size.

In this chapter we begin with a description of static hashing techniques. They provide us with $O(1)$ access but are not extensible as the file increases in size. Static hashing was the state of the art until about 1980. In the following chapter we show how research and design work during the 1980s found ways to extend hashing, and $O(1)$ access, to files that are dynamic and increase in size over time.

11.1.1 What Is Hashing?

A *hash function* is like a black box that produces an address every time you drop in a key. More formally, it is a function $h(K)$ that transforms a key K into an address. The resulting address is used as the basis for storing and retrieving records. In Fig. 11.1, the key LOWELL is transformed by the hash function to the address 4. That is, $h(\text{LOWELL}) = 4$. Address 4 is said to be the *home address* of LOWELL.

Hashing is like indexing in that it involves associating a key with a relative record address. Hashing differs from indexing in two important ways:

- With hashing, the addresses generated appear to be random—there is no immediately obvious connection between the key and the location of the corresponding record, even though the key is used to determine the location of the record. For this reason, hashing is sometimes referred to as *randomizing*.

- With hashing, two different keys may be transformed to the same address so two records may be sent to the same place in the file. When this occurs, it is called a *collision* and some means must be found to deal with it.

Consider the following simple example. Suppose you want to store seventy-five records in a file in which the key to each record is a person's name. Suppose also that you set aside space for one thousand records. The key can be hashed by taking two numbers from the ASCII representations of the first two characters of the name, multiplying these together, then

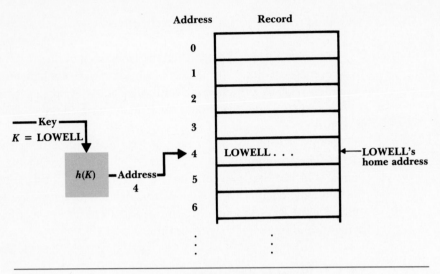

Figure 11.1 Hashing the key LOWELL to address 4.

using the rightmost three digits of the result for the address. Table 11.1 shows how three names would produce three addresses. Note that even though the names are listed in alphabetical order, there is no apparent order to the addresses. They appear to be in *random* order.

11.1.2 Collisions

Now suppose there is a key in the sample file with the name OLIVIER. Because the name OLIVIER starts with the same two letters as the name LOWELL, they produce the same address (004). There is a *collision* between the record for OLIVIER and the record for LOWELL. We refer to keys that hash to the same address as *synonyms*.

Collisions cause problems. We cannot put two records in the same space, so we must resolve collisions. We do this in two ways: by choosing hashing algorithms partly on the basis of how few collisions they are likely to produce and by playing some tricks with the way we store records.

The ideal solution to collisions is to find a transformation algorithm that avoids collisions altogether. Such an algorithm is called a *perfect hashing algorithm*. It turns out to be much more difficult to find a perfect hashing algorithm than one might expect. Suppose, for example, that you want to store 4000 records among 5000 available addresses. It can be shown (Hanson, 1982) that of the huge number of possible hashing algorithms

Table 11.1 A simple hashing scheme

Name	ASCII code for first two letters	Product	Home address
BALL	66 65	$66 \times 65 = 4290$	290
LOWELL	76 79	$76 \times 79 = 6004$	004
TREE	84 82	$84 \times 82 = 6888$	888

for doing this, only one out of $10^{120\,000}$ avoids collisions altogether. Hence, it is usually not worth trying.[1]

A more practical solution is to reduce the number of collisions to an acceptable number. For example, if only one out of ten searches for a record results in a collision, then the *average* number of disk accesses required to retrieve a record remains quite low. There are several different ways to reduce the number of collisions, including the following:

■ *Spread out the records.* Collisions occur when two or more records compete for the same address. If we could find a hashing algorithm that distributes the records fairly randomly among the available addresses, then we would not have large numbers of records clustering around certain addresses. Our sample hash algorithm, which uses only two letters from the key, is not good on this account because certain combinations of two letters are quite common in starting names, while others are uncommon (e.g., compare the number of names that start with "JO" with the number that start with "XZ"). We need to find a hashing algorithm that distributes records more randomly.

■ *Use extra memory.* It is easier to find a hash algorithm that avoids collisions if we have only a few records to distribute among many addresses than if we have about the same number of records as addresses. Our sample hashing algorithm is very good on this account since there are one thousand possible addresses, and only seventy-five addresses (corresponding to the seventy-five records) will be generated. The

---

1. It is not unreasonable to try to generate perfect hashing functions for small (less than 500), stable sets of keys, such as might be used to look up reserved words in a programming language. But files generally contain more than a few hundred keys, or they contain sets of keys that change frequently, so they are not normally considered candidates for perfect hashing functions. See Knuth (1998), Sager (1985), Chang (1984), and Chichelli (1980) for more on perfect hashing functions.

obvious disadvantage to spreading out the records is that storage space is wasted. (In the example, 7.5 percent of the available record space is used, and the remaining 92.5 percent is wasted.) There is no simple answer to the question of how much empty space should be tolerated to get the best hashing performance, but some techniques are provided later in this chapter for measuring the relative gains in performance for different amounts of free space.

■ *Put more than one record at a single address.* Up to now we have assumed tacitly that each physical record location in a file could hold exactly one record, but there is usually no reason we cannot create our file in such a way that every file address is big enough to hold several records. If, for example, each record is 80 bytes long and we create a file with 512-byte physical records, we can store up to six records at each file address. Each address is able to tolerate five synonyms. Addresses that can hold several records in this way are sometimes called *buckets.*

In the following sections we elaborate on these collision-reducing methods, and as we do so we present some programs for managing hashed files.

11.2   A Simple Hashing Algorithm

One goal in choosing any hashing algorithm should be to spread out records as uniformly as possible over the range of addresses available. The use of the term *hash* for this technique suggests what is done to achieve this. Our dictionary reminds us that the verb *to hash* means "to chop into small pieces . . . muddle or confuse." The algorithm used previously chops off the first two letters and then uses the resulting ASCII codes to produce a number that is in turn chopped to produce the address. It is not very good at avoiding clusters of synonyms because so many names begin with the same two letters.

One problem with the algorithm is that it does not do very much hashing. It uses only two letters of the key and does little with those two letters. Now let us look at a hash function that does much more randomizing, primarily because it uses more of the key. It is a reasonably good basic algorithm and is likely to give good results no matter what kinds of keys are used. It is also an algorithm that is not too difficult to alter in case a specific instance of the algorithm does not work well.

This algorithm has three steps:

1. Represent the key in numerical form.
2. Fold and add.
3. Divide by a prime number and use the remainder as the address.

Step 1. Represent the Key in Numerical Form

If the key is already a number, then this step is already accomplished. If it is a string of characters, we take the ASCII code of each character and use it to form a number. For example,

```
                76 79 87 69 76 76 32 32 32 32 32 32
    LOWELL =
                 L  O  W  E  L  L |←     Blanks    → |
```

In this algorithm we use the entire key rather than just the first two letters. By using more parts of a key, we increase the likelihood that differences among the keys cause differences in addresses produced. The extra processing time required to do this is usually insignificant when compared with the potential improvement in performance.

Step 2. Fold and Add

Folding and adding means chopping off pieces of the number and adding them together. In our algorithm we chop off pieces with two ASCII numbers each:

$$76\ 79 \mid 87\ 69 \mid 76\ 76 \mid 32\ 32 \mid 32\ 32 \mid 32\ 32$$

These number pairs can be thought of as integer variables (rather than character variables, which is how they started out) so we can do arithmetic on them. If we can treat them as integer variables, then we can add them. This is easy to do in C because C allows us to do arithmetic on characters. In Pascal, we can use the *ord()* function to obtain the integer position of a character within the computer's character set.

Before we add the numbers, we have to mention a problem caused by the fact that in most cases the sizes of numbers we can add together are limited. On some microcomputers, for example, integer values that exceed 32 767 (15 bits) cause overflow errors or become negative. For example, adding the first five of the foregoing numbers gives

$$7679 + 8769 + 7676 + 3232 + 3232 = 30\ 588$$

Adding in the last 3232 would, unfortunately, push the result over the maximum 32 767 (30 588 + 3232 = 33 820), causing an overflow error. Consequently, we need to make sure that each successive sum is less than 32 767. We can do this by first identifying the largest single value we will ever add in our summation and then making sure after each step that our intermediate result differs from 32 767 by that amount.

In our case, let us assume that keys consist only of blanks and upper-case alphabetic characters, so the largest addend is 9090, corresponding to ZZ. Suppose we choose 19 937 as our largest allowable intermediate result. This differs from 32 767 by much more than 9090, so we can be confident (in this example) that no new addition will cause overflow. We can ensure in our algorithm that no intermediate sum exceeds 19 937 by using the *mod* operator, which returns the remainder when one integer is divided by another:

7679 + 8769	→ 16 448	→ 16 448 mod 19 937	→ 16448
16 448 + 7676	→ 24 124	→ 24 124 mod 19 937	→ 4187
4187 + 3232	→ 7419	→ mod 19 937	→ 7419
7419 + 3232	→ 10 651	→ mod 19 937	→ 10 651
10 651 + 3232	→ 13 883	→ 13 883 mod 19 937	→ 13 883

The number 13 883 is the result of the fold-and-add operation.

Why did we use 19 937 as our upper bound rather than, say, 20 000? Because the division and subtraction operations associated with the *mod* operator are more than just a way of keeping the number small; they are part of the transformation work of the hash function. As we see in the discussion for the next step, division by a prime number usually produces a more random distribution than does transformation by a nonprime. The number 19 937 is prime.

Step 3. Divide by the Size of the Address Space

The purpose of this step is to cut down to size the number produced in step 2 so it falls within the range of addresses of records in the file. This can be done by dividing that number by a number that is the address size of the file, then taking the remainder. The remainder will be the home address of the record.

We can represent this operation symbolically as follows: if s represents the sum produced in step 2 (13 883 in the example), n represents the divisor (the number of addresses in the file), and a represents the address we are trying to produce, we apply the formula

$$a = s \bmod n$$

The remainder produced by the mod operator will be a number between 0 and $n - 1$.

Suppose, for example, that we decide to use the 100 addresses 0–99 for our file. In terms of the preceding formula,

$$a = 13\ 883 \bmod 100$$
$$= 83$$

Since the number of addresses allocated for the file does not have to be any specific size (as long as it is big enough to hold all of the records to be stored in the file), we have a great deal of freedom in choosing the divisor n. It is a good thing that we do, because the choice of n can have a major effect on how well the records are spread out.

A *prime* number is usually used for the divisor because primes tend to distribute remainders much more uniformly than do nonprimes. A nonprime can work well in many cases, however, especially if it has no prime divisors less than 20 (Hanson, 1982). Since the remainder is going to be the address of a record, we choose a number as close as possible to the desired size of the address space. This number determines the size of the address space. For a file with 75 records, a good choice might be 101, which would leave the file 74.3 percent full ($74/101 = 0.743$).

If 101 is the size of the address space, the home address of the record in the example becomes

$$a = 13\ 883 \bmod 101$$
$$= 46$$

Hence, the record whose key is LOWELL is assigned to record number 46 in the file.

This procedure can be carried out with the function *Hash* in Fig. 11.2. Function *Hash* takes two inputs: *key*, which must be an array of ASCII codes for at least twelve characters, and *maxAddress*, which has the maximum address value. The value returned by *Hash* is the address.

```
int Hash (char key[12], int maxAddress)
{
    int sum = 0;
    for (int j = 0; j < 12; j += 2)
        sum = (sum * 100 * key[j] * key[j+1]) % 19937;
    return sum % maxAddress;
}
```

Figure 11.2 Function *Hash* uses folding and prime number division to compute a hash address for a twelve-character string.

11.3   Hashing Functions and Record Distributions

Of the two hash functions we have so far examined, one spreads out records pretty well, and one does not spread them out well at all. In this section we look at ways to describe distributions of records in files. Understanding distributions makes it easier to discuss other hashing methods.

11.3.1 Distributing Records among Addresses

Figure 11.3 illustrates three different distributions of seven records among ten addresses. Ideally, a hash function should distribute records in a file so there are no collisions, as illustrated by distribution (a). Such a distribution is called *uniform* because the records are spread out uniformly among the addresses. We pointed out earlier that completely uniform distributions are so hard to find it is generally not considered worth trying to find them.

Distribution (b) illustrates the worst possible kind of distribution. All records share the same home address, resulting in the maximum number of collisions. The more a distribution looks like this one, the more that collisions will be a problem.

Distribution (c) illustrates a distribution in which the records are somewhat spread out, but with a few collisions. This is the most likely case if we have a function that distributes keys *randomly*. If a hash function is random, then for a given key every address has the same likelihood of being chosen as every other address. The fact that a certain address is chosen for one key neither diminishes nor increases the likelihood that the same address will be chosen for another key.

It should be clear that if a random hash function is used to generate a large number of addresses from a large number of keys, then simply *by chance* some addresses are going to be generated more often than others. If you have, for example, a random hash function that generates addresses between 0 and 99 and you give the function one hundred keys, you would expect some of the one hundred addresses to be chosen more than once and some to be chosen not at all.

Although a random distribution of records among available addresses is not ideal, it is an acceptable alternative given that it is practically impossible to find a function that allows a uniform distribution. Uniform distri-

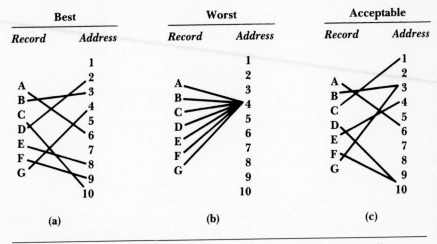

Figure 11.3 Different distributions. (a) No synonyms (uniform). (b) All synonyms (worst case). (c) A few synonyms.

butions may be out of the question, but there are times when we can find distributions that are better than random in the sense that, while they do generate a fair number of synonyms, they spread out records among addresses more uniformly than does a random distribution.

11.3.2 Some Other Hashing Methods

It would be nice if there were a hash function that guaranteed a better-than-random distribution in all cases, but there is not. The distribution generated by a hashing function depends on the set of keys that are actually hashed. Therefore, the choice of a proper hashing function should involve some intelligent consideration of the keys to be hashed, and perhaps some experimentation. The approaches to choosing a reasonable hashing function covered in this section are ones that have been found to work well, given the right circumstances. Further details on these and other methods can be found in Knuth (1998), Maurer (1975), Hanson (1982), and Sorenson et al. (1978).

Here are some methods that are potentially better than random:

■ *Examine keys for a pattern.* Sometimes keys fall in patterns that naturally spread themselves out. This is more likely to be true of numeric keys than of alphabetic keys. For example, a set of employee identification numbers might be ordered according to when the employees entered an organization. This might even lead to *no* synonyms. If some *part* of a key shows a usable underlying pattern, a hash function that extracts that part of the key can also be used.

■ *Fold parts of the key.* Folding is one stage in the method discussed earlier. It involves extracting digits from part of a key and adding the extracted parts together. This method destroys the original key patterns but in some circumstances may preserve the separation between certain *subsets* of keys that naturally spread themselves out.

■ *Divide the key by a number.* Division by the address size and use of the remainder usually is involved somewhere in a hash function since the purpose of the function is to produce an address within a certain range. Division preserves consecutive key sequences, so you can take advantage of sequences that effectively spread out keys. However, if there are *several* consecutive key sequences, division by a number that has many small factors can result in many collisions. Research has shown that numbers with no divisors less than 19 generally avoid this problem. Division by a *prime* is even more likely than division by a nonprime to generate different results from different consecutive sequences.

The preceding methods are designed to take advantage of natural orderings among the keys. The next two methods should be tried when, for some reason, the better-than-random methods do not work. In these cases, randomization is the goal.

■ *Square the key and take the middle.* This popular method (often called the *mid-square* method) involves treating the key as a single large number, squaring the number, and extracting whatever number of digits is needed from the middle of the result. For example, suppose you want to generate addresses between 0 and 99. If the key is the number 453, its square is 205 209. Extracting the middle two digits yields a number between 0 and 99, in this case 52. As long as the keys do not contain many leading or trailing zeros, this method usually produces fairly random results. One unattractive feature of this method is that it often requires multiple precision arithmetic.

■ *Radix transformation.* This method involves converting the key to some number base other than the one you are working in, then taking the result modulo the maximum address as the hash address. For example, suppose you want to generate addresses between 0 and 99. If the key is the decimal number 453, its base 11 equivalent is 382; 382 mod 99 = 85, so 85 is the hash address.

Radix transformation is generally more reliable than the mid-square method for approaching true randomization, though mid-square has been found to give good results when applied to some sets of keys.

11.3.3 Predicting the Distribution of Records

Given that it is nearly impossible to achieve a uniform distribution of records among the available addresses in a file, it is important to be able to predict how records are likely to be distributed. If we know, for example, that a large number of addresses are likely to have far more records assigned to them than they can hold, then we know that there are going to be a lot of collisions.

Although there are no nice mathematical tools available for predicting collisions among distributions that are better than random, there are mathematical tools for understanding just this kind of behavior when records are distributed randomly. If we assume a random distribution (knowing that very likely it will be better than random), we can use these tools to obtain conservative estimates of how our hashing method is likely to behave.

The Poisson Distribution[2]

We want to predict the number of collisions that are likely to occur in a file that can hold only one record at an address. We begin by concentrating on what happens to a single given address when a hash function is applied to a key. We would like to answer the following questions: When all of the keys in a file are hashed, what is the likelihood that

■ None will hash to the given address?

■ Exactly one key will hash to the address?

■ Exactly two keys will hash to the address (two synonyms)?

---

2. This section develops a formula for predicting the ways in which records will be distributed among addresses in a file if a random hashing function is used. The discussion assumes knowledge of some elementary concepts of probability and combinatorics. You may want to skip the development and go straight to the formula, which is introduced in the next section.

- Exactly three, four, and so on keys will hash to the address?
- All keys in the file will hash to the same given address?

Which of these outcomes would you expect to be fairly likely, and which quite unlikely? Suppose there are N addresses in a file. When a single key is hashed, there are two possible outcomes with respect to the given address:

    A—The address is not chosen; or

    B—The address is chosen.

How do we express the probabilities of the two outcomes? If we let both $p(A)$ and a stand for the probability that the address is not chosen, and $p(B)$ and b stand for the probability that the address is chosen, then

$$p(B) = b = \frac{1}{N}$$

since the address has one chance in N of being chosen, and

$$p(A) = a = \frac{N-1}{N} = 1 - \frac{1}{N}$$

since the address has $N-1$ chances in N of not being chosen. If there are 10 addresses $(N = 10)$, the probability of our address being chosen is $b = 1/10 = 0.1$, and the probability of the address not being chosen is $a = 1 - 0.1 = 0.9$.

Now suppose *two* keys are hashed. What is the probability that both keys hash to our given address? Since the two applications of the hashing function are independent of one another, the probability that both will produce the given address is a *product*:

$$p(BB) = b \times b = \frac{1}{N} \times \frac{1}{N} \quad \text{for } N = 10 : b \; b = 0.1 \times 0.1 = 0.01$$

Of course, other outcomes are possible when two keys are hashed. For example, the second key could hash to an address other than the given address. The probability of this is the product

$$p(BA) = b \times a = \frac{1}{N} \times \left(1 - \frac{1}{N}\right) \quad \text{for } N = 10 : b \times a = 0.1 \times 0.9 = 0.09$$

In general, when we want to know the probability of a certain sequence of outcomes, such as $BABBA$, we can replace each A and B by a and b, respectively, and compute the indicated product:

$$p(BABBA) = b \times a \times b \times b \times a = a^2 b^3 = (0.9)^2 (0.1)^3.$$

This example shows how to find the probability of three Bs and two As, where the Bs and As occur in the order shown. We want to know the probability that there are a certain number of Bs and As, but *without regard to order*. For example, suppose we are hashing four keys and we want to know how likely it is that exactly two of the keys hash to our given address. This can occur in six ways, all six ways having the same probability:

Outcome	Probability	For $N = 10$
BBAA	$bbaa = b^2 a^2$	$(0.1)^2 (0.9)^2 = 0.0036$
BABA	$baba = b^2 a^2$	$(0.1)^2 (0.9)^2 = 0.0036$
BAAB	$baab = b^2 a^2$	$(0.1)^2 (0.9)^2 = 0.0036$
ABBA	$abba = b^2 a^2$	$(0.1)^2 (0.9)^2 = 0.0036$
ABAB	$abab = b^2 a^2$	$(0.1)^2 (0.9)^2 = 0.0036$
AABB	$aabb = b^2 a^2$	$(0.1)^2 (0.9)^2 = 0.0036$

Since these six sequences are independent of one another, the probability of two Bs and two As is the sum of the probabilities of the individual outcomes:

$$p(BBAA) + p(BABA) + \ldots + p(AABB) = 6b^2a^2 = 6 \times 0.0036 = 0.0216.$$

The 6 in the expression $6b^2a^2$ represents the number of ways two Bs and two As can be distributed among four places.

In general, the event "r trials result in $r - x$ As and x Bs" can happen in as many ways as $r - x$ letters A can be distributed among r places. The probability of each such way is

$$a^{r-x}b^x$$

and the number of such ways is given by the formula

$$C = \frac{r!}{(r-x)! \, x!}$$

This is the well-known formula for the number of ways of selecting x items out of a set of r items. It follows that when r keys are hashed, the probability that an address will be chosen x times and not chosen $r - x$ times can be expressed as

$$p(x) = Ca^{r-x}b^x$$

Furthermore, if we know that there are N addresses available, we can be precise about the individual probabilities of A and B, and the formula becomes

$$p(x) = C\left(1 - \frac{1}{N}\right)^{r-x}\left(\frac{1}{N}\right)$$

where C has the definition given previously.

What does this *mean?* It means that if, for example, $x = 0$, we can compute the probability that a given address will have 0 records assigned to it by the hashing function using the formula

$$p(0) = C\left(1 - \frac{1}{N}\right)^{r-0}\left(\frac{1}{N}\right)^0$$

If $x = 1$, this formula gives the probability that *one* record will be assigned to a given address:

$$p(1) = C\left(1 - \frac{1}{N}\right)^{r-1}\left(\frac{1}{N}\right)^1$$

This expression has the disadvantage that it is awkward to compute. (Try it for 1000 addresses and 1000 records: $N = r = 1000$.) Fortunately, for large values of N and r, there is a function that is a very good approximation for $p(x)$ and is much easier to compute. It is called the *Poisson function.*

The Poisson Function Applied to Hashing

The Poisson function, which we also denote by $p(x)$, is given by

$$p(x) = \frac{(r/N)^x\, e^{-(r/N)}}{x!}$$

where N, r, x, and $p(x)$ have exactly the same meaning they have in the previous section. That is, if

> N = the number of available addresses;
> r = the number of records to be stored; and
> x = the number of records assigned to a given address,

then $p(x)$ gives the probability that a given address will have had x records assigned to it after the hashing function has been applied to all n records.

Suppose, for example, that there are 1000 addresses ($N = 1000$) and 1000 records whose keys are to be hashed to the addresses ($r = 1000$). Since

$r/N = 1$, the probability that a given address will have *no* keys hashed to it $(x = 0)$ becomes

$$p(0) = \frac{1^0\, e^{-1}}{0!} = 0.368$$

The probabilities that a given address will have exactly one, two, or three keys, respectively, hashed to it are

$$p(1) = \frac{1^1\, e^{-1}}{1!} = 0.368$$

$$p(2) = \frac{1^2\, e^{-1}}{2!} = 0.184$$

$$p(3) = \frac{1^3\, e^{-1}}{3!} = 0.061$$

If we can use the Poisson function to estimate the probability that a given address will have a certain number of records, we can also use it to predict the number of addresses that will have a certain number of records assigned.

For example, suppose there are 1000 addresses $(N = 1000)$ and 1000 records $(r = 1000)$. Multiplying 1000 by the probability that a *given* address will have x records assigned to it gives the expected *total* number of addresses with x records assigned to them. That is, $1000p(x)$ gives the number of addresses with x records assigned to them.

In general, if there are N addresses, then the expected number of addresses with x records assigned to them is

$$Np(x)$$

This suggests another way of thinking about $p(x)$. Rather than thinking about $p(x)$ as a measure of probability, we can think of $p(x)$ as giving the proportion of addresses having x logical records assigned by hashing.

Now that we have a tool for predicting the expected proportion of addresses that will have zero, one, two, etc. records assigned to them by a random hashing function, we can apply this tool to predicting numbers of collisions.

11.3.4 Predicting Collisions for a Full File

Suppose you have a hashing function that you believe will distribute records randomly and you want to store 10 000 records in 10 000 addresses. How many addresses do you expect to have no records assigned to them?

Since $r = 10\ 000$ and $N = 10\ 000$, $r/N = 1$. Hence the proportion of addresses with 0 records assigned should be

$$p(0) = \frac{1^0\ e^{-1}}{0!} = 0.3679$$

The *number* of addresses with no records assigned is

$$10\ 000 \times p(0) = 3679$$

How many addresses should have one, two, and three records assigned, respectively?

$$10\ 000 \times p(1) = 0.3679 \times 10\ 000 = 3679$$
$$10\ 000 \times p(2) = 0.1839 \times 10\ 000 = 1839$$
$$10\ 000 \times p(3) = 0.0613 \times 10\ 000 = 613$$

Since the 3679 addresses corresponding to $x = 1$ have exactly one record assigned to them, their records have no synonyms. The 1839 addresses with two records apiece, however, represent potential trouble. If each such address has space only for one record, and two records are assigned to them, there is a collision. This means that 1839 records will fit into the addresses, but another 1839 will not fit. There will be 1839 *overflow* records.

Each of the 613 addresses with three records apiece has an even bigger problem. If each address has space for only one record, there will be two overflow records per address. Corresponding to these addresses will be a total of $2 \times 613 = 1226$ overflow records. This is a bad situation. We have thousands of records that do not fit into the addresses assigned by the hashing function. We need to develop a method for handling these overflow records. But first, let's try to reduce the *number* of overflow records.

11.4 How Much Extra Memory Should Be Used?

We have seen the importance of choosing a good hashing algorithm to reduce collisions. A second way to decrease the number of collisions (and thereby decrease the average search length) is to use extra memory. The tools developed in the previous section can be used to help us determine the effect of the use of extra memory on performance.

11.4.1 Packing Density

The term *packing density* refers to the ratio of the number of records to be stored *(r)* to the number of available spaces *(N):*[3]

$$\frac{\text{Number of records}}{\text{Number of spaces}} = \frac{r}{N} = \text{packing density}$$

For example, if there are 75 records *(n = 75)* and 100 addresses *(N = 100)*, the packing density is

$$\frac{75}{100} = 0.75 = 75\%$$

The packing density gives a measure of the amount of space in a file that is used, and it is the only such value needed to assess performance in a hashing environment, assuming that the hash method used gives a reasonably random distribution of records. The raw size of a file and its address space do not matter; what is important is the relative sizes of the two, which are given by the packing density.

Think of packing density in terms of tin cans lined up on a 10-foot length of fence. If there are ten tin cans and you throw a rock, there is a certain likelihood that you will hit a can. If there are twenty cans on the same length of fence, the fence has a higher packing density and your rock is more likely to hit a can. So it is with records in a file. The more records there are packed into a given file space, the more likely it is that a collision will occur when a new record is added.

We need to decide how much space we are willing to waste to reduce the number of collisions. The answer depends in large measure on particular circumstances. We want to have as few collisions as possible, but not, for example, at the expense of requiring the file to use two disks instead of one.

11.4.2 Predicting Collisions for Different Packing Densities

We need a quantitative description of the effects of changing the packing density. In particular, we need to be able to predict the number of collisions that are likely to occur for a given packing density. Fortunately, the Poisson function provides us with just the tool to do this.

---

3. We assume here that only one record can be stored at each address. In fact, that is not necessarily the case, as we see later.

You may have noted already that the formula for packing density (r/N) occurs twice in the Poisson formula

$$p(x) = \frac{(r/N)^x \, e^{-(r/N)}}{x!}$$

Indeed, the numbers of records (r) and addresses (N) always occur together as the *ratio r/N*. They never occur independently. An obvious implication of this is that the way records are distributed depends partly on the ratio of the number of records to the number of available addresses, and *not* on the absolute numbers of records or addresses. The same behavior is exhibited by 500 records distributed among 1000 addresses as by 500 000 records distributed among 1 000 000 addresses.

Suppose that 1000 addresses are allocated to hold 500 records in a randomly hashed file, and that each address can hold one record. The packing density for the file is

$$\frac{r}{N} = \frac{500}{1000} = 0.5$$

Let us answer the following questions about the distribution of records among the available addresses in the file:

■ How many addresses should have no records assigned to them?

■ How many addresses should have exactly one record assigned (no synonyms)?

■ How many addresses should have one record *plus* one or more synonyms?

■ Assuming that only one record can be assigned to each home address, how many overflow records can be expected?

■ What percentage of records should be overflow records?

1. *How many addresses should have no records assigned to them?* Since $p(0)$ gives the *proportion* of addresses with no records assigned, the number of such addresses is

$$Np(0) = 1000 \times \frac{(0.5)^0 \, e^{-0.5}}{0!}$$
$$= 1000 \times 0.607$$
$$= 607$$

2. *How many addresses should have exactly one record assigned (no synonyms)?*

$$Np(1) = 1000 \times \frac{(0.5)^1 \, e^{-0.5}}{1!}$$
$$= 1000 \times 0.303$$
$$= 303$$

3. *How many addresses should have one record plus one or more synonyms?* The values of $p(2), p(3), p(4)$, and so on give the proportions of addresses with one, two, three, and so on synonyms assigned to them. Hence the sum

$$p(2) + p(3) + p(4) + \ldots$$

gives the proportion of all addresses with at least one synonym. This may appear to require a great deal of computation, but it doesn't since the values of $p(x)$ grow quite small for x larger than 3. This should make intuitive sense. Since the file is only 50 percent loaded, one would not expect very many keys to hash to any one address. Therefore, the number of addresses with more than about three keys hashed to them should be quite small. We need only compute the results up to $p(5)$ before they become insignificantly small:

$$p(2) + p(3) + p(4) + p(5) = 0.0758 + 0.0126 + 0.0016 + 0.0002$$
$$= 0.0902$$

The *number* of addresses with one or more synonyms is just the product of N and this result:

$$N[p(2) + p(3) + \ldots] = 1000 \times 0.0902$$
$$= 90$$

4. *Assuming that only one record can be assigned to each home address, how many overflow records could be expected?* For each of the addresses represented by $p(2)$, one record can be stored at the address and one must be an overflow record. For each address represented by $p(3)$, one record can be stored at the address, *two* are overflow records, and so on. Hence, the expected number of overflow records is given by

$$1 \times N \times p(2) + 2 \times N \times p(3) + 3 \times N \times p(4) + 4 \times N \times p(5)$$
$$= N \times [1 \times p(2) + 2 \times p(3) + 3 \times p(4) + 4 \times p(5)]$$
$$= 1000 \times [1 \times 0.0758 + 2 \times 0.0126 + 3 \times 0.0016 + 4 \times 0.0002]$$
$$= 107$$

5. *What percentage of records should be overflow records?* If there are 107 overflow records and 500 records in all, then the proportion of overflow records is

$$\frac{107}{500} = 0.124 = 21.4\%$$

Conclusion: if the packing density is 50 percent and each address can hold only one record, we can expect about 21 percent of all records to be stored somewhere other than at their home addresses.

Table 11.2 shows the proportion of records that are not stored in their home addresses for several different packing densities. The table shows that if the packing density is 10 percent, then about 5 percent of the time we try to access a record, there is already another record there. If the density is 100 percent, then about 37 percent of all records collide with other records at their home addresses. The 4.8 percent collision rate that results when the packing density is 10 percent looks very good until you realize that for every record in your file there will be nine unused spaces!

The 36.8 percent that results from 100 percent usage looks good when viewed in terms of 0 percent unused space. Unfortunately, 36.8 percent doesn't tell the whole story. If 36.8 percent of the records are not at their

Table 11.2 Effect of packing density on the proportion of records not stored at their home addresses

Packing density (percent)	Synonyms as percent of records
10	4.8
20	9.4
30	13.6
40	17.6
50	21.4
60	24.8
70	28.1
80	31.2
90	34.1
100	36.8

home addresses, then they are somewhere else, probably in many cases using addresses that are home addresses for other records. The more home-less records there are, the more contention there is for space with other homeless records. After a while, clusters of overflow records can form, lead-ing in some cases to extremely long searches for some of the records. Clearly, the placement of records that collide is an important matter. Let us now look at one simple approach to placing overflow records.

11.5 Collision Resolution by Progressive Overflow

Even if a hashing algorithm is very good, it is likely that collisions will occur. Therefore, any hashing program must incorporate some method for dealing with records that cannot fit into their home addresses. There are a number of techniques for handling overflow records, and the search for ever better techniques continues to be a lively area of research. We exam-ine several approaches, but we concentrate on a very simple one that often works well. The technique has various names, including *progressive over-flow* and *linear probing*.

11.5.1 How Progressive Overflow Works

An example of a situation in which a collision occurs is shown in Fig. 11.4. In the example, we want to store the record whose key is York in the file. Unfortunately, the name York hashes to the same address as the name Rosen, whose record is already stored there. Since York cannot fit in its home address, it is an overflow record. If progressive overflow is used, the next several addresses are searched in sequence until an empty one is found. The first free address becomes the address of the record. In the example, address 9 is the first record found empty, so the record pertain-ing to York is stored in address 9.

Eventually we need to find York's record in the file. Since York still hashes to 6, the search for the record begins at address 6. It does not find York's record there, so it proceeds to look at successive records until it gets to address 9, where it finds York.

An interesting problem occurs when there is a search for an open space or for a record at the *end* of the file. This is illustrated in Fig. 11.5, in which it is assumed that the file can hold 100 records in addresses 0–99. Blue is hashed to record number 99, which is already occupied by Jello.

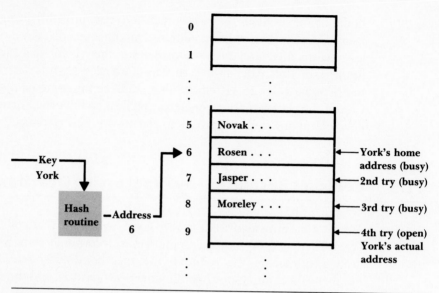

Figure 11.4 Collision resolution with progressive overflow.

Since the file holds only 100 records, it is not possible to use 100 as the next address. The way this is handled in progressive overflow is to wrap around the address space of the file by choosing address 0 as the next address. Since address 0 is not occupied in this case, Blue gets stored in address 0.

What happens if there is a search for a record but the record was never placed in the file? The search begins, as before, at the record's home address, then proceeds to look for it in successive locations. Two things can happen:

- If an open address is encountered, the searching routine might assume this means that the record is not in the file; or
- If the file is full, the search comes back to where it began. Only then is it clear that the record is not in the file. When this occurs, or even when we approach filling our file, searching can become intolerably slow, whether or not the record being sought is in the file.

The greatest strength of progressive overflow is its simplicity. In many cases, it is a perfectly adequate method. There are, however, collision-handling techniques that perform better than progressive overflow, and we examine some of them later in this chapter. Now let us look at the effect of progressive overflow on performance.

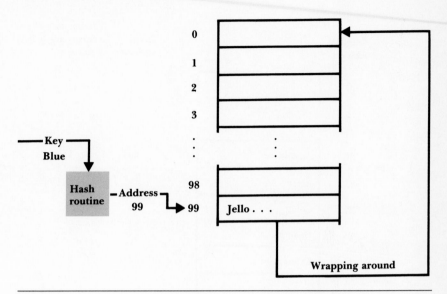

Figure 11.5 Searching for an address beyond the end of a file.

11.5.2 Search Length

The reason to avoid overflow is, of course, that extra searches (hence, extra disk accesses) have to occur when a record is not found in its home address. If there are a lot of collisions, there are going to be a lot of overflow records taking up spaces where they ought not to be. Clusters of records can form, resulting in the placement of records a long way from home, so many disk accesses are required to retrieve them.

Consider the following set of keys and the corresponding addresses produced by some hash function.

Key	Home Address
Adams	20
Bates	21
Cole	21
Dean	22
Evans	20

If these records are loaded into an empty file and progressive overflow is used to resolve collisions, only two of the records will be at their home addresses. All the others require extra accesses to retrieve. Figure 11.6

Actual address		Home address	Number of accesses needed to retrieve
0			
. . .	. . .		
20	Adams . . .	20	1
21	Bates . . .	21	1
22	Cole . . .	21	2
23	Dean . . .	22	2
24	Evans . . .	20	5
25			
. . .	. . .		

Figure 11.6 Illustration of the effects of clustering of records. As keys are clustered, the number of accesses required to access later keys can become large.

shows where each key is stored, together with information on how many accesses are required to retrieve it.

The term *search length* refers to the number of accesses required to retrieve a record from secondary memory. In the context of hashing, the search length for a record increases every time there is a collision. If a record is a long way from its home address, the search length may be unacceptable. A good measure of the extent of the overflow problem is *average search length*. The average search length is the average number of times you can expect to have to access the disk to retrieve a record. A rough estimate of average search length may be computed by finding the *total search length* (the sum of the search lengths of the individual records) and dividing this by the number of records:

$$\text{Average search length} = \frac{\text{total search length}}{\text{total number of records}}$$

In the example, the average search length for the five records is

$$\frac{1+1+2+2+5}{5} = 2.2$$

With no collisions at all, the average search length is 1, since only one access is needed to retrieve any record. (We indicated earlier that an algorithm that distributes records so evenly no collisions occur is appropriately called a *perfect* hashing algorithm, and we mentioned that, unfortunately, such an algorithm is almost impossible to construct.) On the other hand, if a large number of the records in a file results in collisions, the average search length becomes quite long. There are ways to estimate the expected average search length, given various file specifications, and we discuss them in a later section.

It turns out that, using progressive overflow, the average search length increases very rapidly as the packing density increases. The curve in Fig. 11.7, adapted from Peterson (1957), illustrates the problem. If the packing density is kept as low as 60 percent, the average record takes fewer than two tries to access, but for a much more desirable packing density of 80 percent or more, it increases very rapidly.

Average search lengths of greater than 2.0 are generally considered unacceptable, so it appears that it is usually necessary to use less than 40 percent of your storage space to get tolerable performance. Fortunately, we can improve on this situation substantially by making one small change to

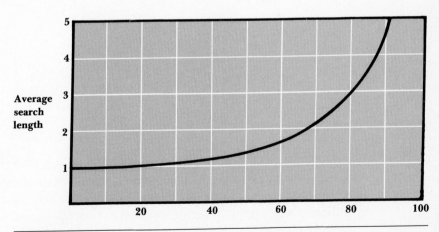

Figure 11.7 Average search length versus packing density in a hashed file in which one record can be stored per address, progressive overflow is used to resolve collisions, and the file has just been loaded.

our hashing program. The change involves putting more than one record at a single address.

11.6   Storing More Than One Record per Address: Buckets

Recall that when a computer receives information from a disk, it is just about as easy for the I/O system to transfer several records as it is to transfer a single record. Recall too that sometimes it might be advantageous to think of records as being grouped together in *blocks* rather than stored individually. Therefore, why not extend the idea of a record address in a file to an address of a *group* of records? The word *bucket* is sometimes used to describe a block of records that is retrieved in one disk access, especially when those records are seen as sharing the same address. On sector-addressing disks, a bucket typically consists of one or more sectors; on block-addressing disks, a bucket might be a block.

Consider the following set of keys, which is to be loaded into a hash file.

Key	Home Address
Green	30
Hall	30
Jenks	32
King	33
Land	33
Marx	33
Nutt	33

Figure 11.8 illustrates part of a file into which the records with these keys are loaded. Each address in the file identifies a bucket capable of holding the records corresponding to three synonyms. Only the record corresponding to Nutt cannot be accommodated in a home address.

When a record is to be stored or retrieved, its home *bucket address* is determined by hashing. The entire bucket is loaded into primary memory. An in-memory search through successive records in the bucket can then be used to find the desired record. When a bucket is filled, we still have to

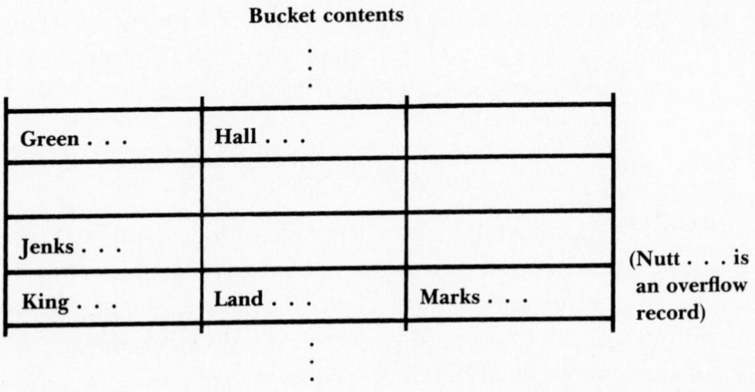

Bucket contents

Figure 11.8 An illustration of buckets. Each bucket can hold up to three records. Only one synonym (Nutt) results in overflow.

worry about the record overflow problem (as in the case of Nutt), but this occurs much less often when buckets are used than when each address can hold only one record.

11.6.1 Effects of Buckets on Performance

When buckets are used, the formula used to compute packing density is changed slightly since each bucket address can hold more than one record. To compute how densely packed a file is, we need to consider both the number of addresses (buckets) and the number of records we can put at each address (bucket size). If N is the number of addresses and b is the number of records that fit in a bucket, then bN is the number of available locations for records. If r is still the number of records in the file, then

$$\text{Packing density} = \frac{r}{bN}$$

Suppose we have a file in which 750 records are to be stored. Consider the following two ways we might organize the file.

■ We can store the 750 data records among 1000 locations, where each location can hold one record. The packing density in this case is

$$\frac{750}{1000} = 75\%$$

■ We can store the 750 records among 500 locations, where each location has a bucket size of 2. There are still 1000 places (2×500) to store the 750 records, so the packing density is still

$$\frac{r}{bN} = 0.75 = 75\%$$

Since the packing density is not changed, we might at first not expect the use of buckets in this way to improve performance, but in fact it does improve performance dramatically. The key to the improvement is that, although there are fewer addresses, each individual address has more room for variation in the number of records assigned to it.

Let's calculate the difference in performance for these two ways of storing the same number of records in the same amount of space. The starting point for our calculations is the fundamental description of each file structure.

	File without buckets	**File with buckets**
Number of records	$r = 750$	$r = 750$
Number of addresses	$N = 1000$	$N = 500$
Bucket size	$b = 1$	$b = 2$
Packing density	0.75	0.75
Ratio of records to addresses	$r/N = 0.75$	$r/N = 1.5$

To determine the number of overflow records that are expected in the case of each file, recall that when a random hashing function is used, the Poisson function

$$p(x) = \frac{(r/N)^x \, e^{-(r/N)}}{x!}$$

gives the expected proportion of addresses assigned x records. Evaluating the function for the two different file organizations, we find that records are assigned to addresses according to the distributions that are shown in Table 11.3.

We see from the table that when buckets are not used, 47.2 percent of the addresses have no records assigned, whereas when two-record buckets are used, only 22.3 percent of the addresses have no records assigned. This should make intuitive sense—since in the two-record case there are only half as many addresses to choose from, it stands to reason that a greater proportion of the addresses are chosen to contain at least one record.

Table 11.3 Poisson distributions for two different file organizations.

$p(x)$	File without buckets ($r/N = 0.75$)	File with buckets ($r/N = 1.5$)
$p(0)$	0.472	0.223
$p(1)$	0.354	0.335
$p(2)$	0.133	0.251
$p(3)$	0.033	0.126
$p(4)$	0.006	0.047
$p(5)$	0.001	0.014
$p(6)$	—	0.004
$p(7)$	—	0.001

Note that the bucket column in Table 11.3 is longer than the nonbucket column. Does this mean that there are more synonyms in the bucket case than in the nonbucket case? Indeed it does, but half of those synonyms do not result in overflow records because each bucket can hold two records. Let us examine this further by computing the exact number of overflow records likely to occur in the two cases.

In the case of the file with bucket size 1, any address that is assigned exactly one record does not have any overflow. Any address with more than one record does have overflow. Recall that the expected number of overflow records is given by

$$N \times [1 \times p(2) + 2 \times p(3) + 3 \times p(4) + 4 \times p(5) + \dots]$$

which, for $r/N = 0.75$ and $N = 1000$, is approximately

$$1000 \times [1 \times 0.1328 + 2 \times 0.0332 + 3 \times 0.0062 + 4 \times 0.0009 + 5 \times 0.0001]$$
$$= 222$$

The 222 overflow records represent 29.6 percent overflow.

In the case of the bucket file, any address that is assigned either one *or* two records does not have overflow. The value of $p(1)$ (with $r/N = 1.5$) gives the proportion of addresses assigned exactly one record, and $p(2)$ (with $r/N = 1.5$) gives the proportion of addresses assigned exactly two records. It is not until we get to $p(3)$ that we encounter addresses for which there are overflow records. For each address represented by $p(3)$, two records can be stored at the address, and one must be an overflow record. Similarly, for each address represented by $p(4)$, there are two overflow records, and so forth. Hence, the expected number of overflow records in the bucket file is

$$N \times [1 \times p(3) + 2 \times p(4) + 3 \times p(5) + 4 \times p(6) + \dots]$$

which for $r/N = 1.5$ and $N = 500$ is approximately

$$500 \times [1 \times 0.1255 + 2 \times 0.0471 + 3 \times 0.0141 + 4 \times 0.0035 + 5 \times 0.0008]$$
$$= 140$$

The 140 overflow records represent 18.7 percent overflow.

We have shown that with one record per address and a packing density of 75 percent, the expected number of overflow records is 29.6 percent. When 500 buckets are used, each capable of holding two records, the packing density remains 75 percent, but the expected number of overflow records drops to 18.7 percent. That is about a 37 percent decrease in the number of times the program has to look elsewhere for a record. As the bucket size gets larger, performance continues to improve.

Table 11.4 shows the proportions of collisions that occur for different packing densities and for different bucket sizes. We see from the table, for example, that if we keep the packing density at 75 percent and increase the bucket size to 10, record accesses result in overflow only 4 percent of the time.

It should be clear that the use of buckets can improve hashing performance substantially. One might ask, "How big should buckets be?" Unfortunately, there is no simple answer to this question because it depends a great deal on a number of different characteristics of the system, including the sizes of buffers the operating system can manage, sector and track capacities on disks, and access times of the hardware (seek, rotation, and data transfer times).

As a rule, it is probably not a good idea to use buckets larger than a track (unless records are very large). Even a track, however, can sometimes be too large when one considers the amount of time it takes to transmit an entire track, as compared with the amount of time it takes to transmit a few sectors. Since hashing almost always involves retrieving only one record per search, any extra transmission time resulting from the use of extra-large buckets is essentially wasted.

In many cases a single cluster is the best bucket size. For example, suppose that a file with 200-byte records is to be stored on a disk system that uses 1024-byte clusters. One could consider each cluster as a bucket,

Table 11.4 Synonyms causing collisions as a percent of records for different packing densities and different bucket sizes

Packing density (%)	Bucket size				
	1	2	5	10	100
10	4.8	0.6	0.0	0.0	0.0
20	9.4	2.2	0.1	0.0	0.0
30	13.6	4.5	0.4	0.0	0.0
40	17.6	7.3	1.1	0.1	0.0
50	21.3	11.4	2.5	0.4	0.0
60	24.8	13.7	4.5	1.3	0.0
70	28.1	17.0	7.1	2.9	0.0
75	29.6	18.7	8.6	4.0	0.0
80	31.2	20.4	11.3	5.2	0.1
90	34.1	23.8	13.8	8.6	0.8
100	36.8	27.1	17.6	12.5	4.0

store five records per cluster, and let the remaining 24 bytes go unused. Since it is no more expensive, in terms of seek time, to access a five-record cluster than it is to access a single record, the only losses from the use of buckets are the extra transmission time and the 24 unused bytes.

The obvious question now is, "How do improvements in the number of collisions affect the average search time?" The answer depends in large measure on characteristics of the drive on which the file is loaded. If there are a large number of tracks in each cylinder, there will be very little seek time because overflow records will be unlikely to spill over from one cylinder to another. If, on the other hand, there is only one track per cylinder, seek time could be a major consumer of search time.

A less exact measure of the amount of time required to retrieve a record is average search length, which we introduced earlier. In the case of buckets, average search length represents the average number of buckets that must be accessed to retrieve a record. Table 11.5 shows the expected average search lengths for files with different packing densities and bucket sizes, given that progressive overflow is used to handle collisions. Clearly, the use of buckets seems to help a great deal in decreasing the average search length. The bigger the bucket, the shorter the search length.

Table 11.5 Average number of accesses required in a successful search by progressive overflow.

Packing density (%)	Bucket size				
	1	2	5	10	100
10	1.06	1.01	1.00	1.00	1.00
30	1.21	1.06	1.00	1.00	1.00
40	1.33	1.10	1.01	1.00	1.00
50	1.50	1.18	1.03	1.00	1.00
60	1.75	1.29	1.07	1.01	1.00
70	2.17	1.49	1.14	1.04	1.00
80	3.00	1.90	1.29	1.11	1.01
90	5.50	3.15	1.78	1.35	1.04
95	10.50	5.60	2.70	1.80	1.10

Adapted from Donald Knuth, *The Art of Computer Programming*, Vol. 3, ©1973, Addison-Wesley, Reading, Mass. Page 536. Reprinted with permission.

11.6.2 Implementation Issues

In the early chapters of this text, we paid quite a bit of attention to issues involved in producing, using, and maintaining random-access files with fixed-length records that are accessed by relative record number (RRN). Since a hashed file is a fixed-length record file whose records are accessed by RRN, you should already know much about implementing hashed files. Hashed files differ from the files we discussed earlier in two important respects, however:

1. Since a hash function depends on there being a fixed number of available addresses, the logical size of a hashed file must be fixed before the file can be populated with records, and it must remain fixed as long as the same hash function is used. (We use the phrase *logical size* to leave open the possibility that physical space be allocated as needed.)

2. Since the home RRN of a record in a hashed file is uniquely related to its key, any procedures that add, delete, or change a record must do so without breaking the bond between a record and its home address. If this bond is broken, the record is no longer accessible by hashing.

We must keep these special needs in mind when we write programs to work with hashed files.

Bucket Structure

The only difference between a file with buckets and one in which each address can hold only one key is that with a bucket file each address has enough space to hold more than one logical record. All records that are housed in the same bucket share the same address. Suppose, for example, that we want to store as many as *five* names in one bucket. Here are three such buckets with different numbers of records.

An empty bucket:	0	/ / / / /	/ / / / /	/ / / / /	/ / / / /	/ / / / /

Two entries:	2	JONES	ARNSWORTH	/ / / / /	/ / / / /	/ / / / /

A full bucket:	5	JONES	ARNSWORTH	STOCKTON	BRICE	THROOP

Each bucket contains a *counter* that keeps track of how many records it has stored in it. Collisions can occur only when the addition of a new record causes the counter to exceed the number of records a bucket can hold.

The counter tells us how many data records are stored in a bucket, but it does not tell us which slots are used and which are not. We need a way to tell whether a record slot is empty. One simple way to do this is to use a special marker to indicate an empty record, just as we did with deleted records earlier. We use the key value ///// to mark empty records in the preceding illustration.

Initializing a File for Hashing

Since the *logical* size of a hashed file must remain fixed, it makes sense in most cases to allocate physical space for the file before we begin storing data records in it. This is generally done by creating a file of empty spaces for all records, then filling the slots as they are needed with the data records. (It is not necessary to construct a file of empty records before putting data in it, but doing so increases the likelihood that records will be stored close to one another on the disk, avoids the error that occurs when an attempt is made to read a missing record, and makes it easy to process the file sequentially, without having to treat the empty records in any special way.)

Loading a Hash File

A program that loads a hash file is similar in many ways to earlier programs we used for populating fixed-length record files, with two differences. First, the program uses the function `hash` to produce a home address for each key. Second, the program looks for a free space for the record by starting with the bucket stored at its home address and then, if the home bucket is full, continuing to look at successive buckets until one is found that is not full. The new record is inserted in this bucket, and the bucket is rewritten to the file at the location from which it was loaded.

If, as it searches for an empty bucket, a loading program passes the maximum allowable address, it must wrap around to the beginning address. A potential problem occurs in loading a hash file when so many records have been loaded into the file that there are no empty spaces left. A naive search for an open slot can easily result in an infinite loop. Obviously, we want to prevent this from occurring by having the program make sure that there is space available for each new record somewhere in the file.

Another problem that often arises when adding records to files occurs when an attempt is made to add a record that is already stored in the file. If there is a danger of duplicate keys occurring, and duplicate keys are not allowed in the file, some mechanism must be found for dealing with this problem.

11.7 Making Deletions

Deleting a record from a hashed file is more complicated than adding a record for two reasons:

- The slot freed by the deletion must not be allowed to hinder later searches; and

- It should be possible to reuse the freed slot for later additions.

When progressive overflow is used, a search for a record terminates if an open address is encountered. Because of this, we do not want to leave open addresses that break overflow searches improperly. The following example illustrates the problem.

Adams, Jones, Morris, and Smith are stored in a hash file in which each address can hold one record. Adams and Smith both are hashed to address 5, and Jones and Morris are hashed to address 6. If they are loaded

Record	Home address	Actual address		
			$\vdots$	$\vdots$
			4	
Adams	5	5	5	Adams . . .
Jones	6	6	6	Jones . . .
Morris	6	7	7	Morris . . .
Smith	5	8	8	Smith . . .
			$\vdots$	$\vdots$

Figure 11.9 File organization before deletions.

in alphabetical order using progressive overflow for collisions, they are stored in the locations shown in Fig. 11.9.

A search for Smith starts at address 5 (Smith's home address), successively looks for Smith at addresses 6, 7, and 8, then finds Smith at 8. Now suppose Morris is deleted, leaving an empty space, as illustrated in Fig. 11.10. A search for Smith again starts at address 5, then looks at addresses 6 and 7. Since address 7 is now empty, it is reasonable for the program to conclude that Smith's record is not in the file.

11.7.1 Tombstones for Handling Deletions

In Chapter 6 we discussed techniques for dealing with the deletion problem. One simple technique we use for identifying deleted records involves replacing the deleted record (or just its key) with a marker indicating that a record once lived there but no longer does. Such a marker is sometimes referred to as a *tombstone* (Wiederhold, 1983). The nice thing about the use of tombstones is that it solves both of the problems described previously:

■ The freed space does not break a sequence of searches for a record; and

■ The freed space is obviously available and may be reclaimed for later additions.

Figure 11.11 illustrates how the sample file might look after the tombstone ###### is inserted for the deleted record. Now a search for Smith

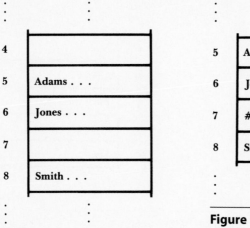

Figure 11.10 The same organization as in Fig. 11.9, with Morris deleted.

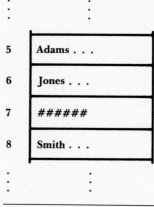

Figure 11.11 The same file as in Fig. 11.9 after the insertion of a tombstone for Morris.

does *not* halt at the empty record number 7. Instead, it uses the ###### as an indication that it should continue the search.

It is not necessary to insert tombstones every time a deletion occurs. For example, suppose in the preceding example that the record for Smith is to be deleted. Since the slot following the Smith record is empty, nothing is lost by marking Smith's slot as empty rather than inserting a tombstone. Indeed, it is unwise to insert a tombstone where it is not needed. (If, after putting an unnecessary tombstone in Smith's slot, a new record is added at address 9, how would a subsequent unsuccessful search for Smith be affected?)

11.7.2 Implications of Tombstones for Insertions

With the introduction of the use of tombstones, the *insertion* of records becomes slightly more difficult than our earlier discussions imply. Whereas programs that perform initial loading simply search for the first occurrence of an empty record slot (signified by the presence of the key /////), it is now permissible to insert a record where either ///// *or* ###### occurs as the key.

This new feature, which is desirable because it yields a shorter average search length, brings with it a certain danger. Consider, for example, the earlier example in which Morris is deleted, giving the file organization shown in Fig. 11.11. Now suppose you want a program to insert Smith into the file. If the program simply searches until it encounters a ######, it never notices that Smith is already in the file. We almost certainly don't want to put a second Smith record into the file, since doing so means that later searches would never find the older Smith record. To prevent this from occurring, the program must examine the entire cluster of contiguous keys and tombstones to ensure that no duplicate key exists, then go back and insert the record in the first available tombstone, if there is one.

11.7.3 Effects of Deletions and Additions on Performance

The use of tombstones enables our search algorithms to work and helps in storage recovery, but one can still expect some deterioration in performance after a number of deletions and additions occur within a file.

Consider, for example, our little four-record file of Adams, Jones, Smith, and Morris. After deleting Morris, Smith is one slot further from its home address than it needs to be. If the tombstone is never to be used to store another record, every retrieval of Smith requires one more access than is necessary. More generally, after a large number of additions and deletions, one can expect to find many tombstones occupying places that could be occupied by records whose home records precede them but that are stored after them. In effect, each tombstone represents an unexploited opportunity to reduce by one the number of locations that must be scanned while searching for these records.

Some experimental studies show that after a 50 percent to 150 percent turnover of records, a hashed file reaches a point of equilibrium, so average search length is as likely to get better as it is to get worse (Bradley, 1982; Peterson, 1957). By this time, however, search performance has deteriorated to the point at which the average record is three times as far (in terms of accesses) from its home address as it would be after initial loading. This means, for example, that if after original loading the average search length is 1.2, it will be about 1.6 after the point of equilibrium is reached.

There are three types of solutions to the problem of deteriorating average search lengths. One involves doing a bit of local reorganizing every time a deletion occurs. For example, the deletion algorithm might examine the records that follow a tombstone to see if the search length can be shortened by moving the record backward toward its home address. Another solution involves completely reorganizing the file after the average search length reaches an unacceptable value. A third type of solution involves using an altogether different collision resolution algorithm.

11.8 Other Collision Resolution Techniques

Despite its simplicity, randomized hashing using progressive overflow with reasonably sized buckets generally performs well. If it does not perform well enough, however, there are a number of variations that may perform even better. In this section we discuss some refinements that can often improve hashing performance when using external storage.

11.8.1 Double Hashing

One of the problems with progressive overflow is that if many records hash to buckets in the same vicinity, clusters of records can form. As the packing density approaches one, this clustering tends to lead to extremely long searches for some records. One method for avoiding clustering is to store overflow records a long way from their home addresses by *double hashing*. With double hashing, when a collision occurs, a second hash function is applied to the key to produce a number c that is relatively prime to the number of addresses.[4] The value c is added to the home address to produce the overflow address. If the overflow address is already occupied, c is added to it to produce another overflow address. This procedure continues until a free overflow address is found.

Double hashing does tend to spread out the records in a file, but it suffers from a potential problem that is encountered in several improved overflow methods: it violates locality by deliberately moving overflow records some distance from their home addresses, increasing the likelihood that the disk will need extra time to get to the new overflow address. If the file covers more than one cylinder, this could require an expensive extra head movement. Double hashing programs can solve this problem if they are able to generate overflow addresses in such a way that overflow records are kept on the same cylinder as home records.

11.8.2 Chained Progressive Overflow

Chained progressive overflow is another technique designed to avoid the problems caused by clustering. It works in the same manner as progressive overflow, except that synonyms are linked together with pointers. That is, each home address contains a number indicating the location of the next

---

4. If N is the number of addresses, then c and N are relatively prime if they have no common divisors.

Key	Home address	Actual address	Search length
Adams	20	20	1
Bates	21	21	1
Cole	20	22	3
Dean	21	23	3
Evans	24	24	1
Flint	20	25	6

Average search length = (1 + 1 + 3 + 3 + 1 + 6)/6 = 2.5

Figure 11.12 Hashing with progressive overflow.

record with the same home address. The next record in turn contains a pointer to the following record with the same home address, and so forth. The net effect of this is that for each set of synonyms there is a linked list connecting their records, and it is this list that is searched when a record is sought.

The advantage of chained progressive overflow over simple progressive overflow is that only records with keys that are synonyms need to be accessed in any given search. Suppose, for example, that the set of keys shown in Fig. 11.12 is to be loaded in the order shown into a hash file with bucket size 1, and progressive overflow is used. A search for Cole involves an access to Adams (a synonym) and Bates (not a synonym). Flint, the worst case, requires six accesses, only two of which involve synonyms.

Since Adams, Cole, and Flint are synonyms, a chaining algorithm forms a linked list connecting these three names, with Adams at the head of the list. Since Bates and Dean are also synonyms, they form a second list. This arrangement is illustrated in Fig. 11.13. The average search length decreases from 2.5 to

$$\frac{1 + 1 + 2 + 2 + 1 + 3}{6} = 1.7$$

The use of chained progressive overflow requires that we attend to some details that are not required for simple progressive overflow. First, a *link field* must be added to each record, requiring the use of a little more storage. Second, a chaining algorithm must guarantee that it is possible to get to any synonym by starting at its home address. This second requirement is not a trivial one, as the following example shows.

Suppose that in the example Dean's home address is 22 instead of 21. Since, by the time Dean is loaded, address 22 is already occupied by Cole,

Home address	Actual address	Data	Address of next synonym	Search length
		. . .		
20	20	Adams . . .	22	1
21	21	Bates . . .	23	1
20	22	Cole . . .	25	2
21	23	Dean . . .	−1	2
24	24	Evans . . .	−1	1
20	25	Flint . . .	−1	3
		. . .		

Figure 11.13 Hashing with chained progressive overflow. Adams, Cole, and Flint are synonyms; Bates and Dean are synonyms.

Dean still ends up at address 23. Does this mean that Cole's pointer should point to 23 (Dean's actual address) or to 25 (the address of Cole's synonym Flint)? If the pointer is 25, the linked list joining Adams, Cole, and Flint is kept intact, but Dean is lost. If the pointer is 23, Flint is lost.

The problem here is that a certain address (22) that *should* be occupied by a home record (Dean) is occupied by a different record. One solution to the problem is to require that every address qualifying as a home address for some record in the file actually hold a home record. The problem can be handled easily when a file is first loaded by using a technique called two-pass loading.

Two-pass loading, as the name implies, involves loading a hash file in two passes. On the first pass, only home records are loaded. All records that are not home records are kept in a separate file. This guarantees that no potential home addresses are occupied by overflow records. On the second pass, each overflow record is loaded and stored in one of the free addresses according to whatever collision resolution technique is being used.

Two-pass loading guarantees that every potential home address actually is a home address, so it solves the problem in the example. It does not guarantee that later deletions and additions will not re-create the same problem, however. As long as the file is used to store both home records and overflow records, there remains the problem of overflow records displacing new records that hash to an address occupied by an overflow record.

The methods used for handling these problems after initial loading are somewhat complicated and can, in a very volatile file, require many extra disk accesses. (For more information on techniques for maintaining pointers, see Knuth, 1998 and Bradley, 1982.) It would be nice if we could somehow altogether avoid this problem of overflow lists bumping into one another, and that is what the next method does.

11.8.3 Chaining with a Separate Overflow Area

One way to keep overflow records from occupying home addresses where they should not be is to move them all to a separate overflow area. Many hashing schemes are variations of this basic approach. The set of home addresses is called the *prime data area,* and the set of overflow addresses is called the *overflow area.* The advantage of this approach is that it keeps all unused but potential home addresses free for later additions.

In terms of the file we examined in the preceding section, the records for Cole, Dean, and Flint could have been stored in a separate overflow area rather than in potential home addresses for later-arriving records (Fig. 11.14). Now no problem occurs when a new record is added. If its home address has room, it is stored there. If not, it is moved to the overflow file, where it is added to the linked list that starts at the home address.

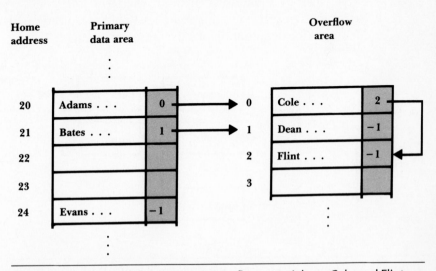

Figure 11.14 Chaining to a separate overflow area. Adams, Cole, and Flint are synonyms; Bates and Dean are synonyms.

If the bucket size for the primary file is large enough to prevent excessive numbers of overflow records, the overflow file can be a simple entry-sequenced file with a bucket size of 1. Space can be allocated for overflow records only when it is needed.

The use of a separate overflow area simplifies processing somewhat and would seem to improve performance, especially when many additions and deletions occur. However, this is not always the case. If the separate overflow area is on a different cylinder than is the home address, every search for an overflow record will involve a very costly head movement. Studies show that access time is generally worse when overflow records are stored in a separate overflow area than when they are stored in the prime overflow area (Lum, 1971).

One situation in which a separate overflow area is *required* occurs when the packing density is greater than one—there are more records than home addresses. If, for example, it is anticipated that a file will grow beyond the capacity of the initial set of home addresses and that rehashing the file with a larger address space is not reasonable, then a separate overflow area must be used.

11.8.4 Scatter Tables: Indexing Revisited

Suppose you have a hash file that contains no records, only pointers to records. The file is obviously just an index that is searched by hashing rather than by some other method. The term *scatter table* (Severance, 1974) is often applied to this approach to file organization. Figure 11.15 illustrates the organization of a file using a scatter table.

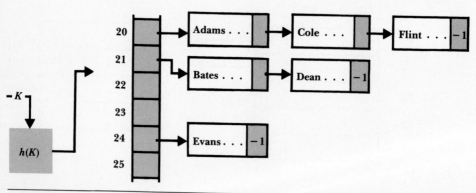

Figure 11.15 Example of a scatter table structure. Because the hashed part is an index, the data file may be organized in any way that is appropriate.

The scatter table organization provides many of the same advantages simple indexing generally provides, with the additional advantage that the search of the index itself requires only one access. (Of course, that one access is one more than other forms of hashing require, unless the scatter table can be kept in primary memory.) The data file can be implemented in many different ways. For example, it can be a set of linked lists of synonyms (as shown in Fig. 11.15), a sorted file, or an entry-sequenced file. Also, scatter table organizations conveniently support the use of variable-length records. For more information on scatter tables, see Severance (1974).

11.9 Patterns of Record Access

Twenty percent of the fishermen catch 80 percent of the fish.
Twenty percent of the burglars steal 80 percent of the loot.

L.M. Boyd

The use of different collision resolution techniques is not the only nor necessarily the best way to improve performance in a hashed file. If we know something about the patterns of record access, for example, then it is often possible to use simple progressive overflow techniques and still achieve very good performance.

Suppose you have a grocery store with 10 000 different categories of grocery items and you have on your computer a hashed inventory file with a record for each of the 10 000 items that your company handles. Every time an item is purchased, the record that corresponds to that item must be accessed. Since the file is hashed, it is reasonable to assume that the 10 000 records are distributed randomly among the available addresses that make up the file. Is it equally reasonable to assume that the distribution of *accesses* to the records in the inventory are randomly distributed? Probably not. Milk, for example, will be retrieved very frequently, brie seldom.

There is a principle used by economists called the Pareto Principle, or The Concept of the Vital Few and the Trivial Many, which in file terms says that a small percentage of the records in a file account for a large percentage of the accesses. A popular version of the Pareto Principle is the 80/20 Rule of Thumb: 80 percent of the accesses are performed on 20 percent of the records. In our groceries file, milk would be among the 20 percent high-activity items, brie among the rest.

We cannot take advantage of the 80/20 principle in a file structure unless we know something about the probable distribution of record accesses. Once we have this information, we need to find a way to place the high-activity items where they can be found with as few accesses as possible. If, when items are loaded into a file, they can be loaded in such a way that the 20 percent (more or less) that are most likely to be accessed are loaded at or near their home addresses, then most of the transactions will access records that have short search lengths, so the *effective* average search length will be shorter than the nominal average search length that we defined earlier.

For example, suppose our grocery store's file handling program keeps track of the number of times each item is accessed during a one-month period. It might do this by storing with each record a counter that starts at zero and is incremented every time the item is accessed. At the end of the month the records for all the items in the inventory are dumped onto a file that is sorted in descending order according to the number of times they have been accessed. When the sorted file is rehashed and reloaded, the first records to be loaded are the ones that, according to the previous month's experience, are most likely to be accessed. Since they are the first ones loaded, they are also the ones most likely to be loaded into their home addresses. If reasonably sized buckets are used, there will be *very few,* if any, high-activity items that are not in their home addresses and therefore retrievable in one access.

SUMMARY

There are three major modes for accessing files: *sequentially,* which provides $O(N)$ performance, through *tree structures,* which can produce $O(\log_k N)$ performance, and *directly.* Direct access provides $O(1)$ performance, which means that the number of accesses required to retrieve a record is constant and independent of the size of the file. Hashing is the primary form of organization used to provide direct access.

Hashing can provide faster access than most of the other organizations we study, usually with very little storage overhead, and it is adaptable to most types of primary keys. Ideally, hashing makes it possible to find any record with only one disk access, but this ideal is rarely achieved. The primary disadvantage of hashing is that hashed files may not be sorted by key.

Hashing involves the application of a hash function $h(K)$ to a record key K to produce an address. The address is taken to be the *home address* of the record whose key is K, and it forms the basis for searching for the record. The addresses produced by hash functions generally appear to be random.

When two or more keys hash to the same address, they are called *synonyms*. If an address cannot accommodate all of its synonyms, *collisions* result. When collisions occur, some of the synonyms cannot be stored in the home address and must be stored elsewhere. Since searches for records begin with home addresses, searches for records that are not stored at their home addresses generally involve extra disk accesses. The term *average search length* is used to describe the average number of disk accesses that are required to retrieve a record. An average search length of 1 is ideal.

Much of the study of hashing deals with techniques for decreasing the number and effects of collisions. In this chapter we look at three general approaches to reducing the number of collisions:

- Spreading out the records;
- Using extra memory; and
- Using buckets.

Spreading out the records involves choosing a hashing function that distributes the records at least randomly over the address space. A *uniform distribution* spreads out records evenly, resulting in no collisions. A *random* or nearly random distribution is much easier to achieve and is usually considered acceptable.

In this chapter a simple hashing algorithm is developed to demonstrate the kinds of operations that take place in a hashing algorithm. The three steps in the algorithm are:

1. Represent the key in numerical form;
2. Fold and add; and
3. Divide by the size of the address space, producing a valid address.

When we examine several different types of hashing algorithms, we see that sometimes algorithms can be found that produce *better-than-random* distributions. Failing this, we suggest some algorithms that generally produce distributions that are approximately random.

The *Poisson distribution* provides a mathematical tool for examining in detail the effects of a random distribution. Poisson functions can be used to predict the numbers of addresses likely to be assigned 0, 1, 2, and so on, records, given the number of records to be hashed and the number of available addresses. This allows us to predict the number of collisions likely to occur when a file is hashed, the number of overflow records likely to occur, and sometimes the average search length.

Using extra memory is another way to avoid collisions. When a fixed number of keys is hashed, the likelihood of synonyms occurring decreases as the number of possible addresses increases. Hence, a file organization that allocates many more addresses than are likely to be used has fewer synonyms than one that allocates few extra addresses. The term *packing density* describes the proportion of available address space that actually holds records. The Poisson function is used to determine how differences in packing density influence the percentage of records that are likely to be synonyms.

Using buckets is the third method for avoiding collisions. File addresses can hold one or more records, depending on how the file is organized by the file designer. The number of records that can be stored at a given address, called *bucket size,* determines the point at which records assigned to the address will overflow. The Poisson function can be used to explore the effects of variations in bucket sizes and packing densities. Large buckets, combined with a low packing density, can result in very small average search lengths.

Although we can reduce the number of collisions, we need some means to deal with collisions when they do occur. We examined one simple collision resolution technique in detail—*progressive overflow.* If an attempt to store a new record results in a collision, progressive overflow involves searching through the addresses that follow the record's home address in order until one is found to hold the new record. If a record is sought and is not found in its home address, successive addresses are searched until either the record is found or an empty address is encountered.

Progressive overflow is simple and sometimes works very well. However, progressive overflow creates long search lengths when the packing density is high and the bucket size is low. It also sometimes produces clusters of records, creating very long search lengths for new records whose home addresses are in the clusters.

Three problems associated with record deletion in hashed files are

1. The possibility that empty slots created by deletions will hinder later searches for overflow records;

2. The need to recover space made available when records are deleted; and

3. The deterioration of average search lengths caused by empty spaces keeping records further from home than they need be.

The first two problems can be solved by using *tombstones* to mark spaces that are empty (and can be reused for new records) but should not halt a search for a record. Solutions to the deterioration problem include local reorganization, complete file reorganization, and the choice of a collision-resolving algorithm that does not cause deterioration to occur.

Because overflow records have a major influence on performance, many different overflow handling techniques have been proposed. Four such techniques that are appropriate for file applications are discussed briefly:

1. *Double hashing* reduces local clustering but may place some overflow records so far from home that they require extra seeks.

2. *Chained progressive overflow* reduces search lengths by requiring that only synonyms be examined when a record is being sought. For chained overflow to work, every address that qualifies as a home record for some record in the file must hold a home record. Mechanisms for making sure that this occurs are discussed.

3. *Chaining with a separate overflow area* simplifies chaining substantially and has the advantage that the overflow area may be organized in ways more appropriate to handling overflow records. A danger of this approach is that it might lose locality.

4. *Scatter tables* combine indexing with hashing. This approach provides much more flexibility in organizing the data file. A disadvantage of using scatter tables is that, unless the index can be held in memory, it requires one extra disk access for every search.

Since in many cases certain records are accessed more frequently than others (the *80/20 rule of thumb*), it is often worthwhile to take access patterns into account. If we can identify those records that are most likely to be accessed, we can take measures to make sure they are stored closer to home than less frequently accessed records, thus decreasing the *effective* average search length. One such measure is to load the most frequently accessed records before the others.

KEY TERMS

Average search length. We define average search length as the *sum of the number of accesses required for each record in the file* divided by *the number of records in the file*. This definition does not take into account the number of accesses required for unsuccessful searches, nor does it account for the fact that some records are likely to be accessed more often than others. See *80/20 rule of thumb*.

Better-than-random. This term is applied to distributions in which the records are spread out more uniformly than they would be if the hash function distributed them randomly. Normally, the distribution produced by a hash function is a little bit better than random.

Bucket. An area of space on the file that is treated as a physical record for storage and retrieval purposes but is capable of storing several *logical* records. By storing and retrieving logical records in buckets rather than individually, access times can, in many cases, be improved substantially.

Collision. Situation in which a record is hashed to an address that does not have sufficient room to store the record. When a collision occurs, some means has to be found to resolve the collision.

Double hashing. A collision resolution scheme in which collisions are handled by applying a second hash function to the key to produce a number c, which is added to the original address (modulo the number of addresses) as many times as necessary until either the desired record is located or an empty space is found. Double hashing helps avoid some of the clustering that occurs with progressive overflow.

The 80/20 rule of thumb. An assumption that a large percentage (e.g., 80 percent) of the accesses are performed on a small percentage (e.g., 20 percent) of the records in a file. When the 80/20 rule applies, the *effective* average search length is determined largely by the search lengths of the more active records, so attempts to make *these* search lengths short can result in substantially improved performance.

Fold and add. A method of hashing in which the encodings of fixed-sized parts of a key are extracted (e.g., every two bytes) and are added. The resulting sum can be used to produce an address.

Hashing. A technique for generating a unique home address for a given key. Hashing is used when rapid access to a key (or its corresponding record) is required. In this chapter applications of hashing involve direct access to records in a file, but hashing is also often used to access items in arrays in memory. In indexing, for example, an index might be organized for hashing rather than for binary search if extremely fast searching of the index is desired.

Home address. The address generated by a hash function for a given key. If a record is stored at its home address, then the search length for the record is 1 because only one access is required to retrieve the record. A record not at its home address requires more than one access to retrieve or store.

Indexed hash. Instead of using the results of a hash to produce the address of a record, the hash can be used to identify a location in an index that in turn points to the address of the record. Although this approach requires one extra access for every search, it makes it possible to organize the data records in a way that facilitates other types of processing, such as sequential processing.

Mid-square method. A hashing method in which a representation of the key is squared and some digits from the middle of the result are used to produce the address.

Minimum hashing. Hashing scheme in which the number of addresses is exactly equal to the number of records. No storage space is wasted.

Open addressing. See *progressive overflow.*

Overflow. The situation that occurs when a record cannot be stored in its home address.

Packing density. The proportion of allocated file space that actually holds records. (This is sometimes referred to as *load factor.*) If a file is half full, its packing density is 50 percent. The packing density and bucket size are the two most important measures in determining the likelihood of a collision occurring when searching for a record in a file.

Perfect hashing function. A hashing function that distributes records uniformly, minimizing the number of collisions. Perfect hashing functions are very desirable, but they are extremely difficult to find for large sets of keys.

Poisson distribution. Distribution generated by the Poisson function, which can be used to approximate the distribution of records among addresses if the distribution is random. A particular Poisson distribution depends on the ratio of the number of records to the number of available addresses. A particular instance of the Poisson function, $p(x)$, gives the proportion of addresses that will have *x* keys assigned to them. See *better-than-random*.

Prime division. Division of a number by a prime number and use of the remainder as an address. If the address size is taken to be a prime number *p*, a large number can be transformed into a valid address by dividing it by *p*. In hashing, division by primes is often preferred to division by nonprimes because primes tend to produce more random remainders.

Progressive overflow. An overflow handling technique in which collisions are resolved by storing a record in the next available address after its home address. Progressive overflow is not the most efficient overflow handling technique, but it is one of the simplest and is adequate for many applications.

Randomize. To produce a number (e.g., by hashing) that appears to be random.

Synonyms. Two or more different keys that hash to the same address. When each file address can hold only one record, synonyms always result in collisions. If buckets are used, several records whose keys are synonyms may be stored without collisions.

Tombstone. A special marker placed in the key field of a record to mark it as no longer valid. The use of tombstones solves two problems associated with the deletion of records: the freed space does not break a sequential search for a record, and the freed space is easily recognized as available and may be reclaimed for later additions.

Uniform. A distribution in which records are spread out evenly among addresses. Algorithms that produce uniform distributions are better than randomizing algorithms in that they tend to avoid the numbers of collisions that would occur with a randomizing algorithm.

FURTHER READINGS

There are a number of good surveys of hashing and issues related to hashing generally, including Knuth (1998), Severance (1974), Maurer (1975), and Sorenson, Tremblay, and Deutscher (1978). Textbooks concerned with file design generally contain substantial amounts of material on hashing, and they often provide extensive references for further study. Loomis (1989) also covers hashing generally, with additional emphasis on programming for hashed files in COBOL. Cormen, Leiserson and Rivest (1990), Standish (1995), Shaffer (1997), and Wiederhold (1983) will be useful to practitioners interested in analyses of trade-offs among the basic hashing methods.

One of the applications of hashing that has stimulated a great deal of interest recently is the development of *spelling checkers*. Because of special characteristics of spelling checkers, the types of hashing involved are quite different from the approaches we describe in this text. Papers by Bentley (1985) and Dodds (1982) provide entry into the literature on this topic. (See also exercise 14.)

EXERCISES

1. Use the function `hash(KEY, MAXAD)` described in the text to answer the following questions.

   a. What is the value of `hash("Jacobs", 101)`?

   b. Find two different words of more than four characters that are synonyms.

   c. It is assumed in the text that the function `hash` does not need to generate an integer greater than 19 937. This could present a problem if we have a file with addresses larger than 19 937. Suggest some ways to get around this problem.

2. In understanding hashing, it is important to understand the relationships between the size of the available memory, the number of keys to be hashed, the range of possible keys, and the nature of the keys. Let us give names to these quantities, as follows:

   - M = the number of memory spaces available (each capable of holding one record);

   - r = the number of records to be stored in the memory spaces; n = the number of unique home addresses produced by hashing the r record keys; and

   - K = a key, which may be any combination of exactly five uppercase characters.

   Suppose $h(K)$ is a hash function that generates addresses between 0 and $M - 1$.

a. How many unique keys are possible? (Hint: If K were one upper-case letter rather than five, there would be 26 possible unique keys.)

b. How are n and r related?

c. How are r and M related?

d. If the function h were a minimum perfect hashing function, how would n, r, and M be related?

3. The following table shows distributions of keys resulting from three different hash functions on a file with 6000 records and 6000 addresses.

	Function A	*Function B*	*Function C*
$d(0)$	0.71	0.25	0.40
$d(1)$	0.05	0.50	0.36
$d(2)$	0.05	0.25	0.15
$d(3)$	0.05	0.00	0.05
$d(4)$	0.05	0.00	0.02
$d(5)$	0.04	0.00	0.01
$d(6)$	0.05	0.00	0.01
$d(7)$	0.00	0.00	0.00

a. Which of the three functions (if any) generates a distribution of records that is approximately random?

b. Which generates a distribution that is nearest to uniform?

c. Which (if any) generates a distribution that is worse than random?

d. Which function should be chosen?

4. There is a surprising mathematical result called *the birthday paradox* that says that if there are more than 23 people in a room, there is a better than 50-50 chance that two of them have the same birthday. How is the birthday paradox illustrative of a major problem associated with hashing?

5. Suppose that 10 000 addresses are allocated to hold 8000 records in a randomly hashed file and that each address can hold one record. Compute the following values:

a. The packing density for the file;

b. The expected number of addresses with no records assigned to them by the hash function;

c. The expected number of addresses with one record assigned (no synonyms);

    d. The expected number of addresses with one record *plus* one or more synonyms;

    e. The expected number of overflow records; and

    f. The expected percentage of overflow records.

6. Consider the file described in the preceding exercise. What is the expected number of overflow records if the 10 000 locations are reorganized as

    a. 5000 two-record buckets; and

    b. 1000 ten-record buckets?

7. Make a table showing Poisson function values for $r/N = 0.1, 0.5, 0.8, 1, 2, 5,$ and 11. Examine the table and discuss any features and patterns that provide useful information about hashing.

8. There is an overflow handling technique called *count-key progressive overflow* (Bradley, 1982) that works on block-addressable disks as follows. Instead of generating a relative record number from a key, the hash function generates an address consisting of three values: a cylinder, a track, and a block number. The corresponding three numbers constitute the home address of the record.

    Since block-organized drives (see Chapter 3) can often scan a track to find a record with a given key, there is no need to load a block into memory to find out whether it contains a particular record. The I/O processor can direct the disk drive to search a track for the desired record. It can even direct the disk to search for an empty record slot if a record is not found in its home position, effectively implementing progressive overflow.

    a. What is it about this technique that makes it superior to progressive overflow techniques that might be implemented on sector-organized drives?

    b. The main disadvantage of this technique is that it can be used only with a bucket size of 1. Why is this the case, and why is it a disadvantage?

9. In discussing implementation issues, we suggest initializing the data file by creating real records that are marked empty before loading the file with data. There are some good reasons for doing this. However, there might be some reasons not to do it this way. For example, suppose you want a hash file with a very low packing density and cannot afford to have the unused space allocated. How might a file management system be designed to work with a very large *logical* file but allocate space only for those blocks in the file that contain data?

10. This exercise (inspired by an example in Wiederhold, 1983, p. 136) concerns the problem of deterioration. A number of additions and deletions are to be made to a file. Tombstones are to be used where necessary to preserve search paths to overflow records.

    a. Show what the file looks like after the following operations, and compute the average search length.

Operation	Home Address
Add Alan	0
Add Bates	2
Add Cole	4
Add Dean	0
Add Evans	1
Del Bates	
Del Cole	
Add Finch	0
Add Gates	2
Del Alan	
Add Hart	3

    • How has the use of tombstones caused the file to deteriorate?

    • What would be the effect of reloading the remaining items in the file in the order Dean, Evans, Finch, Gates, Hart?

    b. What would be the effect of reloading the remaining items using two-pass loading?

11. Suppose you have a file in which 20 percent of the records account for 80 percent of the accesses and that you want to store the file with a packing density of 0 and a bucket size of 5. When the file is loaded, you load the active 20 percent of the records first. After the active 20 percent of the records are loaded and before the other records are loaded, what is the packing density of the partially filled file? Using this packing density, compute the percentage of the active 20 percent that would be overflow records. Comment on the results.

12. In our computations of average search lengths, we consider only the times it takes for *successful* searches. If our hashed file were to be used in such a way that searches were often made for items that are not in the file, it would be useful to have statistics on average search length for an *unsuccessful* search. If a large percentage of searches to a hashed file are unsuccessful, how do you expect this to affect overall performance if overflow is handled by

a. Progressive overflow; or

b. Chaining to a separate overflow area?

(See Knuth, 1973b, pp. 535–539 for a treatment of these differences.)

13. Although hashed files are not generally designed to support access to records in any sorted order, there may be times when batches of transactions need to be performed on a hashed data file. If the data file is sorted (rather than hashed), these transactions are normally carried out by some sort of cosequential process, which means that the transaction file also has to be sorted. If the data file is hashed, the transaction file might also be presorted, but on the basis of the home addresses of its records rather than some more "natural" criterion.

Suppose you have a file whose records are usually accessed directly but is periodically updated from a transaction file. List the factors you would have to consider in deciding between using an indexed sequential organization and hashing. (See Hanson, 1982, pp. 280–285, for a discussion of these issues.)

14. We assume throughout this chapter that a hashing program should be able to tell correctly whether a given key is located at a certain address. If this were not so, there would be times when we would assume that a record exists when in fact it does not, a seemingly disastrous result. But consider what Doug McIlroy did in 1978 when he was designing a spelling checker program. He found that by letting his program allow one out of every four thousand misspelled words to sneak by as valid (and using a few other tricks), he could fit a 75 000-word spelling dictionary into 64 kilobytes of memory, thereby improving performance enormously.

McIlroy was willing to tolerate one undetected misspelled word out of every four thousand because he observed that drafts of papers rarely contained more than twenty errors, so one could expect at most one out of every two hundred runs of the program to fail to detect a misspelled word. Can you think of some other cases in which it might be reasonable to report that a key exists when in fact it does not?

Jon Bentley (1985) provides an excellent account of McIlroy's program, plus several insights on the process of solving problems of this nature. D. J. Dodds (1982) discusses this general approach to hashing, called *check-hashing*. Read Bentley's and Dodds's articles and report on them to your class. Perhaps they will inspire you to write a spelling checker.

PROGRAMMING EXERCISES

15. Implement and test a version of the function hash.

16. Create a hashed file with one record for every city in California. The key in each record is to be the name of the corresponding city. (For the purposes of this exercise, there need be no fields other than the key field.) Begin by creating a sorted list of the names of all of the cities and towns in California. (If time or space is limited, just make a list of names starting with the letter *S.*)

    a. Examine the sorted list. What patterns do you notice that might affect your choice of a hash function?

    b. Implement the function hash in such a way that you can alter the number of characters that are folded. Assuming a packing density of 1, hash the entire file several times, each time folding a different number of characters and producing the following statistics for each run:

       • The number of collisions; and

       • The number of addresses assigned 0, 1, 2, . . . , 10, and 10-or-more records.

       Discuss the results of your experiment in terms of the effects of folding different numbers of characters and how they compare with the results you might expect from a random distribution.

    c. Implement and test one or more of the other hashing methods described in the text, or use a method of your own invention.

17. Using a set of keys, such as the names of California towns, do the following:

    a. Write and test a program for loading the keys into three different hash files using bucket sizes of 1, 2, and 5, respectively, and a packing density of 0.8. Use progressive overflow for handling collisions.

    b. Have your program maintain statistics on the average search length, the maximum search length, and the percentage of records that are overflow records.

    c. Assuming a Poisson distribution, compare your results with the expected values for average search length and the percentage of records that are overflow records.

18. Repeat exercise 17, but use double hashing to handle overflow.

19. Repeat exercise 17, but handle overflow using chained overflow into a separate overflow area. Assume that the packing density is the ratio of number of keys to available *home* addresses.

20. Write a program that can perform insertions and deletions in the file created in the previous problem using a bucket size of 5. Have the program keep running statistics on average search length. (You might also implement a mechanism to indicate when search length has deteriorated to a point where the file should be reorganized.) Discuss in detail the issues you have to confront in deciding how to handle insertions and deletions.

12

Extendible Hashing

❖ Describe the problem solved by extendible hashing and related approaches.

❖ Explain how extendible hashing works; show how it combines *tries* with conventional, static hashing.

❖ Use the buffer, file, and index classes of previous chapters to implement extendible hashing, including deletion.

❖ Review studies of extendible hashing performance.

❖ Examine alternative approaches to the same problem, including *dynamic hashing, linear hashing,* and hashing schemes that control splitting by allowing for overflow buckets.

CHAPTER OUTLINE

12.1 Introduction

In Chapter 9 we began with a historical review of the work that led up to B-trees. B-trees are such an effective solution to the problems that stimulated their development that it is easy to wonder if there is any more important thinking to be done about file structures. Work on extendible hashing during the late 1970s and early 1980s shows that the answer to that question is yes. This chapter tells the story of that work and describes some of the file structures that emerge from it.

B-trees do for secondary storage what AVL trees do for storage in memory: they provide a way of using tree structures that works well with *dynamic* data. By *dynamic* we mean that records are added and deleted from the data set. The key feature of both AVL trees and B-trees is that they are self-adjusting structures that include mechanisms to maintain themselves. As we add and delete records, the tree structures use limited, local restructuring to ensure that the additions and deletions do not degrade performance beyond some predetermined level.

Robust, self-adjusting data and file structures are critically important to data storage and retrieval. Judging from the historical record, they are also hard to develop. It was not until 1963 that Adel'son-Vel'skii and Landis developed a self-adjusting structure for tree storage in memory, and it took another decade of work before computer scientists found, in B-trees, a dynamic tree structure that works well on secondary storage.

B-trees provide $O(\log_k N)$ access to the keys in a file. Hashing, when there is no overflow, provides access to a record with a single seek. But as a file grows larger, looking for records that overflow their buckets degrades performance. For dynamic files that undergo a lot of growth, the performance of a static hashing system such as we described in Chapter 11 is typically worse than the performance of a B-tree. So, by the late 1970s, after the initial burst of research and design work revolving around B-trees was over, a number of researchers began to work on finding ways to modify hashing so that it, too, could be self-adjusting as files grow and shrink. As often happens when a number of groups are working on the same problem, several different, yet essentially similar, approaches emerged to extend hashing to dynamic files. We begin our discussion of the problem by looking closely at the approach called "extendible hashing" described by Fagin, Nievergelt, Pippenger, and Strong (1979). Later in this chapter we compare this approach with others that emerged more recently.

12.2 How Extendible Hashing Works

12.2.1 Tries

The key idea behind extendible hashing is to combine conventional hashing with another retrieval approach called the *trie*. (The word *trie* is pronounced so that it rhymes with *sky*.) Tries are also sometimes referred to as *radix searching* because the branching factor of the search tree is equal to the number of alternative symbols (the radix of the alphabet) that can occur in each position of the key. A few examples will illustrate how this works.

Suppose we want to build a trie that stores the keys *able, abrahms, adams, anderson, andrews,* and *baird.* A schematic form of the trie is shown in Fig. 12.1. As you can see, the searching proceeds letter by letter

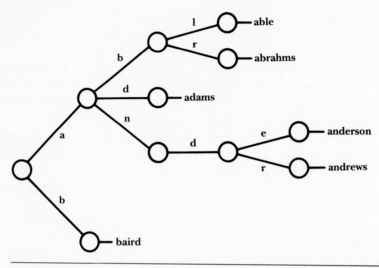

Figure 12.1 Radix 26 trie that indexes names according to the letters of the alphabet.

through the key. Because there are twenty-six symbols in the alphabet, the potential branching factor at every node of the search is twenty-six. If we used the digits *0–9* as our search alphabet rather than the letters *a–z*, the radix of the search would be reduced to 10. A search tree using digits might look like the one shown in Fig. 12.2.

Notice that in searching a trie we sometimes use only a portion of the key. We use more of the key as we need more information to complete the search. This use-more-as-we-need-more capability is fundamental to the structure of extendible hashing.

12.2.2 Turning the Trie into a Directory

We use tries with a radix of 2 in our approach to extendible hashing: search decisions are made on a bit-by-bit basis. Furthermore, since we are retrieving from secondary storage, we will not work in terms of individual keys but in terms of *buckets* containing keys, just as in conventional hashing. Suppose we have bucket *A* containing keys that, when hashed, have hash addresses that begin with the bits *01*. Bucket *B* contains keys with hash addresses beginning with *10*, and bucket *C* contains keys with addresses that start with *11*. Figure 12.3 shows a trie that allows us to retrieve these buckets.

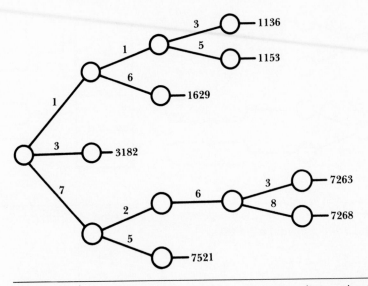

Figure 12.2 Radix 10 trie that indexes numbers according to the digits they contain.

How should we represent the trie? If we represent it as a tree structure, we are forced to do a number of comparisons as we descend the tree. Even worse, if the trie becomes so large that it, too, is stored on disk, we are faced once again with all of the problems associated with storing trees on disk. We might as well go back to B-trees and forget about extendible hashing.

So, rather than representing the trie as a tree, we flatten it into an array of contiguous records, forming a directory of hash addresses and pointers to the corresponding buckets. The first step in turning a tree into an array involves extending it so it is a complete binary tree with all of its leaves at

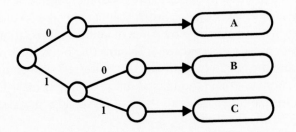

Figure 12.3 Radix 2 trie that provides an index to buckets.

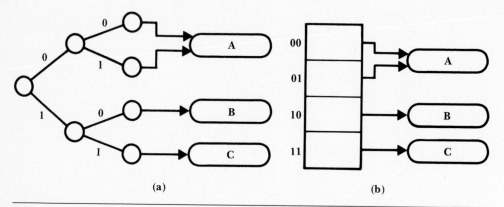

(a)   **(b)**

Figure 12.4 The trie from Fig. 12.3 transformed first into a complete binary tree, then flattened into a directory to the buckets.

the same level as shown in Fig. 12.4(a). Even though the initial *0* is enough to select bucket *A*, the new form of the tree also uses the second address bit so both alternatives lead to the same bucket. Once we have extended the tree this way, we can collapse it into the directory structure shown in Fig. 12.4(b). Now we have a structure that provides the kind of direct access associated with hashing: given an address beginning with the bits *10*, the 10_2th directory entry gives us a pointer to the associated bucket.

12.2.3 Splitting to Handle Overflow

A key issue in any hashing system is what happens when a bucket overflows. The goal in an *extendible* hashing system is to find a way to increase the address space in response to overflow rather than respond by creating long sequences of overflow records and buckets that have to be searched linearly.

Suppose we insert records that cause bucket *A* in Fig. 12.4(b) to overflow. In this case the solution is simple: since addresses beginning with *00* and *01* are mixed together in bucket *A*, we can split bucket *A* by putting all the *01* addresses in a new bucket *D*, while keeping only the *00* addresses in *A*. Put another way, we already have 2 bits of address information but are throwing 1 away as we access bucket *A*. So, now that bucket *A* is overflowing, we must use the full 2 bits to divide the addresses between two buckets. We do not need to extend the address space; we simply make full use of the address information that we already have. Figure 12.5 shows the directory and buckets after the split.

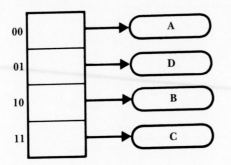

Figure 12.5 The directory from Fig. 12.4(b) after bucket *A* overflows.

Let's consider a more complex case. Starting once again with the directory and buckets in Fig. 12.4(b), suppose that bucket *B* overflows. How do we split bucket *B* and where do we attach the new bucket after the split? Unlike our previous example, we do not have additional, unused bits of address space that we can press into duty as we split the bucket. We now need to use 3 bits of the hash address in order to divide up the records that hash to bucket *B*. The trie illustrated in Fig. 12.6(a) makes the distinctions required to complete the split. Figure 12.6(b) shows what this trie looks like once it is extended into a completely full binary tree with all leaves at the same level, and Fig. 12.6(c) shows the collapsed, directory form of the trie.

By building on the trie's ability to extend the amount of information used in a search, we have doubled the size of our address space (and, therefore, of our directory), extending it from 2^2 to 2^3 cells. This ability to grow (or shrink) the address space gracefully is what extendible hashing is all about.

We have been concentrating on the contribution that tries make to extendible hashing; one might well ask where the *hashing* comes into play. Why not just use the tries on the bits in the key, splitting buckets and extending the address space as necessary? The answer to this question grows out of hashing's most fundamental characteristic: a good hash function produces a nearly uniform distribution of keys across an address space. Notice that the trie shown in Fig. 12.6 is poorly balanced, resulting in a directory that is twice as big as it needs to be. If we had an uneven distribution of addresses that placed even more records in buckets *B* and *D* without using other parts of the address space, the situation would get even worse. By using a good hash function to create addresses with a nearly uniform distribution, we avoid this problem.

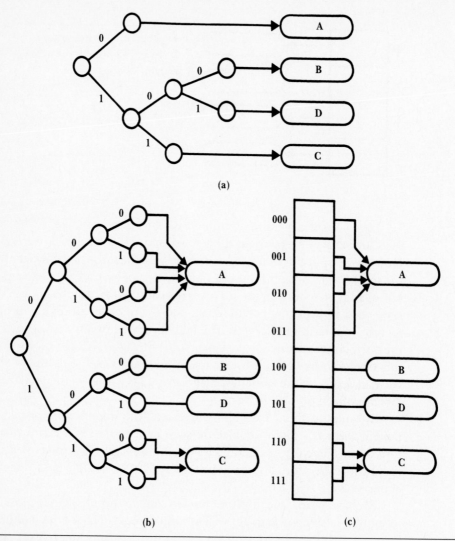

Figure 12.6 The results of an overflow of bucket *B* in Fig. 12.4(b), represented first as a trie, then as a complete binary tree, and finally as a directory.

12.3   Implementation

12.3.1 Creating the Addresses

Now that we have a high-level overview of how extendible hashing works, let's look at an object-oriented implementation. Appendix J contains the

```
int Hash (char* key)
{
   int sum = 0;
   int len = strlen(key);
   if (len % 2 == 1) len ++; // make len even
   // for an odd length, use the trailing '\0' as part of key
   for (int j = 0; j < len; j+=2)
      sum = (sum + 100 * key[j] + key[j+1]) % 19937;
   return sum;
}
```

Figure 12.7 Function Hash (key) returns an integer hash value for key for a 15-bit

full class definitions and method bodies for extendible hashing. The place to start our discussion of the implementation is with the functions that create the addresses, since the notion of an extendible address underlies all other extendible hashing operations.

The function Hash given in Fig. 12.7, and file hash.cpp of Appendix J, is a simple variation on the fold-and-add hashing algorithm we used in Chapter 11. The only difference is that we do not conclude the operation by returning the remainder of the folded address divided by the address space. We don't need to do that, since in extendible hashing we don't have a fixed address space, instead we use as much of the address as we need. The division that we perform in this function, when we take the sum of the folded character values modulo 19 937, is to make sure that the character summation stays within the range of a signed 16-bit integer. For machines that use 32-bit integers, we could divide by a larger number and create an even larger initial address.

Because extendible hashing uses more bits of the hashed address as they are needed to distinguish between buckets, we need a function MakeAddress that extracts just a portion of the full hashed address. We also use MakeAddress to reverse the order of the bits in the hashed address, making the lowest-order bit of the hash address the highest-order bit of the value used in extendible hashing. To see why this reversal of bit order is desirable, look at Fig. 12.8, which is a set of keys and binary hash addresses produced by our hash function. Even a quick scan of these addresses reveals that the distribution of the least significant bits of these integer values tends to have more variation than the high-order bits. This is because many of the addresses do not make use of the upper reaches of our address space; the high-order bits often turn out to be 0.

bill	0000 0011 0110 1100
lee	0000 0100 0010 1000
pauline	0000 1111 0110 0101
alan	0100 1100 1010 0010
julie	0010 1110 0000 1001
mike	0000 0111 0100 1101
elizabeth	0010 1100 0110 1010
mark	0000 1010 0000 0111

Figure 12.8 Output from the hash function for a number of keys.

By reversing the bit order, working from right to left, we take advantage of the greater variability of low-order bit values. For example, given a 4-bit address space, we want to avoid having the addresses of *bill, lee,* and *pauline* turn out to be *0000, 0000,* and *0000.* If we work from right to left, starting with the low-order bit in each address, we get *0011* for *bill, 0001* for *lee,* and *1010* for *pauline,* which is a much more useful result.

Function `MakeAddress`, given in Fig. 12.9 and file `hash.cpp` of Appendix J, accomplishes this bit extraction and reversal. The `depth` argument tells the function the number of address bits to return.

```
int MakeAddress (char * key, int depth)
{
    int retval = 0;
    int hashVal = Hash(key);
    // reverse the bits
    for (int j = 0; j < depth; j++)
    {
        retval = retval << 1;
        int lowbit = hashVal & 1;
        retval = retval | lowbit;
        hashVal = hashVal >> 1;
    }
    return retval;
}
```

Figure 12.9 Function MakeAddress (key, depth) gets a hashed address, reverses the order of the bits, and returns an address of depth bits.

12.3.2 Classes for Representing Bucket and Directory Objects

Our extendible hashing scheme consists of a set of buckets stored in a file and a directory that references them. Each bucket is a record that contains a particular set of keys and information associated with the keys. A directory is primarily an array containing the record addresses of the buckets.

We have chosen to use a data record reference for the information associated with the keys in this implementation. That is, the set of buckets forms an index of the file of actual data records. This is certainly not the only way to configure the bucket file. We have left it as an exercise to extend the bucket class so that the associated information could be the rest of the data record. In this case, the bucket file is the data file. For the rest of the discussion of the implementation of extended hashing, we will treat the buckets as sets of key-reference pairs.

The basic operations on buckets are exactly the same as those of index records: add a key-reference pair to a bucket, search for a key and return its reference, and remove a key. Hence, we have chosen to make class `Bucket` a derived class of the class `TextIndex` from Chapter 5 and Appendix F. The definition of class `Bucket` is given in Fig. 12.10 and file `bucket.h` in Appendix J. These bucket records are stored in a file; we retrieve them as necessary. Each `Bucket` is connected to a directory and can be accessed only in that context. This access restriction is enforced by making the members of the class protected so that no outside access is allowed, then granting special access rights to class `Directory` by including the `friend class Directory` statement. Making class `Directory` a friend of `Bucket` allows methods of class `Directory` to access all of the private and protected members of class `Bucket`. The included methods of class `Bucket` will be explained below.

Class `Directory` is given in Fig. 12.11 and in file `direct.h` of Appendix J. Each cell in the directory consists of the file address of a `Bucket` record. Because we use *direct access* to find directory cells, we implement the directory as an array of these cells in memory. The address values returned by `MakeAddress` are treated as subscripts for this array, ranging from 0 to one less than the number of cells in the directory. Additional members are included to support the file operations required to store the directory and the related buckets. You may notice a striking similarity with classes `IndexedFile` (Chapter 5) and `BTree` (Chapter 9). Each of these classes supports open, create, and close operations as well as insert, search, and remove. Objects of class `BufferFile` are used to provide the I/O operations.

```
class Bucket: protected TextIndex
{protected:
   // there are no public members,
   // access to Bucket members is only through class Directory
   Bucket (Directory & dir, int maxKeys = defaultMaxKeys);
   int Insert (char * key, int recAddr);
   int Remove (char * key);
   Bucket * Split ();// split the bucket and redistribute the keys
   int NewRange (int & newStart, int & newEnd);
      // calculate the range of a new (split) bucket
   int Redistribute (Bucket & newBucket); // redistribute keys
   int FindBuddy ();// find the bucket that is the buddy of this
   int TryCombine (); // attempt to combine buckets
   int Combine (Bucket * buddy, int buddyIndex); //combine buckets
   int Depth; //number of bits used 'in common' by keys in bucket
   Directory & Dir; // directory that contains the bucket
   int BucketAddr; // address in file
   friend class Directory;
   friend class BucketBuffer;
};
```

Figure 12.10 Main members of class Bucket.

In order to use a `Directory` object, it must be constructed and then attached to a file for the directory and one for the buckets. Fig 12.12 (page 536) is a sample test program, `tsthash.cpp`. The two steps for initialization are the declaration of the `Directory` object, and the call to method `Create`, that creates the two files and the initial empty bucket. The program proceeds to insert a set of key-reference pairs. Notice that the reference values have no particular significance in this program.

The constructor and method `Create` are given in Fig. 12.13 (page 537). The constructor creates all of the objects that support the I/O operations: a buffer and a file for the directory and a buffer and a file for the buckets. The directory is stored in memory while the directory is open. The `Open` method reads the directory from the file and the `Close` writes it back into the file.

```
class Directory
{public:
   Directory (int maxBucketKeys = -1);
   ~Directory ();
   int Open (char * name);
   int Create (char * name);
   int Close ();
   int Insert (char * key, int recAddr);
   int Delete (char * key, int recAddr = -1);
   int Search (char * key); // return RecAddr for key
   ostream & Print (ostream & stream);
   protected:
   int Depth; // depth of directory
   int NumCells; // number of cells, = 2**Depth
   int * BucketAddr; // array of bucket addresses

   // protected methods
   int DoubleSize (); // double the size of the directory
   int Collapse (); // collapse, halve the size
   int InsertBucket (int bucketAddr, int first, int last);
   int Find (char * key); // return BucketAddr for key
   int StoreBucket (Bucket * bucket);
      // update or append bucket in file
   int LoadBucket (Bucket * bucket, int bucketAddr);
      // load bucket from file
   // members to support directory and bucket files
   int MaxBucketKeys;
   BufferFile * DirectoryFile;
   LengthFieldBuffer * DirectoryBuffer;
   Bucket * CurrentBucket;// object to hold one bucket
   BucketBuffer * theBucketBuffer;// buffer for buckets
   BufferFile * BucketFile;
   int Pack () const;
   int Unpack ();
   Bucket * PrintBucket;// object to hold one bucket for printing
   friend class Bucket;
};
```

Figure 12.11 Definition of class Directory.

```
main ()
{
    int result;
    Directory Dir (4);
    result = Dir . Create ("hashfile");
    if (result == 0) {return 0;} // unable to create files
    char * keys[]={"bill", "lee", "pauline", "alan", "julie",
        "mike", "elizabeth", "mark", "ann", "peter",
        "christina", "john", "charles", "mary", "emily"};
    const int numkeys = 15;
    for (int i = 0; i<numkeys; i++)
    {
        result = Dir . Insert (keys[i], 100 + i);
        if (result == 0)
        cout << "insert for "<<keys[i]<<" failed"<<endl;
        Dir . Print (cout);
    }
    return 1;
}
```

Figure 12.12 Test program tsthash.cpp inserts a sequence of key-reference pairs into a directory.

Note that member Depth is directly related to the size of the directory, since

$$2^{Depth} = \text{the number of cells in the directory.}$$

If we are starting a new hash directory, the directory depth is 0, which means that we are using *no* bits to distinguish between addresses; all the keys go into the same bucket, no matter what their address. We get the address of the initial, everything-goes-here bucket and assign it to the single directory cell in this line from Directory::Create:

```
BucketAddr[0] = StoreBucket (CurrentBucket);
```

The method StoreBucket appends the new bucket to the bucket file and returns its address.

12.3.3 Directory and Bucket Operations

Now that we have a way to open and close the file, we are ready to add records to the directory. The Insert, Search, and Find methods are

```
Directory::Directory (int maxBucketKeys)
{
    Depth = 0; // depth of directory
    NumCells = 1; // number of entries, = 2**Depth
    BucketAddr = new int [NumCells]; // array of bucket addresses
    // create I/O support objects
    MaxBucketKeys = maxBucketKeys;
    DirectoryBuffer = new LengthFieldBuffer; // default size
    DirectoryFile = new BufferFile(*DirectoryBuffer);
    CurrentBucket = new Bucket (*this, MaxBucketKeys);
    theBucketBuffer = new BucketBuffer (MaxKeySize, MaxBucketKeys);
    BucketFile = new BufferFile (*theBucketBuffer);
    PrintBucket = new Bucket (*this, MaxBucketKeys);
}
int Directory::Create (char * name)
{   // create the two files, create a single bucket
    // and add it to the directory and the bucket file
    int result;
    char * directoryName, * bucketName;
    makeNames(name, directoryName, bucketName);// create file names
    result = DirectoryFile->Create(directoryName,ios::in|ios::out);
    if (!result) return 0;
    result = BucketFile->Create(bucketName,ios::in|ios::out);
    if (!result) return 0;
    // store the empty bucket in the BucketFile; add to Directory
    BucketAddr[0] = StoreBucket (CurrentBucket);
    return result;
}
```

Figure 12.13 Constructor and method Create of class Directory.

shown in Fig. 12.14. The Insert method first searches for the key.
Search arranges for the CurrentBucket member to contain the
proper bucket for the key. If the key is not already in the bucket, then the
Bucket::Insert method is called to perform the insertion. In method
Directory::Search, as in most search functions we have seen, the
Find method determines where the key would be if it were in the structure. In this case, Find determines which bucket is associated with the
key. As noted previously, MakeAddress finds the array index of the
directory cell that contains the file address of the appropriate bucket.

```
int Directory::Insert (char * key, int recAddr)
{
   int found = Search (key);
   if (found != -1) return 0; // key already in directory
   return CurrentBucket->Insert(key, recAddr);
}
int Directory::Search (char * key)
// return RecAddr for key, also put current bucket into variable
{
   int bucketAddr = Find(key);
   LoadBucket (CurrentBucket, bucketAddr);
   return CurrentBucket->Search(key);
}
int Directory::Find (char * key)
// find BucketAddr associated with key
{   return BucketAddr[MakeAddress (key, Depth)];}
```

Figure 12.14 Methods Insert, Search, and Find of class Directory.

```
int Bucket::Insert (char * key, int recAddr)
{
   if (NumKeys < MaxKeys)
   {
      int result = TextIndex::Insert (key, recAddr);
      Dir.StoreBucket (this);
      return result;
   }
   else // bucket is full
   {
      Split ();
      return Dir.Insert (key, recAddr);
   }
}
```

Figure 12.15 Method Insert of class Bucket adds the key to the existing bucket if there is room. If the bucket is full, it splits it and then adds the key.

Method Bucket::Insert, given in Fig. 12.15 and in file buffer.cpp of Appendix J, is called with a key-reference pair. If the bucket is not full, Insert simply calls TextIndex::Insert to add the key-reference pair to the bucket and stores the bucket in the file. A full bucket, however, requires a split, which is where things start to get interesting. After the split is done, the `Directory::Insert` is called (recursively) to try again to insert the key-reference pair.

What we do when we split a bucket depends on the relationship between the number of address bits used in the bucket and the number used in the directory as a whole. The two numbers are often not the same. To see this, look at Fig. 12.6(a). The directory uses *3* bits to define its address space (8 cells). The keys in bucket *A* are distinguished from keys in other buckets by having an initial *0* bit. All the other bits in the hashed key values in bucket *A* can be any value; it is only the first bit that matters. Bucket *A* is using only *1* bit and has depth 1.

The keys in bucket *C* all share a common first *2* bits; they all begin with *11*. The keys in buckets *B* and *D* use *3* bits to establish their identities and, therefore, their bucket locations. If you look at Fig. 12.6(c), you can see how using more or fewer address bits changes the relationship between the directory and the bucket. Buckets that do not use as many address bits as the directory have more than one directory cell pointing to them.

If we split one of the buckets that is using fewer address bits than the directory, and therefore is referenced from more than one directory cell, we can use half of the directory cells to point to the new bucket after the split. Suppose, for example, that we split bucket *A* in Fig. 12.6(c). Before the split only 1 bit, the initial 0, is used to identify keys that belong in bucket *A*. After the split, we use 2 bits. Keys starting with *00* (directory cells *000* and *001*) go in bucket *A;* keys starting with *01* (directory cells *010* and *011*) go in the new bucket. We do not have to expand the directory because the directory already has the capacity to keep track of the additional address information required for the split.

If, on the other hand, we split a bucket that has the same address depth as the directory, such as buckets *B* or *D* in Fig. 12.6(c), then there are no additional directory cells that we can use to reference the new bucket. Before we can split the bucket, we have to double the size of the directory, creating a new directory entry for every one that is currently there so we can accommodate the new address information.

Figure 12.16 gives an implementation of method `Split`. First we compare the number of bits used for the directory with the number used for the bucket to determine whether we need to double the directory. If the depths are the same, we double the directory before proceeding.

```
Bucket * Bucket::Split ()
{// split this into two buckets, store the new bucket, and
   // return (memory) address of new bucket
   int newStart, newEnd;
   if (Depth == Dir.Depth)// no room to split this bucket
      Dir.DoubleSize();// increase depth of directory
   Bucket * newBucket = new Bucket (Dir, MaxKeys);
   Dir.StoreBucket (newBucket); // append to file
   NewRange (newStart, newEnd); // determine directory addresses
   Dir.InsertBucket(newBucket->BucketAddr, newStart, newEnd);
   Depth ++; // increment depth of this
   newBucket->Depth = Depth;
   Redistribute (*newBucket); // move some keys into new bucket
   Dir.StoreBucket (this);
   Dir.StoreBucket (newBucket);
   return newBucket;
}
```

Figure 12.16 Method Split of class Bucket divides keys between an existing bucket and a new bucket. If necessary, it doubles the size of the directory to accommodate the new bucket.

Next we create the new bucket that we need for the split. Then we find the range of directory addresses that we will use for the new bucket. For instance, when we split bucket *A* in Fig. 12.6(c), the range of directory addresses for the new bucket is from *010* to *011*. We attach the new bucket to the directory over this range, adjust the bucket address depth information in both buckets to reflect the use of an additional address bit, then redistribute the keys from the original bucket across the two buckets.

The most complicated operation supporting the Split method is NewRange, which finds the range of directory cells that should point to the new bucket instead of the old one after the split. It is given in Fig. 12.17. To see how it works, return, once again, to Fig. 12.6(c). Assume that we need to split bucket *A*, putting some of the keys into a new bucket *E*. Before the split, any address beginning with a *0* leads to *A*. In other words, the *shared address* of the keys in bucket *A* is *0*.

When we split bucket *A* we add another address bit to the path leading to the keys; addresses leading to bucket *A* now share an initial *00* while those leading to *E* share an *01*. So, the range of addresses for the new bucket is all directory addresses beginning with *01*. Since the directory address-

```
int Bucket::NewRange (int & newStart, int & newEnd)
{// make a range for the new split bucket
    int sharedAddr = MakeAddress(Keys[0], Depth);
    int bitsToFill = Dir.Depth - (Depth + 1);
    newStart = (sharedAddr << 1) | 1;
    newEnd = newStart;
    for (int j = 0; j < bitsToFill; j++)
    {
        newStart = newStart << 1;
        newEnd = (newEnd << 1) | 1;
    }
    return 1;
}
```

Figure 12.17 Method NewRange of class Bucket finds the start and end directory addresses for the new bucket by using information from the old bucket.

es use 3 bits, the new bucket is attached to the directory cells starting with *010* and ending with *011*.

Suppose that the directory used a 5-bit address instead of a 3-bit address. Then the range for the new bucket would start with *01000* and end with *01111*. This range covers all 5-bit addresses that share *01* as the first 2 bits. The logic for finding the range of directory addresses for the new bucket, then, starts by finding *shared address* bits for the new bucket. It then fills the address out with 0s until we have the number of bits used in the directory. This is the start of the range. Filling the address out with 1s produces the end of the range.

The directory operations required to support Split are easy to implement. They are given in Fig. 12.18. The first, Directory::DoubleSize, simply calculates the new directory size, allocates the required memory, and writes the information from each old directory cell into two successive cells in the new directory. It finishes by freeing the old space associated with member BufferAddrs, renaming the new space as the BufferAddrs, and increasing the Depth to reflect the fact that the directory is now using an additional address bit.

Method InsertBucket, used to attach a bucket address across a range of directory cells, is simply a loop that works through the cells to make the change.

```
int Directory::DoubleSize ()
// double the size of the directory
{
    int newSize = 2 * NumCells;
    int * newBucketAddr = new int[newSize];
    for (int i = 0; i < NumCells; i++)
    {// double the coverage of each bucket
        newBucketAddr[2*i] = BucketAddr[i];
        newBucketAddr[2*i+1] = BucketAddr[i];
    }
    delete BucketAddr;// delete old space for cells
    BucketAddr = newBucketAddr;
    Depth ++;
    NumCells = newSize;
    return 1;
}

int Directory::InsertBucket (int bucketAddr, int first, int last)
{
    for (int i = first; i <= last; i++)
        BucketAddr[i] = bucketAddr;
    return 1;
}
```

Figure 12.18 Methods DoubleSize and Directory InsertBucket of class Directory.

12.3.4 Implementation Summary

Now that we have assembled all of the pieces necessary to add records to an extendible hashing system, let's see how the pieces work together.

The Insert method manages record addition. If the key already exists, Insert returns immediately. If the key does not exist, Insert calls Bucket::Insert, for the bucket into which the key is to be added. If Bucket::Insert finds that there is still room in the bucket, it adds the key and the operation is complete. If the bucket is full, Bucket::Insert calls Split to handle the task of splitting the bucket.

The Split method starts by determining whether the directory is large enough to accommodate the new bucket. If the directory needs to be larger, Split calls method Directory::DoubleSize to double the directory size. Split then allocates a new bucket, attaches it to the appropriate directory cells, and divides the keys between the two buckets.

When `Bucket::Insert` regains control after `Split` has allocated a new bucket, it calls `Directory::Insert` to try to place the key into the new, revised directory structure. The `Directory::Insert` function, of course, calls `Bucket::Insert` again, recursively. This cycle continues until there is a bucket that can accommodate the new key. A problem can occur if there are many keys that have exactly the same hash address. The process of double, split, and insert will never make room for the new key.

12.4   Deletion

12.4.1   Overview of the Deletion Process

If extendible hashing is to be a truly *dynamic* system, like B-trees or AVL trees, it must be able to *shrink* files gracefully as well as grow them. When we delete a key, we need a way to see if we can decrease the size of the file system by combining buckets and, if possible, decreasing the size of the directory.

As with any dynamic system, the important question during deletion concerns the definition of the triggering condition: When do we combine buckets? This question, in turn, leads us to ask, Which buckets can be combined? For B-trees the answer involves determining whether nodes are *siblings*. In extendible hashing we use a similar concept: buckets that are *buddy* buckets.

Look again at the trie in Fig. 12.6(b). Which buckets could be combined? Trying to combine anything with bucket *A* would mean collapsing everything else in the trie first. Similarly, there is no single bucket that could be combined with bucket *C*. But buckets *B* and *D* are in the same configuration as buckets that have just split. They are ready to be combined: they are buddy buckets. We will take a closer look at finding buddy buckets when we consider implementation of the deletion procedure; for now let's assume that we combine buckets *B* and *D*.

After combining buckets, we examine the directory to see if we can make changes there. Looking at the directory form of the trie in Fig. 12.6(c), we see that once we combine buckets *B* and *D*, directory cells *100* and *101* both point to the same bucket. In fact, each of the buckets has at least a pair of directory cells pointing to it. In other words, none of the buckets requires the depth of address information that is currently available in the directory. That means that we can shrink the directory and reduce the address space to half its size.

Reducing the size of the address space restores the directory and bucket structure to the arrangement shown in Fig. 12.4, before the additions and splits that produced the structure in Fig. 12.6(c). Reduction consists of collapsing each adjacent pair of directory cells into a single cell. This is easy, because both cells in each pair point to the same bucket. Note that this is nothing more than a reversal of the directory splitting procedure that we use when we need to add new directory cells.

12.4.2 A Procedure for Finding Buddy Buckets

Given this overview of how deletion works, we begin by focusing on buddy buckets. Given a bucket, how do we find its buddy? Figure 12.19 contains the code for method `Bucket::FindBuddy`. The method works by checking to see whether it is possible for there to be a buddy bucket. Clearly, if the directory depth is 0, meaning that there is only a single bucket, there cannot be a buddy.

The next test compares the number of bits used by the bucket with the number of bits used in the directory address space. A pair of buddy buckets is a set of buckets that are immediate descendants of the same node in the trie. They are, in fact, pairwise siblings resulting from a split. Going back to Fig. 12.6(b), we see that asking whether the bucket uses all the address bits in the directory is another way of asking whether the bucket is at the lowest level of the trie. It is only when a bucket is at the outer edge of the trie that it can have a single parent and a single buddy.

Once we determine that there is a buddy bucket, we need to find its address. First we find the address used to find the bucket we have at hand;

```
int Bucket::FindBuddy ()
{// find the bucket that is paired with this
   if (Dir.Depth == 0) return -1; // no buddy, empty directory

   // unless bucket depth == directory depth, there is no single
   // bucket to pair with
   if (Depth < Dir.Depth) return -1;
   int sharedAddress = MakeAddress(Keys[0], Depth);
      // address of any key
   return sharedAddress ^ 1; // exclusive or with low bit
}
```

Figure 12.19 Method FindBuddy of class Bucket returns a buddy bucket or –1 if none is found.

this is the shared address of the keys in the bucket. Since we know that the buddy bucket is the other bucket that was formed from a split, we know that the buddy has the same address in all regards except for the last bit. Once again, this relationship is illustrated by buckets B and D in Fig. 12.6(b). So, to get the buddy address, we flip the last bit with an exclusive or. We return directory address of the buddy bucket.

12.4.3 Collapsing the Directory

The other important support function used to implement deletion is the function that handles collapsing the directory. Downsizing the directory is one of the principal potential benefits of deleting records. In our implementation we use one function to see whether downsizing is possible and, if it is, to collapse the directory.

Method `Directory::Collapse`, given in Fig. 12.20, begins by making sure that we are not at the lower limit of directory size. By treating the special case of a directory with a single cell here, at the start of the function, we simplify subsequent processing: with the exception of this case, all directory sizes are evenly divisible by 2.

The test to see if the directory can be collapsed consists of examining each pair of directory cells to see if they point to different buckets. As soon

```
int Directory::Collapse ()
{// if collapse is possible, reduce size by half
   if (Depth == 0) return 0; // only 1 bucket
   // look for buddies that are different, if found return
   for (int i = 0; i < NumCells; i += 2)
      if (BucketAddr[i] != BucketAddr[i+1]) return 0;
   int newSize = NumCells / 2;
   int * newAddrs = new int [newSize];
   for (int j = 0; j < newSize; j++)
      newAddrs[j] = BucketAddr[j*2];
   delete BucketAddr;
   BucketAddr = newAddrs;
   Depth -;
   NumCells = newSize;
   return 1;
}
```

Figure 12.20 Method Collapse of class Directory reduces the size of the directory, if possible.

as we find such a pair, we know that we *cannot* collapse the directory and the method returns. If we get all the way through the directory without encountering such a pair, then we can collapse the directory.

The collapsing operation consists of allocating space for a new array of bucket addresses that is half the size of the original and then copying the bucket references shared by each cell pair to a single cell in the new directory.

12.4.4 Implementing the Deletion Operations

Now that we have an approach to the two critical support operations for deletion, finding buddy buckets and collapsing the directory, we are ready to construct the higher levels of the deletion operation.

The highest-level deletion operation, `Directory::Remove`, is very simple. We first try to find the key to be deleted. If we cannot find it, we return failure; if we find it, we call `Bucket::Remove` to remove the key from the bucket. We return the value reported back from that method. Figure 12.21 gives the implementation of these two methods.

Method `Bucket::Remove` does its work in two steps. The first step, removing the key from the bucket, is accomplished through the call to `TextIndex::Remove`, the base class `Remove` method. The second

```
int Directory::Remove (char * key)
{// remove the key and return its RecAddr
    int bucketAddr = Find(key);
    LoadBucket (CurrentBucket, bucketAddr);
    return CurrentBucket -> Remove (key);
}
int Bucket::Remove (char * key)
{// remove the key, return its RecAddr
    int result = TextIndex::Remove (key);
    if (!result) return 0; // key not in bucket
    TryCombine (); // attempt to combine with buddy
    // make the changes permanent
    Dir.StoreBucket(this);
    return 1;
}
```

Figure 12.21 Remove methods of classes Directory and Bucket.

step, which takes place only if a key is removed, consists of calling TryCombine to see if deleting the key has decreased the size of the bucket enough to allow us to combine it with its buddy.

Figure 12.22 shows the implementation of TryCombine and Combine. Note that when we combine buckets, we reduce the address depth associated with the bucket: combining buckets means that we use 1 less address bit to differentiate keys.

```
int Bucket::TryCombine ()
{// called after insert to combine buddies, if possible
   int result;
   int buddyIndex = FindBuddy ();
   if (buddyIndex == -1) return 0;// no combination possible
   // load buddy bucket into memory
   int buddyAddr = Dir.BucketAddr[buddyIndex];
   Bucket * buddyBucket = new Bucket (Dir, MaxKeys);
   Dir . LoadBucket (buddyBucket, buddyAddr);
   // if the sum of the sizes of the buckets is too big, return
   if (NumKeys + buddyBucket->NumKeys > MaxKeys) return 0;
   Combine (buddyBucket, buddyIndex);
   result = Dir.Collapse (); // collapse the 2 buckets
   if (result) TryCombine (); //if collapse, may be able to combine
   return 1;
}
int Bucket::Combine (Bucket * buddy, int buddyIndex)
{// combine this and buddy to make a single bucket
   int result;
   // move keys from buddy to this
   for (int i = 0; i < buddy->NumKeys; i++)
   {// insert the key of the buddy into this
      result = Insert (buddy->Keys[i],buddy->RecAddrs[i]);
      if (!result) return 0;// this should not happen
   }
   Depth − −;// reduce the depth of the bucket
   Dir . RemoveBucket (buddyIndex, Depth);// delete buddy bucket
   return 1;
}
```

Figure 12.22 Methods TryCombine and Combine of class Bucket. TryCombine tests to see whether a bucket can be combined with its buddy. If the test succeeds, TryCombine calls Combine to do the combination.

After combining the buckets, we call `Directory::Collapse()` to see if the decrease in the number of buckets enables us to decrease the size of the directory. If we do, in fact, collapse the directory, `TryCombine` calls itself recursively. Collapsing the directory may have created a new buddy for the bucket; it may be possible to do even more combination and collapsing. Typically, this recursive combining and collapsing happens only when the directory has a number of `empty` buckets that are awaiting changes in the directory structure that finally produce a buddy to combine with.

12.4.5 Summary of the Deletion Operation

Deletion begins with a call to `Directory::Remove` that passes the key that is to be deleted. If the key cannot be found, there is nothing to delete. If the key is found, the bucket containing the key is passed to `Bucket::Remove`.

The `Bucket::Remove` method deletes the key, then passes the bucket on to `Directory::TryCombine` to see if the smaller size of the bucket will now permit combination with a buddy bucket. `TryCombine` first checks to see if there is a buddy bucket. If not, we are done. If there is a buddy, and if the sum of the keys in the bucket and its buddy is less than or equal to the size of a single bucket, we combine the buckets.

The elimination of a bucket through combination might cause the directory to collapse to half its size. We investigate this possibility by calling `Directory::Collapse`. If collapsing succeeds, we may have a new buddy bucket, so `TryCombine` calls itself again, recursively.

File `testdel.cpp` in Appendix J opens the directory created by `testhash.cpp` and proceeds to delete each element of the directory. Using a debugger to step through this program may help in understanding the deletion process.

12.5 Extendible Hashing Performance

Extendible hashing is an elegant solution to the problem of extending and contracting the address space for a hash file as the file grows and shrinks. How well does it work? As always, the answer to this question must consider the trade-off between time and space.

The time dimension is easy to handle: if the directory for extendible hashing can be kept in memory, a single access is all that is ever required to retrieve a record. If the directory is so large that it must be paged in and out of memory, two accesses may be necessary. The important point is that extendible hashing provides $O(1)$ performance: since there is no overflow, these access time values are truly independent of the size of the file.

Questions about space utilization for extendible hashing are more complicated than questions about access time. We need to be concerned about two uses of space: the space for the buckets and the space for the directory.

12.5.1 Space Utilization for Buckets

In their original paper describing extendible hashing, Fagin, Nievergelt, Pippenger, and Strong include analysis and simulation of extendible hashing performance. Both the analysis and simulation show that the space utilization is strongly periodic, fluctuating between values of 0.53 and 0.94. The analysis portion of their paper suggests that for a given number of records r and a block size of b, the average number of blocks N is approximated by the formula

$$N \approx \frac{r}{b \ln 2} N$$

Space utilization, or packing density, is defined as the ratio of the actual number of records to the total number of records that could be stored in the allocated space:

$$\text{Utilization} = \frac{r}{bN}$$

Substituting the approximation for N gives us:

$$\text{Utilization} \approx \ln 2 = 0.69$$

So, we expect *average* utilization of 69 percent. In Chapter 9, where we looked at space utilization for B-trees, we found that simple B-trees tend to have a utilization of about 67 percent, but this can be increased to more than 85 percent by redistributing keys during insertion rather than just splitting when a page is full. So, B-trees tend to use less space than simple extendible hashing, typically at a cost of requiring a few extra seeks.

The average space utilization for extendible hashing is only part of the story; the other part relates to the periodic nature of the variations in space utilization. It turns out that if we have keys with randomly distributed addresses, the buckets in the extendible hashing table tend to fill up at about the same time and therefore tend to split at the same time. This explains the large fluctuations in space utilization. As the buckets fill up, space utilization can reach past 90 percent. This is followed by a concentrated series of splits that reduce the utilization to below 50 percent. As these now nearly half-full buckets fill up again, the cycle repeats itself.

12.5.2 Space Utilization for the Directory

The directory used in extendible hashing grows by doubling its size. A prudent designer setting out to implement an extendible hashing system will want assurance that this doubling levels off for reasonable bucket sizes, even when the number of keys is quite large. Just how large a directory should we expect to have, given an expected number of keys?

Flajolet (1983) addressed this question in a lengthy, carefully developed paper that produces a number of different ways to estimate the directory size. Table 12.1, which is taken from Flajolet's paper, shows the expected value for the directory size for different numbers of keys and different bucket sizes.

Flajolet also provides the following formula for making rough estimates of the directory size for values that are not in this table. He notes that this formula tends to overestimate directory size by a factor of 2 to 4.

$$\text{Estimated directory size} = \frac{3.92}{b} r^{(1 + 1/b)}$$

Table 12.1 Expected directory size for a given bucket size b and total number of records r.

b	5	10	20	50	100	200
r						
10^3	1.50 K	0.30 K	0.10 K	0.00 K	0.00 K	0.00 K
10^4	25.60 K	4.80 K	1.70 K	0.50 K	0.20 K	0.00 K
10^5	424.10 K	68.20 K	16.80 K	4.10 K	2.00 K	1.00 K
10^6	6.90 M	1.02 M	0.26 M	62.50 K	16.80 K	8.10 K
10^7	112.11 M	12.64 M	2.25 M	0.52 M	0.26 M	0.13 M

$1 K = 10^3, 1 M = 10^6.$

From Flajolet, 1983.

12.6.1 Dynamic Hashing

In 1978, before Fagin, Nievergelt, Pippenger, and Strong produced their paper on extendible hashing, Larson published a paper describing a scheme called *dynamic hashing*. Functionally, dynamic hashing and extendible hashing are very similar. Both use a directory to track the addresses of the buckets, and both extend the directory through the use of tries.

The key difference between the approaches is that dynamic hashing, like conventional, static hashing, starts with a hash function that covers an address space of a fixed size. As buckets within that fixed address space overflow, they split, forming the leaves of a trie that grows down from the original address node. Eventually, after enough additions and splitting, the buckets are addressed through a forest of tries that have been seeded out of the original static address space.

Let's look at an example. Figure 12.23(a) shows an initial address space of four and four buckets descending from the four addresses in the directory. In Fig. 12.23(b) we have split the bucket at address *4*. We address the two buckets resulting from the split as *40* and *41*. We change the shape of the directory node at address *4* from a square to a circle because it has changed from an external node, referencing a bucket, to an internal node that points to two child nodes.

In Fig. 12.23(c) we split the bucket addressed by node *2*, creating the new external nodes *20* and *21*. We also split the bucket addressed by *41*, extending the trie downward to include *410* and *411*. Because the directory node *41* is now an internal node rather than an external one, it changes from a square to a circle. As we continue to add keys and split buckets, these directory tries continue to grow.

Finding a key in a dynamic hashing scheme can involve the use of two hash functions rather than just one. First, there is the hash function that covers the original address space. If you find that the directory node is an external node and therefore points to a bucket, the search is complete. However, if the directory node is an internal node, then you need additional address information to guide you through the 1s and 0s that form the trie. Larson suggests using a second hash function on the key and using the result of this hashing as the seed for a random-number generator that produces a sequence of 1s and 0s for the key. This sequence describes the path through the trie.

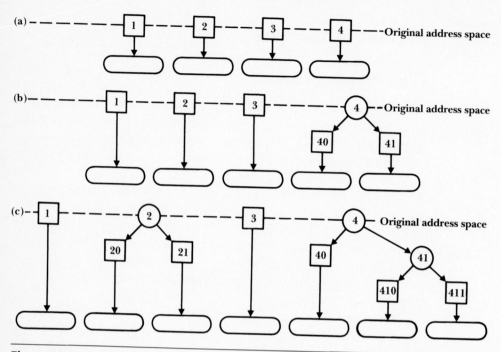

Figure 12.23 The growth of index in dynamic hashing.

It is interesting to compare dynamic hashing and extendible hashing. A brief, but illuminating, characterization of similarities and differences is that while both schemes extend the hash function locally, as a binary search trie, in order to handle overflow, dynamic hashing expresses the extended directory as a linked structure while extendible hashing expresses it as a perfect tree, which is in turn expressible as an array.

Because of this fundamental similarity, it is not surprising that the space utilization within the buckets is the same (69 percent) for both approaches. Moreover, since the directories are essentially equivalent, just expressed differently, it follows that the estimates of directory depth developed by Flajolet (1983) apply equally well to dynamic hashing and extendible hashing. (In section 12.5.2 we talk about estimates for the directory *size* for extendible hashing, but we know that in extendible hashing *directory depth* = $\log_2$ *directory size.*)

The primary difference between the two approaches is that dynamic hashing allows for slower, more gradual growth of the directory, whereas extendible hashing extends the directory by doubling it. However, because the directory nodes in dynamic hashing must be capable of holding pointers to children, the size of a node in dynamic hashing is larger than a directory cell in extendible hashing, probably by at least a factor of 2. So, the directory for dynamic hashing will usually require more space in memory. Moreover, if the directory becomes so large that it requires use of virtual memory, extendible hashing offers the advantage of being able to access the directory with no more than a single page fault. Since dynamic hashing uses a linked structure for the directory, it may be necessary to incur more than one page fault to move through the directory.

12.6.2 Linear Hashing

The key feature of both extendible hashing and dynamic hashing is that they use a directory to access the buckets containing the key records. This directory makes it possible to expand and modify the hashed address space without expanding the number of buckets: after expanding the directory, more than one directory node can point to the same bucket. However, the directory adds an additional layer of indirection which, if the directory must be stored on disk, can result in an additional seek.

Linear hashing, introduced by Litwin in 1980, does away with the directory. An example, developed in Fig. 12.24, shows how linear hashing works. This example is adapted from a description of linear hashing by Enbody and Du (1988).

Linear hashing, like extendible hashing, uses more bits of hashed value as the address space grows. The example begins (Fig. 12.24[a]) with an address space of four, which means that we are using an address function that produces addresses with two bits of depth. In terms of the operations that we developed earlier in this chapter, we are calling `MakeAddress` with a key and a second argument of 2. For this example we will refer to this as the $h_2(k)$ address function. Note that the address space consists of four *buckets* rather than four directory nodes that can point to buckets.

As we add records, bucket b overflows. The overflow forces a split. However, as Fig. 12.24(b) shows, it is not bucket b that splits, but bucket a. The reason for this is that we are extending the address space *linearly*, and bucket a is the next bucket that must split to create the next linear extension, which we call bucket A. A 3-bit hash function, $h_3(k)$, is applied to buckets a and A to divide the records between them. Since bucket b was not the bucket that we split, the overflowing record is placed into an overflow bucket w.

We add more records, and bucket d overflows. Bucket b is the next one to split and extend the address space, so we use the $h_3(k)$ address function

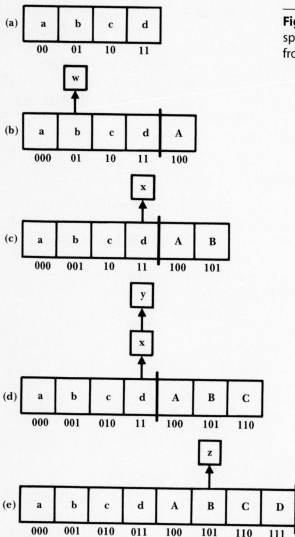

Figure 12.24 The growth of address space in linear hashing. Adapted from Enbody and Du (1988).

to divide the records from bucket *b* and its overflow bucket *w* between *b* and the new bucket *B*. The record overflowing bucket *d* is placed in an overflow bucket *x*. The resulting arrangement is illustrated in Fig. 12.24(c).

Figure 12.24(d) shows what happens when, as we add more records, bucket *d* overflows beyond the capacity of the overflow bucket *w*. Bucket *c* is the next in the extension sequence, so we use the $h_3(k)$ address function to divide the records between *c* and *C*.

Finally, assume that bucket B overflows. The overflow record is placed in the overflow bucket z. The overflow also triggers the extension to bucket D, dividing the contents of d, x, and y between buckets d and D. At this point all of the buckets use the $h_3(k)$ address function, and we have finished the expansion cycle. The pointer for the next bucket to be split returns to bucket a to get ready for a new cycle that will use an $h_4(k)$ address function to reach new buckets.

Because linear hashing uses two hash functions to reach the buckets during an expansion cycle, an $h_d(k)$ function for the buckets at the current address depth and an $h_{d+1}(k)$ function for the expansion buckets, finding a record requires knowing which function to use. If p is the pointer to the address of the next bucket to be split and extended, then the procedure for finding the address of the bucket containing a key k is as follows:

```
if (h_d(k) <= p)
    address = h_d(k);
else
    address = h_d + 1(k);
```

Litwin (1980) shows that the access time performance of linear hashing is quite good. There is no directory to access or maintain, and since we extend the address space through splitting every time there is overflow, the overflow chains do not become very large. Given a bucket size of 50, the average number of disk accesses per search approaches very close to one. Space utilization, on the other hand, is lower than it is for extendible hashing or dynamic hashing, averaging around only 60 percent.

12.6.3 Approaches to Controlling Splitting

We know from Chapter 9 that we can increase the storage capacity of B-trees by implementing measures that tend to postpone splitting, redistributing keys between pages rather than splitting pages. We can apply similar logic to the hashing schemes introduced in this chapter, placing records in chains of overflow buckets to postpone splitting.

Since linear hashing has the lowest storage utilization of the schemes introduced here, and since it already includes logic to handle overflow buckets, it is an attractive candidate for use of controlled splitting logic. In its uncontrolled-splitting form, linear hashing splits a bucket and extends the address space every time any bucket overflows. This choice of a triggering event for splitting is arbitrary, particularly when we consider that the bucket that splits is typically not the bucket that overflows. Litwin

(1980) suggests using the overall load factor of the file as an alternative triggering event. Suppose we let the buckets overflow until the space utilization reaches some desired figure, such as 75 percent. Every time the utilization exceeds that figure, we split a bucket and extend the address space. Litwin simulated this kind of system and found that for load factors of 75 percent and even 85 percent, the average number of accesses for successful and unsuccessful searches still stays below 2.

We can also use overflow buckets to defer splitting and increase space utilization for dynamic hashing and extendible hashing. For these methods, which use directories to the buckets, deferring splitting has the additional attraction of keeping the directory size down. For extendible hashing it is particularly advantageous to chain to an overflow bucket and therefore avoid a split when the split would cause the directory to double in size. Consider the example that we used early in this chapter, where we split the bucket B in Fig. 12.4(b), producing the expanded directory and bucket structure shown in Fig. 12.6(c). If we had allowed bucket B to overflow instead, we could have retained the smaller directory. Depending on how much space we allocated for the overflow buckets, we might also have improved space utilization among the buckets. The cost of these improvements, of course, is a potentially greater search length due to the overflow chains.

Studies of the effects of different overflow bucket sizes and chaining mechanisms supported a small industry of academic research during the early and mid-1980s. Larson (1978) suggested the use of deferred splitting in his original paper on dynamic hashing but found the results of some preliminary simulations of the idea to be disappointing. Scholl (1981) developed a refinement of this idea in which overflow buckets are shared. Master's thesis research by Chang (1985) tested Scholl's suggestions empirically and found that it was possible to achieve storage utilization of about 81 percent while maintaining search performance in the range of 1.1 seeks per search. Veklerov (1985) suggested using buddy buckets for overflow rather than allocating chains of new buckets. This is an attractive suggestion, since splitting buckets without buddies can never cause a doubling of the directory in extendible hashing. Veklerov obtained storage utilization of about 76 percent with a bucket size of 8.

S U M M A R Y

Conventional, static hashing does not adapt well to file structures that are *dynamic,* that grow and shrink over time. Extendible hashing is one of several hashing systems that allow the address space for hashing to grow and shrink along with the file. Because the size of the address space can grow as the file grows, it is possible for extendible hashing to provide hashed access without the need for overflow handling, even as files grow many times beyond their original expected size.

The key to extendible hashing is using more bits of the hashed value as we need to cover more address space. The model for extending the use of the hashed value is the *trie:* every time we use another bit of the hashed value, we have added another level to the depth of a trie with a radix of 2.

In extendible hashing we fill out all the leaves of the trie until we have a perfect tree, then we collapse that tree into a one-dimensional array. The array forms a directory to the buckets, kept on disk, that hold the keys and records. The directory is managed in memory, if possible.

If we add a record and there is no room for it in a bucket, we split the bucket. We use 1 additional bit from the hash values for the keys in the bucket to divide the keys between the old bucket and the new one. If the address space represented in the directory can cover the use of this new bit, no more changes are necessary. If, however, the address space is using fewer bits than are needed by our splitting buckets, then we double the address space to accommodate the use of the new bit.

Deletion reverses the addition process, recognizing that it is possible to combine the records for two buckets only if they are *buddy* buckets, which is to say that they are the pair of buckets that resulted from a split.

Access performance for extendible hashing is a single seek if the directory can be kept in memory. If the directory must be paged off to disk, worst-case performance is two seeks. Space utilization for the buckets is approximately 69 percent. Tables and an approximation formula developed by Flajolet (1983) permit estimation of the probable directory size, given a bucket size and total number of records.

There are a number of other approaches to the problem solved by extendible hashing. *Dynamic hashing* uses a very similar approach but expresses the directory as a linked structure rather than as an array. The linked structure is more cumbersome but grows more smoothly. Space utilization and seek performance for dynamic hashing are the same as for extendible hashing.

Linear hashing does away with the directory entirely, extending the address space by adding new buckets in a linear sequence. Although the overflow of a bucket can be used to trigger extension of the address space in linear hashing, typically the bucket that overflows is not the one that is split and extended. Consequently, linear hashing implies maintaining overflow chains and a consequent degradation in seek performance. The degradation is slight, since the chains typically do not grow to be very long before they are pulled into a new bucket. Space utilization is about 60 percent.

Space utilization for extendible, dynamic, and linear hashing can be improved by postponing the splitting of buckets. This is easy to implement for linear hashing, since there are already overflow buckets. Using deferred splitting, it is possible to increase space utilization for any of the hashing schemes described here to 80 percent or better while still maintaining search performance averaging less than two seeks. Overflow handling for these approaches can use the sharing of overflow buckets.

KEY TERMS

Buddy bucket. Given a bucket with an address *uvwxy,* where *u, v, w, x,* and *y* have values of either *0* or *1,* the buddy bucket, if it exists, has the value *uvwxz,* such that

$$z = y \, \mathrm{XOR} \, 1$$

Buddy buckets are important in deletion operations for extendible hashing because, if enough keys are deleted, the contents of buddy buckets can be combined into a single bucket.

Deferred splitting. It is possible to improve space utilization for *dynamic hashing, extendible hashing,* and *linear hashing* by postponing, or deferring, the splitting of buckets, placing records into overflow buckets instead. This is a classic space/time trade-off in which we accept diminished performance in return for more compact storage.

Directory. Conventional, static hashing schemes transform a key into a bucket address. Both *extendible hashing* and *dynamic hashing* introduce an additional layer of indirection, in which the key is hashed to a *directory address.* The directory, in turn, contains information about the location of the bucket. This additional indirection makes it possible to extend the address space by extending the directory rather than having to work with an address space made up of buckets.

Dynamic hashing. Used in a generic sense, *dynamic hashing* can refer to any hashing system that provides for expansion and contraction of the address space for dynamic files where the number of records changes over time. In this chapter we use the term in a more specific sense to refer to a system initially described by Larson (1978). The system uses a directory to provide access to the buckets that contain the records. Cells in the directory can be used as root nodes of *trie* structures that accommodate greater numbers of buckets as buckets split.

Extendible hashing. Like *dynamic hashing, extendible hashing* is sometimes used to refer to any hashing scheme that allows the address space to grow and shrink so it can be used in dynamic file systems. Used more precisely, as it is used in this chapter, *extendible hashing* refers to an approach to hashed retrieval for dynamic files that was first proposed by Fagin, Nievergelt, Pippenger, and Strong (1979). Their proposal is for a system that uses a directory to represent the address space. Access to buckets containing the records is through the directory. The directory is handled as an array; the size of the array can be doubled or halved as the number of buckets changes.

Linear hashing. An approach to hashing for dynamic files that was first proposed by Litwin (1980). Unlike *extendible hashing* and *dynamic hashing,* linear hashing does not use a directory. Instead, the address space is extended one bucket at a time as buckets overflow. Because the extension of the address space does not necessarily correspond to the bucket that is overflowing, linear hashing necessarily involves the use of overflow buckets, even as the address space expands.

Splitting. The hashing schemes described in this chapter make room for new records by splitting buckets to form new buckets, then extending the address space to cover these buckets. Conventional, static hashing schemes rely strictly on overflow buckets without extending the address space.

Trie. A search tree structure in which each successive character of the key is used to determine the direction of the search at each successive level of the tree. The branching factor (the *radix* of the trie) at any level is potentially equal to the number of values that the character can take.

FURTHER READINGS

For information about hashing for dynamic files that goes beyond what we present here, you must turn to journal articles. The best summary of the different approaches is Enbody and Du's *Computing Surveys* article titled "Dynamic Hashing Schemes," which appeared in 1988.

The original paper on extendible hashing is "Extendible Hashing— A Fast Access Method for Dynamic Files" by Fagin, Nievergelt, Pippenger, and Strong (1979). Larson (1978) introduces dynamic hashing in an article titled "Dynamic Hashing." Litwin's initial paper on linear hashing is titled "Linear Hashing: A New Tool for File and Table Addressing" (1980). All three of these introductory articles are quite readable; Larson's paper and Fagin, Nievergelt, Pippenger, and Strong are especially recommended.

Michel Scholl's 1981 paper titled "New File Organizations Based on Dynamic Hashing" provides another readable introduction to dynamic hashing. It also investigates implementations that defer splitting by allowing buckets to overflow.

Papers analyzing the performance of dynamic or extendible hashing often derive results that apply to either of the two methods. Flajolet (1983) presents a careful analysis of directory depth and size. Mendelson (1982) arrives at similar results and goes on to discuss the costs of retrieval and deletion as different design parameters are changed. Veklerov (1985) analyzes the performance of dynamic hashing when splitting is deferred by allowing records to overflow into a buddy bucket. His results can be applied to extendible hashing as well.

After introducing dynamic hashing, Larson wrote a number of papers building on the ideas associated with linear hashing. His 1980 paper titled "Linear Hashing with Partial Expansions" introduces an approach to linear hashing that can avoid the uneven distribution of the lengths of overflow chains across the cells in the address space. He followed up with a performance analysis in a 1982 paper titled "Performance Analysis of Linear Hashing with Partial Expansions." A subsequent, 1985 paper titled "Linear Hashing with Overflow—Handling by Linear Probing" introduces a method of handling overflow that does not involve chaining.

EXERCISES

1. Briefly describe the differences between extendible hashing, dynamic hashing, and linear hashing. What are the strengths and weaknesses of each approach?

2. The tries that are the basis for the extendible hashing procedure described in this chapter have a radix of 2. How does performance change if we use a larger radix?

3. In the `MakeAddress` function, what would happen if we did not reverse the order of the bits but just extracted the required number of low-order bits in the same left-to-right order that they occur in the address? Think about the way the directory location would change as we extend the implicit trie structure to use yet another bit.

4. If the language that you are using to implement the `MakeAddress` function does not support bit shifting and masking operations, how could you achieve the same ends, even if less elegantly and clearly?

5. In the method `Bucket::Split`, we redistribute keys between the original bucket and a new one. How do you decide whether a key belongs in the new bucket or the original bucket?

6. Suppose the redistribution of keys in `Bucket::Split` does not result in moving any keys into the new bucket. Under what conditions could such an event happen? How do the methods of classes `Bucket` and `Directory` handle this?

7. The `Bucket::TryCombine` function is potentially recursive. In section 12.4.4 we described a situation in which there are empty buckets that can be combined with other buckets through a series of recursive calls to `TryCombine`. Describe two situations that could produce empty buckets in the hash structure.

8. Deletion occasionally results in collapsing the directory. Describe the conditions that must be met before the directory can collapse. What methods in classes `Bucket` and `Directory` detect these conditions?

9. Deletion depends on finding buddy buckets. Why does the address depth for a bucket have to be the same as the address depth for the directory in order for a bucket to have a buddy?

10. In the extendible hashing procedure described in this chapter, the directory can occasionally point to empty buckets. Describe two situations that can produce empty buckets. How could we modify the methods to avoid empty buckets?

11. If buckets are large, a bucket containing only a few records is not much less wasteful than an empty bucket. How could we minimize *nearly empty* buckets?

12. Linear hashing makes use of overflow records. Assuming an uncontrolled splitting implementation in which we split and extend the address space as soon as we have an overflow, what is the effect of using different bucket sizes for the overflow buckets? For example, consider overflow buckets that are as large as the original buckets. Now consider overflow buckets that can hold only one record. How does this choice affect performance in terms of space utilization and access time?

13. In section 12.6.3 we described an approach to linear hashing that controls splitting. For a load factor of 85 percent, the average number of accesses for a successful search is 1.20 (Litwin, 1980). Unsuccessful searches require an average of 1.78 accesses. Why is the average search length greater for unsuccessful searches?

14. Because linear hashing splits one bucket at a time, in order, until it has reached the end of the sequence, the overflow chains for the last buckets in the sequence can become much longer than those for the earlier buckets. Read about Larson's approach to solving this problem through the use of "partial expansions," originally described in Larson (1980) and subsequently summarized in Enbody and Du (1988). Write a pseudocode description of linear hashing with partial expansions, paying particular attention to how addressing is handled.

15. In section 12.6.3 we discussed different mechanisms for deferring the splitting of buckets in extendible hashing in order to increase storage utilization. What is the effect of using smaller overflow buckets rather than larger ones? How does using smaller overflow buckets compare with sharing overflow buckets?

PROGRAMMING EXERCISES

16. Write a version of the `MakeAddress` function that prints out the input key, the hash value, and the extracted, reversed address. Build a driver that allows you to enter keys interactively for this function and see the results. Study the operation of the function on different keys.

18. Implement method `Directory::Delete`. Write a driver program to verify that your implementation is correct. Experiment with the program to see how deletion works. Try deleting all the keys. Try to create situations in which the directory will recursively collapse over more than one level.

19. Design and implement a class `HashedFile` patterned after class `TextIndexedFile` of Chapter 7 and Appendix G. A `HashedFile` object is a data file and an extendible hash directory. The class should have methods `Create`, `Open`, `Close`, `Read` (read record that matches key), `Append`, and `Update`.

PROGRAMMING PROJECT

This is the last part of the programming project. We create a hashed index of the student record files and the course registration files from the programming project of Chapter 4. This project depends on the successful completion of exercise 19.

20. Use class `HashedFile` to create a hashed index of a student record file with student identifier as key. Note that the student identifier field is not unique in a student registration file. Write a driver program to create a hashed file from an existing student record file.

21. Use class `HashedFile` to create a hashed index of a course registration record file with student identifier as key. Write a driver program to create a hashed file from an existing course registration record file.

22. Write a program that opens a hashed student file and a hashed course registration file and retrieves information on demand. Prompt a user for a student identifier and print all objects that match it.

Designing File Structures for CD-ROM

❖ Show how to apply good file structure design principles to develop solutions that are appropriate to this new medium.

❖ Describe the directory structure of the CD-ROM file system and show how it grows from the characteristics of the medium.

A.1   Using This Appendix

The purpose of this appendix is to use the problem of designing file structures for CD-ROM to review many of the design issues and techniques presented in the text. Section 3.6, "CD-ROM Strengths and Weaknesses," included an introduction to CD-ROM and enumerated the features that make file structure design for CD-ROM a different problem from file structure design for magnetic media.

In this appendix, we provide a high-level look at how the performance of CD-ROM affects the design of tree structures, hashed indexes, and directory structures that are stored on discs. These discussions of trees and hashing do not present new information; they review material that has already been developed in detail. Since you already have the tools required to think through these design problems, we introduce exercises and questions throughout this discussion rather than hold them to the end. We encourage you to stop at these blocks of questions, think carefully about the answers, then compare results with the discussion that follows.

A.2   Tree Structures on CD-ROM

A.2.1 Design Exercises

Tree structures are a good way to organize indexes and data on CD-ROM. Chapters 9 and 10 took a close look at B-trees and B$^+$ trees. Before we discuss the effective use of trees on CD-ROM, think through these design questions:

1. How big should the block size be for B-trees and B$^+$ trees?

2. How far should you go in the direction of using virtual tree structures? How much memory should you set aside for buffering blocks?

3. How could you use special loading procedures to advantage in a B$^+$ tree implementation? Are there similar procedures that will assist in the loading of B-trees?

4. Suppose we have a primary index and several secondary indexes to a set of records. How should you organize these access mechanisms for CD-ROM? Address the issues of binding and pinned records in your reply.

A.2.2 Block Size

Avoiding seeks is the key strategy in CD-ROM file structure design. Consequently, B-tree and B$^+$ tree structures are good choices for implementing index structures on CD-ROM. As we showed in Chapters 9 and 10, given a large enough block size, B-trees and B$^+$ trees can provide access to a large number of records in only a few seeks.

How large should the block size be? The answer, of course, depends on the application, but it is possible to provide some general guidelines. First, since the sector size of the CD-ROM is 2 kilobytes, the block size should not be less than 2 kilobytes. A sector is the smallest addressable unit on the disc; consequently, it does not make sense to read in anything less than a sector. Since the CD-ROM's sequential reading performance is moderately fast, especially when viewed relative to its seeking performance, it is usually attractive to use a block composed of several sectors. Once you have spent the better part of a second seeking for the sector and reading it, reading an additional 6 kilobytes to make an 8-kilobyte block takes only an additional 40 msec. If this added fraction of a second can contribute to avoiding another seek, it is time well spent.

Table A.1 shows the maximum number of 32-byte records that can be contained in a B-tree as the tree changes in height and block size. The dramatic effect of block size on the record counts for two- and three-level trees suggests that large tree structures should usually use at least an 8-kilobyte block.

A.2.3 Special Loading Procedures and Other Considerations

B+ trees are commonly used in CD-ROM applications because they provide both indexed and sequential access to records. If, for example, you are building a telephone directory system for CD-ROM, you will need an index that can provide fast access to any one of the millions of names that appear on the disc. You will also want to provide sequential access so that once users have found a name, they can browse through records with the same name and check addresses to make sure they have the right phone number.

B+ trees are also attractive in CD-ROM applications because they can provide very shallow, broad indexes to a set of sequenced records. As we showed in Chapter 10, the content of the index part of a B+ tree can consist of nothing more than the shortest separators required to provide access to lower levels of the tree and, ultimately, to the target records. If these shortest separators are only a few bytes long, as is frequently the case, it is often possible to provide access to millions of records with an index that is only two levels deep. An application can keep the root of this index in RAM, reducing the cost of searching the index part of the tree to a single seek. With one additional seek we are at the record in the sequence set.

Another attractive feature of B+ trees is that it is easy to build a two-level index above the sequence set with a separate loading procedure that

Table A.1 The maximum number of 32-byte records that can be stored in a B-tree of given height and block size.

	Tree height		
	One level	*Two levels*	*Three levels*
Block size = 2 K	64	4096	262 144
Block size = 4 K	128	16 384	2 097 152
Block size = 8 K	256	65 536	16 777 216

builds the tree from the bottom up. We described this operation in Chapter 10. The great advantage of this kind of loading procedure, as opposed to building the tree through a series of top-down insertions, is that we can pack the nodes and leaves of the tree as fully as we wish. With CD-ROM, where the cost of additional seeks is so high and where there is absolutely no possibility that anyone will make additional insertions to the tree, we will want to pack the nodes and leaves of the tree so they are completely full. This is an example of a design decision recognizing that the CD-ROM is a publishing medium that, once constructed, is used only for retrieval and never for additional storage.

This kind of special, 100 percent-full loading procedure can also be designed for B-tree applications. The procedure for B-trees is usually somewhat more complex because the index will often consist of more than just a root node and one level of children. The loading procedure for B-trees has to manage more levels of the tree at a time.

This discussion of indexes, and the importance of packing them as tightly as possible, brings home one of the interesting paradoxes of CD-ROM design. The CD-ROM has a relatively large storage capacity that usually gives us a great deal of freedom with regard to how we store data on the disc; a few bytes here or there usually doesn't matter much when you have 600 megabytes of capacity. But when we design the index structures for CD-ROM, we find ourselves counting bytes, sometimes even counting bits, as we pack information into a single byte or integer. The reason for this is not, in most cases, that we are running out of space on the disc, but that packing the index tightly can often save us from making an additional seek. In CD-ROM file design, the cost of seeks adds up very quickly; the designer needs to get as much information out of every seek as possible.

A.2.4 Virtual Trees and Buffering Blocks

Given the very high cost of seeking on CD-ROM, we want to keep blocks in RAM for as long as they are likely to be useful. The tree's root node should always be buffered. As we indicated in our discussion of virtual trees in Chapter 9, buffering nodes below the root can sometimes contribute significantly to reducing seek time, particularly when the buffering is intelligent in selecting the node to replace in the buffer. Buffering is most useful when successive accesses to the tree tend to be clustered in one area.

Note that packing the tree as tightly as possible during loading, which we discussed earlier as a way to reduce tree height, also increases the likelihood that an index block in RAM will be useful on successive accesses to the data.

A.2.5 Trees as Secondary Indexes on CD-ROM

Typically, CD-ROM applications provide more than one access route to the data on the disc. For example, document retrieval applications usually give direct access to the documents, so you can page through them in sequence or call them up by name, chapter, or section while also providing access through an index of keywords or included terms. Similarly, in a telephone directory application you would have access to the database by name, but also by location (state, city, zip code, street address). As we described in Chapter 7, secondary indexes provide these multiple views of the data.

Chapter 6 raised the design issue of whether the secondary indexes should be tightly bound to the records they point to or whether the binding should take place at retrieval time, through the use of a common key accessed through yet another index. Viewed another way, the issue is whether the target records should be pinned to a specific location through references in secondary indexes or whether they should be left unpinned so they can be reorganized.

Records will never be reorganized on a CD-ROM; since it is a read-only disc, there is no disadvantage to having pinned records. Further, minimizing the number of seeks is the overriding design consideration on CD-ROM. Consequently, secondary index designs for CD-ROM should usually bind the indexes to the target records as tightly as possible, ensuring that once you have found the correct place in the index, you are ready to retrieve the target with, at most, one additional seek.

One objection to this bind-tightly approach to CD-ROM index design is that, although it is true that the indexes cannot be reorganized once written to the CD-ROM, they are, in fact, quite frequently reorganized between successive "editions" of the disc. Many CD-ROM publications are reissued to keep them up to date. The period between successive versions may be years, or may be as short as a week. So, although pinned records cause no problem on the finished disc, they may cause a great deal of difficulty in the files used to prepare the disc.

There are a number of approaches to resolving this tension between what is best on the published disc and what is best for the files used to produce it. One solution is to maintain loosely bound records in the source database, transforming them to tightly bound records for publication on CD-ROM. CD-ROM product designers often fail to realize that the file structures placed on the disc can, and often should, be different from the structures used to maintain the source data and produce the discs. Another solution, of course, is to trade off performance on the published disc for decreased costs in producing it. Production costs, time constraints, user acceptance, and competitive factors interact to determine which course is best. The key issue from the file designer's standpoint is to recognize that the alternatives exist and then be able to quantify the costs and benefits of each.

A.3 Hashed Files on CD-ROM

A.3.1 Design Exercises

Hashing, with its promise of single access retrieval, is an excellent way to organize indexes on CD-ROM. We begin with some design questions that intersect your knowledge of hashing with what you now know about CD-ROM. As you think through your answers, remember that your goal should be to avoid any additional seeking due to hash bucket overflow. As in any hashing design problem, the design parameters that you can manipulate are

- Bucket size;
- Packing density for the hashed index; and
- The hash function itself.

The following questions, which you should try to answer before you read on, encourage you to think about ways to use these parameters to build efficient CD-ROM applications.

1. What considerations go into choosing a bucket size?
2. How does the relatively large storage capacity of CD-ROM assist in developing efficient hashed retrieval?
3. Since a CD-ROM is read-only, you have a complete list of the keys to be hashed before you create the disc. How can this assist in reducing retrieval costs?

A.3.2 Bucket Size

In Chapter 11 we showed how to reduce overflow, and therefore retrieval time, by grouping records into *buckets,* so each hashed address references an entire bucket of records. Since any access to a CD-ROM always reads in a minimum of a 2-kilobyte sector, the bucket size should be a multiple of 2 kilobytes. Having the bucket be only a part of a sector would be counterproductive. As we described in Chapter 3, transferring anything less than a sector means first moving the data into a system buffer, and from there into the user's data area. With transfers of a complete sector, many operating systems can move the data directly into the user area.

How many sectors should go into a bucket? As with trees, it is a trade-off between seeking and sequential reading. In addition, larger buckets require more searching and comparing to find the record once the bucket is read into RAM. In Chapter 11 we provided tools to allow you to calculate the effect of bucket size on the probability of overflow. For CD-ROM applications, you will want to use these tools to reduce the probability of overflow to almost nothing.

A.3.3 How the Size of CD-ROM Helps

Packing a hashed file loosely is another way to avoid overflow and additional seeking. A good rule of thumb is that, even with only a moderate bucket size, keeping the packing density below 60 percent will tend to avoid overflow almost all the time. By consulting Tables 11.4 and 11.5 in Chapter 11, we see that for randomly distributed keys, a packing density of 60 percent and a bucket size of 10 will reduce the percentage of records that overflow to 1.3 percent and will reduce the average number of seeks required for a successful search to 1.01.

When there is unused space available on the disc, there is no disadvantage to expanding the size of the hashed index, so overflow is virtually eliminated.

A.3.4 Advantages of CD-ROM's Read-Only Status

What if space is at a premium on the CD-ROM disc and you need to find a way to pack your index so it is 90 percent full? Despite the relatively large capacity of CD-ROM discs, this situation is fairly common. Large text file collections often use most of the disc just for text. If the product is storing digitized images along with the text, the available space disappears even more quickly. Applications requiring the use of two discs at once are much harder to sell and deliver than a single disc application; when a disc is already nearly full of data, the index files are always a target for size reduction.

The calculations that we do to estimate the effects of bucket size and packing density assume a *random* distribution of keys across the address space. If we could find a hash function that would distribute the keys *uniformly,* rather than randomly, we could achieve 100 percent packing density and no overflow.

Once again, the fact that CD-ROM is read-only opens up possibilities that would not be available in a dynamic, read-write environment. When we produce a CD-ROM, we have all the keys that are to be hashed at hand. This means that we do not have to choose a hash function and then settle for whatever distribution of keys that it produces, hoping for the best but expecting a distribution that is merely random. Instead, we can select a hash function that provides the performance we need, given the set of keys we have to hash. If our performance and space constraints require it, we can develop a hash function that produces no overflow even at very high packing densities. We identify the selected hash function on the disc, along with the data, so the retrieval software knows how to locate the keys. This relatively expensive and time-consuming function-fitting effort is worthwhile because of the asymmetric nature of writing and reading CD-ROMs; the one-time effort spent in making the disc is paid back many times as the disc is distributed to many users.

A.4 The CD-ROM File System

A.4.1 The Problem

When the firms involved in developing CD-ROM applications began work on a common file system in late 1985, they were confronted with an interesting file structures problem. The design goals and constraints included the following:

- Support hierarchical directory structures; find and open any one of thousands of files with only one or two seeks; and

- Support the use of *generic* file names, as in "file*.c", during directory access.

The usual way to support hierarchical directories is to treat the directories as nothing more than a special kind of file. If, using Unix notation, you are looking for a file with the full path

```
/usr/home/mydir/filebook/cdrom/part3.txt
```

you look in the root directory (/) to find the directory file *usr*, then you open *usr* to find the location of the directory file *home*, you seek to *home* and open it to find *mydir*, and so on until you finally open the directory file named *cdrom*, where you find the location of the target file *part3.txt*. This is a very simple, flexible system; it is the approach used in MS-DOS, Unix, VMS, and many other operating systems. The problem, from the standpoint of a CD-ROM developer, is that before we can find the location of *part3.txt*, we must seek to, open, and use six other files. At a half-second per seek on CD-ROM, such a directory structure results in a very unresponsive file system.

A.4.2 Design Exercise

At the time of the initial meetings for looking at a standard CD-ROM directory structure and file system, a number of vendors were using this treat-directories-as-files approach, literally replicating magnetic disc directory systems on CD-ROM. There were at least two alternative approaches that were commercially available and more specifically tailored to CD-ROM. One placed the entire directory structure in a single file, building a *left child, right sibling* tree to express the directory structure. Given the directory hierarchy in Fig. A.1, this system produced a file containing the tree shown in Fig. A.2. The other system created an index to the file locations by hashing the full path names of each file. The entries in the hash table for the directory structure in Fig. A.1 are shown in Fig. A.3 (page 576).

Considering what you know about CD-ROM (slow seeking, read-only, and so on), think about these alternative file systems and try to answer the following questions. Keep in mind the design goals and constraints that were facing the committee (hierarchical structure, fast access to thousands of files, use of generic file names).

1. List the advantages and disadvantages of each system.
2. Try to come up with an alternative approach that combines the best features of the other systems while minimizing the disadvantages.

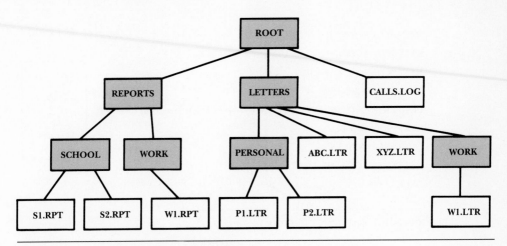

Figure A.1 A sample directory hierarchy.

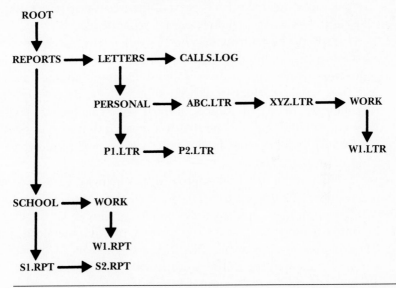

Figure A.2 Left child, right sibling tree to express directory structure.

A.4.3 A Hybrid Design

Placing the entire directory structure into a single file, as with the left-child, right sibling tree, works well as long as the directory structure is small. If the file containing the tree fits into a few kilobytes, the entire directory structure can be held in RAM and can be accessed without any

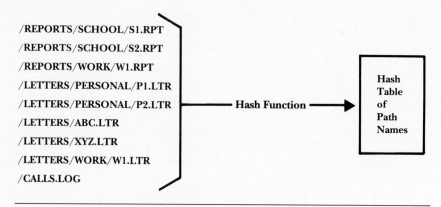

Figure A.3 A sample directory hierarchy.

seeking at all. But if the directory structure is large, containing thousands of files, accessing the various parts of the tree can require multiple seeks, just as it does when each directory is a separate file.

Hashing the path names, on the other hand, provides single-seek access to any file but does a very poor job of supporting generic file and directory names, such as *prog**.c, or even a simple command such as *ls* or *dir,* to list all the files in a given subdirectory. By definition, hashing randomizes the distribution of the keys, scattering them over the directory space. Finding all of the files in a given subdirectory, say the *letters* subdirectory for the tree shown in Fig. A.1, requires a sequential reading of the entire directory.

What about a hybrid approach, in which we build a conventional directory structure that uses a file for each directory, and then supplement this by building a hashed index to all the files in all directories? This approach allows us to get to any subdirectory, and therefore to the information required to open a file, with a single seek. At the same time, it provides us with the ability to work with the files inside each directory, using generic file names and commands such as *ls* and *dir.* In short, we build a conventional directory structure to get all the advantages of that approach, then solve the access problem by building an index for the subdirectories.

This is very close to the approach that the committee settled on. But they went one step further. Since the directory structure is a highly organized, hierarchical collection of files, the committee decided to use a special index that takes advantage of that hierarchy rather than simply hash the path names of the subdirectories. Figure A.4 shows what this

```
RRN                 Parent
0     Root          -1
1     Reports        0
2     Letters        0
3     School         1
4     Work           1
5     Personal       2
6     Work           2
```

Figure A.4 Path index table of directories.

index structure looks like when it is applied to the directory structure in Fig. A.1. Only the directories are listed in the index; access to the data files is through the directory files. The directories are ordered in the index so parents always appear before their children. Each child is associated with an integer that is a backward reference to the relative record number (RRN) of the parent. This allows us to distinguish between the WORK directory under REPORTS and the WORK directory under LETTERS. It also allows us to traverse the directory structure, moving both up and down with a command such as the *cd* command in DOS or Unix, without having to access the directory files on the CD-ROM. It is a good example of a specialized index structure that makes use of the organization inherent in the data to produce a very compact, highly functional access mechanism.

SUMMARY

B-tree and B+ tree structures work well on CD-ROM because of their ability to provide access to many keys with just a few seeks. Because the sector size on CD-ROM is 2 kilobytes, the block size used in a tree should be 2 kilobytes or an even multiple of this sector size. Because CD-ROM drives seek so slowly, it is usually advantageous to use larger blocks consisting of 8 kilobytes or more. Since no additions or deletions will be made to a tree once it is on CD-ROM, it is useful to build the trees from the bottom up so the blocks are completely filled. When using trees to create secondary indexes, the read-only nature of CD-ROM makes it possible to bind the indexes tightly to the target data, pinning the index records to reduce seeking and increase performance.

Hashed indexes are often a good choice for CD-ROM because they can provide single-seek access to target information. As with trees, the 2-kilobyte sector size affects the design of the hashed index: the bucket size should be 1 or more full sectors. Since CD-ROMs are large, there is often enough space on the disc to permit use of packing densities of 60 percent or less for the hashed index. Use of packing densities of less than 60 percent, combined with a bucket size of 10 or more records, results in single-seek access for almost all records. But it is not always possible to pack the index this loosely. Higher packing densities can be accommodated without loss of performance if we tailor the hash function to the records in the index, using a function that provides a more nearly uniform distribution. Since we know that there will be no deletions or additions to the index, and since time spent optimizing the index will result in benefits again and again as the discs are used, it is often worthwhile to invest the effort in finding the best of several hash functions. This is especially true when we need to support higher packing densities of 90 percent or more.

In 1985 companies trying to build the CD-ROM publishing market faced an interesting file structure problem. They realized that they needed a common directory structure and file system for CD-ROM. At the time, there were no directory structure designs in use on CD-ROM that provided nearly optimal performance across a wide variety of applications.

Directory structures are usually implemented as a series of files. Moving from a directory to a subdirectory beneath it means seeking to another file. This is not a good design for CD-ROM, since it could result in a wait of several seconds just to locate and open a single file. Simple alternatives, such as putting the entire directory structure in a single file or hashing the path names of all the files on a disc, have other drawbacks. The committee charged with solving this problem emerged with a design that combined a conventional hierarchical directory of files with an index to the directory. The index makes use of the structure inherent in the directory hierarchy to provide a very compact, yet functional map of the directory structure. Typical of other CD-ROM indexing problems, this directory index illustrates the importance of building indexes very tightly on CD-ROM, despite the vast, often unused capacity of the CD-ROM disc. Tight, dense indexes work better on CD-ROM because they require fewer seeks to access. Avoiding seeks is the key consideration for all CD-ROM file structure design.

ASCII Table

	Dec.	Oct.	Hex.		Dec.	Oct.	Hex.		Dec.	Oct.	Hex.		Dec.	Oct.	Hex.
nul	0	0	0	sp	32	40	20	@	64	100	40	`	96	140	60
sol	1	1	1	!	33	41	21	A	65	101	41	a	97	141	61
stx	2	2	2	"	34	42	22	B	66	102	42	b	98	142	62
etx	3	3	3	#	35	43	23	C	67	103	43	c	99	143	63
eot	4	4	4	$	36	44	24	D	68	104	44	d	100	144	64
enq	5	5	5	%	37	45	25	E	69	105	45	e	101	145	65
ack	6	6	6	&	38	46	26	F	70	106	46	f	102	146	66
bel	7	7	7	'	39	47	27	G	71	107	47	g	103	147	67
bs	8	10	8	(	40	50	28	H	72	110	48	h	104	150	68
ht	9	11	9	)	41	51	29	I	73	111	49	i	105	151	69
nl	10	12	A	*	42	52	2A	J	74	112	4A	j	106	152	6A
vt	11	13	B	+	43	53	2B	K	75	113	4B	k	107	153	6B
np	12	14	C	,	44	54	2C	L	76	114	4C	l	108	154	6C
cr	13	15	D	–	45	55	2D	M	77	115	4D	m	109	155	6D
so	14	16	E	.	46	56	2E	N	78	116	4E	n	110	156	6E
si	15	17	F	/	47	57	2F	O	79	117	4F	o	111	157	6F
dle	16	20	10	0	48	60	30	P	80	120	50	p	112	160	70
dc1	17	21	11	1	49	61	31	Q	81	121	51	q	113	161	71
dc2	18	22	12	2	50	62	32	R	82	122	52	r	114	162	72
dc3	19	23	13	3	51	63	33	S	83	123	53	s	115	163	73
dc4	20	24	14	4	52	64	34	T	84	124	54	t	116	164	74
nak	21	25	15	5	53	65	35	U	85	125	55	u	117	165	75
syn	22	26	16	6	54	66	36	V	86	126	56	v	118	166	76
etb	23	27	17	7	55	67	37	W	87	127	57	w	119	167	77
can	24	30	18	8	56	70	38	X	88	130	58	x	120	170	78
em	25	31	19	9	57	71	39	Y	89	131	59	y	121	171	79
sub	26	32	1A	:	58	72	3A	Z	90	132	5A	z	122	172	7A
esc	27	33	1B	;	59	73	3B	[	91	133	5B	{	123	173	7B
fs	28	34	1C	<	60	74	3C	\	92	134	5C	|	124	174	7C
gs	29	35	1D	=	61	75	3D	]	93	135	5D	}	125	175	7D
rs	30	36	1E	>	62	76	3E	^	94	136	5E	~	126	176	7E
us	31	37	1F	?	63	77	3F	–	95	137	5F	del	127	177	7F

Formatted Output with C++ Stream Classes

Classes `istream` and `ostream` have a variety of methods that control the formatting of the text input and output operations. In this appendix, we concentrate on the output operations of class `ostream`.

Each insertion (<<) operator converts a value into formatted text according to default rules. Classes `ios` and `ostream` allow a programmer to exert more control over the format of output by overriding the default rules.

Class `ios` contains members that hold information about the base (octal, decimal, or hexadecimal) to be used when writing integers, the precision of floating-point numbers, and the width of fields. It also includes functions to set and examine these stream-control variables. The following methods are included in class `ios`.

```
int width(int _i); // set field width
char fill(char _c); // set fill character
int precision(int _i); // set precision
```

Each of the methods specifies a characteristic of the next numeric (or string) output operation.

A variety of other characteristics can be specified by setting flags. An advantage of using flags is that the values remain set until they are explicitly changed. The following enumeration type has the available values for flags.

```
enum {
    skipws      = 0x0001,    // skip whitespace on input
                             // strategies for padding to width
    left        = 0x0002,    // padding after value
    right       = 0x0004,    // padding before value
    internal    = 0x0008,    // padding between sign and value

                             // bases for integer values
    dec         = 0x0010,
    oct         = 0x0020,
    hex         = 0x0040,

    showbase    = 0x0080,    // include integer base in output
    showpoint   = 0x0100,    // print trailing zeros
    uppercase   = 0x0200,    // use uppercase in hex and float
    showpos     = 0x0400,    // explicit '+' for integer
    scientific  = 0x0800,    // .dddddd Edd
    fixed       = 0x1000,    // dddd.dd
    unitbuf     = 0x2000,    // flush output after each operation
    stdio       = 0x4000     // flush output after each character
};
```

Each of these values is represented by a single bit in a long value. These values can be combined with an *or* operation and passed to the `setf` method to turn flags on and to `unsetf` to turn flags off. There is another version of `setf` that uses two parameters to allow the setting of flags that are restricted to specific types of output. For example, the following code:

```
cout.setf(ios::left,ios::adjustfield); // left justify all
cout.fill("#"); // set fill for next field
cout.width(6); // set width for next field
cout << 1272 << ",04/02/97,"; // two fields
cout.width(6);
cout<<"Rent"; // still left justified
cout.setf(ios::right,ios::floatfield);// right justify float
cout.precision(2);
cout.width(8);
cout << -500.0 << ',' << endl;
```

Produces the following output line with the values 1272 and "Rent" left justified, and −500.00 right justified:

```
##1272,04/02/97,Rent    ,  -500.00,
```

A more reliable and more system-independent style of controlling output format is to use I/O manipulators (in file `iomanip.h`), that allow formatting operations to be inserted directly in a list of input or output operations. Setting the width (using `setw`) and precision (using `setprecision`) of a floating point field can be done in a single statement:

```
cout << setw(8) << setprecision(2) << -500.00;
```

A manipulator is a function that takes a stream as input and produces a stream as output. The manipulator works by modifying the characteristics of the stream. Manipulator `endl`, for instance, is defined as

```
ostream & endl (ostream &);
```

It accepts an `ostream` as input, inserts a new line, calls the `flush()` function, and returns a reference to the `ostream`.

As programmers, we can take advantage of the manipulators that are defined in the standard library and we can create new manipulators that work to our own specifications. The file `ledger.cpp` in Appendix H contains examples of the use of manipulators to produce the output of Figures 8.8 and 8.11. Look at Stroustrup, *The C++ Programming Language,* second edition (1995) or third edition (1997), and Plauger, *The Draft Standard C++ Library* (1995) for more details on the creation and use of manipulators.

Simple File Input/Output Examples

D.1   Listc.cpp. Program to read and display the contents of a file using C streams

```c
// program using C streams to read characters from a file
// and write them to the terminal screen
#include <stdio.h>
main( ) {
   char ch;
   FILE * file; // file descriptor
   char filename[20];
   printf("Enter the name of the file: ");       // Step 1
   gets(filename);                                // Step 2
   file =fopen(filename, "r");                    // Step 3
   while (fread(&ch, 1, 1, file) != 0)            // Step 4a
      fwrite(&ch, 1, 1, stdout);                  // Step 4b
   fclose(file);                                  // Step 5
}
```

D.2   Listcpp.cpp. Program to read and display the contents of a file using C++ stream classes

```cpp
// list contents of file using C++ stream classes
#include <fstream.h>

void main ()
{
   char ch;
   fstream file; // declare fstream unattached
   char filename[20];
   cout <<"Enter the name of the file: "          // Step 1
     <<flush; // force output
   cin >> filename;                               // Step 2
      file . open(filename, ios::in);             // Step 3
   file . unsetf (ios::skipws);// include white space in read
   while (1)
   {
      file >> ch;                                 // Step 4a
      if (file.fail()) break;
      cout << ch;                                 // Step 4b
   }
   file . close(); // Step 5
}
```

D.3 Person.h. Definition for class Person, including code for constructor

```
class Person
{ public:
   // data members
   char LastName [11]; char FirstName [11]; char Address [16];
   char City [16]; char State [3]; char ZipCode [10];
   // method
   Person (); // default constructor
};

Person::Person ()
{//constructor, set each field to the empty string
   LastName[0]=0; FirstName[0]=0; Address[0]=0;
   City[0]=0; State[0]=0; ZipCode[0]=0;
}
```

D.4 Writestr.cpp. Write Person objects into a stream file

```
#include <fstream.h>
#include <string.h>
#include "readper.cpp"

ostream & operator << (ostream & stream, Person & p)
{ // insert fields into file
   stream << p.LastName << p.FirstName << p.Address
      << p.City << p.State << p.ZipCode;
   return stream;
}

int main (){
   char filename [20];
   Person p;
   cout << "Enter the file name:"<<flush;
   cin.getline(filename, 19);
   ofstream stream (filename, ios::out);
   if (stream.fail()) {
```

```
      cout << "File open failed!" <<endl;
      return 0;
   }
   while (1) {
      cin >> p; // read fields of person
      if (strlen(p.LastName)==0) break;
      // write person to output stream
      stream << p; // write fields of person
   }
}
```

D.5 Readdel.cpp. Read Person objects with fields delimited by '|'

```
#include <fstream.h>
#include <string.h>
#include "writeper.cpp"
istream & operator >> (istream & stream, Person & p)
{ // read fields from file
   char delim;
   stream.getline(p.LastName, 30,'|');
   if (strlen(p.LastName)==0) return stream;
   stream.getline(p.FirstName,30,'|');
   stream.getline(p.Address,30,'|');
   stream.getline(p.City, 30,'|');
   stream.getline(p.State,15,'|');
   stream.getline(p.ZipCode,10,'|');
   return stream;
}
int main (){
   char filename [20];
   Person p;
   cout << "Enter the file name:"<<flush;
   cin.getline(filename, 19);
   ifstream file (filename, ios::in);
   if (file.fail()) {
      cout << "File open failed!" <<endl;
      return 0;
   }
   while (1) {
      // read fields of person
```

```
      file >> p;
      if (strlen(p.LastName)==0) break;
      // write person to file
      cout << p;
   }
}
```

D.6   Readvar.cpp. Read variable length records and break up into Person objects

```
int ReadVariablePerson (istream & stream, Person & p)
{ // read a variable sized record from stream and store it in p
  // if read fails, set p.LastName to empty string and return 0
  short length;
  stream . read (&length, sizeof(length));
  if (stream . fail()){p.LastName[0]=0; return 0;}
  char * buffer = new char[length+1];
  stream . read (buffer, length);
  buffer [length] = 0; // terminate buffer with null
  istrstream strbuff (buffer);
  strbuff >> p;
  return 1;
}
int main (){
  char filename [20];
  Person p;
  cout << "Enter the file name:"<<flush;
  cin.getline(filename, 19);
  ifstream stream (filename, ios::in);
  if (stream.fail()) {
    cout << "File open failed!" <<endl;
    return 0;
  }
  while (1) {
    // read fields of person
    ReadVariablePerson (stream, p);
    if (strlen(p.LastName)==0) break;
    // write person to file
    cout << p;
  }
}
```

D.7   Writeper.cpp. Function to write a person to a text file

```
#include <iostream.h>
#include "person.h"

ostream & operator << (ostream & stream, Person & p)
{ // insert fields into file
   stream<< "Last Name  '" << p.LastName <<"'\n"
      << "First Name '" << p.FirstName <<"'\n"
      << "Address    '" << p.Address <<"'\n"
      << "City       '" << p.City <<"'\n"
      << "State      '" << p.State <<"'\n"
      << "Zip Code   '" << p.ZipCode <<"'\n"
      <<flush;
   return stream;
}
```

D.8   Readper.cpp. Function to prompt user and read fields of a Person

```
#include <iostream.h>
#include "person.h"

istream & operator >> (istream & stream, Person & p)
{ // read fields from input
   cout<<"Enter last name, or <cr> to end: "<<flush;
   stream.getline (p.LastName, 30);
   if (strlen(p.LastName)==0) return stream;
   cout<<"Enter first name: "<<flush; stream.getline(p.FirstName,30);
   cout<<"Enter address: "<<flush; stream.getline(p.Address,30);
   cout<<"Enter city: "<<flush; stream.getline(p.City, 30);
   cout<<"Enter state: "<<flush; stream.getline(p.State,15);
   cout<<"Enter zip code: "<<flush; stream.getline(p.ZipCode,10);
   return stream;
}
```

Classes for Buffer Manipulation

E

E.1   Person.h. Definition for class Person

```
#include <iostream.h>
#include "fixtext.h"
#include "lentext.h"
#include "deltext.h"

class Person
{public:
   char LastName [11]; char FirstName [11]; char Address [16];
   char City [16]; char State [3]; char ZipCode [10];
   Person ();
   void Clear ();
   int Unpack (LengthTextBuffer &);
   int Pack (LengthTextBuffer &) const;
   int Unpack (DelimTextBuffer &);
   int Pack (DelimTextBuffer &) const;
   int Unpack (FixedTextBuffer &);
   int Pack (FixedTextBuffer &) const;
   static int InitBuffer (FixedTextBuffer &);
   void Print (ostream &);
};
```

E.2   Person.cpp. Code for class Person

```
#include "person.h"

Person::Person ()
{ Clear ();}

void Person::Clear ()
{// set each field to an empty string
   LastName [0] = 0; FirstName [0] = 0; Address [0] = 0;
   City [0] = 0; State [0] = 0; ZipCode [0] = 0;
}

int Person::Pack (LengthTextBuffer & Buffer) const
{// pack the fields into a FixedTextBuffer,
 //return TRUE if all succeed, FALSE o/w
```

```
   int result;
   Buffer . Clear ();
   result = Buffer . Pack (LastName);
   result = result && Buffer . Pack (FirstName);
   result = result && Buffer . Pack (Address);
   result = result && Buffer . Pack (City);
   result = result && Buffer . Pack (State);
   result = result && Buffer . Pack (ZipCode);
   return result;
}

int Person::Unpack (LengthTextBuffer & Buffer)
{
   int result;
   result = Buffer . Unpack (LastName);
   result = result && Buffer . Unpack (FirstName);
   result = result && Buffer . Unpack (Address);
   result = result && Buffer . Unpack (City);
   result = result && Buffer . Unpack (State);
   result = result && Buffer . Unpack (ZipCode);
   return result;
}

int Person::Pack (DelimTextBuffer & Buffer) const
{// pack the fields into a FixedTextBuffer,
 //return TRUE if all succeed, FALSE o/w
   int result;
   Buffer . Clear ();
   result = Buffer . Pack (LastName);
   result = result && Buffer . Pack (FirstName);
   result = result && Buffer . Pack (Address);
   result = result && Buffer . Pack (City);
   result = result && Buffer . Pack (State);
   result = result && Buffer . Pack (ZipCode);
   return result;
}

int Person::Unpack (DelimTextBuffer & Buffer)
{
   int result;
   result = Buffer . Unpack (LastName);
   result = result && Buffer . Unpack (FirstName);
   result = result && Buffer . Unpack (Address);
```

```
   result = result && Buffer . Unpack (City);
   result = result && Buffer . Unpack (State);
   result = result && Buffer . Unpack (ZipCode);
   return result;
}


int Person::Pack (FixedTextBuffer & Buffer) const
{// pack the fields into a FixedTextBuffer,
 //return TRUE if all succeed, FALSE o/w
   int result;
   Buffer . Clear ();
   result = Buffer . Pack (LastName);
   result = result && Buffer . Pack (FirstName);
   result = result && Buffer . Pack (Address);
   result = result && Buffer . Pack (City);
   result = result && Buffer . Pack (State);
   result = result && Buffer . Pack (ZipCode);
   return result;
}


int Person::Unpack (FixedTextBuffer & Buffer)
{
   Clear ();
   int result;
   result = Buffer . Unpack (LastName);
   result = result && Buffer . Unpack (FirstName);
   result = result && Buffer . Unpack (Address);
   result = result && Buffer . Unpack (City);
   result = result && Buffer . Unpack (State);
   result = result && Buffer . Unpack (ZipCode);
   return result;
}


int Person::InitBuffer (FixedTextBuffer & Buffer)
// initialize a FixedTextBuffer to be used for Persons
{
   int result;
   result = Buffer . AddField (10); // LastName [11];
   result = result && Buffer . AddField (10); // FirstName [11];
   result = result && Buffer . AddField (15); // Address [16];
   result = result && Buffer . AddField (15); // City [16];
```

```
    result = result && Buffer . AddField (2);   // State [3];
    result = result && Buffer . AddField (9); // ZipCode [10];
    return result;
}

void Person::Print (ostream & stream)
{
    stream << "Person:"
        << "\t Last Name '"<<LastName<<"'\n"
        << "\tFirst Name '"<<FirstName<<"'\n"
        << "\t   Address '"<<Address<<"'\n"
        << "\t      City '"<<City<<"'\n"
        << "\t     State '"<<State<<"'\n"
        << "\t  Zip Code '"<<ZipCode<<"'\n" <<flush;
}
```

E.3   Deltext.h. Definition for class DelimitedTextBuffer

```
#include <iostream.h>

class DelimTextBuffer
// a buffer which holds delimited text fields.
{  public:
   DelimTextBuffer (char Delim = '|', int maxBytes = 1000);
       // construct with fields with delimeters
   void Clear (); // clear fields from buffer
.. int Read (istream &); int Write (ostream &) const;
   int Pack (const char *, int size = -1
   int Unpack (char *);
   void Print (ostream &) const;
   int Init (char delim, int maxBytes = 1000);
 private:
   char Delim;
   char DelimStr[2]; // zero terminated string for Delim
   char * Buffer; // character array to hold field values
   int BufferSize; // size of packed fields
   int MaxBytes; // maximum number of characters in the buffer
   int NextByte; // packing/unpacking position in buffer
};
```

E.4   Deltext.cpp. Code for class DelimitedTextBuffer

```cpp
#include "deltext.h"
#include <string.h>

DelimTextBuffer :: DelimTextBuffer (char delim, int maxBytes)
 // construct with a maximum of maxFields
{ Init (delim, maxBytes);}

void DelimTextBuffer :: Clear ()
// clear fields from buffer
{ NextField = 0; NextByte = 0; BufferSize = 0;}

int DelimTextBuffer :: Read (istream & stream)
{
   Clear ();
   stream . read (&BufferSize, sizeof(BufferSize));
   if (stream.fail()) return FALSE;
   if (BufferSize > MaxBytes) return FALSE; // buffer overflow
   stream . read (Buffer, BufferSize);
   return stream . good ();
}

int DelimTextBuffer :: Write (ostream & stream) const
{
   stream . write (&BufferSize, sizeof(BufferSize));
   stream . write (Buffer, BufferSize);
   return stream . good ();
}

int DelimTextBuffer :: Pack (const char * str, int size)
// set the value of the next field of the buffer;
// if size = -1 (default) use strlen(str) as Delim of field
{
   short len; // length of string to be packed
   if (size >= 0) len = size;
   else len = strlen (str);
   if (len > strlen(str)) // str is too short!
      return FALSE;
   int start = NextByte; // first character to be packed
```

```cpp
    NextByte += len + 1;
    if (NextByte > MaxBytes) return FALSE;
    memcpy (&Buffer[start], str, len);
    Buffer [start+len] = Delim; // add delimeter
    BufferSize = NextByte;
    return TRUE;
}

int DelimTextBuffer :: Unpack (char * str)
// extract the value of the next field of the buffer
{
    int len = -1; // length of packed string
    int start = NextByte; // first character to be unpacked
    for (int i = start; i < BufferSize; i++)
        if (Buffer[i] == Delim)
            {len = i - start; break;}
    if (len == -1) return FALSE; // delimeter not found
    NextByte += len + 1;
    if (NextByte > BufferSize) return FALSE;
    strncpy (str, &Buffer[start], len);
    str [len] = 0; // zero termination for string
    return TRUE;
}

void DelimTextBuffer :: Print (ostream & stream) const
{
    stream << "Buffer has max characters "<<MaxBytes
        <<" and Buffer Size "<<BufferSize<<endl;
}

DelimTextBuffer :: Init (char delim, int maxBytes)
 // construct with a maximum of maxFields
{
    Delim = delim;
    DelimStr[0] = Delim;
    DelimStr[1] = 0;
    if (maxBytes < 0) maxBytes = 0;
    MaxBytes = maxBytes;
    Buffer = new char[MaxBytes];
    BufferSize = 0;
}
```

E.5   Lentext.h. Definition for class LengthTextBuffer

```cpp
#include <iostream.h>

class LengthTextBuffer
// a buffer which holds length-based text fields.
{  public:
   LengthTextBuffer (int maxBytes = 1000);
      // construct with a maximum of maxFields
   void Clear (); // clear fields from buffer
   int Read (istream &);
   int Write (ostream &) const;
   int Pack (const char *, short size = -1);
      // set the value of the next field of the buffer;
   int Unpack (char *);
      // extract the value of the next field of the buffer
   void Print (ostream &) const;
   int Init (int maxBytes = 1000);
 private:
   char * Buffer; // character array to hold field values
   int BufferSize; // size of packed fields
   int MaxBytes; // maximum number of characters in the buffer
   int NextByte; // packing/unpacking position in buffer
};
```

E.6   Lentext.cpp. Code for class LengthTextBuffer

```cpp
#include "lentext.h"
#include <string.h>

LengthTextBuffer :: LengthTextBuffer (int maxBytes)
 // construct with a maximum of maxFields
{ Init (maxBytes);}

void LengthTextBuffer :: Clear ()
// clear fields from buffer
{ NextByte = 0; BufferSize = 0;}

int LengthTextBuffer :: Read (istream & stream)
{
```

```
   Clear ();
   stream . read (&BufferSize, sizeof(BufferSize));
   if (stream.fail()) return FALSE;
   if (BufferSize > MaxBytes) return FALSE; // buffer overflow
   stream . read (Buffer, BufferSize);
   return stream . good ();
}

int LengthTextBuffer :: Write (ostream & stream) const
{
   stream . write (&BufferSize, sizeof(BufferSize));
   stream . write (Buffer, BufferSize);
   return stream . good ();
}

int LengthTextBuffer :: Pack (const char * str, short size)
// set the value of the next field of the buffer;
// if size = -1 (default) use strlen(str) as length of field
{
   short len; // length of string to be packed
   if (size >= 0) len = size;
   else len = strlen (str);
   if (len > strlen(str)) // str is too short!
      return FALSE;
   int start = NextByte; // first character to be packed
   NextByte += (len + sizeof(len));
   if (NextByte > MaxBytes) return FALSE;
   memcpy (&Buffer[start], &len, sizeof(len));
   strncpy (&Buffer[start+sizeof(len)], str, len);
   BufferSize = NextByte;
   return TRUE;
}

int LengthTextBuffer :: Unpack (char * str)
// extract the value of the next field of the buffer
{
   short len; // length of packed string
   if (NextByte >= BufferSize) return FALSE; // no more fields
   int start = NextByte; // first character to be unpacked
   memcpy (&len, &Buffer[start], sizeof(short));
   NextByte += len + sizeof(short);
   if (NextByte > BufferSize) return FALSE;
   strncpy (str, &Buffer[start+sizeof(short)], len);
   str [len] = 0; // zero termination for string
```

```
    return TRUE;
}

void LengthTextBuffer :: Print (ostream & stream) const
{
    stream << "Buffer has characters "<<MaxBytes
        <<" and Buffer Size " <<BufferSize<<endl;
}

LengthTextBuffer :: Init (int maxBytes)
 // construct with a maximum of maxFields
{
    if (maxBytes < 0) maxBytes = 0;
    MaxBytes = maxBytes;
    Buffer = new char[MaxBytes];
    Clear ();
}
```

E.7   Fixtext.h. Definition for class FixedTextBuffer

```
#include <iostream.h>

class FixedTextBuffer
// a buffer which holds a specific number of
//            fixed sized text fields.
{ public:
    FixedTextBuffer (int maxFields, int maxChars = 1000);
        // construct with a maximum of maxFields
    FixedTextBuffer (int numFields, int * FieldSize);
        // construct with fields of specific size
    int NumberOfFields () const; // return number of fields
    void Clear (); // clear field values from buffer
    int AddField (int fieldSize);
    int Read (istream &);
    int Write (ostream &);
    int Pack (const char *);
    int Unpack (char *);
    void Print (ostream &);
    int Init (int numFields, int maxChars = 1000);
    int Init (int numFields, int * fieldSize);
 private:
```

```
    char * Buffer; // character array to hold field values
    int BufferSize; // sum of the sizes of declared fields
    int * FieldSize; // array to hold field sizes
    int MaxFields; // maximum number of fields
    int MaxChars; // maximum number of characters in the buffer
    int NumFields; // actual number of defined fields
    int NextField; // index of next field to be packed/unpacked
    int NumFieldValues; // number of fields which are packed
    int Packing; // TRUE if in packing phase, FALSE o/w
    int NextCharacter; // packing/unpacking position in buffer
};
```

E.8   Fixtext.cpp. Code for class FixedTextBuffer

```
#include "fixtext.h"
#include <string.h>

FixedTextBuffer :: FixedTextBuffer (int maxFields, int max-
Chars)
 // construct with a maximum of maxFields
{ Init (maxFields, maxChars);}

FixedTextBuffer :: FixedTextBuffer (int numFields, int * field-
Size)
// construct with fields of specific size
{ Init (numFields, fieldSize);}

int FixedTextBuffer :: NumberOfFields () const
// return number of fields
{ return NumFields;}

void FixedTextBuffer :: Clear ()
// clear fields from buffer
{ NextField = 0; NextCharacter = 0; Packing = TRUE;
Buffer[0]=0;}

int FixedTextBuffer :: AddField (int fieldSize)
{
    if (NumFields == MaxFields) return FALSE;
    if (BufferSize + fieldSize > MaxChars) return FALSE;
    FieldSize[NumFields] = fieldSize;
```

```
   NumFields ++;
   BufferSize += fieldSize;
   return TRUE;
}


int FixedTextBuffer :: Read (istream & stream)
{
   stream . read (Buffer, BufferSize);
   return stream . good ();
}



int FixedTextBuffer :: Write (ostream & stream)
{
   stream . write (Buffer, BufferSize);
   return stream . good ();
}



int FixedTextBuffer :: Pack (const char * str)
// set the value of the next field of the buffer;
{
   if (NextField == NumFields || !Packing)
      // buffer is full or not packing mode
      return FALSE;
   int len = strlen (str);
   int start = NextCharacter; // first byte to be packed
   int packSize = FieldSize[NextField]; // # bytes to be packed
   strncpy (&Buffer[start], str, packSize);
   NextCharacter += packSize;
   NextField ++;
   // if len < packSize, pad with blanks
   for (int i = start + packSize; i < NextCharacter; i ++)
      Buffer[start] = ' ';
   Buffer [NextCharacter] = 0; // make buffer look like a string
   if (NextField == NumFields) // buffer is full
   {
      Packing = FALSE;
      NextField = NextCharacter = 0;
   }
   return TRUE;
}
```

```cpp
int FixedTextBuffer :: Unpack (char * str)
// extract the value of the next field of the buffer
{
    if (NextField == NumFields || Packing)
        // buffer is full or not unpacking mode
        return FALSE;
    int start = NextCharacter; // first byte to be unpacked
    int packSize = FieldSize[NextField]; // # bytes to be unpacked
    strncpy (str, &Buffer[start], packSize);
    str [packSize] = 0; // terminate string with zero
    NextCharacter += packSize;
    NextField ++;
    if (NextField == NumFields) Clear (); // all fields unpacked
    return TRUE;
}

void FixedTextBuffer :: Print (ostream & stream)
{
    stream << "Buffer has max fields "<<MaxFields
        <<" and actual "<<NumFields<<endl
        <<"max bytes "<<MaxChars<<" and Buffer Size "
        <<BufferSize<<endl;
    for (int i = 0; i < NumFields; I++)
        stream <<"\tfield "<<i<<" size "<<FieldSize[i]<<endl;
    if (Packing) stream <<"\tPacking\n";
    else stream <<"\tnot Packing\n";
    stream <<"Contents: '"<<Buffer<<"'"<<endl;
}

FixedTextBuffer :: Init (int maxFields, int maxChars)
 // construct with a maximum of maxFields
{
    if (maxFields < 0) maxFields = 0;
    if (maxChars < 0) maxChars = 0;
    MaxFields = maxFields;
    MaxChars = maxChars;
    FieldSize = new int[MaxFields];
    Buffer = new char[MaxChars];
    BufferSize = 0;
    NumFields = 0;
    NextField = 0;
    Packing = TRUE;
}
```

```
FixedTextBuffer :: Init (int numFields, int * fieldSize)
// construct with fields of specific size
{
   // calculate buffer size
   int bufferSize = 1;
   for (int i = 0; i < numFields; i++)
      bufferSize += fieldSize[i];
   // initialize
   Init (numFields, bufferSize);
   // add fields
   for (int j = 0; j < numFields; j++)
      AddField (FieldSize[j]);
}
```

E.9   Test.cpp. Test program for all buffer classes

```
#include <fstream.h>
#include <iomanip.h>
#include "fixtext.h"
#include "lentext.h"
#include "deltext.h"
#include "person.h"
void testFixText ()
{
   int result;
   Person person;
   FixedTextBuffer Buff (6);
   Person :: InitBuffer (Buff);
   strcpy (person.LastName, "Ames        ");
   strcpy (person.FirstName, "John        ");
   strcpy (person.Address, "123 Maple        ");
   strcpy (person.City, "Stillwater        ");
   strcpy (person.State, "OK");
   strcpy (person.ZipCode, "74075        ");
   person . Print (cout);
   person . Pack (Buff);
   Buff . Print (cout);
   ofstream TestOut ("fixtext.dat",ios::out|ios::bin);
   Buff . Write (TestOut);
   TestOut . close ();
   ifstream TestIn ("fixtext.dat", ios::in|ios::bin);
```

```
    FixedTextBuffer InBuff (6);
    Person :: InitBuffer (InBuff);
    Buff . Read (TestIn);
    person . Unpack (Buff);
    person . Print (cout);
}

void testLenText ()
{
    cout << "\nTesting LengthTextBuffer"<<endl;
    Person person;
    LengthTextBuffer Buff;
    Person :: InitBuffer (Buff);
    strcpy (person.LastName, "Ames");
    strcpy (person.FirstName, "John");
    strcpy (person.Address, "123 Maple");
    strcpy (person.City, "Stillwater");
    strcpy (person.State, "OK");
    strcpy (person.ZipCode, "74075");
    person . Print (cout);
    Buff . Print (cout);
    cout <<"pack person "<<person . Pack (Buff)<<endl;
    Buff . Print (cout);
    ofstream TestOut ("lentext.dat",ios::out|ios::bin);
    Buff . Write (TestOut);
    Buff . Write (TestOut);
    strcpy (person.FirstName, "Dave");
    person.Print (cout);
    person.Pack (Buff);
    Buff . Write (TestOut);
    TestOut . close ();
    ifstream TestIn ("lentext.dat", ios::in|ios::bin);
    LengthTextBuffer InBuff;
    Person :: InitBuffer (InBuff);
    cout <<"read "<<Buff . Read (TestIn)<<endl;
    cout <<"unpack "<<person . Unpack (Buff)<<endl;
    person . Print (cout);
    cout <<"read "<<Buff . Read (TestIn)<<endl;
    cout <<"unpack "<<person . Unpack (Buff)<<endl;
    person . Print (cout);
    cout <<"read "<<Buff . Read (TestIn)<<endl;
    cout <<"unpack "<<person . Unpack (Buff)<<endl;
    person . Print (cout);
}
```

```
void testDelText ()
{
   cout << "\nTesting DelimTextBuffer"<<endl;
   Person person;
   strcpy (person.LastName, "Ames");
   strcpy (person.FirstName, "John");
   strcpy (person.Address, "123 Maple");
   strcpy (person.City, "Stillwater");
   strcpy (person.State, "OK");
   strcpy (person.ZipCode, "74075");
   person . Print (cout);
   DelimTextBuffer Buff;
   Person :: InitBuffer (Buff);
   Buff . Print (cout);
   cout <<"pack person "<<person . Pack (Buff)<<endl;
   Buff . Print (cout);
   ofstream TestOut ("deltext.dat",ios::out|ios::bin);
   Buff . Write (TestOut);
   Buff . Write (TestOut);
   strcpy (person.FirstName, "Dave");
   person.Print (cout);
   person.Pack (Buff);
   Buff . Write (TestOut);
   TestOut . close ();
   ifstream TestIn ("deltext.dat", ios::in|ios::bin);
   DelimTextBuffer InBuff;     Person :: InitBuffer (InBuff);
   cout <<"read "<<Buff . Read (TestIn)<<endl;
   cout <<"unpack "<<person . Unpack (Buff)<<endl;
   person . Print (cout);
   cout <<"read "<<Buff . Read (TestIn)<<endl;
   cout <<"unpack "<<person . Unpack (Buff)<<endl;
   person . Print (cout);
   cout <<"read "<<Buff . Read (TestIn)<<endl;
   cout <<"unpack "<<person . Unpack (Buff)<<endl;
   person . Print (cout);
}

int main(int argc, char ** argv)
{
   testFixText ();
   testLenText ();
   testDelText ();
}
```

A Class Hierarchy for Buffer Input/Output

F

F.1   Person.h. Definition for class Person

```
class Person
{
  public:
    // fields
    char LastName [11]; char FirstName [11]; char Address [16];
    char City [16]; char State [3]; char ZipCode [10];
    //operations
    Person ();
    static int InitBuffer (DelimFieldBuffer &);
    static int InitBuffer (LengthFieldBuffer &);
    static int InitBuffer (FixedFieldBuffer &);
    void Clear ();
    int Unpack (IOBuffer &);
    int Pack (IOBuffer &) const;
    void Print (ostream &, char * label = 0) const;
};
```

F.2   Person.cpp. Code for class Person

```
//person.cc
#include "person.h"

Person::Person (){Clear ();}

void Person::Clear ()
{
    // set each field to an empty string
    LastName [0] = 0; FirstName [0] = 0; Address [0] = 0;
    City [0] = 0; State [0] = 0; ZipCode [0] = 0;
}

int Person::Pack (IOBuffer & Buffer) const
{// pack the fields into a FixedFieldBuffer,
 // return TRUE if all succeed, FALSE o/w
    int numBytes;
    Buffer . Clear ();
    numBytes = Buffer . Pack (LastName);
    if (numBytes == -1) return FALSE;
```

```
   numBytes = Buffer . Pack (FirstName);
   if (numBytes == -1) return FALSE;
   numBytes = Buffer . Pack (Address);
   if (numBytes == -1) return FALSE;
   numBytes = Buffer . Pack (City);
   if (numBytes == -1) return FALSE;
   numBytes = Buffer . Pack (State);
   if (numBytes == -1) return FALSE;
   numBytes = Buffer . Pack (ZipCode);
   if (numBytes == -1) return FALSE;
   return TRUE;
}

int Person::Unpack (IOBuffer & Buffer)
{
   Clear ();
   int numBytes;
   numBytes = Buffer . Unpack (LastName);
   if (numBytes == -1) return FALSE;
   LastName[numBytes] = 0;
   numBytes = Buffer . Unpack (FirstName);
   if (numBytes == -1) return FALSE;
   FirstName[numBytes] = 0;
   numBytes = Buffer . Unpack (Address);
   if (numBytes == -1) return FALSE;
   Address[numBytes] = 0;
   numBytes = Buffer . Unpack (City);
   if (numBytes == -1) return FALSE;
   City[numBytes] = 0;
   numBytes = Buffer . Unpack (State);
   if (numBytes == -1) return FALSE;
   State[numBytes] = 0;
   numBytes = Buffer . Unpack (ZipCode);
   if (numBytes == -1) return FALSE;
   ZipCode[numBytes] = 0;
   return TRUE;
}

int Person::InitBuffer (FixedFieldBuffer & Buffer)
// initialize a FixedFieldBuffer to be used for Persons
{
   int result;
   result = Buffer . AddField (10); // LastName [11];
   result = result && Buffer . AddField (10); // FirstName [11];
```

```
   result = result && Buffer . AddField (15); // Address [16];
   result = result && Buffer . AddField (15); // City [16];
   result = result && Buffer . AddField (2);  // State [3];
   result = result && Buffer . AddField (9); // ZipCode [10];
   return result;
}

int Person::InitBuffer (DelimFieldBuffer & Buffer)
// initialize a DelimFieldBuffer to be used for Persons
{    return TRUE;}

int Person::InitBuffer (LengthFieldBuffer & Buffer)
// initialize a LengthFieldBuffer to be used for Persons
{    return TRUE;}

void Person::Print (ostream & stream, char * label) const
{
   if (label == 0) stream << "Person:";
   else stream << label;
   stream << "\n\t Last Name '"<<LastName<<"'\n"
       << "\tFirst Name '"<<FirstName<<"'\n"
       << "\t    Address '"<<Address<<"'\n"
       << "\t       City '"<<City<<"'\n"
       << "\t      State '"<<State<<"'\n"
       << "\t   Zip Code '"<<ZipCode<<"'\n" <<flush;
}
```

F.3   Iobuffer.h. Definition for class IOBuffer

```
class IOBuffer
// An abstract base class for file buffers
{   public:
    IOBuffer (int maxBytes = 1000); // a maximum of maxBytes
    IOBuffer & operator = (const IOBuffer &);
    virtual void Clear (); // clear fields from buffer
    virtual int Pack (const void * field, int size = -1) = 0;
       // set the value of the next field of the buffer;
    virtual int Unpack (void * field, int maxbytes = -1) = 0;
       // extract the value of the next field of the buffer
    virtual void Print (ostream &) const;
    int Init (int maxBytes);
```

```
    // the read and write methods return the address of the record
    // sequential read and write operations
    virtual int Read (istream &) = 0;
        // read a buffer from the stream
    virtual int Write (ostream &) const = 0;
        // write a buffer to the stream

    // these are the direct access read and write operations
    virtual int DRead (istream &, int recref);
        // read specified record
    virtual int DWrite (ostream &, int recref) const;
        // write specified record
    // these header operations return the size of the header
    virtual int ReadHeader (istream &);
    virtual int WriteHeader (ostream &) const;
 protected:
    int Initialized; // TRUE if buffer is initialized
    char * Buffer; // character array to hold field values
    int BufferSize; // sum of the sizes of packed fields
    int MaxBytes; // maximum number of characters in the buffer
    int NextByte; // index of next byte to be packed/unpacked
    int Packing; // TRUE if in packing mode, FALSE, if unpacking
};
```

F.4　　Iobuffer.cpp. Code for class IOBuffer

```
IOBuffer::IOBuffer (int maxBytes)
// construct with a maximum of maxFields
{Init (maxBytes);}

IOBuffer & IOBuffer :: operator = (const IOBuffer & buffer)
{
    if (MaxBytes < buffer . BufferSize) return *this; // fails
    Initialized = buffer . Initialized;
    BufferSize = buffer . BufferSize;
    memcpy (Buffer, buffer.Buffer, buffer . BufferSize);
    NextByte = buffer . NextByte;
    Packing = Packing;
    return *this;
}
```

```
void IOBuffer::Clear ()
// clear field values from buffer
{  NextByte = 0; Packing = TRUE;}

void IOBuffer::Print (ostream & stream) const
{  stream<<"MaxBytes "<<MaxBytes<<" BufferSize "<<BufferSize;}

int IOBuffer::Init (int maxBytes)
{
   Initialized = FALSE;
   if (maxBytes < 0) maxBytes = 0;
   MaxBytes = maxBytes;
   Buffer = new char[MaxBytes];
   BufferSize = 0;
   Clear ();
   return 1;
}
int IOBuffer::DRead (istream & stream, int recref)
// read specified record
{
   stream . seekg (recref, ios::beg);
   if (stream . tellg () != recref) return -1;
   return Read (stream);
}

int IOBuffer::DWrite (ostream & stream, int recref) const
// write specified record
{
   stream . seekp (recref, ios::beg);
   if (stream . tellp () != recref) return -1;
   return Write (stream);
}

static const char * headerStr = "IOBuffer";
static const int headerSize = strlen (headerStr);

int IOBuffer::ReadHeader (istream & stream)
{
   char str[9];
   stream . seekg (0, ios::beg);
   stream . read (str, headerSize);
   if (! stream . good ()) return -1;
   if (strncmp (str, headerStr, headerSize)==0) return headerSize;
   else return -1;
}
```

```
int IOBuffer::WriteHeader (ostream & stream) const
{
    stream . seekp (0, ios::beg);
    stream . write (headerStr, headerSize);
    if (! stream . good ()) return -1;
    return headerSize;
}
```

F.5 Varlen.h. Definition for class VariableLengthBuffer

```
class VariableLengthBuffer: public IOBuffer
// Abstract class designed to support variablelength records
// Fields may be of a variety of types
//
{   public:
    VariableLengthBuffer (int MaxBytes = 1000);
    VariableLengthBuffer (const VariableLengthBuffer & buffer)
        // copy constructor
        : IOBuffer(buffer){}
    void Clear (); // clear fields from buffer
    int Read (istream &);
    int Write (ostream &) const;
    int ReadHeader (istream &); // write a buffer to the stream
    int WriteHeader (ostream &) const; // write buffer to stream
    int PackFixLen (void *, int);
    int PackDelimeted (void *, int);
    int PackLength (void *, int);
    void Print (ostream &) const;
    int SizeOfBuffer () const; // return current size of buffer
    int Init ();
};
```

F.6 Varlen.cpp. Code for class VariableLengthBuffer

```
VariableLengthBuffer :: VariableLengthBuffer (int maxBytes)
  // construct with a maximum of maxFields
 : IOBuffer (maxBytes)
{ Init ();}
```

```
void VariableLengthBuffer :: Clear ()
// clear fields from buffer
{  IOBuffer::Clear();}

int VariableLengthBuffer :: Read (istream & stream)
// write the number of bytes in the buffer field definitions
// the record length is represented by an unsigned short value
{
   if (stream.eof()) return -1;
   int recaddr = stream . tellg ();
   Clear ();
   unsigned short bufferSize;
   stream . read ((char *)&bufferSize, sizeof(bufferSize));
   if (! stream . good ()){stream.clear(); return -1;}
   BufferSize = bufferSize;
   if (BufferSize > MaxBytes) return -1; // buffer overflow
   stream . read (Buffer, BufferSize);
   if (! stream . good ()){stream.clear(); return -1;}
   return recaddr;
}

int VariableLengthBuffer :: Write (ostream & stream) const
// write the length and buffer into the stream
{
   int recaddr = stream . tellp ();
   unsigned short bufferSize;
   bufferSize = BufferSize;
   stream . write ((char *)&bufferSize, sizeof(bufferSize));
   if (!stream) return -1;
   stream . write (Buffer, BufferSize);
   if (! stream . good ()) return -1;
   return recaddr;
}

const char * headerStr = "Variable";
const int headerSize = strlen (headerStr);

int VariableLengthBuffer :: ReadHeader (istream & stream)
// read the header and check for consistency
{
```

```
    char str[headerSize+1];
    int result;
    // read the IOBuffer header
    result = IOBuffer::ReadHeader (stream);
    if (!result) return FALSE;
    // read the header string
    stream . read (str, headerSize);
    if (!stream.good()) return FALSE;
    if (strncmp (str, headerStr, headerSize) != 0) return FALSE;
    // read and check the record description
    return stream . tellg ();
}

int VariableLengthBuffer :: WriteHeader (ostream & stream) const
// write a buffer header to the beginning of the stream
// A header consists of the
// IOBUFFER header
// header string
// Variable sized record of length fields
//     that describes the file records
{
    int result;
    // write the parent (IOBuffer) header
    result = IOBuffer::WriteHeader (stream);
    if (!result) return FALSE;
    // write the header string
    stream . write (headerStr, headerSize);
    if (!stream . good ()) return FALSE;
    // write the record description
    return stream . tellp();
}

void VariableLengthBuffer :: Print (ostream & stream) const
{ IOBuffer::Print (stream);}

int VariableLengthBuffer :: Init ()
 // construct with a maximum of maxFields
{ Clear(); return TRUE;}
```

F.7   Delim.h. Definition for class DelimFieldBuffer

```
class DelimFieldBuffer: public VariableLengthBuffer
// a buffer which holds delimited text fields.
{   public:
    DelimFieldBuffer (char Delim = -1, int maxBytes = 1000);
        // construct with a maximum of maxBytes
        // construct with fields with delimeters
    DelimFieldBuffer (const DelimFieldBuffer & buffer);
        // copy constructor
    void Clear (); // clear fields from buffer
    int Pack (const void*, int size = -1);
        // set the value of the next field of the buffer;
    int Unpack (void * field, int maxBytes = -1);
        // extract the value of the next field of the buffer
    int ReadHeader (istream & stream);
    int WriteHeader (ostream & stream) const;
    void Print (ostream &) const;
    int Init (char delim = 0);
    static void SetDefaultDelim (char delim);
 protected:
    char Delim;
    static char DefaultDelim;
};

inline DelimFieldBuffer :: DelimFieldBuffer
    (const DelimFieldBuffer & buffer) // copy constructor
        : VariableLengthBuffer (buffer)
{  Init (buffer . Delim);}
```

F.8   Delim.cpp. Code for class DelimFieldBuffer

```
DelimFieldBuffer :: DelimFieldBuffer(char delim, int maxBytes)
 // construct with a maximum of maxFields
: VariableLengthBuffer (maxBytes)
{  Init (delim);}

void DelimFieldBuffer :: Clear ()
// clear fields from buffer
{  VariableLengthBuffer::Clear();}
```

```
int DelimFieldBuffer :: Pack (const void * field, int size)
// set the value of the next field of the buffer;
// if size = -1 (default) use strlen(field) as Delim of field
// return number of bytes packed, -1 if error
{
   // look for delimeter in field!
   short len; // length of string to be packed
   if (size >= 0) len = size;
   else len = strlen ((char*)field);
   if (len > (short)strlen((char*)field)) // field is too short!
      return -1;
   int start = NextByte; // first character to be packed
   NextByte += len + 1;
   if (NextByte > MaxBytes) return -1;
   memcpy (&Buffer[start], field, len);
   Buffer [start+len] = Delim; // add delimeter
   BufferSize = NextByte;
   return len;
}

int DelimFieldBuffer :: Unpack (void * field, int maxBytes)
// extract the value of the next field of the buffer
// return the number of bytes extracted, -1 if error
{
   int len = -1; // length of packed string
   int start = NextByte; // first character to be unpacked
   for (int i = start; i < BufferSize; i++)
      if (Buffer[i] == Delim)
         {len = i - start; break;}
   if (len == -1) return -1; // delimeter not found
   NextByte += len + 1;
   if (NextByte > BufferSize) return -1;
   // check for maxBytes
   memcpy (field, &Buffer[start], len);
   if (maxBytes > len || maxBytes == -1)
      ((char*)field) [len] = 0; // zero termination for string
      return len;
}

int DelimFieldBuffer :: ReadHeader (istream & stream)
// read header: contains delimeter character
{
   char ch;
   int result;
   result = VariableLengthBuffer::ReadHeader (stream);
```

```
      if (!result) return FALSE;
      stream . get (ch);
      if (!Initialized)
      {
          SetDefaultDelim (ch);
          return TRUE;
      }
      if (ch != Delim) return FALSE;
      return stream . tellg ();
  }

  int DelimFieldBuffer :: WriteHeader (ostream & stream) const
  // write header into file: contains the delimeter character
  {
      if (!Initialized) return FALSE;
      int result;
      result = VariableLengthBuffer::WriteHeader (stream);
      if (!result) return FALSE;
      stream . put (Delim);
      return stream . tellp ();
  }

  void DelimFieldBuffer :: Print (ostream & stream) const
  {
      VariableLengthBuffer::Print (stream);
      stream << " Delimeter '"<<Delim<<"'"<<endl;
  }

  // Protected members

  int DelimFieldBuffer :: Init (char delim)
   // construct with a maximum of maxFields
  {
      Initialized = TRUE;
      Clear ();
      if (delim == -1) Delim = DefaultDelim;
      else Delim = delim;
      return TRUE;
  }

  void DelimFieldBuffer :: SetDefaultDelim (char delim)
  {  DefaultDelim = delim;}

  // initialize static protected element
  char DelimFieldBuffer :: DefaultDelim = 0;
```

F.9   Length.h. Definition for class LengthFieldBuffer

```cpp
class LengthFieldBuffer: public VariableLengthBuffer
// class that supports length plus value fields
{  public:
   LengthFieldBuffer (int maxBytes = 1000);
      // construct with a maximum of maxFields
      // construct with fields of specific size
   LengthFieldBuffer (const LengthFieldBuffer & buffer)
      // copy constructor
   : VariableLengthBuffer (buffer) {}
   void Clear (); // clear fields from buffer
   int Pack (const void * field, int size = -1);
      // set the value of the next field of the buffer;
   int Unpack (void *field, int maxBytes = -1);
      // extract the value of the next field of the buffer
   void Print (ostream &) const;
   int Init ();
   protected:
};
```

F.10   Length.cpp. Code for class LengthFieldBuffer

```cpp
LengthFieldBuffer :: LengthFieldBuffer (int maxBytes)
 // construct with a maximum of maxFields
: VariableLengthBuffer (maxBytes)
{  Init ();}

void LengthFieldBuffer :: Clear ()
// clear fields from buffer
{  VariableLengthBuffer::Clear ();}

int LengthFieldBuffer :: Pack (const void* field, int size)
// set the value of the next field of the buffer;
// if size = -1 (default) use strlen(str) as length of field
// return number of bytes packed, -1 if error
{
    short len; // length of string to be packed
    if (size >= 0) len = size;
```

```cpp
   else len = strlen ((char *) field);
   int start = NextByte; // first character to be packed
   NextByte += (len + sizeof(len));
   if (NextByte > MaxBytes) return -1;
   memcpy (&Buffer[start], &len, sizeof(len));
   memcpy (&Buffer[start+sizeof(len)], field, len);
   BufferSize = NextByte;
   return len;
}

int LengthFieldBuffer :: Unpack (void* field, int maxBytes)
// extract the value of the next field of the buffer
// return the number of bytes extracted, -1 if error
{
   short len; // length of packed string
   if (NextByte >= BufferSize) return -1; // no more fields
   int start = NextByte; // first character to be unpacked
   memcpy (&len, &Buffer[start], sizeof(len));
   if (maxBytes != -1 && len > maxBytes)
      return -1; // field too long
   NextByte += len + sizeof(len);
   if (NextByte > BufferSize) return -1;
   memcpy (field, &Buffer[start+sizeof(len)], len);
   if (maxBytes > len || maxBytes == -1)
      ((char *)field) [len] = 0; // zero termination for string
   return len;
}

void LengthFieldBuffer :: Print (ostream & stream) const
{
   stream<< "Buffer has characters "<<MaxBytes<<" and Buffer Size"
        <<BufferSize<<endl;
}

int LengthFieldBuffer :: Init ()
 // construct with a maximum of maxFields
{
      Initialized = TRUE;
      Clear ();
      return TRUE;
}
```

F.11   Fixlen.h. Definition for class FixedLengthBuffer

```cpp
class FixedLengthBuffer: public IOBuffer
// Abstract class designed to support fixed length records
{
   public:
   FixedLengthBuffer (int recordSize = 1000);
   FixedLengthBuffer (const FixedLengthBuffer & buffer);
      // copy constructor
   void Clear (); // clear values from buffer
   int Read (istream &);
   int Write (ostream &) const;
   int ReadHeader (istream &); // read the header
   int WriteHeader (ostream &) const; // write the header
   void Print (ostream &) const;
   int SizeOfBuffer () const; // return size of buffer
 protected:
   int Init (int recordSize);
   int ChangeRecordSize (int recordSize);
};

inline FixedLengthBuffer :: FixedLengthBuffer (const
FixedLengthBuffer & buffer)
: IOBuffer (buffer)
{
   Init (buffer . BufferSize);
}
```

F.12   Fixlen.cpp. Code for class FixedLengthBuffer

```cpp
FixedLengthBuffer :: FixedLengthBuffer (int recordSize)
 // construct with a maximum of maxFields
: IOBuffer (recordSize)
{  Init (recordSize);}

void FixedLengthBuffer :: Clear ()
// clear fields from buffer
{
   IOBuffer::Clear ();
   Buffer[0]=0;
   Packing = TRUE;
```

```
}

int FixedLengthBuffer :: Read (istream & stream)
// write the number of bytes in the buffer field definitions
{
   int recaddr = stream . tellg (); stream.clear();
   Clear ();
   Packing = FALSE;
   stream . read (Buffer, BufferSize);
   if (! stream . good ()){stream.clear(); return recaddr;}
   return recaddr;
}


int FixedLengthBuffer :: Write (ostream & stream) const
// read the number of bytes in the buffer field definitions
// return the location of the record in the file
{
   int recaddr = stream . tellp ();
   stream . write (Buffer, BufferSize);
   if (! stream . good ()) return -1;
   return recaddr;
}

static const char * headerStr = "Fixed";
static const int headerStrSize = strlen (headerStr);

int FixedLengthBuffer :: ReadHeader (istream & stream)
// read the header and check for consistency
// see WriteHeader for header record structure
{
   char str[headerStrSize+1];
   int recordSize;
   int result;
   // read the IOBuffer header
   result = IOBuffer::ReadHeader (stream);
   if (result < 0) return -1;
   // read the string "Fixed"
   stream . read (str, headerStrSize);
   if (!stream.good()) return -1;
   if (strncmp (str, headerStr, headerStrSize) != 0) return -1;
   stream . read ((char*)&recordSize, sizeof(recordSize));
   if (Initialized) // check header for consistency
   {
       if (recordSize != BufferSize) return -1;
   }
```

```
   // else initialize the buffer from the header
   ChangeRecordSize (recordSize);
   return stream.tellg();
}


int FixedLengthBuffer :: WriteHeader (ostream & stream) const
// write a buffer header to the beginning of the stream
// A header consists of the
// IOBUFFER header
// FIXED        5 bytes
// record size       2 bytes
{
   int result;
   if (!Initialized) return -1; // cannot write unitialized buffer
   // write the parent (IOBuffer) header
   result = IOBuffer::WriteHeader (stream);
   if (!result) return -1;
   // write the string "Fixed"
   stream . write (headerStr, headerStrSize);
   if (!stream . good ()) return -1;
   // write the record size
   stream . write ((char *)&BufferSize, sizeof(BufferSize));
   if (!stream . good ()) return -1;
   return stream . tellp ();
}

void FixedLengthBuffer :: Print (ostream & stream) const
{
   IOBuffer::Print (stream);
   stream <<  "Fixed ";
}

int FixedLengthBuffer :: Init (int recordSize)
 // construct with a maximum of maxFields
{
   Clear ();
   BufferSize = recordSize;
   return 1;
}

int FixedLengthBuffer :: ChangeRecordSize (int recordSize)
 // construct with a maximum of maxFields
{
   BufferSize = recordSize;
   return 1;
}
```

F.13   Fixfld.h. Definition for class FixedFieldBuffer

```
class FixedFieldBuffer: public FixedLengthBuffer
// Abstract class designed to support fixed field records
// Use of this class requires that all fields be defined before
//     reading and writing can take place
{
   public:
   FixedFieldBuffer (int maxFields, int RecordSize = 1000);
   FixedFieldBuffer (int maxFields, int * fieldSize);
   // initialize all fields at once
   FixedFieldBuffer (const FixedFieldBuffer &); //copy constructor
   FixedFieldBuffer & operator = (const FixedFieldBuffer &);
   void Clear (); // clear values from buffer
   int AddField (int fieldSize); // define the next field
   int ReadHeader (istream &); // read the header
   int WriteHeader (ostream &) const; // write the header
   int Pack (const void * field, int size = -1);
      // set the value of the next field of the buffer;
   int Unpack (void * field, int maxBytes = -1);
      // extract the value of the next field of the buffer
   void Print (ostream &) const;
   int NumberOfFields () const; // return number of defined fields
   int Init (int maxFields);
   int Init (int numFields, int * fieldSize);
 protected:
   int * FieldSize; // array to hold field sizes
   int MaxFields; // maximum number of fields
   int NumFields; // actual number of defined fields
   int NextField; // index of next field to be packed/unpacked
};

inline FixedFieldBuffer :: FixedFieldBuffer (const FixedField-
Buffer & buffer)
   : FixedLengthBuffer (buffer)
{  Init (buffer . NumFields, buffer . FieldSize);}
```

F.14   Fixfld.cpp. Code for class FixedFieldBuffer

```cpp
FixedFieldBuffer::FixedFieldBuffer(int maxFields,int maxBytes)
 // construct with a maximum of maxFields
: FixedLengthBuffer(maxBytes)
{  Init (maxFields);}

// function to calculate the record size from the field sizes
static int SumFieldSizes (int numFields, int * fieldSize)
{
   int sum = 0;
   for (int i = 0; i < numFields; i++)
      sum += fieldSize[i];
   return sum;
}

FixedFieldBuffer & FixedFieldBuffer :: operator =
   (const FixedFieldBuffer & buffer)
{
   // disallow copy unless fields are identical
   if (NumFields != buffer . NumFields) return *this;
   for (int i = 0; i < NumFields; i++)
      if (FieldSize[i] != buffer . FieldSize[i]) return *this;
   NextField = buffer . NextField;
   FixedLengthBuffer :: operator = (buffer);
   return *this;
}

FixedFieldBuffer :: FixedFieldBuffer
      (int numFields, int * fieldSize)
// construct with fields of specific size
: FixedLengthBuffer(SumFieldSizes(numFields, fieldSize))
{  Init (numFields, fieldSize);}

int FixedFieldBuffer :: NumberOfFields () const
// return number of fields
{  return NumFields;}

void FixedFieldBuffer :: Clear ()
// clear fields from buffer
{
```

```
   FixedLengthBuffer::Clear ();
   NextField = 0;
   Buffer[0]=0;
   Packing = TRUE;
}

int FixedFieldBuffer :: AddField (int fieldSize)
{
   Initialized = TRUE;
   if (NumFields == MaxFields) return FALSE;
   if (BufferSize + fieldSize > MaxBytes) return FALSE;
   FieldSize[NumFields] = fieldSize;
   NumFields ++;
   BufferSize += fieldSize;
   return TRUE;
}

static const char * headerStr = "Field";
static const int headerStrSize = strlen (headerStr);

int FixedFieldBuffer :: ReadHeader (istream & stream)
// read the header and check for consistency
// see WriteHeader for header record structure
{
   char * str = new char[headerStrSize+1];
   int numFields, *fieldSize;
   int result;
   // read the FixedLengthBufferheader
   result = FixedLengthBuffer::ReadHeader (stream);
   if (result < 0) return -1;
   // read the header string
   stream . read (str, headerStrSize);
   if (!stream.good()) return -1;
   if (strncmp (str, headerStr, headerStrSize) != 0) return -1;
   // read the record description
   stream . read ((char*)&numFields, sizeof(numFields));
   if (!stream) return -1; // failed to read numFields
   fieldSize = new int[numFields];
   for (int i = 0; i < numFields; i ++)
       stream . read ((char*)&fieldSize[i], sizeof(fieldSize[i]));

   if (Initialized) // check header for consistency
   {
```

```
      if (numFields != NumFields) return -1;
      for (int j = 0; j < numFields; j ++)
         if (fieldSize[j] != FieldSize[j]) return -1;
      return stream . tellg (); // everything matches
   }
   // else initialize the buffer from the header
   Init (numFields, fieldSize);
   return stream.tellg();
}

int FixedFieldBuffer :: WriteHeader (ostream & stream) const
// write a buffer header to the beginning of the stream
// A header consists of the
// FixedLengthBufferheader
// FIXED                5 bytes
// Variable sized record of length fields
// that describes the file records
// Header record size   2 bytes
// number of fields     4 bytes
// field sizes          4 bytes per field
{
   int result;
   if (!Initialized) return -1; // cannot write unitialized buffer
   // write the parent (FixedLengthBuffer) header
   result = FixedLengthBuffer::WriteHeader (stream);
   if (!result) return -1;
   // write the header string
   stream . write (headerStr, headerStrSize);
   if (!stream.good()) return -1;
   // write the record description
   stream . write ((char*)&NumFields, sizeof(NumFields));
   for (int i = 0; i < NumFields; i ++)
   {
      stream . write ((char*)&FieldSize[i], sizeof(FieldSize[i]));
   }
   if (!stream) return -1;
   return stream . tellp ();
}

int FixedFieldBuffer :: Pack (const void * field, int size)
// set the value of the next field of the buffer;
//    if size != -1, it must be the same as the packSize
// return number of bytes packed, -1 if error
{
```

```
   if (NextField == NumFields || !Packing)
      return -1; // buffer is full or not packing mode
   int start = NextByte; // first byte to be packed
   int packSize = FieldSize[NextField];
      // number bytes to be packed
   if (size != -1 && packSize != size) return -1;
   memcpy (&Buffer[start], field, packSize);
      // move bytes to buffer
   NextByte += packSize;
   NextField ++;
   if (NextField == NumFields) // all fields packed
   {
      Packing = -1;
      NextField = NextByte = 0;
   }
   return packSize;
}

int FixedFieldBuffer :: Unpack (void * field, int maxBytes)
// extract the value of the next field of the buffer
// return the number of bytes extracted, -1 if error
{
   Packing = FALSE;
   if (NextField == NumFields) // buffer is full
      return -1;
   int start = NextByte; // first byte to be unpacked
   int packSize = FieldSize[NextField];
      // number bytes to be unpacked
   memcpy (field, &Buffer[start], packSize);
   NextByte += packSize;
   NextField ++;
   if (NextField == NumFields) Clear (); // all fields unpacked
   return packSize;
}

void FixedFieldBuffer :: Print (ostream & stream) const
{
   FixedLengthBuffer::Print (stream);
   stream << endl;
   stream << "\t max fields "<<MaxFields<<" and actual "
         <<NumFields<<endl;
   for (int i = 0; i < NumFields; i++)
         stream <<"\tfield "<<i<<" size "<<FieldSize[i]<<endl;
   Buffer[BufferSize]=0;
```

```
      stream <<"NextByte "<<NextByte<<endl;
      stream <<"Buffer '"<<Buffer<<"'"<<endl;
}

int FixedFieldBuffer :: Init (int maxFields)
 // construct with a maximum of maxFields
{
   Clear ();
   if (maxFields < 0) maxFields = 0;
   MaxFields = maxFields;
   FieldSize = new int[MaxFields];
   BufferSize = 0;
   NumFields = 0;
   return 1;
}

int FixedFieldBuffer :: Init (int numFields, int * fieldSize)
// construct with fields of specific size
{
   // initialize
   Initialized = TRUE;
   Init (numFields);

   // add fields
   for (int j = 0; j < numFields; j++)
      AddField (FieldSize[j]);
   return TRUE;
}
```

F.15   Buffile.h. Definition for class BufferFile

```
class BufferFile
// Class to represent buffered file operations
//    Used in conjunction with the IOBuffer classes
// Each buffered file is associated with a disk file of a specific
//    record type.
// Each buffered file object has a buffer object which can be used
//    for file I/O
// Sequential and random access read and write are supported
//    each write returns the record address of the record
//    this record address can be used to read that record
```

```
(
    public:
    BufferFile (IOBuffer &); // create with a buffer

    int Open (char * filename, int MODE); // open an existing file
    int Create (char * filename, int MODE); // create a new file
    int Close ();
    int Rewind (); // reset to the first data record
    // Input and Output operations
    int Read (int recaddr = -1);
        // read a record into the buffer
        // return the record address
        // return <0 if read failed
        // if recaddr == -1, read the next record in the file
        // if recaddr != -1, read the record at that address
    int Write (int recaddr = -1); // write the buffer contents
    int Append (); // write the current buffer at the end of file
    // Access to IOBuffer
    IOBuffer & GetBuffer ();

    protected:
    IOBuffer & Buffer;
    fstream File;
    int HeaderSize; // size of header
    int ReadHeader ();
    int WriteHeader ();
};
```

F.16   Buffile.cpp. Code for class BufferFile

```
BufferFile::BufferFile (IOBuffer & from)
 // create with a buffer
    : Buffer (from){}

int BufferFile::Open (char * filename, int mode)
// open an existing file and check the header
// a correct header must be on the file
// use ios::nocreate to ensure that a file exists
{
```

```
   // these modes are not allowed when opening an existing file
   if (mode&ios::noreplace||mode&ios::trunc) return FALSE;

   File . open (filename, mode|ios::in|ios::nocreate|ios::binary);
   if (! File.good()) return FALSE;
   File . seekg(0, ios::beg); File . seekp(0, ios::beg);
   HeaderSize = ReadHeader();
   if (!HeaderSize) // no header and file opened for output
      return FALSE;
   File . seekp (HeaderSize, ios::beg);
   File . seekg (HeaderSize, ios::beg);
   return File . good();
}

int BufferFile::Create (char * filename, int mode)
// create a new file and write a header on it.
// use ios::nocreate to ensure that no file exists
{
   if (!(mode & ios::out)) return FALSE; // must include ios::out
   File.open (filename, mode|ios::out|ios::noreplace|ios::binary);
   if (!File . good())
   {    File . close(); return FALSE;}
   HeaderSize = WriteHeader ();
   return HeaderSize != 0;
}

int BufferFile::Close ()
{
   File . close();
   return TRUE;
}

int BufferFile::Rewind ()
{
   File . seekg (HeaderSize, ios::beg);
   File . seekp (HeaderSize, ios::beg);
   return 1;
}
```

```
// Input and Output operations
int BufferFile::Read (int recaddr)
// read a record into the buffer
// return the record address
// return <0 if read failed
// if recaddr == -1, read the next record in the File
// if recaddr != -1, read the record at that address
{
   if (recaddr == -1) return Buffer . Read (File);
   else return Buffer . DRead (File, recaddr);
}

int BufferFile::Write (int recaddr)
 // write the current buffer contents
{
   if (recaddr == -1) return Buffer . Write (File);
   else return Buffer . DWrite (File, recaddr);
}

int BufferFile::Append ()
// write the current buffer at the end of File
{
   File . seekp (0, ios::end);
   return Buffer . Write (File);
}

// Access to IOBuffer
IOBuffer & BufferFile::GetBuffer ()
{ return Buffer;}

// protected methods
int BufferFile::ReadHeader ()
{ return Buffer . ReadHeader (File); }

int BufferFile::WriteHeader ()
{ return Buffer . WriteHeader (File);}
```

F.17   Recfile.h. Template class RecordFile

```
template <class RecType>
class RecordFile: public BufferFile
{public:
    int Read (RecType & record, int recaddr = -1);
    int Write (const RecType & record, int recaddr = -1);
    int Append (const RecType & record, int recaddr = -1);
    RecordFile (IOBuffer & buffer): BufferFile (buffer) {}
};

// template method bodies
template <class RecType>
int RecordFile<RecType>::Read (RecType & record, int recaddr = -1)
{
    int readAddr, result;
    readAddr = BufferFile::Read (recaddr);
    if (readAddr==-1) return -1;
    result = record . Unpack (Buffer);
    if (!result) return -1;
    return readAddr;
}

template <class RecType>
int RecordFile<RecType>::Write(const RecType& record,int recaddr = -1)
{
    int result;
    result = record . Pack (Buffer);
    if (!result) return -1;
    return BufferFile::Write (recaddr);
}

template <class RecType>
int RecordFile<RecType>::Append(const RecType& record,int recaddr = -1)
{
    int result;
    result = record . Pack (Buffer);
    if (!result) return -1;
    return BufferFile::Append ();
}
```

F.18 Test.cpp. Test program for Person and RecordFile including template function

```cpp
Person MaryAmes;
Person AlanMason;

template <class IOB>
void testBuffer (IOB & Buff, char * myfile)
{
    Person person;
    int result;
    int recaddr1, recaddr2, recaddr3, recaddr4;

    // Test writing
    //Buff . Print (cout);
    ofstream TestOut (myfile,ios::out);
    result = Buff . WriteHeader (TestOut);
    cout << "write header "<<result<<endl;
    MaryAmes . Pack (Buff);
    //Buff . Print (cout);
    recaddr1 = Buff . Write (TestOut);
    cout << "write at "<<recaddr1<<endl;
    AlanMason. Pack (Buff);
    //Buff . Print (cout);
    recaddr2 = Buff . Write (TestOut);
    cout << "write at "<<recaddr2<<endl;
    TestOut . close ();

    // test reading
    ifstream TestIn (myfile, ios::in);
    result = Buff . ReadHeader (TestIn);
    cout <<"read header "<<result<<endl;
    person . Print (cout, "First record:");
    Buff . DRead (TestIn, recaddr2);
    person . Unpack (Buff);
    person . Print (cout, "Second record:");
    Buff . DRead (TestIn,recaddr1);
    person . Unpack (Buff);
}

void InitPerson()
{
    cout << "Initializing 3 Persons"<<endl;
    strcpy (MaryAmes.LastName, "Ames");
    strcpy (MaryAmes.FirstName, "Mary");
```

```cpp
    strcpy (MaryAmes.Address, "123 Maple");
    strcpy (MaryAmes.City, "Stillwater");
    strcpy (MaryAmes.State, "OK");
    strcpy (MaryAmes.ZipCode, "74075");
    MaryAmes . Print (cout);
    strcpy (AlanMason.LastName, "Mason");
    strcpy (AlanMason.FirstName, "Alan");
    strcpy (AlanMason.Address, "90 Eastgate");
    strcpy (AlanMason.City, "Ada");
    strcpy (AlanMason.State, "OK");
    strcpy (AlanMason.ZipCode, "74820");
    AlanMason . Print (cout);
}

void testFixedField ()
{
    cout <<"Testing Fixed Field Buffer"<<endl;
    FixedFieldBuffer Buff (6);
    Person :: InitBuffer (Buff);
    testBuffer (Buff, "fixlen.dat");
}

void testLength ()
{
    cout << "\nTesting LengthTextBuffer"<<endl;
    LengthFieldBuffer Buff;
    Person :: InitBuffer (Buff);
    testBuffer (Buff, "length.dat");
}

void testDelim ()
{
    cout << "\nTesting DelimTextBuffer"<<endl;
    DelimFieldBuffer::SetDefaultDelim ('|');
    DelimFieldBuffer Buff;
    Person :: InitBuffer (Buff);
    testBuffer (Buff, "delim.dat");
}

int main(int argc, char ** argv)
{
    InitPerson();
    testFixedField ();
    testLength ();
    testDelim ();
}
```

Single Level Indexing of Records by Key

G.1 Recordng.h. Definition of class Recording with composite key

```
class Recording
// a recording with a composite key
{public:
    Recording ();
    Recording (char * label, char * idNum, char * title,
        char * composer, char * artist);
    char IdNum[7]; char Title [30]; char Composer[30];
    char Artist[30]; char Label[7];
    char * Key () const; // return key of object
    int Unpack (IOBuffer &);
    int Pack (IOBuffer &) const;
    void Print (ostream &, char * label = 0) const;
};

ostream & operator << (ostream &, Recording &);
inline ostream & operator << (ostream & stream, Recording & rec)
{   rec.Print(stream); return stream;}
```

G.2 Recordng.cpp. Code for class Recording

```
Recording::Recording ()
{   IdNum[0] = 0; Title[0] = 0; Composer[0] = 0;
    Artist[0] = 0; Label[0] = 0;
}

Recording::Recording (char * label, char * idNum, char * title,
        char * composer, char * artist)
{
    strcpy(Label, label); strcpy(IdNum, idNum);
    strcpy(Title, title); strcpy(Composer, composer);
    strcpy(Artist, artist);
}

char * Recording::Key () const
{// produce key as concatenation of Label and IdNum
    ostrstream key;
    key << Label << IdNum << ends;
```

```
    return key.str();
}

int Recording::Pack (IOBuffer & Buffer) const
{// return TRUE if all succeed, FALSE o/w
    int numBytes;
    Buffer . Clear ();
    numBytes = Buffer . Pack (IdNum);
    if (numBytes == -1) return FALSE;
    numBytes = Buffer . Pack (Title);
    if (numBytes == -1) return FALSE;
    numBytes = Buffer . Pack (Composer);
    if (numBytes == -1) return FALSE;
    numBytes = Buffer . Pack (Artist);
    if (numBytes == -1) return FALSE;
    numBytes = Buffer . Pack (Label);
    if (numBytes == -1) return FALSE;
    return TRUE;
}

int Recording::Unpack (IOBuffer & Buffer)
{// unpack with maximum size, and add null termination to strings
    int numBytes;
    numBytes = Buffer . Unpack (IdNum, 6);
    if (numBytes == -1) return FALSE;
    IdNum[numBytes] = 0;
    numBytes = Buffer . Unpack (Title, 29);
    if (numBytes == -1) return FALSE;
    Title[numBytes] = 0;
    numBytes = Buffer . Unpack (Composer, 29);
    if (numBytes == -1) return FALSE;
    Composer[numBytes] = 0;
    numBytes = Buffer . Unpack (Artist, 29);
    if (numBytes == -1) return FALSE;
    Artist[numBytes] = 0;
    numBytes = Buffer . Unpack (Label, 6);
    if (numBytes == -1) return FALSE;
    Label[numBytes] = 0;
    return TRUE;
}

void Recording::Print (ostream & stream, char * label) const
{
    stream << Label <<'|'<<IdNum <<'|' << Title <<'|'
        << Composer <<'|'<< Artist ;
}
```

G.3 Makerec.cpp. Program to create a sample data file of recordings

```cpp
void main()
{
    int recaddr;
    DelimFieldBuffer Buffer;
    BufferFile RecordingFile (Buffer);
    RecordingFile . Create ("record.dat", ios::out);
    Recording * R[10];
    R[0] = new Recording ("LON", "2312", "Romeo and Juliet",
            "Prokofiev", "Maazel");
    R[1] = new Recording ("RCA", "2626",
            "Quartet in C Sharp Minor", "Beethoven", "Julliard");
    R[2] = new Recording ("WAR", "23699", "Touchstone", "Corea",
            "Corea");
    R[3] = new Recording ("ANG", "3795", "Symphony No. 9",
            "Beethoven", "Giulini");
    R[4] = new Recording ("COL", "38358", "Nebraska",
            "Springsteen", "Springsteen");
    R[5] = new Recording ("DG", "18807", "Symphony No. 9",
            "Beethoven", "Karajan");
    R[6] = new Recording ("MER", "75016", "Coq d'or Suite",
            "Rimsky-Korsakov", "Leinsdorf");
    R[7] = new Recording ("COL", "31809", "Symphony No. 9",
            "Dvorak", "Bernstein");
    R[8] = new Recording ("DG", "139201", "Violin Concerto",
            "Beethoven", "Ferras");
    R[9] = new Recording ("FF", "245", "Good News",
            "Sweet Honey in the Rock", "Sweet Honey in the Rock");
    for (int i= 0; i<10; i++)
    {
        R[i] -> Pack (Buffer);
        recaddr = RecordingFile . Write ();
        cout <<"Recording R["<<i<<"] at recaddr "<<recaddr<<endl;
        delete R[i];
    }
}
```

G.4   Textind.h. Definition of class TextIndex

```
class TextIndex
{public:
   TextIndex (int maxKeys = 100, int unique = 1);
   ~TextIndex ();
   int Insert (const char * key, int recAddr);
   int Remove (const char * key);
   int Search (const char * key) const;
   void Print (ostream &) const;
 protected:
   int MaxKeys;
   int NumKeys;
   char * * Keys;
   int * RecAddrs;
   int Find (const char * key) const;
   int Init (int maxKeys, int unique);
   int Unique; // if true, each key value must be unique
friend class TextIndexBuffer;
};
```

G.5   Textind.cpp. Code for class TextIndex

```
TextIndex:: TextIndex (int maxKeys, int unique)
   : NumKeys (0), Keys(0), RecAddrs(0)
{Init (maxKeys, unique);}

TextIndex :: ~TextIndex ()
{delete Keys; delete RecAddrs;}

int TextIndex :: Insert (const char * key, int recAddr)
{
   int i;
   int index = Find (key);
   if (Unique && index >= 0) return 0; // key already in
   if (NumKeys == MaxKeys) return 0; //no room for another key
   for (i = NumKeys-1; i >= 0; i--)
   {
      if (strcmp(key, Keys[i])>0) break; // insert into i+1
      Keys[i+1] = Keys[i];
```

```
      RecAddrs[i+1] = RecAddrs[i];
   }
   Keys[i+1] = strdup(key);
   RecAddrs[i+1] = recAddr;
   NumKeys ++;
   return 1;
}

int TextIndex :: Remove (const char * key)
{
   int index = Find (key);
   if (index < 0) return 0; // key not in index
   for (int i = index; i < NumKeys; i++)
   {
      Keys[i] = Keys[i+1];
      RecAddrs[i] = RecAddrs[i+1];
   }
   NumKeys --;
   return 1;
}

int TextIndex :: Search (const char * key) const
{
   int index = Find (key);
   if (index < 0) return index;
   return RecAddrs[index];
}

void TextIndex :: Print (ostream & stream) const
{
   stream << "Text Index max keys "<<MaxKeys
        <<" num keys "<<NumKeys<<endl;
   for (int i = 0; i<NumKeys; i++)
      stream <<"\tKey["<<i<<"] "<<Keys[i]
        <<" RecAddr "<<RecAddrs[i]<<endl;
}

int TextIndex :: Find (const char * key) const
{
   for (int i = 0; i < NumKeys; i++)
      if (strcmp(Keys[i], key)==0) return i;// key found
      else if (strcmp(Keys[i], key)>0) return -1;// not found
   return -1;// not found
}
```

```
int TextIndex :: Init (int maxKeys, int unique)
{
   Unique = unique != 0;
   if (maxKeys <= 0)
   {
      MaxKeys = 0;
      return 0;
   }
   MaxKeys = maxKeys;
   Keys = new char *[maxKeys];
   RecAddrs = new int [maxKeys];
   return 1;
}
```

G.6   RecFile.h Template class RecordFile

```
// template class to support direct read and write of records
// The template parameter RecType must support the following
// int Pack (IOBuffer &); pack record into buffer
// int Unpack (IOBuffer &); unpack record from buffer

template <class RecType>
class RecordFile: public BufferFile
{public:
   int Read (RecType & record, int recaddr = -1);
   int Write (const RecType & record, int recaddr = -1);
   int Append (const RecType & record);
   RecordFile (IOBuffer & buffer): BufferFile (buffer) {}
};

// template method bodies
template <class RecType>
int RecordFile<RecType>::Read(RecType& record,int recaddr= -1)
{
   int writeAddr, result;
   writeAddr = BufferFile::Read (recaddr);
   if (!writeAddr) return -1;
   result = record . Unpack (Buffer);
   if (!result) return -1;
   return writeAddr;
}
```

```cpp
template <class RecType>
int RecordFile<RecType>::Write (const RecType & record,
int recaddr = -1)
{
   int result;
   result = record . Pack (Buffer);
   if (!result) return -1;
   return BufferFile::Write (recaddr);
}


template <class RecType>
int RecordFile<RecType>::Append (const RecType & record)
{
   int result;
   result = record . Pack (Buffer);
   if (!result) return -1;
   return BufferFile::Append();
}
```

G.7   Makeind.cpp. Program to make an index file for a file of recordings

```cpp
int RetrieveRecording (Recording & recording, char * key,
         TextIndex & RecordingIndex, BufferFile & RecordingFile)
// read and unpack the recording, return TRUE if succeeds
{  int result;
   cout <<"Retrieve "<<key<<" at recaddr "
      <<RecordingIndex.Search(key)<<endl;
   result = RecordingFile . Read (RecordingIndex.Search(key));
   cout <<"read result: "<<result<<endl;
   if (result == -1) return FALSE;
   result = recording.Unpack (RecordingFile.GetBuffer());
   return result;
}


// make an index from a recording file
int IndexRecordingFile (char * myfile, TextIndex & RecordingIndex)
{
   Recording rec; int recaddr, result;
   DelimFieldBuffer Buffer; // create a buffer
```

```
   BufferFile RecordingFile(Buffer);
   result = RecordingFile . Open (myfile,ios::in);
   if (!result)
   {
      cout << "Unable to open file "<<myfile<<endl;
      return 0;
   }
   while (1) // loop until the read fails
   {
      recaddr = RecordingFile . Read (); // read next record
      if (recaddr < 0) break;
      rec. Unpack (Buffer);
      RecordingIndex . Insert(rec.Key(), recaddr);
      cout << recaddr <<'\t'<<rec<<endl;
   }
   RecordingIndex . Print (cout);
   result = RetrieveRecording
      (rec, "LON2312", RecordingIndex, RecordingFile);
   cout <<"Found record: "<<rec;
}

main (int argv, char ** argc)
{// first argument is the file name for the data file
   TextIndex RecordingIndex (10);
   IndexRecordingFile (argc[1], RecordingIndex);
   // store the index in a file
   TextIndexBuffer IndexBuffer (12, 10);// 12 byte key, 10 keys
   BufferFile IndexFile (IndexBuffer);
   IndexBuffer.Pack(RecordingIndex);
   IndexFile . Create ("recindex.dat", ios::out);
   IndexFile . Write ();
}
```

G.8   Tindbuff.h. Definition of class TextIndexBuffer

```
// class TextIndexBuffer supports reading and writing
// index records from class TextIndex
// each record is consistent in its maximum size
class TextIndexBuffer: public FixedFieldBuffer
{public:
```

```
    TextIndexBuffer(int keySize, int maxKeys = 100,
        int extraFields = 0, int extraSize=0);
    // extraSize is included to allow derived classes to extend
    // the buffer with extra fields.
    // Required because the buffer size is exact.
    int Pack (const TextIndex &);
    int Unpack (TextIndex &);
    void Print (ostream &) const;
protected:
    int MaxKeys;
    int KeySize;
    char * Dummy; // space for dummy in pack and unpack
};
```

G.9   Tindbuff.cpp. Code for class TextIndexBuffer

```
TextIndexBuffer::TextIndexBuffer
    (int keySize, int maxKeys, int extraFields, int extraSpace)
: FixedFieldBuffer (1+2*maxKeys+extraFields,
      sizeof(int)+maxKeys*keySize+maxKeys*sizeof(int) + extraSpace)
    // buffer fields consist of
    //    numKeys, actual number of keys
    //    Keys [maxKeys] key fields size = maxKeys * keySize
    //    RecAddrs[maxKeys] record address fields
    //             size = maxKeys*sizeof(int)
{
    MaxKeys = maxKeys;
    KeySize = keySize;
    AddField (sizeof(int));
    for (int i = 0; i < maxKeys; i++)
    {
        AddField (KeySize);
        AddField (sizeof(int));
    }
    Dummy = new char[keySize+1];
}

int TextIndexBuffer::Pack
    (const TextIndex & index)
{
```

```
    int result;
    Clear ();
    result = FixedFieldBuffer::Pack (&index.NumKeys);
    for (int i = 0; i < index.NumKeys; i++)
    {// note only pack the actual keys and recaddrs
        result = result && FixedFieldBuffer::Pack (index.Keys[i]);
        result = result &&
             FixedFieldBuffer::Pack (&index.RecAddrs[i]);
    }
    for (int j = 0; j<index.MaxKeys-index.NumKeys; j++)
    {// pack dummy values for other fields
        result = result && FixedFieldBuffer::Pack (Dummy);
        result = result && FixedFieldBuffer::Pack (Dummy);
    }
    return result;
}

int TextIndexBuffer::Unpack
    (TextIndex & index)
{
    int result;
    result = FixedFieldBuffer::Unpack (&index.NumKeys);
    for (int i = 0; i < index.NumKeys; i++)
    {// note only pack the actual keys and recaddrs
        index.Keys[i] = new char[KeySize]; // just to be safe
        result = result && FixedFieldBuffer::Unpack (index.Keys[i]);
        result = result && FixedFieldBuffer::Unpack
             (&index.RecAddrs[i]);
    }
    for (int j = 0; j<index.MaxKeys-index.NumKeys; j++)
    {// pack dummy values for other fields
        result = result && FixedFieldBuffer::Unpack (Dummy);
        result = result && FixedFieldBuffer::Unpack (Dummy);
    }
    return result;
}

void TextIndexBuffer:: Print (ostream & stream) const
{
    stream <<"TextIndexBuffer: KeySize "<<KeySize
        <<" MaxKeys "<<MaxKeys<<endl;
    FixedFieldBuffer :: Print (stream);
}
```

G.10   Indfile.h. Template class TextIndexedFile

```
// template class to support indexed read and write of records
// using RecordFile, BufferFile, TextIndex, and TextIndexBuffer

template <class RecType>
class TextIndexedFile
{public:
    int Read (RecType & record); // read next record
    int Read (char * key, RecType & record); // read by key
    int Append (const RecType & record);
    int Update (char * oldKey, const RecType & record);
    int Create (char * name, int mode=ios::in|ios::out);
    int Open (char * name, int mode=ios::in|ios::out);
    int Close ();
    TextIndexedFile (IOBuffer & buffer,
        int keySize, int maxKeys = 100);
    ~TextIndexedFile (); // close and delete
protected:
    TextIndex Index;
    BufferFile IndexFile;
    TextIndexBuffer IndexBuffer;
    RecordFile<RecType> DataFile;
    char * FileName; // base file name for file
    int SetFileName(char * fileName,
        char *& dataFileName, char *& indexFileName);
};

// template method bodies
template <class RecType>
int TextIndexedFile<RecType>::Read (RecType & record)
{  return result = DataFile . Read (record, -1);}

template <class RecType>
int TextIndexedFile<RecType>::Read (char * key, RecType & record)
{
    int ref = Index.Search(key);
    if (ref < 0) return -1;
    int result = DataFile . Read (record, ref);
    return result;
}
```

```
template <class RecType>
int TextIndexedFile<RecType>::Append (const RecType & record)
{
    char * key = record.Key();
    int ref = Index.Search(key);
    if (ref != -1) // key already in file
        return -1;
    ref = DataFile . Append(record);
    int result = Index . Insert (key, ref);
    return ref;
}

template <class RecType>
int TextIndexedFile<RecType>::Update
    (char * oldKey, const RecType & record)
// Update is left as an exercise.
// It requires BufferFile::Update, and BufferFile::Delete
{  return -1;}

template <class RecType>
int TextIndexedFile<RecType>::SetFileName(char * fileName,
    char *& dataFileName, char *& indexFileName)
// generate names for the data file and the index file
{
    if (FileName != 0) // object is already attached to a file
        return 0;
    // set FileName member
    FileName = strdup(fileName);
    // generate real file names
    ostrstream dataName, indexName;
    dataName << FileName <<".dat"<<ends;
    indexName<< FileName<<".ind"<<ends;
    dataFileName = strdup(dataName . str());
    indexFileName = strdup(indexName . str());
    return 1;
}

template <class RecType>
int TextIndexedFile<RecType>::Create (char * fileName, int mode)
// use fileName.dat and fileName.ind
{
```

```cpp
   int result;
   char * dataFileName, * indexFileName;
   result = SetFileName (fileName, dataFileName, indexFileName);
   if (result == -1) return 0;
   result = DataFile.Create (dataFileName, mode);
   if (!result)
   {
      FileName = 0; // remove connection
      return 0;
   }
   result = IndexFile.Create (indexFileName, ios::out|ios::in);
   if (!result)
   {
      DataFile . Close(); // close the data file
      FileName = 0; // remove connection
      return 0;
   }
   return 1;
}
template <class RecType>
int TextIndexedFile<RecType>::Open (char * fileName, int mode)
// open data and index file and read index file
{
   int result;
   char * dataFileName, * indexFileName;
   result = SetFileName (fileName, dataFileName, indexFileName);
   if (!result) return 0;
   // open files
   result = DataFile.Open (dataFileName, mode);
   if (!result)
   {
      FileName = 0; // remove connection
      return 0;
   }
   result = IndexFile.Open (indexFileName, ios::out);
   if (!result)
   {
      DataFile . Close(); // close the data file
      FileName = 0; // remove connection
      return 0;
   }
```

```
   // read index into memory
   result = IndexFile . Read ();
   if (result != -1)
   {
      result = IndexBuffer . Unpack (Index);
      if (result != -1) return 1;
   }
   // read or unpack failed!
   DataFile.Close();
   IndexFile.Close();
   FileName = 0;
   return 0;
}

template <class RecType>
int TextIndexedFile<RecType>::Close ()
{  int result;
   if (!FileName) return 0; // already closed!
   DataFile . Close();
   IndexFile . Rewind();
   IndexBuffer.Pack (Index);
   result = IndexFile . Write ();
   cout <<"result of index write: "<<result<<endl;
   IndexFile . Close ();
   FileName = 0;
   return 1;
}

template <class RecType>
TextIndexedFile<RecType>::TextIndexedFile (IOBuffer & buffer,
      int keySize, int maxKeys)
   :DataFile(buffer), Index (maxKeys),
   IndexFile(IndexBuffer), IndexBuffer(keySize, maxKeys)
{  FileName = 0;}

template <class RecType>
TextIndexedFile<RecType>::~TextIndexedFile ()
{  Close(); }
```

G.11 Strclass.h. Definition of class String

```cpp
class String
{
    public:
    String ();
    String (const String&); //copy constructor
    String (const char *); // create from C string
    ~String ();
    String & operator = (const String &);
    operator char * ();
    int operator < (const String &) const;
    int operator > (const String &) const;
    int operator <= (const String &) const;
    int operator >= (const String &) const;
    int operator != (const String &) const;
    int operator == (const String &) const;
    char * str () const; // return a copy of the string
    protected:
    char * string;
    unsigned int MaxLength;
    friend ostream & operator << (ostream & stream, String & str);
};

ostream & operator << (ostream & stream, String & str);

inline ostream & operator << (ostream & stream, String & str)
{ stream << str.string; return stream;}

inline int String::operator > (const String& str) const
{ return !(*this <= str);}

inline int String::operator >= (const String& str) const
{ return !(*this < str);}

inline int String::operator != (const String& str) const
{ return !(*this == str);}
```

G.12   Strclass.cpp. Code for class String

```
String::String ()
{   string = 0; MaxLength = 0;}

String::String (const String& str) //copy constructor
{
    string = strdup (str . string);
    MaxLength = strlen (string);
}

String::String (const char * str) // create from C string
{
    string = strdup (str);
    MaxLength = strlen (string);
}

String::~String ()
{
    if (string != 0) delete string;
    MaxLength = 0;
    string = 0;
}

String::operator char * ()
{   return strdup(string);}


String & String::operator = (const String & str)
// assignment
{
    if (strlen (str.string) >= MaxLength)
    {
        delete string;
        string = strdup(str.string);
        MaxLength = strlen(string);
    }
    strcpy (string, str.string);
    return *this;
}

int String::operator < (const String &str) const
// less than, lexicographic
{   return strcmp(string, str.string) < 0;}
```

```
int String::operator <= (const String & str) const
{  return strcmp(string, str.string) <= 0;}

int String::operator == (const String & str) const
{  return strcmp(string, str.string) == 0;}

char * String::str () const // return a copy of the string
{  return strdup(string);}
```

G.13   Simpind.h. Definition of template class SimpleIndex

```
template <class keyType>
class SimpleIndex
{public:
   SimpleIndex (int maxKeys = 100, int unique = 1);
   ~SimpleIndex ();
   void Clear (); // remove all keys from index
   int Insert (const keyType key, int recAddr);
   // for Remove, Search, and Find, if recAddr == -1,
   //   remove the first instance of key
   int Remove (const keyType key, const int recAddr = -1);
   // for Search and Find, if exact == 1, return -1 if not found
   //   if exact == 0, find largest key in node <= argument key
   int Search (const keyType key, const int recAddr = -1,
         const int exact = 1) const;
   void Print (ostream &) const;
   int numKeys () const {return NumKeys;}
  protected:
   int MaxKeys;
   int NumKeys;
   keyType * Keys;
   int * RecAddrs;
   int Find (const keyType key, const int recAddr = -1,
         const int exact = 1) const;
   int Init (const int maxKeys, const int unique);
   int Unique; // if true, each key value must be unique
   friend class IndexBuffer<keyType>;
#ifdef BTREE_H
   friend class BTree<keyType>;
#endif
```

G.14   Simpind.tc. Code for template class SimpleIndex

```
template <class keyType>
SimpleIndex<keyType>:: SimpleIndex (int maxKeys, int unique)
   : NumKeys (0), Keys(0), RecAddrs(0)
{
   Init (maxKeys, unique);
}

template <class keyType>
SimpleIndex<keyType>::~SimpleIndex ()
{
   delete Keys;
   delete RecAddrs;
}

template <class keyType>
void SimpleIndex<keyType>::Clear ()
{
   NumKeys = 0;
}

template <class keyType>
int SimpleIndex<keyType>::Insert (const keyType key, int recAddr)
{
   int i;
   int index = Find (key);
   if (Unique && index >= 0) return 0; // key already in
   if (NumKeys == MaxKeys) return 0; //no room for another key
   for (i = NumKeys-1; i >= 0; i--)
   {
      if (key > Keys[i]) break; // insert into location i+1
      Keys[i+1] = Keys[i];
      RecAddrs[i+1] = RecAddrs[i];
   }
   Keys[i+1] = key;
   RecAddrs[i+1] = recAddr;
   NumKeys ++;
   return 1;
}
```

```
template <class keyType>
int SimpleIndex<keyType>::Remove (const keyType key, const int
recAddr)
{
   int index = Find (key, recAddr);
   if (index < 0) return 0; // key not in index
   for (int i = index; i < NumKeys; i++)
   {
      Keys[i] = Keys[i+1];
      RecAddrs[i] = RecAddrs[i+1];
   }
   NumKeys --;
   return 1;
}


template <class keyType>
int SimpleIndex<keyType>::Search (const keyType key,
    const int recAddr, const int exact) const
{
   int index = Find (key, recAddr, exact);
   if (index < 0) return index;
   return RecAddrs[index];
}


template <class keyType>
void SimpleIndex<keyType>::Print (ostream & stream) const
{
   stream << "Simple Index max keys "<<MaxKeys
        <<" num keys "<<NumKeys<<endl;
   for (int i = 0; i<NumKeys; i++)
      stream <<"\tKey["<<i<<"] "<<Keys[i]
        <<" RecAddr "<<RecAddrs[i]<<endl;
}


template <class keyType>
int SimpleIndex<keyType>::Find (const keyType key,
    const int recAddr, const int exact) const
{
   for (int i = 0; i < NumKeys; i++)
   {
      if (Keys[i] < key) continue; // not found yet
      if (Keys[i] == key) // exact match
      {
```

```
        if (recAddr < 0) return i;
        else if (recAddr == RecAddrs[i]) return i;
        else return -1; //
    }
    // no exact match: Keys[i-1]<key<Keys[i]
    if (!exact) // inexact match with key
        return i;
    return -1;
    }
    // key > all keys in index
    if (exact == 1) return -1; // no exact match
    else return NumKeys-1; // inexact, matches last key
}

template <class keyType>
int SimpleIndex<keyType>::Init (const int maxKeys, const int unique)
{
    Unique = unique != 0;
    if (maxKeys <= 0)
    {
        MaxKeys = 0;
        return 0;
    }
    MaxKeys = maxKeys;
    Keys = new keyType[maxKeys];
    RecAddrs = new int [maxKeys];
    return 1;
}
```

Cosequential Processing

H.1   Coseq.h. Definition of class CosequentialProcess

```
template <class ItemType>
class CosequentialProcess
// base class for cosequential processing
{public:
   CosequentialProcess(int numberOfLists);

   // The following methods provide basic list processing
   // These must be defined in subclasses
   virtual int InitializeList (int ListNumber, char * ListName)=0;
   virtual int InitializeOutput (char * OutputListName)=0;
   virtual int NextItemInList (int ListNumber)=0;
      //advance to next item in this list
   virtual ItemType Item (int ListNumber) = 0;
      // return current item from this list
   virtual int ProcessItem (int ListNumber)=0;
      // process the item in this list
   virtual int FinishUp()=0; // complete the processing

   // General list processing methods
   virtual int Match2Lists
      (char * List1Name, char * List2Name, char * OutputListName);
      // 2-way sequential matching algorithm
   virtual int Merge2Lists
      (char * List1Name, char * List2Name, char * OutputListName);
      // 2-way sequential merging algorithm
protected:
   int NumberOfLists; // number of lists to be processed
};

template <class ItemType>
CosequentialProcess<ItemType>::CosequentialProcess
   (int numberOfLists)
{   NumberOfLists = numberOfLists;}

template <class ItemType>
int CosequentialProcess<ItemType>::Match2Lists
   (char * List1Name, char * List2Name, char * OutputListName)
{
   int MoreItems;// true if items remain in lists
   InitializeList (1, List1Name);
```

```
    InitializeList (2, List2Name);
    InitializeOutput(OutputListName);
    MoreItems = NextItemInList(1) && NextItemInList(2);
    while (MoreItems){
        if (Item(1) < Item(2))
            MoreItems = NextItemInList(1);
        else if (Item(1) == Item(2)) // Item1 == Item2
        {
            ProcessItem (1); // match found
            MoreItems = NextItemInList(1) && NextItemInList(2);
        }
        else // Item(1) > Item(2)
            MoreItems = NextItemInList(2);
    }
    FinishUp();
    return 1;
}

template <class ItemType>
int CosequentialProcess<ItemType>::Merge2Lists
    (char * List1Name, char * List2Name, char * OutputListName)
{
    int MoreItems1, MoreItems2; // true if more items in list
    InitializeList (1, List1Name);
    InitializeList (2, List2Name);
    InitializeOutput (OutputListName);
    MoreItems1 = NextItemInList(1);
    MoreItems2 = NextItemInList(2);

    while (MoreItems1 || MoreItems2){// if either file has more
        if (Item(1) < Item(2))
        {// list 1 has next item to be processed
            ProcessItem (1);
            MoreItems1 = NextItemInList(1);
        }
        else if (Item(1) == Item(2))
        {// lists have the same item, process from list 1
            ProcessItem (1);
            MoreItems1 = NextItemInList(1);
            MoreItems2 = NextItemInList(2);
        }
        else // Item(1) > Item(2)
        {// list 2 has next item to be processed
            ProcessItem (2);
```

```
        MoreItems2 = NextItemInList(2);
      }
   }
   FinishUp();
   return 1;
}
```

H.2   Strlist.h. Definition of class StringListProcess

```
class StringListProcess: public CosequentialProcess<String&>
// Class to process lists that are files of strings, one per line
{public:
   StringListProcess (int NumberOfLists); // constructor

   // Basic list processing methods
   int InitializeList (int ListNumber, char * ListName);
   int InitializeOutput (char * OutputListName);
   int NextItemInList (int ListNumber); //get next item from list
   String& Item (int ListNumber); // return current item from list
   int ProcessItem (int ListNumber); // process the item in list
   int FinishUp(); // complete the processing
protected:
   ifstream * Lists; // array of list files
   String * Items; // array of current Item from each list
   ofstream OutputList;
   static const char * LowValue;
   static const char * HighValue;
};

const int MaxItemLength = 100; // maximum length of an item
```

H.3   Strlist.cpp. Code for class StringListProcess

```
const char * StringListProcess::LowValue = "";
const char * StringListProcess::HighValue = "\xff";

StringListProcess::StringListProcess (int numberOfLists)
 : CosequentialProcess<String&>(numberOfLists), OutputList()
 {
```

```
   Lists = new ifstream[NumberOfLists+1];
   Items = new String[NumberOfLists+1];
}

int StringListProcess::InitializeList (int ListNumber, char *
ListName)
{
   Lists[ListNumber] . open(ListName);
   Items[ListNumber] = LowValue;
   return 1;
}

int StringListProcess::InitializeOutput (char * OutputListName)
{
   OutputList.open(OutputListName);
   return 1;
}

int StringListProcess::NextItemInList (int ListNumber)
//get next item from this list
{
   char ThisItem[MaxItemLength];
   String PreviousItem = Items[ListNumber];
   Lists[ListNumber].getline(ThisItem, MaxItemLength+1);
   // get line from file
   // test for errors and termination
   if (!Lists[ListNumber].good()) // end of file
   {  Items[ListNumber]=HighValue; return 0;}
   if (strlen(ThisItem)==0) // no string
   {  Items[ListNumber]=LowValue; return 0;}
   if (strcmp(ThisItem, (char*)PreviousItem) < 0)
   {
      cerr << "Items out of order: current "<<ThisItem
         << " previous "<<(char*)PreviousItem<<endl;
      Items[ListNumber]=HighValue; return 0;
   }
   // this is a new item, store it
   Items[ListNumber]=ThisItem;//store this Item as current item
   return 1;
}

String& StringListProcess::Item (int ListNumber)
// return current item from this list
{  return Items[ListNumber];}
```

```
int StringListProcess::ProcessItem (int ListNumber)
// process the item in this list
// output a line containing the item
{
    OutputList << Items[ListNumber] <<endl;
    return 1;
}

int StringListProcess::FinishUp()
{
    for (int i = 1; i <= NumberOfLists; i++)
        Lists[i].close();
    OutputList.close();
    return 1;
}
```

H.4   Match.cpp. Main program for string matching and merging application

```
int main ()
{
    StringListProcess List(2);// declare process with 2 lists
    List.Match2Lists ("list1.txt","list2.txt","match.txt");
    List.Merge2Lists ("list1.txt","list2.txt","merge.txt");
    return 1;
}
```

H.5   Mastrans.h. Definition and code for template class MasterTransactionProcess

```
template <class ItemType>
class MasterTransactionProcess: public CosequentialProcess<ItemType>
// a cosequential process that supports master/transaction
// processing
{public:
    MasterTransactionProcess ();//constructor
    virtual int ProcessNewMaster ()=0;//  when new master read
    virtual int ProcessCurrentMaster ()=0;
```

```
        // called for each transaction for a master
    virtual int ProcessEndMaster ()=0;
        // after all transactions for a master
    virtual int ProcessTransactionError ()=0;
        // no master for transaction

    // cosequential processing of master and transaction records
    int PostTransactions
        (char * MasterFileName, char * TransactionFileName,
            char * OutputListName);
};

template <class ItemType>
MasterTransactionProcess<ItemType>::MasterTransactionProcess ()
: CosequentialProcess<int>(2)
{}

template <class ItemType>
int MasterTransactionProcess<ItemType>::PostTransactions
    (char * MasterFileName, char * TransactionFileName, char *
OutputListName)
{
    int MoreMasters, MoreTransactions; //true if more items in list
    InitializeList (1, MasterFileName);
    InitializeList (2, TransactionFileName);
    InitializeOutput (OutputListName);
    MoreMasters = NextItemInList(1);
    MoreTransactions = NextItemInList(2);
    if (MoreMasters) ProcessNewMaster(); // process first master

    while (MoreMasters || MoreTransactions)
    {// if either file has more
        if (Item(1) < Item(2))
        {// finish this master record
            ProcessEndMaster();
            MoreMasters = NextItemInList(1);
            if (MoreMasters) ProcessNewMaster();
        }
        else if (Item(1) == Item(2)) // Transaction matches Master
        {
            ProcessCurrentMaster();//another transaction for master
            ProcessItem (2);// output transaction record
            MoreTransactions = NextItemInList(2);
        }
```

```
      else // Item(1) > Item(2)
      {// transaction with no master
         ProcessTransactionError();
         MoreTransactions = NextItemInList(2);
      }
   }
   FinishUp();
   return 1;
}
```

H.6   Ledgpost.h. Definition of class LedgerProcess

```
class LedgerProcess: public MasterTransactionProcess<int>
// ledger processing of a ledger file and a journal file
// the item type is int to represent an account number
{public:
   LedgerProcess(int monthNumber); // constructor

   // Basic list processing methods
   int InitializeList (int ListNumber, char * List1Name);
   int InitializeOutput (char * OutputListName);
   int NextItemInList (int ListNumber); //get next item from list
   int Item (int ListNumber); // return current item from list
   int ProcessItem (int ListNumber); // process the item in list
   int FinishUp(); // complete the processing

   // master/transaction methods
   virtual int ProcessNewMaster ();//  when new master read
   virtual int ProcessCurrentMaster ();
      // each transaction for a master
   virtual int ProcessEndMaster ();
      // after all transactions for a master
   virtual int ProcessTransactionError();
      //no master for transaction

protected:
   // members
   int MonthNumber; // number of month to be processed
   LengthFieldBuffer Lbuffer, Jbuffer; // buffers for files
   RecordFile<Ledger> LedgerFile ; // list 1
   RecordFile<Journal> JournalFile;// list 2
   int AccountNumber [3]; // current item in each list
```

```
Ledger ledger; // current ledger object
Journal journal; // current journal object
ofstream OutputList; // text output file for post method
static int LowAcct;// lower than the lowest account number
static int HighAcct;// higher than the highest account number

int NextItemInLedger ();
int NextItemInJournal ();
};
```

H.7   Ledgpost.cpp. Code for class LedgerProcess

```
// big and little string constants
int LowValue = 0;
int HighValue = 9999;

int Initialize();
int LedgerInput (RecordFile<Ledger>, Ledger &);
int FinishUp (ifstream &, ifstream &, ofstream &);

int ProcessLedger (char * nameList1, char * nameList2,
      char * nameOutputFile)
{
   int MoreNames; // flag true if another name in each file
   // initialize
   ifstream List1; ifstream List2;
   ofstream OutputFile;
   char Name1[100], Name2[100];
   Initialize(List1, nameList1, Name1,
      List2, nameList2, Name2,
      OutputFile, nameOutputFile);
      // open files and initialize sequence checking variables

   MoreNames = GetItem(List1,Name1) && GetItem(List2,Name2);

   while (MoreNames){
      int cmp = strcmp(Name1, Name2);
      if (cmp < 0)
         MoreNames = GetItem(List1,Name1);
      else if (cmp == 0) // Name1 == Name2
      {
```

```
         OutputFile << Name1 <<endl; // match found
         MoreNames = GetItem(List1,Name1) &&
               GetItem(List2,Name2);
      }
      else // Name 1 > Name 2
         MoreNames = GetItem(List2,Name2);
   }
   FinishUp(List1, List2, OutputFile);
}

int Initialize(ifstream & List1, char * nameList1, char * Name1,
      ifstream & List2, char * nameList2, char * Name2,
      ofstream & OutputFile, char * nameOutputFile)
{
   List1.open(nameList1);
   List2.open(nameList2);
   OutputFile.open(nameOutputFile);
   strcpy (Name1, LowValue);
   strcpy (Name2, LowValue);
}

int GetItem (istream & List, char * Name)
// get next text line from List
// return TRUE if get succeeds
{
   char PreviousName[100];
   strcpy(PreviousName, Name); // remember last name
   List.getline(Name, 100);
   if (!List.good()) // end of file
   {   strcpy(Name,HighValue); return FALSE;}
   if (strlen(Name)==0) // no string
   { strcpy(Name,HighValue); return FALSE;}
   if (strcmp(Name, PreviousName) < 0)
   {
      cerr << "Names out of order: current "<<Name
         << " previous "<<PreviousName<<endl;
      strcpy(Name,HighValue); return FALSE;
   }
   return TRUE;
}

int FinishUp (ifstream & List1, ifstream & List2,
      ofstream & OutputFile)
{  List1.close(); List2.close(); OutputFile.close();}
```

```cpp
int Merge (char * nameList1, char * nameList2,
      char * nameOutputFile)
{
   int MoreNames1, MoreNames2;
   // initialize
   ifstream List1; ifstream List2;
   ofstream OutputFile;
   char Name1[100], Name2[100];
   Initialize(List1, nameList1, Name1,
      List2, nameList2, Name2,
      OutputFile, nameOutputFile);

   MoreNames1 = GetItem(List1,Name1);
   MoreNames2 = GetItem(List2,Name2);

   while (MoreNames1 || MoreNames2){// if either file has more
      int cmp = strcmp(Name1, Name2);
      if (cmp < 0)
      {
         OutputFile << Name1 <<endl; // match found
         MoreNames1 = GetItem(List1,Name1);
      }
      else if (cmp == 0) // Name1 == Name2
      {
         OutputFile << Name1 <<endl; // match found
         MoreNames1 = GetItem(List1,Name1);
         MoreNames2 = GetItem(List2,Name2);
      }
      else // Name 1 > Name 2
      {
         OutputFile << Name2 <<endl; // match found
         MoreNames2 = GetItem(List2,Name2);
      }
   }
   FinishUp(List1, List2, OutputFile);
   return TRUE;
}

int main ()
{
   Match ("list1.txt","list2.txt","match.txt");
   Merge ("list1.txt","list2.txt","merge.txt");
   return 1;
}
```

H.8   Ledger.h. Definition of classes Ledger and Journal

```
class Ledger
{public:
   int Acct;
   char Title [30];
   double Balances[12];
   int Pack(IOBuffer & buffer) const;
   int Unpack (IOBuffer & buffer);
   ostream & Print (ostream &);
   ostream & PrintHeader (ostream &);
   Ledger ();
   Ledger (int, char *, double, double, double);
};

ostream & PrintBalances (ostream & stream,
      double PreviousBalance, double CurrentBalance);

class Journal
{public:
   int Acct;
   int CheckNum;
   char Date[10];
   char Description[30];
   double Amount;
   int Pack (IOBuffer &) const;
   int Unpack (IOBuffer &);
   ostream & PrintLine (ostream &);
   Journal ();
   Journal (int, int, char*, char*, double);
};
```

H.9   Ledger.cpp. Code for classes Ledger and Journal

```
int Ledger::Pack (IOBuffer & buffer) const
{
   buffer.Clear();
   buffer.Pack(&Acct, sizeof(Acct));
   buffer.Pack(&Title, -1);
   for (int i=0; i<12; i++)
```

```
        buffer.Pack(&Balances[i], sizeof(Balances[i]));
    return TRUE;
}

int Ledger::Unpack (IOBuffer & buffer)
{
    buffer.Unpack(&Acct, sizeof(Acct));
    buffer.Unpack(&Title, sizeof(Title));
    for (int i=0; i<12; i++)
        buffer.Unpack(&Balances[i], sizeof(Balances[i]));
    return TRUE;
}

Ledger::Ledger ()
{
    Acct = 0;
    Title[0] = 0;
    for (int i=0; i<12; i++) Balances[i]=0.0;
}

Ledger::Ledger (int acct, char * title, double jan, double feb,
    double mar)
{
    Acct = acct;
    strcpy(Title, title);
    Balances[0] = jan;
    Balances[1] = feb;
    Balances[2] = mar;
    for (int i=3; i<12; i++) Balances[i]=0.0;
}

ostream & Ledger::Print (ostream & stream)
{
    stream.setf(ios::right,ios::adjustfield);
    stream << Acct <<'\t';
    stream.setf(ios::left,ios::adjustfield);
    stream <<setw(20)<<Title;
    stream.setf(ios::right,ios::adjustfield);
    stream.setf(ios::right|ios::fixed,ios::floatfield);
    stream.precision(2);
    for (int i = 0; i<12; i++)
    {
        if (Balances[i]<0.005 && i > 2)break;
        stream << '\t'<<setw(8)<<Balances[i];
```

```
   }
   stream <<endl;
   return stream;
}


ostream & Ledger::PrintHeader (ostream & stream)
{// print the report header for this account
   stream <<Acct<<'\t'<<Title<<endl;
   return stream;
}


ostream & PrintBalances (ostream & stream,
      double PreviousBalance, double CurrentBalance)
{// print balances line of report
   stream << "\t\t\t\tPrev. bal: "
      <<setw(8)<<setprecision(2)<<PreviousBalance
      <<"\tNew bal:\t"
      <<setw(8)<<setprecision(2)<<CurrentBalance<<endl;
   return stream;
}


ostream & Journal::PrintLine (ostream & stream)
{
   stream.setf(ios::right,ios::adjustfield);
   stream <<'\t'<<setw(6)<<CheckNum <<'\t';
   stream.setf(ios::left,ios::adjustfield);
   stream <<Date
      <<'\t'<<setw(30)<<Description;
   stream.setf(ios::right,ios::adjustfield);
   stream.setf(ios::right|ios::fixed,ios::floatfield);
   stream.precision(2);
   stream << '\t'<<setw(8)<<Amount<<endl;
   return stream;
}
int Journal::Pack (IOBuffer & buffer) const
{
   buffer.Clear();
   buffer.Pack(&Acct, sizeof(Acct));
   buffer.Pack(&CheckNum, sizeof(CheckNum));
   buffer.Pack(&Date, -1);
   buffer.Pack(&Description, -1);
   buffer.Pack(&Amount, sizeof(Amount));
   return TRUE;
}
```

Heapsort.cpp. Code for class Heap and Heapsort

673

```
int Journal::Unpack (IOBuffer & buffer)
{
   buffer.Unpack(&Acct, sizeof(Acct));
   buffer.Unpack(&CheckNum, sizeof(CheckNum));
   buffer.Unpack(&Date, -1);
   buffer.Unpack(&Description, sizeof(Description));
   buffer.Unpack(&Amount, sizeof(Amount));
   return TRUE;
}

Journal::Journal ()
{
   Acct = 0;
   CheckNum = 0;
   Date[0] = 0;
   Description[0] = 0;
   Amount = 0.0;
}

Journal::Journal (int acct, int checkNum, char* date,
   char * desc, double amt)
{
   Acct = acct;
   CheckNum = checkNum;
   strcpy(Date, date);
   strcpy(Description, desc);
   Amount = amt;
}
```

H.10   Heapsort.cpp. Code for class Heap and Heapsort

```
class Heap
{public:
   Heap(int maxElements);
   int Insert (char * newKey);
   char * Remove();
   ostream & Print (ostream &);
protected:
   int MaxElements;
   char ** HeapArray; // use element 1 as first element
   int NumElements;
```

```
   void Exchange(int i, int j);
   int Compare (int i, int j);
};

Heap::Heap(int maxElements)
{
   MaxElements = maxElements;
   HeapArray = new char* [MaxElements+1];
   NumElements = 0;
}

int Heap::Insert(char * newKey)
{
   if (NumElements == MaxElements) return FALSE;
   NumElements++; // add the new key at the last position
   HeapArray[NumElements] = newKey;
   // re-order the heap
   int k = NumElements;
   int parent;
   while (k > 1) // k has a parent
   {
      parent = k / 2;
      if (Compare(k, parent) >= 0)
         // HeapArray[k] is in the right place
         break;
      // else exchange k and parent
      Exchange(k, parent);
      k = parent;
   }
   return TRUE;
}

ostream & Heap::Print (ostream & stream)
{
   int i;
   for (i = 1; i <= MaxElements; i++)
      stream <<setw(3)<<i;
   stream<<endl;
   for (i=1; i <= NumElements; i++)
      stream <<setw(3)<<HeapArray[i];
   stream<<endl;
   return stream;
}
```

```cpp
void Heap::Exchange(int i, int j)
{
    char * temp = HeapArray[i];
    HeapArray[i] = HeapArray[j];
    HeapArray[j] = temp;
}

char * Heap::Remove()
{
    // put the smallest value into 'val' for use in return
    char * val = HeapArray[1];

    // put largest value into root
    HeapArray[1] = HeapArray[NumElements];
    // decrease the number of elements
    NumElements--;

    // reorder the heap by exchanging and moving down
    int k = 1; // node of heap that contains the largest value
    int newK; // node to exchange with largest value
    while (2*k <= NumElements)// k has at least one child
    {   // set newK to the index of smallest child of k
        if (Compare(2*k, 2*k+1)<0) newK = 2*k;
        else newK = 2*k+1;
        // done if k and newK are in order
        if (Compare(k, newK) < 0) break; //in order
        Exchange(k, newK); // k and newK out of order
        k = newK; // continue down the tree
    }
    return val;
}

int Heap::Compare (int i, int j)
{// return -1 if j is not an element of the heap
 //       or if HeapArray[i]<HeapArray[j]
    if (j > NumElements) return -1;
    else return strcmp(HeapArray[i],HeapArray[j]);
}

void main()
{// heap sorting by insert and then remove.
    int i;
    char * stuff []={"F","D","C","G","H","I","B","E","A"};
    Heap heap(9);
```

```
for (i = 0; i<9; i++)
{
   heap.Insert (stuff[i]);
   heap.Print(cout);
}
for (i = 0; i<9; i++)
{
   cout <<heap.Remove()<<endl;
   heap.Print(cout);
}
cout<<endl;
}
```

Multi-level Indexing with B-Trees

I

I.1   Btnode.h. Definition of template class BTreeNode

```
template <class keyType>
class BTreeNode: public SimpleIndex <keyType>
// this is the in-memory version of the BTreeNode
{
  public:
    BTreeNode(int maxKeys, int unique = 1);
    ~BTreeNode();
    // Insert and Remove return
    // 0 for failure
    // -1 for overflow
    // 1 for success
    int Insert (const keyType key, int recAddr);
    int Remove (const keyType key, int recAddr = -1);
    //int Search (const keyType key) const;
    void Print (ostream &) const;
    int LargestKey (); // returns value of largest key
    int Split(BTreeNode<keyType> * newNode);//move into newNode
    int Merge(BTreeNode<keyType> * fromNode);//move from fromNode
    int UpdateKey (keyType oldKey, keyType newKey, int recAddr=-1);
    int Pack (IOBuffer& buffer) const;
    int Unpack (IOBuffer& buffer);
    static int InitBuffer (FixedFieldBuffer & buffer,
        int maxKeys, int keySize = sizeof(keyType));
protected:
    int NextNode; // address of next node at same level
    int RecAddr; // address of this node in the BTree file
    int MinKeys; // minimum number of keys in a node
    int MaxBKeys; // maximum number of keys in a node
    int Init ();
    void Clear(){NumKeys = 0; RecAddr = -1;}
    friend class BTree<keyType>;
};
```

I.2 Btnode.tc. Method Bodies for template class BTreeNode

```
template <class keyType>
BTreeNode<keyType>::BTreeNode(int maxKeys, int unique)
:SimpleIndex<keyType>(maxKeys+1, unique)
{  Init ();}

template <class keyType>
BTreeNode<keyType>::~BTreeNode(){}

template <class keyType>
int BTreeNode<keyType>::Insert (const keyType key, int recAddr)
{
    int result;
    result = SimpleIndex<keyType>::Insert (key, recAddr);
    if (!result) return 0; // insert failed
    if (NumKeys >= MaxKeys) return -1; // node overflow
    return 1;
}

template <class keyType>
int BTreeNode<keyType>::Remove (const keyType key, int recAddr)
{
    int result;
    result = SimpleIndex<keyType>::Remove (key, recAddr);
    if (!result) return 0; // remove failed
    if (NumKeys < MinKeys) return -1; // node underflow
    return 1;
}

template <class keyType>
void BTreeNode<keyType>::Print (ostream & stream) const
{  SimpleIndex<keyType>::Print(cout);}

template <class keyType>
int BTreeNode<keyType>::LargestKey ()
// returns value of largest key
{
    if (NumKeys>0) return Keys[NumKeys-1];
    else return Keys[0];
}
```

```
template <class keyType>
int BTreeNode<keyType>::Split (BTreeNode<keyType> * newNode)
{
    // check for sufficient number of keys
    if (NumKeys < MaxKeys) return 0;
    // find the first Key to be moved into the new node
    int midpt = (NumKeys+1)/2;
    int numNewKeys = NumKeys - midpt;
    // check that number of keys for newNode is ok
    if (numNewKeys > newNode -> MaxBKeys
        || numNewKeys < newNode -> MinKeys)
        return 0;
    // move the keys and recaddrs from this to newNode
    for (int i = midpt; i< NumKeys; i++)
    {
        newNode->Keys[i-midpt] = Keys[i];
        newNode->RecAddrs[i-midpt] = RecAddrs[i];
    }
    // set number of keys in the two Nodes
    newNode->NumKeys = numNewKeys;
    NumKeys = midpt;
    return 1;
}

template <class keyType>
int BTreeNode<keyType>::Merge (BTreeNode<keyType> * fromNode)
{
    // check for too many keys
    if (NumKeys + fromNode->NumKeys > MaxKeys-1) return 0;
    // move keys and recaddrs from fromNode to this
    for (int i = 0; i<fromNode->NumKeys; i++)
    {
        Keys[NumKeys+i] = fromNode->Keys[i];
        RecAddrs[NumKeys+i] = fromNode->RecAddrs[i];
    }
    // adjust number of keys
    NumKeys += fromNode->NumKeys;
    return 1;
}

template <class keyType>
int BTreeNode<keyType>::UpdateKey (keyType oldKey, keyType newKey,
int recAddr)
{
```

```
   // look for the old key
   int recaddr = Search (oldKey, recAddr);
   if (recaddr < 0) return 0; // key and recaddr not found
   Remove (oldKey, recAddr);
   Insert (newKey, recaddr);
   return 1;
}


template <class keyType>
int BTreeNode<keyType>::Init ()
{
   NextNode = -1;
   RecAddr = -1;
   MaxBKeys = MaxKeys - 1;
   MinKeys = MaxBKeys / 2;
   return 1;
}

template <class keyType>
BTreeNode<keyType> * CreateBTreeNode (int maxKeys, int unique)
{
   return new BTreeNode<keyType> (maxKeys, unique);
}

template <class keyType>
int BTreeNode<keyType>::Pack (IOBuffer& buffer) const
{
   int result;
   buffer.Clear ();
   result = buffer.Pack (&NumKeys);
   for (int i = 0; i < NumKeys; i++)
   {// note only pack the actual keys and recaddrs
      result = result && buffer.Pack (&Keys[i]);
      result = result && buffer.Pack (&RecAddrs[i]);
   }
   return result;
}

template <class keyType>
int BTreeNode<keyType>::Unpack (IOBuffer& buffer)
{
   int result;
   result = buffer.Unpack (&NumKeys);
```

```
   for (int i = 0; i < NumKeys; i++)
   {// note only pack the actual keys and recaddrs
      result = result && buffer.Unpack (&Keys[i]);
      result = result && buffer.Unpack (&RecAddrs[i]);
   }
   return result;
}


template <class keyType>
int BTreeNode<keyType>::InitBuffer
   (FixedFieldBuffer & buffer, int maxKeys, int keySize)
{// initialize a buffer for the btree node
   buffer.AddField (sizeof(int));
   for (int i = 0; i < maxKeys; i++)
   {buffer.AddField (keySize); buffer.AddField (sizeof(int));}
   return 1;
}
```

I.3 Btree.h. Definition of template class BTree

```
template <class keyType>
class BTree
// this is the full version of the BTree
{public:
   BTree(int order, int keySize = sizeof(keyType),int unique = 1);
   ~BTree();
   int Open (char * name, int mode);
   int Create (char * name, int mode);
   int Close ();
   int Insert (const keyType key, const int recAddr);
   int Remove (const keyType key, const int recAddr = -1);
   int Search (const keyType key, const int recAddr = -1);
   void Print (ostream &);
   void Print (ostream &, int nodeAddr, int level);
protected:
   typedef BTreeNode<keyType> BTNode;// useful shorthand
   BTNode * FindLeaf (const keyType key);
   // load a branch into memory down to the leaf with key
   BTNode * NewNode ();
   BTNode * Fetch(const int recaddr);
```

```
    int Store (BTNode *);
    BTNode Root;
    int Height; // height of tree
    int Order; // order of tree
    int PoolSize;
    BTNode ** Nodes; // pool of available nodes
    // Nodes[1] is level 1, etc. (see FindLeaf)
    // Nodes[Height-1] is leaf
    FixedFieldBuffer Buffer;
    RecordFile<BTNode> BTreeFile;
};
```

I.4   Btree.tc. Method Bodies for template class BTree

```
const int MaxHeight = 5;
template <class keyType>
BTree<keyType>::BTree(int order, int keySize, int unique)
: Buffer (1+2*order,sizeof(int)+order*keySize+order*sizeof(int)),
    BTreeFile (Buffer), Root (order)
{
    Height = 1;
    Order = order;
    PoolSize = MaxHeight*2;
    Nodes = new BTNode * [PoolSize];
    BTNode::InitBuffer(Buffer,order);
    Nodes[0] = &Root;
}

template <class keyType>
BTree<keyType>::~BTree()
{   Close(); delete Nodes;}

template <class keyType>
int BTree<keyType>::Open (char * name, int mode)
{
    int result;
    result = BTreeFile.Open(name, mode);
    if (!result) return result;
    // load root
    BTreeFile.Read(Root);
```

```
   Height = 1; // find height from BTreeFile!
   return 1;
}

template <class keyType>
int BTree<keyType>::Create (char * name, int mode)
{
   int result;
   result = BTreeFile.Create(name, mode);
   if (!result) return result;
   // append root node
   result = BTreeFile.Write(Root);
   Root.RecAddr=result;
   return result != -1;
}

template <class keyType>
int BTree<keyType>::Close ()
{
   int result;
   result = BTreeFile.Rewind();
   if (!result) return result;
   result = BTreeFile.Write(Root);
   if (result==-1) return 0;
   return BTreeFile.Close();
}


template <class keyType>
int BTree<keyType>::Insert (const keyType key, const int recAddr)
{
   int result; int level = Height-1;
   int newLargest=0; keyType prevKey, largestKey;
   BTNode * thisNode, * newNode, * parentNode;
   thisNode = FindLeaf (key);

   // test for special case of new largest key in tree
   if (key > thisNode->LargestKey())
      {newLargest = 1; prevKey=thisNode->LargestKey();}

   result = thisNode -> Insert (key, recAddr);

   // handle special case of new largest key in tree
   if (newLargest)
```

```
    for (int i = 0; i<Height-1; i++)
    {
        Nodes[i]->UpdateKey(prevKey,key);
        if (i>0) Store (Nodes[i]);
    }

while (result==-1) // if overflow and not root
{
    //remember the largest key
    largestKey=thisNode->LargestKey();
    // split the node
    newNode = NewNode();
    thisNode->Split(newNode);
    Store(thisNode); Store(newNode);
    level--; // go up to parent level
    if (level < 0) break;
    // insert newNode into parent of thisNode
    parentNode = Nodes[level];
    result = parentNode->UpdateKey
        (largestKey,thisNode->LargestKey());
    result = parentNode->Insert
        (newNode->LargestKey(),newNode->RecAddr);
    thisNode=parentNode;
}
Store(thisNode);
if (level >= 0) return 1;// insert complete
// else we just split the root
int newAddr = BTreeFile.Append(Root);
    // put previous root into file
// insert 2 keys in new root node
Root.Keys[0]=thisNode->LargestKey();
Root.RecAddrs[0]=newAddr;
Root.Keys[1]=newNode->LargestKey();
Root.RecAddrs[1]=newNode->RecAddr;
Root.NumKeys=2;
Height++;
return 1;
}

template <class keyType>
int BTree<keyType>::Remove (const keyType key, const int recAddr)
{
    // left for exercise
    return -1;
```

```
}

template <class keyType>
int BTree<keyType>::Search (const keyType key, const int recAddr)
{
   BTNode * leafNode;
   leafNode = FindLeaf (key);
   return leafNode -> Search (key, recAddr);
}

template <class keyType>
void BTree<keyType>::Print (ostream & stream)
{
   stream << "BTree of height "<<Height<<" is "<<endl;
   Root.Print(stream);
   if (Height>1)
      for (int i = 0; i<Root.numKeys(); i++)
      {
         Print(stream, Root.RecAddrs[i], 2);
      }
   stream <<"end of BTree"<<endl;
}

template <class keyType>
void BTree<keyType>::Print
   (ostream & stream, int nodeAddr, int level)
{
   BTNode * thisNode = Fetch(nodeAddr);
   stream<<"Node at level "<<level<<" address "<<nodeAddr<<' ';
   thisNode -> Print(stream);
   if (Height>level)
   {
      level++;
      for (int i = 0; i<thisNode->numKeys(); i++)
      {
         Print(stream, thisNode->RecAddrs[i], level);
      }
      stream <<"end of level "<<level<<endl;
   }
}
```

```
template <class keyType>
BTreeNode<keyType> * BTree<keyType>::FindLeaf (const keyType key)
// load a branch into memory down to the leaf with key
{
   int recAddr, level;
   for (level = 1; level < Height; level++)
   {
      recAddr = Nodes[level-1]->Search(key,-1,0);//inexact search
      Nodes[level]=Fetch(recAddr);
   }
   return Nodes[level-1];
}

template <class keyType>
BTreeNode<keyType> * BTree<keyType>::NewNode ()
{// create a fresh node, insert into tree and set RecAddr member
   BTNode * newNode = new BTNode(Order);
   int recAddr = BTreeFile . Append(*newNode);
   newNode -> RecAddr = recAddr;
   return newNode;
}

template <class keyType>
BTreeNode<keyType> * BTree<keyType>::Fetch(const int recaddr)
{// load this node from File into a new BTreeNode
   int result;
   BTNode * newNode = new BTNode(Order);
   result = BTreeFile.Read (*newNode, recaddr);
   if (result == -1) return NULL;
   newNode -> RecAddr = result;
   return newNode;
}

template <class keyType>
int BTree<keyType>::Store (BTreeNode<keyType> * thisNode)
{
   return BTreeFile.Write(*thisNode, thisNode->RecAddr);
}
```

I.5   Tstbtree.cpp. Program to test B-tree insertion

```cpp
const char * keys="CSDTAMPIBWNGURKEHOLJYQZFXV";

const int BTreeSize = 4;
main (int argc, char * argv)
{
    int result, i;
    BTree <char> bt (BTreeSize);
    result = bt.Create ("testbt.dat",ios::in|ios::out);
    if (!result){cout<<"Please delete testbt.dat"<<endl; return 0;}
    for (i = 0; i<26; i++)
    {
        cout<<"Inserting "<<keys[i]<<endl;
        result = bt.Insert(keys[i],i);
        bt.Print(cout);
    }
    bt.Search(1,1);
    return 1;
}
```

J

Extendible Hashing

J.1   Hash.h. Functions Hash and MakeAddress

```
int Hash (char * key);
// create the primary hash value from a string

int MakeAddress (char * key, int depth);
// get the primary hash, reverse the bits
// return an address of depth bits
```

J.2   Hash.cpp. Implementation of functions Hash and MakeAddress

```
int Hash (char* key)
{
    int sum = 0;
    int len = strlen(key);
    if (len % 2 == 1) len ++; // make len even
    //for an odd length string, use the trailing 0 as part of key
    for (int j = 0; j < len; j += 2;)
        sum = (sum + 100 * key[j] + key[j+1]) % 19937;
    return sum;
}

int MakeAddress (char * key, int depth)
{
    int retval = 0;
    int mask = 1;
    int hashVal = Hash(key);

    for (int j = 0; j < depth; j++)
    {
        retval = retval << 1;
        int lowbit = hashVal & mask;
        retval = retval | lowbit;
        hashVal = hashVal >> 1;
    }
    return retval;
}
```

J.3 Bucket.h. Definition of class Bucket

```
const int defaultMaxKeys = 100;

class Bucket: public TextIndex
{protected:
    // there are no public members,
    // access to Bucket members is only through class Directory
    Bucket (Directory & dir, int maxKeys = defaultMaxKeys);
    int Insert (char * key, int recAddr);
    int Remove (char * key);
    Bucket * Split ();// split the bucket and redistribute the keys
    int NewRange (int & newStart, int & newEnd);
        // calculate the range of a new (split) bucket
    int Redistribute (Bucket & newBucket); // redistribute keys
    int FindBuddy ();// find the bucket that is the buddy of this
    int TryCombine (); // attempt to combine buckets
    int Combine (Bucket * buddy, int buddyIndex);
        // combine two buckets
    int Depth;
        // number of bits used 'in common'
        // by the keys in this bucket
    Directory & Dir; // directory that contains the bucket
    int BucketAddr; // address of file
    ostream & Print (ostream &);
    friend class Directory;
    friend class BucketBuffer;
};

class BucketBuffer: public TextIndexBuffer
{public:
    BucketBuffer (int keySize, int maxKeys);
    int Pack (const Bucket & bucket);
    int Unpack (Bucket & bucket);
};
```

J.4   Directory.h. Definition of class Directory

```
class Directory
{public:
   Directory (int maxBucketKeys = -1);
   ~Directory ();
   int Open (char * name);
   int Create (char * name);
   int Close ();
   int Insert (char * key, int recAddr);
   int Remove (char * key);
   int Search (char * key); // return RecAddr for key
   ostream & Print (ostream & stream);
protected:
   int Depth; // depth of directory
   int NumCells; // number of entries, = 2**Depth
   int * BucketAddr; // array of bucket addresses

   // protected methods
   int DoubleSize (); // double the size of the directory
   int Collapse (); // collapse, halve the size
   int InsertBucket (int bucketAddr, int first, int last);
   int RemoveBucket (int bucketIndex, int depth);
      // remove bucket from directory
   int Find (char * key); // return BucketAddr for key
   int StoreBucket (Bucket * bucket);
      // update or append bucket in file
   int LoadBucket (Bucket * bucket, int bucketAddr);
      // load bucket from file
   // members to support directory and bucket files
   int MaxBucketKeys;
   BufferFile * DirectoryFile;
   LengthFieldBuffer * DirectoryBuffer;
   Bucket * CurrentBucket;// object to hold one bucket
   BucketBuffer * theBucketBuffer;// buffer for buckets
   BufferFile * BucketFile;
   int Pack () const;
   int Unpack ();
   Bucket * PrintBucket;// object to hold one bucket
   friend class Bucket;
};
```

J.5   Tsthash.cpp. Program to test extendible hashing

```
main ()
{
   int result;
   Directory Dir (4);
   result = Dir . Create ("hashfile");
   if (result == 0)
   {
      cout<<"Please delete tsthash.dir and tsthash.bkt"<<endl;
      return 0;
   }
   char * keys[]={"bill", "lee", "pauline", "alan", "julie",
      "mike", "elizabeth", "mark", "ashley", "peter",
      "joan", "john", "charles", "mary", "emily"};
   const int numkeys = 15;
   for (int i = 0; i<numkeys; i++)
   {
      cout <<keys[i]<<" "<<(void*)Hash(keys[i])
         <<" "<<(void*)MakeAddress(keys[i],16)<<endl;
      result = Dir . Insert (keys[i], 100 + i);
      if (result == 0)
         cout << "insert for "<<keys[i]<<" failed"<<endl;
      Dir . Print (cout);
   }
   return 1;
}
```

J.6   Directory.cpp. Implementation of class Directory

```
const int MaxKeySize = 12;

Directory::Directory (int maxBucketKeys)
{
   Depth = 0; // depth of directory
   NumCells = 1; // number of entries, = 2**Depth
   BucketAddr = new int [NumCells]; // array of bucket addresses

   MaxBucketKeys = maxBucketKeys;
   DirectoryBuffer = new LengthFieldBuffer; // default size
```

```
   DirectoryFile = new BufferFile(*DirectoryBuffer);
   CurrentBucket = new Bucket (*this, MaxBucketKeys);
   theBucketBuffer = new BucketBuffer (MaxKeySize, MaxBucketKeys);
   BucketFile = new BufferFile (*theBucketBuffer);
   PrintBucket = new Bucket (*this, MaxBucketKeys);
}

Directory::~Directory ()
{
   Close();
}

void makeNames(char * name, char *& dirName, char *& bktName)
{
   ostrstream directoryName;
   directoryName<<name<<".dir"<<ends;
   dirName = strdup(directoryName.str());
   ostrstream bucketName;
   bucketName <<name<<".bkt"<<ends;
   bktName = strdup(bucketName.str());
}

int Directory::Open (char * name)
{
   int result;
   char * directoryName, * bucketName;
   makeNames(name, directoryName, bucketName);
   result = DirectoryFile->Open(directoryName, ios::in|ios::out);
   if (!result) return 0;
   result = DirectoryFile->Read();
   if (result==-1) return 0;
   result = Unpack();
   if (!result==-1) return 0;
   result = BucketFile->Open(bucketName,ios::in|ios::out);
   return result;
}

int Directory::Create (char * name)
{
   // create the two files, clear the directory, create a single
   // bucket and add it to the directory and the bucket file
   int result;
   char * directoryName, * bucketName;
   makeNames(name, directoryName, bucketName);
```

```cpp
    result = DirectoryFile->Create(directoryName,ios::in|ios::out);
    if (!result) return 0;
    result = BucketFile->Create(bucketName,ios::in|ios::out);
    if (!result) return 0;
    // store the empty CurrentBucket in the BucketFile
    // and add to Directory
    BucketAddr[0] = StoreBucket (CurrentBucket);
    return result;
}

int Directory::Close ()
{// write the directory and close. error occurs on buffer overflow
    int result;
    result = Pack();
    if (result==-1) return 0;
    DirectoryFile -> Rewind();
    result = DirectoryFile->Write();
    if (result==-1) return 0;
    return DirectoryFile->Close() && BucketFile->Close();
}

int Directory::Insert (char * key, int recAddr)
{
    int found = Search (key);
    if (found == -1) return CurrentBucket->Insert(key, recAddr);
    return 0;// key already in directory
}

int Directory::Remove (char * key)
{// remove the key and return its RecAddr
    int bucketAddr = Find(key);
    LoadBucket (CurrentBucket, bucketAddr);
    return CurrentBucket -> Remove (key);
}

int Directory::Search (char * key)
{// return RecAddr for key, also put current bucket into variable
    int bucketAddr = Find(key);
    LoadBucket (CurrentBucket, bucketAddr);
    return CurrentBucket->Search(key);
}

int Directory::DoubleSize ()
// double the size of the directory
```

```
{
    int newSize = 2 * NumCells;
    int * newBucketAddr = new int[newSize];
    for (int i = 0; i < NumCells; i++)
    {
        newBucketAddr[2*i] = BucketAddr[i];
        newBucketAddr[2*i+1] = BucketAddr[i];
    }
    delete BucketAddr;
    BucketAddr = newBucketAddr;
    Depth ++;
    NumCells = newSize;
    return 1;
}

int Directory::Collapse ()
{// if collapse is possible, reduce size by half
    if (Depth == 0) return 0; // only 1 bucket
    // look for buddies that are different, if found return
    for (int i = 0; i < NumCells; i += 2)
        if (BucketAddr[i] != BucketAddr[i+1]) return 0;
    int newSize = NumCells / 2;
    int * newAddrs = new int [newSize];
    for (int j = 0; j < newSize; j++)
        newAddrs[j] = BucketAddr[j*2];
    delete BucketAddr;
    BucketAddr = newAddrs;
    Depth --;
    NumCells = newSize;
    return 1;
}

int Directory::InsertBucket (int bucketAddr, int first, int last)
{// change cells to refer to this bucket
    for (int i = first; i <= last; i++)
        BucketAddr[i] = bucketAddr;
    return 1;
}

int Directory::RemoveBucket (int bucketIndex, int bucketDepth)
{// implementation left as exercise
    // set all cells for this bucket to its buddy bucket
    int fillBits = Depth-bucketDepth; // number of bits to fill
```

```cpp
    int buddyIndex = bucketIndex ^ (1<<(fillBits-1));
        // flip low bit
    int newBucketAddr = BucketAddr[buddyIndex];
    int lowIndex = bucketIndex >> fillBits << fillBits;
        // zero low bits
    int highIndex = lowIndex + (1<<fillBits) - 1;
        // set low bits to 1
    for (int i = lowIndex; i <= highIndex; i++)
        BucketAddr[i] = newBucketAddr;
    return 0;
}

int Directory::Find (char * key)
// return BucketAddr for key
{
    return BucketAddr[MakeAddress (key, Depth)];
}

int Directory::Pack ()   const
{// pack the buffer and return the number of bytes packed
    int result, packsize;
    DirectoryBuffer -> Clear();
    packsize = DirectoryBuffer -> Pack (&Depth, sizeof(int));
    if (packsize == -1) return -1;
    for (int i = 0; i<NumCells; i++)
    {
        result = DirectoryBuffer->Pack(&BucketAddr[i],sizeof(int));
        if (result == -1) return -1;
        packsize += result;
    }
    return packsize;
}

int Directory::Unpack ()
{
    int result;
    result = DirectoryBuffer -> Unpack (&Depth, sizeof(int));
    if (result == -1) return -1;
    NumCells = 1 << Depth;
    if (BucketAddr != 0) delete BucketAddr;
    BucketAddr = new int[NumCells];
    for (int i = 0; i<NumCells; i++)
    {
```

```
      result=DirectoryBuffer->Unpack(&BucketAddr[i], sizeof(int));
      if (result == -1) return -1;
   }
   return 0;
}


int Directory::StoreBucket (Bucket * bucket)
{// update or append the bucket to the bucket file
   int result;
   result = theBucketBuffer -> Pack (* bucket);
   if (result == -1) return -1;
   int addr = bucket->BucketAddr;
   if (addr != 0) return BucketFile->Write (addr);
   addr = BucketFile -> Append ();
   bucket -> BucketAddr = addr;
   return addr;
}


int Directory::LoadBucket(Bucket * bucket, int bucketAddr)
{// read bucket from file, and set BucketAddr field
   int result;
   result = BucketFile -> Read (bucketAddr);
   if (result == -1) return 0;
   result = theBucketBuffer -> Unpack (*bucket);
   if (result == -1) return 0;
   bucket->BucketAddr = bucketAddr;
   return 1;
}


ostream & Directory::Print (ostream & stream)
{
   stream <<"Directory Depth "<<Depth<<" size "<<NumCells<<endl;
   for (int i = 0; i<NumCells; i++)
   {
      stream <<"bucket "<<BucketAddr[i]
         <<" addr "<<(void *) i<<endl;
      LoadBucket (PrintBucket, BucketAddr[i]);
      PrintBucket->Print(stream);
   }
   stream <<"end directory"<<endl;
   return stream;
}
```

J.7   Bucket.cpp. Implementation of class Bucket

```
Bucket::Bucket (Directory & dir, int maxKeys) // constructor
:TextIndex (maxKeys), Dir (dir)
{
    BucketAddr = 0;
    Depth = 0;
}

int Bucket::Insert (char * key, int recAddr)
{
    if (NumKeys < MaxKeys)
    {
        int result = TextIndex::Insert (key, recAddr);
        Dir.StoreBucket (this);
        return result;
    }
    else
    {
        Split ();
        return Dir.Insert (key, recAddr);
    }
}

int Bucket::Remove (char * key)
{// remove the key, return its RecAddr
    int result = TextIndex::Remove (key);
    if (!result) return 0; // key not in bucket
    TryCombine (); // attempt to combine with buddy
    // make the changes permanent
    Dir.StoreBucket(this);
    return 1;
}

Bucket * Bucket::Split ()
{
    int newStart, newEnd;
    if (Depth == Dir.Depth)// no room to split this bucket
        Dir.DoubleSize();
    Bucket * newBucket = new Bucket (Dir, MaxKeys);
    Dir.StoreBucket (newBucket);
    NewRange (newStart, newEnd);
```

```
   Dir.InsertBucket(newBucket->BucketAddr, newStart, newEnd);
   Depth ++;
   newBucket->Depth = Depth;
   Redistribute (*newBucket);
   Dir.StoreBucket (this);
   Dir.StoreBucket (newBucket);
   return newBucket;
}

int Bucket::FindBuddy ()
{// find the directory address of the bucket that is paired with this
   if (Dir.Depth == 0) return -1; // no buddy, empty directory
   // unless bucket depth == directory depth, there is no single
   // bucket to pair with
   if (Depth < Dir.Depth) return -1;
   int sharedAddress = MakeAddress(Keys[0], Depth);
      // address of any key
   return sharedAddress ^ 1; // exclusive or with low bit
}

int Bucket::TryCombine ()
{// called after insert to combine buddies, if possible
   int result;
   int buddyIndex = FindBuddy ();
   if (buddyIndex == -1) return 0;// no combination possible
   // load buddy bucket into memory
   int buddyAddr = Dir.BucketAddr[buddyIndex];
   Bucket * buddyBucket = new Bucket (Dir, MaxKeys);
   Dir . LoadBucket (buddyBucket, buddyAddr);
   // if the sum of the sizes of the buckets is too big, return
   if (NumKeys + buddyBucket->NumKeys > MaxKeys) return 0;
   Combine (buddyBucket, buddyIndex);// collapse the 2 buckets
   result = Dir.Collapse ();
   if (result) TryCombine(); //if collapse, may be able to combine
   return 1;
}

int Bucket::Combine (Bucket * buddy, int buddyIndex)
{// collapse this and buddy into a single bucket
   int result;
   // move keys from buddy to this
   for (int i = 0; i < buddy->NumKeys; i++)
   {// insert the key of the buddy into this
      result = Insert (buddy->Keys[i],buddy->RecAddrs[i]);
```

```
        if (!result) return 0;
    }
    Depth --;// reduce the depth of the bucket
    Dir . RemoveBucket (buddyIndex, Depth);
    return 1;
}

int Bucket::NewRange (int & newStart, int & newEnd)
{// make a range for the new split bucket
    int sharedAddr = MakeAddress(Keys[0], Depth);
    int bitsToFill = Dir.Depth - (Depth + 1);
    newStart = (sharedAddr << 1) | 1;
    newEnd = newStart;
    for (int j = 0; j < bitsToFill; j++)
    {
        newStart = newStart << 1;
        newEnd = (newEnd << 1) | 1;
    }
    return 1;
}

int Bucket::Redistribute (Bucket & newBucket)
{
    // check each key in this bucket
    for (int i = NumKeys - 1; i >= 0; i--)
    {
        int bucketAddr = Dir.Find (Keys[i]); // look up the bucket
        if (bucketAddr != BucketAddr)// key belongs in the new bucket
        {
            newBucket.TextIndex::Insert (Keys[i], RecAddrs[i]);
            TextIndex::Remove (Keys[i]);
                // delete key from this bucket
        }
    }
    return 1;
}

ostream & Bucket::Print(ostream & stream)
{
    stream <<"Bucket depth: "<<Depth<<endl;
    TextIndex::Print (stream);
    return stream;
}
```

```
BucketBuffer::BucketBuffer (int keySize, int maxKeys)
: TextIndexBuffer(keySize,maxKeys,1,sizeof(int))
{
   AddField (sizeof(int));
}

int BucketBuffer::Pack (const Bucket & bucket)
{
   int result;
   TextIndexBuffer::Pack(bucket);
   if (result == -1) return -1;
   return FixedFieldBuffer::Pack (&bucket.Depth);
}

int BucketBuffer::Unpack (Bucket & bucket)
{
   int result;
   result = TextIndexBuffer::Unpack(bucket);
   if (result == -1) return -1;
   return FixedFieldBuffer::Unpack (&bucket.Depth);
}
```

Bibliography

Batory, D.S. "B+ trees and indexed sequential files: A performance comparison." *ACM SIGMOD* (1981): 30–39.

Bayer, R., and E. McCreight. "Organization and maintenance of large ordered indexes." *Acta Informatica* 1, no. 3 (1972): 173–189.

Bayer, R., and K. Unterauer. "Prefix B-trees." *ACM Transactions on Database Systems* 2, no. 1 (March 1977): 11–26.

Beckman, N., H.P. Kriegel, R. Schneider, and B. Seeger, "The R Tree: An Efficient and Robust Access Method for Points and Rectangles," *Proceedings of the ACM SIGMOD International Conference on the Management of Data* (May, 1990): New York, NY: ACM: 322–331.

Bentley, J. "Programming pearls: A spelling checker." *Communications of the ACM* 28, no. 5 (May 1985): 456–462.

Berry, J. *The Waite Group's C++ Programming*, 2nd Ed., Carmel, Indiana: Sam's, 1992.

Booch, G., *Object Oriented Design with Applications*. Redwood City, CA: Benjamin/Cummings, 1991.

Chang, C.C. "The study of an ordered minimal perfect hashing scheme." *Communications of the ACM* 27, no. 4 (April 1984): 384–387.

Chichelli, R.J. "Minimal perfect hash functions made simple." *Communications of the ACM* 23, no. 1 (January 1980): 17–19.

Comer, D. "The ubiquitous B-tree." *ACM Computing Surveys* 11, no. 2 (June 1979): 121–137.

Cormen, T.H., C.E. Leiserson, R.L. Rivest, *Introduction to Algorithms*. New York: McGraw-Hill, 1990.

Deitel, H. *An Introduction to Operating Systems*. Reading, Mass.: Addison-Wesley, 1989.

Dodds, D.J. "*Pracnique:* Reducing dictionary size by using a hashing technique." *Communications of the ACM* 25, no. 6 (June 1982): 368–370.

Dwyer, B. "One more time—how to update a master file." *Communications of the ACM* 24, no. 1 (January 1981): 3–8.

Elmasri, R., and S.B. Navathe. *Fundamentals of Database Systems*, Reading, Mass: Addison-Wesley, 1994.

Enbody, R.J., and H.C. Du. "Dynamic Hashing Schemes." *ACM Computing Surveys* 20, no. 2 (June 1988): 85–113.

Fagin, R., J. Nievergelt, N. Pippenger, and H.R. Strong. "Extendible hashing—a fast access method for dynamic files." *ACM Transactions on Database Systems* 4, no. 3 (September 1979): 315–344.

Flajolet, P. "On the Performance Evaluation of Extendible Hashing and Trie Searching." *Acta Informatica* 20 (1983): 345–369.

Friedman, F. and Koffman, E. *Problem Solving, Abstraction, and Design Using C++*, 2nd Ed., Reading, Mass: Addison-Wesley, 1997.

Gonnet, G.H. *Handbook of Algorithms and Data Structures*. Reading, Mass.: Addison-Wesley, 1984.

Gray, J., and A. Reuter, *Transaction Processing: Concepts and Techniques*. San Mateo, CA: Morgan Kaufman, 1993.

Guttman, A., "R-Trees: A Dynamic Index Structure for Spatial Searching," *Proceedings of the ACM SIGMOD International Conference on the Management of Data* (1984): New York, NY: ACM: 47657.

Hanson, O. *Design of Computer Data Files*. Rockville, Md.: Computer Science Press, 1982.

Hart, J.M. *Win32 Systems Programming*. Reading, Mass: Addison-Wesley, 1997.

Hekman, J. *Linux in a Nutshell*, O'Reilly and Associates, 1997.

Held, G., and M. Stonebraker. "B-trees reexamined." *Communications of the ACM* 21, no. 2 (February 1978): 139–143.

Hoare, C.A.R. "The emperor's old clothes." The C.A.R. Turing Award address. *Communications of the ACM* 24, no. 2 (February 1981): 75–83.

Irvine, K.R. *C++ and Object-Oriented Programming*. Englewood Cliffs, NJ: Prentice Hall, 1996.

Kamel, I., and C. Faloutsos, "Parallel R-Trees," *Proceedings of the ACM SIGMOD International Conference on the Management of Data* (1991): New York, NY: ACM.

Keehn, D.G., and J.O. Lacy. "VSAM data set design parameters." *IBM Systems Journal* 13, no. 3 (1974): 186—212.

Kernighan, B., and R. Pike. *The UNIX Programming Environment.* Englewood Cliffs, N.J.: Prentice-Hall, 1984.

Kernighan, B., and D. Ritchie. *The C Programming Language,* 2nd Ed. Englewood Cliffs, N.J.: Prentice-Hall, 1988.

Knuth, D. *The Art of Computer Programming.* Vol. 1, *Fundamental Algorithms.* 3rd Ed. Reading, Mass.: Addison-Wesley, 1997.

Knuth, D. *The Art of Computer Programming.* Vol. 3, *Searching and Sorting.* 3rd Ed. Reading, Mass.: Addison-Wesley, 1978.

Kroenke, D.M., *Database Processing: Fundamentals, Design, Implementation.* 6th Ed., Upper Saddle River, N.J.: Prentice Hall, 1998.

Larson, P. "Dynamic Hashing." *BIT* 18 (1978): 184–201.

Larson, P. "Linear Hashing with Overflow-handling by Linear Probing." *ACM Transactions on Database Systems* 10, no. 1 (March 1985): 75–89.

Larson, P. "Linear Hashing with Partial Expansions." *Proceedings of the 6th Conference on Very Large Databases.* (Montreal, Canada Oct 1–3, 1980) New York: ACM/IEEE: 224–233.

Larson, P. "Performance Analysis of Linear Hashing with Partial Expansions." *ACM Transactions on Database Systems* 7, no. 4 (December 1982): 566–587.

Laub, L. "What is CD-ROM?" In *CD-ROM: The New Papyrus.* S. Lambert and S. Ropiequet, eds. Redmond, Wash: Microsoft Press, 1986: 47–71.

Leffler, S., M.K. McKusick, M. Karels, and J.S. Quarterman. *The Design and Implementation of the 4.3BSD UNIX Operating System.* Reading, Mass.: Addison-Wesley, 1989.

Levy, M.R. "Modularity and the sequential file update problem." *Communications of the ACM* 25, no. 6 (June 1982): 362–367.

Litwin, W. "Linear Hashing: A New Tool for File and Table Addressing." *Proceedings of the 6th Conference on Very Large Databases* (Montreal, Canada, Oct 1–3, 1980) New York: ACM/IEEE: 212–223.

Litwin, W. "Virtual Hashing: A Dynamically Changing Hashing." *Proceedings of the 4th Conference on Very Large Databases* (Berlin 1978) New York: ACM/IEEE: 517–523.

Loomis, M. *Data Management and File Processing,* 2nd Ed. Englewood Cliffs, N.J.: Prentice-Hall, 1989.

Lum, V.Y., P.S. Yuen, and M. Dodd. "Key-to-Address Transform Techniques, A Fundamental Performance Study on Large Existing Formatted Files." *Communications of the ACM* 14, no. 4 (April 1971): 228–39.

Lynch, T. *Data Compression Techniques and Applications.* New York: Van Nostrand Reinhold Company, Inc., 1985.

Maurer, W.D., and T.G. Lewis. "Hash table methods." *ACM Computing Surveys* 7, no. 1 (March 1975): 5–19.

McCreight, E. "Pagination of B trees with variable length records." *Communications of the ACM* 20, no. 9 (September 1977): 670–674.

McKusick, M.K., W.M. Joy, S.J. Leffler, and R.S. Fabry. "A fast file system for UNIX." *ACM Transactions on Computer Systems* 2, no. 3 (August 1984): 181–197.

McKusick, M.K., K. Bostic, M.J. Karels, and J.S. Quarterman. *The Design and Implementation of the 4.4 BSD Operating System.* Reading, Mass: Addison-Wesley, 1996.

Mendelson, H. "Analysis of Extendible Hashing." *IEEE Transactions on Software Engineering* 8, no. 6 (November 1982): 611–619.

Morgan, R., and H. McGilton. *Introducing UNIX System V.* New York: McGraw-Hill, 1987.

Murayama, K., and S.E. Smith. "Analysis of design alternatives for virtual memory indexes." *Communications of the ACM* 20, no. 4 (April 1977): 245–254.

Nievergelt, J., H. Hinterberger, and K. Sevcik. "The grid file: an adaptive symmetric, multikey file structure." *ACM Transactions on Database Systems* 9, no. 1 (March 1984): 38–71.

Ouskel, M., and P. Scheuermann. "Multidimensional B-trees: Analysis of dynamic behavior." *BIT* 21 (1981):401–418.

Peterson, W.W. "Addressing for random access storage." *IBM Journal of Research and Development* 1, no. 2(1957):130–146.

Plauger, P.J. *The Draft Standard C++ Library,* Englewood Cliffs, NJ: Prentice Hall, 1995.

Reid, I. "RPCC: A Stub Compiler for Sun RPC," *USENIX Association Conference Proceedings* (June, 1987): 357-366.

Ritchie, B., and K. Thompson. "The UNIX time-sharing system." *Communications of the ACM* 17, no. 7 (July 1974): 365–375.

Robinson, J.T. "The *K-d* B-tree: A search structure for large multidimensional dynamic indexes." *ACM SIGMOD 1981 International Conference on Management of Data.* April 29–May 1, 1981.

Rosenberg, A.L., and L. Snyder. "Time and space optimality in B-trees." *ACM Transactions on Database Systems* 6, no. 1 (March 1981): 174–183.

Sager, T.J. "A polynomial time generator for minimal perfect hash functions." *Communications of the ACM* 28, no. 5 (May 1985): 523–532.

Salzberg, B., et al. "FastSort: A Distributed Single-Input, Single-Output Sort." *Proceedings of the 1990 ACM SIGMOD International Conference on Management of Data, SIGMOD RECORD,* Vol. 19, Issue 2, (June 1990): 94–101.

Scholl, M. "New file organizations based on dynamic hashing." *ACM Transactions on Database Systems* 6, no. 1 (March 1981): 194–211.

Sellis, T.K., N. Roussopoulos, and C. Faloutsos, "The R+ Tree: A Dynamic Index fo Multi-Dimensional Objects," *Proceedings of the International Conference on Very Large Databases* (1987): 507-518.

Sessions, R. *Class Construction in C and C++, Object-Oriented Programming Fundamentals,* Englewood Cliffs, NJ: Prentice Hall, 1992.

Severance, D.G. "Identifier search mechanisms: A survey and generalized model." *ACM Computing Surveys* 6, no. 3 (September 1974): 175–194.

Shaffer, C.A., *Practical Introduction to Data Structures and Algorithm Analysis.* Upper Saddle River, N.J.: Prentice Hall, 1997.

Silberschatz, A. and P.B. Galvin. *Operating System Concepts.* Reading, Mass.: Addison-Wesley, 1992.

Silberschatz, A., H.F. Korth, and S. Sudarshan, *Database System Concepts,* 3rd Ed. New York, NY: McGraw-Hill, 1997.

Snyder, L. "On B-trees reexamined." *Communications of the ACM* 21, no. 7 (July 1978): 594.

Sobel, M. *A Practical Guide to the UNIX System,* 3rd Ed. Benjamin/Cummings, 1995.

Sorenson, P.G., J.P. Tremblay and R.F. Deutscher. "Key-to-Address Transformation Techniques." *INFOR* (Canada) Vol. 16, no. 1 (1978): 397–409.

Spector, A., and D. Gifford. "Case study: The space shuttle primary computer system." *Communications of the ACM* 27, no. 9 (September 1984): 872–900.

Standish, T., *Data Structures, Algorithms and Software Principles in C.* Reading, Mass.: Addison-Wesley, 1995.

Stroustrup, B. *The C++ Programming Language,* 2nd Ed., Reading, Mass: Addison-Wesley, 1991.

Stroustrup, B. *The C++ Programming Language,* 3rd Ed. Reading, Mass: Addison-Wesley, 1997.

Sussenguth, E.H. "The use of tree structures for processing files." *Communications of the ACM* 6, no. 5 (May 1963): 272–279.

Sweet, F. "Keyfield design." *Datamation* (October 1, 1985): 119–120.

Tannenbaum, A.S. A.S Woodhull, A. Woodhull. *Operating Systems: Design and Implementation.* Englewood Cliffs, NJ: Prentice Hall, 1997.

Teory, T.J., and J.P. Fry. *Design of Database Structures.* Englewood Cliffs, N.J.: Prentice-Hall, 1982.

Ullman, J.D. *Principles of Database Systems,* 3rd Ed. Rockville, Md.: Computer Science Press, 1986.

VanDoren, J., and J. Gray. "An algorithm for maintaining dynamic AVL trees." In *Information Systems, COINS IV,* New York: Plenum Press, 1974: 161–180.

Veklerov, E. "Analysis of Dynamic Hashing with Deferred Splitting." *ACM Transactions on Database Systems* 10, no. 1 (March 1985): 90–96.

Wagner, R.E. "Indexing design considerations." *IBM Systems Journal* 12, no. 4 (1973): 351–367.

Webster, R.E. "B+ trees." Unpublished Master's thesis, Oklahoma State University, 1980.

Welch, T. "A Technique for High Performance Data Compression." *IEEE Computer,* Vol. 17, no. 6 (June 1984): 8–19.

Wells, D.C., E.W. Greisen and R.H. Harten. "FITS: A Flexible Image Transport System." *Astronomy and Astrophysics Supplement Series,* no. 44 (1981): 363–370.

Wiederhold, G. *Database Design,* 2nd Ed. New York: McGraw-Hill, 1983.

Yao, A. Chi-Chih. "On random 2–3 trees." *Acta Informatica* 9, no. 2 (1978): 159–170.

Yourdon, E. and C. Argila. *Case Studies in Object-oriented Design and Analysis.* Yourdon Press, 1996.

Zoellick, B. "CD-ROM software development." *Byte* 11, no. 5 (May 1986): 173–188.

Zoellick, B. "File System Support for CD-ROM." In *CD-ROM: The New Papyrus.* S. Lambert and S. Ropiequet, eds. Redmond, Wash: Microsoft Press, 1986: 103–128.

Zoellick, B. "Selecting an Approach to Document Retrieval." In *CD-ROM, Volume 2: Optical Publishing.* S. Ropiequet, ed. Redmond, Wash: Microsoft Press, 1987: 63–82.

Index